Juvenile Delinquency in a Diverse Society

Second Edition

Juvenile Delinquency
in a Diverse Society
Second Edition

DEDICATION

To William and Christopher, my little delinquents —KB

To Bryce, Avary, Gavin, and Olivia —RS

Juvenile Delinquency in a Diverse Society

Second Edition

Kristin A. Bates

California State University,
San Marcos

Richelle S. Swan

California State University,
San Marcos

Los Angeles | London | New Delhi
Singapore | Washington DC | Melbourne

FOR INFORMATION:

SAGE Publications, Inc.
2455 Teller Road
Thousand Oaks, California 91320
E-mail: order@sagepub.com

SAGE Publications Ltd.
1 Oliver's Yard
55 City Road
London EC1Y 1SP
United Kingdom

SAGE Publications India Pvt. Ltd.
B 1/I 1 Mohan Cooperative Industrial Area
Mathura Road, New Delhi 110 044
India

SAGE Publications Asia-Pacific Pte. Ltd.
3 Church Street
#10-04 Samsung Hub
Singapore 049483

Acquisitions Editor: Jessica Miller
eLearning Editor: Laura Kirkhuff
Editorial Assistant: Jennifer Rubio
Production Editor: David C. Felts
Copy Editor: Diana Breti
Typesetter: C&M Digitals (P) Ltd.
Proofreader: Victoria Reed-Castro
Indexer: Karen Wiley
Cover Designer: Scott Van Atta
Marketing Manager: Amy Lammers

Printed in Great Britain by Bell & Bain Ltd, Glasgow

Library of Congress Cataloging-in-Publication Data

Names: Bates, Kristin Ann, author. | Swan, Richelle S., author.

Title: Juvenile delinquency in a diverse society / Kristin A. Bates, Richelle S. Swan.

Description: Second edition. | Los Angeles : SAGE, [2018] | Includes bibliographical references and index.

Identifiers: LCCN 2016038632 | ISBN 978-1-5063-4749-3 (pbk. : alk. paper)

Subjects: LCSH: Juvenile delinquency. | Juvenile delinquents. | Juvenile justice, Administration of.

Classification: LCC HV9069 .B38 2017 | DDC 364.36—dc23
LC record available at https://lccn.loc.gov/2016038632

This book is printed on acid-free paper.

18 19 20 21 10 9 8 7 6 5 4 3

BRIEF CONTENTS

CONTENTS

PREFACE

My husband and I joke a lot about our sons. One of our sons is easily influenced by the threat of punishment. He will pretty much do anything to not receive a time-out. He is our gentle giant. Our other son is unconcerned by punishment, and we refer to him as our mafia don. I have a sneaking suspicion we may be bailing him out of juvie one day. Or he will become the next Zen Master—it could go either way. I love to watch these two kids and wonder what their futures will hold. Will they be into theater? And sports? Will they love school, like I did? Or rather spend all day outside talking each other into jumping off the roof of the house like my husband and his brother did? Will we hit a rough patch where they won't want to talk to us? Will they come out the other side of their teenage years happy and healthy, with a strong dose of empathy for their fellow citizens?

One of the things I wonder most about my kids is whether they will engage in delinquency—or actually, more to the point, whether they will be caught and end up in the juvenile justice system. As you will see (and as you know, if you have ever been a teenager), almost everyone engages in some form of juvenile delinquency, or status offense, or ends up being a victim of it. The reasons for this are many, but two of the largest are that, first, the term *juvenile delinquency* (in addition to *status offense*) covers such a large array of behaviors and, second, we are constantly redefining behaviors that in the past were not considered delinquency and making them so. As the mother of two amazing boys, this scares the heck out of me and at the same time makes me certain that the study of juvenile delinquency and our societal responses to it is one of the most important academic endeavors a sociologist, a criminologist, or you, an undergraduate student, faces. I have taught juvenile delinquency for almost two decades. I never tire of the opportunity to explore this topic with undergraduates, but I have always wished that there were a text more dedicated to diversity that made central discussions of race, class, gender, and sexuality issues (or, in many instances, an acknowledgment of the lack of research in these areas). Enter my colleague and friend, Richelle Swan.

The two of us wrote this book. And throughout the text you will see examples and stories that come from our lives and scenarios based on the lives of others. At times, we have written these in the first person—some are from Kristin, some from Richelle— but all illustrate the importance of a critical understanding of juvenile delinquency in a diverse society. So why did we write this book? While teaching juvenile delinquency we have observed several things: (1) Most books take a mainstream approach to juvenile delinquency and fail to emphasize the social diversity that explains varying experiences and behavior; (2) many students have never been introduced to a systematic critical approach to evaluating social behavior and social institutions such as juvenile delinquency and the juvenile justice system; (3) students learn more from real-world examples (of both delinquency and public policy) than they do from purely theoretical discussions; and (4) after taking a juvenile delinquency course, students are often more inspired to "do more" or "get involved" than they are at the end of almost any other course in the area of criminology.

This textbook is written from a critical perspective. It offers several innovative features that set it apart from other textbooks on the market. First, it offers a systematic critical understanding of juvenile delinquency, focusing on issues of race, class, and gender. Second, it substantively links theories of delinquency, not only to existing public policies but to existing community programs that focus on a critical response to juvenile delinquency and social control. And, finally, it guides you, the student, to explore the diversity in your own community and what this means for juvenile delinquency and social control where you live.

WHAT'S NEW?

Preparing a new edition of a book is both a rewarding and scary prospect. Rewarding because it suggests that the previous editions have been well-received and students and colleagues see some merit in the book. However, if the previous editions have been well-received, it is scary to change what we and others have grown to love. We wish to emphasize again how great the reviewers of our earlier efforts were. They helped guide several new substantive directions and also helped us maintain the philosophy and heart of the book as one that explores juvenile delinquency in a diverse society:

- We reorganized each chapter to remove the spotlight boxes and, where appropriate, incorporate this information into the body of the text.

- This allowed us to add a new textbox, On the Media, to each chapter that explores the impact of social media and new technologies on our understanding of juvenile delinquency.

- Throughout the book, we updated the research and, where possible, included more extensive discussions of LGBTQ youth, American Indian youth, and Asian and Pacific Islander youth.

- We also added tables in the theory chapters of the book (Chapters 4, 5, and 6) that summarize the theories' main points.

- In Chapter 1, we added a new section on the juvenile justice system and diversity to introduce the topics that are found in the last four chapters of the book.

- In Chapter 2, we expanded the discussion of media panics about delinquency to include more on gaming and delinquency and the Internet and delinquency.

- In Chapter 3, we updated all the tables and figures to include the new trends that have developed in official and self-reported data on juvenile delinquency.

- In Chapter 4, we included extensive discussions of pre-classical, classical, biological, biosocial, and psychological theories. In addition, we offer a current example of the Flint, Michigan water crisis in the context of these theories.

- In Chapter 5, we updated the research on macro-structural theories and added an analysis of social disorganization and mass incarceration.

- In Chapter 6, we added consideration of gendered pathways theory.

- In Chapter 7, we added a new section on foster care and foster youth.

- In Chapter 8, we added a section on the school and student rights with a discussion of Supreme Court cases.

- In Chapter 9, we significantly expanded the section on the use of technology as a means of peer interaction and updated the discussion of sexting.

- In Chapter 10, we incorporated information about family drug use and significantly updated data related to the use of legal products and youth substance use patterns. We also added an expanded analysis of the war on drugs and an analysis of the effects of marijuana legalization on youth.

- In Chapter 11, we added the most recent decisions on juvenile justice by the U.S. Supreme Court and updated the section on the future of juvenile justice.

- In Chapter 12, we included an extensive discussion of the police and juveniles.

- In Chapter 13, we added to the discussion of life without parole and solitary confinement for juveniles.

- In Chapter 14, we revised the prevention section to have stronger emphasis on the structural factors needed for effective delinquency prevention, added a consideration of diverting victims of sexual exploitation from detention, and added a new section on restorative justice and LGBT youth.

- Finally, we created pretests with answers for each chapter.

SPECIAL TOOLS FOR LEARNING

Our goals are made evident in each chapter and throughout the text through a variety of specific learning features:

- Juvenile Delinquency Vignette: Each chapter opens with a vignette that illustrates the concepts of the chapter from a diverse or critical perspective. These vignettes are used throughout the chapters to illustrate chapter concepts.

- In the News: One of the most successful parts of our juvenile delinquency courses is making the concepts of juvenile delinquency come alive to students by linking them to current events. Each chapter offers an example of a current event (in box format) that links a main concept from that chapter to a "real world" example.

- From the Classroom to the Community: This box will focus on how social science can influence/shape public policy and community experiences. We highlight examples of collaborative learning and community action and/or specific public policies addressing juveniles and juvenile delinquency.

- A Focus on Research: Each chapter highlights an influential piece of research that focuses on the experiences of a diverse population with juvenile delinquency and/or social control. For example, we focus on research on foster children, runaways, LGBTQ youth, youth of color, poor youth, and girls (among other diverse populations).

- On the Media: Each chapter will include a consideration of how different forms of traditional or social media are used to convey ideas about delinquency or to publicize acts of delinquency.

- Eye on Diversity Exercise: While each chapter will have woven throughout its main text a sociological discussion of the relationship between a diverse society and juvenile delinquency, each chapter will also end with a very specific class exercise or service learning example that can be used as either a starting point for class discussion or a class activity/assignment.

- Discussion Questions: Each chapter additionally has a set of thought-provoking questions that can be used as the basis of in-class or online discussions. These questions draw upon material from the entire chapter and serve as good review tools.

- Chapter Pretest: Each chapter starts with a True/False pretest that allows students to test their knowledge before reading the chapter, to help address misconceptions up front. The answers are found at the end of the chapter.

DIGITAL RESOURCES

SAGE edge offers a robust online environment featuring an impressive array of tools and resources for review, study, and further exploration, keeping both instructors and students on the cutting edge of teaching and learning. SAGE edge content is open access and available on demand. Learning and teaching has never been easier!

edge.sagepub.com/bates2e

Instructor Teaching Site

SAGE edge for Instructors supports teaching by making it easy to integrate quality content and create a rich learning environment for students.

These resources include an extensive test bank, chapter-specific PowerPoint presentations, lecture notes, sample syllabi for semester and quarter courses, SAGE journal articles with accompanying review questions, video links, and web resources.

Student Study Site

SAGE edge for Students provides a personalized approach to help students accomplish their coursework goals in an easy-to-use learning environment.

This site includes mobile-friendly eFlashcards and web quizzes, SAGE journal articles with accompanying review questions, video links, and web resources.

In the end, what we wanted to write was a text that sparks your critical sociological imaginations; that helps you understand our diverse society and the connections between individual experiences, social institutions, and power; and that helps you see there are important questions (and continuing questions) about how we define and how we respond to juvenile delinquency. But, most importantly, we hope this text inspires you to wonder about the future of the children around you and inspires you to act for those children. As you will see, there is a lot to do.

However this text inspires you, we wish you the best in your explorations.

ACKNOWLEDGMENTS

Our deepest appreciation to Jerry Westby at SAGE Publications. Jerry championed our vision with sincerity, warmth, and humor. Special thanks to Jerry's team for help with our second edition: Jessica Miller, Laura Kirkhuff, Jennifer Rubio, David Felts, and Diana Breti. We also thank Theresa Accomazzo and Megan Krattli, MaryAnn Vail, Rachael Leblond, Laura Barrett, Melinda Masson, and Scott Van Atta for their help on the first edition of this book. The team at SAGE was devoted to creating a text that was true to our vision and that would speak to both instructors and students.

We want to especially thank the California State University, San Marcos Department of Sociology. Our colleagues are truly outstanding. They support our professional endeavors, but, even more important, they support us personally. Their open hearts and critical perspective enrich our lives in and outside of work. It is wonderful to be inspired and to learn from our colleagues and friends. Hard to believe we are lucky enough to build careers here! We would also like to thank all of our students—they know that we often run ideas for our books by them in class and we really appreciate their feedback. In addition, we would like to thank the student research assistants who helped us stay up to date on the latest findings related to juvenile delinquency: Lexus Criswell, Jennifer Seidlitz, Olivia Victory, Sharghi Jami, Miranda Mendez, Emely Yanagida, Claudia Caywood, and Xochitl Palacios. Big thanks to Jeff Henson and Allen Lanese for all the computing help they provided us during moments of desperation. We would also like to thank the individuals who contributed to our online resource sites: Dawn Lee, Olivia Victory, Robbin Brooks and Rachael Zeller, Rita Naranjo, Diego Avalos, and Leo Sanchez.

Kristin would like to thank her graduate school mentors and friends from the University of Washington Department of Sociology: Bob Crutchfield, George Bridges, Joe Weis, Michelle Inderbitzin, Randy Gainey, Charis Kubrin, Sara Steen, Rod Engen, Edie Simpson, Ed Day, Chris Bader, and Tim Wadsworth. I am told our time at the UW is not the usual graduate school experience—all I know is seeing you guys is like coming home to family. Speaking of family, a big sloppy kiss to my parents (Bill and Dee Ann) and sisters (Laurie and Julie) who taught me that a fierce love and a great sense of humor are the best foundations for a happy life. I owe much of my sanity to the Friday night group: I hope when we are 80 we are still dedicated to a Friday night of carbs, good beer, and an ardent protection of the no-fun zone. Special thanks to Sharon Elise, Marisol Clark-Ibáñez, Kim Knowles-Yanez, Deirdre Lowell-Caldera, and Heather Craig, the women in my life who remind me to stop and breathe and take a little time with friends. And to Richelle Swan, my daytime partner: I understand how lucky I am to have a colleague (but, more important, a friend) who I can talk into crazy projects, to whom I feel comfortable reading my first drafts and unorganized thoughts, and who is so gentle with her critiques and lessons. I am not sure where I would be without you, and I know I wouldn't have had half the fun getting there. Finally, all my love to Jeff, my nighttime partner: the yin to my yang, the type B to my type A, the up to my down. Thank you for making me laugh about doing all my work while crying.

Richelle would like to thank her mentors and professors from her two graduate programs at Arizona State University (Justice Studies) and the University of California at Irvine (Criminology, Law and Society) who sparked her interest in issues of law, delinquency, and social justice: John Dombrink, Kitty Calavita, Valerie Jenness, and Diego Vigil. In particular, I would like to thank Peg Bortner as the inspiration for much of the writing about youth that I am doing today. In addition, I'd like to express an enormous amount of appreciation and gratitude to Kristin Bates, my research and writing partner. I am so lucky to have met such a generous and intelligent friend and mentor. I am very thankful for all of your ingenious ideas and plans that you share with me and know there will be many more to come! I would also like to thank my parents, Sharon and Richard, for their unbelievable generosity and support through this and every other project I've ever pursued. Similarly, I'd like to thank my sister, Alicia, and all the other members of my family for the encouragement they gave me throughout the process. In particular, I'd like to thank Chendo for always being there for me, for his patience with my work schedule, and for the laughter he provided when I needed it the most. The valuable support of Maricela Chaídez, Marisol Clark-Ibáñez, Mercedes Ibáñez, Fay McGrew, Theresa Suarez, and Sharon Elise also helped me during both stages of this project. Thanks to all of you!

We are particularly grateful to the reviewers who provided valuable feedback on the manuscript.

Reviewers for the Second Edition

Margie Ballard-Mack, South Carolina State University

Amanda Barrientez, University of Colorado Boulder

James Blair, South Texas College

Michael D. Collins, William Penn University

Brandi Copenhaver, Somerset Community College

Nancy A. Horton, Kaplan University

James M. Stewart, Calhoun Community College

Reviewers for the First Edition

Kathryn Branch, University of Tampa–Tampa

Robbin Brooks, Arizona State University–Downtown Phoenix

Adam Langsam, Northwestern Oklahoma State University–Enid

Shanell Sanchez-Smith, University of Nebraska–Lincoln

Miyuki Tedor, Cleveland State University–Cleveland

Shela Van Ness, University of Tennessee–Chattanooga

Elizabeth Legerski, University of North Dakota School of Law–Grand Forks

Gregory Lindsteadt, Missouri Western State College–Saint Joseph

Tamara Lynn, Fort Hays State University–Hays

Mónica Herrera Pérez, Holyoke Community College—Holyoke

Edward Powers, University of Central Arkansas–Conway

Martine Wehr, Saddleback College–Mission Viejo

Justin Pickett, State University of New York–Albany

Verna Jones, Jackson State University–Jackson

Jeri Kirby, West Virginia University–Morgantown

Lisa Kort-Butler, University of Nebraska–Lincoln

Lois Presser, University of Tennessee–Knoxville

Victor Shaw, California State University–Northridge

Julie White, University of Massachusetts–Boston

Kareem Jordan, University of Central Florida–Orlando

Keith Durkin, Ohio Northern University–Ada

Kristen DeVall, University of North Carolina–Wilmington

Nadine Connell, University of Texas at Dallas–Richardson

SAGE was founded in 1965 by Sara Miller McCune to support the dissemination of usable knowledge by publishing innovative and high-quality research and teaching content. Today, we publish over 900 journals, including those of more than 400 learned societies, more than 800 new books per year, and a growing range of library products including archives, data, case studies, reports, and video. SAGE remains majority-owned by our founder, and after Sara's lifetime will become owned by a charitable trust that secures our continued independence.

Los Angeles | London | New Delhi | Singapore | Washington DC | Melbourne

PART 1:
UNDERSTANDING JUVENILE DELINQUENCY

THINKING ABOUT JUVENILE DELINQUENCY IN A DIVERSE SOCIETY

CHAPTER OBJECTIVES ·····················

After reading this chapter, you should be able to

- Describe why juveniles are treated differently than adults

- Explain the difference between juvenile delinquency and status offenses

- Summarize the three conceptions of delinquency and how they relate to our responses to juvenile delinquency

- Identify the social context in which juveniles are living and its effect on the well-being of children

- Compare and contrast the concepts of individual and institutional racism, classism, and sexism

- Explain why intersectionality is important

- Describe the role of the sociological imagination in explaining the societal response to juvenile delinquency

Michael was in trouble, again, for stealing cigarettes from the store (this was the sixth time he had been caught). He was only 10 years old, and it was suspected that his father had made Michael steal. He had been referred to juvenile court. Michael was a quiet child, with a younger sister at home. He lived part-time with his father and part-time with his mother and qualified for a pilot program of the juvenile court that provided transportation to his court hearings because his mother had no means of taking him herself. He met with his probation officer and attended his hearings, but never really participated in the court activities. Michael did not appear remorseful for his actions. In fact, he did not appear to care about much except his younger sister. One day his probation officer bought him a hamburger, but the boy wouldn't eat it in the car. The probation officer thought he was worried about getting the car dirty, but the boy said he was saving it to share with his sister. The next time the probation officer met with Michael, he asked him how he and his sister had liked the burger. Michael told him that the little girl had dropped her half in the dirt, so Michael had given her his half of the burger and eaten nothing himself. So yesterday, Michael was picked up a sixth time for stealing cigarettes at the corner store. What should happen to Michael?

Anthony had never been in trouble. He was also 10 years old. He was caught yesterday beating a neighborhood boy with a large stick. He broke the boy's nose and his arm and chipped a tooth. Anthony claimed that the boy started it by always calling him names and bullying him and his friend. Anthony says that while he was walking home alone the boy started to call him names again and throw rocks at him. Anthony did have multiple bruises, but no one could tell if these bruises came from the rocks or the boy defending himself from Anthony's attack. When the police approached Anthony, he immediately started to cry and say he was sorry. He asked for his parents, whom the police called. Anthony had never mentioned the bullying to his parents, or any other adults in his life, but both his parents said that since school started this year, Anthony had been a bit more withdrawn about school. What should happen to Anthony?

● ● ●

the general policy is that juveniles should not be arrested or formally treated by the juvenile court for behavior that falls in this category. But, in reality, sometimes they are, especially if they are considered "chronic status offenders." Chronic status offenders are those who engage in repeated and systematic behavior even after the behavior has been addressed by school, family, or a social service agency.

CONCEPTIONS OF JUVENILE DELINQUENCY

Normative Conception of Delinquency

How we define juvenile delinquency is also dependent on our general conceptions of misbehavior and deviance. Many believe that juvenile delinquency is a social construct, and even those who believe in a more normative conception of delinquency acknowledge that race, class, and gender (among other such concepts as age, sexual orientation, nationality, and ability) are somehow connected to delinquency.

●●●

Normative conception of delinquency:
A conception that assumes that there is a general set of norms of behavior, conduct, and conditions with which we can agree.

It is more likely deviance textbooks than delinquency textbooks that discuss conceptions of deviance and delinquency, but it is important to understand that our definitions of delinquency are not black-and-white. They are based on conceptual orientations about how definitions are created. Rubington and Weinberg argue that there are generally two ways of conceptualizing deviance and delinquency as either "objectively given" or "subjectively problematic."[3] Clinard and Meier also suggest two general conceptions, the reactionist or relativist conception and the normative conception.[4] Thio argues that we can view deviance from a positivist perspective or a constructionist perspective.[5]

While none of these authors are using the same language, they are defining similar ways of conceptualizing "misbehavior." The first conception—that of an "objectively given," normative, or positivist conception of deviance—assumes that there is a general set of norms of behavior, conduct, and conditions with which we can all agree. Norms are rules of behavior that guide people's actions. W. G. Sumner broke norms down into three categories: folkways, mores, and laws. Folkways are everyday norms that do not generate much uproar if they are violated.[6] Think of them as behaviors that might be considered rude if engaged in—like standing too close to someone while speaking or picking one's nose. Mores are "moral" norms that may generate more outrage if broken. In a capitalist society, homelessness and unemployment can elicit outrage if the person is considered unworthy of sympathy. Similarly, drinking too much or alcoholism may be seen as a lapse in moral judgment. Finally, the third type of norm is the law, which is considered the strongest norm because it is backed by official sanctions (or a formal response). In this conception, then, deviance and delinquency becomes a violation of a rule understood by the majority of the group. This rule may be minor, in which case the individual is seen as fairly harmless, or the rule may be major, in which case the individual is seen as "criminal." The obvious problem with this conceptualization goes back to the earlier example of Michael and Anthony. It is unlikely you and your classmates agree on the definition of delinquency and crime in those two cases. This leads to the second conception.

Many behaviors that are not considered crimes for adults are still considered wrong for juveniles. These acts are called status offenses.

Social Constructionist Conception of Delinquency

The second conception of delinquency—the "subjectively problematic," reactionist/relativist, social constructionist conception—assumes that the definition of deviance and delinquency is constructed based on the interactions of those in society. According to this conception, behaviors or conditions are not inherently deviant; they become so when the definition of deviance is applied to them. The study of deviance is not about why certain individuals violate norms, but instead about how those norms are constructed. Social constructionists believe that our understanding of the world is in constant negotiation between actors. Those who have a relativist conception define deviance and delinquency as those behaviors that elicit a definition or label of deviance:

> Social groups create deviance by making the rules whose infraction constitutes deviance, and by applying those rules to particular people and labeling them as outsiders. For this point of view, deviance is not a quality of the act the person commits but rather a consequence of the application by others of rules and sanctions to an "offender." The deviant is one to whom that label has successfully been applied; deviant behavior is behavior that people so label.[7]

This is a fruitful conceptualization, but is also problematic. What about very serious violations of norms that are never known or reacted to? Some strict reactionists/relativists would argue that these acts (beliefs or attitudes) are not deviant. Most of us would agree that killing someone and making it look like he simply skipped the country is deviant; however, there may be no reaction.

Folkways: Everyday norms that do not generate much uproar if they are violated.

Mores: "Moral" norms that may generate more outrage if broken.

Laws: The strongest norms because they are backed by official sanctions.

Social constructions of delinquency: Popular ideas about delinquency that are created and influenced by social, political, and economic factors and that change over time.

Critical Conception of Delinquency

A third conception of deviance and delinquency that has not been advanced in many text-books is a critical conception.[8] Those working from a critical conception argue that the normative understanding of deviance and delinquency is established by those in power to maintain and enhance their power. It suggests that explorations of both have focused on a white, male, middle- to upper-class understanding of society that implies that people of color, girls, and youth from working poor neighborhoods are, by definition, delinquent. Instead of focusing on individual types of deviance or delinquency, this conception critiques the social system that exists that creates such norms in the first place. This too is a useful approach, but, frankly, there are many things that the vast majority of society agrees are immoral, unethical, and deviant and should be illegal, and the system actually serves to protect society's interests. This book adopts a critical approach to crime and delinquency, but offers a discussion of the theories that fall under both the normative conception and the social constructionist conception of delinquency (see Table 1.1).

THE WELL-BEING OF CHILDREN

In order to better understand juvenile behavior (delinquent and nondelinquent) in the United States, it is important to understand the social context in which juveniles are living. Since 1994, the Office of Management and Budget (OMB) has partnered with several other federal agencies to track the well-being of children in the United States. Its priorities were to foster better collection of data and communication between agencies and the community on the state of children and childhood. Part of this effort is a yearly report, *America's Children in Brief: Key National Indicators of Well-Being.*[9] The report tracks seven key areas of well-being, including family and social environment, economic circumstances, health care, physical environment and safety, behavior, education, and health.

The most recent study reports that there were 73.6 million children (ages 0–17) in the United States in 2014. These numbers are projected to increase over the next 30 years. Approximately one third of those children fall in the age range of 12–17 (25 million, 2014 numbers). While the overall number of children has been increasing in recent years (and the increase is projected to continue), the proportion of children to adults has been decreasing, down from 36% in 1964 to 23.1% in 2014. This decrease in proportion of the entire population is due largely to the decrease in the mortality rate (i.e., people are living longer).

TABLE 1.1 Summary of Conceptions of Delinquency

CONCEPTIONS OF DELINQUENCY	DELINQUENCY IS . . .	KEY PROPOSITIONS
Normative	A violation of norms, rules, or the law	Delinquency is caused by biological, psychological, environmental, or social factors that impact individuals or communities.
Social Constructionist	Constructed by society	Behaviors are not inherently delinquent, but they become so once society determines that they are delinquent.
Critical	Established by those in power to maintain and enhance their power	Previous explorations of delinquency have focused on a white, male, middle- to upper-class understanding of society that implies that people of color, girls, and youth from working poor neighborhoods are, by definition, delinquent. Instead, this conception critiques the social system that establishes these beliefs and norms in the first place.

● ● ●

Critical conception of delinquency: A conception that critiques the existing social system that creates norms of oppression.

A Focus on Research

Samuel Phillips Day's "Juvenile Crime: Its Cause, Character, and Cure"

In 1858, Samuel Phillips Day wrote an article on juvenile delinquents, titled "Juvenile Crime: Its Cause, Character, and Cure." Day argued that examining juvenile crime is even more important that examining adult crime, because the juvenile is the embodiment of the future and the past. Day listed the causes of delinquency as "pauperism, compulsion, evil example, temptation, and hereditary predisposition; incommodious dwellings and low lodging-houses; ignorance, intemperance, minor theatres, penny gaffs, dancing and singing saloons, gaming and betting."[10]

As to the cure for delinquency, Day lamented the misdirection of "current" programs and policies, the waste of resources put toward these misguided programs, and the indifference he felt that much of society had for saving children. "There is more wisdom, more care, more knowledge applied in England, if not elsewhere, to the origin and growth of animals than to human beings; the latter owe their origin and growth to fortuitous circumstances, the former to intelligent care and scientific foresight. It is to this unpardonable neglect and stultified apathy that are due the horrible crimes and miseries set forth."[11]

Day concluded that while the "old" are beyond training, society should focus on the young because the young can still be saved from bad families and bad social training.

DISCUSSION QUESTION

1. As you read the chapters in this book, think about Day's characterization of juveniles and the causes of juvenile delinquency. Do we still characterize juveniles and juvenile delinquency this way?

Racial and ethnic diversity is also increasing among children. In 2014, 51.9% of children were white (non-Hispanic), 24.4% were Hispanic, 13.8% were black, 4.8% were Asian, 0.9% were American Indian or Alaskan Native, 0.2% were Native Hawaiian or Other Pacific Islander, and 4.1% were two or more races.[12] It is projected that by 2050, Latino children will be 32% of children, with white children making up 39% of the child population.

Economic Circumstances

The report offers several indicators of the economic well-being of children. The percentage of children living in poverty has increased in the last decade from its low in 2000 and 2001 of 16% to 20% in 2013. But what is most striking is the link between race and ethnicity and the likelihood of living in poverty. In 2013, 39% of black, non-Hispanic children; 30% of Hispanic children; and 11% of white, non-Hispanic children lived in poverty. This means that the poverty rate was 3.5 times higher for black than for white youth and almost 3 times higher for Latino children than for white children. And as for a statistic that might be an indicator of the growing gap between those at the bottom and those at the top, both the percentage of children living in extreme poverty and the percentage of those living in households with very high incomes increased (extreme poverty increased from 7% to 9% between 2000 and 2013, and very high-income households increased from 7% to 13% between 1991 and 2013). In addition, 21% of children (15.8 million) lived in a household that was considered food insecure in 2013. Food insecurity is defined as reduced food intake; difficulty obtaining food, including a poor-quality diet because food cannot be obtained; and anxiety about obtaining food. While some food-insecure households managed to keep the effects from the children in the household (the adults reported they went without food so that the children did not have to), a majority of the households reported that children's eating patterns and diets were affected, too.

One of the most troubling conditions in the United States is the number of children living in poverty. Almost 1 in 4 children live below the poverty level, with proportionally more youth of color than white youth living in poverty.

Physical Environment and Safety

Although the percentage of children living in polluted conditions has decreased, in 2013, approximately 50% of all children still lived in an area where at least one air pollutant was above the allowable levels. Water pollutants have also decreased since these reports were first created. The percentage of children who lived in areas where the community drinking water did not meet health-based standards decreased from 18% in 1993 to 6% in 2013 (although it has fluctuated between 5% and 11% over the past 15 years). Although air and water pollutants have been decreasing, inadequate housing has been increasing for children. Inadequate housing is measured by crowding, physical inadequateness, and cost burden (greater than 30% of family income). Forty percent of households with children suffer from at least one of these housing problems. In addition, "during 2009, an estimated 346,000 children utilized homeless shelters or transitional housing services, a rate of 4.6 per 1,000 children."[13] And, an estimated 138,000 children, or 2 per 1,000 children, were found to be homeless during at least one night in 2013.

Education

Educational attainment has also been increasing for juveniles. The percentage of children graduating with a diploma or GED increased from 84% to 92% between 1980 and 2013. But these levels were not the same for all children. White children increased their graduation rate from 87% in 1980 to 94% in 2013, while black children increased their rate from 75% in 1980 to 92% in 2013. Latino children had the greatest percentage increase, but they had consistently lower graduation rates than either white or black children: 57% in 1980 and 85% in 2013.

In addition to high school graduation rates, the percentage of those who enroll in college right after high school has increased (although it has fluctuated) from 49% in 1980 to 66% in 2013. These percentages have also been dependent on race and ethnicity. White youth are more likely to immediately enroll in college (67%) compared to black (57%) and Latino (66%) youth. Gender also influences this likelihood. In 2013, 64% of males, but 68% of females, immediately enrolled in college. Although the percentages by gender fluctuate significantly, for many years there was no statistical difference in the likelihood to enroll by gender. It is interesting to note that the likelihood to enroll in college decreased for all groups (except Latinos) between 2009 and 2013, perhaps due to the impact of the economic challenges in the United States and their effect on the affordability of college.

The Cradle-to-Prison Pipeline

A black boy born in 2001 has a 1 in 3 chance of going to prison in his lifetime; a Latino boy a 1 in 6 chance; and a white boy a 1 in 17 chance. A black girl born in 2001 has a 1 in 17 chance of going to prison in her lifetime; a Latina girl a 1 in 45 chance; and a white girl a 1 in 111 chance.[14]

While many well-being indicators for youth are decreasing, educational attainment is increasing; however, compared to other countries (see Chapter 8, on schools and delinquency), the United States still lags behind.

The Children's Defense Fund, a nonprofit organization, has identified a phenomenon it refers to as the cradle-to-prison pipeline (see Figure 1.1; in Chapter 8 you will learn about the school-to-prison pipeline). The cradle-to-prison pipeline refers to the many issues for children that make it more likely they will become incarcerated at some stage in their lives. These issues include pervasive poverty, inadequate access to health coverage, gaps in early childhood development, disparate educational opportunities, intolerable abuse and neglect, unmet mental and emotional problems, substance abuse, and overburdened, ineffective educational and juvenile justice systems that focus on zero tolerance and other suppression policies.[15]

What do these indicators tell us about the overall health and well-being of juveniles in this country? For the most part, indicators tell us that children are doing better in many ways now than they were 40 years ago—children are less likely to be living in a polluted area and more likely to have clean drinking water, more likely to graduate from high school, and more likely to enroll immediately in college. However, there are several things of which to be cautious. First, even though conditions are getting better for youth in some arenas, economic conditions are actually worse for children; more youth live in economic uncertainty now, insecure about both shelter and food. And both the gains and the losses made for children are dependent on race and ethnicity, gender, and class. In other words, whether a juvenile is black, Latino, white, Native American, or Asian, and whether the juvenile is male or female, or from a working poor or well-off family, impacts his or her experiences in the United States.

THE UNITED STATES AS A PLACE WHERE RACE, CLASS, GENDER, AND SEXUALITY ARE IMPORTANT

What does it mean when we say that in the United States race, class, and gender still matter? It means that in the United States we have different experiences based on our race/ethnicity, class, and gender (we also have different experiences based on our age,

FIGURE 1.1   The Cradle-to-Prison Pipeline

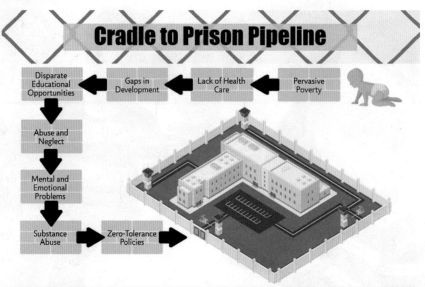

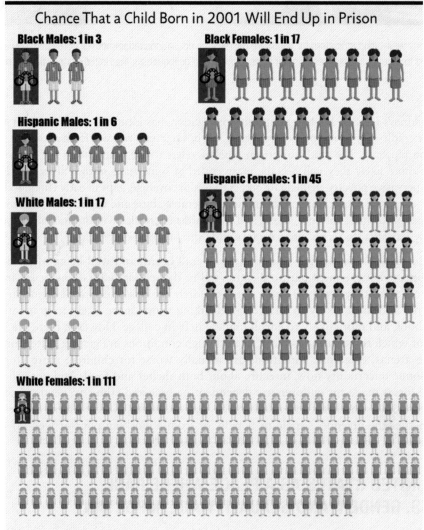

Source: Created using piktochart.com.

from the CLASSROOM to the COMMUNITY

Center on Wrongful Convictions of Youth

The Center on Wrongful Convictions of Youth is a project at the Northwestern University School of Law that investigates convictions of youth who have some credible basis for a claim of innocence. It is the only innocence project in the country that focuses on juveniles (instead of adults). The center believes that age may be a contributing factor to a wrongful conviction.

Among the leading contributors to wrongful convictions are false confessions. While it seems unlikely to many of us that we would ever falsely confess to a serious crime we did not commit, this has happened in numerous cases. Youth are overrepresented in false confession wrongful convictions. There are several reasons this is the case. First, law enforcement interrogation tactics are designed to be unbearable; police emphasize that the individual is already caught, and there is little to no hope that the accused will go free. In addition, the techniques include long periods of interrogation and, oftentimes, false information about the state of the case. These tactics are allowed to be used on juveniles. Second, youth are socialized to respect authority and authority figures such as the police. The combination of harsh tactics and youth who often trust and want to please the police means that false confessions can be likely. Youth who made false confessions and were finally exonerated report that they thought if they told the police what they wanted to hear they would be able to go home to their families.

In addition, juveniles are unsophisticated and are, therefore, less aware of their rights and less likely to be able to understand the long-term consequences of their confessions. Even when read their *Miranda* rights juveniles often do not understand the intricacies of those rights (for example, that they are allowed to actually remain silent and not answer police questions). The combination of not understanding their rights and failing to recognize the long-term consequences of confessing means that youth will falsely confess in hopes of getting out of the interrogation room. As of 2016, more than 100 individuals convicted as youth have had their cases overturned as wrongful convictions, and some of these individuals spent more than 20 years in prison before they were exonerated.

DISCUSSION QUESTIONS

1. What are the reasons that youth might offer a false confession to a crime they did not commit? How is it that juveniles might be more susceptible to these confessions than adults?

2. What safeguards could be put in place to ensure that juveniles do not engage in false confessions?

Source: Center on Wrongful Convictions of Youth. (2009). Northwestern University School of Law. Retrieved from http://cwcy .org/Default.aspx

sexual orientation, nationality, and abilities). One of the reasons we have these different experiences is because in the United States we define, describe, and distinguish people based on these different categories. This process is called social differentiation.[16] Some categories are ascribed, meaning you are born into them and cannot change them; your race is an example of this. Some categories are achieved, meaning that they are more flexible, or that you have a better chance of changing them if you wish (or you can try to change them); your social class and religion are examples of these. Social differentiation leads to ranking; in other words, as we differentiate between people based on certain categories, we tend to rank the levels of these categories. For example, is it better to be rich or poor, educated or not educated, an adult or a child? These rankings are what form social inequality. Once the levels of a category such as age, race, gender, or class have had values placed on them (i.e., they have been ranked), we have placed "judgments of inequalities" on them.[17] We have implicitly or explicitly decided it is better to be one value in that category than another. These value judgments may be more implicit than

Social differentiation: The process by which we define, describe, and distinguish people based on different categories.

Ascribed category: A category that an individual is born into and cannot change.

explicit, but that doesn't mean they don't exist. For example, no one comes right out and says it is better to be an adult than a child, and, in fact, some who have an idealized sense of childhood may argue that being a child is better. But when you examine the level of power that is conferred on adulthood and childhood, it is easy to see that juveniles have much less power than adults have. They are more oppressed and rely on the "kindness of strangers" more than adults.

Individual Versus Institutional Racism, Classism, and Sexism

Individual racism, classism, or sexism occur when individuals hold personal attitudes of prejudice based on race, class, or gender and act on these attitudes in a discriminatory fashion.[18] This prejudice and discrimination can appear as the stereotyping of individuals based on their race, class, or gender. An example of this is the stereotype that girls are more delicate and prone to crying and hysteria than boys so they should not be trusted to do certain jobs or be in charge of important events. Sometimes individual racism, classism, and sexism are most evident in a person's speech; especially among young people they might manifest themselves in name-calling and bullying. But individual acts of racism, classism, and sexism can have a strong impact on the juvenile experience beyond bullying. For example, a teacher who assumes that most young, Latino men are in gangs has made a racist assumption that might impact the education that young Latinos receive in his classroom. A police officer who has classist beliefs about who is most likely to use drugs (she believes that working-class juveniles use drugs more than wealthy juveniles) might focus her policing in poor neighborhoods or handle teens from rich neighborhoods informally by taking them home to their parents if they get in trouble, while handling poorer teens formally and arresting them for their bad behavior.

Although racism, sexism, and classism were more overt in the past (e.g., schools—and other institutions—were segregated), there are still many examples of race, class, and gender impacting individual experiences in the United States. How might the experiences of these children differ over time?

• • •

Achieved category: A flexible category that individuals may be able to move in and out of.

Social inequality: Unequal distribution of resources, services, and positions.

Individual classism: Prejudice or discrimination based solely on someone's class.

Individual racism: The belief in the inferiority of certain racial or ethnic groups, often accompanied by discrimination.

Individual sexism: Prejudice or discrimination based solely on someone's sex.

Institutional classism: Classism that occurs when individuals are disadvantaged or oppressed because of their class because of the routine workings of social institutions.

Institutional racism: Racism that occurs when individuals are disadvantaged or oppressed because of their race because of the routine workings of social institutions.

In the News

The Income Gap

A lot has been heard in the news lately about the income gap in the United States and the world. The United States ranks worse than most of Europe and Asia, including India and China, and large parts of Africa. While no country has income equality, the gap has been increasing significantly in the United States over the last 30 years. The average household income (adjusted for inflation) has not changed over the last three decades while the average household income for the top 1% has almost quadrupled (see Figure 1.2). The gap is puz-

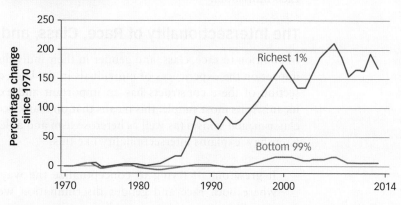

FIGURE 1.2 The Income Gap in the United States, 1970–2014

Source: Gilson and Perot (2011).

zling to some economists who see industrialized countries as the least likely to experience an income gap. The idea is that a gap forms and exists for a while with a transition from one economic system, say agrarian to industrialized, but eventually those at the bottom start to catch up as everyone moves into better-paying jobs. However, this has not happened this time. One of the speculations is that education is not affordable for all households in the United States, so those in the bottom percentiles do not have the resources and therefore the opportunity to advance, while those at the top continue to accumulate wealth. We expect this will have a detrimental effect on juveniles in the United States if education remains out of reach for a portion of them.

DISCUSSION QUESTION

1. In addition to a lack of education, what might be other reasons that the income gap in the United States is increasing instead of decreasing? When coming up with your answers, determine whether you are focusing on characteristics of those in the upper or lower economic groups or on broader, macro concerns, such as institutional characteristics.

Individual racism, classism, and sexism are important aspects of the juvenile experience in the United States, but institutional racism, classism, and sexism probably have a far greater impact on the juvenile experience. Institutional racism, classism, and/or sexism occur when individuals are disadvantaged because of their race, class, or gender because of the routine workings of institutions in the United States.[19] Institutions refer to organizational structures such as the political system, the legal system, media, and education. For the purposes of this book, we are most concerned with institutional racism, classism, and sexism that might exist in the criminal and juvenile justice systems and the educational system.

For example, the adult criminal justice system is still a very classist system of justice. How so? In its simplest terms, individuals will have a very different experience in the system based on how much money they have. Requiring bail means that those who can afford to pay will spend their time before trial at home, while those who cannot

●●●
Institutional sexism: Sexism that occurs when individuals are disadvantaged or oppressed because of their sex or gender because of the routine workings of social institutions.

pay will spend their time before trial in a jail. Don't ever underestimate the benefit of living at home, instead of jail, while waiting for trial. Those who are at home can participate in their legal defense in a way that those in jail cannot. Those at home have the benefit of friends and family around them in a way that those in jail do not. Those at home arrive at their trial in street clothes, better fed, better rested, and better prepared in a way than those in jail. All else being equal between the individual who can pay bail and the one who cannot, the ability to make bail affects the experience of each individual.

The Intersectionality of Race, Class, and Gender

In addition to race, class, and gender in their individual constructs having an important impact on the experiences of individuals in the United States, many argue that the intersection of these constructs has an important and exponential impact. What does this mean? At its most simple, this means that on many occasions we are impacted by racism, classism, and sexism (as well as heterosexism and ableism) all at the same time. Kimberlé Crenshaw explains intersectionality like this:

> It grew out of trying to conceptualize the way the law responded to issues where both race and gender discrimination were involved. What happened was like an accident, a collision. Intersectionality simply came from the idea that if you're standing in the path of multiple forms of exclusion, you are likely to get hit by both. These women are injured, but when the race ambulance and the gender ambulance arrive at the scene, they see these women of color lying in the intersection and they say, "Well, we can't figure out if this was just race or just sex discrimination. And unless they can show us which one it was, we can't help them."[20]

People will come to different conclusions about what the roots of a given act of delinquency (such as shoplifting) are, depending on what theoretical lens they use to examine it.

While Crenshaw is specifically examining the differential experience that one might have with the law, the idea of intersectionality can be applied in many more instances than just this. One of the central considerations of intersectionality is that a power hierarchy exists in social relations. In other words, a system of power exists in which some hold more power than others based on the social groups they identify with. Hill Collins calls this power hierarchy a "matrix of domination."[21] The farther down the matrix an individual is situated, the more inequality that individual experiences. These experiences are not additive but exponential.[22] For example, if we examine the illustration by Crenshaw above, it isn't just that being black and a woman means that you are discriminated against based upon your race and gender. It can also mean that the system does not know how to alleviate those multiple oppressions and often compounds them.

In addition to the fact that intersectionalities can reinforce inequality, Hill Collins and Burgess-Proctor argue that these intersectionalities can mean that individuals experience both oppression and privilege.[23] They argue that no individual or group can be entirely oppressed or privileged and that the social location on this matrix of domination means that at times individuals and groups can be either oppressed or privileged over one another.

THE SOCIOLOGICAL IMAGINATION

As you begin your investigation of juvenile delinquency in this book, it is important for you to turn on your "sociological imagination." This idea comes from the work of C. Wright Mills, who argued that the only way to truly understand the experiences of the individual is to first understand the societal, institutional, historical conditions that individual is living under. In other words, Mills believed that no man, woman, or child is an island. Below are excerpts from his profound book.

Men do not usually define the troubles they endure in terms of historical change and institutional contradiction. The well-being they enjoy, they do not usually impute to the big ups and downs of the societies in which they live. Seldom aware of the intricate connection between the patterns of their own lives and the course of world history, ordinary men do not usually know what this connection means for the kinds of men they are becoming and for the kinds of history-making in which they might take part. They do not possess the quality of mind essential to grasp the interplay of man and society, of biography and history, of self and world. They cannot cope with their personal troubles in such ways as to control the structural transformations that usually lie behind them.

The sociological imagination enables its possessor to understand the larger historical scene in terms of its meaning for the inner life and the external career of a variety of individuals. It enables him to take into account how individuals, in the welter of their daily experience, often become falsely conscious of their social positions. With that welter, the framework of modern society is sought, and within that framework the psychologies of a variety of men and women are formulated. By such means the personal uneasiness of individuals is focused upon explicit troubles and the indifference of publics is transformed into involvement with public issues.

The first fruit of this imagination—and the first lesson of the social science that embodies it—is the idea that the individual can understand his own experience and gauge his own fate only by locating himself within his period, that he can know his own chances in life only by becoming aware of those of all individuals in his circumstances. In many ways it is a terrible lesson; in many ways a magnificent one.

In these terms, consider unemployment. When, in a city of 100,000, only one man is unemployed, that is his personal trouble, and for its relief we properly look to the character of the man, his skills, and his immediate opportunities. But when in a nation of 50 million employees, 15 million men are unemployed, that is an issue, and we may not hope to find its solution within the range of opportunities open to any one individual. The very structure of opportunities has collapsed. Both the correct statement of the problem and the range of possible solutions require us to consider the economic and political institutions of the society, and not merely the personal situation and character of a scatter of individuals.

What we experience in various and specific milieu, I have noted, is often caused by structural changes. Accordingly, to understand the changes of many personal milieu we are required to look beyond them. And the number and variety of such structural changes increase as the institutions within connected with one another. To be aware of the idea of social structure and to use it with sensibility is to be capable of tracing such linkages among a great variety of milieu. To be able to do that is to possess the sociological imagination.[24]

We have an example that might help explain the importance of a sociological imagination that should resonate with college students. In the United States, one of the persistent philosophies is individualism and personal responsibility. Under this philosophy, individuals are assumed to be solely responsible for their successes and failures. This philosophy relies heavily on the notion that individuals are rational actors who weigh the cost and benefit of their actions, can see the consequences of their behavior, and have perfect information. This example helps individuals who rely heavily on this conception of the individual to see the importance of social structure to individual behavior.

As a college student, you are often reminded that you are responsible for your own work and your own grades. As professors we expect that you come to class, study at least 2 hours a week outside of class for each unit you are taking, start your papers for class early in the semester, don't plagiarize, and stay awake in class. We expect you to pick a major in your sophomore year, that you know what general education courses you need to take, and that you make appointments with your advisor when you have questions. If you put in this effort, ask for extra help when needed, come to office hours, and study hard, we expect you will graduate in a timely manner with a degree in your intended major. But is this always the case?

During hard economic times when state and federal budgets are uncertain, your experience as a college student is different than when economic times are better. As university budgets become tighter, it may be harder to get the major you want. Even if you do get the major you want, the courses to complete that major are fewer and farther between, and class sizes increase, which means it is harder to get one-on-one time with your professor. All of a sudden the degree that you expected to earn in four years (if you are going full time) takes six years because you cannot get classes, and because tuition has increased and you need to go part time so that you may work more hours to pay that tuition. The economy has an impact on the educational system and through this has a very real and personal impact on you. This impact will not be uniform across populations or categories of people. For example, working-class students may be impacted sooner or more strongly by some of the economic forces than wealthier students.

Your Sociological Imagination Put to the Test: Five Vignettes

It may be easy as a college student to see how a stagnant economy affects your experiences as you earn your degree, but now we turn to the experiences of juveniles, their behavior, and the juvenile justice system. How do social forces and the social structure affect individual juveniles?

Vignette 1: The Problem of Jesse

Jesse is 6 years old. He is in the first grade at a public elementary school in a medium-sized city. While in kindergarten and now the first grade, Jesse has gotten into a fair amount of trouble. His mother and father have been called more than once to come get him from school. Most of Jesse's behavior can be considered "youthful": While in kindergarten, he hid under the table while other children were doing their work; he was disruptive in the classroom, laughing and running around when he should have been working; he hugged kids on the playground "enthusiastically"; and on occasion he would play "war" with other little boys, and he would hit or kick them during the game. He does not listen well to his teachers. But some of his behavior is a bit more troublesome. He is openly defiant with his teacher and the playground supervisor. If he is told to stop doing something, he often takes this as a challenge to go further. His rough behavior has hurt several kids on the playground (nothing serious, but both children started to cry).

The school that Jesse attends is an excellent one in the district. It receives Title I money, which means that a large percentage of its children qualify for free lunches, it earns very good test scores, and it can count on heavy participation from the parents and PTA. However, the budget has suffered a series of blows for the whole district. Teachers have been threatened with layoffs. The music teacher, PE teacher, and librarian have been laid off. The class size has increased every year over the past 5 years. This year, Jesse's class has 32 children in it, with one teacher, no aides, and intermittent help from parents.

Jesse's teacher admits that she has a problem with Jesse. She says that she cannot teach the other 31 children if she has to focus so much attention on him. She estimates that about 10%–15% of every day is spent somehow dealing with Jesse. She is frustrated with the situation, feeling pressure from the school to keep up with her coursework and achieve good test scores, and frustrated with the number of children in the classroom.

Jesse's most recent run-in happened when he drew a stick figure of a man who looked like he might be naked. Jesse's mom was called and asked to come to the principal's office. The principal showed the picture to Jesse's mom and explained that the school had a zero-tolerance policy for such things and that if Jesse drew any more pictures ever of stick figures whose "private parts" were showing he would be suspended from the school.

Can this situation be resolved? If so, how should it be resolved? What are the main problems you see in the scenario? What factors are contributing to these problems? How might these problems be resolved?

What did you define as the problems in this scenario? Did you focus on Jesse's behavior? Admittedly, Jesse is disruptive. He clearly does not know how to interact with the children around him in a manner that the school expects. And his openly defiant behavior with his teacher disrupts the learning environment, making her job harder and taking away from the educational time she has with the rest of the class. Besides, let's face it, it is *really* irritating to be around a child who is disruptive and defiant.

But is this all that is going on? Using your sociological imagination, what might be contributing to the focus on Jesse's behavior?

The first issue is the budgetary problems for the school. The school has had to lay off the librarian, the PE teacher, and the music teacher. This means that those activities, PE, music, and visiting the library, fall to the teacher to organize and supervise. In other words, the teacher is being asked to do her job, *and* the job of three other professionals. In addition, she is being told to do her job with more students in the classroom (32 this year) with no increase in professional help (no additional aide). Instead, the teacher must rely on the help of her students' parents. In this context, Jesse's behavior is even more disruptive. If the teacher had an aide or fewer children (for example, in California there was a program to maintain class size for grades K–3 at 20 students, which has been scrapped in many districts because of the budget problems), she might be able to work with Jesse and help him understand how to change his disruptive behavior.

The second issue is the school's zero-tolerance policy. This policy often catches incidents that no one would expect would lead to suspension. In the case of the picture that Jesse drew, a stick figure was determined to be naked, and though that may or may not have been Jesse's intention, a zero-tolerance policy does not leave room for discretion in many of these instances. Instead, if someone defines the juvenile's behavior as wrong, the child automatically receives the punishment. It probably would not help Jesse and his behavior to be suspended over the drawing of a stick figure.

Vignette 2: Theories of Delinquency—Normative, Social Constructionist, and Critical

Jessica and Alicia are 13-year-old twins starting the eighth grade at Parkside Elementary. They live with their mother, Andrea, in a house several blocks from the school. They moved into the house about a year ago, and Andrea works extra shifts and overtime whenever she gets the chance so that they can make the house payments. Prior to moving into the house, they had lived across town in a school district that was underfunded and dangerous. The street they lived on had experienced repeated violence. Even though Andrea must work extra shifts, she is less worried about her kids in this neighborhood than the one they were in previously.

But because of the increased house payment, Jessica and Alicia often come home to an empty house. Recently, they have met a young girl, Laurie. Laurie shoplifts candy from the convenience store near their house, sticks sugar in the gas tanks of cars she doesn't like (she particularly does not like Acuras because her mother drives one), and has been known to torture small animals.

Recently, Jessica and Alicia were caught stealing Butterfingers from the convenience store (Laurie had left the store about five minutes earlier and was not caught taking anything). The police were called, and they called Andrea. She came and picked the girls up and took them home. The next afternoon, Jessica, Alicia, and Laurie went back to the store. They were told that they were not allowed back in because they had been caught stealing the day before. Jessica and Alicia were very embarrassed, and Laurie was very mad about being denied entry. Laurie suggested they put sugar in the convenience store clerk's gas tank. Neither Jessica nor Alicia wanted to and had started to walk away, but Laurie pulled sugar out of her backpack and was prying open the gas tank when the same police officer pulled up to the back of the convenience store. She stopped Laurie and detained all three girls for attempted vandalizing.

What are the problems that you see in this scenario? What might be the solutions that could address these problems?

If you focus on the shoplifting behavior of Jessica and Alicia, and the vandalizing and torturous treatment that Laurie engages in, you have approached this scenario from a certain conceptualization, normative. What might be the reasons for Jessica, Alicia, and Laurie's behavior? Some may suggest that because Jessica and Alicia are left alone at home, they are not getting supervised as well as they should be, while some might argue this is because they come from a single-parent household. Others might point to Jessica and Alicia's new friendship with Laurie. They might argue that Jessica and Alicia are learning this delinquent behavior from their new friend. Finally, those who focused on Laurie's delinquency might argue that she seems to have very few good coping mechanisms for strain in her life; she clearly has a strained relationship with her mother, and being denied entrance to the convenience store pushed her to vandalize the convenience store clerk's car.

Those of you who identified the major problem in this scenario as the fact that Jessica and Alicia have just been arrested for an act they did not engage in, vandalizing the car, may be approaching this scenario from a social constructionist's conceptualization. Social constructionists may argue that Jessica and Alicia have been labeled because of their past behavior and their friendship with Laurie. Given that the police officer had just interacted with Jessica and Alicia the day before, it is likely that she may expect that they were involved in the vandalization, too. Even though Jessica and Alicia did not vandalize the car, the expectation of the police officer is that they were a part of the act. This expectation impacts the interaction that the police officer has with them and the treatment (getting arrested) that Jessica and Alicia experience.

Finally, a few of you might have identified the main problem of the scenario as the fact that Andrea had to move her children to a whole new neighborhood in order to help them receive a good education with a decreased likelihood they would be hurt while walking home from school or playing in their yard. Those of you who focused on this are taking a critical conceptualization. Instead of focusing on the minor delinquency, this conceptualization focuses on the structure of the system that requires that an individual actually move in order to remain safe and get a decent education. Those following this conception would also critique a system that had required that an individual work two jobs in order to make rent and support her family. This conception would be less interested in the behavior in which each girl engaged.

Vignette 3: The Problem of Appropriate Policies

The members of the South State Legislature have come close to finishing their proposed budget for the fiscal year. However, they find themselves with something of a predicament. For the first time in 30 years they do not have enough programs to spend money on. For this reason, they find they have $25 million (which is a lot less than you think it is) that they can allocate to a special program or project. The drawback is that this money may only be available this one time—there is no guarantee that future budgets could provide continued support. There has been a proposal that this money be used on the children of South State to show a renewed commitment to the next generation at the turn of the century. Two proposals have been put forth for the one-time allotment of funds.

Rebecca Hanlin has suggested that the money be used to increase the bed size at two South State detention centers. This would include building or adding on to several buildings in each facility, and supplying the needed infrastructure, such as beds, bedding, and food, for the increase in inmates. The existing facilities are well made, but nearing their maximum capacities, and Hanlin has made an argument that it is likely, given the demographics of the area and a predicted increase in teenagers in the area in the next 10 years, that there will also be an increase in delinquency rates. She wants to be ready with larger detention facilities.

Richard Harring has suggested that the money be used to create five new community facilities in underserved areas that would include small libraries as well as sports equipment. These facilities would be open after school and on weekends for children under the age of 18 to use. The five areas he has suggested have little available for juveniles at the present time.

Both proposals have been reviewed by the South State Legislature and have been determined to be within the proposed budget of $25 million. It is your job to decide which of the above proposals should be sponsored and receive the $25 million. The money can be spent on only one project. Spend a moment deciding which one you would choose. What are your reasons for making this choice?

These two proposals come from fundamentally different philosophies about how to approach juveniles and juvenile delinquency (which we will discuss further in the last section of the book). If you chose Rebecca Hanlin's proposal, it might be argued that you are supporting a deterrent or punishment philosophy, in which you expect that delinquency will increase and that the only way to combat delinquency is to be ready to punish those who have engaged in it. Over the last 30 years, this philosophy has been argued for and supported (with increased funds) in many jurisdictions in the United States. We have increased our budgets for the criminal justice system, increased our laws that address juvenile misbehavior, and increased our policies that socially control juveniles.

In contrast, if you chose Richard Harring's proposal, it could be argued that you are supporting a preventative philosophy toward juvenile delinquency. This philosophy focuses on offering resources and support to juveniles *before* they engage in misbehavior and are picked up by the police. Prevention can focus on areas or juveniles who society suspects might be more likely to engage in delinquency (or who have less personal resources) such as Richard Harring's proposal, which focuses on underserved communities. Or prevention programs can focus on the juvenile population as a whole (such as California's push to lower class sizes to a manageable 20 students per classroom; while this program's first intent was to support better performance in the classroom, a secondary outcome might be less delinquency as juveniles get more rewards out of their educational experiences).

Vignette 4: Unequal Enforcement—Class

Lillyburg has had an increasing homeless problem, especially homeless youth. In order to curb this problem, a new law has just been suggested in Lillyburg, making it a misdemeanor to sit on public sidewalks or in nondesignated sitting areas, between the hours of 9 a.m. and 9 p.m. Opponents of this proposal point out that this law may be differentially enforced because Lillyburg is a large tourist town and often tourists can be found sitting on sidewalks and in nondesignated sitting areas. Proponents of the bill insist it will solve the homeless youth problem and that because it is only a misdemeanor, the law is not meant to be overly punitive. Most individuals will only be fined for breaking the law by sitting on sidewalks between 9 a.m. and 9 p.m. Should this proposal be made into a law? What are the ramifications of such a law? Who is most likely to be affected by a law like this?

Randall Kennedy discussed the impact of unequal enforcement in his book *Race, Crime, and the Law*.[25] While he focused his attention on the detrimental effects of unequal enforcement of the law on communities of color, his ideas can be applied in this example, too. Unequal enforcement is the idea either that the law is written in a manner that focuses attention on one group disproportionately over another, or that supposedly neutral laws are applied in a manner that oppresses one group more than another. The law in Lillyburg can be used as an example. In its language, this law is class, race,

©iStockphoto.com/Juanmonino;

Loitering and public nuisance laws are rarely uniformly applied. What is considered loitering, and what is considered the proper use of a public park bench?

and gender neutral. It merely stipulates that it is illegal to sit on the sidewalk between 9 a.m. and 9 p.m. However, the discourse around this law shows that it was written for a less neutral purpose. Homeless youth are the target of this law. And it is likely in the application of this law (who it is used against) that homeless juveniles will more likely be arrested. It is unlikely that a tourist family with a couple of kids will be arrested for sitting in a nondesignated sitting area.

In addition, while the punishment (sentence) attached to this law is minimal in the eyes of most individuals (someone arrested for sitting would be fined), given that the law is aimed at homeless youth (by definition, juveniles who have so little resources they are living on the street), even a small fine can mean jail time because they will have no way of paying. Finally, a policy such as this, focused on individuals who will probably habitually break it (in other words, homeless youth have very few choices about where they can go; it is likely they will still live on the streets and sit on the sidewalks), will likely mean that the homeless youth will be considered chronic offenders, and, as we will see, chronic juvenile offenders are treated differently in the juvenile justice system than nonchronic offenders.

Vignette 5: Unequal Enforcement—Race and Gender

Maria is a 16-year-old Latina who has just gotten in trouble with the police. She was with her cousin in their neighborhood (a working-poor, Latino neighborhood near Tempe, Arizona) while he was holding 10 ounces of methamphetamine (meth), which is the minimum amount to be charged with selling drugs (instead of possession of meth). Maria claims she did not know her cousin had the drugs and he was not selling at the time they were caught. Because it is Maria's first offense, she was charged with possession (because she was with her cousin), but charged in the juvenile court. The court adjudicated her true (found her guilty of drug possession) and gave her a disposition (sentence) of three days in detention. Upon completing her disposition, Maria received probation and must comply with a list of rules in order to remain out of trouble. Included on this list is that Maria must improve her grades in school, comply with a 7 p.m. curfew, and have no contact with her boyfriend (whom her probation officer has decided, because of several conversations with Maria's mother, is a bad influence on her).

Last week Maria came home at 7:15 p.m. and her mom called her probation officer, telling him that Maria had been late home and that she suspected Maria had been out with her boyfriend. Maria does not dispute that she came home 15 minutes late, but says she was late because the bus she takes from work did not show up, so she had to start to walk home, and catch a later bus that finally happened by. She could not call her mom to tell her because her mom took away her cell phone when she got in trouble in the first place.

The probation officer considers this to be a violation of her probation, and Maria is now back in court for this violation. The court has no evidence that Maria saw her boyfriend, but they do have Maria's admission that she was 15 minutes late coming home. The judge hearing the case admonishes Maria for violating her curfew and not listening to her mother about who she should date and gives her 30 days of detention for the violation.

What are the main problems you see in the scenario? What factors are contributing to these problems? How might these problems be resolved?

This case might be considered harsh and unlikely, but it was a real case witnessed by the authors. In this case, Maria has found herself in trouble. She is hanging out with individuals who are getting in trouble with the police and dragging her into that trouble. But what does our sociological imagination and a critical perspective help us observe about her experiences? First, Maria and her cousin live in Arizona in a predominantly Latino community. It is likely that this community experiences a stronger police presence than other communities in Tempe because of the strong, declared focus on immigration in Arizona. In other words, had Maria and her cousin been from a different neighborhood her cousin may not have been caught (which is a whole separate discussion, but given that Maria was unaware of her cousin's possession of meth, it certainly would have benefitted her to not get caught).

Now that Maria has been caught up in the juvenile justice system, she must contend with a new issue. While status offenses should not be used to arrest a juvenile, once a juvenile has been arrested and brought into the system, behaviors that are considered status offenses are often listed on probation agreements. The dating and sexual behavior of girls is often managed and controlled through these agreements,[26] as it is for Maria. Over the years, the juvenile justice system has focused more attention on the sexual behavior of girls than that of boys.[27] In this instance, with very little concrete proof of interaction between Maria and her boyfriend, it appears the judge has taken this into consideration when deciding on the disposition that Maria will serve for violating her curfew.

This case can be used as an example of the importance of the intersections of race and gender for the experiences of many juveniles in the juvenile justice system. It could be argued that Maria has more likely been caught up in the system in the first place because of the community she was in when arrested, and certainly her experiences once in the system are somewhat dependent on her gender.

These vignettes are examples of the issues that this book will explore. They represent our focus on theory and contextual concerns such as family and school. They illustrate the importance of thinking beyond personal responsibility and agency to include an understanding of social forces and social structure when examining juvenile delinquency and the societal responses to it. And, they illustrate the importance of examining juvenile delinquency through an intersectional lens, which highlights the effects of race, class, and gender and other social variables on juvenile delinquency and the societal responses to it.

THE JUVENILE JUSTICE SYSTEM AND DIVERSITY

This chapter, so far, has explored the importance of diversity in the United States and the impact that such characteristics as race, gender, or sexual orientation may have on juveniles. We see that it can impact their educational experiences or their likelihood to be in poverty. We also see from the vignettes above that race, gender, class, and other characteristics, such as sexual orientation and age, can impact the experiences that juveniles have as they go through the juvenile justice system.

Figure 1.3 illustrates the stages of the juvenile justice system in comparison to the adult system. We spend a significant amount of time in Chapters 2, 11, 12, 13, and 14 discussing the history, stages, and philosophy of the system from policing to corrections, but we want to spend the next several paragraphs introducing the system and emphasizing the importance of diversity and inequality for juvenile experiences in this system. As you will learn in Chapters 2 and 11, the juvenile system was created under a different philosophy than the adult system. While the adult system focuses on punishment, the juvenile system was created under a philosophy that children are savable and thus rehabilitation, not punishment, should be the focus. This meant that the system for many years operated with a lack of formal legal procedures (in other words, the system did not follow a systematic set of rules, but instead relied on "informal" justice) and judicial discretion.[28] This informality and discretion was based on the idea that the system needed to pay attention to the child as an individual and offer what was best for each child's circumstances. The problem with that system was that often the treatment looked very much like punishment (children were kept for long periods of time with little focus on rehabilitation), and the discretion meant that children were vulnerable to the decision-making practices of individual workers in the system.[29] And certain children were found to be even more vulnerable than children in general. For example, girls who were suspected of sexual behavior were kept in detention facilities until a marriageable age, while boys who were found to be engaging in sexual behavior were not held in detention.

In the 1960s and 1970s, the Supreme Court made several changes as a result of the realizations that discretion in the system and a lack of formal protections for youth meant that youth were vulnerable to unequal treatment. These changes instituted formal rules, the most important of which were that juveniles had the right to an attorney, a notice of the charges against them, to confront their accuser, and to not incriminate themselves. If these rights sound familiar, it is because they are from the Fifth and Sixth Amendments to the U.S. Constitution. Juveniles were not afforded these constitutional rights until 1967. The introduction of these rules is known as the due process era because juveniles were given many of the same due process rights as adults. In order to assure these rights, though, the juvenile justice system had to create formal procedures (e.g., creating the role of prosecuting and defense attorney for all court cases).

The irony is that with the formalization of the system came a similarity to the adult system. Remember that the juvenile justice system was created to be *different* from the

FIGURE 1.3 Comparing the Juvenile and Adult Justice Systems

What is the sequence of events in the criminal justice system?

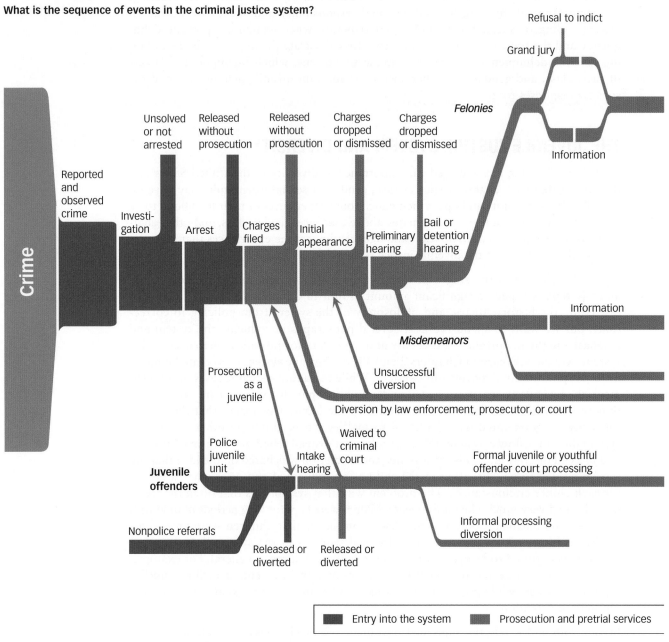

Source: Bureau of Justice Statistics. (1997). *Criminal Justice System Flowchart.* Retrieved from http://www.bjs.gov/content/largechart.cfm

adult system, and yet, with the introduction of these constitutional rights, the juvenile system became more similar to the adult system.[30] Now both systems follow similar legal rules, and often their outcomes (punishments) look very similar, too. So similar that some researchers argue that maybe it is time for a single criminal justice system for both juveniles and adults.[31]

A second irony of this formalization is that it did not protect juveniles from being treated differently based on their personal characteristics. The adult and juvenile justice systems both experienced an increased focus on rules and guidelines meant, in part, to decrease

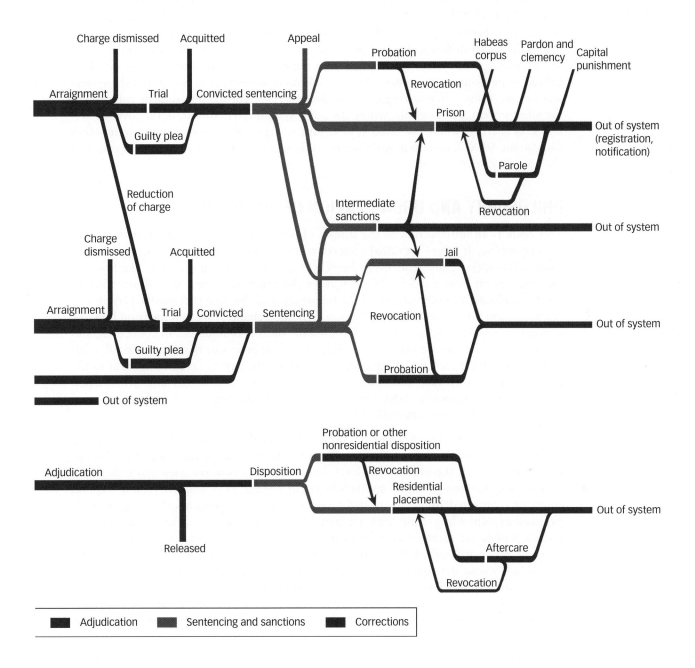

the discrimination that was found to exist when judicial discretion (the practice of having judges make the decisions about how long an individual should be sentenced) was in play. However, many researchers found that when judicial discretion was limited through such practices as sentencing guidelines, the discretion did not disappear but merely moved to an early stage.[32] For example, prosecutorial discretion became much more influential because the decision of how to charge an individual was now more important.

Figure 1.3 illustrates the five main stages of both the adult and juvenile systems: (1) entry into the system, (2) prosecution and pretrial services, (3) adjudication, (4) sentencing and sanctions, and (5) corrections. Both the juvenile and adult systems have these five general stages, but as the figure illustrates, within these five general stages there are slight differences. The top two lines of the figure show the adult process for felony and misdemeanor arrests; the bottom line shows the juvenile process through the system. While much of the experience is becoming more similar between the systems, on its surface this figure shows one of the bigger differences that stems from the initial philosophy of the juvenile system at its creation. The system was created with the belief that juveniles could be saved, so instead of punishment the system should focus on treatment. This meant that the system was created using different language that did not represent the punishment language of the adult system. For example, where the adult system refers to a trial, the juvenile system says hearing; where the adult system says sentence, the juvenile system refers to a disposition. We will go into much more detail in Chapters 12 and 13 about the stages of the juvenile justice system.

PHILOSOPHY AND ORGANIZATION OF THE BOOK

This book is an introduction to the study of juvenile delinquency written from a critical perspective. It offers a critical understanding of juvenile delinquency, focusing on issues of race, class, and gender. The book is organized into four sections. The first section focuses on how we define and measure delinquency, paying special attention to the historical progression of juvenile delinquency and the role that media play in our contemporary understanding of delinquency. In these chapters we will focus on how the concept of juvenile delinquency was first used to control communities of color, girls, and the working poor, and we will compare this to current processes that may be similar. We will examine the trends in delinquency since the 1980s, paying special attention to the relationship between race and ethnicity and delinquency and gender and delinquency. And we will ask ourselves, "Does the type of data we use impact our understanding of delinquency and these relationships?"

Our second and third sections of the book focus on the contexts of delinquency and theoretical explanations of delinquency. We will start by offering three theoretical chapters on micro-level theories, macro-level theories, and critical theories that either help predict the likelihood than an individual might engage in delinquency; help explain changing trends in delinquency, or delinquency rates for neighborhoods and communities; and explain why certain laws are created, certain communities are focused on, or certain groups are targeted as delinquent. In section three, we will examine the relationship between family, schools, peers and gangs, and drugs and our understanding and beliefs about delinquency. What are the contexts in which juvenile delinquency seems more prevalent? Do our societal beliefs about family, school, peers and gangs, or drugs impact our beliefs about delinquency? And do juveniles' social location, as youth of color, boys or girls, and/or youth with or without resources, affect the contexts of delinquency?

Our fourth section of the book examines societal responses to delinquency. We will examine why we have a separate juvenile justice system, the process of the system, the correctional stage, and prevention, rehabilitation, and restorative approaches to delinquency. In these chapters we will focus on the impact of race, class, and gender and other social variables on both the creation and maintenance of these various policies and programs, and the impact that race, class, and gender have on the experiences of youth in these arenas.

When finished with this book, you should be better prepared to apply your sociological imagination to the connections between juveniles, their behaviors, and the world in which they live.

The study of delinquency is more complex than you might think at the outset. Not only must we understand the context in which youth exist, but we must understand the changing societal definitions of acceptable and unacceptable behavior. We think this makes this area exciting and full of possibilities for advancing the understanding of youth behavior. As you start your exploration of juvenile delinquency, we will end this chapter with a final story to illustrate the complexity of youth behavior. One of us has a son who has an anxiety disorder. He is almost paralyzed with worry that he is violating the rules. I have found that allowing him to swear gives him a bit of power over his anxiety. And, let me tell you, the only people better at swearing are truck drivers and his mother. So yes, when he gets anxious, I hear him whisper the F word under his breath (and yes, he is still in elementary school).

So the questions are this: should parents OK epic swearing for elementary school children? Is he more likely to engage in delinquency because his parents allow him to break the norms on swearing for young children? How do I manage his anxiousness and swearing outside the household? If he engages in delinquent behavior down the road, is it my fault because I allowed the swearing? If I told you that much of his anxiousness stems from being bullied at school, would it change your answers above? In the long run, if he turns out to be a rule-following adult, does any of his youth behavior matter?

We are not sure that this book will answer all of these questions for you, or that the book is even meant to, but we hope that it helps you prepare yourself to think critically about these questions and stand behind whatever answer you arrive at.

EYE ON DIVERSITY EXERCISE: SOCIAL CONSTRUCTION AND MEDIA

Two of the themes in this chapter are the characterization of the juvenile and the social construction of juvenile delinquency. In this activity, try your hand at investigating how the media portray juveniles and juvenile delinquency.

1. Search the Internet for media pieces on juveniles and/or juvenile delinquency. Is there a difference in how print media presents these topics compared to television news?

2. Using LexisNexis, find five articles on juvenile delinquency. What are the behaviors that are being described in these articles? Do the articles suggest a reason for the delinquent behavior being reported? What are the conceptions of delinquency that the media reports are using? Is one conception used more than others? If so, why might this be the case?

3. Finally, what are the characteristics (categories) of the youth who are being portrayed as delinquent in these articles? Are certain categories overrepresented in the news articles?

DISCUSSION QUESTIONS

1. Explain the conceptions of delinquency. Using each conception of delinquency, explain juvenile gangs and the societal reaction to them.

2. Explain the current well-being of children. What is their economic, physical, and educational well-being? Are they currently better off than they were a decade or two ago?

3. What is the difference between individual and institutional racism, classism, and sexism? Give an example of each.

4. How are intersectionality and the matrix of domination important to our understanding of the impact of race, class, and gender on the experiences of juveniles?

5. What is the sociological imagination? How might it be used to help understand juvenile delinquency?

KEY TERMS

Achieved category 13

Ascribed category 12

Critical conception of delinquency 8

Folkways 7

Individual classism 14

Individual racism 14

Individual sexism 14

Institutional classism 14

Institutional racism 14

Institutional sexism 14

Laws 7

Mores 7

Normative conception of delinquency 6

Social constructionist conception of delinquency 7

Social differentiation 13

Social inequality 13

Status offenses 5

CHAPTER PRETEST ANSWERS

1. True

2. False

3. True

4. True

5. False

6. False

7. False

STUDENT STUDY SITE

$SAGE edge™

edge.sagepub.com/bates2e

Sharpen your skills with SAGE edge!

SAGE edge for students provides a personalized approach to help you accomplish your coursework goals in an easy-to-use learning environment. You'll find action plans, mobile-friendly eFlashcards, and quizzes, as well as videos, web resources, and links to SAGE journal articles to support and expand on the concepts presented in this chapter. Check out the website for original videos of former offenders discussing their experiences as juveniles.

U.S. National Archives and Records Administration

THE CREATION OF DELINQUENCY

CHAPTER OBJECTIVES

After reading this chapter, you should be able to

- Describe how the concept of juvenile delinquency developed over the course of U.S. history before culminating in the creation of the first juvenile justice system

- Explain how different forms of popular culture have been the focus of moral panics about delinquency

- Analyze the connections between social constructions of youth and mainstream ideas about juvenile misbehavior

- Compare and contrast ideas about youth and juvenile delinquency related to one's race, ethnicity, social class, gender, and sexuality

To Hon. Caleb S. Woodhull, Mayor of the City of New York (1849)

I deem it to be my duty to call the attention of your honor to a deplorable and growing evil which exists amid this community, and which is spread over the principal business parts of the city. It is an evil and a reproach to our municipality, for which the laws and ordinances afford no adequate remedy.

I allude to the constantly increasing numbers of vagrant, idle and vicious children of both sexes, who infest our public thoroughfares, hotels, docks, &c. Children who are growing up in ignorance and profligacy, only destined to a life of misery, shame and crime, and ultimately to a felon's doom. Their numbers are almost incredible, and to those whose business and habits do not permit them a searching scrutiny, the degrading and disgusting practices of these almost infants in the schools of vice, prostitution and rowdyism, would certainly be beyond belief. The offspring of always careless, generally intemperate, and oftentimes immoral and dishonest parents, they never see the inside of a school-room. . . . Left, in many instances to roam day and night wherever their inclination leads them, a large proportion of these juvenile vagrants are in the daily practice of pilfering wherever opportunity offers, and begging where they cannot steal. In addition to which, the female portion of the youngest class, those who have only seen some eight or twelve summers, are addicted to immoralities of the most loathsome description. Each year makes fearful additions to the ranks of these prospective recruits of infamy and sin, and from this corrupt and festering fountain flows on a ceaseless stream to our lowest brothels—to the Penitentiary and the State Prison.

In presenting these disagreeable facts for the consideration of Your Honor, I trust that I may be pardoned for the suggestion, in conclusion, that in my opinion some method by which these children could be compelled to attend our schools regularly, or be apprenticed to some suitable occupation, would tend in time more to improve the morals of the community, prevent crime, and relieve the City from its onerous burden of expenses for the Alms-House and Penitentiary.

—Respectfully submitted, Geo. W. Matsell, [NYC] Chief of Police[1]

CHAPTER PRETEST

Test your knowledge of this chapter's material by determining whether the following statements are true or false. Be sure to compare your answers with the answers on page 56.

1. The primary vision of delinquency that developed in Western societies resulted in the similar labeling of youth across all social statuses.

2. In ancient times and during the Middle Ages, there was no formal concept known as juvenile delinquency.

3. The age at which youth were thought to be capable of having a "guilty mind" has changed over time.

4. Houses of Refuge and other institutions housed children in need of care along with those labeled delinquent or predelinquent in an effort to "save" them.

5. The creation of the first juvenile court was based on the philosophy of retribution.

6. In the 21st century, it is clear that moral panics about violent music, websites, and films as causes of delinquency are justified by scientific research.

7. Youth of color, particularly boys, are often portrayed by the media as people to fear, rather than people to protect.

In 2010, New York City Mayor Michael Bloomberg indicated that he was concerned about the numbers of young people being detained in juvenile institutions and the fact that they were often placed far from their homes and families.[2] He noted that juveniles placed in institutions tend to recommit acts of delinquency after release and to return to those same institutions, which is, ultimately, an unproductive cycle. Bloomberg stated that it would be best for young people who engage in nonviolent delinquency to be treated under a rehabilitative model and to have access to services within their own communities.[3] As a result, Mayor Bloomberg eliminated the Department of Juvenile Justice in December 2010 and subsumed it within the Administration for Children's Services in order to break the cycle of delinquency and treat juvenile misbehavior, first and foremost, as a child welfare issue.[4]

●●●

THE SOCIAL CONSTRUCTION OF YOUTH AND DELINQUENCY

As the opening writings about juvenile delinquency in New York City written over a century apart demonstrate, social constructions of youth and delinquency or mainstream ideas about youth and misbehavior, and what to do about youth and misbehavior, change over time. In order to understand how the concept of juvenile delinquency developed and culminated in the creation of the juvenile justice system, it is important to consider how differing ideas about youth have emerged over the course of history. These ideas about youth are difficult to generalize about because they are socially constructed differently in different places and cultures around the world.[5] Although in Western countries we tend to automatically think of teenagers when we think about juvenile delinquency, this concept is not recognized in a similar way in all cultures of the world, nor do Western countries themselves frame the years of adolescence in exactly the same way. As we will discuss in this chapter, the very notion of adolescence did not always exist—it was created in light of social and economic changes that necessitated a new, more extended, experience of childhood.

Social constructions of youth and delinquency:
Popular ideas about delinquency that are created and influenced by social, political, and economic factors and that change over time.

The concept of juvenile delinquency emerged out of a particular Western vision of what it is to be a child or a young adult, and entire systems of justice were developed to address the special needs of youth labeled as "juvenile delinquents." And, even within a given Western society, we can observe that the labeling of youth as juvenile delinquents occurs much more in certain segments of our communities than in others. As Mennel explains, "When considered a violation of mores, juvenile delinquency becomes less a fixed concept and more a description of certain kinds of behavior by certain kids living in certain places."[6] Popular ideas about youth and their behaviors have been shaped by raced, classed, and gendered biases and concerns. In this chapter we will highlight the historical ideas about juveniles and their behavior that eventually led to the creation of the first juvenile court in the United States in 1899. In addition, we will consider the role of popular culture (music, films, books, games, etc.) in moral panics about delinquency both preceding and following the creation of state juvenile justice systems in the United States.

Ancient Times and the Middle Ages (776 BCE–1400 CE)

Young people certainly acted up or misbehaved prior to being labeled juvenile delinquents by society. Consider this description of an event experienced by one young man named Ariston (estimated to be 17–19 years of age) at the hands of another young man, Ktesias, and his father, Kronon, in Ancient Greece (4th century BCE):

> First they tore my cloak off of me, and then, tripping me up and pushing me into the mud, they struck me so violently that they split my lip and caused my eye to close up. They left me in this sorry condition, so that I could neither get up or utter a word. While I was lying there, I heard them making a number of abusive comments, much of which was so offensive that I would shrink from repeating some of it in your presence. . . . After this I was picked up naked by some passers-by, for my assailants had carried off my cloak.[7]

As explained by Garland, although this act involved violence of one youth against another (with the *help of his father*, something we generally do not see too much of today), it would not have been labeled as delinquency because such behaviors were not seen as related to age at that point in history.[8] The acts committed were fueled by the consumption of alcohol on the part of both Ktesias and his father, and they took place within the context of military service. Based upon the historical data available, it appears as though Greek society at that time encouraged misbehavior among male youth and that this example was not an isolated one. There was even a law at that time that stated that young men should not beat their parents, which indicates that parental beating by children must have raised the concern of at least a few lawmakers. There are limited sources of data for scholars to explore specifically related to juvenile misbehavior in ancient cultures, but data related to other social practices of the time indicate that youth were often treated and punished in ways that were comparable to those of their adult counterparts.[9] Youth were treated as the property of their fathers, corporal punishment was common, and youth were often beaten harshly.

If we skip ahead in history to examine a period on which scholars have had more luck finding information, the Middle Ages (5th century CE–15th century) in Europe, we can see that still very little distinction was made between human beings based upon age.[10] At that time and place in history, society was heavily interdependent, living and working together in large groups. This was because the economy was agricultural, and lots of bodies, young and old, were needed to prepare and work the crops. Because of this, the biggest age-based distinction that played a role in the process was whether a child had mastered the basic physiological and emotional functions needed in order to work in the fields. Usually, once children turned 7 years of age, they were for all intents and purposes considered adults. Seven-year-olds could usually speak well (they had no need to know how to read because there was not yet any printed

Although young people engaged in behaviors that we would label as delinquent today, they were not labeled as such in ancient times.

material), and their oral communication skills were considered sufficient preparation for many of the daily tasks of the adult world.

Life was not easy for children of this period, and they were often subjected to practices of abuse and neglect that resulted in short life spans.[11] Those who did survive engaged in many of the same activities as adults, including drinking alcohol, gambling, and engaging in sexual behavior. These behaviors were accepted among youth, and adults did not see any need to shelter their children from what are seen today as adult behaviors; extended families and communities lived very closely together, and there was very little privacy to be had, even if it was desired. Everyone had an eye on one another, and this informal social control kept a lot of young people from misbehaving.

The Colonial and Revolutionary Period (late 1400s–1800)

As the Europeans began to colonize North America, the ideas about childhood that they employed in the "New World" were similar to those that they employed prior to the Colonial period. Youth were seen as developing over time, but there still was not a tradition that emphasized age in the manner that we have today. There was a notable labor shortage during this period, so the tradition of youth working at a young age was especially helpful to adults. Gender-based distinctions developed further at this time, and boys were encouraged to develop their skill sets as apprentices in the working world, while girls were encouraged to learn to serve and care for others by becoming domestic servants or wives.[12] The raising of children and young adults remained a group project, as the people for whom the youth worked or apprenticed had a large role in their upbringing. There was no sense of the nuclear family in the manner that is emphasized today, but extended families were seen as the primary source for disciplining and educating youth.

In the Middle Ages and in most of the Colonial era, legal assumptions were made about young people that mirrored the idea that young people were not that different from adults. The English common law tradition that was employed focused upon whether youth were capable of *mens rea*, or having the guilty mind needed to preplan an act of wrongdoing. Once again, the 7-year mark was seen as an important one. Generally speaking, individuals under 7 years of age were seen as too young to be able to rationally plan an act of harm in advance. But once people turned 7, their capacities for such forethought and planning were debated. This held true for all individuals between 7 and 14 years of age; they were assumed not to have the capability to plan a crime, but exceptions were made to that assumption on a case-by-case basis. (An age within this period that was considered important was 10.5 years of age—before that it was deemed less likely that a youth would be a rational planner, but after that it was seen as more likely.) After individuals turned 14, they were considered to be basically adults and were held to have the same abilities to reason and make decisions, and to have a brain mature enough to harbor a guilty mind.[13] There were no medical technologies available at that time to measure physiological development accurately, so that assumption went largely unquestioned. Over the course of this time in history, juries were very wary of convicting white youth and sending them to jail with adults, because the jurors believed they would simply be dooming these youth to lives of crime. One critic of this approach in the early 1800s, John Pintard, embodied this common sentiment in his description of prisons as a place where "little Devils are instructed to become great ones and at the expiration of their terms turn out accomplished villains."[14] As we will demonstrate later in this chapter, youth of color were not treated with the same concern by juries.[15]

As society began shifting from an agrarian to an industrial economy, a shift in ideas about youth followed. The development and spread of the printing press inspired a major transformation in the idea of what it meant to be a child or an adult, which gradually

Mens rea:
A Latin term meaning "guilty mind."

established a stronghold between the 16th and 18th centuries.[16] Once the printing press was put into use, an assortment of books, newspapers, and other materials were printed. The mainstream of society suddenly had access to a wealth of ideas, but people's access to these ideas depended on their ability to read. It takes time to learn to read, and thus adults began to recognize that young people needed a period of time to do so. Parents who were literate began teaching their children at home, or enlisting the help of neighbors to teach their children. The initial efforts to create schools in which children received a more formalized education began during this period, but at that point schools did not separate students into different classes by age; they were all included in the same classroom. Children generally did not attend school consistently because they had to balance school and work. Yet, a shift away from seeing children as mini-adults early on in their lives was clearly under way because of the perceived need for formalized education. In addition, the loosening of informal controls that came from urbanization and industrialization changed the habits of working-class youth in ways that were visible and that garnered attention by the media. For example, a newspaper article from 1791 in Philadelphia, Pennsylvania, noted,

> The custom of permitting boys to ramble about the streets at night, is productive of the most serious and alarming consequences to their morals. Assembled in corners, and concealed from every eye, they can securely indulge themselves in mischief of every kind.[17]

As more youth from the lower social ranks began spending time on the streets, adults from privileged social classes became concerned about the number of youth who appeared to be without adult protection. The concept of juvenile delinquency began

The development of the printing press brought about a major shift in many societies' ideas about childhood and the needs of young people.

to take a particular shape at this time. As Mennel (1973) explains, "Thus, during the eighteenth century, juvenile delinquency slowly ceased to mean a form of misbehavior common to all children and became instead a euphemism for the crimes and conditions of poor children."[18]

The "Child-Saving" Era, the Industrial Revolution, and the Creation of the Juvenile Court (1800s–early 1900s)

In order to address what some saw as serious social problems, large-scale organized efforts to address the issue of neglected and abandoned youth, as well as delinquent youth, were undertaken by religious and social reformers, such as those associated with the Religious Society of Friends (commonly known as the Quakers). Beginning in the 1820s, a number of different institutions were created in the United States to provide youth with the discipline that founders believed they were no longer experiencing in their own families, to keep youth out of adult prisons, and as a means for reformists to deal with what they perceived as the negative aftereffects and threats posed by immigration,[19] which they framed primarily as an issue of begging or pauperism. The institutions that were created included almshouses or "poor farms," in which poor children and adults were housed; asylums, farm schools, and labor schools for homeless and/or delinquent youth; and houses of refuge that were assigned by state and local courts to take in youth ruled to be in need of care (dependent or neglected children) or deemed delinquent or predelinquent. It is important to note that youth labeled as either poor or in need of discipline were treated as one and the same in these institutions, conceived of as a means for "saving" youth who had not yet been fully corrupted.[20] These institutions were aimed at teaching youth the value of hard work and individual responsibility, typically by means of religious and moral instruction. The development of the first houses of refuge in New York (1825), Boston (1826), and Philadelphia (1828) was followed by the opening of many other such institutions in the Northeast and Mideast in the years prior to the Civil War.[21]

The superintendent of the Chicago Reform School annually wrote reports about the state of the boys who were part of the institution. In this report, he included a number of tables that addressed a variety of topics, such as those in Table 2.1, in which he enumerated what he saw as the causes of each boy's history of delinquency. Some of his categories are still used today. A few are indicative of the period in which he wrote. We would not, for example, expect to see the categories "naturally ugly" (which he used the most), "hereditary criminality," and "love of a wandering life" utilized by administrators dealing with youth today.

Once a large number of children in society were deemed in need of special care, there was an accompanying shift in the ways in which reformers characterized their parents as well. Typically, the characterization was that the parents of the children in the institutions were lazy, incompetent, or otherwise deficient human beings. Oftentimes parents wanted their children removed from an institution, but they met with resistance in legal justification rooted in *parens patriae*, the concept that in some cases the state is justified to step in and serve as a substitute parent. In the precedent-setting case of *Ex parte Crouse* (1838), the Pennsylvania Supreme Court refused to let the father of Mary Ann Crouse remove her from a house of refuge:

> The object of charity is reformation, by training its inmates to industry; by imbuing their minds with principles of morality and religion; by furnishing them with the means to earn a living; and above all, by separating them from the corrupting influence of improper associates. To this end, may not the natural parents, when unequal to the task of education, or unworthy of it, be superseded by the *parens patriae*, or common guardian of the community?[22]

● ● ●

Houses of refuge: Institutions developed in the United States in the early 19th century to house children who were poor and steer them away from pursuing a life of crime.

***Parens patriae*:** A Latin term signifying that the state should serve as a substitute parent in cases in which children's actual parents either neglect or abuse them, or simply cannot control their behavior.

Youth placed in houses of refuge were subject to days full of moral and religious training, and a great deal of labor. Boys would make goods such as shoes, nails, or furniture, and the folks running the houses of refuge would receive small sums of money from contactors for the labor of each boy who helped them run the institution.[23] Children were often placed in apprenticeships outside of the institution; boys were placed on farms away from the city, on whaling or merchant ships, and with tradespersons, and for girls the only type of apprenticeship deemed acceptable was to be indentured as maids. All of these practices separated youth from their families and worked to weaken the bonds formed by everyday interaction; sometimes parents were not even notified where their children were sent.[24] Although they were touted as places of treatment and labeled as houses of refuge, scholars of these institutions note that sometimes little actual refuge was found, and instead youth were often subjected to abusive conditions, lack of adequate food and water, and essentially prison-like conditions.[25]

The development of houses of refuge and other institutions was driven by different ideas about white male youth and white girls, as well as of youth of color in general.[26] Those who ran institutions treated youth of color and girls as inferior beings.[27] For example, during the years of slavery in the southern United States, black youth who misbehaved were disciplined within that system and the delinquency of white youth generally was ignored.[28] Black children in free states were generally not admitted to the houses of refuge, but in the cases in which they were, they were segregated and treated as less important than the white youth.[29] Unlike the shift in ideas of youth that white youth experienced in the early 1800s, black youth were still treated as virtual adults and were typically housed in adult prisons.[30] Not until 1850 was a house of refuge designed specifically for black children created, the House of Refuge for Colored Children in Philadelphia, Pennsylvania. As Frey (1981) explains, there were racialized and classed motives behind its construction:

TABLE 2.1   Hypothesized Causes of Juvenile Delinquency (in 1859)

Intemperance of parents	91	Half-orphans	25
Bad company	33	Cruelty of parents	14
Want of parental control	24	Bad occupation	31
Orphanage	48	Bad home	21
Parental neglect	33	Truancy from school	13
Stepparents	9	Familiarity with vice	13
Hereditary criminality	10	Squalid poverty	6
Naturally ugly	193	Love of a wandering life	9
Love of strong drink	0	Idleness	12
Improper recreations	6	Total number included in this table	428

Source: Nicols, D. B. (1970). Fourth annual report of the officers of the Chicago Reform School . . . for the year ending September 30, 1859. In W. B. Sanders (Ed.), *Juvenile offenders for a thousand years: Selected readings from Anglo-Saxon times to 1900* (pp. 395–397). Chapel Hill: University of North Carolina Press.

Note: Table shows the probable cause of delinquency as ascertained from the facts of the inmates' previous history.

Since reformers believed that early habit formation of a child could make him into either a good citizen or a criminal, and since they believed that the earlier a child was admitted to the House of Refuge, the better were his chances for reformation, it follows that they also believed that the early admission of black children to such an institution could transform these children from potential criminals into law-abiding citizens who would accept the white, middle class values of the Managers.[31]

White girls of this period were not placed into institutions as frequently as white boys were, but when they were it was often because they were judged to be "fallen women" who were engaging in sexual behavior,[32] behaviors that were generally ignored when engaged in by boys. Gendered notions of what it was to be a girl made it a commonly held perception (arguably still held by many today) that girls were weaker and more vulnerable to temptation than boys. Some went as far as to say girls and women needed to be watched over more closely than their male counterparts because they were innately more sinful. Based upon these presumptions, reformers thought it was important to intervene in suspected girls' lives as early as possible and to watch over them for as long as possible.[33] Girls of poor and working-class European immigrant families were considered much more likely to be delinquent and were more likely to find themselves in an institution than native-born white girls.[34] When girls were put into institutions with boys, they were segregated within the institution. In 1856 the first reform school specifically for girls, the Lancaster Industrial School for Girls, opened in Massachusetts. It housed delinquent girls from 7 to 16 years of age. After a girl in the school turned 16, she was indentured to serve a family outside of the institution until her 18th birthday.[35]

Although the stated intent behind houses of refuge was to positively influence young people through discipline and labor, scholars today note that the outcomes of institutionalization were often negative ones.

Large-scale shifts in society came to the United States with the advent of the Industrial Revolution. Most notable are the development of machines and technology that changed the economic base of the society from agricultural to industrial, and a significant rise in the rate at which people were immigrating to the United States. People were needed to work in the factories that had been established, and the labor force began shifting away from the fields and farther from home. As capitalism took hold, opportunities for wage labor unrelated to the apprenticeship system multiplied. Requirements for factory labor were not high, and a young person could obtain a job quite easily. Over a million children between the ages of 10 and 15 were workers, according to the 1880 census.[36]

The predominant social construction of what it meant to be young during this period was in transition. In the late 1800s, the concept of adolescence began to be utilized as an extended period of childhood.[37] Upper- and middle-class Anglo American adults began to consider children as delicate people in need of protection and began organizing their family lives in a way that focused on their home and their immediate family. This conceptualization was at odds with child labor, a practice that involved low-income and immigrant youth who were forced to work to help their families make ends meet. Movements for social change gained momentum as activists, often middle- and upper-class white women and men, considered how to best address the role of youth in society's institutions and to spread their ideals about childhood and parenting in light of the challenges being posed by modernization, immigration, and the rise of technology.[38] Their actions became known as those of the Progressive movement, a social movement that began in roughly the 1890s and lasted until the beginning of World War I in 1914, and one in which reformers believed that they could utilize the expert knowledge provided by science to improve society. In order to protect youth and to allow them a longer period to develop and to be nurtured into well-rounded adults, reformers successfully campaigned for mandatory, and eventually age-graded, public schooling, which was put into effect by most Northern and Midwestern states by 1900,[39] and for child labor laws that resulted in the establishment of minimum age requirements for jobs and restrictions on the number of hours that youth could work. These changes were attempts to force parents to exclude their children from contributing in any significant way to the economic stability of their families, and to take what were seen as adult responsibilities out of the hands of youth.[40]

The idea of adolescence reinforced ideas about youth and delinquency that had been developing over the course of the 18th century. The psychiatrist who coined the term *adolescence*, G. Stanley Hall, stated, "A period of semicriminality is normal for all healthy boys . . . those whose surroundings are bad will continue it, but others will grow away from it as they reach maturity."[41] The idea that youth were redeemable, and that minor acts of delinquency did not doom an offending youth to a life of crime, fueled reformers' desires to address youth misbehavior in new ways. The houses of refuge, reform schools, and industrial schools established until that point began to be criticized by observers in light of acts of violence and abuse exposed there.[42] Reformers became less enthusiastic about the ability for these institutions to be the primary means of shaping wayward youths' behavior and began campaigning for a more substantial change—the separation of the adult and juvenile justice systems.

The first juvenile court was created in 1899, in Cook County, Illinois, and it marked one of the most important historical changes in the treatment of juveniles. By 1925, all but two states had established their own juvenile courts (Center for Juvenile & Criminal Justice, n.d.). We will examine the common characteristics of the various state juvenile justice systems that were developed near the turn of the 20th century in detail in the last section of the book. For now, it is sufficient to note that the development of the juvenile

A Focus on Research

Chávez-García's Intelligence Testing at
Whittier State School, 1890–1920

How did child savers and reformers make distinctions between the children whom they thought were worth saving and those whom they did not? Miroslava Chávez-García conducted a socio-historical study on the ways in which administrators of one reform school in California, the Whittier State School, utilized preconceived notions about youth of color, as well as intelligence testing, which often led to their removal from the reformatory.[43] In her article, "Intelligence Testing at Whittier State School, 1890–1920," she examines how popular scientific ideas at the turn of the 20th century shaped the decisions that were made about young males in the institution. Quite popular at that time was the field of eugenics and the idea that intelligence and criminality were genetic traits that could be scientifically identified.

The Whittier State School began as a place for the reform of delinquents from the ages of 10 to 16 who had not been placed in San Quentin, California's first adult prison. The Whittier youth would be released by the age of 21 according to the law. When the state of California created the school, it also created the Preston School of Industry, primarily for older males from 16 to 20 years of age. In 1912, businessman Fred Nelles came to take over the Whittier State School, and attempted to change it to reflect the day's philosophy about delinquency—that youth would respond to nurturing rather than harsh punishment. He emphasized athletics and schooling as a means of reforming youth, and many of them responded to the approach. He also hired a psychological researcher, J. Harold Williams, to conduct intelligence testing on each of the youth because he believed such tests could reveal a boy's mental abilities and the reason for his delinquency.

Although Nelles and his testing assistants were aware of the critiques of the Stanford-Binet test that they administered—that it did not accurately measure the intelligence of people who were not thoroughly familiar with the English language, or who had not been formerly schooled—they persisted with their approach. At the end of the process, Williams claimed that 28% of the boys were feebleminded and that 25% were borderline feebleminded. He additionally claimed that there were racial and ethnic differences in the intelligence of the boys and that the most notable issue with feeblemindedness was among youth from Mexico (60% of the boys were considered feebleminded), followed by African-American boys (48%) and lastly European American boys (6%). He attributed what he considered the deficiencies of the Mexican-origin youth to their "Indian blood."

Williams and Nelles recommended that the mentally defective boys be separated from the rest of the youth and sterilized, as to never pass on what they thought were genetic abnormalities that would prevent youth from becoming productive members of society. They encouraged the development of a second state hospital for the feebleminded that would allow for sterilization of wards without their consent, which was created in 1917 (the Pacific Colony). They released a disproportionate number of boys of color from the Whittier State School as a result of their intelligence test scores—some of them ended up in the industrial school and were tracked into vocational programs, and some ended up in the Pacific Colony, and possibly sterilized. The approach used at the Whittier State School for classifying its youth and segregating those deemed unintelligent was replicated at reform schools across the country.

DISCUSSION QUESTION

1. According to Chávez-García's historical research findings, intelligence testing of the young people in reform schools was motivated by a societal interest in eugenics at the time. What does the term *eugenics* signify? How might recent or future scientific approaches to delinquency and criminality be used to support eugenics campaigns? Should such approaches be supported and developed if they can be used to "weed out" people who are thought to be inferior?

Source: Chávez-García, M. (2007). Intelligence testing at Whittier State School, 1890–1920. *Pacific Historical Review, 76,* 193–228.

court was predicated upon the notion that youth are markedly different from adults, and that they are developing and are in need of protection by and from adults. The first court employed a rehabilitative philosophy, the idea that children who had engaged in misbehavior could be influenced to change their behaviors to more socially acceptable ones. **Rehabilitation** was a popular philosophy during the Progressive era, and it was linked to the acceptance of psychological and sociological theories of crime and delinquency at that time—theories that located the reasons for misbehavior not as purely rational choices for which the offender was fully responsible, but as factors outside of the conscious control of the actor. In other words, if physical, psychological, and/or social factors were related to the creation of delinquency and crime, they could be scientifically identified, and then changed or eliminated (see also Chapter 11).

The creation of juvenile courts at the turn of the 20th century marked a new era in how youth were dealt under the law.

The stated purpose of the juvenile court was to address the needs and behaviors of youth who had allegedly misbehaved (delinquent youth) and those who were in need of care because they had been neglected, abandoned, or abused (dependent and/or neglected youth). In order to distinguish between the juvenile court and the adult court, a completely different language for every stage in the process was created—cemented in an idea that had been percolating for some time: that juvenile *delinquents* should not be equated with adult *criminals*.[44] It served as response to arguments made by parents of youth institutionalized indefinitely in cases such as that of Mary Ann Crouse, discussed above, and made it so youth could have their time in court. Scholars have cautioned against looking back on the child savers' creation of the juvenile court as a purely benevolent or kind move as the operation of the courts favored white boys who were thought to have the potential to be reformed and molded into valuable citizens, unlike girls of all races and boys of color.[45] In addition, the juvenile courts made it possible for the state to intrude upon family life in ways that were previously never allowed, and juvenile court actors created a whole other category of offenses known as status offenses (acts labeled inappropriate for youth, simply because of their age, such as drinking alcohol, running away from home, truancy, and walking outside at night; see also Chapters 1 and 6) that expanded the number of youth who would one day find themselves wrapped up in the juvenile justice system.

Views of Youth and Delinquency in the Juvenile Court (1899–Present)

The views about youth upon which the juvenile court was based were not questioned in any substantial way until the 1960s.[46] The 1960s were a time of a rise in the teenage population as the large population of children born after World War II (i.e., the generation known as the baby boomers) entered adolescence. This generation garnered quite a bit of attention, and as a subset experimented openly with drugs, protested against social and legal institutions, and rose up against the status quo. The group's actions were often tied to the many movements for social change that had grabbed the attention of the public during this period of U.S. history. Large numbers of people had become active in social movements such as the civil rights movement, the peace movement (also known as the anti–Vietnam War movement), and the feminist movement, all which shared concerns

● ● ●

Rehabilitation:
The idea that youth who engage in delinquency and misbehavior should be taught how to change their ways in order to develop prosocial behaviors.

about legal fairness and equality. Urbanization had resulted in racial and ethnic diversity in major cities, and increased attention to the legacy of discrimination that remained even after the abolishment of segregation in 1954 and other Jim Crow laws (laws that allowed for a two-tiered social system in which black Americans were disadvantaged) with the 1964 Civil Rights Act. Frustration with racism and classism led to several uprisings as people became more conscious of the injustices that they faced. There were over 164 of these uprisings or "race riots" in just the first six months of 1967, along with protests at college campuses across the country.[47] These events brought social tensions to public awareness, and it became apparent that the U.S. justice system was seen by many to target communities of color and the poor and working class. Less discussed, but present as well, were the numerous ways that juvenile justice courts and detention centers were used to deviantize and abuse LGBT youth and to attempt to "cure" them of their sexual orientation and/or gender identity through rehabilitation programs.[48] Others were threatened by the social unrest and were looking to get tougher on juvenile misbehavior. As we will examine in Chapter 11, this era marked the beginning of a due process revolution in which young people who were accused and/or adjudicated delinquent gained additional legal rights.

POPULAR CULTURE: A TARGET OF MORAL PANICS ABOUT DELINQUENCY

Now that we have taken an in-depth look at some of the major changes in the way that youth and juvenile delinquency were defined historically prior to the development of the juvenile justice system, it is revealing to look at some of the accompanying **moral panics** or scares about delinquency that have occurred over the course of U.S. history.[49] These scares typically share a number of elements: The news and/or entertainment media spread exaggerated information about the prevalence and seriousness of delinquency and/or an alleged source of juvenile delinquency in the community, interested community members pick up on the information, and attempts are made to fuel some sort of change or reform to the system. Regardless of whether any meaningful change is accomplished, the particular characterization of the juvenile delinquency problem tends to fade away, and subsequently reemerges in another form.[50] What is interesting about these scares is that they often involve competing images about youth simultaneously: the idea of youth as vulnerable and impressionable and the idea of youth as mini-adults ready to pounce on any opportunity to engage in something dangerous.

These panics not only are fueled by the publicity generated by media sources, such as television shows, news stories, and print journalism, but often the very focus of the scares is the *consumption and/or use* of different means of communication and entertainment and how they allegedly lead to delinquency. In this section of the chapter we will focus on some of the means of communication and entertainment that have grabbed the attention of politicians, scholars, newsmakers, and the general public because of their alleged links with juvenile delinquency. There have been other sorts of scares related to juvenile delinquency as well; scares about youth drug use and youth weapon use are also popular, and will be discussed in other chapters in this book.

When we examine these historical panics about delinquency and popular culture, it helps us place current moral panics about delinquency in the proper context. Then, when we consider, for example, heightened concerns about the effect of Internet use on youth delinquency in the 21st century, we can attempt to be more objective about the issues at hand. Are such concerns deserving of serious attention, or are they simply the result of overzealous adults targeting a trend because it is popular with young people or because they misunderstand it?

● ● ●

Moral panic:
Heightened concern over an issue that is not in line with its seriousness or frequency of occurrence in the world.

Ahmed Mohamed and the Clock That Started a Panic

In September 2015 in Irving, Texas, 14-year-old Ahmed Mohamed, a student of Sudanese ancestry who is Muslim, was suspended from his high school after he brought a homemade clock to school to show his engineering teacher. Ahmed aims to be an engineer and likes creating different devices. His English teacher was upset after the alarm on the clock went off in class and she reported him to the principal, who then called law enforcement. They said they suspected that the clock was a bomb. The police searched Ahmed and escorted him out of school in handcuffs to a juvenile detention facility. He was fingerprinted, made to take a mug shot, and then suspended for three days after release. Widespread publicity of the event started a social media campaign on Twitter—#IStandWithAhmed—that highlighted the discrimination that Muslim youth face when they are assumed to be involved in terrorism. Ahmed received messages of support from around the world, including from President Obama. His experience is focused upon in a "trap transmedia" project created by Jamel Mims, which includes a rap and video named after Ahmed and aims to draw attention to the discrimination faced by Muslim Americans.

The panic that ensued when Ahmed Mohamed brought a homemade clock to school was the result of negative stereotyping of Muslim American youth.

DISCUSSION QUESTIONS

1. How does the panic around Ahmed's clock reflect how many non-Muslim adults perceive and stereotype Muslim American youth?

2. How did the social media response in support of Ahmed challenge this social construction?

Sources: Rao, S. (2015, Sept. 17). Zuckerberg, Obama and more stand with Ahmed. *Colorlines*. Retrieved from https://www.colorlines.com/articles/zuckerberg-obama-and-more-stand-ahmed; Rao, S. (2016, June 1). Watch: The story of Ahmed Mohamed told via trap music and magical realism. *Colorlines*. Retrieved from https://www.colorlines.com/articles/watch-story-ahmed-mohamed-told-trap-music-and-magical-realism

Some of the first scares about the influence of music and the arts came early in the history of the United States. In the late 1700s there was a burgeoning concern about the dangers of "explicit" songs and photos as inspirations for juvenile delinquency, as explained in the words of an English doctor of the time:

> Even ballad singers and street musicians are useful in their spheres to promote vice. . . . Observe who listen to and buy those lewd ballads, you will find that young people of both sexes, particularly apprentice boys, servant maids, and gentleman servants, are the purchasers. They read them with the greatest avidity, and thereby poison their morals, by affording them fuel to their turbulent passions.[51]

Hardly imaginable in today's world, silent movies were seen as a likely source of delinquency by some adults in the United States in the early 1900s.

The concerns about music and photography were followed with a related concern—acting and drama, and their purported negative influence upon youth. The concern was that youth would be corrupted not only by watching acting, but by engaging in acting. An administrator in the Philadelphia House of Refuge described his perception of this threat:

> A new source of juvenile corruption has been opened in the city, which deserves to be noticed. They allude to what for want of a more appropriate phrase may be called children's theatres . . . the actors and the audience are minors of both sexes, though it is supposed that the whole is under the direction and for the benefit of adults. They are established in obscure places, the price of admission is low, and there is unlimited license in them for every sort of vicious indulgence.[52]

In the early decades of the 1900s, there were concerns about all forms of media as delinquency instigators. Dime novels, small, cheap books that tended to have extreme plots full of action, were thought to be full of bad ideas that would tempt young people into wrongdoing.[53] As one delinquency theorist of the time noted, "It is not unknown to find counterfeiting and even murder springing from bad reading."[54] The "flaming youth" era of the silent films of the 1920s and the "talking films" of the 1930s were seen by some adults as providing youth with easy exposure to provocative and dangerous ideas.[55] During this period, a lot of negative attention was focused on jazz music as well. Magazine articles with titles such as "Does Jazz Put the Sin in Syncopation?" were written as a means of raising awareness about the dangers of jazz.[56] The music form was accused of bringing out evil in the listener. Jazz dancing and jazz music were considered to be dangerous for the youth, and part of the concern was rooted in racism because jazz was closely associated with black musicians. Claims about jazz and delinquency typically had the following tone:

> Anyone who says that "youths of both sexes can mingle in close embrace"—with limbs intertwined and torso in contact—without suffering harm lies. Add to this position the wriggling movement and sensuous stimulation of the abominable jazz orchestra with its voodoo-born minors and its direct appeal to the sensory center, and if you can believe youth is the same after this experience as before, then God help your child.[57]

Communities across the country passed laws prohibiting jazz music in public dance halls as a result of this scare.

Another mass medium began getting a lot of attention in the 1930s and 1940s, and in the 1950s reached a peak in terms of the popular attention it was given as a possible source of the corruption of youth.[58] This source of fear was the comic book. Comic books were thought to be very influential during the early 20th century, and by the 1950s all sorts of comics were being printed weekly—those considered relatively innocent such as *Donald Duck* and *Archie*, and then a variety of others that raised the concern of many adults, such as comics having to do with romance, crime, and horror. (*Tales From the Crypt* was one that garnered quite a bit of negative attention in the horror genre.) J. Edgar Hoover used comics to advertise the crime fighting of the Federal Bureau of Investigation, but by the 1950s the main concern discussed among social scientists, government officials, law enforcement agents, and members of the Catholic Church was that comic books were being used as tools to learn how to commit acts of delinquency and crime. These comic books, along with other media, were the focus of a series of televised congressional hearings on the causes of juvenile delinquency in 1954 (known as the Kefauver hearings for one of the senators who helped lead them). Ultimately, a rating system for comics was put into place as a result of these concerns, the Comics Code Authority, and comic books stamped with approval were ones deemed safe for young people to read.[59]

••• *on the* MEDIA

Award-Winning Perspectives on Juvenile Justice Issues

Every year, the National Council for Crime and Delinquency (NCCD) announces their choices for the Annual Media for a Just Society Awards (http://www.nccdglobal.org/newsroom/media-for-a-just-society-awards).

The NCCD analyzes a number of types of media—books, films, magazines, newspapers, radio, TV/video, and web sources—before they choose which pieces have done the best job of spreading accurate information about the juvenile and adult justice systems in the United States. Some examples of winners that focused upon juvenile justice issues are the film *The Central Park Five* by Ken Burns; the newspaper article "Will Juvenile Lifers Get a Second Chance?" by Alan Prendergast of *Westword;* the book *Burning Down the House: The End of the Juvenile Prison*; and episodes 1–3 in the VICE news documentary series *Last Chance High.* In 2015, the NCCD's Just Society Youth Media Award went to Marlo Scott for his online article in *Represent,* "My Looking-Glass Self."[60]

In the article, Marlo, a former foster youth, describes his path through high school and college and the way he consciously changed his self-concept and presentation of self in order to change his life.

He acknowledges that he was a smart kid in middle school but he felt he needed to act tough to gain the respect of his peers. Mario explains that although he enjoyed his image as a "thug" for a while, he knew during his first year of high school that he wanted to change his image in order to accomplish his goal of going to college one day and becoming an accountant. Marlo's story is a reflexive look at how one young person put the concept of Cooley's looking glass self (see Chapter 6) into use in his own life.

DISCUSSION QUESTIONS

1. What are the benefits of new forms of media that provide outlets for first-person accounts of delinquency? What can we learn from them?

2. What do you think it would take for there to be more socially just depictions of youth and their behaviors in the media? Explain the reasoning behind your answer.

Music continued to be targeted throughout the decades as a cause of delinquency—in the 1950s with rock music and worries about the influence of a gyrating Elvis Presley—and in the 1960s and 1970s with concerns over "hippies" and the influence of groups such as the Grateful Dead. In the 1980s and 1990s, more scares about music entertainment garnered attention. This time, the concern was not with jazz or mainstream rock music, but with heavy metal rock music and rap music.[61] The concern with heavy metal music occurred in the mid-1980s, and at its root was the idea that its lyrics might corrupt youth. Indicative of this argument was that the "lyrics glamorize drug and alcohol use, and glorify death and violent rebellion, ranging from hatred of parents and teachers to suicide—the ultimate act of violence to oneself."[62] In 1985, the issue of what was called "porn rock" was investigated by the U.S. Senate, and the Parents' Music Resource Center (PMRC), a group led by women who were tied to the political power structure in Washington, DC, at the time (e.g., Tipper Gore, who was married to Senator Al Gore, and Susan Baker, who was married to Treasury Secretary Al Baker), was asked to participate in the hearing. A psychiatrist working with the PMRC claimed that

> the individual identified in the newspapers as the Night Stalker has been said to be into hard drugs and the music of the heavy metal band AC/DC. . . . Young people who are seeking power over others through the identification with the power of evil find a close identification. The lyrics become a philosophy of life. It becomes a religion.

The PMRC also claimed that listening to heavy metal music would lead children to violence against others: teachers, parents, and women.[63] They claimed that a good deal of heavy metal music was linked to Satanism, and worship of the devil would certainly lead teenagers to nothing but negative behavior. According to their argument, youth needed to be protected from the threats posed by such music. Many record companies began to put parental advisory stickers to signify explicit lyrics on albums that same year.

Beginning in the early 1990s, delinquency and crime became associated in the mainstream media with rap music. As Binder explains, the concerns about rap music immediately were framed differently than those around the predominantly white genre of heavy metal music—rap and rap listeners were almost always characterized as a danger to society.[64] When the PMRC or others voiced concerns about rap music's effect on youth, they tended not to ever voice concern about the young men of color who might be "corrupted" by the lyrics, as they did with heavy metal, but instead considered the threats these young men might pose to others in society in the form of hanging out together and possibly raping women or threatening others.[65] A particular form of rap, "gangsta rap," became popular in the early 1990s with groups such as N.W.A. and rappers such as Snoop Dogg and Dr. Dre at the top of music sales. These rappers garnered a lot of negative attention from concerned adults because of their songs' explicit lyrics, gang references, and use of violent and sexist language.[66] The concern was once again that the music would provoke delinquency, but delinquency on the part of young men of color, particularly young black men, was at the crux of the uproar. This concern has remained until the present day. In fact, in spite of all the concern about rap music in the 1990s, it was not until 2007 that a congressional subcommittee conducted a hearing on the issues of language and violence in rap music. Lawmakers quoted rapper 50 Cent's lyrics and analyzed the role of the explicit music on young listeners.[67] In the 21st century, concerns about the dangers of some forms of cultural consumption, such as listening to electronic and other forms of music at raves, are not always characterized by moral outrage; instead, they are highly bureaucratized efforts at "quiet regulation."[68] In spite of the different form of claims-making present in these regulatory efforts, like moral panics, they ultimately facilitate the social control of media and cultural forms, as well as their consumers.

from the CLASSROOM to the COMMUNITY

The Campaign for Youth Justice—"Because the Consequences Aren't Minor"

The Campaign for Youth Justice (CYJ) is a social action group based in Washington, D.C., that is actively challenging the misconceptions about youth and their experiences in the justice system. The CYJ motto, "Because the consequences aren't minor," reflects the group's primary concerns, which are the results that come from prosecuting and imprisoning youth in the adult justice system. One of the many campaigns that the CYJ is behind is National Youth Justice Awareness Month; a Missouri mother named Tracy McClard whose son killed himself during his incarceration in the adult system started an advocacy campaign in which the facts about youth justice are focused upon in cities across the United States yearly during activities in October. Since 2008, activities such as 5k run/walks, art exhibits, poetry slams, and film screenings have been undertaken during National Youth Justice Awareness month as a means of pointing out that youth who are punished within the juvenile justice system are less likely to reoffend than those who have been incarcerated in the adult system. In spite of popular notions of youth, CYJ argues that youth are not yet mature adults, but developing children in need of different punishments than their adult counterparts.

DISCUSSION QUESTION

1. Are you familiar with CYJ's or similar campaigns in your own community? What types of activities do you think best get the word out about information related to treating youth who have committed acts of delinquency as adults? Are any of your ideas different from those used by CYJ?

Sources: Campaign for Youth Justice. (n.d.). *Current campaigns.* Retrieved from http://www.campaignforyouthjustice.org/change-the-system/current-campaigns.html; Campaign for Youth Justice. (n.d.). *National youth justice awareness month.* Retrieved from http://www.campaignforyouthjustice.org/change-the-system/national-youth-justice-awareness-month.html

Another moral panic about media effects on youth occurred in the 2000s, and this panic was focused on playing video games or "gaming." Although videogames played at home on a TV or computer have been popular since the 1980s, the concern about violent or sexually suggestive video games and their effects on youth's behavior did not become a major concern until the 1990s. In 1992, a videogame called *Night Trap* ignited the fears of many adults who misconstrued its content as gratuitous violence that could lead to aggression among the youth who played it, particularly boys. Uproar over the concern led to yet another set of congressional hearings on offensive video game content, and ultimately, by 1994, the video game industry began a rating system to indicate which games were appropriate for which age groups. In spite of this "solution," adult concern over violent video games as a gateway to violent acts of delinquency continued. In the 2000s the games became increasingly realistic due to sophisticated technology. Claims that playing games such as *Grand Theft Auto*, which has 3D graphics and players who assume roles as characters who engage in virtual crimes, led teenagers to engage in such acts themselves began being heard in courtrooms across the United States. Politicians led the charge yet again against the video game industry in an effort to protect youth gamers. In 2010, California, following several other states,[69] attempted to pass a law stating that "extremely violent video games" could no longer be sold to minors. The U.S. Supreme Court in *Brown v. Entertainment Merchants Association* (2011) agreed with a lower court that ruled that the law was unconstitutional.[70] The majority decision made reference to the many moral panics about delinquency and youth that had come prior to the violent video game scare before claiming that such a restriction violated the right to free speech.

In December of 2012, the shooting of 20 children and six staff members at Sandy Hook Elementary School in Newtown, Connecticut renewed interest in the effects of violent video games on youth and young adults. The 20-year-old shooter, Adam Lanza, was barely out of his teenage years when he shot his mother at home, took three of her guns, went to Sandy Hook Elementary to commit a mass shooting, and then killed himself.[71] Some news stories that followed the tragedy claimed that Lanza spent a lot of time playing violent video games, like *Call of Duty*, in his basement.[72] Although these claims were ultimately disputed, public concern about violent video games gained international attention as the vice president of the United States, Joseph Biden, met with gaming industry executives to encourage them to think twice about the promotion of violence for entertainment.[73] Legislation was proposed in the House of Representatives to ban the sale of violent video games to minors, and President Obama encouraged Congress to dedicate $10 million to the study of the connection between violent video games and societal violence.[74] In Southington, Connecticut there were efforts to gather and burn a bunch of violent video games as a statement of outrage (that never came to pass).[75] Less than six months later, Nathon Brooks, a 14-year-old from Moses Lake, Washington, received widespread attention beginning in March 2013 when he was accused of shooting both of his parents after his parents took his video games away.[76] He told police that he was playing video games "24/7" until he was grounded and his parents took his electronic devices away. Brooks took a pistol out of the family safe and shot both of his parents, who survived. He was first charged with two counts of attempted murder, but ultimately, he pled guilty to two charges of assault, a lesser punishment for which his parents argued.[77]

Amidst all the heightened attention given to a possible video game–violence connection, there were some opposing voices. For example, psychologist and video game scholar Christopher Ferguson noted in an editorial for the *Hartford Courant* newspaper,

> Of course most young males play at least some violent video games; by this standard it would be possible to link almost any crime by men under 40 to them. That's about as meaningful as linking crime to anything else almost everybody does — watching *Sesame Street* as a kid, wearing sneakers, drinking soda. Newtown was an opportunity for moral crusaders to harrumph over violent video games as they did over rock music in the 1980s and comic books in the 1950s.
>
> By focusing, uselessly, on violent video games, these debates suck the air out of discussions of real issues such as tackling mental illness before it can do harm. During the past 20 years in which video games have soared in popularity, youth violence has dropped by almost 90 percent. We would do well to remember this, concentrate on more pressing matters such as poverty, and forgo discussion of cultural issues, if we are really serious about crime.[78]

Ferguson's points reflect the findings of one arm of recent video game research that do not support the assertion that violent video games lead to real-life violence and claim that the harmfulness of video games is often assumed by clinicians and researchers, in part because of a generational divide.[79] Adachi and Willoughby found that the *competitive element of* video game play is linked to an increase in aggression over time, not necessarily the violent content of a given game.[80] They also claimed that it is important to shift the attention from the negative effects of video games to the more positive—such as the role of strategic video games in developing pro-social skills that help adolescent gamers do well academically.[81]

As the use of the Internet becomes increasingly integrated in the lives of young people, other forms of online expression have come under public scrutiny as possible inspirations for delinquent acts. One of these forms is online storytelling, such as on the website Creepypasta, which is a compilation of scary stories and urban legends that have been cut and pasted to the website or have been created on the Creepypasta Wiki.[82] The stories are often ghost stories or horror stories, and although they may include stories of murder and suicide, website founders state the purpose of the website is a literary one. They had to defend their website repeatedly in the 2010s after the commission of violent acts by teens who said characters on Creepypasta motivated them. In the most publicized example, two 12-year-olds in Wisconsin, Morgan Geyser and Anissa Weier, went with their mutual friend, Payton Leutner, into the woods and allegedly stabbed her 19 times.[83] They claimed that they did so in order to please a character known as Slender Man that they had read about on Creepypasta Wiki: a tall, thin, faceless character who wears a suit, has tentacles on his back, and abducts children.[84] The girls noted that they had hoped to gain his favor through the blood sacrifice of killing their friend and, ultimately, to be protected from any harm that he might otherwise do to them.[85] In 2015, another incident involving Creepypasta came to light

In recent years online characters like Slender Man have been blamed for influencing serious acts of delinquency.

in Elkhart, Indiana. A 12-year-old girl allegedly stabbed her 50-year-old stepmother, Maria Torres, because she thought a Creepypasta clown named Laughing Jack told her to do so.[86] The Laughing Jack character is portrayed online as a clown that approaches kids, gains their trust, and eventually kills them and stuffs them with candy.[87] In both of these cases of preteen violence, the mental health of the perpetrators has been called into question,[88] yet popular interest in the stories remains fixated on the role played by the words and images on the Internet.

AT THE CROSSROADS: 21ST-CENTURY SOCIAL CONSTRUCTIONS OF YOUTH AND DELINQUENCY

As we have described in this chapter, the treatment of the subject of youth and delinquency has had a long history, full of twists, turns, and repetitions. In contemporary society, adults portray youth in two fundamentally different ways: "Children play a dual role in terms of innocence and brutality, protection and control. We can justify excess in protecting children, and increasingly, we can excuse excess in punishing them, particularly—and paradoxically—if extreme sanctions will protect the innocence of children."[89] In the last decade of the 20th century, following the well-publicized school shooting in Columbine, Colorado, media sources increasingly spread the message that youth were often more frequently people to be afraid of, rather than people to protect.[90] In keeping with our historical past, black and brown youth, particularly young men, were characterized as people law-abiding adults should be afraid of and protected against.[91] Girls, although not seen as quite as threatening as their male counterparts, were also the objects of heightened concern, as claims that they were getting out of control—joining gangs, acting like boys, and being overtly assertive and violent—were publicized.[92] LGBT youth were demonized and abused by the public and in juvenile institutions by adults who were charged with protecting them.[93] These messages about youth have not disappeared in the 21st century. As Henry Giroux explains, "Put bluntly, American society at present exudes a deep-rooted hostility and chilling fear about youth."[94]

In spite of the widespread fears about youth that persist, we can look at the Supreme Court decisions made in the 2000s (as we will in Chapter 11 of this book), and see that the justices are utilizing the same social characterization of young people who engage in delinquency that Progressive reformers did over a century ago—that of youth as people who are developing mentally and socially, deserve time to do so, and can redeem themselves in light of any mistakes that they make during their childhood and adolescent years. Perhaps the balance is slowly shifting, and soon this idea of youth misbehavior will once again predominate.

In the News

The Deaths of Trayvon Martin, Michael Brown, and Tamir Rice

On February 26, 2012, an African-American 17-year-old, Trayvon Martin, was shot to death by a self-appointed neighborhood watchperson, George Zimmerman. Martin was walking back to his father's girlfriend's home in a gated community in Orlando, Florida, after going to the store during a break in the NBA All-Star game that he was watching. He was carrying some Skittles candy and an iced tea from the store.[95] It was raining, and he was wearing the hood of his sweatshirt up to keep from getting wet. Zimmerman was patrolling the neighborhood

The deaths of Trayvon Martin, Michael Brown, and Tamir Rice resulted in widespread mourning and social protest.

and noticed Martin walking. He confronted Martin for walking through the neighborhood and ultimately shot him, which he claimed was in self-defense, although Martin was unarmed. On July 13, 2013, a jury made up predominantly of white women found Zimmerman not guilty in the death of Martin.[96]

On August 9, 2014, an 18-year-old unarmed African-American young man named Michael Brown was killed as the result of multiple gunshots to his body in Ferguson, Missouri by a white police officer named Darren Wilson.[97] What happened that day was subject to many conflicting accounts, but ultimately what has been shown is that the use of deadly force against Brown was an extreme response, and less fatal police tactics could have been employed. A grand jury of six white men, three white women, one black man, and two black women was convened to consider the case. Nine votes out of twelve were needed to indict Wilson, and the grand jury ultimately did not indict him.[98]

On November 22, 2014 in Columbus, Ohio a 12-year-old African-American boy, Tamir Rice, was shot and killed by a white police officer-in-training, Timothy Loehmann. Loehmann and his supervisor, Frank Garmback, responded to a 911 call from someone near the rec center who stated there was "a guy with a pistol" that was "probably fake." Video of the incident showed that when the police drove up to the area where Rice was standing, Loehmann shot him within seconds of his arrival. While the grand jury deliberated, prosecutors hired their own investigators who wrote reports that the officer's use of lethal force was justified and released them to the public.[99] A grand jury decided not to indict either Loehmann or Garmback on criminal charges.[100] Outrage and controversy has followed the decision, as the Cuyahoga County Prosecutor's Office noted that the grand jury did not actually vote on the issue of indictment, which is highly unusual.[101]

The law enforcement-related deaths of Martin, Brown, and Rice are related to numerous others that have occurred. In the aftermath of these killings, *The Guardian* did a study that revealed that in 2015, "Despite making up only 2% of the total US population, African-American males

between the ages of 15 and 34 comprised more than 15% of all deaths logged this year by an ongoing investigation into the use of deadly force by police. Their rate of police-involved deaths was five times higher than for white men of the same age."[102] This finding was also supported by other studies, such as one published by Amnesty International.[103]

DISCUSSION QUESTIONS

1. The outcry over the deaths of Trayvon Martin, Michael Brown, and Tamir Rice is related to the widespread perception that their deaths were one of the violent outcomes experienced by youth of color after they are stereotyped and assumed to be dangerous. What are some ways that people are challenging these stereotypes and assumptions?

2. What are some additional social changes that you think are necessary to prevent the use of deadly force against youth of color?

Sources: Amnesty International (2015). *Deadly force: Police use of force in the United States.* New York: Amnesty International USA; Associated Press. (2014, August 22). Racial and gender makeup of grand jury revealed in Ferguson case. *CBS News.* Fantz, A., Almasy, S., & Shoichet, C. E. (2015, Dec. 28). Tamir Rice shooting: No charges for officers. *CNN News.* Retrieved from http://www.cnn.com/2015/12/28/us/tamir-rice-shooting; Gutman, M. (2012). Trayvon Martin neighborhood watch shooting: 911 tapes send mom crying from room. *ABC News,* March 16. Retrieved from http://www.abcnews.go.com/US/treyvon-martin-neighborhood-watch-shooting-911-tapes-send/story?id=15937881#.T2vBicyyzQo; Lee, J. (2015, Oct. 28). Outrage is growing over the Tamir Rice investigation. Is the grand jury process stacked in favor of the cop that killed the 12-year-old? *Mother Jones.* Retrieved from http://www.motherjones.com/politics/2015/10/tamir-rice-leaked-reports-grand-jury; Sandy, E. & Grzegorek, V. (2016, Jan. 20). The grand jury in the Tamir Rice case did not take a vote on charges. *Scene.* Retrieved from http://www.clevescene.com/scene-and-heard/archives/2016/01/20/the-grand-jury-in-the-tamir-rice-case-did-not-take-a-vote-on-charges; Swaine, J., Laughland, O., & Lartey, J. (2016, Jan. 2). Young black men killed by police at highest rate in year of 1,134 deaths. Retrieved from http://www.alternet.org/civil-liberties/young-black-men-killed-us-police-highest-rate-year-1134-deaths; Tienabesco, S., Gutman, M., & Wash, S. (2013). George Zimmerman found not guilty and goes free. *ABC News,* July 13. Retrieved from http://abcnews.go.com/US/george-zimmerman-found-guilty-free/story?id=19653300

Adults' ideas about who young people are and how they should be treated have undergone large shifts over time. Social constructions of youth from ancient times to the Middle Ages provided a common understanding that young people over the age of 7 were capable of handling an ever-increasing amount of responsibility, and when children misbehaved they were often treated as an adult would be. The English common law tradition that came to influence the region that is now the United States was one that focused upon *mens rea*, or whether a young person was capable of having a guilty mind and pre-planning an act of wrongdoing in advance. Typically, children from the ages of 7 to 14 were thought to have some ability to do such planning, and those above the age of 14 were assumed to have the same abilities as adults. After the invention of the printing press and with the advent of industrialization, adults began to question their ideas about childhood and decided that some children, particularly white children from middle- and upper-class families, needed to be formally educated over time. Urbanization that accompanied industrialization led to an increase in population in major cities, as well as a more visible presence of children on the streets who were from working-class and/or poor families. Concerns about the seeming lack of supervision of such children fueled reform efforts in the "child saving" era of the 19th and early 20th centuries.

The child saving era brought with it the creation of a number of new institutions that reformers used to address children's behaviors or their family situations: "poor farms," asylums, farm schools, labor schools, and houses of refuge. Most of these institutions functioned to teach lessons about hard work and individual responsibility. The legal justification of *parens patriae*, or the state as a substitute parent for children who were deemed to be abused or neglected, or to have parents who could not control them, led to the increased institutionalization of youth. These institutions treated the young people differently depending on their race, ethnicity, and gender. For example, black youth were not allowed in houses of refuge until 1850 and, unlike white youth, were still treated as adults and housed in adult prisons until that time. Girls from immigrant families and poor and working-class families were much more likely to be placed in an institution for concerns about their immoral behavior than native-born white girls were—and girls in general were watched over more closely and disciplined more often than boys.

In the late 1800s, the concept of adolescence was created, and its increasing acceptance as a stage of human development during the late 19th century culminated in the development of the first juvenile court in Cook County, Illinois, in 1899. This was followed by the creation of juvenile courts across the country, and the founders of such courts claimed that they were based on a rehabilitative philosophy—the idea that young people who had committed an act of delinquency were capable of changing their behavior and staying out of trouble if they were given the support and guidance to do so. Status offenses, acts that are considered problematic because of the age of the person carrying them out (e.g., truancy and curfew violations), were among the many that adult reformers targeted in the day-to-day functioning of the juvenile justice system. Juveniles were considered distinct from adults, and the juvenile justice system was set up to treat them differently from adults; in turn, they were given fewer legal rights than adults. This changed a bit in the due process revolution of the 1960s when a number of significant legal protections were established.

Moral panics about delinquency have accompanied the many shifts in how young people have been viewed over time. These scares typically share a number of elements: The news and/or entertainment media spread exaggerated information about the prevalence and seriousness of delinquency and/or an alleged source of juvenile delinquency in the community, interested community members pick up on the information, and attempts are made to fuel some sort of change or reform to the system. Sometimes media forms themselves are often targeted as the source of delinquency; panics about music, comic books, and video games frequently occur.

The mass media have long played a role in socially constructing delinquency by portraying images of youth and delinquency that can impact the viewer. Typically, images of youth of color, girls, and the working class in the news, on television, and in film have been stereotypical ones that misrepresent the broad range of life experiences of these young people.[104] Just take a quick look at some of the titles of the films that depict delinquency in the mid-20th century—*Good-Time Girl* (1948), *So Young, So Bad* (1950), and *So Evil, So Young* (1961). Although usually films misrepresent the complex realities of children who act out delinquently and/or are wards of the state, documentary films, though not nearly as popular as fictional films, do a better job of showing the true experiences of youth.

For this exercise, explore depictions of youth, delinquency, and dependence in films released in the 21st century. These films may be fictional dramas or documentaries focusing upon actual events and people. It is revealing to compare and contrast depictions of youth and delinquency (and issues of dependency, neglect, and abuse leading to state institutionalization) from countries around the world as well, and thus our list of suggested movies is international in scope.

Some suggestions: *Girlhood* (2015, France); *DOPE* (2015, U.S.); *The Life of a King* (2013); *Fish Tank* (2009, U.K.); *Independent Lens*: "Me Facing Life: Cyntoia's Story" (2011, U.S.); *White Irish Drinkers* (2010, U.S.); *Yelling at the Sky* (2011, U.S.); *Neds* (2010, U.K.); *The Unloved* (2009, U.S.); *Confession* (2005, U.S.); *If I Want to Whistle, I Whistle* (2010, Romania); *The Edukators* (2005, Germany); *The Wild and Wonderful Whites of West Virginia* (2009, U.S.); *Holy Rollers* (2010, U.S.); *Bullet Boy* (2004, U.K.); *The Black Donnellys* (2007, U.S.); *Liberty Kid* (2007, U.S.); *I'm Gonna Explode* (2008, Mexico); *The Glass House* (2009, Iran).

After watching a film, or films, answer the following questions:

1. How do the filmmakers portray the factors that lead to delinquency and dependence on the part of youth?

2. How are issues of race, class, gender, and sexuality portrayed?

3. When filmmakers explicitly or implicitly address the "solutions" to delinquency, what do they focus upon in the film or films you have chosen to analyze?

DISCUSSION QUESTIONS

1. After reading about the history of the social construction of delinquency in this chapter, what three facts about it did you find the most surprising? Explain why you found them surprising. Did they challenge your understanding of how we have come to define delinquency today?

2. Why is it the case that many scholars look back on the houses of refuge and state that they were misnamed?

3. How did considerations of race, ethnicity, social class, gender, and sexuality affect the ways that authorities throughout history handled delinquency and dependency?

4. In what ways did the creation of juvenile courts shift mainstream perceptions about youth and delinquency at the turn of the 20th century? How did the due process cases of the 1960s and early 1970s later affect perceptions about youth and delinquency? Were these similar or dissimilar effects?

5. What can we learn from analyzing the various moral panics or scares about popular culture and delinquency? What are some current issues in popular culture that are garnering excessive attention for being alleged inspirations for delinquency?

KEY TERMS

Houses of refuge 38

Mens rea 36

Moral panic 44

Parens patriae 38

Rehabilitation 43

Social constructions of youth and delinquency 34

CHAPTER PRETEST ANSWERS

1. False

2. True

3. True

4. True

5. False

6. False

7. True

STUDENT STUDY SITE

$SAGE edge™

edge.sagepub.com/bates2e

Sharpen your skills with SAGE edge!

SAGE edge for students provides a personalized approach to help you accomplish your coursework goals in an easy-to-use learning environment. You'll find action plans, mobile-friendly eFlashcards, and quizzes, as well as videos, web resources, and links to SAGE journal articles to support and expand on the concepts presented in this chapter. Check out the website for original videos of former offenders discussing their experiences as juveniles.

CHAPTER 3

UNDERSTANDING DELINQUENCY

Data, Correlates, and Trends

CHAPTER OBJECTIVES ··

After reading this chapter, you should be able to

- Describe what is needed to create a good statistic (gather good data)

- Explain the difference between quantitative and qualitative data

- Explain the correlates of delinquency

- Explain the strengths and weaknesses of each data source

- Explain the trends in delinquency (violence, property, and drug crimes)

- Analyze the race differences in trends in delinquency (violence, property, and drug crimes)

- Analyze the gender differences in trends in delinquency (violence, property, and drug crimes)

- Compare and contrast the type of data used in our understanding of the correlates and trends in delinquency

Our girls are becoming more violent. This was the unsolicited opinion of a stranger in the supermarket line I was standing in. I was surprised by the observation because, frankly, my young sons were creating good-natured havoc in between us, and I wondered how anyone could be focused on girls and delinquency during all of the commotion. The stranger pointed to People magazine and the story of a young American woman accused of murder in Italy. "It's a sad story," I said in reply, which opened the way for more opinion. "Girls didn't used to go around killing people. But now, these days, they are as bad as boys. They fight, and steal, and kill their roommates. I don't know what this world is coming to—it seems like young people are getting scarier and scarier. I expect it from boys," the stranger said, looking down at my sons, "but never girls." This opinion, shared in the traditional media and online,[1] has fueled a debate about the changing nature of female delinquency. This discussion is often accompanied by stories of 8-year-old girls who beat others with bike handlebars, girls who fight with a singular focus, continuing even after adults have arrived to break up the fight.[2] The opinion is spread from news shows, popular magazines, and online websites to average citizens who expect that the stories they hear and the statistics they read represent the "truth."

But research tells us that television and the media tend to distort crime, telling us that there is more of it and that it is more violent than it really is. So, how do we know the "truth"? Should we be worried that there is a female crime spree upon us? Are girls "as bad as boys"? Examining data that chart the trends of delinquency, learning how to interpret those data, and understanding the social context of the times will help us answer these questions.

HOW TO LIE WITH STATISTICS

There is a famous book by Darrell Huff called *How to Lie With Statistics*.[3] In it, Huff discusses many ways that statistics have been improperly used. And it is true: The statistic is a misused and maligned creature. Individuals are often all too willing to quote numbers that cannot be verified, but they may be just as willing to dismiss numbers that legitimately tell a certain story. This is what this chapter is about. It is about helping you, the student, develop a "statistical literacy" about juvenile delinquency that better informs your understanding of the nature and extent of delinquency in the United States.[4] In other words, it is going to help you ask certain questions about the statistics presented to you so that you can better determine which are statistics you might quote to your friends and which are "lies."

What Goes Into a Good Statistic?

We often rely on compelling stories or anecdotes to illustrate what we consider to be trends or "truths" about how the world works. However, while powerful, an anecdote rarely gives us the full understanding of a social fact or event and oftentimes is captivating because of its rarity. For this reason, in order to understand the social world, we need to understand how to best capture its commonalities. For this, we need an understanding of statistics.

Sampling

One of the most important things that goes into a good statistic (one we can reasonably assume is telling us how the world works) is a representative sample.[5] In other words, we do not describe the social world (for example, whether girls are becoming more violent) by interviewing all girls or examining the behavior of all girls. Instead, we take a **sample** (or smaller group) of girls, examine their behaviors, and use this to make inferences about the larger social world. In order to have a representative sample, we must make sure that our sample has the same proportions on important characteristics as the group as a whole (for example, the sample must have the same proportionate gender and racial makeup as the group as a whole). In order to obtain a representative sample, we must engage in a **random sample** process, which means that each individual in the group (population) has the same chance of making it into the sample. In practice, however, it can be difficult to get equal access to all individuals in any population.

If we look back at the stranger who expressed so much worry about girls becoming more violent, we need to ask, what was her sample? In that particular instance, the sample was a single story about an American woman who was charged with murder in Italy. This particular woman was not even under the age of 18 but in her early 20s. In addition, she was not randomly selected from all girls—she was chosen *because* she was accused of engaging in a violent crime. So the sample in question was one woman who was not randomly chosen or representative of juvenile girls because she was over the age of 18.

But this "sample" is also a glaring example of a second important condition of a good representative sample: a sample size large enough to capture the complexity of the group being studied. The more homogeneous a group is (that is, the more group members have similar characteristics), the smaller the sample can be, but as a group gets more and more heterogeneous (that is, more diverse), the sample size should be expanded to capture this diversity in the correct proportions. For this reason, a single story or anecdote cannot tell us about the complexities of the social world, although it could very well spark our interest in asking deeper questions about the social world that statistics from properly collected data could answer.

●●●

Sample:
A smaller group that is representative of the whole.

Random sample:
When each individual in the group (population) has the same chances of making it into the sample as the next individual.

The Tyranny of Small Numbers

In addition to the importance of a proper sample, in order to be confident in the comparisons we make with our statistics we should understand the concept of "the tyranny of small numbers."[6] We often talk about increases and decreases in juvenile crime by comparing the number of youth who engage in crime one year to the number who engage in crime the following year. For example, if 100 youth are caught tagging school property one year and 200 youth are caught tagging the school the next year, we may be tempted to say that tagging has increased by 100% at that school in a single year, and statistically we would be right. But we must be careful when we start to make comparisons using such methods.

from the CLASSROOM to the COMMUNITY

The Children's Defense Fund

The Children's Defense Fund is a nonprofit organization that grew out of the civil rights movement. The goal of the organization is to improve the living conditions and experiences of children in the United States by focusing on improving related policies and programs. To this end, the organization utilizes research from many areas in criminology, sociology, political science, and feminist studies, among others, to identify the best ways to help children. As we saw in Chapter 1, the Children's Defense Fund has identified factors that lead to the cradle-to-prison pipeline. The organization has also identified five key areas and many opportunities to destroy this pipeline:

- Individuals: mentor a child, volunteer at school or in after-school programs, educate others about the pipeline (elected officials and neighbors and family), become involved in the foster care system

- Families: spend quality time with your family, attend school activities, consistently praise your child, create daily routines (homework, meals, quality time), do something fun with your sibling every day

- Communities: start a "Cradle Roll" in your faith-based or other community organization that links every child to a permanent adult mentor who can keep track of the child and help him or her if needed, start a support group for parents, create scholarships for children who need them, create community resource manuals so that parents and children in need know that help is available and how to get it

- Organizations: contribute to prevention and intervention programs, host community fairs that help children get assistance they might need (for example, a health fair to help children get enrolled in state and federal health care programs), encourage alternatives to incarceration that are focused on restorative justice and community involvement

- Government agencies: promote high-quality television programming, expand second-chance programs for youth, stop the criminalization of children, focus on prevention and intervention instead of suppression techniques, fund education

For more ideas, visit the Children's Defense Fund, *Cradle to Prison Pipeline Campaign: Take Action*.[7]

DISCUSSION QUESTION

1. Using the suggestions from the Children's Defense Fund concerning ways to destroy the cradle-to-prison pipeline, give three real-world examples (from three of the five areas) of programs/policies that address this pipeline.

Source: Children's Defense Fund, www.childrensdefense.org

What if in that first year 10 Latino and 90 white students, and then in the next year 30 Latino and 170 white students, were caught tagging. We might be tempted to say that the increase in Latinos caught tagging at the school was 200% while the increase for white students was about 89%, and we would be technically correct. But that discussion would miss an important point, that white students were 85% of those caught for tagging on campus the second year, and that in absolute numbers the increase in white students' tagging was greater than the increase for Latino students for the year.

The tyranny of small numbers means that when dealing with small numbers—especially when comparing them to another group with larger numbers—an increase or decrease in the smaller group is going to cause a greater change than an increase or decrease in the larger group. Reporting that change is *one* way to craft the story, but we should be aware that it is influenced by the tyranny of those small numbers.

QUALITATIVE VERSUS QUANTITATIVE DATA

Up until now we have been talking about our understanding of delinquency in a very quantitative fashion—and we will end the chapter in the same way when we explore the trends in delinquency over the past several decades. However, there is another way, known as qualitative analysis, to explore our understanding of delinquency, and it deserves special attention before we go any further.

Qualitative analyses are different from quantitative in several ways. First, data in quantitative research are in the form of numbers by either counting an event or representing a social fact. Data in qualitative research are represented through words, pictures, objects, songs, and films. Qualitative research often uses inductive reasoning—researchers keep an open mind and may go into their research with few preconceived notions of what they expect to find. The researchers have an interesting research question, but the data are going to guide them to the ultimate story. Quantitative research uses deductive reasoning. A researcher starts with a hypothesis (a relationship between two social facts) and then conducts the research to determine whether that initial hypothesis can be supported by the data. With quantitative research, the researcher often sacrifices contextual detail for generalizability. With qualitative research, the researcher often sacrifices generalizability for contextual detail. Many researchers have a preference for quantitative or qualitative research, arguing that one is better than the other at finding "the answers," but we believe that the research question should dictate the method of gathering data and that neither qualitative nor quantitative research is inherently good or bad.

Quantitative research is good at giving us the general, broad picture of a social phenomenon, such as trends over time, or correlations between two social facts. Quantitative research is good at this because the sampling technique with quantitative work more often allows for generalizability, and quantitative work also allows for a large number of cases to be sampled. You will see us use quantitative data to discuss the trends in delinquency in the last half of this chapter.

But qualitative research gives us the rich texture and deep understanding of groups and social phenomena. We want to spend a bit of time here explaining the importance of qualitative research for our deeper understanding of juvenile delinquency. You will see examples of qualitative work throughout this book.

In the study of juvenile delinquency, two of the most often used forms of qualitative data collection are probably unstructured and semistructured interviews and ethnographic work that utilizes participant observation. The interview is a very popular technique; it allows the researcher to sit down with a participant one-on-one for an in-depth

Inductive reasoning: Reasoning that moves from specific observations (data) to broader generalizations (theory) based on those observations. Qualitative research often uses inductive reasoning.

Deductive reasoning: Reasoning from general ideas (theory) to more specific observations (data). Deductive reasoning is often used in quantitative research.

Hypothesis: A testable supposition or tentative explanation for a phenomenon.

Quantitative data: Data that are measured or identified on a numerical scale.

Qualitative data: Data that are descriptive in nature that can be observed rather than measured.

Participant observation: A qualitative method of data collection in which the researcher studies a group by sharing in its activities and daily life.

discussion. While the researcher may have some set questions in the form of a semistructured interview guide, it is often the case that researchers sit down for a discussion in which they know the topics they want to cover, but really allow the participant to guide the interview. These interviews typically last at least an hour but can go much longer, or can involve a series of interviews that cover a wide variety of topics. The interview is often recorded if the participant agrees. While a survey sample might consist of 100, 1,000, or 5,000 participants, a sample of qualitative interviews for a typical sociological study would include fewer participants (10 to 100). Yet, it is important to note that a single interview is full of data and can yield a transcript (typed-out interview) of tens to hundreds of pages.

One of the ways to get the most in-depth information possible is to conduct one-on-one interviews.

Researchers engaging in participant observation in the form of an **ethnography** work to become accepted members of the group they are studying so they can experience some of the same social phenomena or events as the participants. This method of research, like the use of interviews, allows for an in-depth look at the life of a group, or an individual who participates in delinquency, in ways that quantitative survey data cannot. Researchers can document participant interactions with others, nonverbal communications, group dynamics, and individual behavior because of their involvement in the research field over time. Typically, researchers engage in ethnographic research for at least a year before writing up and publishing their findings. Sometimes, participant observations and ethnographic methods are used together in order to find even more out about the acts or actors under investigation.

Qualitative work is especially useful when studying participants or behaviors in which people do not want to report their activities to survey researchers, or behaviors only represented in data gathered by law enforcement officials or other social control agents (these data do not always allow for a rich description of the factors related to an act of delinquency and do not allow for much understanding of the reasons why delinquency occurred). For example, a rich body of qualitative work on delinquency focuses upon gangs and/or youth of color and their interactions with law enforcement.[8] We will explore many of these studies throughout this book as they offer a rich depiction of youth and their experiences with delinquency and social control.

In sum, qualitative research methods are strong tools for getting to know more about the behavior of youth and the ways in which they make sense out of their social worlds. Because of the small sample size of participants in the research, or people being observed and/or interacted with, qualitative methods do not allow us to make the generalizations we are able to make with quantitative methods. In ethnographies of delinquency and crime, they also involve ethical and moral dilemmas, as researchers must decide how involved to get with the group they are examining—if the group decides to use illegal drugs or commit an act of violence or delinquency, for example, each researcher needs to consider whether she or he will do so as well in order to find out more about the topic.[9]

● ● ●
Ethnography:
A qualitative method that is the scientific description of the customs of a group.

HOW DO WE KNOW WHAT WE KNOW? WHAT DATA SOURCES DO WE USE TO MAP TRENDS?

While qualitative research is excellent at helping us explore a topic in great detail and depth, and often is the best way to gather data on a hard-to-sample group (gang members) or behavior (heroin use), it is not useful at helping us determine correlates or trends in delinquency. Traditionally, three types of data can help us understand the correlates and trends of delinquency and victimization for juveniles: the Uniform Crime Report and National Incident-Based Reporting System, the National Crime Victimization Survey, and self-report data. Each has its strengths and weaknesses and is discussed below.

Data Sources for Correlates and Trends in Delinquency

Data come from many sources. The most common sources for understanding crime and delinquency are the Uniform Crime Report, the National Incident-Based Reporting System, the National Crime Victimization Survey, and self-report surveys.

Uniform Crime Reports

The Uniform Crime Report (UCR) is one of the most widely cited sources of data for crime and delinquency trends. Since 1930, the Federal Bureau of Investigation (FBI) has been collecting data from local law enforcement and compiling a national database whose reports can be accessed by anyone with an Internet connection at www.fbi.gov/stats-services/crimestats, and whose data files can be requested online, too. More than 17,000 law enforcement agencies report every year, but this is not 100%—for the year 2006, it was estimated that 94.6% of eligible data was collected.[10] Many cannot report in a given year for a variety of reasons: for example, computer problems, personnel changes, or a lack of resources dedicated to the gathering and dissemination of data—especially in extremely small agencies.

The UCR collects information at several levels, first on eight offenses commonly referred to as Index crimes or Part I offenses: murder and nonnegligent manslaughter, forcible rape, robbery, aggravated assault, burglary, larceny-theft, motor vehicle theft, and arson. The first four of these (murder to aggravated assault) are often referred to as "person" crimes, while the last four are called property crimes. At this level, the information is collected at the stage where offenses become known to the police and are referred to as "crimes known to police." This means that very little is known about the offense at this stage, just that it happened and where it happened.

• • •

Uniform Crime Report (UCR): Official data in the form of crimes known to the police or arrests collected by the FBI.

Clearance rate: The rate at which a certain crime category is closed because of arrest or exceptional means.

Arrest rate: The number of arrests per 100,000 in the population.

In addition to these Part I offenses, the UCR collects data on 21 additional offenses, referred to as Part II offenses, and amasses these data at the stage where an arrest is made for the crime. These data, referred to as the arrest statistics, include more information. At this stage, the UCR includes gender, age, and race/ethnicity demographics for the alleged offender. In addition, the UCR records the jurisdiction (place) in which the crime occurred. Both Part I and Part II offenses are tracked at the arrest stage. These data record the number of arrests law enforcement has made. For example, Table 3.1 reports 800 juvenile arrests for homicide and/or nonnegligent manslaughter in 2014. This means that 800 arrests were made, but if a single person was arrested more than once in this year for homicide (unlikely, given we are talking about homicide), that person would show up more than once in this statistic, and if more than one person were arrested for a single homicide, all the individuals arrested would show up in this number, too. So the number doesn't tell us the number of homicides in a given year or even the number of people arrested; it merely tells us the number of arrests made in that category.

Clearance Rates. We can determine the clearance rate (the rate that a certain crime category is closed because of arrest or exceptional means) by knowing the arrest rate.

TABLE 3.1 Estimated Arrests of Persons Under Age 18 in the United States (2014)

MOST SERIOUS OFFENSE	NUMBER OF JUVENILE ARRESTS	PERCENT CHANGE		
		2005–14	2010–14	2013–14
Total	1,024,000	−50%	−30%	−6%
Violent Crime Index	53,500	−44%	−29%	1%
Murder and nonnegligent manslaughter	800	−40%	−25%	1%
Rape[1]	3,300			
Robbery	19,400	−33%	−29%	2%
Aggravated assault	30,100	−51%	−33%	−2%
Property Crime Index	234,200	−44%	−36%	−5%
Burglary	40,300	−48%	−38%	−6%
Larceny-theft	178,000	−39%	−37%	−5%
Motor vehicle theft	12,700	−66%	−19%	9%
Arson	3,200	−61%	−31%	−14%
Nonindex				
Other assaults	139,100	−44%	−34%	−5%
Forgery and counterfeiting	1,200	−72%	−31%	10%
Fraud	4,300	−45%	−25%	−4%
Embezzlement	500	−59%	5%	18%
Stolen property (buying, receiving, possessing)	10,400	−53%	−29%	0%
Vandalism	45,200	−57%	−41%	−3%
Weapons (carrying, possessing, etc.)	20,700	−54%	−34%	1%
Prostitution and commercialize vice	700	−54%	−29%	−2%
Sex offenses (except forcible rape and prostitution)	9,400	−44%	−27%	−9%
Drug abuse violations	112,600	−42%	−34%	−4%
Gambling	600	−72%	−57%	−20%
Offenses against the family and children	3,400	−39%	−9%	20%
Driving under the influence	7,000	−61%	−42%	−8%
Liquor low violations	53,300	−57%	−44%	−12%
Drunkenness	6,500	−59%	−49%	−12%
Disorderly conduct	80,800	−61%	−48%	−15%

(Continued)

TABLE 3.1 (Continued)

MOST SERIOUS OFFENSE	NUMBER OF JUVENILE ARRESTS	PERCENT CHANGE		
		2005–14	2010–14	2013–14
Vagrancy	900	–75%	–56%	8%
All other offenses (except traffic)	186,000	–49%	–37%	–5%
Curfew and loitering	53,700	–62%	–43%	–5%
Runaways*	n/a	n/a	n/a	n/a

Source: OJJDP. (2015). *Statistical Briefing Book.* Retrieved from http://www.ojjdp.gov/ojstatbb/crime/qa05101.asp?qaDate=2014

[1] The new definition of rape went into effect in 2013. The revised definition expands rape to include both male and female victims, and reflects the various forms of sexual penetration understood to be rape, especially nonconsenting acts of sodomy, and sexual assaults with objects. The percent change in the number of rape arrests is not displayed since the new definition is not compatible with the prior definition.

* As of 2010, the FBI no longer reports arrests for running away.

The clearance rate tells us the proportion of crimes considered closed because an individual has been arrested for the crime, it can be fairly well documented that the offender is dead, or the victim will not participate in the prosecution of the case. A single arrest does not always close a single case, though. Often more than one arrest is made for a single crime (a single homicide in which four people are alleged to have participated, for example), or a single arrest closes a series of cases (an individual, for example, is arrested on a string of burglaries). It might surprise you as to how much crime is actually cleared in this country. The clearance rate for all homicides in the United States, in 2014, was 64.5% (meaning 64.5% of all homicides reported were closed—due to an arrest or exceptional means). The lowest clearance rate for 2014 was motor vehicle theft at 12.8%. Of the homicides that were cleared (in 2014), 4.3% were juvenile arrests.[11]

Strengths. The UCR data have been collected for more than 80 years (with several policy changes on how and what data were collected during this time). This still allows for quite a rich data set that allows for a longitudinal assessment of crimes known to police and arrest practices across the country. In addition, while there is never 100% reporting, it is quite impressive that so many agencies consistently report their crime statistics. Used properly, these data can be an excellent source and offer quite a bit of information, but that information is not necessarily about crime and delinquency behaviors so much as reporting behaviors and arrest practices.

Limitations. Many of these are not weaknesses so much as cautionary notes about how UCR data should be used. As we have already discussed, the UCR collects data on crimes known to police and arrest practices. These two categories have several drawbacks. Crimes known to police are just that, crimes that have been reported to the police. We know, however, that crime is not systematically reported to the police. Crimes are more likely to be reported if they involve a serious injury or big economic loss.[12] But there may also be other reasons that people do not report an offense. Forcible rape, for example, often goes systematically unreported. Why? Well, rape is often traumatic at a level that other crimes are not. Victims often believe that they are somehow responsible for the attack (they should not feel this way, but the depiction of rape in this country has often put at least partial blame on the victim). In addition to the extreme emotional trauma that rape creates, it is one of the harder crimes to voluntarily discuss with the police. While law enforcement has begun to acknowledge the intricacies of the reporting process by, for example, providing a female officer for a female victim to report to, there is still a long way to go to get accurate counts of rape. Finally, until 2012 male victims were not counted at all because the UCR has defined forcible rape as the "carnal knowledge of a female forcibly and against her will."[13]

In addition to the issue of underreporting, the UCR is *not* a measure of behavior (crime or delinquency), but instead a measure of law enforcement practices. In other words, when examining trends created from UCR statistics, we should remember that these are trends in arrest practices, not crime and delinquency. Agency resources, training, political agendas, individual officer decision-making practices, and agency policies all have an effect on arrest practices and therefore the trends reported using UCR data.

A limitation that we believe is significant is the fact that the UCR does not collect data on

What is the difference between simple and aggravated assault? It depends on the jurisdiction. In general, aggravated assault often includes a weapon and an intent to do bodily harm. In many instances, discretion plays a part in how a crime gets charged.

Latinos (commonly referred to as Hispanics in crime and delinquency data and research). Because *Latino* is considered an ethnic category (based on cultural differences), not a racial category, Latinos are categorized in the racial group they most often identify with (for most Latinos this is either white or black, although Latinos can be of any race). This is a significant drawback given the discourse on race/ethnicity and delinquency in this country.

National Incident-Based Reporting System

The **National Incident-Based Reporting System (NIBRS)** was developed and approved in 1988 to address critiques of the UCR. As law enforcement agencies increased their capabilities to collect data, the summary system designed for the UCR was called into question. A thorough study was conducted to determine if a new system (and what type of system) might be needed. NIBRS is the result.[14]

In some ways, NIBRS is still similar to the UCR—both have the same jurisdictional rules for reporting their data—however, NIBRS differs from the UCR in several important ways.[15] First, the number of offenses that NIBRS reports on is significantly larger than the number reported by the UCR (UCR reports 8 crimes known to police; NIBRS reports 46). Second, the UCR has no way to distinguish between a crime that was attempted and one that was completed, while NIBRS does distinguish between these two. Third, in the UCR, the "hierarchy rule" is enforced, meaning that in instances where more than one crime is committed at the same time (for example, robbery and homicide), only the highest offense is reported (the homicide). NIBRS allows for each incident to be reported whether or not other crimes were committed at the same time. Finally, while the UCR reports in the categories of Crimes Against Persons and Crimes Against Property, NIBRS reports in a third category as well, called Crimes Against Society (for example, drug crimes).

Strengths. NIBRS collects considerably more detailed information than the UCR, which is a significant strength of the new system. Details such as whether a crime was attempted or completed are important for truly understanding the extent of crime in the United States. In addition, cataloguing all the crimes committed (instead of just the most serious as is done in the UCR) also helps with our understanding of the extent of crime in the United States.

Limitations. However, NIBRS still has many of the weaknesses discussed for the UCR. NIBRS still must rely on a crime being reported before it can be tallied. In other words,

● ● ●

National Incident-Based Reporting System: A reporting system that houses data on incidents, both crimes known to police and arrests.

many crimes still go uncounted in NIBRS because they are not initially reported to the police. In addition, NIBRS is not a measure of crime and delinquency behavior (as many often assume it is); it is still a measure of law enforcement policies and practices—just as the UCR is. This makes these data very useful for many research questions concerning policing practices, but the data are not useful for answering questions about the nature and extent of delinquency in the United States. Finally, as of 2012, only 32 states had been certified to collect NIBRS data, which means that national trends concerning arrest practices and crimes known to police are still reported using UCR data because NIBRS does not cover as many states or as large a population as UCR does.[16] This is obviously the biggest weakness of all, if we are interested in using these data to determine trends in delinquency arrests.

on the MEDIA •••

Podcast: Improving Youth Programming: The Role of Research

Social media and research. We were stumped. How were we supposed to explain the use of media to discuss data? But it turns out we should not have feared the topic because there is quite a bit of discussion out there on podcasts, websites, and Twitter, emphasizing the importance of research in our understanding of the social world and juvenile delinquency and the juvenile justice system specifically. One of our favorites is a podcast interview about the importance of being aware of research and listening to research to understand what programs work to help juveniles. According to Angela Irvine of the National Council on Crime and Delinquency,

> Researchers always have a role in identifying which program should be invested in. So if researchers identify programs that effectively reduce recidivism or improve graduation rates, I think that the government, the federal government, state governments always justify their investment in programs based on research. I think that it's really important to think about who the researchers [are who] should be doing this work. I think it's really important that we try to recruit researchers of color who come from the neighborhoods where we are arresting most of the people, so that we can have a richer discussion about what the findings are, but also have a richer discussion about what the possible solutions are because in my experience, researchers who are more familiar with low-income communities

of color come up with more realistic solutions in terms of effectively changing behavior.[17]

One of the challenges of researchers in many areas, but particularly those who study crime and delinquency, is getting their research into the social consciousness because, let's face it, everyone already thinks they know what to do about crime and delinquency. One of the ways that researchers are getting the work out is through Twitter. Below are four organizations that regularly introduce research through Twitter:

- The Equal Justice Initiative @EJI_org
- The Vera Institute @verainstitute
- The Juvenile Justice Information Exchange @JJIEnews
- The Center on Juvenile and Criminal Justice @CJCJmedia

DISCUSSION QUESTION

1. Follow one of the organizations on Twitter. How well do you think they use social media to get their point across? Which recent story most caught your eye, and why?

Source: Adapted from Center for Court Innovation. (2012). *Angela Irvine Interview: Improving Youth Programming: The Role of Research.* Retrieved from http://www.courtinnovation.org/research/improving-youth-programming-role-research-0?url=research%2F9%2Fall&mode=9&type=all&page=4

National Crime Victimization Survey

The **National Crime Victimization Survey** (NCVS) is a nationally representative survey designed to collect data on both household and personal victimization. Conducted since 1973 by the U.S. Census Bureau, the NCVS is administered every six months to approximately 49,000 households (consisting of more than 100,000 individuals 12 and older). The survey focuses on person and property crimes such as rape, sexual assault, robbery, assault (aggravated and simple), domestic violence, purse-snatching and/or pocket-picking, burglary, theft, motor vehicle theft, and vandalism. It, notably, does not focus on crimes in which the victim cannot take the survey (homicide), is not human (arson), or does not exist (drug crimes and prostitution, considered victimless crimes). In addition to the above victimization, the NCVS collects information on the victim, including age, race/ethnicity, gender, marital status, income, and level of education; on the offender, including approximate age, race/ethnicity, gender, and the relationship with the victim; and characteristics of the crime, including the time and place of the crime, whether a weapon was used, the nature of the injury, and economic consequences.[18]

The NCVS was created to do four things: "(1) to develop detailed information about the victims and consequences of crime, (2) to estimate the number and types of crimes not reported to the police, (3) to provide uniform measures of selected types of crimes, and (4) to permit comparisons over time and types of areas."[19] It is used regularly to determine crime rates and often in comparison to the crime rates computed from the UCR.

Strengths. The NCVS was redesigned between 1989 and 1993 to address critiques on the ability of the survey to accurately collect data on sexual assault and domestic violence. While we can never be quite sure of the true numbers of sexually based offenses, it is generally assumed that the NCVS collects more thorough information than the UCR. In other words, it is more likely that individuals will report their sexual victimization to the NCVS than to the police. In general, the NCVS more thoroughly reports on crime/victimization rates than the UCR because it does not rely on victims to proactively approach the police to report their victimization.

Limitations. One of the limitations that students most often argue exists in the NCVS is the likelihood for survey respondents to "lie" or exaggerate about their level of victimization. And, certainly, it is a concern that victims might "overestimate" their victimization. Let's face it—being a victim of crime is an emotional event and one that many individuals may significantly focus on. The NCVS is designed to address this estimation problem by creating "boundaries" for victimization. First, the NCVS is administered every six months because this means that individuals are then asked to only remember back over the last six months of their experiences.[20] Second, the survey is a multistage cluster sample, which means that the survey is administered every six months for several years (three years) to a household before the household rotates out of the sample and a new household rotates in. This is also used to limit overestimation because it means that if individuals say that they have been victimized in the same way two surveys in a row, the survey administrator can specifically ask them if they have indeed been victimized twice or if they are remembering the same incident and reporting it two surveys in a row.

For the purposes of a book on delinquency there is a second limitation of the NCVS. These data are collected on victimization, not crime and delinquency behaviors. This means that, like the UCR and NIBRS, the data being collected are not specific to crime and delinquency behaviors. We can learn important information, but we must remember that this information should not be mistaken for giving us an accurate count of delinquent behavior. In fact, the NCVS does collect data on the offender, but they are estimated from the victim. While the victim might be fairly accurate when giving the

● ● ●

National Crime Victimization Survey (NCVS): The primary U.S. source of data on criminal victimization.

gender of the offender, it is much more likely that victims are not accurate about the age of the offender (unless the victim and offender have a relationship). Finally, the NCVS does not ask about personal victimization for those under 12 in a household, so we cannot use these data to know anything about children under 12 and their level of victimization. A book on juvenile delinquency should also be interested in juvenile victimization, so the NCVS is important, but we must remember the data it does and does not collect!

Self-Report Surveys

A self-report survey is much like the NCVS in that both are surveys that allow individuals to report on some aspect of their life. The NCVS focuses on the individuals' experiences with criminal victimization. Other self-report surveys focus on the offending behaviors that individuals have engaged in themselves (frankly, self-report surveys can focus on just about anything, but for this book we will concentrate on those that allow individuals to report on their delinquent behavior). While self-report surveys can have limitations, which we will discuss shortly, most researchers acknowledge that for the purposes of discussing delinquency trends and delinquent behavior in general, self-report surveys are the most reliable data collection sources.[21]

Several nationally representative self-report surveys offer a comprehensive view of many forms of delinquency. Below we discuss two: Monitoring the Future and the National Longitudinal Survey of Youth.

Monitoring the Future.

This study examines changes in beliefs, attitudes, and behaviors among juveniles. The survey was first administered in 1975, and has been administered yearly ever since. It is not a traditional longitudinal study because each year it surveys a new group of twelfth graders (in 1991, surveys of eighth graders and tenth graders were included). Approximately 16,000 twelfth graders, 17,000 tenth graders, and 18,000 eighth graders are interviewed each year.[22]

In addition to a variety of attitudinal questions, this study asks students about their illicit and over-the-counter drug, cigarette, and alcohol use, and includes six questions about violent behavior the respondents might have engaged in. The data collected by the survey are used for the White House National Drug Control Strategy.

National Longitudinal Survey of Youth.

This study began in 1997 and surveyed approximately 9,000 juveniles between the ages of 12 and 16 and one of each juvenile's parents. The study focuses on school and labor market issues, but also asks a series of questions concerning the juvenile's delinquent behavior. For this reason, the data have been used repeatedly to study the connection between work, school, and delinquent activities.[23]

Strengths.

One of the biggest strengths of self-report surveys is that they are focusing on the actual behaviors of youth, instead of the practices of law enforcement or the likelihood of individuals to report crime to the police. Self-reports were designed specifically to overcome the limitation of the UCR (or arrest statistics in general), getting a better sense of all the crime committed in the United States instead of just that reported to and then "solved" by law enforcement.

In addition to capturing a more extensive proportion of crime and delinquency, self-report surveys can collect a more extensive array of personal and institutional information. In other words, the survey is only limited by the creator's imagination as to what topics might be explored. As you have seen, extensive national surveys focus on family relations, labor relations, and school relations in addition to delinquent behavior.

● ● ●

Self-report survey: A data collection method in which respondents select the responses themselves, usually in questionnaire format.

In the News

A Tyranny of Small Numbers, or Is YouTube the Start of the Next Australian Girls' Violence Epidemic?

A massive spike in violent attacks by young Queensland girls has been blamed on the internet. Authorities say a 44 percent jump in assaults is being driven by the growing popularity of "girl fight sites." Queensland police charged 441 girls aged 10 to 14 with assault last year—up from 307 the previous year. The surge coincided with an explosion in teenage girls filming fights on mobile phones and uploading them on to sites such as YouTube.

Police are still investigating a savage school-girl fight at Ipswich State High School posted on the internet in June. "The internet actually encourages this behaviour because kids from all over the world go on and rate the fights, so even when conflict doesn't exist this particular medium may be encouraging violence." A simple internet search revealed 73 million hits for girls' fighting compared with 31 million for boys, and 24 million girl fight videos on YouTube—eight times more than those featuring boys. "Most people I've shown are shocked when they see them." Queensland police investigated a string of school fights recorded on mobile phones last year, including three other girls bashing a 15-year-old Upper Coomera State College girl.

Violent offences account for about a third of all crimes committed by girls, compared with a quarter or a fifth of the offences committed by boys. Police acknowledged "emerging social networking trends" as a factor in juvenile offences but said statistics showed girls were still more likely to commit property offences than crimes against people. In 2008–09, more than 1700 girls aged 10 to 14 years were arrested for shoplifting. They were second only to girls aged 15 to 19 years, with 2447 shoplifting offences. "If there were no 15-year-old girls, you'd almost eliminate shoplifting completely," a Child Protection Investigation Unit officer said.

DISCUSSION QUESTIONS

1. What else might you want to know to help determine if this is an example of a tyranny of small numbers or a true "violence epidemic"?

2. Critique the language of the article. How are all the numbers in the article used to make the case for a worrisome new trend in female violence?

Source: Ironside, R. (2010). Bad girls: Online fights blamed for frightening rise in violent young females. *The Courier Mail* (Australia), January 12, p. 1.

Limitations. While self-report data are generally considered some of the best ways to find out about delinquency, there are some limitations. First, self-reported delinquency scales may not be equally valid or reliable across race, gender, or age.[24] This means that self-report data may not tell us equally well how white and black youth, or Native American and Asian youth, engage in delinquency. Neither might they tell us equally well how young women and men engage in delinquency.

In addition, there is a worry about inaccuracy of reporting delinquent behavior. In other words, there is a worry that juveniles will under- or overreport their delinquency. Research tells us that there is a likelihood that juveniles will overreport their behavior, especially violent behavior that has occurred in the last year, but knowing this good surveys can compensate with sophisticated survey techniques that take into account the likelihood to overreport behavior.[25]

This means that none of the data we have discussed so far do an exceptionally good job of telling us about race, class, or gender relationships to delinquency—which is ironic, given how much focus there is on the correlations between delinquency and race, class, and gender.

CORRELATES OF DELINQUENCY

Some of our strongest correlates of delinquency are demographic characteristics (for example, age or gender). But a correlate does not have to be a demographic characteristic of an individual. At its most basic, a correlate of delinquency is anything that shows itself to have a relationship to delinquency, which researchers may use to predict the likelihood of an increase or decrease of delinquency in individuals, groups, or communities or to predict the differential experience of an individual in the juvenile justice system or another such social institution as school or family.

The correlates we discuss below go to the heart of the premise of this book. We believe that individuals' *social location* has an impact on their experiences in our society. In other words, in order to understand juvenile delinquency, we must understand how issues of age, gender, race, class, and sexual orientation, to name a few, affect juvenile experiences, juvenile behavior, and societal perceptions and expectations of juveniles. We start by briefly explaining what research tells us is the relationship between each correlate and juvenile delinquency. We spend the rest of the book exploring the reasons these correlations might exist.

Age

Age is one of the strongest correlations to delinquency and crime. The age-delinquency correlation is curvilinear. In other words, as individuals get older, they are more likely to engage in delinquency; then, at a certain age, their likelihood to engage in delinquency decreases. Data from the UCR tell us that the likelihood to engage in property crime peaks at 16, while the likelihood to engage in violent crime peaks at 18.

There is a debate among researchers as to how strong this age-delinquency correlation is. One side of the debate argues that the relationship is almost constant. In other words, everyone gets older and ages out of crime. The other side of the debate, though, argues that some persistent offenders (career offenders) never age out of crime, continuing their criminal behavior well into their adult years. This side of the argument does not deny that age has a relationship to offending, but argues that those who start offending very early in life are more likely to continue to offend later in life (so making a different argument about the correlation between age and delinquency and crime). We will see more of this discussion in Chapter 4, when we discuss the life course and developmental theories of delinquency.

Gender

Another very strong correlate to delinquency is gender. With very few exceptions, boys engage in more delinquency than girls. Arrest statistics show that boys, compared to girls, are four times as likely to engage in violent crime and twice as likely to engage in property crime. But even a relationship this strong (or perhaps because of a relationship this strong), there is quite a bit of disagreement as to the complexities of the gender delinquency relationship. We can see this with the opening vignette illustrating that many think that girls are becoming more delinquent and at a faster rate than boys (we will discuss this relationship in detail later in this chapter), while others argue that this relationship is a function of changing law enforcement and policy practices such as zero-tolerance policies in public schools. Even others argue that our patriarchal focus isn't even necessarily asking the right questions when we examine the gender relationship to delinquent behavior. We should instead, they argue, be examining the gender relationship to social control, abuse, and the social construction of the expectations we place on juveniles (in other words, we often expect girls to act better than boys, and when they don't our response to them can be much more harsh—out of a patriarchal sense that girls need more "protection" than boys). We discuss these various gendered issues throughout the book, from the ability of theory (in Chapters 5 and 6) to help explain gender differences in delinquency to the differential experiences of girls and boys from arrest to the juvenile justice system.

Race and Ethnicity

One of the most controversial relationships to delinquency may be race and ethnicity. A significant amount of research has been conducted on the nature of the relationship between race/ethnicity and delinquency. Official statistics, such as arrest data from the UCR, show a strong correlation between race and arrest. However, this relationship is not replicated in studies using self-report data. There appears to be very little relationship between race/ethnicity and delinquency for many behaviors, including drug use and petty crimes. However, youth of color (specifically black youth) do report engaging in some crimes more than white youth (e.g., using a weapon to steal).[26]

We believe two things make this relationship controversial. The first is the differences between the correlations that official statistics illustrate and those that self-report studies illustrate. Why might it be the case that arrest statistics show such a strong relationship, while self-report data show a moderate to nonexistent relationship (depending on the type of delinquency we are examining)? As we will discuss extensively below, some researchers focus on law enforcement practices as a way to explain the relationship between race and arrests. In other words, these researchers focus on law enforcement practices that single out youth of color, or communities of color, while more likely excluding white youth. Other researchers focus on the fact that arrest data are often capturing behavior that is more severe (for example, aggravated assault) than what self-report data are capturing (self-reports more often focus on drug use and less serious crimes including property crimes). These researchers argue that youth of color may be more likely than white youth to engage in more serious crimes while there is no race/ethnicity difference for less serious crimes. As you will see in our discussions throughout the book, the answer is complex and probably lies somewhere between

Girls engage in less delinquency than boys overall, and a better understanding of the factors influencing their delinquency and how they are related to gender expectations and gendered experiences in contemporary society is needed.

these two explanations. The second is the media and public focus on youth of color as more delinquent when, clearly, the research points to a much more complex relationship between race/ethnicity and delinquency than the arrest statistics alone show. In other words, those who study delinquency are not in agreement as to the exact relationship between race and delinquency, or to the reasons for a relationship, yet youth of color are depicted by many in the public and the media as delinquent. It is our hope that after reading this book you will understand the complexity involved in exploring the relationship between race/ethnicity and delinquency.

Class

Like race and delinquency, social class and delinquency have a complicated relationship. As you will see in Chapters 4, 5, and 6, class has a robust history in theories of delinquency. At the macro level (when looking at neighborhoods or cities), there does appear to be a correlation between class and delinquency. Neighborhoods characterized by poverty or disorganization (see Chapter 5) are more likely to have high rates of delinquency than neighborhoods that are considered more organized or less impoverished. But just as with race, this relationship seems to hold up better when using UCR data (or other official data sources) and not as well once we begin to examine the relationship at the micro level (whether individuals who live in poverty are more likely to engage in delinquency).

One of the problems with this complication is that the public assumes that if impoverished neighborhoods have higher rates of delinquency, then this must mean people living in those neighborhoods have higher rates of delinquency, too. This is what is known as the ecological fallacy—the notion that we can apply what we know at the macro level (neighborhoods) to the micro level (individuals) and find the same correlations. We cannot.

●●●
Ecological fallacy:
The mistake of making an inference about an individual based on aggregate data for the group.

When we explore the relationship at the micro level, we find no strong relationship between class and delinquency.[27] In fact, while numerous studies were conducted between the 1950s and the 1990s on class and delinquency at the micro level, the number of studies conducted since the mid-1990s appears to have dropped off. Hagan and McCarthy argued that one of the reasons no relationship is found between class and individual-level delinquency may be that most studies measure class as a parental income measure (how much do your parents make?), and most self-report studies are conducted in middle or high schools.[28] They argue that an income measure may not be measuring the class-related issues that another measure could (they conducted a study of youth living on the street) and that studies conducted in schools might miss a subsample of youth (e.g., those who have been expelled or dropped out) that may offer an example of class differences.

Spencer Platt/Getty Images News/Getty Images

There is a stronger correlation between class and delinquency at the neighborhood level than the individual level. This means that we should be careful to not engage in the ecological fallacy of assuming that poor individuals engage in crime and delinquency because they live in a neighborhood with high crime rates.

In any event, what we can say from the research to this date is that a relationship between class and delinquency is observed very strongly at the neighborhood level and, at the individual level, depending on the study, it is weak or nonexistent.

A Focus on Research

Sampson's "Immigration and Homicide Trends"

Robert Sampson, in the magazine *Contexts,* shed light on the relationship between immigration and crime (see Figure 3.1).[29] In the past decade, there has been an increasing, urgent, and misinformed focus on immigrants, both documented and undocumented, and their violent behavior. Fred Thompson (at the time a candidate for the Republican presidential nomination) was quoted as saying, "Twelve million illegal immigrants later, we are now living in a nation that is beset by people who are suicidal maniacs and want to kill countless innocent men, women, and children around the world."[30]

While the discourse in many political circles and street corners has been about the "dangerous immigrant," Sampson and other researchers such as Martinez and Valenzuela have found that neighborhoods with large immigrant populations are actually *less violent* than other neighborhoods.[31] For example, New York has a large immigrant population and is also one of the safest cities in the United States, and San Diego is a border town, which also has a low crime rate.

Sampson argues that one of the reasons that violence may decrease with an influx of immigrants is that immigration changes the host city. In other words, immigration might change cultural mores that value violence—effectively assimilating the city into nonviolence.

Contrast these findings with the increasing focus in the popular media and many political discussions about the connection between immigrant groups (most specifically Mexican immigrants), youth gangs, the drug trade, and violence. Sampson's findings that communities with large immigrant populations are actually *less* violent contradicts this popular image.

DISCUSSION QUESTION

1. Using the Uniform Crime Reports and U.S. Census Bureau websites, find the violent crime and immigration rates for 10 cities. Is there a relationship? Can a relationship be documented over time for any of the cities?

THE NATURE OF DELINQUENCY AS MEASURED BY THE UCR

Table 3.1 (pp. 65–66) shows the number of arrests of juveniles in the United States in 2014. There were approximately 1.024 million arrests of juveniles in 2014 (remember, a juvenile can be arrested more than once in the same year). Of those 1.024 million arrests, only 800 were for homicide or non-negligent manslaughter. The largest single category for arrests was all other arrests, with 186,000 arrests, followed by larceny-theft with 178,000 arrests. This means that these two categories accounted for a little more than one third of all juvenile arrests for the year. This is important because often, when discussing the arrest trends, the media refer to the "violent crime rate" or "person crimes," both aggregates of homicide, rape, robbery, aggravated assault, and sometimes even simple assault (also considered a "person crime"). If we look at the table, we see that by far the bulk of the **violent crime index** or person offenses is made up of robbery, aggravated assault, and simple assault. But when we refer to violent crime, most people think of homicide and rape. Given how small the numbers are for homicide and rape, the other categories can easily mask the trends of these two categories (so homicide and rape may decline or remain the same, but the violent crime index will be driven by the trends in robbery and aggravated assault). Why should we care? Aren't robbery and aggravated assault really serious violent crimes, too? They certainly can be, but we will see in later

Violent crime index: Measure of violent crime comprising four offenses: murder and non-negligent manslaughter, forcible rape, aggravated assault, and robbery.

discussions on changing enforcement practices (in Chapters 8 and 11–14) that these categories are not as cut and dried as we would expect. Often our discretion or lack of discretion can impact what we think of as delinquency, and you may be surprised at what "counts" as crime and delinquency sometimes.

GENERAL TRENDS IN DELINQUENCY

Quick. Stop reading this book and text your best friend or sibling, or lean across the library table and ask the student across from you, what has been the trend in juvenile violence over the last 30 years? Is violence increasing, decreasing, or staying the same among juveniles? What about property crime trends? Drug trends? Now continue reading. Did anyone get it right?

Trends Measured by the UCR

First of all, when considering trends, it is important to remember that trends reported from the UCR are arrest trends, not delinquent behavior trends. Figure 3.2 reports the juvenile arrest rate trend for violent crime (measured by the violent crime index, which is homicide, forcible rape, robbery, and aggravated assault) for the years between 1980 and 2014. The rate is measured as number of arrests per 100,000 youth between the ages of 10 and 17. This means that we are only seeing the trends for arrests of juveniles between the ages of 10 and 17, which captures nearly all violent arrests (it is rare for a child under 10 to be arrested).

Figure 3.2 shows us that the violent crime arrest rate decreased slightly in the early 1980s, was stable for the remainder of the 1980s, and then increased sharply until 1994. After 1994, the rate decreased to its lowest point since the early 1980s, in 2003 and 2004, before increasing slightly between 2004 and 2006. As of 2014, the juvenile violent arrest rate was lower than it was in 1980.

Because of the substantial increase (62%) in the late 1980s/early 1990s, there was a much publicized argument that the United States had a juvenile violent crime epidemic

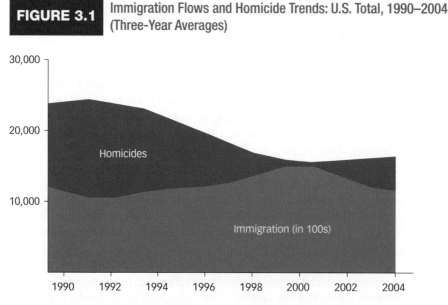

FIGURE 3.1 Immigration Flows and Homicide Trends: U.S. Total, 1990–2004 (Three-Year Averages)

on its hands. Juveniles were characterized as out of control and "super-predators."[32] It was predicted that the United States was on the cusp of a violence outbreak of epic proportions. However, as we can see from the Figure 3.2 arrest statistics, this epidemic did not break out. So what might account for the increase in the violent arrests during the late 1980s/early 1990s? Some of it may be attributed to an increase in violent behavior, but given we are looking at arrest statistics another issue we cannot overlook is the likelihood that law enforcement practice may have had something to do with it. Zimring found evidence that minor juvenile offenses were being charged as more serious offenses between 1988 and 1992 because of an increased intolerance for juvenile misbehavior stemming from the worry over the initial increase.[33] In other words, some of this increase may have been due to a crackdown on juveniles—once more juveniles were arrested and the public began to worry that juveniles were becoming more violent, more attention was paid to juveniles and more were arrested, even for behavior that may not have been considered violent five years prior.

Figure 3.3 shows the property crime index arrest trends for 1980 through 2014. The rate is measured as the number of property crime arrests per 100,000 juveniles between the ages of 10 and 17. Contrary to the juvenile violent crime arrest trends, the juvenile property crime arrest trends do not show a marked increase during the period of 1980 to 2008. The property crime index (which is a composite of the arrest rates for burglary, larceny-theft, motor vehicle theft, and arson) remained fairly stable between 1980 and 1994 before starting a dramatic decline between 1994 and 2005. Between 2005 and 2008 there was a slight increase, but the overall rate remained almost half of what it was at its highest in 1991. Between 2008 and 2014, the rate decreased again. In 2014, it was about one third of what it was in 1980. Given that the trend for the property crime index never increased the way that the trend for the violent crime index increased, the data suggest that violent crime may have had an increased focus from law enforcement that property crimes did not experience.[34]

● ● ●

Property crime index: Measure of property crime comprising four offenses: arson, larceny, burglary, and motor vehicle theft.

FIGURE 3.2 Juvenile Arrest Rates for Violent Crime Index Offenses, 1980–2014

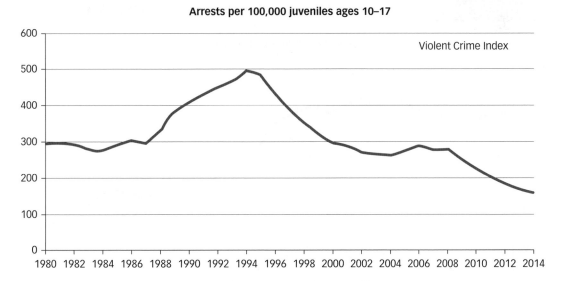

Arrests per 100,000 juveniles ages 10–17

Source: OJJDP. (2015, December 13). *Statistical Briefing Book.* Retrieved from http://www.ojjdp.gov/ojstatbb/crime/JAR_Display.asp?ID=qa05201

Note: Rates are arrests of persons ages 10–17 per 100,000 persons ages 10–17 in the resident population. The violent crime index includes the offenses of murder and nonnegligent manslaughter, forcible rape, robbery, and aggravated assault

Not only do impressions about juvenile behavior fuel arrest practices, but arrest practices fuel how the public and police begin to think about juveniles. If we see increases in violent and property arrest rates for juveniles, we may believe that juveniles are becoming more delinquent. That is one interpretation, but it may be a change in police practices that are also impacting those trends.

The most popular trends reported from the UCR data are the trends from the violent crime and property crime index. Certainly the media focus most of their attention on the violent crime trends. Our next trend does not spend as much time in the limelight, although we argue given the level of resources and public hand-wringing that goes into drug abuse violations it is surprising that we do not discuss this trend more often.

Figure 3.4 shows the drug abuse violation arrest rates for 1980 through 2014. We included an examination of the arrest rate trend because self-report surveys often focus heavily on drug use when measuring delinquency. This trend measured with UCR data will be compared to self-report data later in this chapter.

The arrest rate is measured as the number of arrests per 100,000 juveniles between the ages of 10 and 17 in the population. The trend held steady (with slight variations) between 1980 and 1991 before increasing dramatically between 1991 and 1997. In this six-year time frame, the arrest rate more than doubled from 300 arrests per 100,000 juveniles to more than 700 arrests per 100,000 juveniles. Since 1997 the rate has been decreasing steadily and is now at the 1992 rate. More than any other trend measured by the UCR, this one may be the

FIGURE 3.3 Juvenile Arrest Rates for Property Crime Index Offenses, 1980–2014

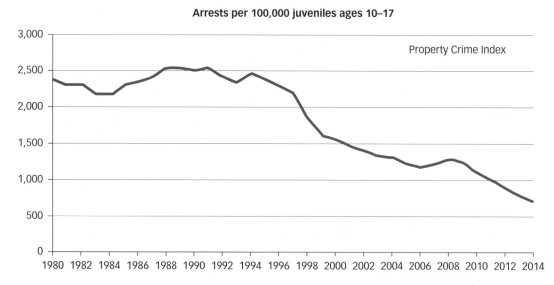

Source: OJJDP. (2015, December 13). *Statistical Briefing Book*. Retrieved from http://www.ojjdp.gov/ojstatbb/crime/JAR_Display.asp?ID=qa05201

Note: Rates are arrests of persons ages 10–17 per 100,000 persons ages 10–17 in the resident population. The property crime index includes the offenses of burglary, larceny-theft, motor vehicle theft, and arson

FIGURE 3.4 Juvenile Arrest Rates for Drug Abuse Violations, 1980–2014

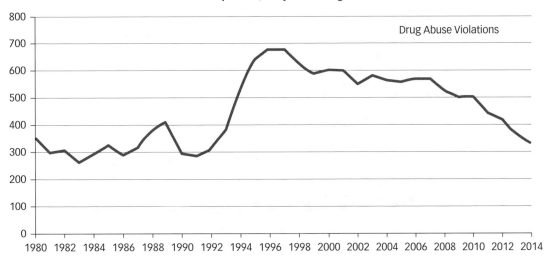

Arrests per 100,000 juveniles ages 10–17

Source: OJJDP. (2015, December 13). *Statistical Briefing Book.* Retrieved from http://www.ojjdp.gov/ojstatbb/crime/JAR_Display.asp?ID=qa05201

Note: Rates are arrests of persons ages 10–17 per 100,000 persons ages 10–17 in the resident population

best example of the impact of a change in law enforcement practices or policies on the arrest rate. The startling increase in the drug abuse violation arrest rate in the 1990s corresponds with a similar increase in reported drug use (as measured by self-report data, to be discussed below), but this time period also corresponds directly with the middle of the "war on drugs," implemented during the Reagan presidency and still in effect today.[35] Given that drug use subsequently declined, yet we see the drug abuse violation trends remain high, it is expected that much of this trend is a product of a persistent focus on drug use and abuse by law enforcement.[36]

Trends Measured by the NCVS

Violent crime trends, as measured by the National Crime Victimization Survey, offer a complementary story of violent crime in the United States. When examining trends using data from the NCVS, the most important consideration is exactly what about crime and delinquency is being measured. Figure 3.5 shows the trend between 1993 and 2014 of violent crime victimization. This figure shows that, similar to the trends from the UCR, violent crime victimization decreased significantly between 1993 and 2010. There was a slight increase in victimization between 2010 and 2013 before it decreased again in 2014. This increase can be attributed to the increase in simple assault at the same time (remember we said that assaults often drive our trends, more than rapes, robberies, or homicides). The most important difference between the trends measured with the UCR and those with the NCVS is that the NCVS is not measuring delinquency at all. This data set is measuring the likelihood to be victimized. So when examining Figure 3.5, we are looking at the rate of juvenile victims, compared to Figure 3.2 where we are looking at the rate of juvenile arrests. The NCVS can only collect the approximate age of offenders because this information is estimated by the victim. This makes the use of these data for estimating juvenile delinquency rather weak. However, data showing the trend in juvenile victimizations are still very important because they show us that juveniles are safer now (as measured by violent victimization) than they have been since prior to 1975.

FIGURE 3.5 Violent Crime Victimization Rate Trend for Juveniles, 1993–2014

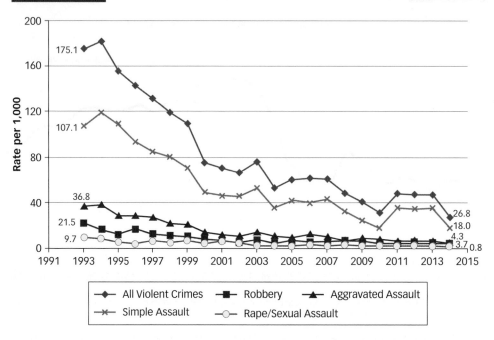

Source: Child trends calculations from U. S. Bureau of Justice Statistics. (2015). *NCVS Victimization Analysis Tool (NVAT)*. Retrieved from http://www.bjs.gov/index.cfm?ty=nvat

Self-Report Data: Monitoring the Future

Figure 3.6 shows the prevalence of illicit drug use by students in Grades 8, 10, and 12. This graph measures prevalence as the percentage of children who have reported trying an illicit drug in the past year, and it shows that at its highest, in 1979, more than 50% of twelfth graders reported trying an illicit drug (data on eighth and tenth grades were not collected until 1990). Examining the twelfth-grade trend line (because it represents about the same years as the UCR and NCVS data, 1975–2015), we see that drug use as measured by self-report data shows a different trend than the UCR data. This trend shows prevalence of illicit drug use increased between 1975 and 1979, then decreased significantly until 1992 before increasing again until 1997 (although this increase did not reach the previous levels of more than 50% of twelfth graders). Finally, between 1997 and 2015 the trend remains relatively stable, hovering just above or below 40%. Although data for tenth and eighth graders have only been collected since 1990, they show similar trends to the twelfth-grade data, although lower overall percentages of juveniles report the usage of illicit drugs at each stage.

How does this compare with the drug abuse violation arrest rate trends reported by the UCR? We see that the increase between 1992 and 1997 is mirrored in the UCR data, although the increase does not appear to be as steep in the self-report data. And, more important, while the UCR data were stable before this increase, the self-report data report a significant decrease in drug use prior to the 1990s. Comparing these trends is important because if we look solely at the UCR data, it appears that there is an epidemic of drug use that sweeps the nation in the 1990s and never really goes away. Looking at the self-report data, however, suggests that although drug use did increase, it was not in epidemic proportions and, in fact, was not as prevalent as in the 1970s and 1980s.

What do the three data sources as a whole tell us about crime, delinquency, and juveniles in the United States? They tell us that the story is more complicated than we may have

Trends in Annual Prevalence of Illicit Drug Use for Grades 8, 10, and 12, 1975–2015

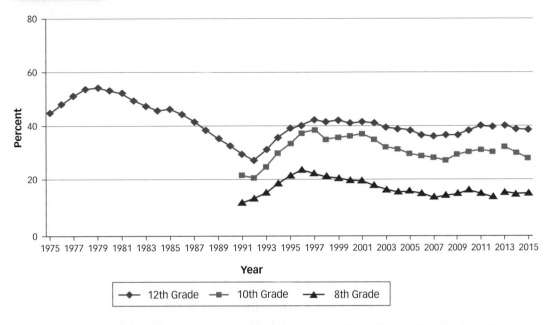

Source: Johnston, L. D., Miech, R. A., O'Malley, P. M., Bachman, J. G., & Schulenberg, J. E. (2015, December 16). Use of ecstasy, heroin, synthetic marijuana, alcohol, cigarettes declined among US teens in 2015. *University of Michigan News Service*. Retrieved from http://www.monitoringthefuture.org

originally suspected. First, contrary to the media discourse and public opinion, crime and delinquency (as measured by arrest rates or self-reported data) are down in the United States. In fact, by some measures they are at a 30-year low. Second, our measures are important for this understanding. Only if we are using self-report data are we actually getting a measure of delinquency; the UCR and NCVS, it can be argued, give us proxy measures (arrest and victimization).

TRENDS IN DELINQUENCY FOR GENDER

So what about the claim of the stranger in the supermarket? Are girls becoming more violent? Are they catching up with boys when it comes to violent, property, or drug crimes?

Official Trends From the UCR

Figure 3.7 shows the juvenile arrest trends for the violent crime index for both males and females, and the answer appears mixed. When Huff cautioned against lying with statistics, he may have had this scenario in mind.[37]

A quick glance at Figure 3.7 shows that the trends appear relatively similar for both males and females. Throughout the 1980s, the trends appear stable; then in 1989 the trends begin to increase for both groups. The trends peak within a year of each other (boys in 1994, girls in 1995) before decreasing rapidly. Although here the trends appear to diverge a bit, the male arrest rate decreases more sharply than the female rate with the male rate falling to levels lower than any other time in the past 30 years. Female rates, on the other hand, also decline, but level off before reaching the levels achieved prior to 1990. In addition to the shape of the trend line, we must be aware of the actual arrest rate reported in each graph. In fact, at every stage on the graph boys are still more likely than girls to be arrested for violent crime, but that gap is shrinking. Between 1980 and 2004, female delinquency arrests (as measured by the violent crime index) went from representing 11% of all arrests to more than 30% of all arrests.[38] Those following these trends worried this change was an indication that girls were becoming more violent.

Gender Trends in Illicit Drug Use From Self-Reports

Illicit drug use trends are very similar for both males and females. Figure 3.8 measures this illicit drug use by reporting the prevalence that an individual has used any illicit drug in the past year. The numbers show that between 30% and 60% of boys over time reported that they had tried at least one illicit drug during the year. Between 25% and 50% of girls reported that they had tried at least one illicit drug during the year. Overall, girls were less likely to engage in illicit drug use than boys, but the trends follow the same increases and decreases over time. Both boys and girls reported an increase in drug use in the late 1970s before a significant decrease throughout the 1980s in use. Use steadily increased for both groups, for most of the 1990s, before leveling off and decreasing slightly. Overall, both boys and girls reported moderate use of illicit drugs (less than the high, but more than the lowest levels that we saw at the beginning of the 1990s).

Comparisons of Gender and Delinquency Between the UCR, the NCVS, and Self-Report Data: The Girls Study Group

In 2004, the Office of Juvenile Justice and Delinquency Prevention brought together its Girls Study Group, a group of researchers focused on examining issues of gender and delinquency.[39] This was in response to the apparent increases in violence trends for girls during the 1990s and 2000s. While boys remained more violent overall, girls were edging up in proportion of arrests (but remember, violence was down overall in both groups during this time). The Girls Study Group compared trends from the UCR, the NCVS, and the **Monitoring the Future study**, to determine whether girls were, indeed, becoming more violent.[40]

The Girls Study Group found that while girls appeared to be becoming more violent (in relation to boys) in the UCR, this trend did not hold up when examining NCVS or self-report data. Both the NCVS and self-report data showed that the proportion of violent behavior between girls and boys had remained fairly steady during this time period. The Girls Study Group concluded that the proportional increase in arrests was probably not due to an increase in violent behavior in relation to boys, but to a change in arrest practices and policies for law enforcement during this time period.

● ● ●

Monitoring the Future study:
A University of Michigan study that surveys around 50,000 youth about their drug use patterns in middle and high schools in Grades 8, 10, and 12 across the United States, and then one more time the year after they graduate.

An increase in mandatory and pro-arrest policies had a stronger effect on the likelihood girls would be arrested than boys (the policies meant it was more likely for both groups to be arrested, but girls more likely than boys). Specifically, it appears that girls are being arrested more often for simple assaults than they were in the past. This probably occurs because of mandatory domestic violence arrest policies and zero-tolerance policies in school (which we will discuss in much greater detail in Chapter 8). It is likely these policies formalize responses to behaviors that girls have been engaging in all along. For example, while it is known that many girls have had to put up with abuse at home and that many may fight back, with domestic violence mandatory arrest policies, now when the police are called they must arrest one or more individuals involved in the dispute. While many of these disputes may have been dealt with informally in the past, this is no longer the case.

FIGURE 3.7 Juvenile Arrest Rates for Violent Crime Index Offenses by Sex, 1980–2014

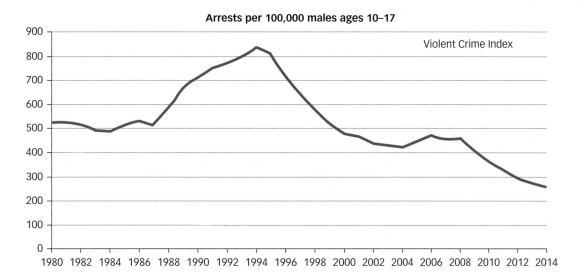

Arrests per 100,000 males ages 10–17

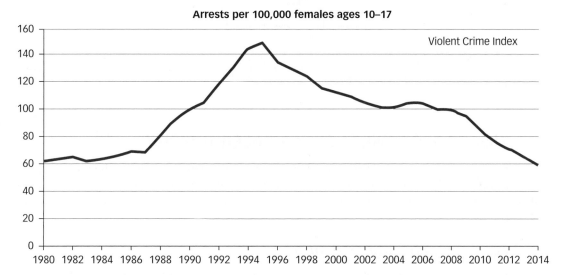

Arrests per 100,000 females ages 10–17

Source: OJJDP. (2015, December 13). *Statistical Briefing Book.* Retrieved from http://www.ojjdp.gov/ojstatbb/crime/JAR_Display.asp?ID=qa05201

Note: Rates are arrests of persons ages 10–17 per 100,000 persons ages 10–17 in the resident population. The violent crime index includes the offenses of murder and nonnegligent manslaughter, forcible rape, robbery, and aggravated assault.

Was our supermarket stranger right, then? Are girls more violent in general these days? Or more violent than boys? While it might be easy to look at some of these trends and worry that there is a kernel of truth there, the answer is no. The data do not support that girls are becoming more violent or that they are gaining on boys and their level of violence. The surge in the proportion of violence that can be linked to girls can be accounted for by the increase in simple assault arrests. And these arrests can be linked to changes in laws and law enforcement policies that increase the likelihood of arrest but not the likelihood of violent behavior. In other words, there is no "national crisis" of female violence.[41]

FIGURE 3.8 Annual Prevalence Rates of Illicit Drug Use for 12th-Grade Males and Females, 1974–2014

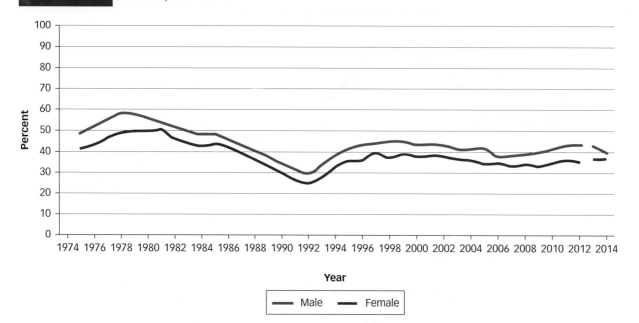

Source: Johnston, L. D., O'Malley, P. M., Miech, R. A., Bachman, J. G., & Schulenberg, J. E. (2015). *Demographic subgroup trends among adolescents in the use of various licit and illicit drugs, 1975–2014* (Monitoring the Future Occasional Paper No. 83). Ann Arbor, MI: Institute for Social Research, The University of Michigan. Retrieved from http://monitoringthefuture.org/pubs/occpapers/mtf-occ83.pdf

TRENDS IN DELINQUENCY FOR RACE/ETHNICITY

Some of the biggest disparities in our understanding of trends comes when we examine trends in delinquency for race and ethnicity between official data and data from such sources as the NCVS and self-reports. In this section, pay special attention to drug trends.

Official Trends From the UCR

Looking at the official statistics for juvenile arrest rates for violent crime by race (Figure 3.9) leaves quite an impression. According to this graph, blacks are significantly more likely to be arrested for violent crimes than whites. In fact, the top graph in Figure 3.9 shows that for 2014, blacks were 5 times more likely to be arrested for violent crimes than whites. But we must take a harder look at this table to see important details that might initially be missed. Looking at just the black trends, we see that between 1980 and 1989, the arrest rate was relatively stable (with a small decrease and subsequent increase that left the rate at the beginning and end of the decade almost the same). Then in the beginning of the 1990s the rate increased by more than 33%. However, in 1995 the trends began to decrease, and from its highest to lowest point (in 2014) it decreased by more than 50% to its lowest point since before the 1980s.

If we looked at the trend line for whites in the same graph, it would appear that whites have remained almost stable over the same period. However, a further examination of white trends in Figure 3.9 tells a slightly different story. The white, Asian, and American Indian trends for violent crime arrests mirror the black trends, just on a smaller scale.

FIGURE 3.9 Juvenile Arrest Rates for Violent Crime Index Offenses by Race, 1980–2014

Arrests per 100,000 juveniles ages 10–17, 1980–2014

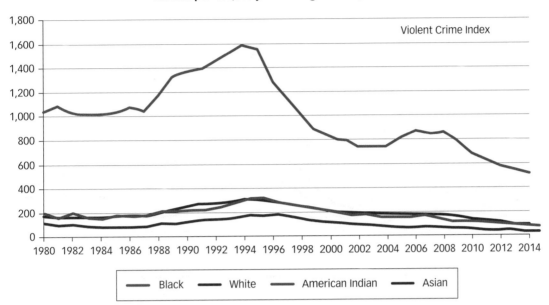

Source: OJJDP. (2015, December 13). *Statistical Briefing Book*. Retrieved from http://www.ojjdp.gov/ojstatbb/crime/JAR_Display.asp?ID=qa05201

Note: Rates are arrests of persons ages 10–17 per 100,000 persons ages 10–17 in the resident population. Persons of Hispanic ethnicity may be of any race (i.e., white, black, American Indian, or Asian). Arrests of Hispanics are not reported separately. The violent crime index includes the offenses of murder and nonnegligent manslaughter, forcible rape, robbery, and aggravated assault.

In fact, white arrest rates actually increased by 50% from their lowest point in 1983 to their highest point in 1993. And while white rates also decreased significantly in the 1990s, they did not decrease at the same rate as black rates, until very recently (they finally fell below their 1980s rates in 2009). American Indians have a very similar trend line to whites, while Asians have a lower rate at all points on the graph but a trend line that looks similar to that of both American Indians and whites.

Figure 3.10 tells a strikingly different story for black, white, American Indian, and Asian arrest rates for drug abuse violations. We can see that in 1980, the black and white rate for drug abuse violations was almost the same, but diverged quickly after this. The black rate increased quickly, more than tripling between 1980 and 1989, and then dropped for a single year before increasing again to its high in 1995 of more than 1,600 arrests per 100,000 black juveniles between the ages of 10 and 17. The rate then decreased by almost 50% in a six-year period between 1996 and 2002, with a moderate increase again in the mid-2000s. In 2014, the rate was down from its highs in the 1990s and was almost to the level of the early 1980s.

Whites, American Indians, and Asians, again, have similar-looking trends, although whites had the highest rates of arrest for the three groups across the entire time period. White arrests decreased almost 50% between 1980 and 1991 (while black rates were skyrocketing). Then between 1991 and 1996, white rates almost tripled (American Indian rates quadrupled but remained below white rates, and Asian rates also tripled

Arrests per 100,000 juveniles ages 10–17

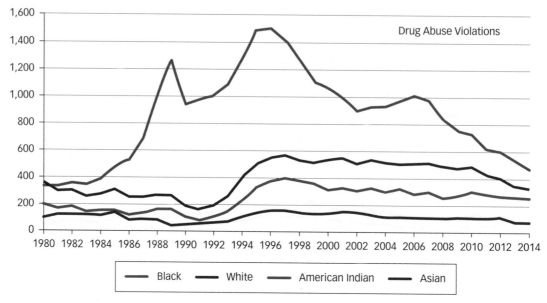

Source: OJJDP. (2015, December 13). *Statistical Briefing Book*. Retrieved from http://www.ojjdp.gov/ojstatbb/crime/JAR_Display.asp?ID=qa05201

Note: Rates are arrests of persons ages 10–17 per 100,000 persons ages 10–17 in the resident population. Persons of Hispanic ethnicity may be of any race (i.e., white, black, American Indian, or Asian). Arrests of Hispanics are not reported separately.

but remained lower than rates for any other racial group). For the last half of the 1990s and the 2000s, the rates for all three groups remained relatively stable, with slight decreases for each.

Race and Ethnicity Trends in Illicit Drug Use From Self-Reports

In contrast to official records of drug abuse violations, self-report data tell a very different story about racial differences in drug use. The data in Figure 3.11, taken from the Monitoring the Future study, track illicit drug use of white, black, and Latino youth in the 12th grade. For this reason, it is not directly comparable to the official data, because we are not tracking the same racial/ethnic groups (we are not tracking Native American and Asian youth in this table, but we are tracking Latino youth). The overall trends for all three groups moderately mirror the official statistical trends of whites, Native Americans, and Asians in Figure 3.10. Illicit drug use decreased throughout the 1980s for all three groups, before increasing for all three groups in the early 1990s. The trends diverged a bit at this stage because black use leveled off sooner than white or Latino use. Latino use then decreased again sharply in the 2000s, while white and black use remained fairly stable. Use in 2010, for all three groups, was lower than the levels measured in the early 1980s.

What is most striking about this figure, though, is that the self-report data show higher rates of illicit drug use for whites (compared to blacks and Latinos) every year between 1977 and 2013 (except for 2000, 2012, and 2013, when Latinos report

FIGURE 3.11 Annual Prevalence of Illicit Drug Use by Race, 1974–2014

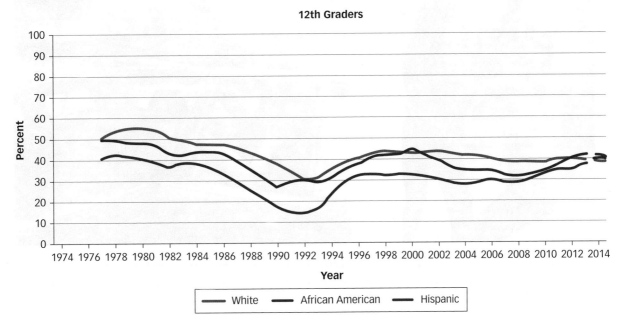

Source: Johnston, L. D., O'Malley, P. M., Miech, R. A., Bachman, J. G., & Schulenberg, J. E. (2015). *Demographic subgroup trends among adolescents in the use of various licit and illicit drugs, 1975–2014* (Monitoring the Future Occasional Paper No. 83). Ann Arbor, MI: Institute for Social Research, The University of Michigan. Retrieved from http://monitoringthefuture.org/pubs/occpapers/mtf-occ83.pdf

higher use). This is a very different story than the official statistics on drug abuse violations tell.

Comparisons of Race/Ethnicity and Delinquency Between Official and Self-Report Data

When looking at Figures 3.9, 3.10, and 3.11, the most pressing question is what contributes to the black arrest rate being so much higher than the arrest rate for other races? Or, put another way, are black juveniles really that much more delinquent than white, Asian, or Native American juveniles? Given that arrest data measure law enforcement practices and not delinquent behavior specifically, we cannot answer that question examining just the arrest trends from the UCR. In order to provide an answer, we need to also know what self-report data tell us about delinquent behavior.

Morenoff examined the differences between official statistics and self-report data.[42] He reported that the Monitoring the Future data do show slight differences between black and white juveniles and both violent and property crimes. But these differences are nowhere near as extreme as we see in the official statistics. Blacks are slightly more likely to engage in violent crimes, while whites are slightly more likely to engage in property crimes. And we have already seen, from Figure 3.11, that whites are more likely than either blacks or Latinos to report illicit drug use.

So which data are "telling the truth"? Frankly, neither. We know that official statistics are measuring more than just delinquent behavior, that institutional racist, sexist, and classist practices make it likely that the racial differences are not due solely to behavior, and we know that clearance rates are so low that we are only getting information on a

Increases in mandatory arrest policies mean that more girls are getting arrested for behaviors that were treated informally in the past. Should it be the case that all physical encounters are treated as assaults, or should some behaviors be treated informally? How would you treat these two girls? Why?

mere fraction of offenders.[43] But we also know that early self-report data did not capture the complexities of delinquency (i.e., did not measure a full range of delinquency, leaving out more serious forms of delinquency) and might have had sampling biases that affected one race more than others (e.g., conducting data collection at school, not accounting for juveniles who were truant or dropped out).[44] Researchers have spent years improving their self-report measures, but enough questions still remain that we cannot accept the findings from one type of data over another.[45]

We started this chapter with a section on how to lie with statistics. One of the best ways is to mischaracterize the relationships and trends that we see. To misquote a famous saying, when it comes to delinquency trends, eventually "what comes down, must go up." Most delinquency trends are decreasing or stable at levels that are lower than we have seen in 30 or 40 years. Eventually it is likely that these trends will tick up. The question is, when they do, how will we characterize this change?

This chapter fosters in you, the student, a "statistical literacy" that can help you understand the many statistics we are presented with in the social world. In order to best understand the data and trends we are presented with, we must be aware of several things. The first is that we must know the data. When trends and relationships about the social world are presented to us, we must ask, where did those data come from, how were they collected, and how do they measure our variables of interest? Second, we must know the strengths and weaknesses of the method used to collect the data. Was the best method used for the research question being asked? Once we have acquainted ourselves with the data, we can be more assured about the trends and relationships we are examining.

We have spent a good deal of this chapter discussing the strengths and weaknesses of data and what we can really know from the trends presented. These critiques are not meant to dismiss the trends that we have examined, and we do know a lot about crime and delinquency based on the data we collect from the UCR, the NCVS, and self-report surveys. Especially when these trends are similar across two or three data sources, we can be confident that our data are telling us something important about the social world. The critiques do suggest, though, that our job as criminologists, researchers, and statisticians is not done. We must continue to strive to improve our data collection techniques and to know more and more about the data we use to explain juvenile delinquency.

EYE ON DIVERSITY EXERCISE: JUVENILE VIOLENT CRIME TREND IN CITY

Research the juvenile violent crime trend in your city. Then create a table charting the general trend for your city over the past 10 years. Create a second table, charting the trend broken down by race and then gender. When creating these tables, make sure you label all the parts appropriately and explain where your data came from.

Once the tables are finished, compare the trends for either race or gender. Make a comparison that illustrates the "tyranny of small numbers" and explain why your example illustrates this phenomenon.

What might be the reason for the trend(s) that you have charted?

DISCUSSION QUESTIONS

1. Compare the trends in drug-related delinquency according to the UCR and self-report surveys. What events or behaviors is each measuring? Are the race and gender differences in these trends the same for the UCR and self-report data?

2. You are interested in finding out whether living on the East or West Coast has an impact on gender differences in delinquency. Which type of data might best answer this question? Why?

3. Explain the strengths and weaknesses of the UCR, the NCVS, and self-report data.

4. While on the bus, you overhear a conversation in which one person is lamenting how much more delinquent juveniles are today than they were 30 years ago. What would you say to this person?

KEY TERMS

CHAPTER PRETEST ANSWERS

1. False

2. False

3. True

4. True

5. False

6. True

7. False

8. False

STUDENT STUDY SITE

SAGE edge™

edge.sagepub.com/bates2e

Sharpen your skills with SAGE edge!

SAGE edge for students provides a personalized approach to help you accomplish your coursework goals in an easy-to-use learning environment. You'll find action plans, mobile-friendly eFlashcards, and quizzes, as well as videos, web resources, and links to SAGE journal articles to support and expand on the concepts presented in this chapter. Check out the website for original videos of former offenders discussing their experiences as juveniles.

PART 2:
THEORIES OF JUVENILE DELINQUENCY

©iStockphoto.com/Christopher Futcher

MICRO-LEVEL THEORIES

After reading this chapter, you should be able to

- Describe the process of differential association

- Describe the difference between differential association and social learning theories

- Explain the social bonds in social control/social bonding theory

- Explain the processes in life course theory

- Analyze the three types of strain in general strain theory

- Analyze the coping strategies in general strain theory and the place of delinquency in those coping strategies

- Compare and contrast differential association, social control, and general strain theories

- Compare and contrast the merits of the theories for explaining these race, class, and gender differences

In Pennsylvania, a rumor was started about a high school junior. Another student from the school made the comment that "he is the type to bring a gun to school," and soon the rumor that this young man had, indeed, made a threat and was planning to bring a gun to school on Monday was flying around on social media sites. During this same time, hateful messages were posted to both the boy's and his sister's Facebook walls. In addition, parents of other students posted to social media sites calling the parenting skills of the boy's parents into question.

In fact, the day of the supposed threat of violence was actually going to be the last day at this school for this young man. He had been continually bullied because of his red hair and medical condition, he was considered an outcast by classmates, and he routinely asked to stay home from school. His parents had decided he might be better served by an alternative school that would take into consideration his medical condition and learning disability.

The police became aware of this rumor and on Sunday afternoon went to the boy's home to interview him and search for weapons. After interviewing the boy and the boy's parents, and searching the family home, the police concluded that the boy did not own a gun, have access to a gun, or have access to any materials that may create a weapon. It was determined that the boy had not made the threat, was not planning to engage in school violence, and instead was the victim of a rumor.

In many ways, this boy might fit the "profile" of a student who would shoot his classmates. He is considered an outcast, and is often bullied by his fellow classmates. His parents may or may not have good parenting skills, and he may or may not have close friends. The bullying he endures may or may not cause him to "snap" and kill classmates.

What we are more sure of is that a rumor got wildly out of hand on a social media site—so out of hand that both parents and students felt they were allowed to post hateful comments to the boy and family in question, and the police showed up at the family home to search for weapons based on nothing more than a rumor.

Throughout this story there are competing assumptions about the reasons for school violence: poor parenting, a lack of friends or not fitting in, and the stress that bullying can add to the bullied child's life. All of these assumptions or "theories" about the causes of school violence are focused upon the individual level.

CHAPTER PRETEST

Test your knowledge of this chapter's material by determining whether the following statements are true or false. Be sure to compare your answers with the answers on page 122.

1. The social contract is the agreement that citizens will follow the rules and laws of society in exchange for protection from harm.

2. According to Beccaria, in order for punishment to work it must be certain, swift, and fair in its severity.

3. The earliest biological theories of crime and delinquency focused on the size and shape of the head to predict bad behavior.

4. Excessive toxins, such as lead, have been linked to delinquency.

5. Poor children and children of color are more likely to be exposed to toxins such as lead.

6. According to differential association theory, it is most likely a juvenile will learn delinquent behavior from a friend.

7. Social bonds keep juveniles from engaging in delinquency.

8. According to Agnew, a coping mechanism for strain may be delinquency.

9. According to Broidy and Agnew, boys and girls may have different issues that trigger strain.

In other words, these explanations for engaging in delinquent acts are focused on the circumstances of the individual's life or personal characteristics of the individual.

Source: Adapted from Leitsinger, M. (2012). When rumor, the Internet and school violence fears collide. *U.S. News on NBCNEWS.com*, March 8. Retrieved from http://usnews.msnbc.msn.com/_news/2012/03/08/10604539-when-rumor-the-internet-and-school-violence-fears-collide

● ● ●

While the theories in the next chapter focus on institutional and community characteristics, and social, cultural, or political processes to explain rates in delinquency, the theories in this chapter are micro-level theories that will focus on the characteristics of the individual, or social processes that have an effect on individual-level behavior. The theories in this chapter can all be considered normative theories, too. A normative theory assumes that there is a standard or agreed-upon set of societal norms that everyone knows and can, therefore, live by. These theories do not question whether a delinquent act should be a delinquent act, who might be defining the delinquency or the delinquent, or what role society or individuals in society play in these definitions (a discussion of those theories will be found in the next chapter). Instead, the theories in this chapter assume that we can all define an act as delinquent when we see it and that we know the difference between right and wrong.

One of the broad critiques of most of the theories and perspectives found in this chapter is that they are "general" in nature, meaning they propose that they can explain delinquency generally. As we saw in Chapter 3, there is a lot of variation in both the societal perceptions and reactions to delinquency, and the nature and extent of that delinquency when examining race, gender, or class, for example. The critique of the theories in this chapter is that they were often created and first tested on boys only (girls were not even in the studies), and in many instances white boys only (although race was included much earlier than gender in eventual studies). Those who critique these theories, then, argue that they can hardly take into consideration the variety of experiences of juveniles based on their race, class, gender, or sexual orientation if none of these characteristics were even taken into consideration when the theories were developed. To some extent, these critiques are valid, but fortunately, in many instances, later researchers have adapted the classic theories to address such limitations. This chapter will examine some of the micro-level theories, such as biological theories, differential association theory, rational choice theory, social control theory, and general strain theory that were designed to explain individual-level juvenile delinquency, and then explore some of the instances in which these theories have been applied or extended to include the diverse experiences of juveniles based on race, gender, and class.

PRE-CLASSICAL IDEAS

There is little literature that focuses on the behavior and punishment of juveniles (as opposed to adults) during the Middle Ages.[1] We know more about general punishments and what society felt were the reasons for bad behavior. We are going to offer a brief overview of these pre-Classical ideas, acknowledging that it is probably the case that juveniles were not often thought of as different or separate from adults.

Micro-level theories: Theories of delinquency that focus on the individual.

Normative theory: Assumes that consensus is a basic fact of organized social life, therefore delinquency is a violation of norms, rules, or the law, caused by any number of individual or societal factors.

During the Middle Ages, behavior that was considered wrong was usually attributed to supernatural or religious factors (e.g., the devil made him do it, or she was a witch). This meant that "punishments" were focused on driving the evil from the individual. Exorcisms were one of the more common policies to stop behavior that was considered harmful or criminal. But, in addition to exorcisms, punishments included torturing, beheading, burning at the stake, drowning, stoning, and quartering.[2]

In addition to evil, such "natural" causes as the cycle of the moon were blamed for bad behavior. Interestingly, we can see many of these beliefs today in our horror stories of vampires, werewolves, and possessions, and most of our understanding of how to deal with that is as violent and brutal as it was in the Middle Ages.

Responding to these beliefs in the supernatural and brutal ways of dealing with those believed to be evil or possessed was Thomas Hobbes, a philosopher with two radical ideas for the time period: (1) individuals are rational beings, and (2) individuals will not give respect or buy into a system of government or a justice system that does not offer a certain degree of respect. In other words, Hobbes was one of the first to formally suggest that harmful behavior was not the product of lunar cycles or satanic possession but was, instead, the product of a choice an individual made, and punishments that were brutally harsh did more harm than good because they delegitimated the entire system.

These two ideas led to Hobbes's claim that citizens would agree to follow the rules or laws set forth by society in return for protection from harm. This exchange is known as the social contract. In addition to this social contract, Hobbes argued that individuals should have a say in the government, especially the justice system. He believed that individuals should be able to help determine who was guilty, as well as determine appropriate punishments for guilty behavior.[3]

These new ideas ushered in the Enlightenment Era and a new way of thinking about crime and punishment.

CLASSICAL THEORIES

During the Enlightenment, with a move toward a reliance on human "rational" thought, some of the first theories about human behavior focused on man's (because, at this stage, women were almost never included in discussions) capacity as a rational actor. These theories eventually focused on crime and became the first attempts to explain criminal behavior. Focusing on free will, Beccaria and Bentham argued that individuals weigh the costs and benefits of all their actions and act when the benefits outweigh the costs. They then explained those who engaged in crime as acting on their free will to satisfy such desires as greed, revenge, or survival.[4]

These early Enlightenment philosophers, such as Beccaria, also did not focus specifically on juveniles and their behavior. But many of his ideas are important because they are the framework for the adult justice system and, increasingly, the juvenile justice system. In addition, the expectations in U.S. society of individualism and rationality in which we raise our children stem from many of these ideas.

One of the most important ideas for dealing with juvenile delinquent behavior and juvenile justice is Beccaria's concept of deterrence. Beccaria believed that people freely choose their destinies, which meant that they freely choose whether or not to engage in bad behavior. Beccaria, then, believed that individuals could be deterred from bad behavior through thoughtful punishments (as opposed to the brutal and unpredictable punishments of the Middle Ages). But according to Beccaria, for punishment to be most useful, it needed to adhere to three elements: certainty, celerity (swiftness), and severity.

●●●

Social contract: Citizens agree to follow the rules or laws set forth by society in return for protection from harm.

Certainty of Punishment. Beccaria considered this the most important of the three elements of deterrence. The more certain an individual is that he will be caught and punished for an action, the more likely he will not engage in that action. Which brings us back to Chapter 3 and our discussion of clearance rates. Remember that in the United States our highest clearance rate in 2014 was 64.5% for homicide (meaning 35.5% of homicides were not solved). Another way of saying this is that about one third of those who kill someone get away with it. So the crime we can say has the *most* certainty of being punished still goes unpunished one third of the time. And these are the crimes known to police (of which homicide is reported most often). Think about all the crimes that go unreported, which all go unsolved. All of this factors into the certainty of punishment, which is very low in U.S. society.

Celerity of Punishment. Beccaria thought celerity of punishment was important for two reasons. One reason was he lived in the 18th century, when individuals could often be imprisoned for years waiting for a trial. Often individuals were imprisoned longer waiting for their trial than their punishment would have been for the crime. The second reason was Beccaria believed that individuals were more likely to link the pain of punishment to their actions if the punishment came swiftly after their act. The farther away a punishment was from the individual's behavior the less likely the individual would link the two and the less likely they would think twice before engaging in the behavior again.

Severity of Punishment. The most complex of the three elements of deterrence is severity of punishment. Beccaria believed that punishments had to be harsh enough so that they outweighed the benefit of committing the crime, but at the same time, Beccaria thought that punishments that were too harsh caused people to believe the system was illegitimate. So he believed that punishments should be equal to, or slightly outweigh, the benefits: "For the punishment to attain its end, the evil which it inflicts has only to exceed the advantage derivable from the crime."[5]

These choice arguments are the early versions of classical criminology and lay the groundwork for rational choice theory.[6] As an extension of these first choice theories, rational choice theory focuses on the rational component of crimes. According to this theory, offenders act deliberately and to maximize their self-interests. However, Cornish and Clarke point out that no one is a completely rational actor. No actor has full or completely accurate information all the time.[7] In addition, they acknowledge that individuals do not have the reasoning skills to be perfectly rational. This is an especially important point (see the prefrontal cortex discussion below) for juveniles who sometimes seem even less capable of truly rational thought. For this reason, this theory has been used to explain adult behavior much more often than juvenile behavior in the research, although elected officials, general citizens, and public policy have all made the argument that juveniles are rational actors and are using a choice argument when they do so.[8]

BIOLOGICAL, PSYCHOLOGICAL, AND BIOSOCIAL THEORIES

Although the Classical school and deterrence theory dominated the discussion of crime and the justice system for many years, criticisms emerged of the theory because it did not predict certain types of crimes or the type of individual who may commit those crimes. Instead theorists started to look at biological factors to predict the likelihood to engage in crime. The view that biology is responsible for criminal behavior is known as

● ● ●

Certainty of punishment: The most important element of deterrence. The assumption that if individuals perceive a high likelihood of being caught and punished for a crime, they will not engage in it.

Celerity of punishment: The element of deterrence that assumes that the faster a punishment occurs, the more likely an individual will not engage in that behavior in the future.

Severity of punishment: The assumption that punishment must be harsh enough to outweigh the benefits of the crime, but not so harsh that it is perceived to be unfair.

biological determinism. Over time these theories were replaced with more sociological (and in some instances psychological) theories of criminal and delinquent behavior. When this view was replaced by one focusing on more environmental (sociological) causes of crime and delinquency, it became known as environmental determinism. Recently, there has been a resurgence in some of these ideas in what are known as biosocial theories (an integration of some of the biological and sociological concepts).

Early Biological Theories

Very early theorists who focused on biology believed that individuals or groups that offended more than others were somehow biologically inferior to general society. This led to the belief that these individuals or groups should be at the very least controlled, if not eliminated. This early work fit within the larger framework of eugenics, which was the general movement to improve the human race through selective reproduction. Eugenics did not focus specifically on crime, but those who focused on inferior biology as a predictor of crime fit within the eugenics movement. These first theorists emphasized such areas as craniometry, the belief that the size of the skull or brain predicts criminality (the smaller the skull or brain the more inferior the individual) and phrenology, the study of the bumps on the skull as an indicator of the shape of the brain.[9] Bumpy skulls were considered to be an indication of an abnormal brain and an indication of someone who may be more likely to engage in crime.[10] The biggest critique of these early works, other than the fact there was little evidence to support them, is that the authors did not create systematic research designs in order to test them. For the most part, the theorists knew ahead of time who was considered a criminal and who was considered "normal" when evaluating the characteristics of the skull and brain (often because these studies were conducted on skulls of criminals who had died). Interestingly, evaluations conducted on the leading theorists in these areas found that the theorists had "abnormal" brains and skulls and might have been considered likely to engage in crime by their own standards.[11] These earliest theories were especially troubling because there was often a racial and class bias that influenced who represented normal and who represented abnormal.

Cesare Lombroso, often referred to as the father of modern criminology, was the first to offer and then systematically collect data to evaluate a biological theory of crime.[12] At its most basic, Lombroso's theory was that criminals were physically different from noncriminals. He believed that it was more likely that criminals were atavistic, or had characteristics that were a throwback to earlier developmental stages in evolution. Basing much of his early work on Darwin's theories, Lombroso argued that criminals were not as evolved as noncriminals and that this primitive stage manifested itself in physical characteristics that he called criminal stigmata: asymmetry of the face, large jaws and cheekbones, unusually large or small ears that stand out from the head, fleshy lips, abnormal teeth, flattened nose, angular form of the skull, scanty beard but a general hairiness of the body, and excessively long arms.[13]

Lombroso did not believe that these physical characteristics caused criminality; he believed merely that they helped identify those individuals who were not as evolved as noncriminals (these physical characteristics could be seen as markers of primitive individuals). At the heart of Lombroso's theory was that individuals were born into their crime and delinquency (it was part of their biology). Later iterations of the theory acknowledged the importance of other factors that might interact with or affect this biology.

Sheldon also believed that physical appearance could predict delinquent behavior. He focused on body type to predict an individual's likelihood to engage in crime.[14] Sheldon

●●●

Biological determinism: The view that biology is responsible for criminal behavior.

Environmental determinism: The view that one's environment or experiences are responsible for criminal behavior.

Eugenics: The movement to improve the human race through selective reproduction.

Craniometry: The belief that the size of the skull or brain predicts criminality.

Phrenology: The belief that the shape of the skull and brain (how bumpy the skull was) could predict criminality.

Atavistic: The belief that individuals may have certain characteristics that are throwbacks to earlier developmental stages of evolution.

Stigmata: The physical signs of atavism, such as asymmetry of the face, large jaw or cheekbones, unusually large or small ears, fleshy lips, abnormal teeth.

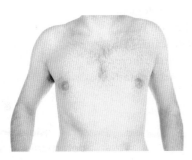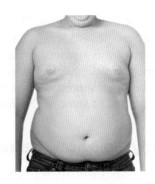

One of the earliest theories of criminal behavior said that we could predict crime based on body type. Does one of these body types seem more likely to engage in criminal behavior than another?

argued that there were three primary body types (*somatotypes*) that were linked to temperament of the individual. The endomorphic body type is soft and round with small bones, short limbs, and soft smooth skin. Those with an endomorphic body, Sheldon believed, were *viscerotonic* in temperament: relaxed and outgoing, with a desire for comfort, food, and affection. The ectomorphic body type is fragile, thin, and delicate, with poor muscles and weak bones. These individuals' temperament is *cerebrotonic*: introverted, shy, restrained, and inhibited. Finally, the mesomorphic body type is muscled and strong, with an upright, hard, sturdy physique. Individuals with this temperament are *somatotonic*: assertive, aggressive, motivated, and insensitive. Glueck and Glueck believed that a majority of delinquents were mesomorphic.[15]

Psychological Theories

One of the most well-known early psychological theories to be adapted to crime and delinquent behavior was psychoanalysis, made popular by Freud.[16] Psychoanalysis is an entire field of psychology that goes well beyond issues of crime and delinquency, but several of Freud's concepts were used by later theorists to explore delinquent behavior specifically. Freud argued that behavior was based on three elements in an individual's personality: the id, ego, and superego. The id (also called the "it") is the instinctual component of the personality, existing from birth. It is considered impulsive and lives completely within the individual's unconscious. This is where passion, pleasure, and aggression reside. The ego (also called the "I") is considered the decision-making element of personality that develops to negotiate the impulsive desires of the id in reality. Theoretically, ego is the rational part of one's personality. The superego (also called "above I") is where an individual's conscience resides. The values learned from society are developed and stored in the superego. The superego can be thought of as an individual's conscience or ideal self. The superego, then, helps the ego be more than just a rational component but instead an ideal, moral self.

August Aichhorn used Freud's ideas to try to explain the unconscious motives of juveniles engaging in delinquency.[17] He believed that there was a difference between manifest and latent delinquency. Manifest delinquency was delinquency that had been acted out (become an action), while latent delinquency had not been performed yet but was still in the mind or unconscious. He was critical of policies that focused on punishment and suppression because he believed these did not help uncover the latent delinquency that could become manifest if not addressed.[18]

●●●

Endomorphic: A body type that is soft and round with small bones, short limbs, and soft smooth skin.

Ectomorphic: A body type that is fragile, thin, and delicate, with poor muscles and weak bones.

Mesomorphic: A body type that is muscled and strong, with an upright, hard, sturdy physique.

●●● *on the* MEDIA

The Viral Blog Post: I Am Adam Lanza's Mother

On December 14, 2012, Adam Lanza walked into Sandy Hook Elementary School and killed 20 students and 6 staff members after killing his mother that morning at home. This textbox is not about him. It is about the blog post that another mother, Liza Long, wrote and posted to her webpage the day of the shooting. There it was called "Thinking the Unthinkable," but it was soon picked up by several websites and retitled "I am Adam Lanza's Mother." In the post, this mother describes the love and fear she has for her 13-year-old son whose behavior is sometimes so uncontrollable she worries that he will one day be another Adam Lanza. She describes how scared she is of him sometimes, the emergency plan her 7- and 9-year-old can automatically implement to get to the car and lock themselves in so her 13-year-old can't hurt them, her frustration that there seems to be no ready help for him. She has been told the only way to get him help is to set up a paper trail by having him arrested, but she wonders if that is the right type of help for a 13-year-old who threatens to kill himself, who threatens to kill her, who one minute can be happy and remorseful and the next angry and out of control.

The blog post set off a national discussion on the resources available for the kids who may be mentally ill. In U.S. society, there is no systematic or institutionalized response to kids with behavioral problems. Often the school is expected to respond, or parents are expected to get the answers to help their kids on their own. Sometimes, if parents are lucky, their insurance covers psychological help; sometimes insurance does not.

Although her blog post was read by millions of people and she got a lot of positive responses to it, she also received a lot of criticism. Some people posted that she was responsible for her son's behavior and that she had violated his rights by talking about it.

"Mother-blaming is as old as Eve though, right, it's really easy for us to blame mothers, and that was exactly the point I was trying to make," Long says. "Families are suffering in shame and silence; I was suffering in shame and silence. So is my child. But when we don't share our stories, there's no chance that we're going to make change."[19]

The good news for this family is that the post also led them to some answers. One persistent reader kept e-mailing to say she thought she knew someone who could help them. Turns out it was a doctor who helped diagnose her son with bipolar disorder and get him on medication that helps him control his rages.

"When I wrote that blog post, I was really concerned that my son's fate was prison or worse, and now we are talking every day about college, about what he'd like to major in," Liza Long says. "I don't think there are any right or wrong answers for Eric. There are just a lot of great opportunities for Eric."[20]

DISCUSSION QUESTION

1. Analyze how this mother reached out to talk about her concerns about her son. How did social media help her (and others)? How might it have hurt her (or others)? What does it say about contemporary society that this was the venue she had readily available for her concerns?

Sources: Adapted from Long, L. (2012, December 14). *Thinking the Unthinkable. The Anarchist Soccer Mom.* Retrieved from http://anarchistsoccermom.blogspot.com; NPR. (2016, April 24). *How Talking Openly Against Stigma Helped a Mother and Son Cope with Bipolar Disorder.* Weekend Edition Sunday. Retrieved from http://www.npr.org/sections/health-shots/2016/04/24/475461959

Biosocial Theories

Contemporary biological theories on crime are considered biosocial theories because they integrate biological, psychological, and social causes.[21] These theories have come a long way from some of the early classical and biological theories, offering a more nuanced approach to the effects of biology, psychology, and environment on juvenile behavior. A variety of theories focus on this integration. For example, some researchers focus on neurological deficits such as natural developmental delays in the prefrontal cortex, given that the frontal lobes do not fully develop until late adolescence. The prefrontal cortex is responsible for planning and reflecting on one's actions. This research suggests that one of the reasons for the impulsivity of children is that their brains are not fully developed. These natural developmental delays have an effect on intelligence, verbal development, and attentiveness and focus. Research has linked these delays to poor self-regulation of emotions and behaviors, including delinquency.[22] Given these developmental delays, Andrews and Bonta ask, "If brain capacity and function is still developing, with frontal lobes developing last, can we hold adolescents responsible for uninhibited, anti-social behavior?"[23]

Another area of research has examined the effect of diet on the likelihood of delinquency.[24] This research has found an effect on several areas in a child's life depending on the type of diet he or she has. Most of this research suggests that diet has an indirect effect on delinquency. In other words, diet affects such things as depression, hyperactivity, or cognitive problems that then might impact the likelihood to engage in delinquency. Diets that are healthy in polyunsaturated fatty acids, minerals such as zinc and iron, and vitamins such as folate, B vitamins, and antioxidants, such as vitamins C and E, are linked to lower levels of attention deficit/hyperactivity disorder (ADHD), depression, schizophrenia, and dementia.

There has also been research on the effect of hormones, specifically testosterone, on delinquent behavior. Testosterone is secreted by both males and females, but in much larger doses by males. Some believe that testosterone is the reason why males are more likely to engage in delinquent behavior than females. It is assumed to be partly responsible for a greater likelihood of aggressive and delinquent behavior in males.[25] However, while testosterone has been linked to aggressive behavior in animals, the research conducted on humans is much less conclusive.[26] Research examining the effect of social factors on the effect of testosterone on aggressive or delinquent behavior has found that social class and environmental conditions may be mediating factors.[27]

Finally, of particular interest recently is the research that links toxins such as lead and manganese to the likelihood of delinquency and crime (see the In the News textbox). This research has found that exposure to high levels of lead is linked to a greater chance of delinquent and criminal behavior. This is especially important for our discussions for two reasons. First, children are much more vulnerable to excessive toxins because they cannot physically fight the exposure as well as adults, and it is likely that they are more exposed (e.g., if there is lead in household paint, kids are more exposed because they rub up against walls and are more likely to come into contact with paint chips). Second, it is more likely that children of color and poor children will be exposed to such toxins because they are more likely to be exposed to a crumbling infrastructure or homes that have not been renovated.[28]

DIFFERENTIAL ASSOCIATION THEORY

Sutherland offered his theory of differential association as a sociological explanation of behavior that crossed social dimensions (e.g., class, race, and gender). While Sutherland focused on white-collar crime, the theory of differential association can be especially useful when explaining delinquency given the fact that such a significant proportion of delinquency happens with friends and acquaintances and across social dimensions (see Chapter 9).

● ● ●

Differential association: The learning of behaviors and norms from the groups with which we have contact.

Sutherland offered his full-fledged model of differential association in his text *Principles of Criminology*.[29] This model included nine propositions:[30]

1. Criminal behavior is learned.

2. Criminal behavior is learned in interaction with other persons in a process of communication.

3. The principal part of the learning of criminal behavior occurs within intimate personal groups.

4. When criminal behavior is learned, the learning includes (a) techniques of committing the crime, which are sometimes very complicated and sometimes very simple, and (b) the specific direction of motives, drives, rationalizations, and attitudes.

5. The specific direction of motives and drives is learned from definitions of the legal code as favorable or unfavorable.

6. A person becomes delinquent because of an excess of definitions favorable to violation of law over definitions unfavorable to violation of the law.

7. Differential associations may vary in frequency, duration, priority, and intensity.

8. The process of learning criminal behavior by association with criminal and anti-criminal patterns involves all of the mechanisms that are involved in any other learning.

9. Although criminal behavior is an expression of general needs and values, it is not explained by those general needs and values because noncriminal behavior is an expression of the same needs and values.

While Sutherland referred to crime (not delinquency) in his propositions and initially applied them to the concept of white-collar crime, it is easy to see how these propositions can be applied to juvenile behavior and the learning of delinquency.

In order to analyze our example of delinquency that we presented at the beginning of the chapter, we will focus on the first seven propositions of differential association, as the last two were discounted in later formulations of the theory.[31] While most people might think to try to explain the likelihood of the young man bringing a gun to school and killing his classmates, we would like to start by focusing on the behavior of the rumormongers. Why is it that a rumor such as this one would become such a sensation on social media sites? Why would so many students (and parents) feel free to spread the rumor with no actual knowledge of the events themselves? Sutherland's theory of differential association and his first seven propositions will help explain these events.

Are you more likely to engage in delinquent behavior yourself if you are around others who engage in delinquency? Would it matter if the others engaging in delinquency were your friends or strangers?

The first proposition suggests that delinquent behavior is learned instead of inherited or the result of some biological trait. Today even those interested in biological predictors of crime and delinquency do not argue that *behavior* is inherited; rather, there may be predispositions that make some folks more likely to engage in behavior.[32] In fact, Sutherland was responding to the early biological and psychological traditions that were fairly deterministic in nature (i.e., individuals were born with some trait or characteristic that

©iStockphoto.com/VBStock

made them "bad"—for example, a mesomorphic body type instead of an ectomorphic or endomorphic one).[33] And even today we speak of "crack babies" as if they are destined to a life of drug use, when studies are starting to tell us that those "crack babies" have few lasting effects from their exposure.[34] By focusing on *learning* acts of delinquency, Sutherland was moving toward a more sociological explanation of delinquent behavior.

From the second and third proposition we can conclude that Sutherland considered learning to be a social process that was most likely to happen with one's friends and family. While current researchers have taken into account new modes of communication such as social media, Sutherland focused more specifically on traditional, direct modes of communication and learning. These two propositions are very useful to our understanding of bullying and the use of social media to spread rumors. The spreading of rumors is, by nature, a communicative act that is done among one's peers. We see our peers telling a story, then see and experience the impact of that story ourselves, and pass the same information on to others. But even bullying is often found to be a social act in which more than one person engages in the bullying of an individual.[35]

The fourth proposition suggests two distinct issues are needed to learn delinquency and continue to engage in delinquent behavior. First, an individual must be taught how to engage in the delinquent act, no matter how simple or complex that act is. For example, we must learn how to use technology before we can use it to spread rumors. Second, we need to know why people would want to engage in the behavior in the first place. Sutherland believed that people change their attitudes to be accepting of the deviant or delinquent behavior in order to initially engage in and then to continue with the behavior. For example, it is likely that most of the kids spreading rumors about the bullied youth had been taught to not talk negatively about others, and it certainly can be expected that the adults understood that spreading rumors is wrong. So why engage in the behavior? Sutherland argues that individuals must change their attitude about the behavior, to decide either that it is not as bad as they were initially taught, or that it is OK to do to the individual in question. In the fifth proposition, Sutherland offers how it might be that individuals listen to these new messages (e.g., it is OK to spread rumors online), rather than the old message (e.g., do not talk negatively about others). He believes that if an individual sees the legal code of a behavior as favorable or unfavorable, then that individual will be more or less likely to engage in the behavior. For example, while spreading rumors is harmful and may be punishable legally, depending on the harm that it causes, if spreading a rumor is seen as the "right" thing to do (in this case, it may stop violence at school), then it is easier to engage in that act.

The sixth proposition is the most important proposition to differential association theory, and it states that an excess of definitions favorable to delinquent behavior over definitions unfavorable to delinquent behavior increases the likelihood of committing delinquent acts. Sutherland believed that if one message is more prevalent or more dominant than the other, then it is likely to be the one that individuals listen to. In this instance, it might be that if an individual is exposed to the rumor enough, he or she will begin to believe that it is OK to pass it on, too. Social media, then, becomes an easy way for rumors to spread because they can blossom so quickly and each time the rumors are passed on they are seen as more legitimate.

The seventh proposition specifies this further and states that differential associations vary in terms of *frequency* (how often exposed), *duration* (how long exposed), *priority* (how early in life one is exposed), and *intensity* (the respect or admiration one holds for the person providing the definitions). Again, one can see that even in a society that rebukes bullying (we generally at least try to teach our children to be nice to others in theory), some people are exposed to definitions favorable to bullying—frequently, for long durations of time, from an early age where youth are impressionable, and from people they are expected to respect (e.g., parents, an older sibling, or media figures)—which makes them more likely to engage in the behavior themselves. It is important to note that Sutherland emphasized not differential association with persons, but rather *differential exposure to definitions,* and that sometimes these messages are contradictory. Although the two variables may be related, they are clearly not the same thing. For example, parents can tell their children to be nice to each other but, at the same time, treat their children harshly themselves; they may also reward behavior, such as "sticking up for oneself or what one believes in," in ways that really seem to condone bullying rather than standing one's ground on principle. In other words, the message itself is important, and in many instances, such as bullying behavior, the message juveniles receive might be mixed (see Figure 4.1 for the general process of differential association).

Sutherland's theory of differential association is perhaps the most long-standing and most popular theory of delinquency in terms of empirical evaluation, and it has made important inroads to policy and programs. It has been instrumental in studying a wide array of criminal and noncriminal delinquent behaviors and has found much support. The theory has also been sharply criticized and challenged on a number of grounds.[36] However, it is still cited widely in the social sciences and has been modified and expanded by Ronald Akers and his colleagues.

Akers introduced the behavioral concepts of operant conditioning, punishment, and reinforcement into Sutherland's differential association theory.[37] Akers argued that learning, at its most basic, did not have to come from social interaction (a major assumption of Sutherland), but could come from rewards and punishments that evolved from the individual behavior itself.[38] According to Akers, behavior is shaped by what follows it (the reaction—the reward or punishment for that behavior). These rewards and punishments are broken into four categories: positive reinforcement, negative reinforcement, positive punishment, and negative punishment. Behavior is strengthened because of reinforcement. A **positive reinforcement** is a reward for that behavior, for example the pleasurable feeling that some might claim they get from doing drugs. A bit harder to understand is **negative reinforcement**, which is an event that *strengthens* behavior because the behavior stops a negative event that an individual wants to stop. For example, a juvenile is getting bullied, and because of the bullying he or she starts to skip school. If skipping school relieves the negative feelings that arise from the bullying, then the juvenile will probably continue to skip school. Given that a reinforcement is likely to increase or strengthen a behavior, a punishment is designed to decrease behavior. A **positive punishment** is a punishment that is introduced or added in order to decrease a behavior. For example, if youth are caught bullying, they may be told to stay after school for detention. In contrast, a **negative punishment** is something that is *taken away,* instead of introduced, as a punishment. In this instance, if juveniles are caught bullying, they may be expelled from school, or might be told they can no longer participate in football, cheerleading, or marching band. In Akers's version of differential association theory, social learning theory, he suggests that whether delinquent behavior will develop and persist for individuals will depend on the differential reinforcement—the level of rewards and punishments that

●●●

Positive reinforcement: A reward for behavior, for example the pleasurable feeling that people might feel they get from doing drugs.

Negative reinforcement: An event that *strengthens* behavior because the behavior stops a negative event that an individual wants to stop.

Positive punishment: A punishment that is introduced or added to decrease a behavior.

Negative punishment: Something that is taken away, instead of introduced, as a punishment.

FIGURE 4.1 The Process of Differential Association

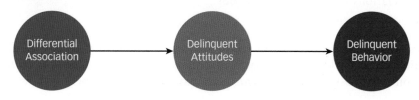

exist in the juvenile's life for that delinquent behavior. But unlike Sutherland's differential association theory, these differential reinforcements (associations) do not just have to be with delinquent or nondelinquent peers. School, family, and religion could all add to the differential reinforcements.

Differential Association Theory and Class, Gender, and Race

Differential association theorists have most often focused on the social learning aspects of the theory and have not focused much attention on how differential association may explain the relationship between class, gender, race, and juvenile delinquency. We offer several specific examples of research that has incorporated class, gender, or race into the explanation, but it is clear that theorists should explore these avenues in more detail.

Class

While the use of differential association theory has most often focused on the association and social learning aspects of the theory, Sutherland and Cressey argued that these differences in association might likely be determined by "differential social organization."[39] Or, put another way, some areas might be more likely to create opportunities for delinquency and crime, and in these areas one would be more likely, then, to associate with individuals who would engage in delinquency and teach that delinquency to others. Like social disorganization theory (Chapter 5), much of the focus was on class-based differences in areas. However, Reinarman and Fagan tested the notion that differential association and/or delinquency might vary by area (focusing on areas differentiated by class), and they found that different socioeconomic areas did not predict individual-level delinquency, nor did these areas have varying levels of differential association.[40]

Gender

While some theorists call for gender-specific theories of delinquency (see Chapter 6), others (who use more general theories such as those found in this chapter) explain that gender differences in delinquency focus on the idea that boys and girls are either differently exposed or differently affected by the same conditions. (In other words, the first perspective might say that in a patriarchal system that devalues girls and overlooks much of the oppression that girls experience, one of their reactions to this oppression might be delinquency. The second perspective would say that while both girls and boys are oppressed as young people in our society, they deal with that oppression in different ways.) Those who use differential association theory to explain gender differences usually focus on the fact either that boys are more likely to be around delinquent peers than girls or that delinquent peers have a different impact on boys than they do on girls.[41] Mears et al. used differential association theory to explain the gender differences in delinquency and found that boys are, indeed, more likely than girls to have delinquent friends.[42] But even more important than the number of delinquent friends, girls seem sheltered from their delinquent associations (friends) by their moral values (the socialization of girls that strongly emphasizes not harming others). In other words, the emphasis on not harming or hurting others to whom girls are exposed may counteract associations with delinquent friends.

Race

Very little research has examined racial differences in delinquency using the differential association or social learning theory.[43] One study that did examine these differences focused on research that suggests that there may be race differences in how juveniles experience "broken homes."[44] While some studies have found no racial differences in the effect of single-headed households on white juveniles or juveniles of color, others have found a difference, and at least in a study completed by Matsueda and Heimer, these differences can be explained by differential association theory.[45] Matsueda and Heimer found that black youth from "broken homes" were more likely to be exposed to and learn definitions favorable to delinquency than white youth—although they also found that the learning of these definitions favorable to delinquency explained *both* black and white delinquency, overall. They also found that differential association theory explained delinquency among these juveniles better than social control theory, the next theory we will explore.

SOCIAL CONTROL THEORY/SOCIAL BONDING THEORY

Social control theories of delinquency got their start from the early classical theories usually associated with Beccaria. Both the classical school and the neoclassical school have, as a basis, a belief in the free will and rationalistic hedonism of the individual.[46] Beccaria, writing in the 18th century, viewed the individual as a rational actor (the popular belief of the time) and sought under this belief system to reform the system of punishment.[47] Most important for modern control theories is Beccaria's overall support for the notion that, being free actors, individuals need control in their lives to keep them from hedonistic action (if that action is harmful to society).

Control theorists assert that human beings are basically antisocial, assuming that delinquency is part of the natural order in society; individuals are attracted to the idea of norm violation and thus motivated to deviate. This leads control theorists to assert that concern for delinquent motivation alone does not account for the forces leading people to deviate—all people are capable of feeling a certain motivation to deviate. "The important question is not 'why do men not obey the rules of society', but rather 'why do men obey the rules of society.'"[48]

Classical Social Control Theory

Theorists of the classical social control theory formulate many of the assumptions of the classical school and early psychological theories into a sociological theory of delinquency and social control. Nye was one of the first theorists to articulate a distinction between *internal* and *external* social control.[49] While later theorists do not always explicate their theories in the same dichotomy of internal and external control, most accept the notion of internal social control (i.e., through thoughtful introspection or a conversation with oneself one decides not to engage in delinquency) and external control (i.e., formal controls placed upon the individual by society in order to keep him or her from engaging in crime).

Travis Hirschi

The person most associated with control theories is Travis Hirschi. Hirschi's version of social control theory is often referred to as **social bonds**.[50] This theory concentrates on indirect controls of behavior. Hirschi's social control theory suggests that delinquency is not a response to learned behavior or stimuli or the strains surrounding an individual (as differential association theory and strain theory suggest). Instead, social control theory assumes that delinquent activity is a given, and it is the absence of delinquency that needs to be explained. In fact, not only are we capable, but we are willing creators and participants in delinquency. The reason we do not engage in delinquency or crime is because we have social bonds to conformity that keep us from engaging in socially unacceptable activities. This social bond comprises four parts—attachment, commitment, involvement, and belief.

● ● ●

Social bonds:
Bonds to conformity that keep us from engaging in socially unacceptable activities.

In the News

The Flint Water Crisis

Lagretta Hinton (C) gets her blood tested for lead poison levels by Lashae Campbell as she holds her grandson Shawn Bozier at a clinic set up to help screen for the effects of the crisis when the city's drinking water became contaminated with dangerously high levels of lead in Flint, Michigan, March 6, 2016.

Flint, Michigan is in the middle of a public health crisis that is predicted to last for decades. The city, a majority black town with 40% of its population living in poverty, is at the center of what most consider to be, at the very least, an example of inept government and, at the most, an example of government crime. But for this chapter, we will focus on the actual public health crisis: heavy levels of lead in the water. How did it come about?

Between June of 2012 and April of 2013, Flint officials explored saving money by switching water providers from the Detroit Water and Sewage Department (DWSD) to the Karegnondi Water Authority (KWA). It was projected that the city would save $200 million over 25 years. In order to make this switch, Flint needed to build a pipeline to connect to the KWA. The DWSD was informed that Flint had decided to join the KWA, and DWSD decided to terminate service to Flint as of April 2014.

The pipeline was not operational by April 2014, though, so the city had to find an alternative source of water, and it decided to use the Flint River as its water source until the pipeline was operational. Flint River was the water source for the city in the 1960s. On April 25, 2014, Flint River water became the water source for the city. City officials decided not to treat the water to ensure that it would not corrode the pipes, instead waiting to see whether problems presented themselves. In May of 2014, the issues with this decision started to materialize (see Figure 4.2).

The continuing problem is that the pipes carrying water to Flint are damaged. The state claims they can be fixed by running treated water through them, but the residents are not using their water (1) because it is poisoned and (2) because they will be charged for water they cannot use. This means the water is not flowing through the pipes. The pipes will need to be fixed before the residents of Flint can use the water again. The question is when and how they will be fixed. As of June 2016, residents were still relying on bottled water.

For a book on juvenile delinquency in a diverse society, there are two issues of importance in this story: the first is the number of children who were exposed to critically high levels of lead in their water, and the second is the disproportionate number of poor children of color who were affected. We have already read that toxins such as lead are strongly correlated to behavioral problems in children, and we will also learn later in the book that children of color are more likely to be held accountable for their behavior by being arrested and formally charged in the juvenile justice system.

What does the water crisis in Flint, Michigan, mean for the children of Flint, then?

DISCUSSION QUESTION

1. If there are increased rates of delinquency in Flint in 10 years, should these children be held accountable for their behavior, or should it be understood that the water crisis is the real offender? Why or why not?

Source: Adapted from Kennedy, M. (2016, April 20). *Lead-Laced Water in Flint: A Step-by Step Look at the Making of a Crisis.* The Two-Way: Breaking news from NPR. Retrieved from http://www.npr.org/sections/thetwo-way/2016/04/20/465545378

FIGURE 4.2 Timeline of the Flint Water Crisis

May 2014
- Flint residents start to complain about the smell and color of the new water.

August 2014
- Residents are advised to boil their water because E.coli and total coliform bacteria are detected in the water.
- The Michigan Department of Environmental Quality (MDEQ) says the problem has been addressed by increasing chlorine in the water.

October 2014
- General Motors stops using Flint River water because of concerns it will corrode their equipment.

January 2015
- Flint water is in violation of the Safe Drinking Water Act.
- The state buys bottled water for its employees at affected government offices, in response.

February 2015
- A city test finds high levels of lead at an area resident's home.
- This same resident reports that her child has been diagnosed with lead poisoning.

April 2015
- Virginia Tech researchers find lead levels in the water of 13,200 ppb (5,000 ppb is considered hazardous waste) at this same resident's house.
- EPA finds out that Flint never implemented corrosion control for its pipes.

July 2015
- The EPA expresses concern over lead levels in Flint water and the MDEQ assures the public that they can relax because there is no extensive problem with lead in the Flint water.

September 2015
- Virginia Tech tests hundreds of homes and finds "serious" levels of lead. Officials at the MDEQ dismiss the results.
- A local medical study finds increased levels of lead in Flint children.
- The city of Flint issues a lead advisory.
- A spokesman for the Michigan governor says that the MDEQ and Department of Community Health believe that some in Flint are trying to blame the state and turn this into a political issue.

October 2015
- The governor's office says the state will supply water filters and water testing to the citizens of Flint.
- Flint switches back to the Detroit Water and Sewage Department (now called the Great Lakes Water Authority).

December 2015
- New mayor of Flint declares a state of emergency because of the lead levels in the city's water. Even though the city had switched back to less corrosive water in October, the pipes had already been severely damaged, so the lead continued to leach into the water.
- The head of the MDEQ resigns.

January 2016
- The state of Michigan and the federal government declare a state of emergency for Flint.

March 2016
- The MDEQ is found to have primary responsibility for the crisis.

April 2016
- Flint water is still unsafe.

Moffitt makes an extended life course argument saying that there are two offender groups.[61] The first is considered a life course–persistent group whose delinquency stems from neurodevelopmental processes—these individuals are predicted to be fairly consistent in their delinquent behavior. In other words, over their life they are more likely to engage in crime. Moffitt considers this to be a fairly small group. The second is called adolescence-limited. This group is much larger, its members' delinquency stems from social processes, and over time it is likely that most will stop engaging in delinquent behavior.[62]

These variations on the life course theory are often used to explain the age-crime curve. The relationship between age and crime is so strong at the aggregate level that many believe it is invariant (meaning that it does not change over era or type of crime, for example), and while this is probably not the case, it is a very strong relationship—we see, in general, that the likelihood for crime rises sharply as one ages into the teenage and late teenage/early adult years and then not quite as swiftly drops off (see Figure 4.3).[63] Steffensmeier, Allan, Harer, and Streifel found that the age-crime relationship was extremely strong, but varied for type of crime (for example, while the relationship between age and property crimes peaks at about 17, the relationship between age and violent crime peaks a bit later).[64]

Theorists who use the life course theory argue that this age-crime relationship exists because as people age they go through stages that allow them to be more or less delinquent. For example, as adolescents become teenagers, they are more likely to pull away from their parents' control, perhaps becoming less attached to their parents and more attached to their peers. Then as individuals become even older, they enter new stages of their life in which delinquent behavior may be less rewarding or available, and thus they begin to engage in less and less delinquency and more and more conformity—we call this "aging out of crime and delinquency."

FIGURE 4.3 Age-Crime Curve

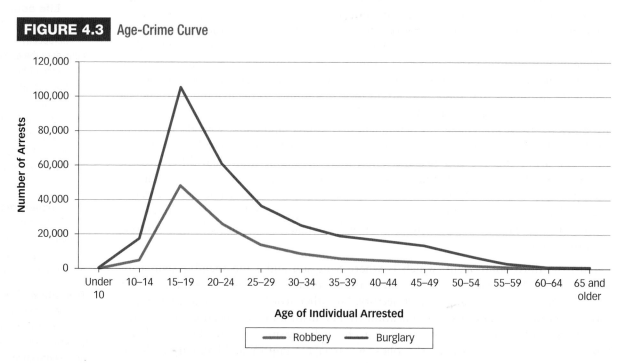

Source: Bureau of Justice Statistics. (2012). *Arrests in the United States, 1990–2010.* Retrieved from http://www.bjs.gov/content/pub/pdf/aus9010.pdf

Note: Most recent data available.

from the CLASSROOM to the COMMUNITY

Helping Kids Make Better Choices: Mujeres Organization

To help youth succeed in school and stay out of trouble, teachers often use strategies related to the main insights of the social process theories covered in this chapter. See if you can identify insights related to differential association theory, social bonding theory, and life course theory in the set of events described in the following newspaper article.

Castro Valley High School senior Bianca Arias plans on becoming a nurse, and she has applied to several universities to achieve her goal. She gives much of the credit for her academic success to the "strong support system" she receives from belonging to Mujeres, a group that meets regularly with school counselor Connie Iglesias.

Many prevention programs focus on boys, instead of girls, which means girls in need of support and guidance fall through the cracks. Mujeres is an example of a program designed to focus on supporting the success of girls.

"Instead of thinking short-term, I'm thinking long-term," says Arias, who is the club's president.

Iglesias founded the club because she saw some female students getting into fights, not succeeding at school, and even dropping out. She worried that they were making choices that might lead to a "rougher life" in adulthood—affecting their future relationships, career choices and overall well-being.

The Castro Valley Teachers Association member wanted to put these girls, mostly Latina, on a better path, and asked some of them to join a group called Mujeres, which is Spanish for "women." Programs reaching out to minority youth, she observes, often focus on boys rather than girls, who may fall through the cracks.

"Traditionally, these kinds of girls don't talk to adults and might be failing in class," she says. "I can be that caring adult who wants them to succeed. I know what it's like. I am a Latina, and some of my family members did not graduate from high school. I call their parents. I do a lot of hand-holding."

Founded three years ago, Mujeres meets weekly for lunch to discuss life, coping skills, and how to be successful in school. During meetings, Iglesias shares advice for taking the PSAT and SAT tests, keeping up with schoolwork, and applying to colleges. There are also meetings to discuss issues such as self-esteem, family, friendships, peer pressure, romantic relationships and gangs.

"I try to connect them with school culture," says Iglesias, who came up with the idea for Mujeres while earning her counseling degree in graduate school. "Sometimes the Latino population has trouble feeling that connection when they are in a big school setting, which is why they have the highest dropout rate. I tell my girls that they need to change the stereotype people have of Latinos by working hard, not fighting, and doing well in school."

While the group is geared toward helping Latinas, it is also open to any female students who wish to join. The goal is to help members close the achievement gap, feel more confident, and make good choices for the future.

(Continued)

(Continued)

Stacey Aguilar, 16, says the club opens both "eyes" and "doors" for its members. Her older sister didn't even know what a UC [University of California] campus was until Iglesias explained to her that "college" could be different from a community college. Today her sister is a freshman at UC Santa Cruz.

"I also want to get into a good school so I can have a good job," says Aguilar, the club's vice president. "This club makes me more serious about my grades, staying motivated and serving as a good example for freshman students."

Iglesias is proud to see the progress and personal growth of her students.

"I love these kids so much, and it's great to see them take up a leadership role within Mujeres," says Iglesias. "If they have a plan—whether it's college or vocational school—they will learn how to take care of themselves, reach their goals, and eventually become role models for others."

DISCUSSION QUESTION

1. Which theory is best represented in this article? Use examples from the article to illustrate.

Source: Posnick-Goodwin, S. (2012). Helping girls make better choices. *California Teachers Association, 16*(6). Retrieved from http://www.cta.org/en/Professional-Development/Publications/2012/03/March-Educator-2012/Helping-girls.aspx Reprinted by permission of the California Teachers Association.

Social Control and Gender: The Example of Power-Control Theory

The control theories presented up to this point have been generalist in nature. In other words, the assumption is that they can predict the likelihood of delinquency across diverse populations. While our examples of the application of differential association theory to race, class, and gender differences in delinquency illustrated the use of general theory, our example here is one in which the ideas of control theory are merged with another perspective (conflict theory, discussed in Chapter 6) to form a new variation on the theory to help explain gender differences in delinquency. John Hagan, A. R. Gillis, and John Simpson developed one of the best known control/neo-Marxist theories of delinquency, known as power-control theory.[65] In their article "Class in the Household: A Power-Control Theory of Gender and Delinquency," Hagan, Simpson et al. claimed that previous theories of delinquency did not pay enough attention to social class and gender, and their theory was an attempt to remedy that problem by blending Marxist or "power" theories that look at the big picture—the macro level—with "control" theories that look at the microstructural level—the day-to-day interactions between individuals.[66] They explained how both types of theory, when used together, can help us better understand different types of *dominance* and how they relate to the creation of delinquency among boys and girls respectively:

Hagan, Simpson et al. theorized that the more freedom people have to act and the less social control upon them, the more likely they will break norms and commit common acts of delinquency (e.g., petty theft, auto theft, grand larceny, battery, vandalism). These authors stated that boys have more freedom than girls to act as they wish in society, and both boys and girls in the highest socioeconomic classes have the most freedom to do what they please. Ultimately, Hagan, Simpson et al. stated that we should expect that boys from the highest social classes have the most ability of youth as a whole to deviate from societal norms, and forwarded a few reasons why they thought this would be the case. First, they stated that youth who are under strict parental control are less likely to acquire a taste for risk taking and more likely to perceive that they will get in trouble if they commit an act of delinquency. Second, the authors hypothesized that girls are more likely than boys to be taught in the home not to break the rules and to be scared of punishment.

Their empirical study of self-reported delinquency as it related to the variables outlined above found that boys in all social classes committed more acts of delinquency than girls. But in the case of the youth coming from homes in which their parents were unemployed or underemployed, there was no difference in delinquency among girls and boys after parental control was taken into account. Overall, youth who were children of business owners were more likely as a whole than youth from other classes to engage in common delinquency. Hagan, Simpson et al. also found that boys from homes whose parents were business owners were less likely to be subjected to parental controls than those in middle-class and working-class homes, which led upper-class boys to engage in more common delinquency. Unlike middle- and working-class boys, upper-class boys did not even need to develop a taste for risk taking—they simply acted out in more delinquency because they could and did not worry about getting in trouble. Hagan, Simpson, et al. noted that their study results, on the whole, supported what early Marxist criminologist Bonger theorized long ago: that the greatest effect of gender on delinquency would be found in the upper social classes of society.[67]

Hagan and his colleagues expanded their theory in subsequent years to consider the degree of power parents had in their jobs outside of the home and how that translated into power and control within the family.[68] Power-control theory was later reconsidered again as a means of addressing feminist critiques that stated it was off the mark by ignoring the role that patriarchal families played in generating girls' delinquency through acts of violence and abuse.[69] Patriarchal families, according to the critique, cannot just be theorized as positive forces that prevent children, especially girls, from committing acts of delinquency. McCarthy, Hagan, and Woodward looked into the effect that women's increasing power and freedom in nonpatriarchal families had on their children as an extension of the power-control theory.[70] One of their primary findings was that in families where mothers had more power in the home, boys were less apt to develop mainstream ideas about gender and risk taking. Thus they were less likely to act out delinquently. The lessening of social control of girls in nonpatriarchal households was met by increased control of boys in such households and a gender egalitarian socialization.

Techniques of Neutralization Model

One of the many questions that stem from such normative theories as differential association and social control/social bonding theory is how individuals can engage in bad behavior when they are aware it is wrong. Sykes and Matza offered an explanation for why individuals might engage in delinquency even though they understand it is wrong.[71] Asking the question "Why would we violate the norms and laws in which we believe?" they suggest that we employ **techniques of neutralization** in order to rationalize away our understanding of the rules. They argue that society is organized for these sorts of rationalizations because much of our understanding of the rules comes with a certain flexibility already. In other words, they point out, while we understand the normative system, we also understand that under certain circumstances those norms do not apply. For example, while killing someone is generally wrong, we know during times of war or in self-defense it is not. As Sykes and Matza pointed out, there are ways that people neutralize or rationalize their wrongdoing at times, even in the face of such a label. They noted five primary psychosocial techniques for doing so:

●●●

Techniques of neutralization: Rationalizations used by individuals in order to engage in delinquency.

**Denial of
responsibility:** The
belief that outside
forces compel a
person's behavior,
and thus the person
refuses to take
responsibility for his or
her actions.

Denial of injury:
A neutralization
technique in which
the person denies
that anyone has been
harmed by her or his
actions.

**Denial of
the victim:**
A neutralization
technique in which
a person justifies
his or her behavior
by stating that the
person who was
victimized deserved
it, or that because
of circumstances,
the delinquent act
committed needed to
occur.

**Condemnation of
the condemners:**
A neutralization
technique in which
a person tries to
turn the tables on
those who condemn
or disapprove of his
or her behavior by
condemning them.

**Appeal to
higher loyalties:**
A neutralization
technique in which
a youth who has
committed a
delinquent act justifies
it on the basis of
a higher calling or
purpose.

1. **Denial of responsibility.** Sykes and Matza stated that this is when a person refuses to claim responsibility for a given act. A person takes on a "billiard ball conception of himself in which he sees himself as helplessly propelled into new situations."[72] The belief that outside forces compel a person's behavior allows him or her to ignore any disapproval from others when breaking norms and also allows the person to avoid feeling bad about any behavior that might be considered wrongdoing.

2. **Denial of injury.** In this technique of neutralization, "the link between acts and their consequences [may] be broken."[73] In other words, the person denies that anyone has been harmed by her or his actions. Sykes and Matza provided examples in which youth may redefine their delinquent acts in terms that are less harmless, such as labeling them as "mischief" in the case of vandalism and "borrowing" in the case of theft. This allows the youth to challenge the legitimacy of social control efforts and, once again, to avoid internalizing a delinquent label.

3. **Denial of the victim.** According to Sykes and Matza, denial of the victim occurs when a person justifies his or her behavior by stating that the person who was victimized deserved it, or that because of circumstances the delinquent act committed needed to occur. The person might actually admit responsibility, but will refuse to acknowledge that anyone harmed by her or his actions did not deserve it. Sykes and Matza explained that "by a subtle alchemy the delinquent moves himself into a position of avenger and the victim is transformed into a wrong-doer."[74] We have all unfortunately heard of the rape myth that many rapists perpetuate: "She deserved it." A less violent example Sykes and Matza provided to illustrate this technique is the figure of Robin Hood, who justified stealing from the rich and giving it to the poor because he saw it as necessary to even the economic playing field. Robin Hood was not defining the rich as victims in those situations in which he was stealing from them. When there is no discernible victim apparent, such as in the case of acts of delinquency against public property, it is even easier for a person to deny a victim and to avoid internalizing negative feelings about norm breaking.

4. **Condemnation of the condemners.** In this technique of neutralization, a person tries to turn the tables on those who condemn or disapprove of his or her behavior by condemning them. People who typically serve social control functions in a young person's life, such as law enforcement officers, parents, and teachers, are labeled by delinquent youth as being corrupt or misguided in their disapproval. "Police it might be said, are corrupt, stupid and brutal. Teachers always show favoritism, and parents always 'take it out' on their children."[75] By engaging in this technique, youth can repress their feelings about their own behavior and motivations and shift them to others.

5. **Appeal to higher loyalties.** This final technique of neutralization is one in which a youth who has committed a delinquent act justifies it on the basis of a higher calling or purpose. Oftentimes, a young person will claim that a close friendship or relationship with a group of peers necessitates some sort of lawbreaking. The youth might not stand in opposition to the rules or laws in general, but feels that in a specific situation norm breaking is necessary to help a friend, a group of friends, or a family member. An example would be when a person helps a friend commit an act of delinquency in order to get money to pay for food, because she feels it is important for her friend to survive.

Sykes and Matza's schema explains the ways that people who have actually done something wrong justify their behavior and talk themselves out of feeling guilty about it. It is basically a psychological consideration of this process. This theory is especially useful in conjunction with social control theory or differential association theory. Since both theories are normative and assume that individuals understand the difference between right and wrong, the techniques of neutralization offer an explanation for why people engage in delinquent behavior when they know it is wrong.

GENERAL STRAIN THEORY

In Chapter 5 you will be introduced to the macro-level versions of anomie and strain theories. As we discussed, these classic strain theories dominated criminological research in the 1950s and 1960s, and their relevance was marked in public policy of the time, particularly in strain theory's impact on the War on Poverty during the 1960s.[76] Strain theory came under attack in the 1970s as relativist theorists shifted the focus to conflict and labeling theories (see Chapter 6), offering a new perspective on societal influences on both crime and punishment. One of the main critiques of the classic theories was the focus on class-based delinquency and crime, given that the assumption was a uniform societal goal of wealth attainment (Merton's version).

Robert Agnew resurrected the tradition with his general strain theory (GST) by expanding the discussion of what may create strain in juvenile's lives (see Figure 4.4).[77] GST focuses on what circumstances lead individuals and groups within a society to engage in delinquent behavior. Agnew suggests that they are "pressured into crime." Along with the failure to achieve valued goals, Agnew argues that strain may also result from negative relationships. Agnew specifies three major types of strain:[78]

1. The anticipated or actual failure to achieve a goal (for example, not achieving a spot on a sports team or achieving popularity with peers).

2. The anticipated or actual loss of a positive stimulus (for example, the death of a parent or breakup of a romantic relationship).

3. The anticipated or actual presentation of a negative stimulus (for example, physical assaults, failing grades, public insults, discrimination, or oppression). Such negative relations will likely lead to anger and frustration, which may then lead to delinquent behavior, such as physical violence, running away from home, illicit drug use, or self-harming behavior.

FIGURE 4.4 Model of General Strain Theory

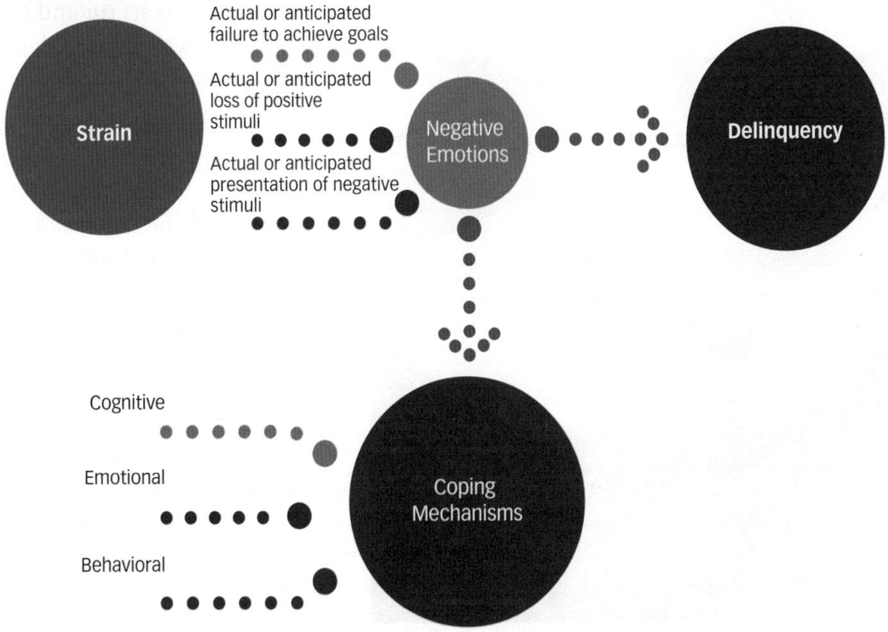

Source: Adapted from Agnew, R. (2001). Building on the foundation of general strain theory: Specifying the types of strain most likely to lead to crime and delinquency. *Journal of Research in Crime and Delinquency, 38*, 319–361.

Agnew argues that some types of strain are more likely to cause crime and delinquency than others.[79] He identifies the following characteristics as most likely to cause crime: The strain is high in magnitude; the strain is seen as unjust; the strain is associated with low self-control; and the strain creates some pressure or incentive for criminal coping. More specifically, examples of strains that are likely to cause crime include parental rejection, erratic or excessively harsh discipline, child abuse and neglect, negative school experiences, abusive peer relationships, criminal victimization, residence in economically deprived neighborhoods, and discrimination based on characteristics such as race/ethnicity and gender.

●●●

Behavioral coping: A type of coping strategy that focuses on actions that might help to reduce the strain itself.

Cognitive coping: A type of coping strategy that involves trying to reinterpret the strain to lessen the impact of that strain.

Emotional coping: A type of coping strategy that is an attempt to lessen the negative emotions that might arise from the strain.

Agnew is careful to point out that not all individuals respond to strains with crime and delinquency, and, in fact, most people cope in legal and conforming ways. There are many possible coping strategies, including behavioral coping, cognitive coping, and emotional coping.[80] **Behavioral coping** strategies focus on actions that might help to reduce the strain itself. **Cognitive coping** strategies involve trying to reinterpret the strain to lessen the impact of that strain. **Emotional coping** strategies are an attempt to lessen the negative emotions that might arise from the strain. Coping strategies can be positive or negative. This means that, according to Agnew, delinquency is seen as a coping strategy, albeit a bad one.

General Strain Theory and Race

Agnew lists several instances of strain that may be specifically linked to the experiences of juveniles of color, including criminal victimization, adverse or negative school experiences, and most specifically the experience of prejudice and discrimination.[81] J. M. Kaufman, Rebellon, Thaxton, and Agnew extend this discussion to specifically examine the strains and coping mechanisms present in the lives of African Americans.[82] They suggest that African Americans are more likely to experience a host of strains including economic, community (neighborhood strains), educational (unfair discipline), discrimination, and victimization. And to the extent that much of this strain may be perceived as unfair (it is one thing to be disciplined because you have actually done something wrong, and another thing to be disciplined because you are singled out), the reaction to strain and coping may be less conventional.

Gabbidon detailed an excellent review of the way that GST might help explain racial and ethnic differences in delinquency.[83] While he reviewed the expanse of studies that examine both crime and delinquency, he highlighted several important studies that focus on delinquency. Simons, Chen, Stewart, and Brody specifically examined the relationship between discrimination, strain, and delinquency among black juveniles.[84] They found that discrimination fostered anger and depression among juveniles and that this anger and depression was a predictor of delinquency. A second study by Perez, Jennings, and

One of the circumstances in which racial discrimination may exist is during pretextual traffic stops. Drivers of color may experience significant strain under these conditions.

©iStockphoto.com/Rich Legg

Gover examined the effect of strain on Hispanic juveniles.[85] This study found that "in both low and high Hispanic concentration areas, as the adolescents' perception of anti-Hispanic discrimination increased so did the likelihood of violent delinquency."[86] Finally, while university students are technically not juveniles anymore, Moon, Hays, and Blurton also found that experiencing race discrimination was a type of strain that led to violent delinquency and crime.[87]

All of these studies put the experiences of juveniles of color into a context. Some differences in delinquency rates between juveniles of color and white juveniles may be attributable to the increased levels of strain that juveniles of color are exposed to, especially strains/stressors coming from discrimination and increased levels of social control that juveniles of color are exposed to in school.

General Strain Theory and Gender

There has been a substantial level of research examining the effect of strain on gender differences in delinquency, too.[88] Broidy and Agnew used general strain theory to answer two questions: (1) How can we explain the higher rate of crime among males? and (2) How can we explain why females engage in crime?[89] To explain the higher rate of criminality among boys than girls, Broidy and Agnew suggest four possible relationships between gender and strain. First, boys might be subject to more stressors or strains than girls. However, after examining the various strains that boys and girls are subjected to, they concluded that girls are subjected to at least as many strains as boys, if not more.

Second, the strains that boys and girls face may be different, and the strains that boys face may be more conducive to delinquency than those faced by girls. Examining the gendered differences in strain, Broidy and Agnew concluded that boys focus more on strains of a material nature and are more likely the victims of aggression and anger, while girls focus on strains that are more interpersonal in nature and focus on issues of procedural justice. For this reason, Broidy and Agnew concluded that strain may explain why boys engage in more violence and property crime.

Third, boys and girls might have different emotional responses to crime. Some studies suggest that boys respond to stress with anger, while girls respond with depression.[90] And it is true that in many instances girls respond to stress with depression, but they also respond with anger. In fact, Mirowsky and Ross found that girls often respond with more anger than boys.[91] However, how boys and girls experience anger is different. Boys are more likely to experience anger in a morally righteous way (they are more likely to blame others for their treatment and to take insult), while girls are conflicted by their anger, feeling guilty that they are angry and worrying it might jeopardize relationships. The way boys experience anger (in an outward rather than inward manner) may mean that their strain and anger are more conducive to delinquency.

Finally, Broidy and Agnew examined whether boys are more likely to respond to their strain and anger with crime than girls. In other words, they examined what coping strategies both boys and girls have available to them. The findings are mixed on gender and coping strategies. Some research suggests that girls have less effective coping resources (because of a lower sense of mastery or self-esteem), while other research suggests that girls have higher levels of coping strategies because they have more emotional social support. In the end, Broidy and Agnew concluded that boys may be more likely to engage in outward-aggressive delinquent coping mechanisms when legitimate ones are not available, while girls may be more likely to engage in self-directed delinquent coping mechanisms, such as alcohol and drug abuse or eating disorders, when legitimate coping mechanisms are not available.

A Focus on Research

General Strain Theory and Delinquency: Extending a Popular Explanation to American Indian Youth

In their *Youth & Society* article, "General Strain Theory and Delinquency: Extending a Popular Explanation to American Indian Youth," Eitle and Eitle examine the ability of general strain theory to predict the delinquent behavior of American Indian youth.[92] The researchers found that general strain theory did predict the likelihood that American Indian youth would engage in general, violent, and property crimes. Those who had experienced criminal victimization, or had recent negative life events, were more likely to engage in delinquency.

In addition, they found that having strong social support decreased the likelihood of delinquency while exposure to substance-using peers increased delinquent behavior. However, they also found that religiosity had an unexpected positive effect on delinquency. In other words, those who were more religious were more likely to engage in delinquency. Eitle and Eitle speculate that their measure of religiosity may, in part, be measuring traditional American Indian spirituality, and given that American Indian culture and religion are not universally supported or accepted in general society, a strong religious presence may actually add strain.

Eitle and Eitle also tested whether personal and social resources could impact the effect of strain on American Indian youth behavior. In other words, could those with personal and social resources basically combat their strain and not engage in delinquency? Their findings were unexpected. Most important, the researchers found that school commitment and school attachment affected youth behavior but not in the expected way. Those with greater school attachment were more likely to have a strong relationship between school-based strain and general delinquency. Again, Eitle and Eitle suggest that this may be because there may be a conflict of culture between American Indian youth and the large urban and suburban schools in which this study was conducted. In other words, large urban and suburban schools have not been known to support American Indian culture in a deep and meaningful way.

According to Eitle and Eitle, these findings suggest that more research needs to be done to examine why strain may be caused by school and religion—two social resources that should be supports to help youth through stressful times. In both instances, if American Indian youth are not feeling the support from mainstream society, they could be compounding their stress.

DISCUSSION QUESTION

1. How might schools help decrease strain for American Indian youth?

Source: Eitle, D. & McNulty Eitle, T. (2016). General strain theory and delinquency: Extending a popular explanation to American Indian youth. *Youth & Society, 48*(4): 470–495.

MICRO-LEVEL THEORIES AND PUBLIC POLICY

One of the most important contributions of theory is that it can inform the public policies that are created to address juvenile delinquency and crime. Given that this chapter has presented theories that explain individual-level behavior, public policies from these theories would also focus on individual-level behavior.

Differential association theory focuses on the learning of delinquency from peers and in the form of social learning theory from reinforcements and punishments that individuals experience in their interactions with friends, family, school, and general society. Public policy created from this theory could focus on several factors. For example, school programs that focus on either decreasing norms that favor delinquency or increasing

TABLE 4.1 Summary of Micro-Level Theories

THEORY	THEORISTS	MAJOR CONCEPTS
Pre-Classical Theory	Hobbes	Individuals are rational beings Social contract
Classical Theories	Beccaria	Deterrence Certainty of punishment Celerity of punishment Severity of punishment
Biological Theories	Lombroso Sheldon	Craniometry Phrenology Atavism Stigmata Endomorphic Ectomorphic Mesomorphic
Psychological	Freud	Id Ego Superego
Biosocial	Beaver Walsh	Neurological deficits Diet Hormones Toxins
Differential Association and Social Learning Theories	Sutherland Akers	Delinquency is learned through interactions with friends. The learning includes techniques of committing the delinquency and attitudes about the behavior. Operant conditioning Punishment Reinforcement
Social Control and Social Bonding Theory	Hirschi	Social bonds of attachment, commitment, involvement, and belief keep youth from engaging in delinquency.
Life Course and Developmental Theories	Sampson and Laub Moffitt	Problem behaviors occur in an orderly, progressive fashion and life events and milestones have an impact on one's behavior.
General Strain Theory	Agnew	Strain from failure to achieve positively valued goals, anticipated or actual loss of positive stimuli, or anticipated or actual presentation of negative stimulus can push juveniles to delinquency.

conventional norms could stem from this theory. While in high school, we both experienced peer groups established by school counselors that emphasized the importance of conventional peer interactions. These groups were populated by "outgoing" students, and students who were seen as leaders or popular by the school administration. The message of these groups mostly revolved around the importance of staying off drugs and alcohol. It was believed that as high school students we would be much more likely to listen to and take this message from our peers than we would from adults in our life.

A public policy from social control/social bonding theory would focus on one or all of the social bonds that must remain strong in order to stop delinquency. For example, this theory would advocate for strong, rich, well-funded after-school programs for juveniles, such as clubs (e.g., Model UN or the chess club), music programs (e.g., marching band or jazz band), sports programs (e.g., field hockey, football, or cheerleading), and non–school-related activities (e.g., girl scouts or boys' and girls' clubs). What bonds would these programs help strengthen? In fact, they have the possibility of strengthening at least two bonds. The involvement bond would be strengthened through the time spent involved in these programs. A juvenile who has Model UN or football practice for two hours after school has two fewer hours in the day to get into mischief. And it is much more likely that when students are done with these after-school activities their parents will be returning home from work, meaning that parental supervision is more likely after these programs than right after school. The commitment bond is also likely strengthened with these programs. As juveniles become more committed to their activities, more bonded with the others in the club or on the team, and more committed to the success of the group or organization, they will be less likely to jeopardize these activities by engaging in delinquent behavior.

Finally, general strain theory (GST) focuses on the likely strains and available coping mechanisms for juveniles. GST emphasizes that strains are likely in most juveniles' lives (we cannot likely avoid all strain in our lives), but that some strains may be more likely in some juveniles' lives than in others (remember, both girls and juveniles of color are more likely to experience discrimination and oppression). Public programs may focus on decreasing strains that certain groups experience more than others or increasing the general coping skills of all juveniles. For example, given the studies that have documented that students of color receive more harsh treatment while at school, a school district may create special training based on these findings that helps teachers identify the differential treatment that some students might experience. Enhanced training for teachers and administrators may help decrease disproportionate social control that targets juveniles of color. While it is extremely important to create programs that address strain and certainly alleviate strain that is more likely placed on one group of juveniles than another, most strain theorists would probably argue that it would be easier to strengthen coping skills in youth than eliminate strain. For example, an emphasis in both home and school settings on appropriate and inappropriate responses to stress (for example, early emphasis with children that responding aggressively, with anger and violence, is not appropriate) and offering alternatives, such as methods of verbally communicating or taking time to let one's anger and stress diminish, may help juveniles identify better coping strategies.

SUMMARY

This chapter has focused on social process theories that explain individual-level behavior. The theories in this chapter are some of the most popular theories used to explain juvenile delinquency, but as we have discussed, they were not created with all types of juveniles in mind, and some are better than others at explaining the diverse experiences of juveniles and differing levels of delinquency that some groups of juveniles engage in. We can see that general strain theory has been used with a fair degree of success to explain gender differences in delinquency, and while few studies have used the theory to examine race differences, those that have started are quite promising. While differential association theory was actually created as a comment on the myopic focus of criminologists up to that time, and their obsession with street crime and "lower class" offenders, the theory has not really been used systematically to move away from a focus on street delinquency or to address systematic differences in levels of delinquency among girls or juveniles of color. The theories in Chapter 6 have been created to expressly examine many of these differences.

Many schools have antibullying programs now that focus on helping students identify traditional bullying and cyberbullying as a way to decrease instances of bullying at school. In addition, there has been an increase in stories in the media about gay and lesbian youth who have been bullied with severe consequences for those experiences.

Contact a local middle or high school. Ask if the school has an antibullying program in place and, if it does, ask if there is a written policy or program you may have access to. Examine this program. Does it seem to follow any of the theories discussed in this chapter? Does it acknowledge that some youth may be bullied more than others? Evaluate the program for its likely ability to decrease bullying on campus.

Finally, choose one of the theories we have examined in this chapter. Using this theory, create your own antibullying program for a middle or high school. Pay special attention to the different experiences that girls, juveniles of color, or gay and lesbian youth may have with bullying and try to create a program that acknowledges these differences.

DISCUSSION QUESTIONS

1. "If brain capacity and function is still developing, with frontal lobes developing last, can we hold adolescents responsible for uninhibited, antisocial behavior?"[93]

2. Thinking about the process of differential association, can you give an example from your life of your associations affecting your likelihood to engage in, or not engage in, delinquency?

3. Which of the social bonds do you think is most important for preventing delinquency? Why?

4. Can you identify three strains/stressors that existed in your middle school or high school that you or other students experienced? Do you think that all students experienced these strains equally? Why or why not?

5. Create a community program to prevent delinquency based on differential association, social control, or general strain theory.

6. Evaluate the process of confining juveniles in detention/correctional facilities using the theories in this chapter. Would any of these theories advocate for detention facilities as a preventative measure for delinquency? Explain why or why not.

KEY TERMS

Appeal to higher loyalties 114

Atavistic 97

Attachment 108

Behavioral coping 116

Belief 108

Biological determinism 97

Certainty of Punishment 96

Celerity of Punishment 96

Cognitive coping 116

Commitment 108

Condemnation of the condemners 114

Craniometry 97

Denial of injury 114

Denial of responsibility 114

CHAPTER PRETEST ANSWERS

1. True

2. True

3. True

4. True

5. True

6. True

7. True

8. True

9. True

STUDENT STUDY SITE

$SAGE edge™

edge.sagepub.com/bates2e

Sharpen your skills with SAGE edge!

SAGE edge for students provides a personalized approach to help you accomplish your coursework goals in an easy-to-use learning environment. You'll find action plans, mobile-friendly eFlashcards, and quizzes, as well as videos, web resources, and links to SAGE journal articles to support and expand on the concepts presented in this chapter. Check out the website for original videos of former offenders discussing their experiences as juveniles.

MACRO-LEVEL THEORIES

After reading this chapter, you should be able to

- Explain why social structural theories of delinquency are considered sociological positivist theories

- Distinguish between Durkheim's and Merton's versions of anomie theory

- Outline the roots of social disorganization theories and their fundamental assumptions

- Identify the primary ways social structural theories of delinquency address race, gender, and class

- Relate social structural theories of delinquency to possible policy interventions

Jason and Alex are teenagers who live on the outskirts of a major city. Their family moved to the apartment that they now live in three years ago when they immigrated to the United States. They can still remember the excitement their parents had before the big move—they could not stop talking about the future and the many opportunities that living in the United States would provide. Jason and Alex didn't know exactly what would happen when they moved, but as young boys they imagined that life might be like they had seen on celebrity Instagram accounts—a life in which a young man could easily strike it rich and have a giant house, many cars, and all sorts of fancy possessions. They were excited about the possibilities because they were tired of seeing their mother and father working so hard to survive.

Now, as teenagers getting close to graduating from high school, Jason and Alex are struggling to figure out what decisions to make. Their living situation does not look at all like what they imagined life might be; they live in a run-down area, there are many homeless people sleeping on the streets near their apartment, and there is quite a bit of street crime, especially at night. Jason and Alex's parents are working long hours in a factory, often on the night shift, to make ends meet, just like most of the adults in the neighborhood who have recently come to the United States from a variety of countries and were able to find jobs. The boys have had a hard time adjusting to the life of teenagers in the United States—it does not seem as though getting good grades in school and playing by the rules pays off in any substantial way, and they were automatically tracked into the lowest level of classes due to the fact English is their second language. They feel unchallenged and bored in school. Alex is pretty close to dropping out, and Jason is barely getting passing grades.

After a big flood damaged their neighborhood last year, things got even worse for everyone. Now, almost all of the businesses that used to attract customers have left, and it's hard for young people who do not have cars to get to another area to find jobs. To Jason and Alex, it appears as though the guys in the neighborhood who are dealing drugs are the only successful ones. They have new, trendy clothes and cars, and are able to spend money on the weekends and still have money to spare to help their parents. Jason and Alex have been approached by some of those guys looking to expand their drug sales in the area and are thinking that it would probably be a smart idea to work with them.

CHAPTER PRETEST

Test your knowledge of this chapter's material by determining whether the following statements are true or false. Be sure to compare your answers with the answers on page 150.

1. Social structural theorists focus upon how factors *inside* of a person's conscious control influence delinquency.

2. According to Durkheim, *anomie* occurs when shared norms are no longer apparent.

3. Merton theorized that there are 10 primary ways by which people adjust to the strain created by societal goals and the legitimate means to obtain those goals.

4. Social disorganization theory is often used to focus on delinquency rates between neighborhoods or geographical regions.

5. According to Park and Burgess's concentric zone model, we can expect that the rate of street delinquency in the commuter zone will be lower than the rate of street delinquency in the zone of transition.

6. Frazier's work on delinquency in the black community focused on the influence of disorganization outside of downtown Chicago on migrants from the South.

7. Most studies have found that collective efficacy makes the social disorganization of a neighborhood worse.

8. According to research, girls may experience the impact of neighborhood effects, such as collective efficacy, in different ways than boys.

SOCIAL STRUCTURAL THEORIES OF DELINQUENCY

Sociological positivist theories: Theories created by scholars using scientific methods (i.e., observation, measurement, and empirical verification).

Determinism: The concept that factors *outside of* the conscious control of individuals, chiefly the social organization of society and/or the environment, influence or determine behavior.

Macro-level theories: Theories of delinquency that focus on the social structure or the big picture of society.

Anomie theory: Durkheim's theory that proposes that rapid social change often results in a state of normlessness that results in the deregulation of people and their behavior.

Social disorganization theory: The theory of delinquency that posits that neighborhoods may become so disorganized that delinquent behavior occurs as a result.

Consensus theorist: A theorist who assumes that society is based upon consensus and that laws generally reflect agreed-upon societal expectations.

In order to understand Alex and Jason's situation, we might want to take the perspective of a macro-level theorist in this chapter to look at the big picture that surrounds it—that is, the overarching social forces that impact not only these two young men, but a number of people around them at the same time. In this chapter we will do just that by examining social structural theories that pinpoint the ways in which large-scale social factors influence delinquency. The theories that we will examine in this chapter are traditional sociological theories that are considered **sociological positivist theories**. This is because scholars coming from this perspective utilize a *positivist* approach, which means that they use scientific methods (i.e., observation, measurement, and empirical verification) to study the social world. Social structural theorists take a **deterministic** position on delinquency; that is, they claim that factors *outside of* the conscious control of individuals, chiefly the social organization of society and/or the environment, influence or determine delinquency (for more on determinism see Chapter 11). As you will see, this means that when we look at the opening scenario of the chapter and try to imagine why Alex and Jason might want to be drug dealers through the perspective of one of the social structural theories, we look to explanations that transcend those based on the micro level or individual level (e.g., those that focus upon mental health [psychological theories] or those that see delinquency as simple choice to pursue pleasure [rational choice theory]).

In this chapter we will focus on two general types of **macro-level theories**: those that come from a tradition of what is known as **anomie theory**, and those that derive from a tradition known as **social disorganization theory**. These theories consider the role of large-scale social change in human behavior, and the effect of the environment on individuals. According to these theories, if we want to figure out why youth are committing acts of delinquency, we will want to step outside and take a look at the world around us!

ANOMIE THEORIES

Anomie theories consider how the society is structured, and how that structure impacts our ability to follow social norms. These theories work from the premise that society is based on a set of norms and that most community members share these norms. When people go against the norms, in the form of either deviance or delinquency, it is typically because they are experiencing forces in their social world that are leading them to do so.

Durkheim's Anomie Theory

Although he did not specifically address the delinquency of young people in his scholarly work, the person who is credited with inspiring anomie theories of delinquency is French theorist Émile Durkheim. Durkheim (1858–1917) was a man of many "firsts"—he earned the first PhD in sociology in France and also taught the first sociology class in France.[1] He was a **consensus theorist** who believed society is best described as being based on a loose consensus in which most people agree on the same basic values. In other words, he assumed that we all share a basic sense of right or wrong and that laws and other rules reflect the values that we share. (This stance can be contrasted with many conflict-based assumptions of the critical theories that will be discussed in Chapter 6.)

One of Durkheim's most famous works, *The Division of Labor in Society*, focused upon the function of the division of labor in society.[2] He decided that division of labor's function is to shore up society's shared moral sense (its **collective conscience**—its sense of right and wrong) because it makes people depend on one another to get anything done. He studied law in industrial society and in preindustrial society to determine what brought people together in times prior to the shift to industrialization. He claimed that in preindustrial (or what he labeled **mechanical**) society, the collective conscience was strong because everyone basically did the same thing all day—for example, worked the fields—and thus people basically had the same outlook on life. Society was close-knit, and the law was repressive at that time; it focused upon punishment for punishment's sake and on the infliction of pain against people who defied society's norms and rules. He claimed that industrial society (what he labeled **organic society**) is more fragmented due to the division of labor, but we now rely on each other to do different jobs out in the world, so the collective conscience still exists, though weakened. Laws in industrial society, according to Durkheim, are restitutive, and stress the restoration of equilibrium and making amends, rather than repression.

Durkheim first referenced anomie in his study of the division of labor in society. He explained that a well-integrated or stable society in industrial times is one in which society's members are dependent upon one another for different purposes, and the division of labor is spontaneous. But when the division of labor is forced, things do not work as harmoniously, and, as he stated, "if the division of labor does not produce solidarity in these cases, it is because the relationship of the organs are not regulated, because they are in a state of *anomy*."[3] In simple terms, shared norms are no longer apparent (the word can be remembered by looking at its roots: *a* signifies "without," and *nomy* is built on *nomos*, meaning "laws or norms"; hence "without norms").

In his work *The Rules of Sociological Method*, Durkheim stated that there are **social facts**, or dimensions of human life that are external to the individual and that restrain individuals—values, cultural norms, and social structures.[4] In *Suicide*, he looked at the social facts related to suicide rates.[5] His work was groundbreaking because it was the first time scholarly attention had been paid to suicide as a social behavior rather than an individual choice. He examined police-recorded suicide rates in Western Europe during the 18th century and found that the suicide rates over time differed according to the characteristics of a given community. Communities in which people were more highly integrated into society and regulated by its various institutions were found to have lower suicide rates. For example, when societies had many people who were members of highly structured religions, such as Catholicism, and many people who were married and over

the age of 20, their members tended to be well integrated and less likely to commit suicide. Particularly relevant to the sociological theories of delinquency that follow in Durkheim's footsteps was the typology of suicide types that Durkheim developed based upon the results of his study. He called one of his four types of suicide **anomic suicide**, building upon his consideration of anomie as it related to the division of labor. Anomic suicide occurs when abrupt changes in a community lead to a loss of integration and a decrease in the shared belief and adherence to societal norms. Abrupt changes that might affect a community include increases in the frequency of divorce or physical and economic disasters that disrupt the very foundation of a community. In an anomic society, there is no effective regulation of its members because a state of normlessness

Anomie theorists state that times of disaster are ones in which extreme social change leads to unexpected behaviors and a likely increase in delinquency and crime.

Colin McDermott/NWS/NOAA

●●●
Collective conscience: Society's shared moral sense or sense of right and wrong according to Durkheim.

Mechanical society: Preindustrial societies that shared a strong collective conscience and had high levels of informal social control.

Organic society: Industrial societies that are fragmented due to the division of labor, yet maintain a sense of collective conscience (although weaker than in mechanical society).

Social facts: Dimensions of social life that are external to the individual and that restrain individuals.

has taken hold. People do not know what to do; there is confusion about how to proceed in life. The dreams and wants of society members are not being met, nor are they being constrained. People's desires are unchecked. The rules are no longer clear, and according to Durkheim's anomie theory this can lead to large violations of social norms, such as taking one's own life. If a Durkheimian anomie theorist were to consider the scenario about Alex and Jason outlined at the beginning of this chapter, she or he would likely pay a great deal of attention to the effects of the recent flood that affected their community, as such an event is likely to result in a number of disruptive events that can weaken a society and its social order. An anomic theorist would not be surprised that Jason and Alex feel adrift in the aftermath of such a disaster, but would instead expect it to be the case. Delinquency, in turn, would be an unsurprising next step for them.

Merton's Strain Theory

Robert Merton built upon Durkheim's concept of anomie when he was a PhD student in sociology at Harvard University, four decades after Durkheim's original formulation. Although attending school at a prestigious Ivy League university, Merton was intimately familiar with life in less privileged circumstances. He grew up in the inner city of Philadelphia, Pennsylvania, as the son of Eastern European Jewish immigrants, and was well aware of the social forces urging everyone in U.S. society to take advantage of opportunities and to become successful adults.[6] Indeed, in Merton's case, he did become quite successful, and his strain theory is one of the best known criminological theories of all time. In his now famous 1938 article "Social Structure and Anomie," Merton created a theory of anomie that focused upon the United States.[7] This theory is still quite popular as an explanation for certain types of youth delinquency.

On first glance, Merton's concept about anomie seems diametrically opposed to Durkheim's. He considers how social norms can be *so strong* that some people become strained and are pushed to break some rules (and some laws) in order to accomplish them. What is important to note is that, like Durkheim, Merton thought that anomie was related to unregulated desires. But, in Merton's case, he explained the unregulated desires were woven into the very fabric of the "American Dream."

What "American Dream" do you think is the predominant one that people are socialized to aim for as they mature? Typically, people think of the image of the heterosexual married couple, 2.5 kids, and the home with the white picket fence. In the 21st century arguably the shape that the familial part of the dream takes comes in many forms. Some might add a bit more glamour to the picture as well—prestige, wealth, maybe even fame. The most common version certainly involves some measure of financial or material success. All of these things are thought to be laudable targets to go after, and if you are exposed to any sort of mass media (or even just your own family), you have probably been the recipient of the message that you can accomplish this if you only work hard and put your mind to it. Merton claimed that in U.S. society to obtain this material and financial wealth is the primary cultural goal. As a result, "social structures *exert a definite pressure* upon certain persons in the society to engage in non-conforming conduct, rather than conformist conduct."[8] In other words, some people will be compelled to deviate rather than to follow the rules in certain circumstances. Merton claimed that the reason why is that although most people believe in the cultural goals of the American Dream, all people do not have access to the legitimate means of accomplishing these goals. These legitimate means, getting an education, deferring gratification while working hard, and ultimately getting a reliable job with potential for growth and promotion, are not equally available to all, and vary depending on one's socioeconomic class. He explained,

● ● ●

Anomic suicide:
One of the types of suicide that Durkheim theorized, which was more likely to occur in societies experiencing rapid social change and a lack of social norms.

Strain theory:
Merton's idea of what happens when social norms of conventional success (i.e., the American Dream) are not accompanied by equally strong or available legitimate means of achieving that success.

The "American Dream" has long invoked certain images of material success.

These goals are to held to *transcend class lines*, not to be bounded by them, yet the actual social organization is such that there exist class differentials in the accessibility of these *common* success-symbols. Frustration and thwarted aspiration lead to the search for avenues of escape from a culturally induced intolerable situation; or unrelieved ambition may eventuate in illicit attempts to achieve the dominant values.[9]

Merton claimed that the gap between the cultural goal of monetary success and the limited opportunities to achieve that goal causes strain. He stated that there are five ways that people adapt to this strain (see Table 5.1).

Conformity is the first and most common way of adapting to strain. Merton considered conformity as the one nondeviant **adaptation to strain**. Conformists have accepted both the goal of the American Dream and the socially legitimate ways of trying to obtain it. They follow the rules and do things they are told; they might go to school, get an advanced education or some additional training after graduation, work part-time jobs, save their earnings, and possibly obtain a good paying job, with some security and promise of advancement. Merton claims that the fact that most of us are conformists is what upholds the stability of society—otherwise it would be impossible to maintain.

Innovation is an adaptation that occurs when people do not accept the legitimate route to obtaining the cultural goal of material and financial wealth, because they either are blocked from accessing legitimate means, or do not believe that they should be limited to those ways of obtaining their goal. This adaptation is the one discussed the most, especially in relationship to the study of delinquency. Innovators include those who break the rules or the law to get their hands on some money or material goods. There are too many examples of this to list here, but innovators can include people who are drug dealing, shoplifting, and burglarizing.

Ritualism is the innovation in which people have abandoned the American Dream but continue to go through the motions of doing what most of society rewards—going to work, and going to school. In other words, these people are just "playing the game" even though they do not believe their actions will lead them to financial wealth or do not care about that cultural goal. Merton claimed this was a deviant adaptation to strain, because to abandon the societally approved striving toward advancement and monetary success is to go against the norms of society. People who go to work and follow every single rule, just to get through the day and survive, are examples of ritualists.

●●●
Adaptations to strain: The five ways that Merton theorized that people adjust to the strain created by the societal goals and the legitimate means by which to achieve those goals: conformity, innovation, ritualism, retreatism, and rebellion.

TABLE 5.1 Merton's Adaptations to Strain

	CULTURAL GOALS	INSTITUTIONALIZED/LEGITIMATE MEANS
Conformity	+ (acceptance)	+ (acceptance)
Innovation	+ (acceptance)	− (nonacceptance or rejection)
Ritualism	− (nonacceptance or rejection)	+ (acceptance)
Retreatism	− (nonacceptance or rejection)	− (nonacceptance or rejection)
Rebellion	+/− (substitution of new goals and means)	+/− (substitution of new goals and means)

Source: Merton, R. K. (1938). Social structure and anomie. *American Sociological Review*, 3(5), 672–682.

Note: In his schema, Merton used + to signify acceptance, − to signify nonacceptance or rejection, and +/− to signify not only rejection but substitution of new goals and means.

Retreatism is the adaptation of those who have rejected the cultural goal of material success and have also rejected the legitimate means of going about such a goal. These folks are seen as those who have "dropped out" of society in some way, perhaps after trying to be materially and financially successful by either legitimate or illegitimate means and, ultimately, failing. Merton thought that some chronic drug users and addicts, homeless people, and some mentally ill people would fall into this category. He claimed this was the least common adaptation.

Rebellion is the last type of adaptation. Rebels not only reject the cultural goals of monetary success promoted as part of the American Dream, but also reject the legitimate means for going about them. Basically, they reject the entire system of cultural goals and acceptable means and want to replace them with new goals and means, what Merton called "a new social order." Not many people fall into this category besides political terrorists and, possibly, the members of some cults.

Differential Opportunity Theory

Merton's theory of anomie was quite popular, and many people have expanded upon it through the years. One of the most successful expansions of the theory was forwarded by Richard Cloward and Lloyd Ohlin in 1960 in *Delinquency and Opportunity: A Theory of Delinquent Gangs*. What they brought to the table was something Merton had not considered in his theory—they focused upon the question of how a person's access to illegitimate means affects the shape of his or her adaptations to anomie and strain.

As Merton stated, we do not all have equal access to legitimate means to success. Yet, Cloward and Ohlin argued that we need to also think about how there is not equal access to *illegitimate means* of obtaining cultural goals as well. For example, if you are a teenager growing up in a Southern California neighborhood and you have resigned yourself to earning some money illegally, it is much more likely that you will be inclined to "innovate" by selling methamphetamine for a white or Latino gang than by dealing heroin for the Italian Mafia. You simply do not have easy access to the Italian Mafia, nor do you have easy entrée into their illegal dealings, because of how your social world is structured.

Cloward and Ohlin studied youth gangs and the neighborhoods in which they formed. They focused on neighborhood conditions and the opportunities available to learn and practice legitimate or illegitimate skills. They found that in some marginalized

Visit edge.sagepub .com/bates2e to view a video clip about community involvement.

neighborhoods, **criminal delinquent subcultures**, or gangs, arose in the face of limited legitimate opportunities. In these neighborhoods there were established ties between young gangs and long-standing criminal subcultures, such that it made sense for gang members to learn the ropes of whatever criminal enterprise in which their elders were involved. Oftentimes these activities were theft-oriented, and tied to organized crime syndicates. Adults involved in criminal activities were visible members of the community, and acted as role models to the boys who wanted to imitate them. The boys learned to stay out of fights and to avoid violence as a way of making sure no extra attention was put on their activities, or those of the adults with whom they were involved.

In other neighborhoods that tend to exist in disorganized areas that are socially unstable (we will discuss such neighborhoods at length later in the chapter), **conflict delinquent subcultures** develop as a result of a lack of both legitimate and illegitimate opportunities for youth. According to Cloward and Ohlin, there is simply not much going on in these neighborhoods, and youth become frustrated. There are few successful role models, and the immediate world around them looks bleak. As a means of expressing their frustration, they often turn to violence. Boys attempt to gain respect through physical force and intimidation.

In other neighborhoods that are poor or working class, Cloward and Ohlin stated that **retreatist delinquent subcultures** would be found. They characterized these youth in these subcultures as those who could not find a place in either the criminal or the conflict subculture. Perhaps a young man is not perceived as tough enough to be accepted by a group of teens who spend most of their days fighting people from other gangs—he might be compelled to adapt to his failure to be part of this group by becoming involved with those others who have been unaccepted and who know how to get and to use illegal substances.

Subcultural Theory of Delinquency

Albert Cohen's **subcultural delinquency theory** was also informed by Merton's anomie theory. In 1955 in his book *Delinquent Boys*, Cohen examined the ways in which boys coming from an economically disadvantaged background deal with the strain that comes from not being able to succeed at institutions perpetuating middle-class standards.[10] These standards, such as individual responsibility, ambition, long-term goal planning, deferred gratification, nonviolent recreation, and respect for others' property, are those taught more commonly in middle-class homes and neighborhoods, and working-class young men are not always exposed to them. Thus, when they go to schools that promote these values, they are not well equipped to succeed in those environments and are typically seen as unsuccessful students—they do not follow rules well, are not punctual, and have problems acting calmly in the classroom. Because of their frustration with their status they take part in what Cohen calls "reaction-formation"—they decide to turn the middle-class values on their head by engaging in and promoting violent behavior, instant gratification, and all-in-all a negative attitude toward authority and society in general. Unlike other responses to strain, Cohen finds that the subcultural responses do not serve a concrete purpose other than satisfying an emotional one; the behaviors that the members of the group engage in typically work against them in a culture that values hard work and the pursuit of long-term goals.

Now that we have examined the basics of Merton's anomie theory, and some of the classic theories inspired by it, we can interpret Alex and Jason's situation by using their concepts. As recent immigrants whose family is struggling to make ends meet, Alex and Jason do not have access to a lot of resources to help them succeed in school, nor do they

●●●
Criminal delinquent subculture: A subculture in which youth commit acts of delinquency as a means to an end— usually to obtain something material or monetary to gain status in the group.

Conflict delinquent subculture: A subculture in which youth oppose the mainstream through violence, underground economies, and/ or gang activity because of a lack of opportunities to succeed.

Retreatist delinquent subculture: A subculture of youth who join together after failing to find a place in either the criminal or the conflict delinquent subculture.

Subcultural delinquency theory: The theory that involvement in small groups of youth in marginalized neighborhoods or social groups arises in the face of limited legitimate opportunities.

from the CLASSROOM to the COMMUNITY

The "I Have a Dream" Foundation

According to Merton, if we want to keep kids out of trouble, one of the things we can do is to encourage conformity. One way to do this is to help youth to stay in school. Yet, it is clear that all youth do not have equal access to the financial resources and social support that could help them graduate from high school and to pursue a higher education. Members of the "I Have a Dream" (IHAD) Foundation recognize this inequity and work with youth who live in low-income communities to improve their chances of staying in school and avoiding opportunities to engage in delinquency. The IHAD program was first developed in 1981 by Eugene Lang after he returned to his elementary school in East Harlem as an adult and found that about 75% of the students were estimated to drop out of school at some point. He was determined to help change this situation. The IHAD Foundation has programs in cities across the United States, and they are offer service in six areas:

1. Academic achievement

2. Knowledge and life skills

3. Mental health and stability

4. Mindset of direction and aspiration

5. Support networks

6. Financial resources and opportunity

There are IHAD-affiliated programs across the United States, and they all follow the same model. Program administrators choose a cohort of students or public housing residents to be part of the program. Those youth who are chosen, called "Dreamers," participate in the program from elementary school until high school graduation. IHAD sponsors provide Dreamers with mentoring, tutoring, financial assistance, and information about college as they continue their studies. Program details differ depending on the particular needs of the youth involved, but all include an acknowledgment that in working-class and economically struggling communities, the high school dropout rate is extremely high, especially for youth of color, and a great deal of encouragement and action is needed to counter that trend. When Dreamers graduate from high school, the IHAD Foundation will provide financial assistance to help them go to college or to a vocational school.

DISCUSSION QUESTIONS

1. The "I Have a Dream" Foundation focuses upon education as a pathway to a conventional life-style. What are the strengths and weaknesses of this approach?

2. What component of Merton's theory does this program work to change: the legitimate means of achieving the American Dream, or the end goal of the American Dream itself? What might the program look like if it set out to change the component it doesn't currently address as well? Would it be possible for program administrators to do so? Why or why not?

Sources: "I Have a Dream" Foundation. (2016). *What we do*. Retrieved from http://www.ihaveadreamfoundation.org/what-we-do/; "I Have a Dream" Foundation—Los Angeles. (2016). *How it works: IHADLA educating children in poverty changes communities*. Retrieved from http://www.ihadla.org/how-it-works

have the means to obtain a part-time job. They do not have the money to buy a car, and they do not have easily accessed transportation to get them outside of their neighborhood where legitimate job opportunities are located. Yet, the boys have long been influenced by the American Dream and the promise of material success that they see all around them on TV and in the movies. An anomie theorist, in the tradition of Merton, would see that their position in the social structure is setting up Alex and Jason to experience strain. Innovative or "creative" ways of earning money by illegal means is a form of delinquency that will likely be generated out of this situation. A differential opportunity theorist would pay special attention to the fact that Jason and Alex have easy access to an illegitimate money-making effort, drug dealing, which makes it highly likely that they will get involved with drug dealing in their neighborhood. The humiliation and disappointment that Jason and Alex feel about not being able to excel in school, or in money-making endeavors in general, is something that we would pay attention to if we were utilizing Cohen's subcultural theory of delinquency; we might expect the young men to adapt an antagonistic attitude toward authority figures in general and to begin to express distaste for school and everything it stands for because of what they experience as failure in the system.

Anomie Theories of Delinquency and Race, Class, and Gender Intersections

Anomie/strain theories of delinquency employ notions of socioeconomic privilege and disadvantage in their conceptualizations of strain. Traditionally, they have not given a great deal of explicit attention to the relevance of race and gender. The bulk of race and gender studies on anomie-related theories has been on Agnew's general strain theory—a theory derived from Mertonian strain theory but with more of a micro- or individual-level focus—and one that we analyzed in the previous chapter.

Anomie Theories and Race

One of the exceptions to the absence of race-oriented research on Merton's anomie theory is Cernkovich, Giordano and Rudolph's work "Race, Crime and the American Dream."[11] They conducted a longitudinal study that compared black and white youth's perceptions of the economic message of the American Dream with their behavior as teenagers and, years later, as young adults. These researchers found that black adults were very committed to the American Dream. They also found that even though they were more likely to have lower-paying jobs or to be unemployed than their white counterparts, they did not experience strain that led to crime. Yet, strain did lead to crime among white adults. They attributed this finding to the possibility that

> Whites are more likely than African Americans to feel frustrated when they are unable to realize the promises of the American dream. . . and such failure, when it does occur among Whites, may generate high levels of anger and frustration and result in criminal behavior in some instances. . . . Because African Americans have been subjected to a long history of racial and economic discrimination, economic failure, while never welcomed, is not entirely unexpected.[12]

In Walters' work, he used Mertonian strain theory to understand hate crimes by white people against people of color and other members of minority groups and came to similar conclusions about race.[13] He theorized that although strain theory is not sufficient to fully understand acts of hate, it is a necessary tool for understanding them. He explained that although socioeconomically marginalized members of dominant groups are likely to experience strain and to scapegoat other members of a racially and ethnically diverse society, socioeconomically privileged people in dominant groups may be in *fear* of strain and also act out in hate.

Anomie Theories and Gender

In terms of gender, a few studies have tested anomie/strain theory by comparing male and female delinquency.[14] Findings are generally mixed. Usually not many differences are found in terms of rates of delinquency of boys and girls related to measures of strain. When differences are found in studies, they do not take a particular pattern—in some studies girls are more affected by some types of strain than boys, and at other times boys are found to be

How can strain theory be used to understand acts of hate against the LGBT community?

more affected by the limited or blocked opportunities related to strain than girls.[15] In one study, Smith and Paternoster looked at whether strain experienced in the educational realm had different effects on marijuana use of male and female youth, and they found that social strain was not significantly related to either group's drug use.[16]

Anomie Theories and Class

Recent studies demonstrate the generalizability of classic strain theory to countries beyond the United States. In a globalized world, many countries now promote financial and material cultural goals in the tradition of the United States. For example, a study of Turkish youth, through the eyes of classic strain theory, found that strain, particularly perceptions of blocked economic opportunities, is related to an increase of delinquency on the part of Turkish female adolescents.[17] The authors of the study explained that the relatively recent onslaught of Western messages about consumption have come to affect Turkish girls more than boys. This is because their lesser position in Turkish society creates more obstacles for them to obtain the education and job-related opportunities required to accomplish financial goals; Turkish boys are more privileged than girls and do not experience this as strongly. Thus, the girls act out in delinquency as a reaction to their perceptions of strain. A study reassessing the role of Merton's strain theory using data from the country of Ukraine found that the *relative strain* of high school students was related to their likelihood to engage in delinquency.[18] The authors assert that in the anomic cultural context of post-Soviet Ukraine, adolescents are more likely to report delinquent behavior if they see their access to legitimate opportunities as limited in comparison to others and have feelings of relative deprivation.

SOCIAL DISORGANIZATION THEORY

Social disorganization theory is a social structural theory of crime and delinquency that was very popular from the 1920s to the 1940s and in the 1980s and 1990s.[19] To put its initial emergence into perspective in relation to the anomie theories just outlined, social disorganization theory was developed after Durkheim's theory and before Merton's. It emerged out of a desire for scholars to study the various changes happening in the urban areas of the United States in the aftermath of World War I. The emergence of social disorganization theory marked a shift away from theories of crime and delinquency that were focused on the individual level (e.g., psychological theories that posited something was wrong internally with an individual causing him or her to commit crimes), to those that looked to external forces as motivations for misbehavior. Social disorganization theory really does not look much at individuals at all, but looks at crime and delinquency rates between neighborhoods or geographical regions. The easiest way to remember the thrust of social disorganization theory is to note that, as real estate agents like to say, "it's all about location, location, location!"

Park and Burgess's Social Disorganization Theory

Social disorganization emerged out of the work of scholars associated with the University of Chicago's Department of Sociology, and thus it is often referred to as a "Chicago School" theory. The main idea of the theory is that society is always in the midst of a cycle of change that shifts from social disorganization to reorganization and back again. In the process, certain neighborhoods become so disorganized that, in order to adapt to them, people must engage in deviant behavior. The theory essentially places humans into the context of the plant and animal world and requires us to think about how our "natural habitats" affect our behavior.

Social disorganization theorists pay a lot of attention to the question of how the state of a neighborhood might increase or decrease the likelihood of street delinquency.

The work of Robert Park and Ernest Burgess played a formative role in the social disorganization theory of delinquency that their colleagues from the University of Chicago later produced. They drew upon ideas derived from popular thought of the day—namely Charles Darwin's ideas about evolution, as well as those related to social ecology, the study of relationships between individuals, social groups, and the environment, to explore the changing world around them. In their 1925 book *The City*, Park and Burgess presented their theory of urban ecology in which they borrowed concepts from plant ecology to explain human behavior in the city. They noted that, like plants, humans generally live in a state of symbiosis in the world, in which we are interdependent and give and take from one another in order to survive. The major changes in a given society—immigration, urbanization (population shifts from rural to urban areas), and the rise of technology—interrupt societal balance from time to time. Because of a rise in heterogeneity or differences among people living in a given area, there is a lack of shared norms. Because of this, there is also a reduction in the amount of informal social control in the affected area—community social ties are weakened, and there is less of a community structure in place to dissuade people from acting out against the societal norms, rules, and laws. Crime rates will increase until a new level of balance is reached. Park and Burgess utilized ecological terms to explain the trajectory of this cyclical process (see Figure 5.1).

Park and Burgess conducted their research of the city of Chicago by going out into the community and mapping "the natural urban areas" of the city. They claimed that once cities were fully developed, they could be mapped as having five different concentric zones emanating out around the city center (see Figure 5.2). The downtown area or city center has the highest degree of land use and feels the impact of large-scale social change very strongly. Typically people with the money to do so decide to move away from the areas near downtown that are highly populated and out into zones where land use is less dense and people have more room to move. They take their money with them, and invest it in the new communities in which they take root. Then, other groups of people in a process called "succession" move into the less desirable area that they left behind. Each natural zone was thought to have its own characteristics. The character of life in these zones was seen to be a function of place and to be unchanging over the years, regardless of any shifts in the demographics of a neighborhood over time.

Social ecology: The study of relationships between individuals, social groups, and the environment.

Symbiosis: A state of interdependence that social disorganization theorists state characterizes the social world.

Heterogeneity: Difference and diversity; in a neighborhood context heterogeneity often reduces informal social control.

Informal social control: The means by which ordinary people exert control over others' behavior through enforcing traditions or norms and by informally punishing those who break such norms through the use of gossip, stigmatization, and disapproval.

FIGURE 5.1 | Arrow Diagram of Park and Burgess's Model of the Cycle of Social Disorganization and Reorganization

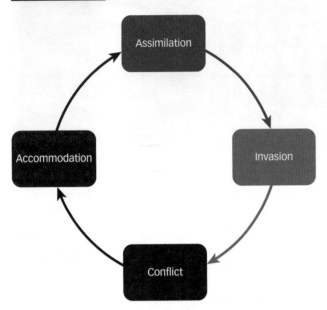

Zone 1: The central business district (CBD)—This zone is typically the center of the city where many businesses are located and the forces of urbanization, immigration, and technological changes have a strong effect.

Zone 2: The zone of transition—The area immediately on the outskirts of the downtown area was where Park and Burgess stated that the most physical deterioration could be seen and where the social problems of the city were most abundant. This is the area where many homeless live on the streets, and where people are living very closely together. People who newly arrive to the city often live in this area because it is affordable. But after living there a bit they are eager to move out of the area. Thus, they focus on working, sometimes multiple jobs, if they can find work, and eventually moving—when they have saved enough money to do so. Typically, there is not a lot of investment in the community on the part of either the government or private agencies, and community residents are not always invested in it either because they see themselves as on the way out soon. According to Park and Burgess, this **zone of transition** is the area where one is most likely to observe street crime, in part because the community is not exerting much informal social control upon one another. As residents move out into areas farther away from the urban center, generally they move into areas that are more privileged. Living density and land use decrease.

Zone 3: Multifamily housing—This zone is characterized by a high amount of group living, in the form of either housing complexes, apartments, and duplexes. In any case, oftentimes generations of families live together in this zone. It is a little removed from the stressors of the innermost city and the transition zone, but still subject to some of them. This is typically a working-class area.

Zone 4: Single-family housing—In Zone 4 there is an abundance of single-family housing. Usually the community is a middle- to upper-class community with lots of room for children to play and lots of green spaces, such as parks to enjoy. Many people live in houses, or, if they live in townhomes or condominiums, they have yards and garages. People in this zone are typically just living by themselves or with a few members of their immediate family.

Zone 5: The commuter zone—This area is characterized by the least density and the most distance from the forces of social change impacting the central business district. Another name for this zone is the suburbs. These areas typically have a lot of community and government invested in them—they are kept clean and have many of the desirable geographical features of Zone 4, and additional ones as well. Because people find this area so attractive and comfortable, if they have the money to do so they may even drive into the central business district to work during the week (hence its name the commuter zone). Social order is often intact in these areas according to Park and Burgess.

● ● ●

Concentric zone model: A model used by social disorganization theorists in which they map an urban area and measure the degree of social disorganization in each.

Zone of transition: The area right outside of the central business district of a city that experiences the most negative effects of the forces of social change and the highest rate of street delinquency.

FIGURE 5.2 The Concentric Zone Model

 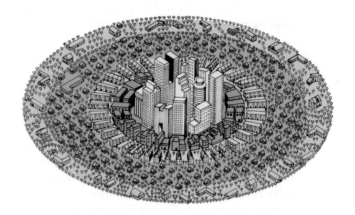

1. Central Business District: Downtown area with many factories and businesses
2. Transition Zone: Characterized by deteriorated housing, factories, and abandoned buildings.
3. Working Class Zone: Multifamily housing such as apartments and duplexes
4. Residential Zone: Single family homes with yards/garages
5. Commuter Zone: Suburbs

Shaw and McKay's Social Disorganization and Delinquency Theory

Clifford Shaw and Henry McKay, researchers associated with the University of Chicago, built upon the social ecological model, by examining how delinquency in Chicago related to the concentric zones. In the research that they describe in their book *Juvenile Delinquency and Urban Areas*, they examined almost 56,000 juvenile court records that spanned over 30 years of juvenile cases in Chicago (beginning in 1900).[20] They then plotted on maps the home addresses of 10- to 16-year-old boys who had been brought into the court for alleged delinquency, who had been committed by the court to a correctional facility, or who had significant interaction with the police related to alleged delinquency.

The findings of their research supported Park and Burgess's model. They found that delinquency rates were the highest in the CBD and Zone 2, the zone of transition, consistently over time. The ethnicity of the groups of people who lived there changed over time, and was not correlated with delinquency. Delinquency appeared to be strongly related to the effect of living in a disorganized neighborhood and decreased with distance from the city center. Neighborhoods with high rates of delinquency had high rates of poverty, residential mobility, and racial and ethnic diversity. In line with Park and Burgess's theory, their study supported the idea that delinquency can be attributed to location, not to individual traits of people. Although in the years following the study's publication, many people cited it as an example of income being negatively correlated to delinquency (i.e., less income and more delinquency), this is an inaccurate summary of Shaw and McKay's findings. Instead, as Bursik explains,

Shaw and McKay did not posit a direct relationship between economic status and rates of delinquency. Rather, areas characterized by economic deprivation tended to have high rates of population turnover and population heterogeneity. . . . Population turnover and population heterogeneity were assumed to increase the likelihood of social disorganization.[21]

Frazier's Ecological Analysis of Delinquency Among Black Youth

E. Franklin Frazier also did groundbreaking work on social disorganization in association with the University of Chicago.[22] He became a doctoral student and began working under Robert Park when he was in his early 30s and focused upon black families and neighborhoods in Chicago. Frazier wrote his dissertation, *The Negro Family in Chicago*, in 1932. Frazier's work served as a serious intellectual challenge and critique of racist theories about black culture and families.[23] Frazier utilized a social disorganization lens to examine many of the issues in which he was interested, which he partnered with a sociohistorical eye on the impact of slavery on black family life and issues of crime and delinquency.[24] Frazier's paternal grandfather was a slave until he bought his freedom and became emancipated, and his mother was born into slavery. His interest in the subjects of which he studied was both personal and political.

Frazier utilized Park and Burgess's concentric zone framework to look at changes in the rates of black delinquency in Chicago over time. He did studies of the cases of black delinquency in Chicago and found that the rate of such delinquency had increased subsequent to the migration of black people to the region from the South during and after World War I. He found that most of this delinquency occurred after youth and their families migrated right outside of Chicago's Central Business District—an area that had long had a high delinquency rate and was socially disorganized. Frazier stated that black families in the disorganized area experienced a breakdown in social control that was markedly different from the experience of black families who lived in more organized zones. Frazier's work on social disorganization and delinquency has received little mainstream attention since the 1960s (when his work was misrepresented by the Moynihan Report and was utilized to blame black people and socioeconomically disadvantaged families for their economic plight), and it is one of the few classic works to explicitly consider race as an important factor related to social disorganization studies.

Sampson and Groves's Model of Social Disorganization

Social disorganization theory experienced a decrease in popularity after the 1940s as people began to focus more on individualistic theories and/or theories that were not focused upon social ecology.[25] It is difficult to invest the time and energy, not to mention financial resources, to carry on types of studies that Shaw and McKay thought were necessary to study social disorganization properly over a span of several years, and there was some confusion about exactly how to measure social disorganization. These longitudinal studies on social disorganization fell out of favor for some time. It was not until the 1980s that several studies about social disorganization were published.

One major study of delinquency and social disorganization that garnered widespread attention in the 1980s was that of Robert Sampson and Walter B. Groves. In their 1989 article "Community Structure and Crime: Testing Social Disorganization Theory," published in the *American Journal of Sociology*, Sampson and Groves developed a variant of Shaw and McKay's theory of social disorganization and delinquency. They worked from a definition of social disorganization as "the inability for the community structure to realize the values of its residents and maintain effective social control."[26] Sampson and Groves then explained what they theorized were the specific ways in which social disorganization affected crime and delinquency. In other words, they discussed the intervening variables, the intermediate steps between social disorganization and its expression in the form of delinquency. They stated there were three intervening factors. Social disorganization leads to (1) sparse local friendship networks, (2) unsupervised teenage peer groups, and (3) low organizational participation (i.e., low community member involvement in formal and voluntary organizations), which facilitate crime and delinquency (see Figure 5.3).

They tested their expanded social disorganization theory by statistically analyzing data on crime in Britain, and found support for their theory. There were higher victimization rates and self-reported incidents of violent and property crimes in neighborhoods that were characterized by their three intervening variables. Subsequently, others have also found support or partial support for the expanded model.[27]

Collective Efficacy Model

In the 1990s, Robert Sampson, Stephen Raudenbush, and Felton Earls added to the social disorganization research by developing the concept of collective efficacy. They define collective efficacy "as social cohesion among neighbors combined with their willingness to intervene on the behalf of the common good."[28]

Sampson et al. theorized that collective efficacy is a factor that may mitigate or lessen the effects of social disorganization on a community and, in turn, lessen violence. Collective efficacy is seen in the everyday ways that people in the community take actions in the name of the community to make it more organized. These researchers looked at the informal ways in which residents work together to create public order, such as by watching children's playgroups, by acting to stop youth in the neighborhood who are trying to "ditch" or skip school or to deal drugs, and by standing up against people who are causing trouble in public spaces in the neighborhood. They found that when communities were severely disadvantaged, had a high proportion of recent newcomers, and had a low number of people who lived there for a long period of time, collective efficacy was negatively affected. As a result, more violence was found to occur in those communities. Their results strongly supported their modified version of social disorganization theory. As Sampson and his colleagues

> ● ● ●
> **Intervening variables:** Variables that change the relationships between other variables because of their existence.
>
> **Collective efficacy:** Social cohesion among neighbors that is characterized by efforts to make positive changes in their neighborhoods.

Some studies have found that if there is a sense of collective efficacy among neighbors in a socially disorganized neighborhood, it helps lessen the likelihood that delinquency will occur.

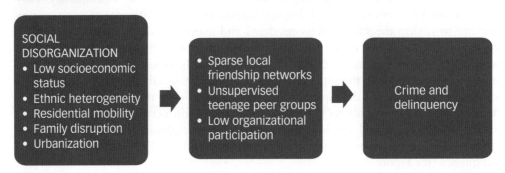

FIGURE 5.3 Sampson and Groves's Model of Social Disorganization

SOCIAL DISORGANIZATION
- Low socioeconomic status
- Ethnic heterogeneity
- Residential mobility
- Family disruption
- Urbanization

→

- Sparse local friendship networks
- Unsupervised teenage peer groups
- Low organizational participation

→

Crime and delinquency

expanded on social disorganization research in the 2000s, they often discovered that collective efficacy was *strengthened* in some immigrant communities, and delinquency and crime rates were lower than in other similarly situated neighborhoods.[29] This was the case even in low-income communities in the inner city. This finding challenged the findings of their previous research and partially challenges the assertions of traditional social disorganization theorists as well.

Social Disorganization Theories of Delinquency and Race, Class, and Gender Intersections

Visit edge.sagepub .com/bates2e to view a video clip about factors that lead to delinquency.

Unlike another body of theories that we will explore later in this book, critical theories of delinquency—issues of race, class, and gender—are not at the forefront of most social disorganization theorizing. This is because the theory focuses on *places*, rather than people. Nevertheless, there has been work done looking at the relationship between race, socioeconomic class, and gender and social disorganization, which we will briefly examine here.

Social Disorganization Theory and Race

The classic works of ecological theory of Park and Burgess, as well as those of Shaw and McKay having to do with delinquency, have long pointed out the irrelevance of race to the misbehavior of people living in disorganized areas. In their work, Shaw and McKay noted that the ethnicity or race of people living in the central business district and the zone of transition didn't matter; rates of delinquency were higher than in the rest of the city there, and this was consistent over time. Of course, they did focus on issues of race and ethnicity in the sense that they thought that when a diverse group of people lived in an area together (when there was ethnic and racial heterogeneity), the neighborhood would be characterized by less social cohesion. As discussed previously, E. Franklin Frazier did look explicitly at issues of how social disorganization affected black communities in Chicago, yet his work is rarely discussed in mainstream considerations of social disorganization theory today.

Social disorganization theory has been used to understand the impact that mass incarceration has on low-income communities of color who live in urban areas, typically in the zone of transition.[30] Although these areas are now not as ethnically or racially heterogeneous as they once were, many of the characteristics of the areas remain the same as the early social disorganization theorists stated. A high degree of social mobility of the residents, concentrated poverty, and a lack of shared norms and values challenges

In the News

residents of these areas when they attempt to make strong community bonds and also makes it harder to control crime and delinquency. The social controls of the state, including incarceration, are geared at controlling individuals, but they may have potentially harmful secondary effects on the community. As explained by Rose and Clear, "at the ecological level, the side effects of policies intended to fight crime by controlling individual criminals may exacerbate problems that lead to crime in the first place."[31]

The impact of mass imprisonment is disproportionately experienced by the poorest communities of color in the United States today and "there is a social dynamic that aggravates and augments the negative consequences to individual inmates when they come from and return to particular neighborhoods in concentrated numbers."[32] In areas that are already socially disorganized, the removal of residents through incarceration creates additional community-level disruption because those residents often have complex ties to their social networks, and their removal from them is disruptive to their families, friends, and neighbors. When these networks are damaged or broken, it is more difficult for communities to develop a sense of collective efficacy, and the relationship between communities and state social control agents additionally becomes contentious. This, in turn, negatively affects a community's ability to receive public services and resources from governmental agencies, which can weaken a neighborhood's social capital and results in concentrated disadvantage.[33]

AP Photo/Brynn Anderson / ASSOCIATED PRESS

Mass incarceration in the United States has a particularly negative effect on low-income communities of color.

Coercive mobility, social mobility inside and outside the neighborhood, is increased each time someone is incarcerated and each time someone is released back into the neighborhood from prison or a detention center.[34] A formerly incarcerated youth or adult re-enters the neighborhood with the added socialization of the prison or detention center subculture, which is said to increase the heterogeneity of community values and lead to further disorganization.[35] Youth of color who are growing up in these socially disorganized neighborhoods that bear the burdens of imprisonment must contend with reduced quality of life along many dimensions, such as public health, access to romantic partners, economic stability, and public safety.[36]

Social Disorganization Theory and Class

Socioeconomic class is considered in social disorganization theory as it relates to neighborhoods. Both classic and modern variations of social disorganization theory look at issues of socioeconomic class in the sense that they link neighborhoods' resource bases to the concepts of social disorganization. In their simplest formulation, social disorganization theories of delinquency see low socioeconomic class as one of several signs of social disorganization, which collectively tend to lead to higher rates of delinquency and crime.

Social disorganization theorists tend to address class issues in cities, but some researchers have begun to utilize the theory to look at rural areas as well. D. Osgood and Chambers did this in their study of social disorganization and rural areas in the southern United States. In their research, they explained that they were testing "the proposition that social disorganization theory is based upon principles of community organization and social relations that are applicable to communities of all types and settings."[37] They looked at violent crime rates across 264 rural counties in Florida, Georgia, South Carolina, and Nebraska. They found that family disruption (which they measured as the proportion of female-headed households), population turnover, and ethnic heterogeneity were all positively related to arrest rates for rape and weapon offenses. Unlike most social disorganization studies, they did not find that in rural communities the socioeconomic status of the neighborhoods under investigation significantly affected these measures of crime.

Contemporary social disorganization research has also expanded to look at how the socioeconomic levels of socially disorganized neighborhoods work in conjunction with other markers of social disorganization (including neighborhood racial diversity) to generate delinquency. Beverly Kingston, David Huizinga, and Delbert S. Elliott looked at adolescent delinquency in high-risk urban neighborhoods, in Denver, Colorado, in an attempt to examine differences between neighborhoods that suffer from numerous social problems and others in terms of the production of delinquency.[38] Kingston et al. found that the structure of a particular neighborhood does indeed affect the social relationships and, ultimately, delinquency rates:

● ● ●

Coercive mobility:
The removal of people from a poor neighborhood as a result of incarceration. A formerly incarcerated youth or adult re-enters the neighborhood with the added socialization of the prison or detention center subculture, which is said to increase the heterogeneity of community values and lead to further disorganization.

In a sample of structurally disadvantaged neighborhoods, variation in neighborhood poverty accounts for variations in the perceived effectiveness of social institutions and youths' perceptions of limited opportunities, even when the sample is quite restricted. Furthermore, neighborhoods with greater racial mix have smaller social networks and lower levels of social control. The poorest Denver neighborhoods also have significantly higher rates of violent offending.[39]

They found that objective poverty (the actual rate of poverty in a region) and *perceptions* on the part of youth that their life chances were negatively affected by living in their neighborhood most strongly predicted rates of juvenile delinquency. The youth who felt the most hopeless about the effects of the environment on them, and those living in particularly rough neighborhoods with even fewer resources than most other high-risk neighborhoods, were apt to engage in delinquency more than other youth.

Social Disorganization Theory and Gender

What about social disorganization theorists' treatment of gender issues?

In general, very little attention has been paid to issues of gender, social disorganization, and delinquency.[40] When scholars have considered gender, they have tended to hypothesize that boys would be more affected by neighborhood social disorganization than girls because they are generally allowed more freedom to be outside in the neighborhood. Nevertheless, many tests of this hypothesis do not support it and instead show that all youth are similarly affected by social disorganization.[41] A study by Abigail Fagan and Emily Wright looked at the neighborhood effects on delinquency for boys and girls in Chicago.[42] Unlike many previous studies, they tested to see if such effects—if differences between youth due to gender—were statistically significant. They examined both the effects of collective disadvantage, the result of social disorganization, and the mediating effect of collective efficacy. Their results were surprising ones. They found that collective efficacy of a neighborhood actually was related to an *increase* in female delinquency in disorganized neighborhoods, rather than a decrease, which is generally predicted by the theory. In addition, concentrated disadvantage was related to a *decrease* in girls' violent delinquency. There were no significant social disorganization effects shown for boys at all in their study. In light of their findings, the authors concluded that social disorganization may work in complex ways at the individual level and that girls may sometimes feel the impact of neighborhood effects such as collective efficacy in different ways and, sometimes, more strongly than boys.

Corina Graif drew upon social disorganization in her study of the role of gender in neighborhood effects on delinquency.[43] Like other researchers before her, she looked at longitudinal data related to the Moving to Opportunity Program, a randomized intervention program that assisted families from public housing in five U.S. inner cities to relocate to neighborhoods with low poverty rates.[44] Graif examined what type of neighborhoods the participants resided in and classified them as one of the following three types of extended neighborhoods, which are immediate neighborhoods and their surrounding areas: (1) neighborhoods of *extended concentrated disadvantage* (extremely disadvantaged neighborhoods whose surrounding neighborhoods were also very disadvantaged), (2) neighborhoods of *localized concentrated disadvantage* (extremely disadvantaged neighborhoods whose surrounding neighbors were not disadvantaged, and (3) neighborhoods of *extended nonconcentrated disadvantage* (neighborhoods of nonextreme disadvantage surrounded by similar neighborhoods). She found that girls who lived in extended neighborhoods with nonconcentrated disadvantage benefitted significantly from the area's organization; they increased their pro-social behavior and experienced the benefits of collective efficacy. Girls who lived in neighborhoods of

A Focus on Research

Huang, Ryan, and Rhoden's "Foster Care, Geographic Neighborhood Change, and the Risk of Delinquency"

In the article "Foster Care, Geographic Neighborhood Change, and the Risk of Delinquency," published in *Children and Youth Services Review* (2016), Hui Huang, Joseph P. Ryan, and Michelle-Ann Rhoden use insights from social disorganization theory to examine the neighborhood factors that influence delinquency in foster youth. They conducted a longitudinal study of foster youth born in 1983 and 1984 in Chicago, Illinois, in which they analyzed census data about the neighborhoods where the youth were placed in foster care, as well as administrative records and court records, to determine their subsequent delinquency. Their sample was predominantly African American (92%) and almost equally divided between girls and boys. Huang et al. discovered that when foster youth are moved from their original home to neighborhoods with higher residential stability, there is a lower risk of delinquency than if they were moved to neighborhoods characterized by lower residential stability. They found this trend specifically for the foster youth who were moved before the age of 12. They also found that neighborhood stability played a more apparent role in the lives of boys than girls; boys who were moved into higher stability neighborhoods had less likelihood of delinquency than those moved to less stable neighborhoods, but this effect was not as apparent for girls. The researchers did not find that change in neighborhood concentrated disadvantage was associated with juvenile delinquency risk among their sample.

DISCUSSION QUESTIONS

1. Given the findings of the study, what sorts of societal changes would help reduce the likelihood that foster youth will engage in delinquency after their placement in a new neighborhood? What sorts of programs and policies would support these changes?

2. What recommendations would you make to foster care administrators about how to place foster youth with foster families? Would you have different recommendations based on gender? Why or why not?

---

extended concentrated disadvantage exhibited the highest degree of risk-taking behavior. On the other hand, boys in localized concentrated disadvantaged neighborhoods showed the most risk-taking behavior. Graif noted that part of this is likely related to a sense of relative deprivation that occurs when boys notice that their neighbors enjoy more privileges, yet she states that even without this sense of injustice, delinquency is more likely because of the ready availability of desirable material goods nearby. She also found gender differences in exposure to risk and protective factors in extended neighborhoods, and that girls' frequent involvement in supervised and structured activities and/or being in the home protected them, while boys' involvement in unsupervised and unstructured activities, often outside of the home, left them more vulnerable to negative extended neighborhood effects.

Let's look back at the opening vignette about Alex and Jason one last time now that we have examined social disorganization theory and its relationship to delinquency. How would a social disorganization theorist analyze their situation? First and foremost, attention would be paid to the location in which the boys are living their lives. As the scenario indirectly indicates, they are likely living in a zone of transition as recent immigrants to a large city—the city in which they live has a lot of street crime, is dilapidated, and has many homeless people sleeping on the streets, which fits the description of Zone 2. Also, it is an area that people work to find a way to move away from as soon as they can,

TABLE 5.2 Overview of Anomie and Social Disorganization Theories

THEORY	THEORISTS	MAJOR CONCEPTS
Anomie Theories		
Anomie Theory	Durkheim	Anomie (normlessness) lessens social control
Strain Theory	Merton	Strain between cultural goals and legitimate means leads to norm breaking
Differential Opportunity Theory	Cloward & Ohlin	Differential social opportunity impacts how people handle strain
Subcultural Theory	Cohen	Working-class youth react to middle-class values and turn them on their head
Social Disorganization Theories		
Social Disorganization Theory	Park & Burgess	Social disorganization influences social behavior
Social Disorganization Theory of Delinquency	Shaw & McKay	Street delinquency is frequent in socially disorganized areas
Ecological Analysis of Black Youth and Delinquency	Frazier	Delinquency among black youth in cities is shaped by social disorganization
Modified Model of Social Disorganization	Sampson & Groves	Social disorganization leads to a number of intervening variables that influence whether delinquency will occur

which is a testament to its disorganization. A social disorganization theorist might note that Alex and Jason are struggling in this environment. There is little sense of community around them, and because their parents and others in the neighborhood are working so hard to make ends meet (or looking for work), and many are recent immigrants from a variety of different countries, there is little informal social control to be found—if Alex and Jason want to deal drugs to make some sense out of their situation, there may not be many people trying to stop them. Their reaction, in this perspective, can be seen as a completely normal response to the world around them.

SOCIAL STRUCTURAL THEORIES AND PUBLIC POLICY

Now that we have considered a number of social structural theories, let's think about their possible applications. There are a number of ways in which the insights of the anomie and social disorganization theories could be used to create public policies geared at reducing or eliminating delinquency.

Anomie

What would social policies on delinquency look like if they were based upon ideas honed from the anomie-related theories? The element that most would have in common would be a focus on reducing anomie and strain among working-class youth. With a reduction of anomie and strain, we can expect there to be a corresponding reduction in delinquency. Policies based upon Durkheim's notion of anomie would focus on messages that tell youth that unlimited aspirations are unrealistic, and that dreams of wealth will only be realized by a segment of the population. Policies based upon Merton's version of anomie might do the same, but because this approach is seen as a somewhat negative take on the very popular American Dream (involving speeches that begin with lines such as "Let's be real, kid—you are never going to be rich"), most policymakers focus on the other elements of Merton's theory. Nevertheless, policymakers could work to shift the message of the cultural goals promoted in the United States (or other countries in which the cultural goals and means are the same). As Einstadter and Henry suggest, "Crime control techniques in such a policy framework might involve limiting the extent that corporations create demand of unnecessary consumption through advertising in the mass media."[45] Campaigns to shift societal messages about what constitutes success could also be implemented, but because they would challenge the mainstream ideas about meritocracy (i.e., a system that rewards hard work), they would be unpopular.

A strain-reducing approach based on Merton's anomie theory that would be more accepted is to focus upon increasing the legitimate opportunities for youth to reach cultural goals and to excel in our society's institutions. Genuine equity in access to opportunities for all would require large-scale overhauls to our capitalistic social structure, but Merton's theory does not explicitly discuss such a major change. Instead, the focus of his work lends itself to a focus on promoting reforms of our existing systems. Policies that take anomie theory insights into account would focus upon **prevention** as a means of addressing the potential for delinquency. Tutoring, affirmative action programs, scholarship programs, and the mentoring of youth in low-income communities are all actions that would promote prevention goals in our social policymaking.

Many people have been inspired to implement similar preventative policy recommendations based on Cloward and Ohlin's and Cohen's work. Beginning in the 1960s, programs such as Head Start, Mobilization for Youth, Job Corps, and the Community Action Partnership were put into place to attempt to bolster marginalized youth's ability to do well in school and in the workplace.[46] Plenty of other groups utilize anomie theories to inform delinquency and crime-related policies today, such as the "I Have a Dream" Foundation (see From the Classroom to the Community, above) and the Boys & Girls Clubs of America.

Prevention efforts are good for those who are not yet caught up in the juvenile justice system. To reduce strain among youth who have been institutionalized and released, reentry programs that teach formerly incarcerated youth skills are needed. Policymakers considering issues of anomie will realize that youth who have delinquent records will experience strain even more than other youth because they are formally stigmatized. Policies that promote and fund adult assistance and peer mentoring will help these youth get back on a conventional path to adulthood.

Social Disorganization

If we were to take the position of a social disorganization theorist and consider how we should best influence social policy, we might decide not to do anything. Remember, some social disorganization theorists originally believed that social disorganization was simply a stage of a community's life that would resolve itself and become organized in time. As Davis explained, many believed that "the melting pot, in time, would eradicate urban pockets of deviance. Even the slum, the lowest point of urban disorganization, would rise from its submerged status and be absorbed into the urban order."[47]

●●●

Prevention: Any number of programs and policies geared at keeping youth on the conventional path and out of delinquency involvement.

Nonetheless, if we take a social disorganization perspective, we may still want to use our energy to contribute to policies for change (perhaps we do not have enough time or patience to wait and see if reorganization will occur on its own). Because social disorganization is a theory that points to neighborhood or community disorganization as a determinant of delinquency, a person who is interested in using policies and programs for change will want to focus on making neighborhoods more organized. If the neighborhood is more organized, then, the reasoning goes, young people will have less of a need to act out in response to a community that leaves them feeling disoriented and desperate. Indeed, policymakers who are concerned about the impact of disorganization

The Interrupters

The *Frontline* documentary "The Interrupters" (often available to view on the PBS website) sheds light on a group of adults who attempted to "interrupt" street violence in some of Chicago's toughest areas. The "interrupters" were people from the communities that they were targeting, often former gang members, who worked for an organization called CeaseFire. Operation CeaseFire was based upon the premise that the spread of violence can be stopped by having people intervene in potentially violent situations and by speaking to people, teens and adults, who appear to be headed down a violent path. Watching the documentary allows the viewer to see the complicated, and sometimes painful, process to strengthen and organize a community that has been shunned and disregarded by many. The city of Chicago quit financially supporting the program in late 2015, and supporters are concerned about the rising crime and delinquency and light of diminishing community support.

DISCUSSION QUESTIONS

1. After watching at least 30 minutes of *The Interrupters* online, what do you see as the strengths and weaknesses of the violence intervention that is shown in the documentary?

2. How does the notion of "interrupting violence" through community outreach relate to social disorganization theory?

Sources: PBS Video. (2012, February 14). The Interrupters. *Frontline*. Retrieved from http://www.pbs.org/wgbh/frontline/film/interrupters/; Associated Press (2015). Anti-violence programs shut down as Chicago shootings climb (Oct. 9). *Chicago Tribune*. Retrieved from http://www.chicagotribune.com/news/ct-ceasefire-funds-frozen-as-chicago-shootings-climb-20151009-story.html

on individuals may want to start programs to clean up the neighborhood, to start a neighborhood crime watch, and to close down brothels or drug houses in an effort to help community organizations.

Some of the originators of the social disorganization perspective were very involved with such policymaking. For example, the Chicago Area Project (CAP) was orchestrated and managed by the Institute for Juvenile Research, where Shaw and McKay did their research for years. The project focused upon improving the zone of transition in Chicago by providing resource centers for residents. Those involved in the project worked to provide services to help youth manage life in the inner city, as well as to facilitate the matching of youths with preexisting services provided by other organizations in the community.[48] The project founders, one of whom was Clifford Shaw, set out to work with the leaders of the community and to help strengthen the existing institutions—churches, youth groups, clubs—rather than to bring in outside groups to "improve" the area. The CAP considered these groups the natural resources of the community and believed they should be built upon to strengthen the community.[49] In addition, they had "curbside counselors" who were present in the neighborhood and talked to youth who were gang involved, or involved in delinquency, in an effort to try and keep them out of trouble. This approach was aimed at helping individuals deal with the disorganization in their community in ways that would not damage their futures. They worked with agencies to divert youth from institutionalization in the event that they were involved in delinquency and worked to reintegrate youth who came back from time in a juvenile institution as well. The CAP still exists today and works to help organize grassroots groups in the area to bring change to their own communities (see www.chicagoareaproject.org).

Another social change approach that supporters have cited as related to social disorganization aims, but that certainly would not be supported by all social disorganization theorists, is the "Operation Weed and Seed" programs that have cropped up across the nation. These programs are focusing on "weeding" an area through collaboration with law enforcement and other government agencies (i.e., shutting down brothels and drug houses, and perhaps arresting the leaders of criminal gangs), then "seeding" the area by investing in it and providing physical and financial resources to help improve the appearance and day-to-day life of the community. Although the seeding component of this approach may be seen as a positive way of strengthening the community, some would argue that any increased presence of the police in the community, or any people from outside of the community coming in to reform it, constitutes a disruptive force that would only lead to more disorganization. Instead the collective efficacy of the community should be strengthened in more organic ways.

A last type of policymaking based upon social disorganization and focused upon delinquency prevention would provide youth with mentorship and activities outside of their immediate neighborhoods to expose them to the possibilities available in other areas in the future. Yet, as Kingston et al. note, it is important not only to help youth to change their perceptions of futility and frustration, but for interventions to actually improve opportunity structures as well.[50]

SUMMARY

Anomie and social disorganization theories require us to shift our focus to elements of the social structure that either facilitate or hinder delinquency. In the case of anomie theories, it is clear that the classic conceptualizations of Durkheim and Merton both focus on the dangers that occur when human beings have unlimited aspirations that go unchecked due to either rapid social change or insistent cultural messages about success. In the latter case, it is clear that when society is structured in ways that do not allow equal access to quality education and jobs, youth will often feel compelled to accomplish material or financial success in whatever means they can. Merton theorized that we can expect to see youth attempt to innovate or "get creative" about the ways they obtain the American Dream in such circumstances in different forms of delinquency that generate money. As elucidated by Cloward and Ohlin, the different forms of delinquency in which strained youth decide to participate are not completely random, but are shaped by the illegitimate activities readily available to them. According to Cohen's theory of delinquent subcultures, it is unsurprising that young men from working-class homes are essentially set up for, if not outright failure, a clash of social norms. Assuming that working-class youth have not been socialized with middle-class norms of behavior and then are placed in school systems that unquestioningly prioritize those middle-class norms, they are likely to experience the process as degrading. Young people in such a situation may choose to develop groups of friends in a similar situation and utilize their own oppositional norms of behavior to express their anger and frustration with the structure, albeit oftentimes unproductively.

Social disorganization theories encourage us to imagine our world as alternating between periods of organization and disorganization in a never-ending cycle. This theory requires us to think about delinquency as a response deriving from the degree of social organization present in our immediate environment, the assumption being that the physical and social class location of our neighborhoods impacts our behavior. The ecological framework of Park and Burgess, later incorporated into Shaw and McKay's social disorganization theory of delinquency, states that geographical distance from the forces of social change that come to bear on the center of cities results in a lower rate of street delinquency than occurs in places and spaces unprotected by social order. Nevertheless, young people who do live in neighborhoods that display markers of disorganization focused upon by the theory may also experience what Sampson and Groves call a sense of collective efficacy—community empowerment and cohesion that shield them from the delinquency-inducing effects that would otherwise be expected. Social disorganization theorists provide evidence that delinquency explanations that focus on the big picture allow us to address large-scale factors that individual-level explanations often cannot.

EYE ON DIVERSITY EXERCISE: A LOOK AT SEXUALITY, HOMELESS YOUTH, AND DELINQUENCY

In this activity we would like you to consider the relationship between sexuality, homeless youth, and delinquency in your vicinity through the lenses of the social structural theories covered in this chapter. Homeless youth are unsurprisingly among some of the most marginalized youth in a given society, and little attention is given to their situations. Homeless or "street youth" have been shown to end up homeless because of reasons such as family conflict and abuse, timing out of the foster care system and having nowhere else to live, and rejection due to identification as a lesbian, gay, bisexual, or transgender teen.[51] When on the streets, they often engage in a number of high-risk behaviors, such as alcohol and illegal drug use, risky sexual behavior (often known as survival sex), and various acts of delinquency.[52] LGBT homeless youth are also very vulnerable to victimization while on the streets, in the form of robbery, assault, and rape, yet they have few community resources tailored to their needs.[53]

Do some research on what resources are available for street youth in your community or the nearest city. Examine online sources or visit a nearby resource center to get your information and to answer the following questions:

- What specific services are provided for LGBT youth who are without permanent shelter in your community?

- How might the resources that are (or are not) available affect LGBT youths' experiences of anomie and/or strain?

DISCUSSION QUESTIONS

1. Assess the relevance of Merton's notion of the American Dream in the 21st century. Do you think that young people still subscribe to a vision of success based upon materialism? Explain why or why not.

2. What are the implications of Merton's categorization of nondeviant and deviant adaptations to social strain? Do you agree with the assumptions on which he based his model?

3. What can community activists and policymakers do to curb delinquency in your neighborhood or one nearby by using the insights from differential opportunity theory?

4. Social disorganization theorists ask us to think about delinquency in terms that draw upon the field of plant ecology, rather than in the psychological terms that dominate popular discussions of deviance. What does this allow us to see that we wouldn't otherwise? If social disorganization were the most popular explanation of juvenile delinquency today, how might that change mainstream responses to juvenile wrongdoing or norm breaking?

5. What are some of the race, class, and/or gender concerns addressed by anomie and social disorganization theories? What race, class, and gender concerns go unaddressed in these theories?

6. Compare and contrast anomie and social disorganization theory explanations for delinquency. Which do you think is the best equipped to deal with delinquency issues today?

KEY TERMS

Adaptations to strain 129

Anomic suicide 127

Anomie theory 126

Coercive mobility 142

Collective conscience 126

Collective efficacy 139

Concentric zone model 135

Conflict delinquent subculture 131

Consensus theorist 126

Criminal delinquent subculture 131

Determinism 126

Heterogeneity 135

Informal social control 135

Intervening variables 139

Macro-level theories 126

Mechanical society 127

Organic society 127

Prevention 146

Retreatist delinquent
 subculture 131

Social disorganization
 theory 126

Social ecology 135

Social facts 127

Sociological positivist
 theories 126

Strain theory 128

Subcultural delinquency
 theory 131

Symbiosis 135

Zone of transition 136

CHAPTER PRETEST ANSWERS

1. False

2. True

3. False

4. True

5. True

6. True

7. False

8. True

STUDENT STUDY SITE

$SAGE edge™

edge.sagepub.com/bates2e

Sharpen your skills with SAGE edge!

SAGE edge for students provides a personalized approach to help you accomplish your coursework goals in an easy-to-use learning environment. You'll find action plans, mobile-friendly eFlashcards, and quizzes, as well as videos, web resources, and links to SAGE journal articles to support and expand on the concepts presented in this chapter. Check out the website for original videos of former offenders discussing their experiences as juveniles.

©iStockphoto.com/Chao Chen Tsun Mei

CRITICAL THEORIES

CHAPTER OBJECTIVES ....

After reading this chapter, you should be able to

- Explain the commonalities of all critical theories

- Summarize labeling theory's origins and key concepts

- Outline the major conflict theories of delinquency and their key concepts

- Identify multiple feminist theories and their respective emphases

- Assess how critical theories address the relationship between race, ethnicity, social class, gender, sexuality, and delinquency

- Analyze the relevance of critical theories of delinquency to public policy

Cecilia, a 17-year-old Latina from Southern California, has lived in the same neighborhood all of her life. She is comfortable in her hometown because nearly all of her extended family live in the same area, and many of the young people there are like her—bilingual Spanish-English speakers and the sons and daughters of recent immigrants. As she was growing up, she could stop by her relatives' homes to have a meal, to babysit her nieces and nephews, and to get emotional support when things got tough. And things did get tough for Cecilia, several times in her life. She was bussed to a middle school out of her area to a school with very few Latinos and when she was there experienced a great deal of bullying and teasing because she was from a "bad" neighborhood and her parents did not have much money to give her for clothes. The teasing escalated, and she was sexually assaulted, in the locker room, one day by two boys from wealthy families. Although she reported it to Mr. Thorton, the principal, the boys were never punished. Cecilia became depressed and dreaded going to school.

As she got older, many of her friends and relatives became part of the neighborhood gang. At first Cecilia was not part of the gang, but after getting put on the official gang list by the gang unit of the local police department (because she sat outside and talked to friends and cousins in the gang sometimes), her life changed. School officials began treating her differently, and teachers began to ignore her, as if they did not believe that she cared about her education. In the neighborhood, the few girls and boys her age who were not in the local gang acted as if they were too busy to hang out with her anymore, and the police officers in her neighborhood frequently accused her of being involved with various gang-related acts of delinquency. The only people who continued reaching out to her were the guys and girls on her block who were involved in the gang. Slowly, she began to spend more time with them, going with them when they were doing things like tagging, drinking in the park, and shoplifting. She figured she had nothing to lose because everyone already treated her as if she were in the gang, and it also helped her forget about the frustrations and pain of her daily life. It was an added plus that it took her away from school, where she felt unsafe.

CHAPTER PRETEST

Test your knowledge of this chapter's material by determining whether the following statements are true or false. Be sure to compare your answers with the answers on page 180.

1. All critical theorists have an interest in understanding how social power affects human behavior.

2. The social critiques that emerge from the critical theories often inspire people to get involved in actions to alleviate social inequities.

3. According to labeling theories, stigmatizing youth after their first act of misbehavior is a good way to prevent them from engaging in secondary deviance.

4. Becker explained that people who are similarly labeled, whether they engage in the same activity or not, will experience similar outcomes.

5. Moral panics about crime and delinquency have resulted in the disproportionate labeling of white youth.

6. Conflict theorists claim that laws often reflect the interests of the working class.

7. According to DuBois, many acts of crime and delinquency can be seen as efforts to resist racial and legal oppression.

8. Some feminist theorists claim that the concept of *intersectionality* helps us understand the complex effects of race, class, gender, sexuality, age, and ability on young people's behaviors.

9. Chesney-Lind and other feminist criminologists state that it is important to look at patriarchy, or male dominance in societal institutions, in order to understand girls' lives.

CRITICAL THEORIES OF DELINQUENCY

What led to Cecilia's delinquency? Clearly, many factors were involved. The critical theories of delinquency that we will examine in this chapter (labeling, conflict theory, and feminist theories) provide us with different lenses we can use to analyze her situation. Although the theorists associated with the three schools of thought we will focus on make sense of delinquency by highlighting different factors, they all share an interest in social **power**, the ability to make things happen, "to realize your wishes, [and] to produce the effects you want to produce."[1] These perspectives require us to look deeply into the world we live in and into the topic of delinquency with a critical eye. Doing so oftentimes results in unexpected answers to questions about delinquency that we might raise—answers that ultimately challenge more popular explanations for delinquency that we hear on the news or that are shown in television shows and movies. The social critiques, or concerns that emerge from these theories, are known for inspiring many to get involved in social actions in their communities in the name of alleviating **social inequities**— unfair distributions of power and social control.

All three types of theories that we examine in this chapter lead us to question how we decide what acts and what people are delinquent. The creation of labeling theory brought attention to race, class, gender, sexuality, and other social variables that we now know are central to the assignment and receipt of labels, but that had previously been underexamined by social scientists.[2] Conflict theories focus on the ways that the benefits and burdens of our economic and class system influence our definitions of delinquency and work to either encourage or discourage delinquency. And feminist theories of delinquency share an interest in the ways in which categories of gender and sexuality are used to socially control youths' behaviors as well as to create and define delinquency.

Labeling Theory

Visit edge.sagepub .com/bates2e to view a video clip about real-life examples of labeling theory.

● ● ●

Power: The ability to make things happen and to exert your will or wishes upon others.

Social inequity: A concept that refers to unfair distributions of power and social control.

The labeling theory of delinquency is often used in conjunction with other theories to explain the process of first calling a particular act a delinquent one and then using that label to justify a particular means of punishing or reacting to the person who has then been labeled. The power of labels is pretty clear to most of us in our daily lives as we were raised with cultural messages about them. The old childhood fable about the "boy who cried wolf"[3] demonstrates the power of labeling as it relates to wrongdoing for young readers. In that story, a boy who was guarding the sheep of his village from wolf attacks yelled out that he saw wolves several times when he had not actually seen any. Because he cried out several times with false information, he was labeled by others in his community as a person who did not tell the truth. Then, when he eventually did see a wolf and yelled out a warning for the townspeople to hear, nobody listened or believed him because the label had stuck—he was no longer considered trustworthy. Although the moral of the story was to be honest, when we look at it through sociological glasses we can see that the labeling ultimately was harmful to both the boy and the greater community. This fable is one in which the boy has actually done something that has resulted in his labeling, yet as you will see the labeling perspective can also be used to analyze acts of wrongdoing in which people have not done anything related to the label that has been placed upon them. For example, the opening scenario of this chapter about Cecilia, a person who was labeled as a juvenile delinquent and gang member at a point when she was not actually doing anything to warrant those labels, can also be analyzed through the lens of labeling theory. Labeling theorists explain that the assignment of a label can have an impact on an individual's future that is worthy of serious examination.

Origins of Labeling Theory

> Differences in the ability to make rules and apply them to other people are essentially power differentials (either legal or extralegal). Those groups whose position gives them weapons and power are best able to enforce their rules. Distinctions of age, sex, ethnicity and class are all related to differences in power, which accounts for the differences in degree to which groups so distinguished can make rules for others.[4]

Labeling theory has its origins in the works of many scholars, but its best known concepts are primarily derived from the work of Edwin Lemert, Howard Becker, and Erving Goffman.[5] Labeling theory became popular in the 1960s and early 1970s, when many people were challenging the status quo and standing up and protesting in the name of civil rights and equality. This makes sense because labeling theory broadens the analysis of delinquency to include a consideration of who is doing the labeling of delinquents, who is being labeled, and to what social groups each delinquent belongs. Early labeling theorists developed ideas about how the assignment of labels may affect the people being labeled, and how those effects might impact the possibility of delinquency on their parts in the future. Ultimately, the perspective generates questions about how legitimate or warranted a given label is and whether its use is productive in preventing future acts of crime and delinquency. Is official labeling of wrongdoing a necessary part of preventing delinquency, or is it simply an exaggerated response to juvenile mischief and what Tannenbaum called the dramatization of evil?[6]

Edwin Lemert's discussion of deviance applies to both juvenile delinquency and adult misbehavior. In his books *Social Pathology* (1951) and *Human Deviance, Social Problems, and Social Control* (1972), Lemert shifted the focus away from earlier theories' focus on the reasons why a person may have originally engaged in an act of deviance (i.e., the subject of **primary deviance**) and introduced and developed the concept of **secondary deviance**.[7] He explained that secondary deviance is the result of other people's negative responses to an individual's original act of "deviance":

> Secondary deviation refers to a special class of social defined responses that people make to problems created by the social reaction to their deviance. These problems are essentially moral problems, which revolve around stigmatization, punishments, segregation, and social control. . . . They become central facts of existence for those experiencing them.[8]

In other words, if people commit an act of deviance and others react in a strongly negative manner toward them, by treating them badly, punishing them, and ultimately telling them they are not worthy to run in the same circles as others in society, the people on the receiving end of such negative messages and behaviors are apt to internalize them. In turn, they may decide to engage in other acts of misbehavior as a way of dealing with the negative experience.

As noted in the words of Lemert above, stigma and **stigmatization** are central to the creation of secondary deviance. Erving Goffman, in his 1963 book *Stigma: Notes on a Spoiled Identity*,[9] explained that stigma refers to a process by which the reactions of others spoil a person's normal identity. In cases in which others label a person as deviant, delinquent, strange, or even just weird, the targeted person has been stigmatized. If the labeling process is widespread and/or perpetuated by especially powerful labelers, it may become hard for the labeled person to hang out with others who are considered normal or members of a "good crowd." As Goffman would put it, for all intents and purposes the labeled person has a **spoiled identity**—it is tainted by the stigmatization.

●●●

Primary deviance: The initial act of deviance or delinquency that a person engages.

Secondary deviance: An act of deviance or delinquency that follows the labeling of a person as a delinquent or troublemaker.

Stigmatization: The process by which a person is marked or labeled as a deviant or a disgrace.

Spoiled identity: Goffman's term for what happens when a person has been labeled as delinquent, criminal, or deviant, and the negative identity sticks, leaving him or her in a perpetual state of stigmatization.

Labeling theorists explain that when young people are labeled negatively, it is likely that they will be excluded and stigmatized by some of their peers.

This stigmatization can lead to a situation in which the label placed on a person comes to be the main thing that people refer to when talking about the person. In other words, it can become a person's **master status**.[10] When this happens in the case of youth, we might see someone referred to by others as a "gang member" or "meth head" or "juvenile delinquent," rather than being discussed in terms of any other qualities, attributes, or labels that could also be applied to them (student, son/daughter, athlete, artist, blogger, etc.). Labeling scholars pay particular attention to the ways that processing of youth through the juvenile and adult justice systems work as *status degradation ceremonies*[11]—processes in which the juveniles are shamed and lose status in the eyes of the community along the way. In some cases a delinquent master status is so powerful that a youth labeled in this manner might go down the road of developing a *criminal career* or long-term delinquent involvement leading to a life of adult crime.

Given that the labeling process was thought to be influential to the future of young people, detailed analyses about what rules labels reflect, how labels are assigned, and the different consequences of labeling were pursued by labeling theorists. Howard Becker, in his 1963 book *Outsiders: Studies in the Sociology of Deviance*, considered who has the power to define the rules that young people are asked to follow:

> Who can, in fact, force others to accept their rules and what are the causes of their success? This is of course a question of political and economic power. . . . By and large, for example, rules are made for young people by their elders. Though the youth of this country exert a powerful influence culturally—the mass media of communication are tailored to their interests, for instance—many important kinds of rules are made for our youth by adults. Rules regarding school attendance and sex behavior are not drawn up with regard to the problems of adolescence.[12]

Becker also explained that many of us assume that official sources, such as juvenile court records, will give us an accurate picture of delinquency in a given year. Although these numbers may reflect the decision making of prosecutors, police, and court administrators, we may need to take a second look at their accuracy. Becker stated that sometimes the numbers are higher than they ought to be. For example, in a case in which a young man has been arrested simply for associating with youth who are committing acts of delinquency, he will also be labeled delinquent. A youth may not have earned that label in the same way that his friend who robbed a liquor store did, yet in the long run the consequences of the labeling may be similar in spite of that fact.

To better understand this idea, think back to the details of the example at the beginning of this chapter. When Cecilia was first labeled as a gang member and a delinquent, she actually was not doing anything substantial to earn that label. But her experience out in the world was the same as if she had been committing acts of gang violence; she was shunned and stigmatized by those in the mainstream of society. Becker created a typology of deviant behavior to address the various ways that behaviors and perceptions of others (or labels of the behavior) were related to one another.[13] He categorized possible scenarios in terms of whether the behavior involved was deviant (i.e., someone was breaking a

● ● ●

Master status:
A status or label that comes to be held as more powerful than others (e.g., "delinquent").

rule) or not, and whether the behavior was labeled by others as deviant or as conforming to society's norms (see Figure 6.1).

In two of the four types that Becker alluded to, the conformist and the pure deviant, the nature of the act a person is engaged in corresponds accurately to the label that others are placing upon the person. The conformist is following societal norms or rules and is not perceived as deviant. For example, many youth go to school, do their homework, and hang out with their friends when they have extra time, and are just considered run-of-the-mill kids. Becker would consider them conformists. The pure deviant is breaking societal norms or rules and is perceived as deviant as a result. An example of this might be the young person who enjoys stealing clothes from the local mall and then is caught and labeled a shoplifter by the local police. Once again, the deviant behavior and the deviant label match.

Where things get complicated is with the other two types, the falsely accused and the secret deviant. The falsely accused person has not done anything deviant, yet is perceived by others who observe her or him as deviant (as is the case of the early stage of Cecilia's example in this chapter). In the case of the secret deviant, a person is doing something that would likely be perceived and labeled as deviant if observed by others, yet is not labeled. According to Becker, this is typically the case with people who are successful in hiding their acts from others. Any number of taboo acts that a person might engage in could motivate a person to try and keep her or his secret deviant status. As we will discuss later in the chapter, not all people have the same ability to maintain a secret deviant status, in part due to the variation in social surveillance that people experience depending on their class, race, and neighborhood. In other words, some people and some neighborhoods are watched more than others, and because of living arrangements, some people have less privacy than others and thus are more likely to have their "secret" acts detected than they would be otherwise.

One of the most important points that Becker made about these different types is that at the end of the day, *people who are similarly labeled, whether they actually have engaged in the activity assumed or not, will experience similar outcomes*. So, the pure deviant and the falsely accused will often experience stigmatization and reduced social opportunities, and the conformist and the secret deviant will go unscathed by negative labeling.

Other important labeling concepts developed in the early stages of labeling theory include the **moral entrepreneur** and moral panic. Moral entrepreneurs are people who

● ● ●
Moral entrepreneur:
People who work to garner attention toward a social issue or group that they have decided amounts to a social problem.

FIGURE 6.1 Becker's Typology of Deviant Behavior

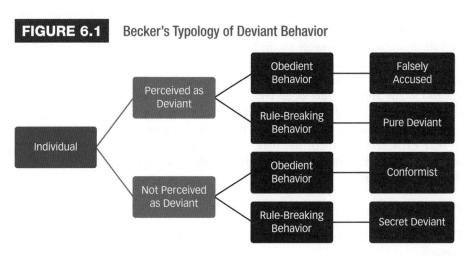

Source: Adapted from Becker, H. S. (1963). *Outsiders: Studies in sociology of deviance*. Glencoe, IL: Free Press.

In the News

Justice-Involved Youth

In April 2016, the U.S. Departments of Justice and Housing and Urban Development announced the Juvenile Reentry Assistance Program, which will help justice-involved youth find jobs and housing after paying back society for any wrongdoing that they have done. The use of the term *justice-involved youth* was intentionally employed in lieu of the term *juvenile delinquent,* which has long been used by government officials.

DISCUSSION QUESTION

1. Why might critical theorists support the creation and use of the new term, *justice-involved youth*?

Source: U.S. Department of Justice. (2016, April 25). *The Departments of Justice and Housing and Urban Development to award $1.75 million to help justice-involved youth find jobs and housing.* Retrieved from https://www.justice.gov/opa/pr/departments-justice-and-housing-and-urban-development-award-175-million-help-justice-involved

work to garner attention toward a social issue or group that they have decided amounts to a social problem; they create deviance, and by extension delinquency, by placing labels on behaviors and actions.[14] As discussed by Gusfield, there is typically a power differential related to how this plays out: "Moral reformism of this type suggests the approach of the dominant class toward those less favorably situated in the economic and social structure."[15] Moral entrepreneurs have launched crusades around a number of issues, such as the temperance movement and the antismoking movement. Sometimes, crusades are fueled by the creation of a moral panic—heightened concern over an issue that is not in line with its seriousness or frequency of occurrence in the world.[16] For example, Chambliss found that in spite of the fact that crime rates were not rising, police, politicians, and the media spread misinformation, beginning in the 1960s, which increased concern about crime among the general public and resulted in the tough-on-crime approach taken since the late 1970s in the United States.[17] The moral panics about crime and delinquency have resulted in the disproportionate labeling of many youth of color, most notably black youth and young black men.[18]

Development of Labeling Theory

Social scientists who have followed in the footsteps of Lemert, Becker, Goffman, and other formative labeling theorists have elaborated upon the processes by which labeling can result in secondary deviance or, in terms of the focus of this book, secondary delinquency. They have done so, in part, in response to the critiques of the theory that were frequently made by scholars in the late 1970s and early 1980s[19]—critiques that the theory was too vague and not developed concretely enough to test scientifically.[20] Some critics interpreted and assessed the proposition that labeling as a delinquent or negative labeling was *always* followed by delinquent behavior.[21] Advocates of labeling theory explained that early labeling theorists always assumed the process to be much more complicated than that and reiterated that secondary deviance depends on multiple factors working in conjunction:

1. The degree to which the label is public,

2. The degree to which others react to the labeled person in a negative or exclusionary manner,

3. A transformation in personal identity, and

4. Support from others who are involved in delinquency or acts popularly thought of as deviant.[22]

The focus of labeling theory in recent decades has been on two factors that help explain why secondary deviance occurs in some cases and not in others after a person has been labeled: **self-concept** and **social exclusion**.[23] Scholars have also looked more closely at who is doing the labeling and how that might affect a person's likelihood of committing an act of breaking the rules or the laws again. As the theory has been tested over time and elaborated upon, most observers have come to agree that it is a useful tool that can work hand in hand with other theories that attempt to focus on the reasons why a person decides to break the rules in the first place (i.e., those that focus upon primary deviance).

Labeling, Self-Concept, and Gender

To understand the relationship between labeling and self-concept, scholars of delinquency typically draw upon insights from the theoretical approach of symbolic interactionism. **Symbolic interactionism** is a framework that examines the way that people make meaning out of symbols, words, and other forms of communication to make sense of the world.[24] One of the most famous symbolic interactionist concepts, Herbert Cooley's **looking-glass self**, plays a role in studies of this type. This concept (which can be summarized in everyday language as "I am what I think you think I am") refers to the idea that people imagine how others perceive them and then internalize that idea as their own.

Being labeled as a delinquent can negatively influence a youth's self-concept—the way that the youth views herself or himself.[25] Scholars have examined this idea in detail by considering how *informal labeling* (labeling by peers, teachers, and parents) and *formal labeling* (labeling by juvenile justice or criminal justice officials) affect youths' thoughts about themselves. Adams et al. studied youths' self-concepts and found that informal sources of labeling played an important role in influencing their future delinquency.[26] When youth perceived that their peers or teachers labeled them negatively, they were more apt to report that they had engaged in delinquent behavior than youth who did not perceive such negative labels. Similarly, Matsueda found that when boys thought that their parents labeled them as rule violators, they were more likely to self-report that they had acted out delinquently than boys who thought otherwise.[27] In addition, although parents were found to quickly assign negative labels to girls who acted out even once, the informal labeling process had a bigger effect on boys' delinquency than on girls'.[28] It seems that this was because when boys recognized that they were seen as rule breakers by their parents, it reinforced their self-concept of being macho or manly—qualities that boys are encouraged to develop by society as a whole. As a result they were more apt to internalize the delinquent label and to engage in future acts of delinquency than girls were.

Along the same lines, research has demonstrated that formal labeling of youth as delinquent by law enforcement agents makes it more likely that a youth will become heavily involved with delinquent peers as well as to join a gang after being labeled.[29] In such cases, delinquent peers provide a sort of shelter from the storm of social stigmatization, as well as the psychological and social tools for committing acts of delinquency. When adolescents are labeled as delinquent by official sources, it directly contributes to a solidification of a delinquent path or career. Labeling theorists attribute this outcome, in part, to the effect of labeling on youths' self-concept.

●●●

Self-concept: A concept that refers to the way in which a person views her- or himself.

Social exclusion: Youth who are negatively labeled as delinquents may later find themselves shut out or excluded from conventional or beneficial opportunities.

Symbolic interactionism: A framework that examines the way that people make meaning out of symbols, words, and other forms of communication.

Looking-glass self: The idea that a person imagines how others perceive her or him and then internalizes that idea as her or his own.

Labeling, Social Exclusion, Race, and Class

A number of different scholars have conducted studies that look at the way in which labeling, particularly formal labeling by actors in the juvenile justice system, affects future delinquency by means of cutting off a number of opportunities or paths that are available for youth to pursue. These studies take a step away from the social-psychological approach of the self-concept studies (although they do not ignore this entirely) just considered and focus primarily on the social structure that a young person labeled as delinquent must navigate. The reality that many labeled youth must deal with is that they are shut out of many legitimate or beneficial opportunities. Studies in this tradition are drawing from life course theory[30] and its consideration of **cumulative disadvantage**: disadvantage that a labeled delinquent youth experiences due to stigmatization in society's primary social institutions, for example family, school, peers, and the government-run juvenile justice system.[31] The negative reaction that a young person who is labeled delinquent experiences may result in a narrowing down of their life options in ways that matter in the long run. This may result in a delinquent or **deviant career** to use the words of labeling theorists: delinquency or deviance that a person pursues over the span of his or her life.

A study that looked at the creation of such a deviant career was conducted by Bernburg and Krohn.[32] They looked at how boys who were labeled delinquents fared over time with an eye toward their social location, in particular their race and social class, and found the following:

1. Juvenile justice intervention during the teenage years lessened the possibility that a youth would graduate from high school;

2. Police labeling during the teenage years increased the probability of unemployment during early adulthood;

3. Juvenile justice intervention also increased the probability of early adult unemployment, but primarily due to its negative effect on youth's educational progress;

4. Youth who were labeled by the police or juvenile justice actors as delinquents were more likely to engage in crime as young adults than other youth, in part because of lack of education and lack of employment; and

5. Young adults who were black (as labeled by juvenile justice officials) and who came from an economically disadvantaged home (as labeled by police or juvenile justice officials) were more likely to engage in crime than other young adults who had been similarly labeled.

In sum, Bernburg and Krohn found that official labeling affected labeled youth in multiple ways. Ultimately, class and race affected the ability of youth to persevere after being labeled delinquent. White youth and those with more financial resources at their disposal were better able to overcome the effects of being labeled as a delinquent and to stay out of trouble after the fact than others were.

Other research that examined the long-term outcomes related to involvement in the juvenile justice system also found that it was related to future association with delinquent youth and illegal behavior.[33] These findings support labeling theory and challenge the notion that formal punishment deters, or prevents, youth from committing future acts of delinquency or crime.

What About Positive Labeling?

As you have seen from the previous examples, the bulk of current labeling research looks at negative reactions to a delinquent or criminal label. A less popular use of the theory

● ● ●

Cumulative disadvantage:
Disadvantage that a labeled delinquent youth experiences due to stigmatization in society's primary social institutions: family, school, peers, and the government-run juvenile justice system.

Deviant career:
Delinquency, crime, or deviance that an individual pursues over the span of his or her life.

twists this approach and considers how "devils in disguise" get away with misbehavior due to positive labeling by others.[34] If you think back to high school, you can probably remember people who were thought to be studious and well-behaved by their parents or other adults, yet their friends knew them to be the life of the party every weekend, drinking alcohol and engaging in other delinquent activities. The youth in these situations understood the power of the positive label and may have actually worked hard to keep the label to get away with what they were doing. They recognized that their wholesome reputation helped distract observers from their delinquent actions. As Brezina and Aragones pointed out,

When you were a teenager, did you know any "devils in disguise" whose delinquency escaped detection?

> the ability to maintain positive labels in the eyes of adults, while engaging in extensive delinquency, is likely to be an important source of reward and reinforcement for many adolescents. And for certain youths, the ability to conceal a delinquent self from conventional others may produce rewards that are large enough to help sustain long-term criminal involvement.[35]

The process of manipulating or shaping the positive labeling process and, in turn, avoiding negative labeling and detection can be quite thrilling to the young person committing undetected acts of delinquency. Successful manipulation is related to race, gender, and class. White, middle or upper-class, females will usually have the easiest time manipulating positive labels and hiding their lawbreaking, while young men of color from low-income neighborhoods will have the most difficult time doing so.[36] This is because widespread stereotypes of juvenile delinquents as young men of color from urban neighborhoods serve as the backdrop for societal impressions of wrongdoing, whether conscious or unconscious.

Resistance to the Delinquent Label

The research on positive labeling, as well as the other more traditional types of labeling research,[37] has demonstrated that youth have an active role in the labeling process. It is important to recognize that some youth resist the negative labels that are placed upon them, by putting them in a bigger political and social context.

Many youth resist labeling because they experience it as unjust targeting by law enforcement and other social control agents. Paul Hirschfield interviewed young adults of color (18–20 years old) about their past delinquent behaviors and their reaction to the labeling process that took place when they were arrested as juveniles.[38] Because they grew up in urban areas subjected to a lot of police activity and attention, it was commonplace for youth to be arrested; as a result, they did not experience much stigmatization or shaming related to that activity. Rather than negatively affecting their self-concepts, the high rate of juvenile arrests for petty acts of delinquency or for acts that the young adults said they did not commit (i.e., false accusations) signaled to the youth that formal labels were not reliable. In other words, they were not considered legitimate or important within the community. At times, the label of delinquent was even thought of as something to be proud of and just part of the process of growing up in the city. As Hirschfield explained, this resistance to labeling as a negative phenomenon is a reaction to being shut out from tangible opportunities:[39]

A Focus on Research

Holsinger and Hodge's "The Experiences of Lesbian, Gay, Bisexual, and Transgender Girls in Juvenile Justice Systems"

In Kristi Holsinger and Jessica P. Hodge's 2016 *Feminist Criminology* article, "The Experiences of Lesbian, Gay, Bisexual and Transgender Girls in Juvenile Justice Systems," they build upon gendered pathway theory as well as labeling theory to examine the perceptions of detained girls and the juvenile justice staff who supervise them.[40] The detained girls that they spoke to in a focus group were African American and identified as either lesbian, gay, or bisexual (LGB). The girls reported being harassed about their sexuality by other detained girls while staff people failed to intervene. They also noted that there was a double standard for LGB girls and other girls—girls who weren't labeled LGB could hold hands or sit close together, but LGB girls were accused of inappropriately crossing boundaries when they did so. In counseling groups, the girls were not allowed to talk about any same-sex relationships because staff were fearful they would inspire heterosexual girls to engage in sexual relationships with them.

Holsinger and Hodge explored themes that emerged in their focus groups with 21 black and white juvenile justice staff one year later.

They found that LGBT girls were assumed to be predatory by many staff people and that they watched them more closely than other detainees. Although some staff noted an understanding of sexuality and had a positive take on LGBT youth, many staff had very little understanding of what it meant for girls to be bisexual. Staff also did not understand the needs of transgender youth. Requests of the girls to be called their preferred name or preferred pronouns were largely ignored. The authors of the article conclude that multiple changes are needed to address the needs of the girls in the facility and to counter the harmful assumptions and practices that drive many of the interactions in juvenile justice facilities today.

DISCUSSION QUESTION

1. Holsinger and Hodge conclude that their findings highlight insights from feminist and labeling theory. According to these theories, what can we expect from the girls who are labeled as troublemakers and surveilled due to their sexuality and/or gender identity when they are released from detention? Why?

The emergent reality in Americans' poorest urban neighborhoods, which sociology has only begun to grasp (but see LeBlanc, 2003), *is that justice system labels are not merely sewn onto individuals, but they are etched into the social fabric of the ghetto* [emphasis added]. . . . The normalization and de-legitimation of official labels are entrenched conditions for poor African-American neighborhoods across the United States, wrought by decades of mass arrests and imprisonment.

The next theoretical tradition we will examine, conflict theory, focuses on the economic issues at the core of modern-day delinquency and the crime control industry.

Conflict theorist:
A theorist who assumes that society is based on class conflict and that laws tend to reflect the interests of the powerful.

CONFLICT THEORY: A FOCUS ON SOCIOECONOMIC CLASS

Conflict or radical theory is closely tied to some variants of labeling theory that we have considered previously in this chapter—in particular the considerations of labeling that stress the role of power and socioeconomic class. If we recall the scenario at the very beginning of the chapter that detailed Cecilia's path to delinquency and attempt to look at it as **conflict theorists**, we will be drawn to the question of how issues of money and material resources affected her life. Theories have emerged from the original formulations of conflict theory that expand it to include social analyses of race and ethnicity. Because of this, we might think about the fact that Cecilia was bussed to another neighborhood, one in which she was teased for being Latina and having little money, and then profiled as a gang member. We might also consider the role that police surveillance and crime control in low-income neighborhoods plays in limiting youths' development of their full potential. In addition, we probably will consider her foray into shoplifting as a reaction to her position in society. As a conflict theorist, we might ultimately see Cecilia's behavior as a means of survival and resistance.

The Origins of Conflict Theory

Conflict theories of delinquency have their roots in the works of theorists who were focused not necessarily on delinquency per se, but rather on macro-structural issues related to the division of power in society; definitions of crime, deviance, and law created by those in power; and the repercussions of those social realities. These theorists were concerned with the big picture and the issues at the forefront of our society today—economics, race relations, and social justice.

This street art in downtown San Diego near a major shopping district embodies one of the messages of conflict theorists, which is to challenge the status quo.

Many variants of conflict theory are related to the work of German scholar Karl Marx and his consideration of social class.[41] Marx theorized that societies were essentially characterized by **class conflict**. In his famous *Communist Manifesto,* co-written with Friedrich Engels, he stated that "the history of all hitherto existing society is the history of class struggles."[42] He was a *historical materialist,* a theorist who believed that if you want to understand any phenomenon in a given society, you must first look specifically at that society at a certain point in time, and examine the material base or economy of that society to understand what is transpiring. He claimed that the economic base of society, the *infrastructure,* influences everything else, which he called the *superstructure.* The superstructure was said to include all other institutions: for example, families, education, religious institutions, and the legal system. Therefore, Marx believed that law reflected the economic base of a society and crime also was related to issues of economics and ownership.

Because of the need to make a profit and create surplus value in a capitalist economic system, there is an automatic class conflict built into the system between the capitalists, or the *bourgeoisie,* the owners of the means of production (e.g., the owners of businesses), and those people who work for the owners, the workers, or the *proletariat* (e.g., factory workers). Marx stated that ultimately law works to reflect the interests of the owners as a means of helping capitalism stay afloat. Otherwise, all of the workers being harmed by the cost-cutting efforts of the owners will eventually realize how they are being oppressed, rise up in **class struggle**, and create a revolution. This revolution will

●●●
Class conflict:
The conflict between owners and workers that Marx and Engels stated was built into the workings of a capitalist economy.

Class struggle:
The outward manifestation of discontent that arises after workers realize that their class interests are being oppressed in a capitalist system.

result in the end of the capitalist system and, according to Marx, a switch to a socialist, and then subsequently a communist, system. (Communism as he envisioned it signified the shared ownership of property among all people.)

Although not as widely recognized as Marx's influence on the field of criminology and delinquency, the ideas of William Edward Burghardt (W. E. B.) Du Bois have also influenced conflict theories of today, especially those that look carefully at the role of race and social class.[43] Like Marx, Du Bois wrote in the late 19th and early 20th centuries about issues of social conflict related to social structure. In works such as "The Negro and Crime," *The Philadelphia Negro: A Social Study, The Spawn of Slavery: The Convict Lease System in the South,* and *Some Notes on Negro Crime, Particularly in Georgia,* he examined issues related to the social position of black people, crime, and social control in the United States in light of the legacy of slavery and other injustices.[44]

Especially relevant to conflict theories of crime and delinquency that follow in his tradition is the idea that racial and class privilege largely experienced by white people in the United States allowed for a system of laws to be written and court decisions to be made that often benefited whites and harmed people of color, "treating the crimes and misdemeanors of negroes with such severity that the lesson of punishment is lost through pity for the punished."[45] He also considered the genesis of crimes committed by a subset of black people and stated that social injustices typically were at the root of these acts—the near destruction of black families after slavery and the various racist social practices that occurred during slavery's aftermath. According to Du Bois, many acts of delinquency and crime can be seen as efforts to resist racial and legal oppression. Whenever we consider the relationship of racism (the systematic subordination of people of color based upon and maintained by stereotypes of inferiority) and delinquency, we are drawing upon his legacy. As we will see later in this chapter, his ideas live on in modern-day conflict theories.

The Development of Conflict Theories of Crime

At the beginning of the 20th century, Willem Bonger, a Dutch scholar, built upon Marxist ideas and explicitly related them to the topic of crime in his book *Criminality and Economic Conditions.*[46] He forwarded the idea that capitalism is a system in which business owners are encouraged to dominate and take advantage of the others in society, the workers and the consumers, to make a profit. Bonger claimed that capitalism basically tears apart the social fabric by making people, especially capitalists, inclined to egotism, or selfishness. Crime, especially economic crime, according to Bonger, is to be expected in a system that dehumanizes and pits people against one another in the name of profit. To minimize criminal activity, he stated that a large step would have to be made—the redistribution of wealth that takes all people's needs into account and a shared ownership of the means of production (i.e., a shift to socialism). These proposed measures would shift the societal emphasis on domination to a focus on cooperation.

● ● ●

Racism: The systematic subordination of people of color based on and maintained by stereotypes of inferiority.

In the 1960s and 1970s, many radical or conflict criminologists picked up on the work of Bonger and his predecessors, as well as the work of labeling theorists, and focused on the role of the economy and class conflict in the production of crime.[47] Before examining some of the conflict theories that deal specifically with delinquency, let's examine one especially influential criminologist's ideas about how conflict theory can be applied to adult crime. This contextualization will allow you to see how the delinquency theories have built upon some of the fundamental ideas of conflict theory's take on crime causation and social control.

Richard Quinney's early works, such as *The Problem of Crime, The Social Reality of Crime, Critique of Legal Order: Crime Control in Capitalist Society, and Class, State, and Crime: On the Theory and Practice of Criminal Justice,*[48] established some of the fundamentals of a conflict theory approach to crime. His ideas, which reflected a basic form of Marxism known as instrumental Marxism, revolve around the idea that

> through the legal system, then, the state forcefully protects its interests and those of the capitalist ruling class. Crime control becomes the coercive means of checking threats to the existing social and economic order, threats that result from a system of oppression and exploitation.[49]

According to Bonger, living in a capitalist economic system encourages us to be greedy, competitive, and to turn against each other through acts of delinquency or crime.

Quinney stated that working-class people who challenge the status quo of society are often labeled dangerous or subversive by government officials. Whenever crime issues are considered by the government, rehabilitation of individuals is emphasized as the way to go (he was writing in the 1970s; in today's language it would surely be punishment), rather than a reconstruction of the capitalist socioeconomic system that actually produces crime.

Under a capitalist system, crimes of domination are committed by the state or government—crimes that involve acts of social control (e.g., police brutality, violations of civil liberties, and illegal surveillance), illegal government acts (e.g., assassinations and crimes of war), economic crimes, and social injustices against basic human rights. Quinney theorized that in the face of domination, some people accommodate, or go along with, the system of oppression at the heart of capitalism by engaging in predatory crimes (e.g., robbery, drug dealing, and burglary). These crimes are done in an effort to get money and to survive economically. People may also engage in personal crimes, or violent crimes (e.g., assault, rape, and murder), which are typically aimed at others who are also oppressed. And yet others consciously choose to oppose their working conditions and the corporations for which they work, through acts of resistance that may or may not be illegal (e.g., sabotaging the production of items on an assembly line or protesting a company). Although the type of Marxism that Quinney utilized in his theory is a basic form of Marxism, many other scholars have built upon his conflict tradition when studying crime and delinquency.

Conflict Theories of Delinquency

There are not many conflict theorists focused specifically on delinquency;[50] many conflict theories have been written to address both adult and juvenile behaviors. David M. Gordon's work is a case in point. In his 1973 article "Capitalism, Class, and Crime in America," he presented a critique of capitalism and its relationship to both crime and delinquency. Gordon discussed society's obsessive focus on youth crimes against property and the disproportionate concern or fear aimed at young black youth. He stated that the oppressed of society, the poor and people of color, are channeled into prisons and eventually into a cycle of parole and recidivism, to stop any potential challenges to the injustice of the capitalist system. Imprisonment accomplishes a number of things:

on the MEDIA •••

Online Analysis of Miscarriages of Youth Justice

The Center for the Wrongful Convictions of Youth, which is part of the Bluhm Legal Clinic at Northwestern Law, uses online resources to communicate information about unjust juvenile sentences in the United States. They have created an interactive map that allows users to learn about laws governing youth around the United States. An especially powerful feature is the ability to click on states that are highlighted to find information about juvenile legal cases that involved false accusations or false confessions and ultimately resulted in punishment for acts that the youths didn't do. They also have posted an online video lecture by the post-conviction lawyers of Brendan Dassey, whose case was featured in the Netflix documentary series, *Making a Murderer*. In the video lecture, "Brendan Dassey: A True Story of a False Confession," attorneys Laura Nirider and Steven Drizin discuss topics such as coerced confessions, pretrial publicity, and how legal documentaries affect the cases of both juveniles and adults.

DISCUSSION QUESTIONS

1. How can labeling theory and conflict theory be used to analyze the topic of false accusations, coerced confessions, and unjust detention of youth?

2. In what ways do you think documentaries on specific legal cases influence their processes and outcomes?

Sources: Center on Wrongful Convictions of Youth. (2016). *CWCY Spotlight* (video lecture). Retrieved from http://www.law.northwestern.edu/legalclinic/wrongfulconvictionsyouth; Center on Wrongful Convictions of Youth. (2016). NationalOutlook: Laws Governing Youth (map). Retrieved from http://www.law.northwestern.edu/legalclinic/wrongfulconvictionsyouth/map

---

first, it limits any acts of resistance that those harmed the most by the system can wage because many voices are silenced; second, it increases any delinquency or criminality on the part of the imprisoned people because they are now part of an angry, violent system in which crime is a part of daily life; and, third, it stigmatizes and shuts people out of jobs and lucrative legitimate opportunities if released from prison. The system breeds class and racial antagonisms and prevents fruitful social movement organizing on the whole. According to Gordon, you can't rise up if the workings of the system are actively keeping you down at every turn.

David F. Greenberg was one of the first scholars to use a Marxist lens to focus specifically on delinquency.[51] In "Delinquency and the Age Structure of Society," Greenberg examined the fact that juvenile delinquency involvement peaked during the early high school years and generally decreased with age. He claimed that this could be explained by looking at juveniles' position in the labor market over time. Greenberg stated that the ability for youth to get jobs in their teenage years was hampered historically by various factors related to the capitalist economy in the United States; labor laws, mandatory schooling laws, and the need to exclude large numbers of possible employees from the economy to keep jobs for adults. Yet in spite of that, the pressure on youth to have the funds to pursue a conventional social life remained high. In the face of social pressures to have money, and little availability of money through paid work, youth were more apt to commit acts of theft. He said that this held true for boys and girls and that an increase in girls' participation in theft in the 1970s was not related to a change in gender roles during that time period as some theorized (as you will see in the liberal feminist section later in this chapter), but instead was simply related to the lessening of youth's economic power at that time. Greenberg claimed that as youth aged they strengthened their self-esteem through other means besides spending money on their social lives and their ability to earn money legitimately expanded as well, leading to a decrease in economically motivated acts of delinquency.

In addition to his focus on theft, Greenberg considered other acts of delinquency (i.e., fighting and vandalism) as responses to school systems that focused on limiting students' freedom to act. He stated that a lot of the school procedures, as well as the content of what the students are taught, are a means of preparing the students to enter a capitalist system that rewards following rules, acting predictably, and following the status quo when they are adults. Acts of delinquency that do not result in any sort of economic value to the youth who engage in them can be seen as a form of rebellion or disengagement with the capitalist system. Although this was traditionally more common among lower-class youth, Greenberg stated it also holds true for youth of all social classes who see the flaws in the capitalist system and are fed up with it. When youth decide to drop out or leave school, they are often happier with the lack of social control, they often feel less controlled and degraded, and as a result they engage in fewer acts of delinquency than they did when they were in school. His discussion of the different effects of this process on white youth and youth of color implicitly picked upon on the observations posed by Du Bois and was later mirrored in the work of other conflict theorists.

What do you think about Greenberg's claim that some acts of theft and other forms of delinquency are related to the fact that youth are shut out of many job opportunities because of their age, yet they are bombarded with societal messages encouraging them to spend money and become consumers?

Mark Colvin and John Pauly developed another Marxist theory of delinquency in 1983. In their article "A Critique of Criminology: Toward an Integrated Structural Marxist Theory of Delinquency Production," Colvin and Pauly considered the ways in which the capitalist economy structures the lives of working adults and their children. They theorized that adults who have working-class jobs are often subjected to coercive authority in their day-to-day lives (e.g., they may be yelled at or micro-managed). These workers, when they go home and parent their own children, may do so in ways that are physical, punitive, and/or "erratic"[52]—fluctuating from a punitive approach to an overly lenient one—which increases the possibility of creating a negative bond between the parent and the child. Children with negative bonds to their parents often feel negatively toward the authority figures in school as well, which translates to poor performance on IQ tests and in the classroom in general. They will then tend to be tracked into low-level, highly coercive classrooms in which children are expected to misbehave. They pick up on these cues, and teachers label them as troublemakers and slow learners. In addition, youth who live in lower-income neighborhoods will be going to schools with fewer resources, and the system of rewards and punishments will not be one that can rely on money or prizes, so coercive systems of social control are more likely to be the norm (i.e., you don't get a prize for behaving, but you do not get humiliated or yelled at if you behave).

These factors in and of themselves prime children to act out in delinquent behaviors. If they are inclined to do so, Colvin and Pauly state, friendship groups can play an important role,[53] and a young person may become part of a **criminal delinquent subculture**, in which youth commit acts of delinquency as a means to an end—usually to obtain something material or monetary to gain status in the group—or a **conflict delinquent subculture**, in which youth oppose the mainstream through violence, underground economies, and/ or gang activity because of a lack of opportunities to succeed. Negative bonding to authority figures plays a role in both delinquent subcultures (first introduced in Chapter 5), but particularly in the conflict subculture.

There has been mixed empirical support for Colvin and Pauly's theory of delinquency.[54] It is difficult to test for a number of reasons, but primarily because it requires getting into the homes of those being studied and examining parenting styles and bonding firsthand. Sally Simpson and Lori Elis broadened the scope of the Colvin and Pauly's original analysis to include a look at how gender and race played a role in relationships to authority in the workplace, the home, and friendship circles.[55] In general, they found experiences with disadvantaged schools, coercive authority, and peer groups were related to serious patterned delinquency in the manner outlined by the theory. At the conclusion of their study, Simpson and Elis surmised that girls and boys, women and men, are subjected to different types of control at the workplace and the home and that this fact needs to be integrated into the structural Marxist theory of delinquency in order for it to be more comprehensive. Social class structure is important, but it plays a more complicated role in youth's lives than Colvin and Pauly imagined.

Many examinations of the conflict tradition in crime and delinquency have continued to examine this complex relationship between social class, race, class, gender, social control, and delinquency.[56] In the next section of this chapter, we will examine a related set of theories that also examines these relationships: feminist theories.

FEMINIST THEORIES: A FOCUS ON GENDER AND INTERSECTIONALITY

As noted at the outset of this chapter, feminist theories share a lot in common with labeling theories and conflict theories. Feminist theories of delinquency are best known for their analysis of the role of gender in delinquency, yet as you can observe from our discussion of the other perspectives earlier in this chapter, modern-day labeling and conflict theories also consider gender as an important factor in creating delinquency. In this section, we will back up a bit and consider some of the most important concepts that have been forwarded in the name of feminist criminology and feminist studies of delinquency. What differentiates theories labeled as feminist is a matter of emphasis—feminist theorists of gender and delinquency not only tend to study the issue of gender but are committed to actively changing the world to be a more just one, for girls and women, as well as for boys and men. It amounts to what feminist scholars have long called "walking the talk" or engaging in real-world practices that go hand in hand with the study of social problems and concerns.

If we go back to the scenario about Cecilia provided at the beginning of this chapter, and consider it from a feminist perspective, we are open to looking at it a number of ways. The reason for this is there is not just a single feminist perspective, but multiple feminist perspectives as we will soon discuss. In spite of their differences, all feminist perspectives share a concern with gender issues and the way in which the social roles of "boy," "girl," "man," and "woman" play out in everyday life to advantage some and disadvantage others. In Cecilia's case, a feminist observer would hone in on the abuse that Cecilia

Criminal delinquent subculture: A group in which youth commit acts of delinquency to obtain something material or monetary to gain status.

Conflict delinquent subculture: A group in which youth oppose the mainstream through violence, undergrounds economies and/or gain activities.

In the News

Teen Computer Hacker Arrested for Targeting U.S. Government Employees

On February 12, 2016 a 16-year-old boy known online by the name of "Cracka" was arrested by British law enforcement because he was suspected of conducting hacks on U.S. intelligence officials in conjunction with a group that calls itself "Crackas With Attitude" (CWA). Cracka, in addition to two of his online companions in CWA, was arrested under suspicion of numerous illegal acts, including breaking into the e-mails of U.S. Central Intelligence Agency Director John Brennan (and sharing his documents on WikiLeaks) and the Direc-

tor of National Intelligence James R. Clapper. In addition, Cracka is suspected of being involved with a hack that resulted in the publishing of the details related to 20,000 Federal Bureau of Investigation employees. He was interviewed by a newspaper in 2015, and he expressed at that time that his hacking was inspired by his dislike of U.S. foreign policy and support for Palestinians. (Of note: He has also been suspected of rerouting the National Intelligence Director's incoming calls to the Free Palestine Movement.)

DISCUSSION QUESTION

1. How would a conflict theorist account for Cracka's behavior and those of his CWA youth colleagues?

Sources: CBS News (2016, Feb. 12). Teen Who Allegedly Hacked CIA Chief's AOL Account in Custody. Retrieved from http://www.cbsnews.com/news/cracka-teen-hacker-cia-director-john-brennan-aol-email-account-custody; Franchesci-Bicchierai, L., & Cox, J. (2016, Feb. 12). Teen Allegedly Behind CIA, FBI Breaches: "They are trying to ruin my life." *Motherboard News.* Retrieved from http://motherboard.vice.com/read/uk-police-arrest-teenage-hacker-cia-john-brennan-fbi-cyberattacks; Perez, E. (2016, Feb. 12). First on CNN: British Police Nab Alleged 'Crackas' Hacker. *CNN News.* Retrieved from http://www.cnn.com/2016/02/11/politics/fbi-british-police-crackas-hacker/

faced at school, and the inadequate response of the school principal, Mr. Thorton, to her victimization. This victimization would be seen as directly related to the delinquency that Cecilia later took part in; because she felt unsafe at school and she was frightened to experience another incident in which she was harmed and ignored, she looked to peers outside of school to keep her company. Eventually, she fell into engaging in acts of delinquency with them. Later in this section, after we describe some of the major feminist traditions, we will refer back to Cecilia's scenario one last time, to consider how feminist scholars might also focus on a variety of other factors in the scenario as being especially important to the creation of delinquency.

The Origins of Feminist Theories

To elaborate on the origins of the many feminist theories that exist would take an entire book itself, so in this part of the chapter we will simply present an abbreviated discussion that frames feminist thinking related to crime and delinquency in its bigger context.

Although feminist theorizing about social life is typically traced back to what is known as the "first wave" of the women's movement, which occurred in the late 1800s and early 1900s, feminist theorists of the "second wave" of the women's movement, in the late 1960s and early 1970s, began garnering a lot of attention to their ideas. That period in history was characterized by a lot of social movement activity—people were working for social change around issues related to causes such as women's rights, civil rights, and the peace movement (as a reaction to the Vietnam War). Today, we are in the period of the "third wave" of feminism, one in which the importance of paying attention to the varied life experiences of women around the world is central to feminist analysis.[57] Although they differ slightly in the way in which they imagine gender concerns to take shape in our world, feminist theories generally agree on the following:

- Gender is not a natural fact but a complex social, historical, and cultural product;

- Gender and gender relations order social institutions in fundamental ways;

- Gender relations and constructs of masculinity and femininity are not symmetrical but are based on an organizing principle of men's superiority and social and political-economic dominance over women;

- Systems of knowledge reflect men's view of the natural and social world; and

- Women should be at the center of intellectual inquiry, not peripheral, invisible, or appendages to men.[58]

There are many different ways to categorize the various types of feminist theories, but one popular way to divide them is into the major groups shown in Table 6.1.

As Amanda Burgess-Proctor explained, in the 21st century, one of the most promising approaches to feminist theorizing is multicultural feminism.[59] Multicultural feminists (e.g., Maxine Baca Zinn and Bonnie Thornton Dill)[60] build upon the work of Patricia Hill Collins and Kimberle Crenshaw by putting the concept of intersectionality at the center of social issues analysis.[61]

Intersectionality (also discussed in Chapter 1) is the idea that to truly understand the social experience of others you have to consider the ways in which they experience race, class, gender, age, sexuality, and ability—all of these variables simultaneously affect a person's experience of the world. By using this sophisticated conceptual lens, we can better understand how a given person can be oppressed in some ways, and be privileged in other ways; it allows for a nuanced investigation of our social reality.[62]

● ● ●

Intersectionality: The ways in which race, ethnicity, class, gender, age, sexuality, and ability (and other social factors) interact to shape a person's social experience.

Now that we have considered some of the types of feminist theories, we can look back on Cecilia's scenario from the beginning of the chapter and think about what feminist theorists might focus on if they were to analyze it. Liberal feminist thinkers would focus on the need for rules to be created and enforced at school to make girls feel safe, and ultimately to prevent delinquency and other harms. Radical feminists would assert that the school's administration needed to be changed to stop the sexist practices of the school principal, and would see Cecilia's delinquency as an unsurprising response to the abuse she experienced. They would advocate for the creation of safe spaces for girls to talk about their concerns and experiences at the school. Marxist and socialist feminists would add a focus

TABLE 6.1 Popular Types of Feminist Theory

FEMINIST THEORY	FOCUS	ADDRESSING INEQUITIES
Liberal feminism	Primarily focuses upon the effects of the different socialization and social treatment of boys and girls and men and women	Equal legal and social rights for all is seen as the way to address gender inequities.
Radical feminism	Primarily focuses upon the effect of the patriarchal society, or a society in which most power is held in the hands of men, on girls and women. **Sexism**, the systematic subordination of girls and women based upon and maintained by ideas about their inferiority, is a primary concern of radical feminists.	Domination of women and girls is thought to be central to gender inequities, and an eradication of patriarchy is thought to be the way to address gender inequities.
Marxist feminism	Focuses upon the role of economics and class issues in society. As we discussed previously in the Marxist section of this chapter, Marxism is concerned with the injustices that occur at the hands of the upper socioeconomic classes and that disproportionately harm the lower socioeconomic classes. Marxist feminists are concerned with how the dynamic often harms women and girls because they are the most vulnerable members of the labor market and are tracked into some of the lowest-paying jobs that can be found in a given society.	Marxist feminists see the end of capitalism and the creation of a socialist society, and then a communist society in which property is commonly owned, as a way to address gender injustice.
Socialist feminism	Brings the ideas of the radical and Marxist feminists together. Thus, there is a focus on the effect of both patriarchy and the capitalist economy on society.	Socialist feminists believe that big changes are needed to address gender inequities and that both patriarchy and capitalism need to be done away with and replaced with systems that share power among classes and genders of people.
Critical race feminism	Primarily focuses on race and its interaction with sexism. Critical race feminists advocate shifting the focus from white, middle-class, or privileged women and looking to the experiences of women of color as a means of understanding the many faces of sexism.	According to critical race feminists, racism and sexism are the core injustices that need to be addressed—the most predominant gender inequities today.
Postmodern feminism	Primarily focuses on "deconstructing," or analyzing, the mainstream idea that there is only one truth. Postmodern feminists emphasize the multiple truths of women and the many different experiences of being a woman and experiencing oppression. Therefore, they are opposed to anyone who claims to know about "women's experience" because it is presumptuous and impossible to generalize.	Although many critics claim that postmodernism makes it difficult to organize people to create social change, postmodern feminists would state that analyzing the language and its ability to be used to give power to some and take away power from others is a method that can aid in the struggle for gender equity.
Lesbian feminism	Primarily focuses on **heterosexism** and how sexism often works hand in hand against lesbians, bisexuals, and transgender people.	Lesbian feminists focus on the need to eradicate both heterosexism and sexism as a path to gender equity.
Transnational feminism	Considers the processes of colonialism and globalization and the manner by which women in developing countries are negatively affected by the economic expansion of developed countries and efforts to superimpose Western ideas upon others in the world. Like Marxist feminism, there is a concern about the injustices of capitalism, along with a concern with challenging militarism—the use of military power to force changes in other countries and to resolve conflicts.	The pursuit of gender equity in this view needs to address Western efforts to make money off the backs of low-wage laborers in less economically privileged regions of the world and to wage wars in other countries as a means of gaining valuable resources. Women and girls are noted to be victimized the most from these endeavors.

According to some feminist theorists, intersectionality helps us understand the complex effects of race, class, gender, sexuality, age, and ability on young people's behaviors.

on the class issues and hone in on the male assailants' connection to money and power and how it influenced the administration to choose to protect the young boys' reputations and sacrifice Cecilia's physical and emotional health. Critical race feminists and multicultural feminists, concerned not only with gender, but with race, ethnicity, class, and sexuality, would also consider the ethnic and class conflict that Cecilia was facing at school. The fact that Cecilia was a Latina who was bussed from her working-class neighborhood, and that she was assaulted by white boys from wealthy families, would be seen as an example of racial, class, and gender privilege all working to victimize Cecilia, and eventually to create a situation from which she needed some sort of reprieve or shelter.

The Development of Feminist Theories of Crime and Delinquency

Feminist theories that focused heavily upon issues of crime and delinquency became prevalent beginning in the 1970s. Much feminist work tries to make sense of youth and adult misbehavior, so we will be highlighting both feminist studies of crime and feminist studies of delinquency in this section. Unlike other traditions covered in this chapter, there are not many feminist theories specifically about delinquency causation, simply because the focus of feminist work is primarily gender injustice, not delinquency specifically.

In 1975, Freda Adler developed one of the best known feminist theories of crime and delinquency, a liberal feminist theory known as the liberation theory of female criminality. In *Sisters in Crime: The Rise of the New Female Criminal*[63] she furthered the argument that female crime was not, as previous generations of scholars had often stated, a function of biology or physiology, but instead was primarily related to social factors. Women were not born to be better behaving, but simply were socialized to be so. She claimed that as the women's liberation movement continued to take hold, female crime continued to rise. Girls and women were being socialized to leave the realm of the home and to venture out into the workplace, and at the same time they were essentially encouraged to act more like boys, and men were encouraged to act assertively, aggressively, and sometimes even greedily.

The theory Adler furthered was that the newfound freedom that many girls and women were experiencing was allowing them to pursue criminal and delinquent opportunities that they would not have experienced earlier in history. She examined crime rates as found in the Federal Bureau of Investigation's Uniform Crime Report and stated that for nearly every type of major crime (except murder and assault) the rates for females increased tremendously since the 1960s, while the rates for males did not. She hypothesized that as women gained more equality with men they would continue to have rapid rates of increase in their official crime rates, and added that female crime tended to be economically motivated and typically was not violent. After the publication of her book,

●●●

Sexism: The systematic subordination of girls and women based on and maintained by stereotypes of inferiority.

Heterosexism: The institutionalized favoritism toward heterosexual people and bias against others.

The Equity Project and Justice for LGBT Youth

Social science research and firsthand observations of the juvenile justice system in action inspired a number of people from across the country to form the Equity Project (www.equityproject.org). This group, which includes justice professionals from groups across the United States, such as the National Center for Lesbian Rights (NCLR), Legal Services for Children (LSC), and the National Juvenile Defender Center, works toward "equity, fairness, and justice" for lesbian, gay, bisexual, and transgender (LGBT) teens who become involved in the juvenile justice system. Because of heterosexism labeling and stigmatization often are a part of daily life for LGBT youth who are forthcoming about their sexuality. As a result, these youth are disproportionately likely to have contact with the juvenile justice system at some point.

The Equity Project cites the following as some of the reasons why this is the case: LGBT youth often become homeless due to unaccepting families; they sometimes participate in acts of delinquency to survive, such as prostitution and theft; they are often made fun of at school and find it hard to excel and may drop out of school; and they often are isolated and depressed, which leads many to abuse substances as a means of coping. When LGBT youth become involved in the system, their due process rights are often violated—people working in the system stereotype and mistreat them; they are verbally, sexually, and/or physically abused while in juvenile institutions; they are unjustly prosecuted for having same-sex relationships; and their psychological and physical safety is often disregarded.

The Equity Project works to conduct research on LGBT youth in the juvenile court system to create positive reforms in the system by sharing data and advocating for youth. The group aims to make sure all youth have proper legal representation, ensure they are protected from harm while in the purview of the juvenile justice system, and help generate conversations and organizing online among concerned parties. As in the tradition of many critical theorists, the group is attempting to use theory and research to create concrete changes in policies and practices. The Equity Project recognizes that the causes of delinquency have roots in injustices linked to our major social institutions.

The Equity Project is working toward the humane treatment of lesbian, gay, bisexual, and transgender youth in the juvenile justice system.

DISCUSSION QUESTION

1. As the Equity Project points out, heterosexism and homophobia can have disastrous results for LGBT youth. Looking back over the course of your teenage and childhood years, what are some experiences that you can now recognize as involving heterosexism and/or homophobia affecting young people? Were there adults who actively addressed these forms of oppression either before or after they occurred? How did the individuals who were targeted respond? In delinquency? What are some groups in your local area that do work similar to that of the Equity Project?

Adler expanded her analysis to look at cross-cultural patterns related to gender and offending in the 1960s and 1970s, and stated that she found similar results in a variety of countries around the world.[64]

Although many feminist observers appreciated the shift in emphasis from theories of female biological and physiological inferiority to a discussion of the social basis of crime and delinquency, Adler's theory was met with a good deal of criticism in the years following its dissemination, particularly from feminists who studied Adler's work and stated that she misinterpreted the data she analyzed or that key parts of the theory were not substantiated, such as the notion that simply filling a particular role in the workplace would be that transformative without a corresponding shift in the power structure.[65] Scholars since have criticized Adler's work for its lack of attention to issues of race and class, as well as its simplistic consideration of gender.[66]

Carol Smart made another breakthrough in the world of feminist criminology with her publication of *Women, Crime and Criminology: A Feminist Critique*.[67] In this book she looked at lack of attention given to women's crimes and at the inaccurate assumptions made about women that were part of some traditional explanations for women's law-breaking. Like Adler, she debunked ideas related to the claim made long ago by biological theorists such as Cesare Lombroso, who stated that either women (and, by extension, girls) committed crimes because they were motivated by physiological factors, such as hormones, or, unlike other girls, they were born biologically defected and geared toward being criminals. Smart pointed out that these ideas about crime causation were flawed, and treated social problems as biological ones, yet allowed girls and women to be treated with especially serious punishments and treatments. To demonstrate that this was in fact the case, and that women and girls were not always given lenient treatment in the justice system as the popular stereotype indicated, she drew on work by a theorist who is perhaps the best known feminist theorist on juvenile delinquency, Meda Chesney-Lind.

Meda Chesney-Lind has done a massive amount of groundbreaking work in the area of feminist theorizing on delinquency, spanning from the 1970s to the current day. She was one of the first feminist scholars to point out the institutionalized bias against girls in criminological theorizing and in justice practices. In her 1989 article, "Girls' Crime and Woman's Place: Toward a Feminist Model of Female Delinquency," she noted that up until the late 1980s most theories of delinquency were **androcentric**, or male-centered.[68] In particular, she noted that theories of delinquency tended to be focused on lower- and working-class boys. She argued that what she called the "add girls and stir approach" was not sufficient to address the greater picture of delinquency—a picture that, for girls, included being arrested quite a bit for noncriminal status offenses, such as being truant from school, being in need of supervision, and running away from home. By ignoring the widening of the net of social control over girls through status offenses, traditional theories of delinquency miss the boat. Chesney-Lind pointed out that although mainstream theories of delinquency have often paid little attention to gender, those creating and maintaining systems of juvenile justice have long been hyper-interested in policing young girls' sexuality, particularly that of immigrant girls and girls of color, and placing these girls in juvenile institutions in the hope that they will not become "promiscuous" or "immoral." Chesney-Lind pointed out that a move toward feminist criminology involved looking at the bigger picture of **patriarchy**, or male dominance, in societal institutions and how variables such as racism and classism interplay with this dominance to affect girls' lives and influence their behaviors.

Chesney-Lind wrote another article around that time with feminist criminologist Kathleen Daly, which has become one of the most commonly recognized discussions of feminism and criminology. In the article "Feminism and Criminology," the authors outlined

● ● ●

Androcentrism:
An approach that places boys' and men's experience at the center of scholarly examination, thereby neglecting or ignoring aspects of girls' and women's experience.

Patriarchy: A social system that is based on "the rule of the father" and a male-dominated power structure that is evident in the majority of social institutions.

the ways in which mainstream criminology failed to address questions of gender in a meaningful way and considered a few of the most popular feminisms at the time, their perspectives of the world, and how those perspectives might be of use to the study of crime and delinquency.[69] (The perspectives that they focused upon at the time were less numerous than those that we discuss in the 2000s and included liberal, radical, Marxist, and socialist approaches.) Daly and Chesney-Lind traced the development of feminist scholarship on crime and noted that two questions had dominated such research in the years before.[70] The first type of research looked at what they labeled "the generalizability problem," whether theories created to explain male delinquency and crime could apply to the acts of girls and women. The second type of research was done in the name of looking at "the gender ratio problem," the question of why males commit more crimes than females. They made the argument that additional topics about why girls committed acts of delinquency needed to be pursued. They pointed out that patriarchal society allows girls, and women, to be exposed to abuse and violence that shape their behaviors. These acts of violence and abuse need to be at the center of analysis. Get rid of those factors, and you will eliminate a large amount of self-defensive delinquency on the part of girls.

● ● ●

Feminisms: The many theories that center on gender and the ways it is constructed and reinforced through laws and social practices.

In her article "Towards Transgression: New Directions in Feminist Criminology," Maureen Cain agreed.[71] She outlined the main concerns that had captured the attention of feminist criminologists historically: studies about gender equity in the criminal justice system and the fact that girls were treated differently than boys in the system, accounts about female offending, and female victimization. She claimed that it was important to utilize a new approach to feminist studies that transcended the typical liberal feminist angle traditionally pursued and to look at the bigger picture, because "what happens to girls and women in courts and prisons connects with what happens in the playground, in the family, and at work."[72] Cain forwarded the idea that the experiences of girls and women needed to be considered on their own—without any reference or comparison to boys and men. She made the argument for what she called a "transgressive criminology," which would shift studies of delinquency and crime away from using males as universal reference points. By doing this, she claimed that the many different standpoints of girls and women could finally be recognized, after decades of being obscured by an unquestioned focus on boys and men. Cain explained that feminist *transgressive* criminologists transgress, or go across the traditional boundaries of, criminology as a discipline; they study the lives of girls and women in their broadest sense first, and only as a result of being interested in big questions about topics such as gender, power, and

Feminist research finds that girls often experience a number of stressors, including trauma and abuse, which precede their delinquency.

violence do they end up studying questions of delinquency and crime. Cain claimed that boys and men should be studied too, but that yet another shift of focus was in order: Scholars needed to analyze society's constructions of maleness and in particular ask, what is it about being a boy or a man in society that is criminogenic or crime producing? The numbers demonstrate that most people involved in crime and delinquency are male, and rather than spending time studying why females are not more involved in crime, Cain argued that the focus needs to be on how ideas of what it is to be a boy or a man shape future behavior.

As Kathleen Daly in "Feminist Thinking About Crime and Justice" explains, in the 2000s feminist scholars are, on the whole, not so interested in creating general theories of crime and delinquency but are interested in developing theories about women's participation in crime and their victimization, considering how crimes and laws are gendered, and analyzing the language of law, policy, and popular discussions in terms of their consideration of gender justice.[73] Among the central questions asked are "How does sex/gender structure women's and men's identities and actions, and how, as active agents, do men and women produce the structures that shape them?" As we know, human beings create the very institutions that we then must answer to. Feminist scholars of delinquency, crime, and the criminal justice system look closely at how we buy into or challenge ideas of sex and gender as well, and how criminal justice institutions reflect these stances. Feminist criminology today has embraced a look at the multiple factors that affect human experience by moving beyond a focus on gender to focusing on race, class, gender, sexuality, and ability—as alluded to previously what critical race scholar and lawyer Kimberle Crenshaw famously termed *intersectionality*.[74] This focus on the complex interactions between social variables allows feminist scholars to counter the backlash against feminist criminology that has manifested in recent years with a body of rich and grounded data.[75]

Feminist studies of delinquency generally find that "the fact that they are less serious delinquents than their male counterparts does not mean that girls have fewer needs; indeed, a close review of their situations reveals a pattern of interconnected troubles that indicate the highly negative contexts and experiences that produce their delinquency."[76] Work that examines these interconnected experiences explores the gendered pathways that differentiate girls' delinquency from boys'.[77] In "Girls' Troubles, Girls' Delinquency, and Gender Responsive Programming: A Review,"[78] factors including trauma, destructive and distraught families, dangerous neighborhoods and unsafe schools, substance abuse, physical and mental health problems, as well as risky sexual behavior and need for special education were highlighted as being central to the creation of delinquency on the part of teenage girls and worthy of serious consideration. Emily Salisbury and Patricia Van Voorhis' quantitative examination of gendered pathways to delinquency found three pathways that led girls to incarceration as adults: childhood victimization that led to mental health challenges and substance abuse; unhealthy intimate relationships that facilitated victimization as adults, a reduction in self-efficacy, and substance abuse and mental health challenges; and challenges in the realm of accumulating social and human capital that result in difficulties with financial issues and employment.[79] The quantitative study of Natalie J. Jones and her colleagues also found that many girls follow gendered pathways to delinquency, yet they additionally found that some of the girls in their sample displayed a path that was in line with the traditional notion of the antisocial youth (i.e., had pro-delinquency attitudes, displayed impulsivity, and acted out more violently than other youth).[80]

In "The Struggle for Heterofeminine Recognition: Bullying, Embodiment, and Reactive Sexual Offending by Adolescent Girls," James Messerschmidt examined the effects of both gender conformity pressure and heterosexual sexual norms on girls (i.e., the effects of pressures of heterofemininity)who did not live up to dominant gender or sexual expectations.[81] He demonstrated that teen girls sometimes sexually offended in response to

● ● ●

Gendered pathways: Pathways to delinquency that are influenced by one's gender.

bullying by others, and because of a desire to satisfy heterofeminine gender expectations and to become sexually experienced, they took advantage of boys who were younger and socially less powerful than they were. Feminist studies, such as those by Messerschmidt and gendered pathways theorists, highlight the need for societal change to focus on violence and the various "isms"—sexism, heterosexism, racism, classism—to decrease the delinquency of both girls and boys.

CRITICAL THEORIES OF DELINQUENCY AND PUBLIC POLICY

As you can see, the various critical theorists all point to large-scale factors in their discussions of delinquency. These macro-level factors are not easily changed through social policies, but piecemeal efforts can be made to chip away at what are seen as unjust institutions, which critical theorists believe will lessen the prevalence of delinquent acts. Social policies that decrease formal labeling of juvenile misconduct are favored by labeling theorists. The least amount of formal intervention possible is seen as ideal by labeling scholars—this can be through informal diversionary measures when young people get in trouble for relatively minor acts of delinquency or decriminalizing or removing harsh punishments from acts that currently are penalized. Labeling theorists, like other macro-oriented thinkers, support policies that allow families and youth access to resources and opportunities to stave off delinquency. According to conflict and Marxist theories, a switch from a capitalist to a socialist economy (an economy that reduces economic disparities between people) would help reduce delinquency. Because this is a very unlikely scenario to occur in the United States today, critical theorists usually support the redistribution of power in whatever way possible, through progressive taxation, minimum-wage laws, comprehensive health care, paid parental leave, and policies to support families in general.[82] Feminist theorists are concerned with promoting just relations not only in terms of gender, but also in terms of race, sexuality, ethnicity, and class. A dismantling of sexism is a primary concern, and although all feminists do not agree on these issues, many will advocate policies that include the equal treatment of men and women, and boys and girls, under the law (e.g., equal pay for equal work), as well as the elimination of patriarchy and gender discrimination through education and affirmative action policies. Many feminists support antiracist and antiheterosexist practices and juvenile justice policies that make these practices real for youth both in and outside of juvenile institutions. An acknowledgment that abuse, neglect, and violence disproportionately affect low-income girls and girls of color is also seen as central to the improvement of delinquency-related policies and practices in order for them to be fully effective.

TABLE 6.2 Overview of Labeling and Conflict Theories and Feminist Theories

THEORY	THEORISTS	MAJOR CONCEPTS
Labeling Theories	Lemert, Becker, Goffman, Cooley	The labeling of youth behavior as delinquent increases the likelihood they will engage in similar acts in the future.
Conflict Theories	Marx, Bonger, Quinney, Greenberg, Colvin & Pauly	Laws reflect the interests of the powerful to the detriment of the working class.
Feminist Theories	Adler, Crenshaw, Chesney-Lind, Smart, Cain, Daly, Belknap, Messerschmidt, Jones, Salisbury & Van Voorhis	The social control of gender though laws and social conventions is related to the behaviors of girls and transgender youth.

As we look back on this chapter of critical theories, it becomes apparent that a wide variety of theoretical attempts to address delinquency and crime come from a critical perspective. Critical theorists are concerned with big questions of power and social control, and although you have seen in this chapter that some theories have been specifically concerned with addressing crime and delinquency, most critical scholars focus their work upon examining and transforming systems of inequity and oppression.

The critical perspectives include labeling theories, which are based on the theoretical contributions of people such as Edwin Lemert, Howard Becker, and Erving Goffman. Labeling theory gained popularity in the 1960s and 1970s, and highlighted the ways that the labeling of youth as delinquents and the corresponding negative reactions to them, such as stigmatization and punishment, could lead to secondary deviance. After youth are labeled with the master status of "delinquent" (or any other similarly negative label), their status becomes degraded in the eyes of others, and it is more likely that they will end up engaging in future delinquent acts (or continue on the path of a "criminal career"). Becker's typology of deviant possibilities outlined the ways that a deviant label placed upon a person may or may not correspond to one's actual behavior, and highlighted the fact that at the end of the day the label itself has negative consequences regardless. Labeling theorists also have pointed out that the control of young people's behavior is related to the efforts of moral entrepreneurs who begin moral panics over an issue and then inspire crusades to get a hold on whatever issue appears to be out of hand. Recent research in the labeling tradition has shown that moral panics related to delinquency often focus upon youth of color and, particularly, black male adolescents. In addition, contemporary labeling research has demonstrated that self-concept, social exclusion, and cumulative disadvantage are important factors to consider in order to understand why some labeled youth engage in secondary deviance and others do not. Considerations of how positive labeling can facilitate delinquency and how youth work to consciously resist labels are also important new areas of labeling theory explorations.

Conflict theories utilize some of the insights from labeling theory in their consideration of how power and socioeconomic class affect the creation of delinquency and the control of both delinquency and youth deemed to be troublesome. These theories are rooted in macro-level or big-picture analyses of economics, race relations, and social justice. Many variants of conflict theory build upon the class-based analyses of Karl Marx and Friedrich Engels and the idea that individuals from the working class, or the unemployed class, are more likely to experience the negative effects of power relations central to the functioning of a given economy. Laws themselves are thought to generally be more reflective of the needs of the economically powerful in a given society (capitalists today), than those of the least powerful in a given society. Many critical theories are also influenced by the race- and class-based analyses of W. E. B. Du Bois. Du Bois pointed out that many laws in the United States have traditionally benefited wealthy white people and harmed poor and working-class people of color. Crime and delinquency, in this perspective, can often be seen as a form of resistance against unjust laws and social practices. Richard Quinney's critical criminological theory of the 1970s is the best known modern articulation of how laws reflect the needs of the privileged. Critical delinquency researchers coming from a critical perspective in the 1970s (e.g., Gordon and Greenberg) emphasized the role of juvenile detention as one that affects communities of color the most seriously, one that helps stem any protest or opposition to capitalism and unjust laws or social practices, and one that increases the likelihood that the youth who are targeted will one day reoffend. The Integrated Structural-Marxist Theory of Delinquency (Colvin and Pauly) forwards the idea that capitalism affects workers in certain ways, and those practices of authority placed upon them in the workplace are replicated in the discipline of their children at home; these factors in turn affect juveniles' experiences of authority and social control and may affect the likelihood of participation in delinquent subcultures.

Feminist theories of delinquency are best known for their consideration of the role of gender in delinquency, and their emphasis on using theory to change the world to a more just one (i.e., praxis). In addition, contemporary feminist theories focus on intersectionality, and the ways in which race, class, gender, sexuality, ethnicity, and other factors work together to influence young people's behaviors. Feminist theories can be traced back to the "first wave" of feminist scholarship in the late 1800s and early 1900s, the "second wave" of the 1960s and 1970s, and the most recent and current "third wave" of feminist scholarship. Feminist scholars of delinquency have noted that there has traditionally been a focus on boys and young men in the research and have worked to analyze the experiences of girls and young women. There are numerous forms of feminist theories that influence delinquency scholarship today: liberal, radical, Marxist, socialist, critical race, postmodern, lesbian, and transnational. Feminist theorists focused on crime and delinquency (e.g., Freda Adler, Carol Smart, Joanne Belknap, Kathleen Daly, and Meda Chesney-Lind) have shifted the focus to girls. The majority of these theorists agree that the abuse and violence that girls are disproportionately exposed to in a patriarchal or male-dominated society need to be central to an analysis of girls' delinquency. Questions about how the experiences of girls in the juvenile justice system mirror the treatment of girls in society as a whole, about the gendered nature of laws and their enforcement, and about the ways in which gender expectations shape youth's delinquent and nondelinquent responses are investigated. Feminist scholars today focus upon the need to eradicate not only sexism, but racism, classism, and heterosexism. Indeed, all critical scholars agree that if such changes were to take place, we could expect to see a corresponding reduction in crime and delinquency.

EYE ON DIVERSITY EXERCISE: ARE CRITICAL THEORIES OF DELINQUENCY BEING PUT INTO ACTION IN YOUR AREA?

Are critical theories of delinquency being put into action in your area? In order to find out, begin by conducting some Internet research on activist groups related to juvenile delinquency and/or juvenile justice issues in the city in which you go to school. Then, take the following steps to collect data on the issue:

1. Count the number of groups that have organized around juvenile delinquency or juvenile justice issues in your city. If you are in a large city and there are many of them, simply start by examining 10 of them. If there are not any in the area of your college or university, examine the county in which your school is located.

2. Analyze their websites and statements of purpose. What do they state is the problem they are setting out to address? How do they define it? Jot down your observations on a piece of paper, and then step back and consider if their statements reflect any of the concepts related to the labeling, conflict, and/or feminist perspectives.

3. Next, consider how they are attempting to address the problem as they have defined it. See if the methods they recommend reflect labeling, conflict, and/or feminist perspectives.

4. Finish the exercise by writing a paper of your findings. If you have analyzed several groups, you may want to create a chart that categorizes the findings to easily gauge if there is a critical presence among activist groups in your region.

DISCUSSION QUESTIONS

1. Labeling theorists' fundamental concern is with secondary deviance rather than primary deviance. What are the strengths and weaknesses of this approach? What other theory do you think would work well with labeling theory to explain primary deviance? Why?

2. Several conflict theories of crime and delinquency were discussed in this chapter. Which one do you think best addresses delinquency today? Explain what elements of the theory made you choose it.

3. The idea of intersectionality is central to many feminist theories today. What does the concept signify? How does the application of this concept help us better understand the experiences of a particular young person?

4. Critical theorists often see youth's involvement in delinquency as a form of resistance against unjust treatment. What do you think of this proposition? Can you think of examples when resistance is related to delinquency? Can you think of examples in which resistance does not explain delinquency? List your examples.

5. In what ways do labeling, conflict, and feminist theories address power disparities? Which approach do you find the most compelling?

KEY TERMS

Androcentrism 174

Class conflict 163

Class struggle 163

Conflict delinquent
   subculture 168

Conflict theorist 162

Criminal delinquent
   subculture 168

Cumulative disadvantage 160

Deviant career 160

Feminisms 175

Gendered pathways 176

Heterosexism 171

Intersectionality 170

Looking-glass self 159

Master status 156

Moral entrepreneur 157

Patriarchy 174

Power 154

Primary deviance 155

Racism 164

Secondary deviance 155

Self-concept 159

Sexism 171

Social exclusion 159

Social inequity 154

Spoiled identity 155

Stigmatization 155

Symbolic interactionism 159

CHAPTER PRETEST ANSWERS

1. True

2. True

3. False

4. True

5. False

6. False

7. True

8. True

9. True

STUDENT STUDY SITE

$SAGE edge™

edge.sagepub.com/bates2e

Sharpen your skills with SAGE edge!

SAGE edge for students provides a personalized approach to help you accomplish your coursework goals in an easy-to-use learning environment. You'll find action plans, mobile-friendly eFlashcards, and quizzes, as well as videos, web resources, and links to SAGE journal articles to support and expand on the concepts presented in this chapter. Check out the website for original videos of former offenders discussing their experiences as juveniles.

PART 3:
THE SOCIAL CONTEXTS OF JUVENILE DELINQUENCY

CHAPTER 7

REUTERS/Mario Anzuoni

FAMILIES IN CONTEXT

CHAPTER OBJECTIVES ···

After reading this chapter, you should be able to

- Describe the nature and extent of family trends, including marriage, divorce, and unmarried birth rates

- Explain the complicated relationship between family structure and delinquency

- Explain the impact of family process on the relationship between family structure and delinquency

- Explain the impact of family process on delinquency

- Explain the nature and extent of child maltreatment

- Analyze the complicated relationship between child maltreatment and delinquency

- Explain the relationship between child maltreatment, parental incarceration, and the experiences in foster care for youth

In 2003 the San Francisco Children of Incarcerated Parents Partnership published a bill of rights for children of incarcerated parents. Based on original work by Gretchen Newby of Friends Outside, a California organization that addresses the special needs of families affected by incarceration, Children of Incarcerated Parents: A Bill of Rights recognizes that children's needs extend well beyond physical comfort and security. The following excerpt is from Parenting Inside Out, an Oregon-based program that advocates for parents' and children's rights while parents are incarcerated, and conducts a parenting program to increase parenting skills for those incarcerated:[1]

1. I have the right to be kept safe and informed at the time of my parent's arrest.

Many children of offenders are introduced to the criminal justice system when their parent is arrested and they see him/her taken away in handcuffs. The majority of police and sheriff's departments do not have protocols for dealing with the children of arrested parents; in too many cases, the resulting experience is terrifying and confusing for the children left behind.

2. I have the right to be heard when decisions are made about me.

When a parent is arrested, children whose chaotic lives may already have left them with little sense of control often feel even more alienated from the events that swirl around them. Adults they have never met remove their parents with little explanation, then decide where the children will go without consulting them.

3. I have the right to be considered when decisions are made about my parent.

Ask the child of an incarcerated mother what might have improved his life and his prospects and you're likely to hear some version of this answer: "Help for my mom." Even after years of trauma and abandonment, young people are likely to see their parents as troubled and in need of support, rather than as bad and in need of punishment.

4. I have the right to be well cared for in my parent's absence.

When a child loses a single parent to incarceration, she also loses a home. In the most extreme cases, children may wind up fending for themselves in a parent's absence.

CHAPTER PRETEST

Test your knowledge of this chapter's material by determining whether the following statements are true or false. Be sure to compare your answers with the answers on page 214.

1. There is a greater percentage of children in two-parent households than any other type of household.

2. Family structure is a stronger predictor of delinquency than family process.

3. Gender, race, class, and age have an impact on how juveniles experience family relationships.

4. An egalitarian household is one in which both partners earn the same amount of money.

5. Older children are more likely to be maltreated than younger children.

6. Neglect is the most likely form of maltreatment that children experience.

7. Black children have the highest rates of maltreatment.

8. Girls who run away from home are more likely to report sexual abuse than boys who run away from home.

9. LGB teens are one of the largest subgroups of teens to run away.

10. Parental incarceration affects all children equally.

11. When a father is incarcerated a significant majority of children are cared for by the other parent.

12. Foster youth are more likely to be absent from school than non-foster youth.

5. I have the right to speak with, see and touch my parent.

Visiting an incarcerated parent can be difficult and confusing for children. If the parent is in a county jail, the child may have to talk to him on a staticky telephone and look at him through scratched Plexiglas. If he is in prison, the child may have to travel a long distance to spend a few hours in a visiting room full of other prisoners and their families.

6. I have the right to support as I struggle with my parent's incarceration.

Children whose parents are imprisoned carry tremendous burdens. Not only do they lose the company and care of a parent, they also must deal with the stigma of parental incarceration and fear for their parent's safety and well-being. Researchers who have interviewed offenders' children have found them prone to depression, anger and shame. Many young children experience a parent's arrest as simple abandonment.

7. I have the right not to be judged, blamed or labeled because of my parent's incarceration.

Incarceration carries with it a tremendous stigma. Because young children identify with their parents, they are likely to internalize this stigma, associating themselves with the labels placed upon their parents and blaming themselves for their parents' absence.

8. I have the right to a lifelong relationship with my parent.

Separation is hard on families—but so, paradoxically, is reunion. Recently released prisoners face an obstacle course of challenges and obligations. They must maintain a relationship with a parole or probation officer; find work and housing despite a criminal record; and struggle to rebuild relationships with friends and family.

Losing a parent to incarceration is a life-changing event. Those who work with children impacted by incarceration can use this Bill of Rights to guide policies and procedures that can help to mitigate some of the trauma and can help children develop the resilience to live positive, prosocial lives.

Source: San Francisco Children of Incarcerated Parents.

This chapter is about family and delinquency. Most people would probably assume that when we say family and delinquency we mean how family life (most often thought of as structure—one parent or two—and process—for example, attachment or supervision) might affect youth behavior. Certainly this is a large component of the discussion, and we devote ample time to it. But there are so many more issues that fall under family. In this chapter we will examine how the family has changed, child maltreatment, parental responsibility laws, the impact and response of running away from home, the growing phenomenon of parents in prison, and the influence these issues have on the lives, experiences, and behavior of our youth. And, as with every chapter, we will examine the diversity of these experiences based on race, class, gender, and sexual orientation.

FAMILY TODAY

You might wonder why we would start a chapter on family and delinquency with a discussion of current trends in the family. We believe it is important to know what is happening in the family today since both the general public and criminologists see a link between the family and delinquency. Much of the discourse about the family and delinquency centers on the impact of divorce, family structure (such as the number of parents in the house), and interactions in the family. We focus on three important-to-know trends—marriage, divorce, and the unmarried birth rate—for the following reasons:

1. Marriage, divorce, and unmarried births impact the family structure in which children live.

2. Divorce rates and unmarried birth rates may be linked to more difficult life challenges.

3. Adolescent unmarried births are also considered to be a form of misbehavior or delinquency for which girls are monitored and socially controlled (you will read about this in the opening story in Chapter 8).

4. In a discussion of delinquency in which the likelihood of delinquency is being linked to characteristics of the family, it becomes important to know what these trends are doing over time.

Trends in the Family—Marriage, Divorce, and Unmarried Birth Rates

According to census data analyzed by the Pew Research Center, a record low number of adults in the United States are currently married.[2] Marriage is on the decline for several reasons in the United States. First, there is an increase in the number of people reporting they have never married (see Figure 7.1), but in addition, even for those who report they are married, the age at first marriage is increasing. In 2015, the median age at first marriage for women was at an all-time high of 27 years, and the median age for men, also at an all-time high, was just over 29 years (see Figure 7.2). Men and women waiting to get married until they are older means that they are married for less time over the course of their lives, and this impacts the percentage of adults who report being married in a given year.

In addition to the marriage rate declining in the United States, the divorce rate has been declining since its high in the late 1970s and early 1980s.[4] While the popular adage is still true that almost "half of all marriages will end in divorce," this is not an accurate accounting of the trend in divorce from year to year in the United States. According to the CDC, the divorce rate has decreased in the United States from 4.7 divorces per 1,000 in the population in 1990 to 3.2 divorces per 1,000 in the population for 2014.

Unmarried birth rates, in general, have been increasing since 1980.[5] For women between the ages of 15 and 44, the unmarried birth rate increased from 29.4 births to 43.9 births per 1,000 women between 1980 and 2014, although the rate is down from the high of 52.5 births per 1,000 women in 2008. But what might be most interesting in the trends of unmarried births is that the only age group whose trend is a steady long-term *decline* is girls aged 15–19. Their rate decreased between 1994 and 2014 from 31.7 per 1,000 to 22 per 1,000. For the purposes of this book, we would want to look at the unmarried birth rate for those between 15 and 17. There has been a long-term

With the median age of first marriage increasing, the median age at first birth is also increasing, from 24.9 years in 2000 to 26.3 years in 2014.[3]

decline for all race/ethnicity groups in this adolescent age range, too, but there are still significant disparities among the birth rate for adolescents aged 15–17. In 2014, Latina adolescents had the highest overall birth rate of 18.6 per 1,000 females (although this is the lowest rate for Latinas since 1989, when data began to be recorded for their ethnicity group). Black adolescents' unmarried birth rate was 16.7 per 1,000 females (off a high in 1991 of 79.9 births per 1,000 females). The unmarried birth rate for white adolescents was 6.3 per 1,000 females. Finally, Asians and Pacific Islanders had the lowest unmarried birth rate for adolescents aged 15–17, which was 3.0 per 1,000 females. It is quite significant that both black and Latino rates declined so substantially between 1991 and 2014, but we should not overlook the important fact that racial and ethnic disparities do still exist. The CDC did not report unmarried birth rates for American Indian and Alaska Native youth, although it did report raw numbers, but those are not comparable.[6]

We can see that these trends in the family offer a mixed assessment of the stability of what we might call the normative, or traditional, family. While marriage rates are decreasing, which some see as a cause for concern, divorce rates are also decreasing, and while the unmarried birth rate has increased substantially for most groups, it is actually decreasing for the group we are probably most interested in—adolescents. How do these trends influence family structure?

Trends in Family Structure/Composition

It is well documented that children, more today than at any other time in the past 100 years, live in a varying degree of alternative family forms.[7] In 2014, the percentage of children ages 0–17 who lived with two married parents decreased to 64% (from 77% in 1980; see Figure 7.3). Of those living in two-parent married households, 91% were

FIGURE 7.1   Current Marital Status, 1960–2014

% of adults 18 or older who are . . .

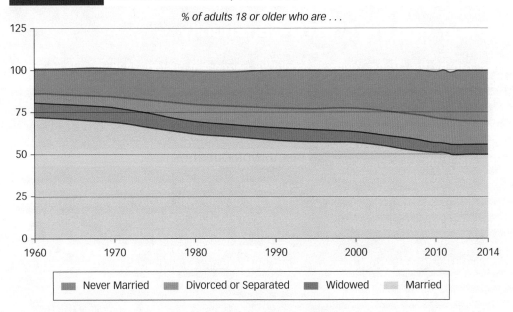

Never Married   Divorced or Separated   Widowed   Married

Source: Pew Research Center analysis of U.S. decennial census (1960–2000) and American Community Survey data (2008, 2010–2014), IPUMS. Retrieved from http://www.pewresearch.org/data-trend/society-and-demographics/marriage/

Note: Based on adults ages 18 and older. Percentages may not total 100% due to rounding.

FIGURE 7.2   Median Age at First Marriage, 1890–2015

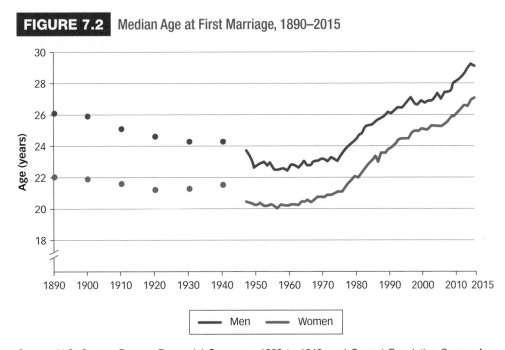

Men   Women

Source: U.S. Census Bureau, Decennial Censuses, 1890 to 1940, and Current Population Survey, Annual Social and Economic Supplements, 1947 to 2015. Retrieved from https://www.census.gov/hhes/families/files/graphics/MS-2.pdf

on the MEDIA ●●●

Podcasts, Parenting, and the LGBTQ Community

Transwaves is a podcast run by the Trans Youth Equality Foundation, a foundation that provides education, advocacy, and support for transgender and gender nonconforming youth and their families. These podcasts cover such topics as parenting a transgender youth through the coming out and transformational process, the legal rights of transgender youth, navigating school, and navigating bullying. Beyond elementary, middle, and high school experiences, this foundation and the podcasts talk about the college experience and what to think about while choosing colleges.

There are also many stories in podcasts about parenting, parenting toddlers, parenting teens, and being gay and lesbian while parenting. One of our favorite stories is about Trystan and John, who were young 20-somethings dating and enjoying a carefree lifestyle when John was told his niece and nephew were going into foster care unless he came to pick them up. So Trystan and John left to pick the kids up and then they

fought for permanent custody of them. It is an amazing story touching on gay and transgender parenting, schools, the foster care system, the medical system, and "flying the plane while you're building it."

DISCUSSION QUESTION

1. Listen to one of the podcasts discussed here or find one of your own on gay and lesbian parenting or parenting gay, lesbian, bisexual, transgender, queer, or questioning youth. What is one thing that was brought up in this podcast that you had not been aware of or made you think about parenting in a way you have not before?

Sources: Adapted from Transwaves. (2015). *Episode 11: On Parents.* Retrieved from https://soundcloud.com/transwaves; Trans Youth Equality Foundation. (2016). Retrieved from http://www.trans youthequality.org; The Longest Shortest Time Podcast. (2015). *Episode #60: The Accidental Gay Parents.* Retrieved from http://longestshortesttime.com/podcast-60-accidental-gay-parents/

in biological or adoptive households, while 9% were in stepfamily households (i.e., one biological parent, one stepparent; see Figure 7.4). The next largest grouping of children was single-mother families, where 24% of children existed. Four percent of children lived with single fathers, and 4% lived with neither their mother nor their father. Race and ethnicity are associated with the type of family structures in which children live. For example, in 2014, 74% of white children lived in two-married-parent households, while 58% of Latino children, and 34% of black children, lived under this family structure.

FAMILY AND DELINQUENCY

When teaching juvenile delinquency we often ask our students what they think contributes to juvenile delinquency. The discussions are always thorough and far-reaching, but one of the prime predictors of delinquency, our students always insist, is the family. When pressed on what they mean by the family, our students focus on two issues—family structure (whether the child is living in what is commonly thought of as a traditional household or in some other arrangement) and family process (or interactions; whether the child is attached to his or her parents or is supervised properly, for example).

It turns out that family has also been at the center of juvenile delinquency research for decades[8] and at the center of public discourse for at least as long (see the *In the News* box below). It is not surprising that both students and researchers would believe that an institution as important as the family would be expected to have an effect on juvenile behavior; what is surprising is that there is still so much we need to learn. For example, there is still some question as to whether or how family structure impacts

●●●

Family structure:
The compositional makeup of the family, such as parental type (for example, single parent or stepparent) or number of children in the household.

Family process:
The interactions and social exchanges that happen within a family.

FIGURE 7.3 Percentage of Children Ages 0–17 by Presence of Parents in Household, 1980–2014

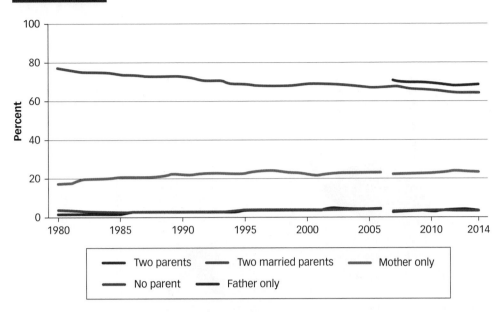

Source: U.S. Census Bureau. (2014). *Current Population Survey, Annual Social and Economic Supplement.* Retrieved from http://www.childstats.gov/americaschildren/family1.asp

Note: Data for 2014 exclude about 229,000 household residents under age 18 who were listed as family reference persons or spouses. The 2014 Annual Social and Economic Supplement (ASEC) of the CPS included redesigned questions for income and health insurance coverage. All of the approximately 98,000 addresses were selected to receive the improved set of health insurance coverage items. The improved income questions were implemented using a split panel design. Approximately, 68,000 addresses were selected to receive a set of income questions similar to those used in the 2013 CPS ASEC. The remaining 30,000 addresses were selected to receive the redesigned income questions. The source of the 2014 data for this figure is the CPS ASEC sample of 98,000 addresses. Prior to 2007, a second parent could only be identified if he or she were married to the first parent on the survey record. Prior to 2007, children with two unmarried parents in the household may be identified as "mother only" or "father only." Starting in 2007, a second parent identifier permits identification of two coresident parents, even if the parents are not married to each other.

juvenile delinquency. Does it have a direct effect? An indirect effect? Or no effect at all, once other family issues such as process are taken into account? Below we examine the different ways that researchers have studied family and delinquency, and—hold on to your hats—there is a lot of research!

Family Structure and Delinquency

Wells and Rankin propose that one of the fundamental problems with much of the research that focuses on structure is its "absence of any systematic conceptual specification of the broken home as a sociological variable."[9] The researchers note that most studies examining family structure define family in biological terms and ask the question "Is the child living with both biological parents?" Studies measuring family structure as the absence of a biological parent have reported differing findings. Some studies have found a relationship between intact (two biological parents) and non-intact (one biological parent) homes and juvenile delinquency.[10] Some researchers have reported a relationship for some forms of delinquency, but not other forms.[11] Finally, a number of researchers have found little effect of family structure,[12] instead reporting that elements of family process (which we will look at next) such as affection, conflict, supervision, and overall home quality are more important predictors of delinquency.[13] Very few of these studies offer a theoretical reason for their conceptualization of family structure. In Table 7.1,

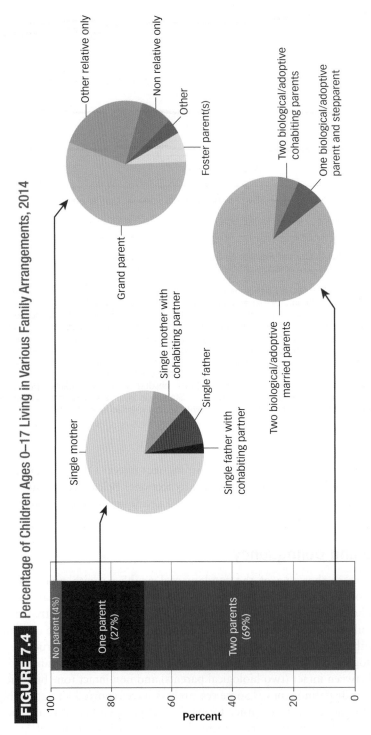

FIGURE 7.4 Percentage of Children Ages 0–17 Living in Various Family Arrangements, 2014

Single mother
Single mother with cohabiting partner
Single father
Single father with cohabiting partner

Grand parent
Other relative only
Non relative only
Other
Foster parent(s)

Two biological/adoptive married parents
Two biological/adoptive cohabiting parents
One biological/adoptive parent and stepparent

No parent (4%)
One parent (27%)
Two parents (69%)

Percent
100
80
60
40
20
0

Source: U.S. Census Bureau. (2014). *Current Population Survey, Annual Social and Economic Supplement.* Retrieved from http://www.childstats.gov/americaschildren/family1.asp

*Includes children living with two stepparents.

Note: Data for 2014 exclude the nearly 229,000 household residents under age 18 who were listed as family reference persons or spouses.

TABLE 7.1 Theories to Potentially Explain the Impact of Family Structure on Juvenile Delinquency

THEORETICAL ORIENTATION	THEORY	DESCRIPTION
Normative orientation: traditional in their approach to a view of family—in other words, they imply that families that stray from our understanding of the normative family are somehow broken or at a disadvantage while raising kids	Strain theory	This theory would suggest that family structure is important because it may represent a stressful event in a youth's life. In this argument, single-parent families might indicate that a youth has experienced the divorce of his or her parents or the death of one parent. Stepfamilies might also be considered stressful, in that there may be conflict between the stepparent and the youth as each learns how to interact with the other. Family structure might also represent a loss of coping mechanisms, if a youth turns to his or her parent for coping strategies but that parent is not living with the youth on a daily basis anymore.
	Social control theory	This theory might argue that family structure is important because it represents a difference or change in formal and informal controls in the family. In this sense, family structure might represent the argument that in some situations parents are less effective at parenting. For example, supervision may become more inconsistent in single-parent or stepfamilies than intact, biological families.
Critical orientation: more critical in their approach to thinking about the relationship between family and delinquency. These theories focus less on the link between youth, their personal families, and delinquency, and more on the structural and cultural contexts that families must navigate in the United States.	Feminist theories	These theories focus on the lack of resources that accompany certain family structures. For example, many single-mother families experience a significant decrease in financial resources after divorce that seems to be linked to lower female labor force participation, lower earning power, differences in human capital investments, and differential child rearing responsibilities.[14] Feminist scholars would argue that differences can be explained by a patriarchal society that privileges the work of men over the work of women. In this argument, it isn't that single mothers are ineffective at parenting; rather, they are disadvantaged by a system that does not value their contributions equally.
	Critical theories	These theories would focus on how family structure might impact the reaction youth receive for their misbehavior. For example, critical scholars might examine the official response to delinquency and whether family structure impacts this official response. Is it the case that youth who are from two-parent households may be more informally handled by the system, while youth from one-parent households are assumed to need the extra supervision and help that the juvenile justice system can provide?

we offer four theories that might help us understand a link between family structure and juvenile delinquency. In each of these instances, family structure may be the focus of the research, but we can see that family structure represents very different arguments for the relationship between family and delinquency in each case.

What Exactly Is Family Structure?

Intact biological families versus non-intact families: While it is sometimes difficult to tell, most research on family structure is of this nature.[15] Research measuring family structure in this manner (in which stepfamilies and single-parent families would be considered non-intact families) has come to a variety of conclusions. Several studies have found very little relationship between family structure and juvenile delinquency,[16] while other research has found that children from non-intact (or "broken") homes are more likely to engage in delinquent behavior than children from intact homes.[17]

Two-parent families versus one-parent families: Research measuring family structure as single-parent families versus two-parent families (in which stepfamilies are considered two-parent families with traditional intact households) has been inconclusive. Some research has found very little relationship between the number of parents in the household and delinquency,[18] while other research has found support for the hypothesis that family structure affects the likelihood of juvenile misbehavior.[19] This measure of family structure has also been correlated more strongly with official delinquency than self-reported delinquency,[20] and found to be a stronger predictor of male than female delinquency.[21]

Intact biological families versus single-parent families versus stepfamilies: This more complex family structure measure has recently been used in delinquency research. Studies using this measure actually offer several variations, taking into account important differences between biological families, single-parent families, and stepfamilies by categorizing them separately.[22] For example, Apel and Kaukinen devised a measure of family structure with *thirteen* categories to take into account intact families, single-parent families, stepfamilies, cohabitation, adoption, and foster families.[23]

The few studies that have extended the family structure variable beyond a dichotomy have reported varying results. Apel and Kaukinen found that family structure was related more closely to delinquency once family structure was more explicitly defined.[24] However, as with previous measures of family structure, some researchers found that while these measures had an effect on official forms of delinquency,[25] they had very little effect on self-reported delinquency.[26] Several such studies found no relationship between family structure and delinquency[27] after the inclusion of such family processes as internal or direct control.[28]

●●●

Attachment:

The degree to which juveniles feel close to a loved one such as a parent or grandparent.

Family Process

When we ask our students what they mean by family issues or interactions, we get a long list of issues in the family that might affect juvenile behavior. Our students talk about how much love children get, how they are disciplined, whether they can learn delinquency from their siblings or parents, if they have a good relationship with their parents, whether their parents watch them or set boundaries, whether they are abused or treated poorly, and the level of support they feel from their parents. We are sure, with only a couple minutes of thought, you could add to this list. Researchers also believe that there are a wide variety of processes within the family that may affect juvenile delinquency. Four of the most often studied are attachment, supervision, conflict, and discipline.

Attachment

Levels of **attachment** in the family have long been successfully linked to juvenile delinquency.[29] In general, studies have found that there is a relationship between attachment to parents and the likelihood to engage in delinquency. In other words, youth who report they are attached to their parents are less likely to misbehave. There are, however, several interesting variations: Attachment to mothers seems to be more important than attachment to fathers, and attachment is more important

©iStockphoto.com/szefei

The physical makeup of a family, such as grandparents as caregivers or guardians, is represented by the term *family structure*, while family process examines the level and type of interaction between family members, including juveniles and their grandparents.

from the CLASSROOM to the COMMUNITY

Parent Responsibility Laws: Should the Parent Be Held Responsible for Youth Behavior?

All 50 states have parent responsibility laws that require parents to pay damages in instances when a youth engages in vandalism or other property damage, and at least 36 states have laws that attach criminal penalties for parents to youth behavior. An example of such a law is California Penal Code Section 270.1, which was signed into law in the fall of 2010 and went into effect on January 1, 2011. Below is the language of that law:

CALIFORNIA EDUCATION CODE SECTION 48263.6 READS AS FOLLOWS:

Any pupil subject to compulsory full-time education or to compulsory continuation education who is absent from school without a valid excuse for 10 percent or more of the school days in one school year, from the date of enrollment to the current date, is deemed a chronic truant, provided that the appropriate school district officer or employee has complied with Sections 48260, 48260.5, 48261, 48262, 48263, and 48291.

CALIFORNIA PENAL CODE SECTION 270.1 READS AS FOLLOWS:

(a) A parent or guardian of a pupil of six years of age or more who is in kindergarten or any of grades 1 to 8, inclusive, and who is subject to compulsory full-time education or compulsory continuation education, whose child is a chronic truant as defined in Section 48263.6 of the Education Code, who has failed to reasonably supervise and encourage the pupil's school attendance, and who has been offered language accessible support services to address the pupil's truancy, is guilty of a misdemeanor punishable by a fine not exceeding two thousand dollars ($2,000), or by imprisonment in a county jail not exceeding one year, or by both that fine and imprisonment. A parent or guardian guilty of a misdemeanor under this subdivision may participate in the deferred entry of judgment program defined in subdivision (b).

DISCUSSION QUESTION

1. While the example of this California law targets "chronic truancy," many of these laws use much broader language, for example, "contributing to the delinquency of a minor"; in these laws, youth misbehavior beyond just truancy could get parents in trouble with the law. What are the pros and cons of such a law? Can you think of any instances in which these laws would be used in an unequal manner? Do you think such laws may be effective in curbing juvenile delinquency?

---

if the parent and child are of the same sex, rather than in a cross-sex relationship. And while, we are sure, parents would love to think how much they report they are attached to their children has an effect on their children's behavior, it seems to only be how much children are attached to their parents, not the other way around, that matters—although we would assume they are somehow related.[30]

Supervision

Supervision is a second extensively researched process within the family that is said to affect the likelihood of delinquency.[31] Supervision can be direct (a parent either is with his or her child or has direct knowledge of what the child is doing or where the child is) or indirect (for example, a parent knows who her or his child hangs out with and has met the child's friends). As with attachment, parents and youth disagree on how much supervision the child is under. It is fairly routine for parents to report they supervise their children more than the child feels he or she is supervised.[32]

● ● ●
Supervision:
A family process in which the juvenile's actions are either directly known or indirectly known by a parent or guardian.

Conflict

There is a fine line between conflict in the family and discipline techniques. Many researchers argue they overlap,[33] and it is true that in a household in which discipline is erratic or harsh there is probably a lot of conflict, too. But, for our purposes, we are going to talk about **family conflict** separately from discipline. Most of the studies examining family conflict have found a relationship between levels of conflict and delinquency,[34] although not all have found a relationship.[35] What is most interesting to note concerning these studies is the varying ways that conflict is measured. Conflict is measured as the level of intermarital conflict (conflict between parents),[36] the level of conflict between parents and adolescents,[37] and the level of conflict between siblings.[38] Juveniles who experience conflict with their parents or are subject to conflict between their parents are more likely to engage in delinquency than those who experience conflict with their siblings.

Discipline

Finally, the relationship between **discipline** and delinquency has been examined.[39] Discipline has an interesting and confusing relationship with delinquency because unlike the previous processes mentioned, we can think about this process in two distinct ways. Generally, discipline is described in one of two ways (these conceptualizations do overlap, but it may be helpful to note the distinctions between the two). First, discipline has been conceptualized as the existence of punishment—a fairly straightforward measure of level of punishment or discipline.[40] Second, discipline has been conceptualized as type of discipline rather than level or existence of discipline. This measure looks at the harshness or predictability of discipline rather than the mere existence of discipline.[41] Both measures of discipline do show a significant relationship with juvenile delinquency—in other words, if a youth experiences harsh discipline or erratic/inconsistent discipline, she or he is more likely to engage in delinquency.

DIVERSITY AND THE FAMILY

Many studies have explored the differing effects that family might have on boys and girls and their delinquent activity. Much of this research posits that boys and girls are differentially affected by family structure or family process, that they experience strain in the family differently, or that they are differentially controlled in the family. Most of these studies are tied to theories we have already discussed in this book—social control theory, strain theory, and power-control theory—but *all* argue that somehow boys and girls experience the family differently.

Gender, Family, and Delinquency

● ● ●

Family conflict: Considered a family process in which there is unrest or bad feelings between either the juvenile in question and his or her parents or siblings, or the juvenile's parents.

Discipline: A process that includes punishment for wrongdoing.

Many studies have examined the effect of family processes such as attachment and supervision on gender differences in delinquency. Some of this research suggests that family is more likely to affect girls' behavior than boys'. Girls have been found to have a stronger attachment to parents[42] and that attachment to parents is more likely to limit female delinquency than male delinquency.[43] But other studies suggest that boys are more strongly attached to parents than girls[44] and that a strong attachment to parents is actually more likely to stop male delinquency.[45]

Monitoring and supervision can also be related to gender in the family. Much of this research suggests that girls are monitored more than boys,[46] although the studies are split on whether supervision is more likely to stop female delinquency[47] or male delinquency.[48]

A. Fagan, Van Horn, Antaramian, and Hawkins found that parents did treat boys and girls differently, but they did not find that girls were always treated *better* (leading to more attachment and better supervision).[49] In fact, they found that girls reported being supervised more consistently and having a strong attachment to their mothers, but they also reported having a much weaker attachment to their fathers and more family conflict. Fagan and his colleagues concluded that socialization is a gendered process in the family and that both the gender of the children and the gender of the parents contribute to the relationship between family and delinquency.

Carter Hay examined the effect of family conflict on gender difference in delinquency using the strain theory to suggest that boys might experience more strain in the family than girls (for example, corporal

While disagreements are a natural part of a relationship, continued or extreme conflict can have a detrimental effect on children. How might parents disagree without negatively impacting children?

punishments, such as hitting or spanking) or that boys might process their strain in the family in different ways than girls (e.g., boys may act out in anger when they feel strain, whereas girls may not).[50] Hay found that boys were more likely physically punished than girls, and this was a strain that increased delinquency (and, more important, Hay controlled for past delinquency, so the boys weren't being physically punished because they were more delinquent than the girls).[51] In addition, Hay found that while both boys and girls experienced a certain level of strain in the family, they were different in how they dealt with that strain. Girls experienced a high degree of guilt with their strain, and guilt is negatively associated with delinquency (i.e., the more guilt, the less delinquency). And, finally, while both boys and girls experienced strain and this had an effect on their behavior, strain had a much stronger effect on the likelihood boys would engage in delinquency than on the likelihood of delinquency for girls.

Intersections of Gender, Class, Family, and Delinquency

Many studies have examined the intersections of gender and class, gender and race, and class and race and the impact of family. In the first chapter, we discussed how the experience that most people have is not based on just their gender or their race or their class, for example, but is based on the intersections of these characteristics—for example, being a young woman in a working-poor home might be different from being a young man in a working-poor home or a young woman in an upper-class house.

One area that has examined these intersections is power-control theory, which looks at the impact of gender and class on how children are supervised and socialized and the impact this has on delinquency. We spent a good deal of time on power control as a theory in Chapter 4, but here we will report the findings of research that has used power-control theory to examine the effect of family on delinquency. Hadjar, Baier, Boehnke, and Hagan examined the usefulness of power-control theory to predict gender differences in delinquency on a cross-cultural sample of youth from Toronto, Ontario, Canada, and East Berlin and West Berlin, Germany (after reunification).[52] This study compared the original model of power-control theory (since women are more likely in the home and men are more likely in the workforce, a patriarchal child-rearing pattern arises in which girls are controlled and expected to follow

In the News

Mothers' Job Curb Urged in Drive on Delinquency

It is 1943, and women in the workforce are being blamed for delinquency. Specifically, legislators are arguing that a "deteriorating" home is the cause of delinquency and that broken homes are the cause of a deteriorating home life.

MOTHERS' JOB CURB URGED IN DRIVE ON DELINQUENCY

Convinced that continued disruption of family life would ultimately lead to the necessity of adopting corrective measures for all children, the State Assembly Interim Committee on Juvenile Delinquency yesterday urged the enactment of laws which would prohibit the employment of mothers unless they could prove proper steps for the care of minor children had been taken.

At the same time the committee adopted a resolution calling upon Governor Warren to proclaim a special session of the Legislature for the enactment of this and other measures which the committee might later recommend.

HOME LAXITY BLAMED

The committee's views were made known at a hearing conducted in the State Building where testimony of more than a dozen representatives of public and private agencies dealing with delinquency was unanimous in the opinion that "deterioration" of home life is the chief cause of juvenile crime.

Most outspoken witness on the subject was Harold A. Slane, member of the California Youth Authority, who reported that more than 80 per cent of the juveniles whose cases have come before his agency are victims of broken homes—broken by divorce, by an attempt of both parents to work outside, or by sheer parental neglect.

Slane also attributed much of the delinquency to use of liquor by minors in spite of the great efforts made by the State Board of Equalization to prevent sales to minors.

Another problem about to fall to California, Slane added, will be forthcoming with the advent of a program initiated with some war industries to employ high school children for interspersed periods of four weeks. During these periods, Slane said, he feared there would not be sufficient supervision for these children outside of actual working hours.

Similar views were given to the committee by Paul J. McKusick, superintendent of the Fred C. Nelles School for Boys at Whittier. He said that of the 390 boys in the school and the 300 more on parole from the institution, the great majority were originally detained on theft charges. These boys, McKusick told the committee, seldom received proper supervision at home.

The committee also heard like views from Dist. Atty. Howser and from the members of the California Business Women's Council, whose members appeared under the direction of the organization's Los Angeles chairman, Mrs. Rosalind G. Bates, an attorney.

Composed of Lorne D. Middough of Long Beach, chairman, and Edward M. Gaffney of San Francisco and Ralph M. Brown of Modesto, the committee will conduct another hearing here today and then will move to Long Beach for a hearing on Wednesday. Thursday and Friday there will be hearings in San Diego. The sessions opened last June 29 in San Francisco.

DISCUSSION QUESTIONS

1. Is there a link between women in the workforce and broken homes?

2. What else was happening in 1943 that might have had an impact on youth and their behavior?

3. Could there be other political reasons linked to the late 1930s and early 1940s that might have caused legislators to want women to curb their workforce participation?

4. Do you think that the state should be able to call on women to not work?

5. Why not call on men to not work?

Source: Mothers' job curb urged in drive on delinquency. (1943). *Los Angeles Times*, July 27.

the rules more than boys, who are encouraged to break the rules more). However, the study acknowledges that in the last part of the 20th century and the first part of the 21st century, female labor force participation has been increasing, and a structural measure of class (that focuses on women remaining out of the labor force) does not accurately portray the realities of parenting today, and therefore an attitudinal measure of patriarchy was also used.

Hadjar et al. found that because of its history, in East Berlin,

> "real socialism" clearly has found its way into structural gender relations: more mothers work in East Berlin, and they work in relatively higher positions than in the West, that is, in Toronto and West Berlin. This difference is reflected in lower preferences for patriarchal gender roles among sons and daughters in East Berlin.[53]

In all three cities, stronger monitoring and control of girls is related to gender differences in delinquency—girls were less likely than boys to act out in delinquency. Class was found to have an interesting impact on patriarchal attitudes, although not the same relationship across all three cities. In East Berlin, structural patriarchy and patriarchal attitudes were linked to the lower class, in which it was much more likely only one parent was working, while in West Berlin, structural patriarchy and patriarchal attitudes were found in the upper class, where the family could afford to have the mother stay home.

Intersections of Race, Gender, Class, Family, and Delinquency

Mack and Leiber examine the intersection of race, class, and gender in their study of family and delinquency.[54] Specifically, they are testing the argument that because there is no adult male in single-mother households, these households by definition cannot have structural patriarchy. According to Hagan, Simpson, and Gillis, single-mother households are a "special kind of egalitarian family type" because "fathers are not an integral part of such households, there should be no manifest power imbalance between parents."[55] However, Mack and Leiber argue that it is too simplistic to think of single-mother households this way. In their study, they find that, instead of boys and girls having similar levels of delinquency (which would be the case in an egalitarian household), both white and black single-mother households have strong gender differences in delinquency. They also argue that given both the historical experience of black families and current social disadvantages, perhaps black single-mother households would be less patriarchal than white single-mother households. In this case we would see fewer gender differences in delinquency in black families than in white families. However, their study found strong gender differences in delinquency in both black single-mother and white single-mother households, thus suggesting that black households may not be less patriarchal. Mack and Leiber conclude that perhaps these gender differences in a household type (single mother) that power-control theory would suggest would see little gender difference can be attributed to strains that exist from the creation or continued existence of the single-mother family.[56] In other words, perhaps in the context of family structure (single families to be specific), strain theory is more equipped to explain gender and race differences in delinquency than power-control theory.

CHILD MALTREATMENT

We can discuss the importance of child maltreatment to many aspects of delinquency. Given its importance to the creation and structure of the juvenile justice system, we have opted to have an extensive discussion of the justice system response to child maltreatment in the last section of the book. In this chapter, we will discuss the nature and extent of child maltreatment as well as the relationship that child maltreatment might have to juvenile delinquency.

Visit edge.sagepub .com/bates2e to view a video clip about families and delinquency.

●●●

Egalitarian household: A household in which both partners (for example, mother and father) have similar levels of power.

The Key National Indicators of Well-Being give us a picture of the likelihood of maltreatment for children in the United States. The definition of **child maltreatment** includes two categories: **abuse** and **neglect**.

- Abuse is characterized by overt aggression, and can be categorized in three ways:
- **Physical abuse** includes kicking, hitting, throwing, burning, stabbing, biting, shaking, or otherwise physically accosting another individual.
- **Emotional abuse** is the constant criticism, rejection, or demeaning of the child.
- **Sexual abuse** refers to rape, molestation, and incest. Familial sexual abuse can be perpetrated by a parent, an older or more powerful sibling, another family member, or a legal guardian and can include both encouraging and rewarding inappropriate sexual behavior or the use of threats or force to engage in sexual acts.
- Neglect is characterized by deprivation or the failure to provide for a child's basic needs, and can also be categorized in three ways:
- **Physical neglect** means the child incurs a physical harm from the deprivation.
- **Educational neglect** is characterized by the failure to meet the child's educational needs, such as neglecting to enroll the child in school or allowing chronic truancy.
- **Emotional neglect** refers to ignoring the child's need for affection or engaging in the abuse of others, such as spousal abuse, in front of the child.[57]

●●●

Child maltreatment: The general term for child abuse that includes both abuse and neglect.

Abuse: Overt aggression that can be categorized in three ways: physical, emotional, and/or sexual abuse.

Neglect: The act of depriving or failing to provide for a child's basic needs.

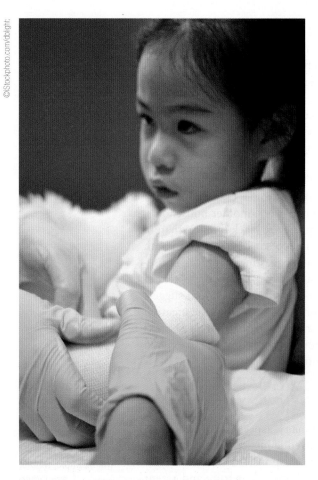

The younger a child is, the more likely he or she is to suffer abuse or neglect. Why might this be the case?

Figure 7.5 shows the gender differences in maltreatment from the National Survey of Children's Exposure to Violence II.[58] While the data explore exposure to many more violent and abusive situations than maltreatment in the family, for our purposes here we can see that boys are more likely to be exposed to physical abuse in the family than girls, while girls are more likely to be exposed to emotional abuse. There is no difference in the exposure to neglect in the family that boys and girls experience.

The data in Figure 7.6 are gathered from state reports to the National Child Abuse and Neglect Data System, and unfortunately not all states report every year. For this reason, we should be skeptical about discussing trends across years. However, the age at which children are most likely to be maltreated is likely more reliable. Figure 7.6 shows that the youngest children (those under 1 year old) have the highest rates of maltreatment (in 2013, 24 per 1,000 children), with the oldest children having the lowest rates of maltreatment (in 2013, 5 per 1,000 children). In addition, higher rates of maltreatment were reported for females than males between the ages of 0–17 (10 incidents per 1,000 for females vs. 9 incidents per 1,000 for males). Finally, black children had the highest rates of maltreatment (16 per 1,000), followed by American Indian and Alaskan Native children (14 per 1,000), Latino children and white children (both at 9 per 1,000), Native Hawaiian and Other Pacific Islander children (8 per 1,000), and Asian children (2 per 1,000).

FIGURE 7.5 Gender Differences in Maltreatment, 2011

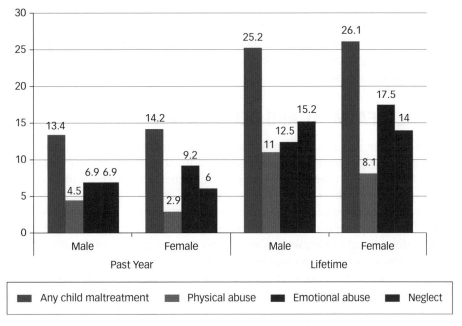

Source: Finkelhor, D., Turner, H., Shattuck, A., Hamby, S., & Kracke, K. (2015). *Children's Exposure to Violence, Crime, and Abuse: An Update.* Office of Juvenile Justice and Delinquency Prevention. Retrieved from http://www.ojjdp.gov/pubs/248547.pdf

FIGURE 7.6 Rate of Substantial Maltreatment Reports of Children Ages 0–17, by Age, 1998–2013

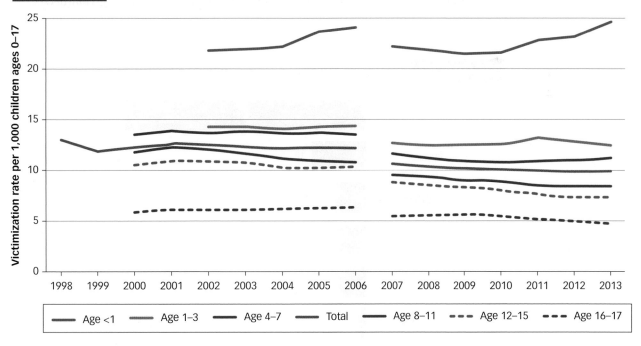

Source: Administration for Children and Families, National Child Abuse and Neglect Data system. Retrieved from http://www.childstats .gov/americaschildren/family7.asp

Note: The count of child victims is based on the number of investigations by Child Protective Services that found the child to be a victim of one or more types of maltreatment. The count of victims is, therefore, a report-based count and a "duplicated count," since an individual child may have been maltreated more than once. The number of states reporting varies from year to year. States vary in their definition of abuse and neglect. Data since 2007 are not directly comparable with prior years as differences may be partially attributed to changes in one state's procedure for determination of maltreatment.

It is expected that younger children are more likely to bear the brunt of maltreatment given that neglect is the most likely form of maltreatment, and those least capable of caring for themselves are the most likely to be neglected. Children are also more likely to be victims of certain types of maltreatment (see Figure 7.7) depending on their age; younger children are more likely to experience physical neglect, while older children are more likely to experience sexual abuse.[59] Figure 7.8 lists some of the signs that may indicate child abuse or neglect.

CHILD MALTREATMENT AND DELINQUENCY

Probably more than any other "family" factor our students believe that abuse in the family has an effect on juvenile delinquency. And much of the research on child maltreatment and later violent behaviors supports this belief. However, we offer a cautionary note at the start of this section. The relationship between child maltreatment and delinquency is more complicated than the most simplistic discussions of the "culture of violence" or intergenerational transmissions of violence offer. Less in the research, and more in the general public, we can see a deterministic quality to the discussions. In these discussions we see students suggesting that "if you are abused you learn to abuse others" or "if your parents hit you, all you know is to hit your kids when you have them." We caution that the relationship is much more complicated than that. While abuse appears to be linked, under certain conditions, to several forms of delinquency, many children who are abused grow up never engaging in violence. Mersky, Topitzes, and Reynolds caution,

> Despite consensus that exposure to maltreatment increases a child's risk of committing future delinquent and criminal acts, it is also recognized that many victims overcome early adversities. Rather than inevitably becoming "murderers and perpetrators of other crimes of violence,"[60] many maltreated children commit

Physical abuse:
Abuse that includes kicking, hitting, throwing, burning, stabbing, biting, shaking, or otherwise physically accosting another individual.

Emotional abuse:
The constant criticism, rejection, or demeaning of a person.

Sexual abuse:
Abuse that consists of rape, molestation, incest, and other sexual assaults.

Physical neglect:
Deprivation that results in physical harm for a child.

FIGURE 7.7 Percentage of Victims by Maltreatment Type, 2013

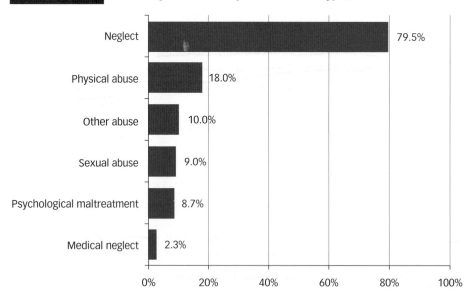

Source: OJJDP. (2016, February 05). *Statistical Briefing Book*. Retrieved from http://www.ojjdp.gov/ojstatbb/victims/qa02108.asp?qaDate=2013

Notes: A child may have been the victim of more than one type of maltreatment, and therefore, the total percent may equal more than 100%. This table is based on sample data reported by a varying number of states.

FIGURE 7.8 Recognizing the Signs of Child Maltreatment and Abuse

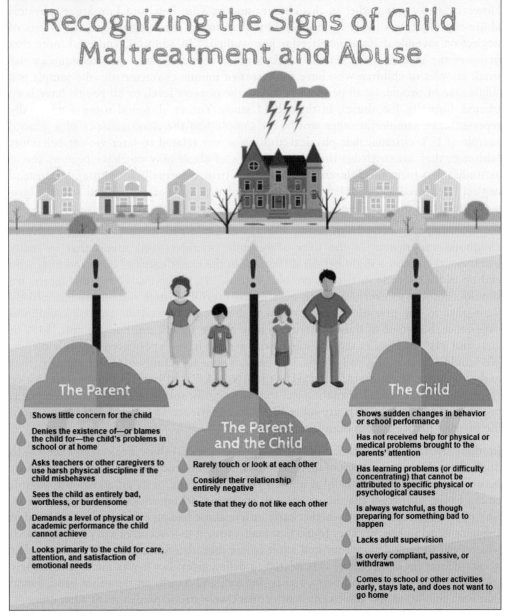

Recognizing the Signs of Child Maltreatment and Abuse

The Parent

- Shows little concern for the child
- Denies the existence of—or blames the child for—the child's problems in school or at home
- Asks teachers or other caregivers to use harsh physical discipline if the child misbehaves
- Sees the child as entirely bad, worthless, or burdensome
- Demands a level of physical or academic performance the child cannot achieve
- Looks primarily to the child for care, attention, and satisfaction of emotional needs

The Parent and the Child

- Rarely touch or look at each other
- Consider their relationship entirely negative
- State that they do not like each other

The Child

- Shows sudden changes in behavior or school performance
- Has not received help for physical or medical problems brought to the parents' attention
- Has learning problems (or difficulty concentrating) that cannot be attributed to specific physical or psychological causes
- Is always watchful, as though preparing for something bad to happen
- Lacks adult supervision
- Is overly compliant, passive, or withdrawn
- Comes to school or other activities early, stays late, and does not want to go home

Created using Piktochart.com

less serious offenses or avoid criminal activity altogether.[61] Therefore, research should aspire to differentiate maltreatment victims who do not offend from victims who commit various types of violent and nonviolent offenses.[62]

So the trick for researchers is to figure out what those conditions might be. And the trick for us, as members of society, is to figure out how to take what is often spoken about as an individual-level problem and elevate the discussion to one that acknowledges the role of our societal beliefs (e.g., the belief that families are private and we should not interfere with child-rearing practices or individual parental decisions except under the most dire of situations), the role of social structures (e.g., the safety nets that American society has in place for families in general or victims of domestic violence in particular), and such institutionalized privileges as patriarchy.

Many studies have focused on the impact that physical abuse has on later exhibitions of violence[63] and report that physical abuse is consistently a predictor of youth violence. However, as we saw earlier in this chapter and as Yun, Ball, and Lim argue, physical abuse is a much less likely form of child maltreatment than neglect, yet the effects of neglect on juvenile delinquency are far less studied.[64] In addition, Yun et al. note that many of the studies that examine a relationship between abuse and delinquency use small samples of children who have some sort of unique characteristic (the sample is a single race of people, or all people live below the poverty level, or all people have been treated, formally, for abuse). In their 2011 study, Yun et al. found using a nationally representative sample (in other words, the sample had the characteristics of a general sample of U.S. citizens) that physical abuse was *not* related to later violent behaviors (although they acknowledge that their measure of abuse may not have been as severe as studies that focus on children who have been treated formally for abuse), but instead neglect (measured as being left home alone and unmet basic needs) and sexual abuse were predictors of later violence.

Baglivio, Epps, Swartz, Huq, Sheer, and Hardt examined the prevalence of adverse childhood experiences in the lives of juvenile offenders and found that in many instances, there was a slight gender difference in the experiences of boys and girls who end up in the juvenile justice system (see Figure 7.9). When evaluating this figure, we should note that in every category, girls in the juvenile justice system are more likely than boys in the juvenile justice system to have experienced an adverse childhood experience, but some of those differences may not be significant. For example, 84% of girls and 81% of boys in the juvenile justice system have experienced family violence. We would say that, basically, girls and boys experience family violence equally (that makes intuitive sense, right?). But 31% of girls and 7% of boys in the juvenile justice system have experienced sexual abuse; that is a significant difference (the difference is big enough to say that girls are more likely to experience sexual abuse and end up in the juvenile justice system than boys).

In addition to the type of maltreatment (physical abuse, sexual abuse, neglect) another way to think about the complications of maltreatment and delinquency is when that maltreatment occurs. Does it matter if a child is abused very early in life or as an adolescent when it comes to the likelihood that he or she will engage in delinquency? Interesting question, isn't it? Mersky et al. studied whether early or late abuse had an effect on the likelihood of engaging in delinquency.[65] They found that maltreatment that occurred early (in childhood) was related to both delinquency and adult crime; they also found that maltreatment that occurred later (in adolescence) was related to delinquency, but it was much less strongly related to adult crime. Thornberry, Henry, Ireland, and Smith, on the other hand, found that both childhood and adolescent maltreatment were strong predictors of adult crime.[66]

Another study by van der Put, Lanctot, de Ruiter, and van Vugt examined child maltreatment and difference in offending behavior among male and female probationers under the age of 18 and found that the type of maltreatment did predict different behaviors in boys and girls.[67] In a study examining juvenile probationers who had either been not mistreated or abused physically, sexually, or in multiple ways, the researchers found that those who had been physically abused or abused in multiple ways were more likely to be arrested for violent offenses that those who were not maltreated. In addition, boys who had been sexually abused were more likely to be probationers for sexual offenses than probationers who had not been sexually abused (note, this study was conducted on probationers in general; both the victims of maltreatment and those who had not been victimized were already in the system, so the study identified the types of crimes they might be in for but not whether they engaged in delinquency in the first place).

Studies suggest, then, that maltreatment and delinquency are related, but we should be mindful of the conditions under which these relationships are more likely to exist.

● ● ●

Educational neglect: Neglect characterized by the failure to meet a child's educational needs, such as neglecting to enroll him or her in school or allowing chronic truancy.

Emotional neglect: Ignoring a child's need for affection or engaging in the abuse of others, such as spousal abuse, in front of a child.

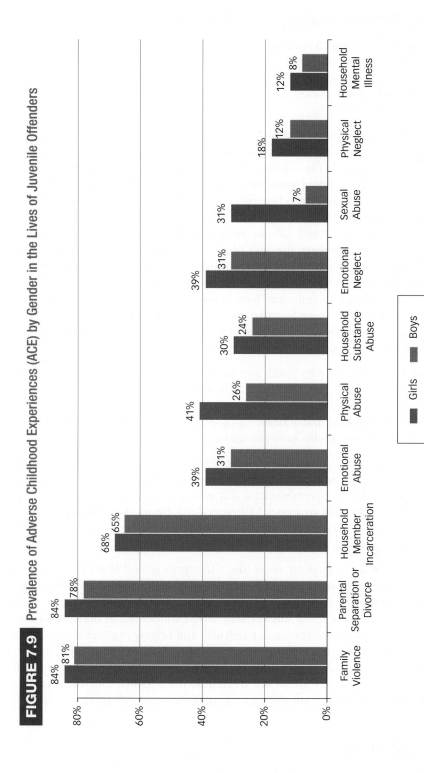

FIGURE 7.9 Prevalence of Adverse Childhood Experiences (ACE) by Gender in the Lives of Juvenile Offenders

Family Violence: 84%, 81%
Parental Separation or Divorce: 84%, 78%
Household Member Incarceration: 68%, 65%
Emotional Abuse: 39%, 31%
Physical Abuse: 41%, 26%
Household Substance Abuse: 30%, 24%
Emotional Neglect: 39%, 31%
Sexual Abuse: 31%, 7%
Physical Neglect: 18%, 12%
Household Mental Illness: 12%, 8%

Girls ■
Boys ■

Source: Baglivio, M. T., Epps, N., Swartz, K., Huq, M., Sheer, A., & Hardt, N. (2014). The Prevalence of Adverse Childhood Experiences (ACE) in the Lives of Juvenile Offenders. *OJJDP Journal of Juvenile Justice, 3*(2), 1–23. Retrieved from http://www.journalofjuvjustice.org/JOJ0302/JOJ0302.pdf

Moving from an examination of individual factors to one in which we assess contextual or larger societal factors, we will examine the special circumstances that have arisen when examining the impact of abuse on girls, specifically.

Girls, Abuse, Running Away, and Delinquency

A substantial amount of research is devoted to the experience of girls and their responses to abuse, especially sexual abuse. One specific response that receives a lot of attention is the relationship between abuse and the likelihood of running away. Are girls more likely to be abused? When they are abused, are they more likely to run away? And how many youth, in general, run away?

Tracking and counting runaways is more of an art form than a science. When we talk about runaways, are we talking about youth who run away to become homeless? Or just leave the house they are in for another, friendlier, dwelling? For the purposes of our discussion, we will assume running away means ending up on the streets. We have only estimates of the number of youth who run away, and those estimates often vary. Greene, Ringwalt, Kelley, Iachan, and Cohen reported that in 1992, approximately 2.8 million youth between the ages of 12 and 17 ran away from home.[68] In 1999, the estimate was that 1.7 million youth between the ages of 7 and 17 had a runaway or throwaway experience.[69] And in 2002, the National Survey on Drug Use and Health estimated that about 1.6 million youth between the ages of 12 and 17 had slept on the street in the previous year because they had run away from home.[70] It is unlikely that the estimates vary that much from year to year because the incidence of running away varies that much—this is much more likely an illustration of exactly how hard it is to get an accurate account of youth who run away and sleep on the street.

While there are many reasons why youth run away from home, family difficulty is the most likely reason that youth run away, and child abuse and sexual abuse are the most prevalent family difficulties linked to running away.[71] While both sexual abuse and other abuse are strongly related to running away,[72] girls who have run away are more likely to report sexual abuse than boys who have run away.[73]

Chesney-Lind argues that this connection between the likelihood of being sexually abused and running away for girls is a pathway to delinquency and continued victimization both on the streets and by the juvenile justice and adult justice systems.[74] Calling it "the criminalization of girls' survival strategies," Chesney-Lind argues that the juvenile justice system heaps added problems onto the shoulders of girls just trying to escape their abuse by arresting them for running away after they have left home.[75]

Beside the fact that runaway girls are more likely to report sexual abuse than runaway boys, why does this issue become a gendered one? We will explore this issue more fully when we examine the experience of girls in the juvenile justice system in the last section of this book, but a quick answer here is that studies tell us that the response to running away from the justice system in particular and society in general is gendered. While estimates suggest that boys and girls are equally likely to run away,[76] girls are more likely to be arrested and punished for running away.[77] This means that girls who are merely looking to end their abuse are treated as delinquents, and running away becomes the first step in a long path through the juvenile and adult justice systems.

● ● ●

Throwaways:
The term used for youth whose parents have kicked them out of the house.

PARENTS IN PRISON

In 2012, approximately 2.6 million children under the age of 18 had an incarcerated parent in federal or state prison (see Figure 7.10). How could it possibly be that so many kids in the United States have to visit a prison to see one of their parents? One of the

A Focus on Research

Rosario, Schrimshaw, and Hunter's Homelessness Among Lesbian, Gay, and Bisexual Youth

It is estimated that 5% of all youth experience homelessness in any given year. These episodes stem from running away or being **"throwaways"** (youth whose parents have kicked them out of the house). One of the largest subpopulations of runaway youth are lesbian, gay, and bisexual (LGB) youth, with estimations between 15% and 36% of all homeless youth being LGB. Rosario, Schrimshaw, and Hunter examined the effect that running away had on LGB youth.[78] In past studies, homeless LGB youth have been found to exhibit more anxiety, depression, substance abuse, and misconduct than homeless heterosexual youth, but the research had never explored whether LGB youth experienced increased strain on the streets that led to more problems, or experienced increased strain prior to becoming homeless. This study compared the experiences of LGB youth who had reported being homeless with those who reported never experiencing homelessness. Of 156 youth interviewed, 75 reported a history of homelessness—57 reported running away, 38 reported being "throwaways," and 20 reported being both. Eighty-one youth reported never being homeless.

The researchers found that homelessness for LGB youth was directly linked to later substance abuse and indirectly linked to misconduct. A useful mediating factor was social support from friends and family. Rosario et al. concluded that

> to the extent that some of the stressors experienced by LGB homeless youth are due to family conflicts, interventions with families

to reduce conflicts (gay-related or otherwise) may serve both to reduce stress and the likelihood of repeated cycles of homelessness (e.g., Milburn et al. 2009; Slesnick & Prestopnik, 2005; see Arnold & Rotheram-Borus, 2009, for review). To the extent that the stressors experienced are due to victimization or harassment by peers, intervention programs that seek to reduce peer victimization (e.g., gay-straight alliances and enforcement of anti-bullying policies in schools) can reduce experiences of anti-gay victimization (Chesir-Teran & Hughes, 2009; Goodenow et al., 2006; Walls et al., 2010). Programs designed to provide social support to LGB youth (e.g., gay straight alliances or gay youth centers) may serve to establish new, more supportive friendships that can replace or counter negative relationships. It is critical that interventions to reduce stress and provide support are accessible to LGB youth with a history of homelessness or who are currently homeless, given the findings demonstrate resources are needed by these youth.[79]

DISCUSSION QUESTION

1. What family interventions might be created in order to lower the risk of LGB youth becoming homeless?

---

strongest factors is the rate at which the United States has been incarcerating its population over the last 30 years. The incarceration rate (also known as the imprisonment rate) has increased significantly, (see Figure 7.11), and as would be expected many of those who have been incarcerated have minor children. A majority of inmates report having minor children—52% of inmates in state facilities and 63% of inmates in federal facilities. These data are limited in several ways. One of the problems with all of these estimates is that they have been collected from surveys of both federal and state inmates. So we only know about the children that inmates want to tell us about. If parents

Incarceration rate: The number of prisoners per 100,000 population (also known as the imprisonment rate).

Gay teens are some of the most vulnerable youth, with many experiencing alienation from family and subsequent homelessness. What might be done, structurally, to reduce the level of homelessness for gay teens?

are worried that their involvement in these surveys will mean they may lose their parental rights or child support payments, come into contact with the child welfare system, or are embarrassed by the stigma of being an incarcerated parent, they may be less likely to truthfully answer the questions.[80]

In addition, these statistics do not capture the diversity of experiences across the states. For example, in California, approximately 9% of children have a parent in prison, in jail, or on probation or parole.[81] Studies conducted in California found that approximately 20% of mothers arrested reported that their children were present during their arrest and that over half of these children were between the ages of 3 and 6.[82]

In addition to the diversity across states, parental incarceration does not affect all children equally. In 2008, 1.8% of white children, 11.4% of black children, and 3.5% of Latino children had at least one parent incarcerated (see Figure 7.12). This means that black children are 6 times more likely to have a parent incarcerated than white children and almost 3 times more likely than Latino children to have a parent incarcerated. Latino children are almost 3 times more likely to have a parent incarcerated than white children. These differences are created by a combination of factors. First, black and Latino adults have a higher rate of incarceration given their population than do white adults, but black and Latino men are also more likely to be parents when incarcerated than white men. Although black, Latina, and white women are all equally likely to be held in state prisons, Latinas are more likely to be mothers in federal prison than are white women.[83]

Western and Wildeman highlighted the significant impact of incarceration on black communities, families, and children in particular:[84]

> The combination of high incarceration rates with a large proportion of fathers among inmates means many children now have incarcerated fathers. . . . Just as incarceration has become a normal life event for disadvantaged young black men, parental incarceration has become commonplace for their children. . . . The prevalence of marriage and fatherhood among prison and jail inmates tells us something about the incapacitation effect of incarceration. Men behind bars cannot fully play the role of father and husband. Single incarcerated men are unlikely to get married while they are locked up. On the outside, the incapacitation effect takes the form of lopsided gender ratios of poor communities. For example, in the high-incarceration neighborhoods of Washington, D.C., there are only sixty-two men for every one hundred women.[85] Studying U.S. counties, William Sabol and James Lynch (1998) quantify the effects of the removal of men to prison.[86] After accounting for educational attainment, welfare receipt, poverty, employment, and crime, Sabol and Lynch find that the doubling of the number of black men admitted to prison between 1980 and 1990 is associated with a 19 percent increase in the number of families headed by black women.

In addition to the impact of race and ethnicity on the experiences of children and incarcerated parents, gender is a factor impacting the experiences of these

One of the challenges for children of incarcerated parents is living arrangements and visitation. While some children can live with their incarcerated mothers (up to a certain age), in other facilities there are no such accommodations. In addition, women, especially, are often housed far away from their children because there are few facility options for women.

FIGURE 7.10 The Number of U.S. Children With an Incarcerated Parent, 1980–2008

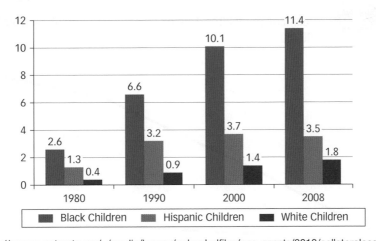

Source: http://www.pewtrusts.org/~/media/legacy/uploadedfiles/pcs_assets/2010/collateralcosts1pdf.pdf

children. Both men and women inmates report that they are parents. In fact, while there are more female inmates in state prison who report being parents than male inmates (61.7% vs. 51.2%), there are actually more men in federal facilities who report being a father than women who report being a mother (63.4% vs. 55.9%). However, there are significant differences in the living arrangements of these parents before incarceration and the living arrangements of their children after incarceration. Mothers were over 3 times more likely to be in a single-parent household before arrest than a two-parent household, while fathers were equally likely to be in a single-parent or two-parent household.[87]

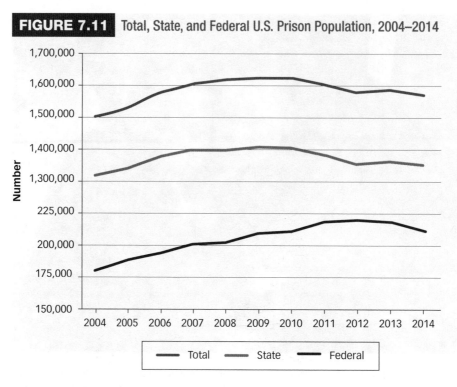

FIGURE 7.11 Total, State, and Federal U.S. Prison Population, 2004–2014

Note: Count based on all prisoners under the jurisdiction of state and federal correctional authorities.

Source: Bureau of Justice Statistics, National Prisoner Statistics, 2004–2014. Retrieved from http://www.bjs.gov/content/pub/pdf/p14.pdf

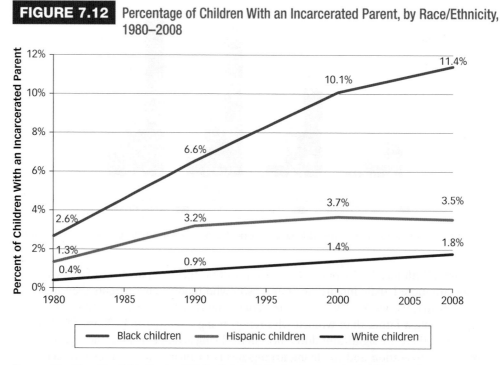

FIGURE 7.12 Percentage of Children With an Incarcerated Parent, by Race/Ethnicity, 1980–2008

Source: The Pew Charitable Trusts. (2010). *Collateral Costs: Incarceration's Effect on Economic Mobility.* Washington, DC: The Pew Charitable Trusts. Retrieved from http://www.pewtrusts.org/~/media/legacy/uploadedfiles/pcs_assets/2010/collateralcosts1pdf.pdf

Why is this important? It is most important for the caregiver implications after a parent has been incarcerated (see Table 7.2). When a father is incarcerated, a significant majority of children are cared for by the other parent (88.4%). This means that although the arrest and incarceration of a parent might be extremely traumatic, it is not compounded by the trauma of also having new caregivers. In contrast, when mothers are incarcerated, only 37% of children remain with the other parent. More children in these situations end up living with a grandparent (44.9%) than their other parent. These gender differences also impact the percentage of children who end up in foster care. Incarcerated mothers are almost five times more likely to have their children end up in foster care than incarcerated fathers. In some states this has quite an impact on parental rights because there can be strict guidelines about how long a child can remain in foster care before his or her parent loses his or her parental rights. In many states, these time limits are so short that even short prison sentences mean that parents may lose their rights (see discussion below under Foster Care and Foster Youth).

The Impact of an Incarcerated Parent

You may be asking yourself why we would spend time discussing parents in prison in a text on juvenile delinquency. We hope at this stage that you see that something like parenting and incarceration has a significant impact on the family and many of the issues we have outlined in this chapter. What do studies say specifically about the effect of parental incarceration on children? The impact of having an incarcerated parent cannot be overemphasized. Studies tell us that children of incarcerated parents experience more upheaval in their lives—they are more likely to live with a caregiver who abuses drugs, experience sexual and physical abuse, and move residences (and caregivers) multiple times.[88] But in addition to violence and upheaval specifically, children were more likely

**Visit edge.sagepub
.com/bates2e to
view a video about
the experiences of a
former foster youth.**

**Visit edge.sagepub
.com/bates2e to
view a video about
the impact of
incarcerated parents.**

Parental rights:
The rights of a parent
to have a say in a
child's legal and
physical custody.

TABLE 7.2	Current Caregiver of Minor Children of Parents in State Prison, by Gender, 2004		
CHILDREN'S CURRENT CAREGIVER[a]	TOTAL	MALE	FEMALE
Other parent	84.2%	88.4%	37.0%
Grandparent Grandmother Grandfather	15.1% 14.0 4.3	12.5% 11.6 3.6	44.9% 42.1 12.0
Other relatives	6.2%	4.7%	22.8%
Foster home or agency	2.9%	2.2%	10.9%
Friends, others[b]	2.9%	2.4%	7.8%
Estimated number of parents in state prison	636,300	585,200	51,100

Source: Glaze, L. E., & Maruschak, L. M. (2010, revised). *Parents in prison and their minor children*. Washington, DC: U.S. Department of Justice, Bureau of Justice Statistics, U.S. Government Printing Office. Retrieved from http://bjs.gov/content/pub/pdf/pptmc.pdf

[a]Includes all parents with minor children. Detail may sum to more than 100% because some prisoners had multiple minor children living with multiple caregivers.

[b]Includes inmate's friends, friends of the inmate's children, cases where the parent reported that the child now lived alone, and others.

to live in poverty, in single-parent households, and with inadequately educated caregivers, and to witness more domestic violence.[89] Many of these children are more likely to exhibit both emotional and behavior problems.[90]

Many of the studies that examine the effect of an incarcerated parent on a child's well-being are small and methodologically limited (for example, early studies did not follow children over a period of time to see what the long-term or lasting effects of parental incarceration might be).[91] These small-scale studies report significant impacts on children. Children of incarcerated parents may experience trauma, anxiety, guilt, sadness, withdrawal, shame, and fear. In addition to these psychological issues, children may experience a decline in school performance, difficulty sleeping, concentration problems, and truancy.[92] Given the significant incarceration rates in the United States, more research on the effect of parental incarceration on child well-being is necessary.

We started this chapter by introducing you to *Children of Incarcerated Parents: A Bill of Rights*.[93] Given what we have discussed in this chapter—the impact of family structure and family process, and the effect of conflict, family stress, and neglect on the behavior of youth—what responsibility do we, as a civil society, have to protect children in this unique position? Should we adopt such a bill of rights?

FOSTER CARE AND FOSTER YOUTH

Finally, we can discuss the impact of the foster care system on the experiences and outcomes of youth who have been removed from their families. We go into extensive detail discussing the foster care system itself in Chapters 12 and 13 while discussing the juvenile justice systems and correctional alternatives, but foster care also has an impact on the experiences of youth that may end in delinquent behavior.

Tracking those in foster care is a tricky thing because each juvenile entering the system has a different journey through. One of the ways to understand the nature and extent of the system is to take a "snapshot" on a given day and describe the system on that day. Each year on September 30 that snapshot is taken. We call this a "point in time" statistic. It is estimated that there were 415,129 children in foster care on September 30, 2014. Of those juveniles in care on that day, there was a goal of reunification with their parents for 55%, a goal of adoption for 25%, a case plan had not been put in place for 5%, emancipation (the right to take care of oneself) was the goal for another 5%, and the last 11% had a goal of some long-term care, either in group homes, with a guardian, or other relative.

Although the goal for 55% of youth is to unify them with one or more of their parents again, this means that 45% of youth are likely to have a different outcome. One of those outcomes is the termination of parental rights so that the child can be adopted or placed in long-term care. Each state has its own standards for the termination of parental rights. The Adoption and Safe Families Act (ASFA) does require that state agencies file a petition to terminate parental rights if a child has been in foster care for 15 of the most recent 22 months, with a few exceptions (one of which is if the child is staying with a relative).[94] Given what we just discussed in the section on incarcerated parents, how does this policy potentially disproportionately impact certain people?

Juveniles can enter foster care between the ages of 0–17 (and may be able to stay beyond the age of 18), but the median age of entry to the system in 2014 was 6.4 years old (see Figure 7.13). Of the estimated 415,129 children in foster care on September 30, 2014, it is estimated that 42% were white, 24% were black, 22% were Latino, 10% were multiracial or other races, and 3% were of an unknown race or ethnicity (see Figure 7.14).

FIGURE 7.13 Age of Foster Youth, 2005 and 2014

Age

Children can enter foster care from infancy up to age 18 years (and sometimes older)[6]

- **Point in Time.** The median age of the children in foster care on September 30, 2014, was 8.0 years.[7]
- **Entries.** The median age of children entering foster care during FY 2014 was 6.4 years.
- **Exits.** The median age of children exiting foster care during FY 2014 was 8.0 years.
- **Trends.** From FY 2006 to FY 2014, the median age decreased for each of the three timeframes (see exhibit 6).

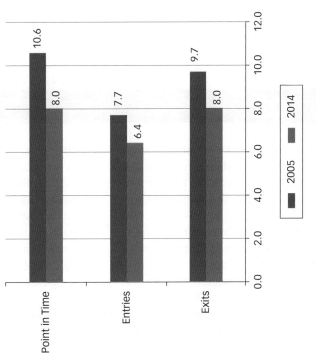

Source: Child Welfare Information Gateway. (2016). *Numbers and Trends: Foster Care Statistics 2014*. Retrieved from https://www.childwelfare.gov/pubs/factsheets/foster/

[6] Some States allow children to remain in foster care to age 19, 20 or 21. The fostering Connections to Success and Increasing Adoptions Act of 2008 gave States the option to extend title IV-E assistance to youth ages 18 to 21, with certain stipulations. For more information, see Information Gateway's web

[7] The median refers to the number in the middle when all numbers are placed in order. In this case, it means that an equal number of children are older and younger than this age.

FIGURE 7.14 Race and Ethnicity of Foster Youth, 2005 and 2014

Race and Ethnicity

AFCARS tracks children's race or ethnicity.

Point in Time. Of the estimated 415,129 children in foster care on September 30, 2014,

- 42 percent were White.
- 24 percent were Black or African-American.
- 22 percent were Hispanic (of any race).
- 10 percent were other races or multiracial.[8]
- 3 percent were unknown or unable to be determined.

Trends. The percentage of Black children in care on September 30 decrease between FY 2005 and FY 2014, while the percentage of Whites children, Hispanic children, children of other races or multiracial children, and children of unknown race increased (See exhibit7)

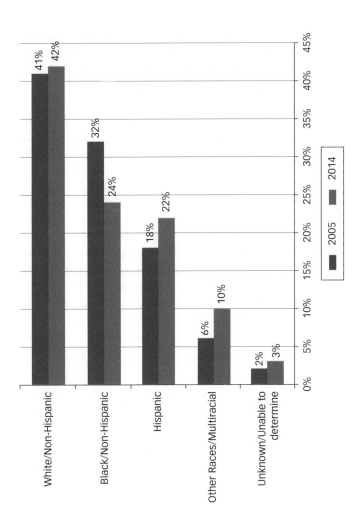

Source: Child Welfare Information Gateway. (2016). *Numbers and Trends: Foster Care Statistics 2014*. Retrieved from https://www.childwelfare.gov/pubs/factsheets/foster/

[8] "Other races or multiracial" includes American Indian/Alaskan Native, Hawaiian/Other Pacific Islander, and two or more races.

Remember that children who end up in the foster care system have often had quite traumatic experiences even before they enter the system. This trauma, in addition to a system that is often bureaucratic at best[95] and abusive at worst,[96] impacts the experiences that juveniles have in school.

When the state intervenes to remove a child from his or her parents or guardian, it does so out of concern for the child's immediate safety and in the wake of an investigation that confirms abuse and/or neglect. Yet even as the safety of foster children is protected by this drastic measure, another set of hazards to their immediate and long-term well-being emerges. Prominent among these is a lack of attention to the education needs and potential of foster youth—a lack of attention that in many ways constitutes another form of damaging neglect.[97]

In fact, compared to other children, foster youth are more likely to be absent from school, more likely to receive disciplinary referrals, and more likely to perform below grade level. This means that more foster youth are likely to be placed in special education (25–52% of foster youth, compared to 10–12% of other students),[98] they are less likely to complete high school (one estimate says that up to 46% of foster youth do not graduate from high school),[99] and they do not attend college (fewer than 3% go to a four-year college).

These educational problems lead to problems as foster youth become adults. Estimates of the outcomes for foster youth just out of foster care find that "within the first 2 to 4 years after aging out of the foster care system, 51% of these young adults are unemployed, 40% are on public assistance, 25% become homeless, and 20% will be incarcerated."[100]

Less research has examined the likelihood of engaging in delinquency as a foster youth. Some research has documented that up to one-third of foster youth end up arrested while in care.[101] A few studies have linked this increase in delinquent behavior to the quality of care while in the system[102] and the strain of an unstable environment.[103] This calls for us to become more aware of the experiences of youth while they are in foster care. It is true that some youth may need to be removed from their families to keep them safe, but if their experiences while in foster care lack stability and attachment, how much good has the system really done?

SUMMARY

The one constant about the family is that it is always changing. Now more than any other time in the last 100 years, children in the United States live in family forms alternative to the traditional two-parent (often assumed biological) family. While the unmarried birth rate in the United States has been increasing since 1980 for most age groups, girls between the ages of 15 and 19 have seen a declining unmarried birth rate. This birth rate is impacted by race and ethnicity. While there has been a long-term decline in the adolescent birth rate for all races and ethnicities, overall there is still a large disparity with Latina girls having the highest birth rate and Asian and Pacific Islander girls having the lowest birth rate in 2009. While we should be skeptical of reporting the trends in child maltreatment because there is not always consistent reporting across states or years in the extent of maltreatment, we can examine the nature of maltreatment and extent by age. We find that neglect is the largest type of maltreatment, and that young children (under the age of 4) are more likely to be neglected than older children.

The relationship between family and delinquency is a complicated one, and one that has been studied extensively. While family structure is often assumed to be strongly linked to delinquency, research highlights several issues about which we must be aware. First, there are many different ways of measuring family structure, and these various definitions (non-intact vs. intact home, single- vs. two-parent homes, or a complicated measure including stepfamilies, foster families, and grandparents) have different relationships to delinquency. Second, if we examine the impact of family structure and family process together on delinquency, it is sometimes the case that family structure is no longer a predictor of delinquency. Third, family process seems to be a strong predictor of delinquency, with such measures as attachment, supervision, conflict, and discipline impacting the likelihood that juveniles will misbehave.

Child maltreatment also has a complicated relationship to delinquency. There is some research that finds a relationship between physical or sexual abuse or neglect and various types of delinquency. However, other researchers are less focused on maltreatment as a predictor of juvenile misbehavior, and more focused on how societal reactions to juveniles who have been maltreated impact their later experiences in the juvenile justice system. These researchers focus on the gendered nature of these reactions, in which girls are often criminalized for their survival techniques that include running away from physical and sexual abuse. Once these girls are arrested for running away, they are much more likely to have an extended history of arrest and interaction with the juvenile justice system.

Finally, the imprisonment of parents has become an increasing problem in the United States. As the incarceration rate in the United States has increased, so has the likelihood that children have a parent in prison. This dynamic of incarcerating parents (and most likely fathers) has a variety of implications for the family, from the likelihood that for certain populations in the United States such as black families, there is a significant increase in the number of single-mother households due to incarceration, to the detrimental effects of watching a parent being arrested, to the impact on youth behavior and misbehavior.

EYE ON DIVERSITY EXERCISE: PARENTING IN PRISON

The policy for visitation or parenting in prison varies by state, and in some instances institutions within the state. Examining the nearest male and female prisons in your state, what is the policy for visitation with children? Are these policies different across the two prisons? Does either prison offer a "parenting in prison" program where children get to come for extended visits or live with their parents while they are incarcerated? If so, what are the parameters of the program? If no such program exists, would you advocate for one, and what would the parameters of your program be? In many states, if juveniles engage in serious crime, they may be sentenced and incarcerated beyond the age of 18. What are the visitation policies of the juvenile correctional facility near you? While there is a bit lower chance that juveniles incarcerated will have children at the time of their incarceration, some might. Are there any juvenile correctional facilities in your state that have "parenting in prison" programs?

DISCUSSION QUESTIONS

1. What is the relationship of family structure and delinquency? Does it matter if we think of family structure as representing a stressful event such as divorce, or if we think of family structure as representing the amount of resources available to a child?

2. What do we mean by family process? What is the impact of family process on delinquency?

3. Explain the intersections of race, gender, and class on the relationship between the family and delinquency.

4. Explain the nature and extent of child maltreatment in the United States. Discuss the relationship between child maltreatment, delinquency, and the juvenile justice system.

5. How does increasing incarceration (mass imprisonment) affect the family in general, youth in particular, and juvenile delinquency?

6. Given the increases in incarceration, and the impact on families and youth, how do you feel about a bill of rights for children of incarcerated parents? Explain.

7. In many states, there are guidelines for how long a child can remain in foster care before the state starts the process of terminating the rights of the parent. What are the guidelines for your state? What are the instances in which you believe that terminating parental rights is warranted? Is going to jail enough to start the termination process? Should it depend on the crime for which the parent is incarcerated? Is there ever a reason to terminate parental rights? How do these policies disproportionately affect people of color and women?

KEY TERMS

Abuse 198	Emotional neglect 198	Physical abuse 198
Attachment 192	Family conflict 194	Physical neglect 198
Child maltreatment 198	Family process 188	Sexual abuse 198
Discipline 194	Family structure 188	Supervision 193
Educational neglect 198	Incarceration rate 205	Throwaways 205
Egalitarian household 197	Neglect 198	
Emotional abuse 198	Parental rights 209	

CHAPTER PRETEST ANSWERS

1. True	5. False	9. True
2. False	6. True	10. False
3. True	7. True	11. True
4. False	8. True	12. True

STUDENT STUDY SITE

⑤SAGE edge™

edge.sagepub.com/bates2e

Sharpen your skills with SAGE edge!

SAGE edge for students provides a personalized approach to help you accomplish your coursework goals in an easy-to-use learning environment. You'll find action plans, mobile-friendly eFlashcards, and quizzes, as well as videos, web resources, and links to SAGE journal articles to support and expand on the concepts presented in this chapter. Check out the website for original videos of former offenders discussing their experiences as juveniles.

CHAPTER

8

©iStockphoto.com/yzak

SCHOOLS IN CONTEXT

After reading this chapter, you should be able to

- Describe the trends in education in the United States

- Explain how gender and race impact these trends

- Explain how a changing budget impacts the educational system, learning, and delinquency

- Explain the impact of school failure on delinquency

- Analyze the contextual factors of tracking, alienation, and social class on failure in school

- Compare and contrast the nature and extent of violence and property crime in schools

- Compare and contrast the nature and extent of bullying and cyberbullying in schools

- Compare and contrast the impact of increased social control in schools on student experiences and delinquency

Shantelle Hicks, a 15-year-old from Gallup, New Mexico, claims she was first forced to leave the Wingate Elementary School and then publicly outed as being pregnant in front of all students and employees, KOB-TV reports. Wingate Elementary is a public boarding school for Native American children from kindergarten through eighth grade.

Now, with the help of the American Civil Liberties Union, Hicks has filed suit against Wingate, claiming the school violated her constitutional rights. According to the complaint, school officials kicked Hicks out after learning of her pregnancy, but readmitted her four days later when the ACLU of New Mexico informed the school that it's illegal to deny a student access to education for being pregnant.

But two weeks after her readmission, a school counselor and the director of the middle school forced the teen to stand before the middle school assembly and announce her condition—allegedly before anyone but her sister knew.

"It was so embarrassing to have all the other kids staring at me as I walked into the gymnasium," said Hicks, according to KOB. "I didn't want the whole school to know I was pregnant because it's not their business, and it wasn't right for my teachers to single me out."

According to the suit, school officials informed Hicks that she would be a "bad example" to other students, and requested she attend another school, a *Washington Post* local report states. "It is outrageous that educators would subject a young woman in their care to such cruelty," ACLU of New Mexico cooperating attorney Barry Klopfer said, according to the Indian Country Today Media Network.

The girl's mother, Vicky Hicks, says her daughter's public humiliation was wrong. "[Students] shouldn't be treated differently because they're pregnant," Hicks told KOAT-TV.

Source: Hibbard, L. (2012). Shantelle Hicks, pregnant 8th grader, outed to New Mexico school assembly. *The Huffington Post*, March 7. Retrieved from http://www.huffingtonpost.com/2012/03/07/staff-out-pregnant-8th-grader-at-school-assembly_n_1327865.html

CHAPTER PRETEST

Test your knowledge of this chapter's material by determining whether the following statements are true or false. Be sure to compare your answers with the answers on page 245.

1. Academic achievement has been decreasing in the United States since 1971.

2. Girls show higher reading scores than boys at all ages and during all years.

3. In 2015, whites were the most proficient in math and reading across all racial and ethnic groups.

4. The educational system is primarily budgeted for at the federal level.

5. Dropping out is correlated to the likelihood to engage in delinquent behavior and delinquent behavior is correlated to the likelihood to drop out.

6. Total number of homicides on campus has been increasing since 1992.

7. Blacks are most likely to be threatened or injured with a weapon on school property.

8. The school-to-prison pipeline is the argument that for some students, school becomes a preparation ground for prison.

9. Zero-tolerance policies first focused on youth who brought firearms to campus.

While one-room schoolhouses were the norm for public education in the 1800s, there has been a trend toward larger middle schools and high schools that can often house several thousand students. What would be the differing experiences of attending a small versus large school?

A significant portion of juvenile life is spent in school with teachers and friends. In fact, during the school year it is estimated that juveniles spend approximately one third of their 24-hour day sleeping and one third at school and in extracurricular activities, meaning that school can have a significant impact on juveniles and their experiences. This was not always the case. As you read in Chapter 2, schools are a recent arrival to child development. Their popularity arose in the shift from an agrarian society to an industry- and service-based economy. Schools existed in the agrarian society, but children were an integral part of the planting and harvesting tasks and only went to school when their parents could afford to let them go. With the Industrial Revolution and the rapid concentration of individuals in urban centers, schools became a place to keep children safe during the day and, some might argue, a place to help mold them into "moral, upstanding citizens." Not only has the importance of school changed in the last 200 years, but the physical characteristics of school have changed, too—in some cases from a one-room schoolhouse with 20 children ranging in age from 5 to 16 to a "super school" that has over 3,000 students ages 14–18. Today there is significant variation in what constitutes a school: Homeschooling, charter schools, private schools, and public schools exist across the nation. In remote parts of Alaska, students may still be in small schools spanning K–12 or homeschooled. In large cities, such as New York and Los Angeles, charter and private schools exist next to large public schools with thousands of children.

This chapter explores the important connection between school and delinquency. We will examine what we know about the types of delinquency that exist in our schools, the link between education and the likelihood to engage in delinquency, and how our schools might help prevent, or hinder the prevention of, delinquency. As always, the answers in this chapter will show that there is a diverse experience for children as they go to school and ponder or experience delinquency.

THE DIVERSE SCHOOL EXPERIENCE

Not all children experience school the same way. Studies have shown us that whether a child is black or white, is a boy or a girl, or lives in a resource-rich or a resource-poor community has an impact on how well the child will do and how he or she will experience the school system. Our opening story shows us an example of how boys and girls might experience school differently. The burgeoning sexuality of girls has been a strong societal focus over the years with more emphasis placed on girls and their sexual experiences than on boys and their sexual experiences. In addition, it is easier for a boy who is sexually active to hide this fact than it is for a girl who becomes pregnant. This means that girls are often treated differently than boys when it is suspected or confirmed that they are sexually active.

Trends in Academic Achievement

The U.S. Department of Education, through its National Center for Education Statistics, measures the nation's educational progress.[1] The National Assessment of Educational Progress (NAEP) regularly administers assessments to school children aged 9, 13, and 17 on their academic achievement in reading and math. These assessments have been administered regularly since 1971. The most current assessment was administered in 2015 to 17-year-olds. These assessments suggest, contrary to the popular story that schools are failing children and children are failing themselves, that reading and math progress increased or remained the same for every group between 1971 and 2012. However, these achievements are not uniform across the country: Figures 8.1 and 8.2 show that there is what we might refer to as "education by geography," with some states clearly offering a better education than others.

Math

The assessments show that 9- and 13-year-olds improved their overall mathematics scores between 1971 and 2012, although 17-year-olds' scores decreased between 2012 and 2015. This trend remains true for gender when the scores are examined for boys and girls separately. Both 9- and 13-year-old boys and girls improved their scores over time, although there is also a gender gap in math scores that opens up over the ages, with boys and girls achieving almost identical scores at age 9 and boys scoring higher on average than girls at ages 13 and 17.

The message is even more mixed when examining the math scores by race and ethnicity. For every age group, Hispanic and black students showed considerable improvement in their math scores between 1971 and 2012. However, there is also a persistent gap in math scores between white students and Hispanic and black students, and although Hispanic and black students have narrowed this gap over time (it was larger in 1971 than in 2012), it still exists for every age group. In 2015, 32% of white students (17-year-olds), 7% of black students, 12% of Hispanic students, 47% of Asian students, 10% of American Indians/Alaska Natives, and 31% of biracial/multiracial students were proficient in math.

Reading

The same general trends can be seen in reading as in math, with 9- and 13-year-olds improving their reading scores between 1971 and 2012, while 17-year-olds saw no significant improvement (through 2015). These trends hold for gender, although the gender gap is in the opposite direction this time. Girls show higher reading scores than boys at all ages and during all years.

And the story is the same for reading scores and race/ethnicity. All racial/ethnic groups improved their scores from the first year of assessment to 2012, but just as with the math scores, while the gap in scores is narrowing, it is still persistent—white students scored higher than black and Hispanic students for all three ages in all years. In 2015, 46% of white students (17-year-olds), 17% of black students, 25% of Hispanic students, 49% of Asian students, 28% of American Indians/Alaska Natives, and 45% of biracial/multiracial students were proficient in reading.

The data in these reports do not allow for class comparisons on reading and math scores. No direct class information was collected on the students. However, the NAEP did collect data on whether the students attended a public, private, or Catholic school.

● ● ●
Academic achievement: The extent to which students achieve their academic goals.

FIGURE 8.1 Comparison Between States of Public School Students at or Above Proficient in Eighth-Grade NAEP Mathematics, 2013

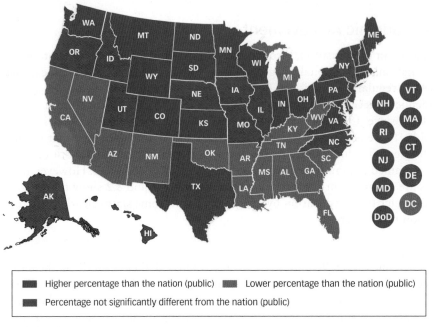

■ Higher percentage than the nation (public)   ■ Lower percentage than the nation (public)
■ Percentage not significantly different from the nation (public)

Source: NAEP. (2016). *The Nation's Report Card*. Retrieved from http://www.nationsreportcard.gov/reading_math_g12_2015/

FIGURE 8.2 Comparison Between States of Public School Students at or Above Proficient in Eighth-Grade NAEP Reading, 2013

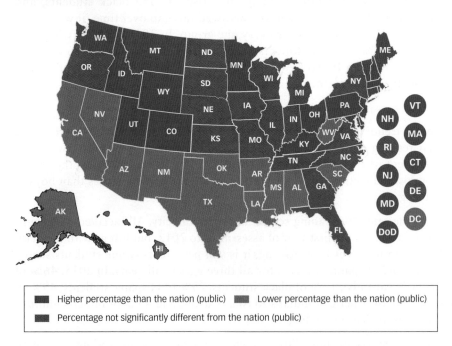

■ Higher percentage than the nation (public)   ■ Lower percentage than the nation (public)
■ Percentage not significantly different from the nation (public)

Source: NAEP. (2016). *The Nation's Report Card*. Retrieved from http://www.nationsreportcard.gov/reading_math_g12_2015/

While the type of school a student attends is not a perfect measure of class, it could be argued one must be able to afford a private or Catholic school, and thus that there are more students whose families can afford to pay for their education in such schools than in public schools. These data also show a persistent gap in both math and reading scores for students who attend public, private, and Catholic schools with public schools consistently showing lower scores in math and reading across all age groups and all years than their private and Catholic counterparts.

While we started this section by suggesting that the educational experience of youth is less dire than sometimes suggested, we end on a cautionary note. While it is energizing to see that, overall, students have improved their math and reading scores since 1971, it is troubling to continue to see gaps in these scores based on gender, race and ethnicity, and type of school.

International Comparisons

While reading and math scores offer one story about the state of education in the United States, another way of examining the state of education is to ask how students in the United States compare to students in other countries. The Organisation for Economic Co-operation and Development (OECD) conducts a study called the Programme for International Student Assessment (PISA) of students in over 60 countries every three years. PISA evaluates the international state of education by examining the skills and knowledge of 15-year-old students. The study focuses on assessing student ability to engage in real-life applications of their knowledge and be full participants in society.

The findings from this study show that the United States, at best, can be considered average in comparison to the other 64 countries that participated in the study.[2] In 2012 (the last year data were published), the United States ranked 24 in reading and 27 in science, with scores that were not statistically different from the OECD average in each area. However, the United States tested below average in mathematics ability, with a rank of 35, and math scores considered statistically significantly below average. In 2012, 18 countries scored higher than the United States in all three categories: Australia, Canada, Chinese Taipei, Estonia, Finland, Germany, Hong Kong-China, Ireland, Japan, Liechtenstein, Macao-China, Netherlands, New Zealand, Poland, Republic of Korea, Shanghai-China, Singapore, and Switzerland.

In addition, these data show that since 2000, the United States has not improved in reading or mathematics, although there has been a slight improvement in science scores during this time.

The educational trends tell us that juveniles have been holding their own or increasing their mastery in reading and math over the last 20 years, but also that in comparison to other countries, the United States is making very little headway and certainly cannot be considered an educational top performer. While we do not know yet, we do have to wonder what the decreasing budgetary support of schools will mean for the success of youth in school.

Comparisons to education internationally show that the United States is rarely at the top of the class when it comes to test scores or critical thinking.

FIGURE 8.3 Per-Student Spending by State

Percent change in state formula funding* per student, inflation-adjusted, fiscal years 2008–2016

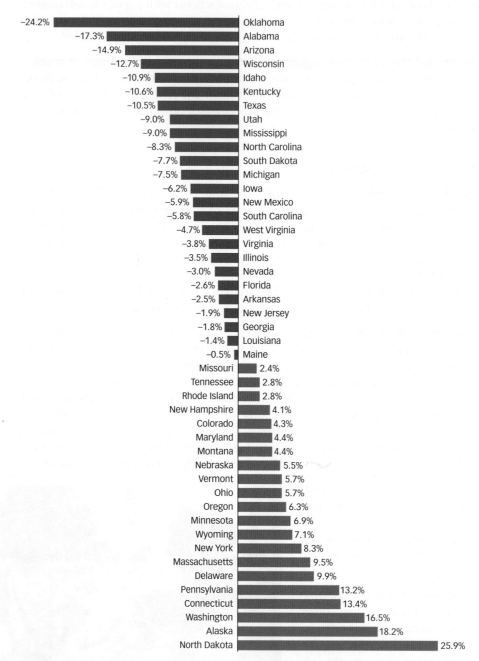

State	Percent change
Oklahoma	-24.2%
Alabama	-17.3%
Arizona	-14.9%
Wisconsin	-12.7%
Idaho	-10.9%
Kentucky	-10.6%
Texas	-10.5%
Utah	-9.0%
Mississippi	-9.0%
North Carolina	-8.3%
South Dakota	-7.7%
Michigan	-7.5%
Iowa	-6.2%
New Mexico	-5.9%
South Carolina	-5.8%
West Virginia	-4.7%
Virginia	-3.8%
Illinois	-3.5%
Nevada	-3.0%
Florida	-2.6%
Arkansas	-2.5%
New Jersey	-1.9%
Georgia	-1.8%
Louisiana	-1.4%
Maine	-0.5%
Missouri	2.4%
Tennessee	2.8%
Rhode Island	2.8%
New Hampshire	4.1%
Colorado	4.3%
Maryland	4.4%
Montana	4.4%
Nebraska	5.5%
Vermont	5.7%
Ohio	5.7%
Oregon	6.3%
Minnesota	6.9%
Wyoming	7.1%
New York	8.3%
Massachusetts	9.5%
Delaware	9.9%
Pennsylvania	13.2%
Connecticut	13.4%
Washington	16.5%
Alaska	18.2%
North Dakota	25.9%

Sources: CBPP budget analysis and National Center for Education Statistics enrollment estimates. Retrieved from http://www.cbpp.org/research/state-budget-and-tax/most-states-have-cut-school-funding-and-some-continue-cutting. Reprinted with permission from the Center on Budget and Policy Priorities, http://www.cbpp.org.

*General or formula funding is the primary form of state K-12 funding. States also typically provide revenue for other, more speicific purposes, such as bus transportation and contributions to school employee pension plans.

Note: California, Hawaii, Indiana, and Kansas are excluded because the data necessary to make a valid comparison are not available.

THE BUDGETING OF EDUCATION

Education is primarily budgeted for at the state level. The federal government budgets about 2% of its overall budget to supplement the educational budgets of the states.[3] State budgets vary widely on the percentage of their overall budgets and the absolute dollars that they make available to education. In addition to this variation, the economic crisis of 2008–2009 significantly affected the educational budgets in all 50 states. Figure 8.3 shows the change in education budgets for the 46 states that offer data to make these comparisons. Of these 46 states, 25 decreased their education budgets between 2008 and the proposed 2016 budget by up to 24.2%. This means that even 8 years after the height of the recession, half of the states in the United States are still cutting education budgets.

While small decreases in educational budgets can probably be absorbed or made up for by finding small efficiencies, school systems that lose large amounts of funding can expect to have to let teachers go, increase class sizes, put off buying up-to-date textbooks, defund extracurricular activities such as sports or band, and forestall much needed repairs to classrooms and school equipment. We will see later in this chapter that these can have an effect on student experiences and, by extension, levels of delinquency.

SCHOOL FAILURE, DROPPING OUT, AND DELINQUENCY

If asked, most individuals would probably agree that there is a connection between failing in school, dropping out, and engaging in delinquency. However, many would be surprised at the complex nature of that relationship.

School Failure

School failure has long been linked to delinquency, although the exact relationship is not a forgone conclusion. There are four ways it has been hypothesized that school failure may be related to delinquency.

1. *Direct relationship*: Students who fail in school are more likely to engage in delinquency. For example, youth who experience school failure become frustrated and angry by their failure and engage in delinquency.

2. *Direct relationship*: Students who are delinquent are more likely to fail in school. This scenario suggests that delinquency may be related to the ability to succeed in school. For example, students who are delinquent on school grounds can be suspended or expelled. Juveniles who are suspended or expelled are much more likely to officially drop out of school than those students who have never been suspended or expelled.

3. *Indirect relationship*: School failure has an indirect effect on the likelihood to engage in delinquency by impacting a mediating event or experience for juveniles. For example, if youth who fail at school become disconnected from their school, this lower level of attachment may have them caring less about getting in trouble and risking their education. It is the failure at school that has an effect on level of attachment to the school, and in the end the level of attachment has an effect on likelihood to engage in delinquency.

4. *Spurious relationship*: A third variable is causing both school failure and delinquency. This is called a spurious relationship because it looks like school failure and delinquency are related, but in reality another variable is affecting both failure and delinquency. For example, if boys were more likely to fail in school and also more likely to engage in delinquency, it would look like school failure and delinquency were related, especially if we did not know about the common connection of gender.

● ● ●

School failure:
A process by which a student falls farther and farther behind his friends and expected level in his or her educational development, gradually disengaging from the school system.

An extensive amount of research explores why juveniles might not be successful in school. Some of this research focuses on individual traits of the juvenile. Is the juvenile depressed? Is she impulsive, or does she have low self-control? Does he have problems at home he is focused on? Is she fighting with friends? Is he angry? And, it is true, middle school and high school (the years in which we see an increased likelihood of school failure and delinquency) are turbulent times in a juvenile's life, and individual life events and characteristics play a part in the successes and failures that young people experience in school.

Beyond these individual traits, though, are several factors that examine how a juvenile's experience in school might affect his or her likelihood to fail or succeed. We consider these factors as macro or contextual factors. Three such factors that we will explore are tracking, alienation, and social class.

Tracking

Fast, average, slow. Cheetahs, rabbits, tortoises. The blue group, the red group, the green group. Tracking occurs when juveniles are placed in classrooms or groups within the classroom based on their perceived intellectual abilities, and chances are, to some extent, many of you were tracked while in school—it is a common characteristic of schools in the United States. In fact, it is estimated that tracking occurs in about 60% of elementary schools and up to 80% of middle and high schools.[4]

While tracking is defended as a way to make teaching more effective, study after study suggests that tracking is detrimental to both the educational achievements and the social experiences of juveniles.[5] Juveniles who learn in mixed-ability classrooms improve in both academic performance and behavior. And tracked students can be hurt socially, too, because their experience with peer groups becomes smaller as they go through school with the same clique of friends. Attending elementary, middle, and high school in the 1970s and 1980s, we can attest to the social impact of tracking. As elementary students, we were both tracked into learning groups, and were taken from our normal classrooms and away from the friendships that we had been establishing. While our learning groups only existed for the first part of the day, the experiences stay with us, even 30 years later, not only because we lost the opportunity to be in a classroom with some of our best friends, but because it became apparent, very early on, that the groups we were each tracked into had something to do with how "smart" we appeared to be. Even as elementary students, we were highly aware of the labels we had been given.

Studies suggest that tracking becomes a self-fulfilling prophecy, in which youth who are tracked into lower groups begin to see themselves as not school oriented or failures at school—and students who are tracked into lower groups are much more likely to fail than students who are tracked into higher groups.

Finally, tracking has also been accused of segregating by both race and class and perpetuating inequality.[6] More students of color and poor students end up in the lower tracks, while more white and upper-class students end up in the higher tracks. Could it be that what we have just learned about the gap in reading and math scores between students of color and white students depends at least partially on a system more likely to challenge one group of students than another?

Alienation

Students' feelings of attachment and commitment to their school can also have an impact on their levels of alienation and their success in school. Those who feel alienated by their experiences in school are more likely to fail. This alienation may be fostered by a variety of school experiences. The tracking we discussed above could cause students to feel alienated if they do not feel their schooling has a purpose or they feel labeled by their teachers or fellow students. But, in addition to tracking, other school characteristics may impact levels of alienation or school connectedness. Positive classroom management styles, participation in extracurricular activities, tolerant disciplinary policies, and small

●●●
Tracking:
A practice that occurs when juveniles are placed in classrooms or groups within the classroom based on their perceived intellectual abilities.

Alienation:
A low degree of integration or high degree of isolation or distance between an individual and another individual, group, community, or institution.

school sizes have all been found to impact levels of alienation and school connectedness.[7] These four factors are especially important given the general trends in education discussed in this chapter: the decreasing education budgets (which increase class sizes) and the trend toward "super schools" to manage budget efficiencies, and the move to zero-tolerance policies in schools, which will be discussed in the last section of this chapter.

Alienation and school connectedness have been linked to the likelihood to become delinquent. Juveniles who report they do not like school are also more likely to report delinquent behavior.[8] Juveniles who reported being connected to school were less likely to engage in physical or relational aggression and also less likely to report that they were victims of aggression at school.[9]

Social Class

Many studies have examined the effect of social class on school failure. Early studies focused on the idea that students from the working class were more likely to have *deficiencies* than students from the middle or upper classes.[10] These studies focused on individual characteristics of students and argued that poorer students were more likely to fail in school because they were less capable of overcoming these deficiencies—for example, they had a lack of verbal skills, or had less time to spend on their schoolwork because they had to be employed to help the family; their parents were less involved in their education; or they did not see the value of an education the way a middle- or upper-class student did.

Other studies have critiqued the educational system as biased in favor of the middle and upper class.[11] These studies have focused on the issue that the educational system is designed to reproduce the culture of the middle and upper classes, and this leaves poorer students disadvantaged in a system that does not value their cultural contributions. In these studies, school failure is not a product of a deficiency in youth, but instead is a product of deficiencies in the educational system, which is not designed to educate all students in the art of reading and math, but instead is focused more on cultural reproduction (for example, a focus on successfully taking a standardized test as opposed to fostering critical thinking).

The Effect on Delinquency

However, the relationship of social class, school failure, and delinquency is murky. Some studies have found that poorer youth are more likely to turn to delinquency when they fail in school.[12] But other research suggests that class does not matter at all—juveniles who do poorly in school turn to delinquency, whether or not they are from the working poor, middle class, or upper class.[13] And, finally, some studies suggest that middle- and upper-class students may become more delinquent upon failing in school because the expectations to succeed are higher for them than for working-class students.[14] Most of these studies, again, focus on failure in school from the individual perspective. They assume that youth are reacting to their failure.

Liazos argues, instead, that working-class youth turn to delinquency when they are "successful" in school.[15] Following the argument that education amounts to cultural reproduction, Liazos argues that the educational system is designed to teach working-class youth how to be good working-class workers—following the rules, not making waves, not questioning authority. Liazos believes that this education is preparing lower-class youth for alienated work and lives, and youth who do not want this alienating existence rebel from their schools and education. Until the expectations of society and an economy that relies on an alienated workforce are changed, Liazos sees no hope for improving education for and decreasing delinquency in juveniles.

Whatever the orientation one takes to school failure, it is an important factor in any discussion on delinquency.

Dropping Out

High school dropout rates are incredibly high in the United States. It is estimated that almost one third of high school students drop out of school or do not graduate on time.[16] Dropout rates also vary by such factors as geography and race/ethnicity. In 2009, Wyoming had a dropout rate of 1.1%, while Illinois had a dropout rate of 11.5%.[17] Stillwell et al. report that black students had the highest dropout rate in 2009 followed closely by American Indian/Alaska Natives and Latinos, while Asian/Pacific Islanders had the lowest rate followed closely by white students.[18]

As with school failure, the predictors of **dropping out** can be separated into two general categories: (1) individual-level characteristics of the juvenile and (2) characteristics of the school. Studies that have focused on the individual suggest that a variety of individual-level characteristics or experiences affect the likelihood of dropping out:[19]

- Students who do not do well academically
- Students who have been tracked into the "low" or "slow" academic tracks
- Students who have been held back a grade
- Students who have issues such as low self-esteem
- Students who feel alienated or disconnected from their school experience
- Students who have a poor attitude about school
- Students who have been previously suspended
- Students who have to work a significant number of hours
- Students with friends who have also dropped out of school

It is often the case that we focus on the individual problems of youth when we ask why they might have dropped out, but if you look over the list of individual predictors, it should be apparent that many of them are impacted by the characteristics or structure of schools and the educational system. Studies that have focused on these structural predictors suggest that the following school characteristics affect the likelihood of an individual dropping out:[20]

Dropping out:
The act of quitting school before graduating.

- Structural characteristics, such as the size of the school, the resources available to the school, and whether the school is public or private

- Organizational characteristics, such as the rules, practices, and decision-making processes in the school

- Climate characteristics, such as the level and type of discipline in the school or the academic emphasis of the school

These structural characteristics could impact individual students in a variety of ways. Exceptionally large schools or schools with exceptionally large classroom sizes may impact how alienated or disconnected students feel from their school; school

Research demonstrates that when students feel alienated, disregarded, and/or disrespected at school, they are less likely to do well in school, and more likely to engage in delinquency than they would be otherwise.

size may also affect the general attitude of students in the school. Tracking has already been discussed as a predictor of student failure in general, and may also affect whether a youth is more likely to drop out. The discipline policies of a school may have an impact on overall student attitudes, students' perceptions of fairness in the school, and suspension and expulsion rates, which we see impact individual-level decisions to drop out.

What is becoming increasingly obvious is that schools have a strong impact on juveniles and their educational trajectories. It is not the case that juveniles exist in a bubble when experiencing school failure and dropping out. Finn, among others, focuses on the fact that dropping out is a "dynamic and cumulative process of disengagement."[21] In

Although doing poorly in school is an individual-level factor related to dropping out, structural, organizational, and climate characteristics of a given school also are related to the likelihood of a student leaving school before completion.

other words, juveniles do not wake up one morning and decide to drop out of school—they have been on a long road of individual and school experiences that begin with individual frustrations and seemingly innocent school decisions and end with failure, withdrawal, and dropping out.

The Effect on Delinquency

What is the impact of dropping out of school on the likelihood of delinquency? An extensive amount of research links dropping out to delinquency. From the statistics gathered on the characteristics of jail and prison inmates alone, one would assume that dropping out is one of the strongest predictors of delinquent and criminal behavior (60% of jail inmates and 68% of state prison inmates do not hold a traditional high school degree).[22] In addition, many studies have linked dropping out to delinquent behavior and drug use.[23] However, Sweeten, Bushway, and Paternoster examined whether dropping out of school was a *cause* of later delinquent behavior or whether both dropping out of school and delinquent behavior were the end result of other life experiences.[24] They concluded that dropping out of school was not the cause of later delinquent behavior, but was more likely a spurious connection to delinquency. For example, Sweeten et al. found that juveniles who had to drop out of school because of work obligations were less likely to engage in delinquency (in other words, dropping out for work reasons did not lead to delinquent behavior). They concluded that we need to investigate the reasons that juveniles drop out of school and recognize that the post-dropout experience of youth matters greatly in their likelihood to engage in delinquency.

DISENGAGEMENT AND DELINQUENCY

While failing and dropping out of school are probably most commonly associated with delinquency, and from our section above we can see that failing and dropping out are complicated issues with many of their own predictors, there is an abundance of other research that focuses on more general experiences in school and the impact on delinquency. Two of the areas most researched are school bonding and school engagement and the effect on delinquency.

School Bonding. School bonding is usually considered to be school attachment, school commitment, and teacher attachment. School attachment is an emotional connection to the school (not necessarily the teacher), while school commitment is considered investment in schoolwork and grades, and teacher attachment is a positive relationship or emotional bond with a teacher. Juveniles who report they are less connected (bonded) to school display more problem behaviors such as delinquency.[25] Liljeberg, Eklund, Fritz, and af Klinteberg examined whether it was school bonding that impacted delinquency or delinquency that impacted school bonding (in other words, do students who are bonded engage in less delinquency or are students who engage in delinquency likely to have their bond to school impacted, for example, through discipline or poor teacher-student relations?).[26] These researchers found that the relationship was actually bidirectional; in other words, the bond to school impacted delinquency and then, in turn, delinquency impacted the bond to school. This study also found that there was a gender difference in school bonding. Boys were impacted by all three types of bonds, while girls were most impacted by their relationship with their teachers.

School Engagement. School engagement is a broader measure that includes school attachment (as emotional engagement) but also includes behavioral engagement, which is involvement in academic activities and participation in school-based social activities,[27] and cognitive engagement, which is the amount of time juveniles spend in challenging activities.[28] Hirschfield and Gasper examined the relationship between all three forms of engagement and the likelihood to engage in delinquency and found that emotional and behavioral engagement predicted decreases in delinquency, while cognitive engagement predicted increases in delinquency (in other words, in this study, students who engaged in challenging activities were also more likely to engage in delinquency).[29]

CRIME AND DELINQUENCY IN SCHOOLS

Schools are often portrayed as a hotbed of violence and crime. And why not? The media attention to some types of crime on school campuses would lead anyone to believe that schools are a dangerous place for their inhabitants. But the reality is slightly different. It is true that crime and delinquency occur at school, but our focus as a nation is not on the actual delinquency that is taking place. In fact, some might argue that our misplaced attention on such events as school shootings has masked other types of delinquency and victimization, including bullying and cyberbullying, for far too long.

Violence at School

School shootings and other violent deaths on campus are tragic events, but remain incredibly rare (see Figure 8.4). In fact, youth homicides at school made up only 1.3% of the total youth homicides in the 2011–2012 school year.

In addition, in Figure 8.5, the middle trend line shows us that although the number of violent deaths is so small (remember our "tyranny of small numbers" discussion in Chapter 3?), it is fairly safe to say that the trend between 1992–1993 (the year data were first kept) and 2009–2010 decreased (with 2009–2010 being the lowest on record), with a slight increase in 2011–2012.

When most people think of violence at school and school shootings they think of Columbine (see *A Focus on Research* textbox), but even within the area of violence and shootings at schools this type of school shooting is very rare. Muschert offers a typology of the five types of shootings that can happen on school grounds (see Table 8.1).[30]

While it is incredibly unlikely that youth will die a violent death while at school, it is actually more likely that they will be a victim of crime on campus than off. In 2010, there

FIGURE 8.4 Number of School-Associated Homicides in Youth Ages 5–18, by Location

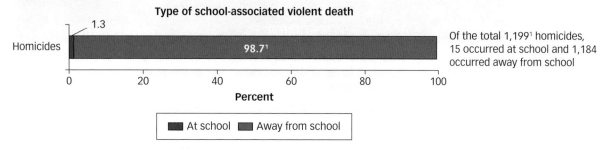

Type of school-associated violent death

Of the total 1,199[1] homicides, 15 occurred at school and 1,184 occurred away from school

Note: "At school" includes on school property, on the way to or from regular sessions at school, and while attending or traveling to or from a school-sponsored event. Estimates were revised and may differ from previously published data.

Source: Data on homicides of youth ages 5–18 at school and total school-associated violent deaths are from the Centers for Disease Control and Prevention (CDC), 2012 School-Associated Violent Deaths Surveillance Study (SAVD), partially funded by the U.S. Department of Education, Office of Safe and Healthy Students, previously unpublished tabulation (February 2015); data on total homicides of youth ages 5–18 for the 2011–12 school year are from the Supplementary Homicide Reports (SHR) collected by the Federal Bureau of Investigation and tabulated by the Bureau of Justice Statistics, preliminary data (June 2014).

FIGURE 8.5 Number of Students, Staff, and Nonstudent School-Associated Violent Deaths at School, 1992–2012

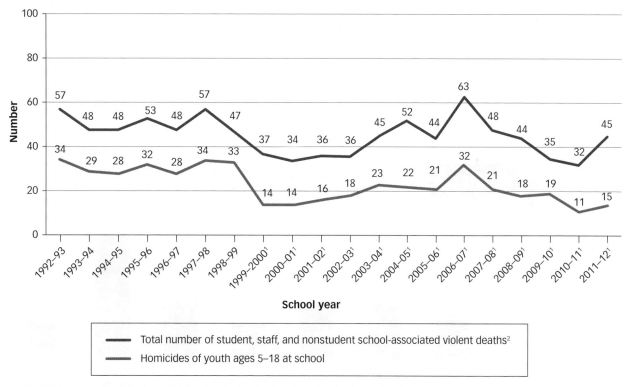

Source: Data on homicides of youth ages 5–18 at school and total school-associated violent deaths are from the Centers for Disease Control and Prevention (CDC), 2012 School-Associated Violent Deaths Surveillance Study (SAVD), partially funded by the U.S. Department of Education, Office of Safe and Healthy Students, previously unpublished tabulation (February 2015); data on total homicides of youth ages 5–18 for the 2011–12 school year are from the Supplementary Homicide Reports (SHR) collected by the Federal Bureau of Investigation and tabulated by the Bureau of Justice Statistics, preliminary data (June 2014).

[1]Data from 1999 -2000 onward are subject to change until interviews with school and law enforcement officials have been completed. The details learned during the interviews can occasionally change the classification of a case.

[2]A school-associated violent death is defined as "a homicide, or legal intervention (involving a law enforcement officer), in which the fatal injury occurred on the campus of a functioning elementary or secondary school in the United States," while the victim was attending or travelling to or from an official school sponsored event. Victims include students, staff members, and others who are not students, from July 1, 1992 through June 30, 2012.

Note: "At school" includes on school property, on the way to or from regular sessions at school, and while attending or travelling to or from a school-sponsored event. Estimates were revised and may differ from previously published data.

TABLE 8.1 Typology of School Shootings and Violence on School Grounds

TYPE OF SHOOTING	PERPETRATOR	REASON/MOTIVE
Rampage shootings	Member or former member of school (student, former student, employee, former employee)	Symbolic significance to exact revenge or gain power
Mass murders	Non-member of school, typically an adult	Symbolic significance, often to gain power
Terrorist attacks	Individuals or groups advancing a political or ideological goal	Politically motivated attack, selected for symbolic importance
Targeted shootings	Member or former member of school (student, former student, employee, former employee)	Targeting an individual or individuals for some real or perceived slight
Government shootings	Military or police	As a response to student protests or riots

were 828,400 incidents of nonfatal victimization (theft and violent crime) at school, while there were 652,500 incidents of nonfatal victimization away from school. This is a victimization rate of 32 incidents at school per 1,000 youth to 26 incidents away from school per 1,000 youth.

Victimization at school also varies depending on who or where you are and what type of victimization we are talking about.[31] In 2013, younger students (6th grade) reported

FIGURE 8.6 Percentage of Students in Grades 9–12 Who Reported Being Threatened or Injured With a Weapon on School Property, by Race/Ethnicity, 2013

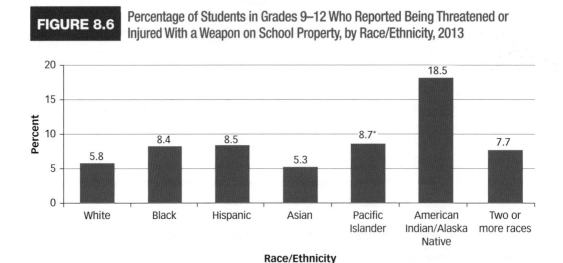

Source: Centers for Disease Control and Prevention, National Center for Chronic Disease Prevention and Health Promotion, Youth Risk Behavior Surveillance System (YRBSS), 2013. Reproduced in Zhang, A., Musu-Gillette, L., and Oudekerk, B.A. (2016). *Indicators of School Crime and Safety: 2015* (NCES 2016-079/NCJ 249758). National Center for Education Statistics, U.S. Department of Education, and Bureau of Justice Statistics, Office of Justice Programs, U.S. Department of Justice. Washington, DC.

*Interpret data with caution. The coefficient of variation (CV) for this estimate is between 30 and 50 percent.

Note: Race categories exclude persons of Hispanic ethnicity. "On school property" was not defined for survey respondents.

In the News

9-Year-Old Tasered

While still relatively uncommon, the use of a Taser (stun gun) on children is not unheard of. A case in Mt. Sterling, Ohio (population 1,800) is an example of the use of a stun gun on a boy accused of skipping school.

A 9-year-old boy, weighing between 200 and 250 pounds, was tased when a police officer came to the child's home investigating a truancy complaint. The boy's mother told her son to comply with the police officer, but the boy dropped to the ground, becoming dead weight. He also refused to be handcuffed, lying on his hands so that the officer could not reach them. The boy was told that if he did not stop resisting arrest he would be shocked by the stun gun.

According to the arresting officer, "He refused any and all orders. I told him if he did not stop flailing and place his hands behind his back, I would deploy the Taser on him. He still did not comply to my orders to stop resisting." The boy was tased twice by the officer before the officer could successfully handcuff him. An ambulance was called to check the boy. Because the boy refused to be handcuffed, he was also charged with resisting arrest (which is a delinquency charge). The truancy charge itself is considered a status offense.

While the police chief was not the officer who tased the boy, he was placed on paid leave for waiting two days before he informed the mayor of the tasing incident. After being placed on leave, the police chief announced he would be resigning due to a problematic budget that he feels keeps him from doing his job. The town is so small that the police chief is its only full-time officer. With the resignation of the police chief, the town basically

Jason Bain

While there is a growing dialogue concerning the use of Tasers on children, there is no systematic policy across jurisdictions as to how the Taser should be used.

has no police force as other officers are either part-time or volunteers. Because the town is without a police force, the Madison County Sheriff's department has been asked to take over patrolling duties.

Some of the residents are up in arms about the tasing incident, while others are worried about the loss of their police force.

DISCUSSION QUESTION

1. This news article illustrates the criminalization of such behaviors as skipping school (truancy) that, in the past, were more often considered status offenses. Are there benefits to treating truancy as a crime? Are there drawbacks to it? How far should an authority figure (police officer, teacher) go to stop truancy?

Source: Adapted from Report: 9-year-old who skipped school is Tasered. (2012). *U.S. News on NBCNews.com*, March 13. Retrieved from http://usnews.msnbc.msn.com/_news/2012/03/13/10669114-report-9-year-old-who-skipped-school-is-tasered

more violent victimization at school than their older counterparts (10–11th grade). Girls had similar rates of general victimization at school as boys (3%, down from 10% for boys and 9% for girls in 1995). And experiencing violent victimization (as measured by threats and injuries with weapons on school property) varied by race and ethnicity, with American Indian/Alaska Native youth most likely to experience violence and Asian youth least likely (see Figure 8.6).

BULLYING AND CYBERBULLYING

While most delinquency and victimization at school is categorized the way we traditionally categorize crime—as property crime or violent crime (just as we have discussed the likelihood of delinquency and victimization above)—some forms of victimization and delinquency are more specific to the school setting. While **bullying** and **cyberbullying** may not always occur on the school campus, they are predominantly linked to the school experience in some way—we go into greater detail with these two behaviors below.

A Focus on Research

●●●
●●●
●●●
●●
●●
●●
●●
●●
●●
●●
●●
●●
●●

Leavy and Maloney's American Reporting of School Violence and "People Like Us": A Comparison of Newspaper Coverage of the Columbine and Red Lake School Shootings

In the article "American Reporting of School Violence and 'People Like Us': A Comparison of Newspaper Coverage of the Columbine and Red Lake School Shootings" published in *Critical Sociology*, Patricia Leavy and Kathryn P. Maloney compare the media coverage of school shootings in Columbine (1999) and Red Lake Indian Reservation (2005).[32] The researchers engaged in a qualitative content analysis of a national paper (the *New York Times*) and a local paper in each community of these two events.

With the shooting at Columbine came national, "saturation" coverage (the coverage of an event on a 24-hour news loop) and headlines such as "Massacre at Columbine" and "Terror in the Rockies." On April 20, 1999, Dylan Klebold and Eric Harris killed 15 people (including themselves, eventually) and wounded 23 during the attack at Columbine. By all accounts, Klebold and Harris planned significant violence, planting bombs that, for the most part, failed. They stalked their victims, and their violence was racialized, including the fatal shooting of a black student who was called "nigger" moments before he was killed. The shooting at Red Lake High School was the largest school shooting since Columbine, but received very little media (in the form of television) attention. On March 21, 2005, Jeff Weise killed his grandfather (a Red Lake police officer) and his grandfather's girlfriend, stole his grandfather's guns, ammunition, vest, and police car, and went to Red Lake High School. He killed an unarmed security guard and then proceeded to shoot at students

Wikimedia Commons

The Columbine massacre received an incredible amount of media coverage including pictures of Dylan Klebold and Eric Harris. In contrast, the Red Lake massacre received local, but very little, national coverage.

and teachers. He killed nine people and injured five before he turned the gun on himself.

In examining the media coverage of these events, Leavy and Maloney found that the Columbine shooting attained a national status and "collective memory" while the Red Lake shooting received minimal national attention. Among other reasons, they point to the differences in race and socioeconomic status of the two schools and surrounding communities. While Columbine is in a middle- to upper-class suburb (Littleton) and Klebold and Harris were white youth, Red Lake is a poverty-stricken Indian reservation and Weise was Native American. While listing several factors for why Columbine created a larger media frenzy, one reporter illuminated the importance of race and class by saying Littleton "is full of what we call PLU, 'People Like Us.'"

Leavy and Maloney find that this made the media narrative of Columbine focus on the "senseless" nature of the shootings. Columbine came to represent an "every city," and the shooting came to be thought of something that could happen "anywhere." In comparison, Red Lake was distinguished from other communities by focusing on the fact that it was a poverty-stricken Indian reservation. Race and class became the central foci of the media coverage of the Red Lake shooting.

Their study concludes that the "overarching message from the newspaper studies was that a white upper-middle class teen needs the media to get the idea to shoot his fellow classmates, while a non-white, poor teen only needs access to weapons to come up with the same idea. The press's narrative implies that violence in poor minority communities is not socially significant and that when white middle-class people/ communities, 'people like us,' are involved in the killing, the event is by nature extraordinary."[33]

DISCUSSION QUESTION

1. This study suggests that when white middle- or upper-class youth engage in violence, it is seen as a senseless, extraordinary act that is both fascinating and in need of explaining. Violence from youth of color and poor youth is presented as expected and not in need of explaining (although may be in need of documenting). Can you find more examples of juvenile violence in the media in which the white juvenile violence is presented as senseless and the juvenile-of-color violence is framed as expected or easy to understand?

Bullying

Bullying is not a behavior that receives much focus in the sociological study of crime and delinquency; a predominant amount of the research appears in educational and psychology journals. However, it has become a global concern,[34] and in the lives of juveniles it might be one of the most prevalent forms of both victimization and delinquent behavior to happen in the school.[35]

One of the main characteristics of bullying is its repeated nature.[36] But in addition to being repetitious, it is aggressive and often focused on individuals who are perceived as different or powerless.[37] In fact, bullying often seems to be used as a way to stigmatize and label someone who is seen as different from the group. Juveniles who offer reasons for bullying talk about the victim as an outsider and misfit, who somehow defies or breaks the social norms established among students. Students who demand conformity see "odd students" as deserving of hostility.[38]

Either bullying can be direct, physical attacks, including the threat of physical harm, or it can be more indirect including such behaviors as slander, the spreading of rumors, social exclusion, and manipulation. Several studies have found a gender relationship to types of bullying, with boys more likely to engage in direct forms of bullying and girls more likely to engage in indirect forms of bullying (although some research has found that boys are more likely to engage in *all* forms of bullying, but if girls bully it is likely indirect).[39]

Homophobic Bullying and Sexual Harassment: Two Specific Types of Bullying

Homophobic Bullying. Homophobic bullying is bullying directed at gay, lesbian, bisexual, transgender, and "questioning" (GLBTQ) students. Bullying victimization is much higher among youth who identify as GLBTQ than youth who identify as heterosexual.[40] In fact, the 2009 National School Climate Survey reports that 40% of GLBTQ students reported being physically bullied over their sexual orientation, and 85% of GLBTQ students reported being verbally bullied because of their sexual orientation.[41] Perhaps because of this pervasive harassment, GLBTQ juveniles are 3 times more likely to miss school than their heterosexual counterparts.

Cyberbullying: The use of technology such as social media sites or texting to intimidate another individual.

School characteristics can affect the likelihood of homophobic bullying. Schools with large populations, a larger percentage of college-bound students, and an urban setting with more class and racial and ethnic diversity have less homophobic bullying than smaller schools or schools that are more homogeneous (meaning students have more similar characteristics). In addition, schools in which teachers receive training or feel empowered to address homophobic bullying are less likely to have such bullying, while schools that have no training or where teachers report that parents, staff, and students react negatively to intervening in homophobic bullying are more likely to encourage (or at least discourage) such bullying. Finally, the presence of social support networks in schools such as clubs or Gay-Straight Alliances are linked to less homophobic bullying in schools.[42]

Sexual Harassment. While sexual harassment and bullying are often thought of and studied separately, they are similar in many ways. The U.S. Department of Education's definition of school sexual harassment offers similarities to bullying:

> Sexual Harassment is defined as unwelcome sexual advances, requests for sexual favors, and other verbal, nonverbal, or physical conduct of a sexual nature by an employee, by another student, or by a third party, that is sufficiently severe, persistent, or pervasive to limit a student's ability to participate in or benefit from an education program or activity, or to create a hostile or abusive educational environment.[43]

A study by the American Association of University Women found that 19% of students reported experiencing systematic sexual harassment (as opposed to occasional sexual harassment) compared to 13% of students who reported being victims of bullying.[44] Sexually harassing behaviors can look very similar to bullying, including sexual comments, gestures, or rumors; sexual graffiti on bathroom and locker room walls; being spied on while dressing or showering at school; being touched, grabbed, or pinched in a sexual manner; having clothes pulled up, off, or down in a sexual way; and being listed in "slam books" that are circulated identifying students and including derogatory sexual comments.[45]

And sexual harassment often has similar consequences to bullying, with individuals who have been harassed reporting more anxiety, depression, fear, and embarrassment, isolation from friends and family, poor school performance, tardiness, skipping, and dropping classes.

The consequences of bullying are significant. Juveniles who are bullied are more anxious, lonely, insecure, and unhappy,[46] and have greater difficulty making friends and poorer relationships with classmates. In addition, juveniles who are bullied see a drop in their grades, perhaps because bullied youth also report more school absenteeism and withdrawals from school.[47] In addition to these immediate problems, individuals who were bullied in school report bullying and increased depression and other mental health problems later in life. Bullied youth are also more likely to commit suicide.

Cyberbullying

Peer interaction has also been transformed by the technological and social act of cyberbullying. Like the bullying that takes place in person, cyberbullying is threatening behavior but occurs over a computer and in cyberspace. There are a variety of mechanisms by which cyberbullying can occur, including the use of social networking sites, cell phones, e-mail, blogs, and chat rooms. What makes a given act of communication cyberbullying is "the willful and repeated harm through the use of computers, cell phones and other electronic devices."[48] The intent of the act is to make the target of cyberbullying feel degraded, insulted, scared, and/or embarrassed.[49] Youth can now very easily decide to take part in bullying someone from afar—it simply takes a few clicks of a computer mouse, a few words typed, or a few images posted or sent. This bullying can have widespread repercussions, because electronic communication between peers is speedy and a rumor, negative post, or picture can be spread to many people with very little effort on the part of the bully. Recent estimates vary, but studies of cyberbullying in the 2000s typically show that between 18% and 36% of youth self-report having been the victim of cyberbullying at some point in time, and between 11% and 20% of youth self-report to have engaged in acts of cyberbullying.[50]

There are a number of different methods of cyberbullying, as shown in Table 8.2.[51] Like person-to-person bullying, cyberbullying has a number of negative effects on the person who is targeted. In any case of bullying, the target feels somewhat helpless to avoid harassment and violence, but these feelings are exacerbated when a person is being targeted online. This is because there are so few rules and laws addressing cyberbullying, and even when they do exist the question becomes, how can adults police cyberspace? Youth victims of cyberbullying react in a number of different ways. Usually their first reaction is to do nothing, because they do not know what to do. Then, gradually, if the bullying continues, they may become depressed, become angry, and/or engage in acts of retaliation or delinquency.[52]

Like traditional bullies, cyberbullies are thought to be attempting to exert some sort of power or superiority over others to feel good about themselves, but are doing it in a more anonymous manner—one might say that they are hiding behind their electronic devices in many cases. Typically, all types of bullies have undergone significant stress before they begin bullying, and they have reacted to this stress by becoming emotionally frustrated and/or angry. Youth who bully have been shown to be much more likely to engage in other acts of delinquency as well and more antisocial behaviors in general. Some research indicates that girls tend to be the victims of cyberbullying more often than boys,[53] which is interesting given that boys are more likely to be bullied in person than girls.[54] When girls cyberbully others it tends to take the form of spreading rumors, and when boys cyberbully it often takes the form of posting videos or pictures aimed to cause harm. In terms of race, it is yet unclear which youth are more apt to be engaged in cyberbullying; there are indications that white youth report it more often, but cyberbullying is common among all racial and ethnic groups.[55]

There is a gendered relationship with bullying. While girls are more likely to engage in indirect bullying, boys are more likely to engage in direct forms of bullying. How might we address both types of bullying, and should our responses be gendered, too?

TABLE 8.2 Methods of Cyberbullying

DIRECT CYBERBULLYING	INDIRECT CYBERBULLYING
Property (e.g., sending a virus-infected file)	Outing of e-mail-entrusted information
Verbal (e.g., using the Internet or mobile phone to insult or threaten)	Masquerading (e.g., deceiving someone by pretending to be someone else)
Nonverbal (e.g., sending threatening or obscene pictures or illustrations)	Spreading gossip by mobile phone, e-mail, or chat
Social (e.g., excluding someone from an online group)	Taking part in voting on a defamatory polling website

Source: Vanderbosch and Van Cleemput (2009, p. 1352).

The expansion of bullying into the cyberspace realm has made educators, parents, and other adults even more concerned about stopping the practice.[56] Both targets and perpetrators of cyberbullying are more likely than other youth to have suicidal thoughts or to commit suicide than youth who have not been bullied.[57] Although he had just reached the age of majority in New Jersey and was considered a legal adult, the tragic results of the incident in which 18-year-old Rutgers student Tyler Clementi was cyberbullied by a roommate, Dharun Ravi, serves as a reminder of the repercussions of cyberbullying upon vulnerable young people. Ravi filmed Clementi having sexual relations with another young man and streamed it live over the Internet. After Clementi found out he felt humiliated and committed suicide. Thirteen-year-old Seth Walsh, a gay teen from Tehachapi, California, was bullied both in person and in cyberspace prior to his suicide in 2010, and 15-year-old Billy Lucas, a gay teen from Greensburg, Indiana, was cyberbullied prior to his suicide as well. These well-publicized cases are among several others in which teens who were cyberbullied or bullied committed suicide in the face of explicit homophobia.[58]

In the face of such potentially serious consequences, adults must contend with the issue of how to curtail vicious acts that are done electronically, and are not linked to a physical place in the same way as traditional bullying. For example, cyberbullying does not always take place on a school computer and thus is not necessarily linked to a school. It can have negative repercussions for a school, however, when a student who is being cyberbullied by another student and the student who is doing the cyberbullying interact with one another on campus. Although students have free speech rights, a 2007 decision by the U.S. Supreme Court, *Morse v. Frederick*, stated that student speech can be restricted if deemed offensive or contrary to the educational purpose of the school. In light of this decision, it appears as though educators and administrators can take steps to restrict speech online that may cause harm or potential violence on school grounds, or that interferes with the educational mission of the school.[59]

One step that schools are taking is enforcing bans on cell phone use in classrooms—adults can then confiscate the phones of youth suspected to be cyberbullying or acting out inappropriately. Yet, this sort of measure can only go so far to stop a much larger problem. Teachers and administrators simply can't jump on any student's cell phone and start searching it for offensive and/or bullying material, because this is a violation of students' Fourth Amendment rights.[60] In addition, cyberbullying takes place off of school grounds quite a bit, which limits intervention of school employees. Not all victims of cyberbullying share their victimization with an adult; many hide it out of shame, or for other reasons such as thinking nobody can help them stop it, fears of having their access to technology limited or taken away, and/or fears about disclosing their sexuality, all of which make it a difficult

on the MEDIA •••

The New Trend: Cyberbullying Laws That Protect Teachers

While many states are turning toward laws that focus on cyberbullying, there is still a ways to go since many of these states do not include criminal punishments or consider behaviors off the school campus. Another type of cyberbullying also lags behind: the bullying of teachers.

North Carolina has passed a bill, the School Violence Prevention Act of 2012, making the cyberbullying of teachers illegal. This law makes it illegal for students to, among other things,

- Build a fake online profile;

- Post a real or doctored image of a school employee online;

- Make a statement, true or false, that is intended to provoke someone into stalking or harassing a school employee; and

- Sign a school employee up for a pornographic website.

Engaging in intimidating or harassing behavior of a school employee online is now a misdemeanor in North Carolina, punishable by a $1,000 fine or jail time.

DISCUSSION QUESTION

1. Instead of passing a law, how might schools help to protect teachers from online bullying from their students?

Source: Choney, S. (2012). Cyberbullying law protects teachers from students. *NBC News,* Technology, September 21. Retrieved from http://www.nbcnews.com/technology/technolog/cyberbullying-law-protects-teachers-students-1B6029252

problem to address. Although schools have created a number of different rules and regulations in schools that address issues of bullying, gender identity, and sexuality, cyberbullying is a topic that is not adequately addressed by the legal and school systems yet.[61]

THE POLICY OF PUNISHMENT IN SCHOOLS: THE SCHOOL-TO-PRISON PIPELINE

The school-to-prison pipeline is the argument that overly harsh rules, security enhancements, and punishments mean that for many students school becomes a preparation ground for prison. Students are trained to accept high levels of social control, and under these policies they are much more likely to be suspended or expelled, which is the first stage in the school-to-prison pipeline. The American Civil Liberties Union calls these policies

> a disturbing national trend wherein children are funneled out of public schools and into the juvenile and criminal justice systems. Many of these children have learning disabilities or histories of poverty, abuse or neglect, and would benefit from additional educational and counseling services. Instead, they are isolated, punished and pushed out. "Zero-tolerance" policies criminalize minor infractions of school rules, while high-stakes testing programs encourage educators to push out low-performing students to improve their schools' overall test scores. Students of color are especially vulnerable to push-out trends and the discriminatory application of discipline . . . children should be educated, not incarcerated.[62]

Nicholson-Crotty, Birchmeier, and Valentine found that out-of-school suspensions were racially disproportionate and that this overrepresentation of youth of color in school suspensions (the study was conducted in Missouri) was linked to an overrepresentation of youth of color in court referrals to the juvenile justice system.[63] We can see in our examples

•••
Dignity in Schools Campaign: A national coalition of grassroots organizations that advocate for human dignity in our schools.

School-to-prison pipeline: An argument that overly harsh rules, security enhancements, and punishments mean that for many students school becomes a preparation ground for prison.

from the CLASSROOM
to the COMMUNITY

The Dignity in Schools Campaign

The Dignity in Schools Campaign is a national coalition of grassroots organizations that advocate for human dignity in our schools and are focused on the detrimental impact of what they call "push out" in these schools.

School pushout refers to the numerous and systemic factors that prevent or discourage young people from remaining on track to complete their education and has severe and lasting consequences for students, parents, schools, and communities. These factors include, among others, the failure to provide essential components of a high quality education, lack of stakeholder participation in decision-making, over-reliance on zero-tolerance practices and punitive measures such as suspensions and expulsions, over-reliance on law enforcement tactics and ceding of disciplinary authority to law enforcement personnel, and a history of systemic racism and inequality. These factors have an impact on all students, but have a disproportionate impact on historically disenfranchised youth.[64]

The coalition is made up of youth, parents, educators, grassroots groups, and policy and legal advocacy groups, and their cause (ending zero-tolerance policies and social control–based responses to student misconduct) has earned so much attention that the U.S. Department of Justice and the U.S. Department of Education hosted a conference titled "Civil Rights and School Discipline: Addressing Disparities to Ensure Equal Educational Opportunity."

The organization:

- Advocate[s] for federal policy change to promote alternatives to zero-tolerance discipline through the reauthorization of the Elementary and Secondary Education Act (ESEA, a.k.a. No Child Left Behind) and other federal initiatives.

- Support[s] state and local campaigns by member groups to end pushout and implement positive approaches to school climate and discipline, such as positive behavior supports, restorative practices, conflict resolution and mediation programs.

- Develop[s] model school policies for school districts and legislators that guarantee fundamental human rights standards for quality education, participation, dignity and freedom from discrimination.[65]

Recently, the coalition has published a Model Code[66] highlighting how schools might move away from zero-tolerance policies that add to the school-to-prison pipeline and instead focus on restorative practices that are tailored to the student, school, and community. This code focuses on five issues in student education and schooling: (1) the academic, social, and emotional development of youth; (2) policies and practices for ensuring the participation of the community, students, and parents and guardians; (3) transformation of the educational system's approach to discipline; (4) policies and practices to address discrimination in education, with a focus on discrimination based on race and ethnicity, national origin, sex, gender identity, sexual orientation, religion, disability, or economic or other statuses; and (5) transparency in data, monitoring, and accountability for all stakeholders, including students, parents and guardians, and the community.

DISCUSSION QUESTION

1. Thinking of your own high school experience, what were the discipline policies at your school? Did your school have policies and practices that addressed discrimination? Were they well known? Were students, parents, guardians, and the community welcomed to participate in school decisions?

Source: Reprinted by permission of Dignity in Schools: http://www .dignityinschools.org

later in this section that other punishments are racially disproportionate across the United States and that school policies are increasingly more socially controlling.

Punishments in Schools: Corporal Punishment, Restraint, and Seclusion

Spanking in schools may seem like something from the distant past (we must admit, before writing this book, we weren't aware that it was actually still being used). However, in 1977 the Supreme Court, in the *Ingraham v. Wright* case, ruled that corporal punishment in schools did not violate the cruel and unusual punishment clause of the 8th Amendment or the due process clause of the 14th Amendment. Thus states have the right to individually determine whether corporal punishment is allowed in schools. This means that 19 states still allow corporal punishment in their schools. These states allow school districts (school boards for those districts) to set the policy as to whether spanking can be a punishment option. There are surprisingly few regulations on the act itself. There are guidelines, but not strict rules, in many of the 19 states about how many times a student can be paddled in a single spanking event. Many states do not require that parents be informed that their child will be spanked prior to the event, although parents do need to be informed that their child has been spanked after the event. In some states, parents may request that their child not be spanked, but if their child is accidentally spanked (e.g., the school administrator does not check the file beforehand to determine whether the parent has given permission), the parent has no legal right to sue the school.[67]

One of the most troubling issues about spanking is the growing racial disproportionality of its implementation. In other words, over the years, a larger percentage of black youth than white youth have been spanked. Table 8.3 shows that in 1976, 29% of the youth who were spanked were black, but the number has risen as high as 39% (through much of the 1990s), and, for the last year that data were reported (2006), 36% of all youth who had been spanked were black. While racial disproportionality is increasing, the overall number of youth being spanked has been decreasing (from 447,314 in 1976 to 79,613 in 2006).

In addition to corporal punishment, the U.S. Department of Education, Office for Civil Rights also tracks the use of restraint and seclusion as forms of punishment. In the 2013–2014 school year, more than 100,000 students were placed in seclusion, involuntarily confined, or physically restrained at school. **Seclusion** refers to involuntary confinement alone in a room they are prevented from leaving (it does not include timeouts, which are an accepted behavior management technique involving a non-locked setting). **Physical restraint** refers to restricting the ability of a student to move his or her head, arms, legs, or torso, and does not include physically escorting a student, which might including holding him or her by the hand or arm. These forms of punishment are also implemented in an unequal manner, with 67% of the students having some form of physical, emotional, or learning impairment (12% of the general student population has an identified impairment), and black and white boys representing 8% and 26% of the general student population but being 18% and 43% of students who are restrained or secluded.[68]

Should there be state or federal policy banning corporal punishment in schools?

Zero Tolerance and Increased Social Control

There has been a growing trend in schools in the United States to rely on increased measures of social control (for example, police and metal detectors) to address perceived increases in delinquency (remember delinquency has generally been on the decline—see Chapter 3). These issues have been framed by school safety issues and the very significant budget cuts, leading to loss of teachers and staff and increased class sizes. One of these social control measures is the zero-tolerance policy.

Zero-tolerance policies popped up across the country in the late 1980s and early 1990s, with some schools enacting harsh penalties for weapons or drugs on campus.[69] The first systematic use of zero tolerance was introduced through the Gun-Free Schools Act of 1994. This federal law required that any school receiving federal money needed to have in place a policy that expelled students who brought a firearm to school campus. The law was reauthorized in 2001 with the No Child Left Behind Act. Because the Gun-Free Schools Act demanded that states put in place a policy for the possession of firearms on school property, all states at least enacted a policy that addressed the possession of firearms, although many states went much farther than this.

While the initial policy was designed to focus on youth who brought firearms to school (who one might assume are more dangerous than youth who do not bring guns to school),[70] the extensions of this initial act went far beyond firearms to include such weapons as daggers, knives with blades of more than 3 inches, knives that open mechanically, and brass knuckles.[71] And, in addition to weapons, some states and/or school districts have extended the policy to include drugs or "problematic" behaviors such as insubordination or disruption.[72] These extensions, it might be argued, are one of the central concerns with a zero-tolerance policy.

Opponents of zero-tolerance policies argue that they are rigid, criminalize childish behavior at worst, and, even when used on behaviors that might be considered delinquent, offer a punishment approach when a rehabilitative approach may be more appropriate. It is hard to disagree when we see some of the behaviors that have been "caught" under zero tolerance:

- The parents of a 9-year-old boy in New York were called, and he was threatened with suspension for bringing a 2-inch LEGO character to school. The character was a police officer, and it carried a tiny plastic gun.[73]

- A 7-year-old boy in New Jersey was charged with carrying an imitation gun onto school grounds for bringing a Nerf-type gun that fired soft Ping-Pong–sized balls. The charge is a criminal misdemeanor.[74]

- A sophomore in Texas was suspended from school for answering his cell phone when his dad called. His dad was deployed in Iraq, and the boy, who was going through something rough, had asked his mother to get in contact with his dad and have him call when he could. Answering the phone violated the school's zero-tolerance policy on cell phones.[75]

- In New York, a 12-year-old girl was arrested and led away from her school in handcuffs for doodling her name on her desk in erasable marker. The school admitted that handcuffing the girl was excessive, but still carried through with her suspension.[76]

- A 6-year-old boy in Delaware, who had just joined the Cub Scouts, was suspended for 45 days for bringing his camping utensil to school to eat his lunch. The utensil is a

Visit edge.sagepub .com/bates2e to view a video about policing in schools.

• • •

Zero-tolerance policy:
The ideology of most U.S. government-funded drug prevention programs that states that no drug usage whatsoever is acceptable without serious consequences and all drugs are equally as harmful.

TABLE 8.3 Number of Students Struck Each Year in U.S. Public Schools

YEAR	# WHITE	%	# BLACK	%	TOT. KIDS HIT	%
1976	992,675	65	447,314	29	1,521,896	3.5
1978	940,467	65	411,271	29	1,438,317	3.4
1980	901,032	64	403,386	29	1,408,303	3.4
1982	no statistical projection was made this year					
1984	852,427	64	374,315	28	1,332,317	3.3
1986	659,224	60	345,411	31	1,099,731	2.7
1988	549,572	61	255,296	28	898,370	2.2
1990	346,488	56	208,543	34	613,760	1.5
1992	295,050	53	215,684	39	555,531	1.3
1994	256,363	54	182,394	39	470,683	1.1
1997	241,406	53	178,114	39	457,754	1.0
1998	199,572	55	135,523	37	365,058	0.8
2000	181,689	53	132,065	39	342,038	0.7
2003	159,446	53	115,819	38	301,016	0.6
2004	143,002	53	104,620	38	272,028	0.57
2006	119,339	53	79,613	36	223,190	0.46

Sources: The U.S. Department of Education, Office for Civil Rights (http://ocrdata.ed.gov).

combination spoon, fork, and knife, and the school district has a zero-tolerance policy for knives on school grounds.[77]

- There are also documented cases of suspension and expulsion from school for bringing aspirin, organic cough drops, nail files, paper clips, a model rocket, an inhaler for asthma, and a kitchen knife in a lunch box to cut chicken.[78]

While zero-tolerance policies have been in place since the early 1990s, they are not the only form of increased social control on school campuses. In addition to these policies, many schools have authorized the use of drug-sniffing dogs, hired private security details (overseen by the school), increased the police presence with officers (overseen by the local police departments) patrolling the perimeter of school grounds, and installed metal detectors and surveillance cameras.[79] All of these policies are part of the larger concern that schools are conditioning students to accept more social control in their lives and, in the case of youth of color especially, creating a pipeline from the classroom to juvenile detention facilities and finally prisons. The expectation that students live up to higher behavioral standards and the increasingly formal treatment for their bad behavior (and in some instances, behavior that many might not agree is bad) means that there is an increasing concern that school often does not mean a gateway to prosperity, but instead means a gateway prison.

In his book *Homeroom Security*, Kupchik examines discipline in American schools. He argues that this move toward hypersecurity and intolerance is counterproductive for five reasons:[80]

1. **Schools are overreacting:** While delinquency and crime exist in schools (as we saw earlier in this chapter), a focus on increasing security is both a detriment to other programs schools should be focusing on (after-school programs, counseling) and overly severe for most of the behaviors that are addressed (most are misbehavior at best, and often not even considered illegal behaviors).

2. **Real student problems are often ignored:** By focusing so intently on finding and punishing bad behavior, the *reasons why* students misbehave are going unexamined.

3. **Students are being taught the wrong lessons:** By focusing on zero-tolerance policies with no room for debate, students are taught their voices do not matter, and are discouraged from thinking critically about power relations. They learn they are powerless to contest how they are treated or to change the environment around them. In addition, students are socialized to accept exaggerated forms of social control in other areas of their lives, which decreases the healthy debate about issues of liberty and security in the United States.

4. **Student misbehavior is likely to get worse with these policies:** One of the strongest reasons why individuals opt to follow the rules is because they perceive them as fair. When rules become rigid, their application unreasonable, and their punishments too severe, individuals lose faith in the system and question the legitimacy of both the rules and the punishments. Under these conditions students may decide to, at best, ignore the rules and, at worst, openly defy a system they see as unfair.

5. **At-risk students are at greater risk:** These policies have been shown to increase the likelihood that kids already at risk for suspension, expulsion, or dropping out will go down that road. While some might argue that this is just catching the kids who we already know are going to be bad, there is evidence that many kids are unfairly targeted, and these enhanced policies exacerbate that problem.

What are the daily experiences for juveniles who attend schools with security guards or police officers in place? Are there other policies or practices that could be instituted that would offer some of the same benefits as security guards without focusing on suppression and social control?

These policies, critics argue, make the journey from school to prison more likely.

THE SCHOOL AND STUDENT RIGHTS

As must of the discussion in this chapter suggests, students do not always have the same rights in school that we might expect outside of school (but as we have been noting throughout this book, juveniles, in general, do not have the same rights and are not treated the same way as adults). Below are six Supreme Court cases that have an impact on juveniles while in school.

Tinker v. Des Moines Independent School District (1969). Three students protested the Vietnam war with black armbands at school and were suspended. The Supreme Court ruled that students (and teachers) do not "shed their constitutional rights to freedom of speech or expression at the schoolhouse gate." But this was not an unlimited right. The Supreme Court ruled that this right to expression needed to be balanced against the school's need to keep order. In other words, the activities cannot be disruptive to the learning environment.

Goss v. Lopez (1975). Ten youth were suspended for a disturbance in the lunchroom. One of the youth argued that he was a bystander and was denied his due process when he was automatically suspended. The Supreme Court agreed that a 10-day suspension was significant and that the school was required to establish a formal process in which students had the right to (1) oral or written notice of the suspension, (2) an explanation of the evidence the officials have, and (3) an opportunity to present his or her side of the story. Essentially, this means notice of the charges and a hearing to defend oneself. While it would be most likely the hearing would take place before the student was suspended, a student could be removed if it was thought he or she was an ongoing threat, but the hearing must take place during the suspension time.

Ingraham v. Wright (1977). A 14-year-old boy was paddled in the principal's office 20 times for initially being disruptive then refusing the first punishment of 5 paddles. He subsequently needed medical attention and was out of school for 10 days with bruising. The Supreme Court ruled that this event was not cruel and unusual punishment and that it was within the school's prerogative to use corporal punishment, although the justices cautioned school administrators to be thoughtful in their use of corporal punishment.

New Jersey v. T.L.O. (1985). A 14-year-old girl was found smoking in the bathroom at school by a teacher and was taken to the principal's office. The principal asked to see her purse and searched it, finding cigarettes, rolling papers, and marijuana. The police were called and the girl was found guilty of possession of marijuana. The girl appealed, arguing it was an unreasonable search and seizure. The Supreme Court ruled that while students have a legitimate expectation of privacy, this must be weighed against the school's need for "maintaining an environment in which learning can take place." This case established that the standard for searching student property on campus was "reasonable suspicion" instead of "probable cause."

Vernonia School District v. Acton (1995). A 12-year-old wanted to play football on his school team. The school required a random drug test, in which the 12-year-old was required to participate. His parents refused to allow him to be tested because they argued that there was no evidence he engaged in drug use. The school refused to allow him to play sports. He and his parents sued the school, arguing that it was an unreasonable search and seizure on the part of the school without a suspicion of illegal activity. The Supreme Court ruled that "students who voluntarily participate in school athletics have reason to expect intrusions upon normal rights and privileges, including privacy." In some ways an extension of the *T.L.O.* case, this case determined that "suspicion-less" searches were also allowed by the school in certain instances, in order to keep the school safe and student athletes off drugs.

Safford Unified School District v. Redding (2009). Officials received a report that a 13-year-old girl had given a classmate four prescription-strength ibuprofen and one over-the-counter naproxen. Based on this report, the officials searched her purse and, finding nothing, had her strip to her underwear and pull her bra and elastic of her underpants out and shake them to see if anything fell out. No contraband was found and the school did not contact the girl's parents during the investigation. The parents sued the school, saying that the strip search was an unreasonable search. The Supreme Court agreed that the strip search had gone too far, given the evidence that was available at the time and the danger presented by the pills weighed against the degradation that results from a strip search.

While schooling has not always been a large part of youth life, over the last 200 years its importance has grown in both youth development and socialization. Today youth spend a significant portion of their day in school or on school-related activities. Within the United States over the past 30 years, reading and math scores have increased, although there are differences in academic achievement based on gender and race. And, compared to other countries, the United States is average or below average in critical thinking and application of knowledge in the areas of reading, math, and science.

School has a strong link to delinquency and victimization in several ways. First, although school shootings are extremely rare, youth are more likely to be victimized at school than at other times during their day. Second, several school-related events (school failure and dropping out) and school experiences (tracking, alienation, and issues with social class) impact a youth's likelihood to engage in delinquency. Finally, some behaviors, which we are finding may be increasingly common in schools, have received less attention than they should in both the media and school policies. Two of these behaviors are bullying and cyberbullying. We see that many youth have experience with one or both of these, and certain subgroups (such as the GLBTQ population) report significant bullying and cyberbullying while at school.

Finally, schools are increasing their responses to crime and delinquency on campus, with the introduction of security guards—also called resource officers— tougher policies on behavior deemed delinquent or harmful (most popular is the zero-tolerance policy), and increased physical security such as metal detectors, video surveillance, and closed campuses with fences and/or security dogs. Those who study these changes in school safety policies argue that many of these security measures increase the likelihood of a school-to-prison pipeline, in which students are taught to accept increased social control in their lives, becoming desensitized to these forms of surveillance, and where minor forms of misbehavior increasingly become criminalized leading to more school suspensions, expulsions, and formal referrals to the juvenile justice system.

EYE ON DIVERSITY EXERCISE: EXAMINING SCHOOL DATA ON DELINQUENCY

This chapter has highlighted the relationship between school and delinquency, and our societal response to it. We have learned that while violence in the form of school shootings is a focus of the media, youth are quite unlikely to ever experience an event like this. However, other forms of delinquency are more likely to happen on school grounds than off, even though many of those acts are not focused on by the media or the public.

Some states require that public schools collect and report all crime and delinquency that happen on school grounds, while other states have no such requirement.

1. Does your state require that these data be collected? If so, how are these data reported? By school? By district? Are the data collected by gender or race, for example? What delinquency and victimization are reported (e.g., are sexual assaults or bullying reported)?

2. If you cannot find data for your state, this is interesting in and of itself. Is it because the data are not systematically collected (in which case, how do schools know how much security they need?), or is it that they are not required to tell the public?

3. Find crime/delinquency data from a state that is required to report (hint: North Carolina requires its public schools to report such data). What crime/delinquency is reported, and what is not?

4. Many more schools are required to make their school safety plans available to the public. Find a report for a school in the state for which you found data. How do its authors discuss crime and delinquency on their campus? How do they talk about safety? Is safety merely linked to physical safety, or do they discuss making their school a place where students can safely learn? Do they focus on the importance of after-school activities

or merely school safety officers? Does the school specifically discuss bullying or cyberbullying? Is there any place in the report where the school acknowledges the diversity of the student body?

5. If you were to create a school safety plan, what would you want to address? What makes

a "safe" school? What behaviors would you focus on? Should the focus be social control? Informal control? Education? Dignity? How would you work to acknowledge the diversity of the student body? Write your own school safety plan.

DISCUSSION QUESTIONS

1. What is the relationship between gender, race, and academic achievement in the United States? How might the issues of tracking and alienation impact these differences in academic achievement?

2. How might educational budgets impact the school experience and juvenile delinquency?

3. Explain the impact of bullying and cyberbullying on school campuses. Who is most likely to be bullied or cyberbullied? How might schools go about addressing the issues of bullying?

4. The members of your local school board have announced that they are very worried about school shootings on local middle school and high school campuses. For this reason, they have decided to increase school security, with metal detectors and armed security guards for each of the schools in the district. Given what you have learned in this chapter, comment on the school board's plan.

KEY TERMS

Academic achievement 219

Alienation 224

Bullying 232

Cyberbullying 232

Dignity in Schools Campaign 237

Dropping out 226

School failure 223

School-to-prison pipeline 237

Tracking 224

Zero-tolerance policy 240

CHAPTER PRETEST ANSWERS

1. False

2. True

3. False

4. False

5. True

6. False

7. False

8. True

9. True

$SAGE edge™

edge.sagepub.com/bates2e

Sharpen your skills with SAGE edge!

SAGE edge for students provides a personalized approach to help you accomplish your coursework goals in an easy-to-use learning environment. You'll find action plans, mobile-friendly eFlashcards, and quizzes, as well as videos, web resources, and links to SAGE journal articles to support and expand on the concepts presented in this chapter. Check out the website for original videos of former offenders discussing their experiences as juveniles.

PEERS AND GANGS IN CONTEXT

After reading this chapter, you should be able to

- List the two primary hypotheses about how peers and friends matter to delinquency

- Explain how gender matters to patterns of peer relationships and delinquency

- Outline the impact of a lack of friends on delinquency

- Discuss the different ways youth are using new technologies and their relevance to delinquency

- Analyze the consequences of labeling a group of youth as a gang

- Identify how race, ethnicity, class, gender, and sexuality play a role in gang formation and dynamics

- Recognize the most common societal responses to youth gangs and their consequences

Exclusive: "Escondido Police Crack Down on Juggalos"

Zealous fans of a decades-old rap duo have been the target of a crackdown by Escondido gang detectives after a string of street robberies and assaults. The group, whose members call themselves Juggalos, are devoted to the Insane Clown Posse and the facepaint-wearing rappers' label, Psychopathic Records. Many of the band's fans have said they're a nonviolent "family" of underdogs and social rejects, not a gang. But they admit a few young Juggalos have been causing trouble.

A handful of Juggalos in Escondido were reportedly committing strong-arm robberies and "pocket checks"—surrounding kids in the park and ordering them to empty their pockets and turn over valuables. In late May or early June, Juggalos allegedly beat and robbed someone and reportedly punched a woman and held her at knifepoint.

After that, detectives cracked down and frequently visited Grape Day Park—a gathering point for the group's members. The intense police attention has since driven most of the active Juggalos into hiding, detectives and friends of the group said. But the violence seemed confined to a small subset of the group in Escondido, said gang Detective Erik Witholt. Out of about 100 people in Escondido who identified themselves as Juggalos, only about a dozen or so have been causing serious trouble. The rest of the crimes tend to be minor, involving marijuana, alcohol or curfew violations, Witholt said.

"We don't want to keep them from exploring life," he said. "There's nothing wrong with being part of a group as long as it's not based on criminal enterprise.". . .

Juggalos typically wear red and black. If they have a logo, it's the "hatchet man," a cartoonish silhouette of a man running with a hatchet. Some have been arrested carrying actual hatchets or found wearing black-and-white face paint, Witholt said. They sometimes flash gang-like hand signs and shout out code words and sounds to greet one another. Tattoos and other symbols tend to fit with the Insane Clown Posse's theme, a blend of horror and carnivals. . . .

CHAPTER PRETEST

Test your knowledge of this chapter's material by determining whether the following statements are true or false. Be sure to compare your answers with the answers on page 274.

1. The teen years are considered the most "friendship intense" years of a person's life.

2. The socialization hypothesis of delinquency states that the amount of time that youth spend with friends away from parents, teachers, and other authority figures influences them to engage in delinquency.

3. Being friends with boys tends to increase the likelihood that girls will be involved in delinquency.

4. Children who experience rejection by their peers have a decreased risk of engaging in delinquency.

5. Research demonstrates that African-American teen girls living in cities with violence sometimes engage in relational isolation, a situated survival strategy.

6. Young people today live their lives in front of electronic devices, big and little, which allow them to communicate in ways that were not possible in previous generations.

7. There is one definition of what a gang is that is used by law enforcement officers and social scientists.

8. To understand gang formation it is important to understand large-scale issues such as immigration, migration, economic marginalization, racism, and sexism.

9. Civil gang injunctions are used to help gang-involved youth find jobs and shelter and form strong social connections.

In Escondido, Juggalos and police have said there have been scuffles between Juggalos and established Latino gangs in the area. None of the incidents resulted in serious injuries. Most Juggalos are white, but the group is not racially exclusive nor supremacist, authorities and members said.

Other law enforcement agencies in California and throughout the nation—including the Los Angeles County Sheriff's Department—have labeled Juggalos a gang, according to detectives and written reports. Escondido police officials stopped short of applying that label, saying they hope to prevent the group from getting to that point.

Source: Lowrey, Brandon. Exclusive: Escondido police crack down on Juggalos. *North County Times*, August 6, 2011. Reprinted with permission of the author.

● ● ●

Young people often tend to be drawn to and spend time with others who share similarities with them.

As the scenario described in the news story above demonstrates, there is a fine line involved when it comes to the question of whether a group of young people is simply a friendship group or a gang that commits delinquent acts together, and the label that is chosen has important consequences for the young people involved. The people with the power to officially decide (e.g., law enforcement officers) make judgments about youth groups based on their looks, behaviors, and location. And once these judgments are made there is often public disagreement with them—not everyone will agree that the labels chosen are appropriate. We will analyze the Juggalo scenario in detail in the latter half of this chapter, but for now we'd like you to begin thinking about your own involvement in peer groups as a young person.

We have all heard the famous saying "Birds of a feather flock together" and understand that it refers to the idea that people who think alike tend to be drawn to one another. Certainly, this seems to be the case for many people who choose to spend time with others like themselves. But, then again, some people are initially drawn to people very unlike themselves and fall into the "opposites attract" camp and may become more alike over time. Think back to your peer group during your teenage years. Who were your closest friends? How often did you spend time with them? What sorts of activities did you do together? Who decided? Did your friends introduce you to new behaviors or activities? Were any of these activities labeled delinquent, or could they have been? When you were in public together, did others perceive your group as a group of friends or a gang? How do you think that perception or label of your group affected your life? All of these questions raise ideas that we will consider in this chapter as we examine the topics of peers, technological innovations in youth communication and delinquency, and gangs.

When we discuss the issue of peers and friendship groups and their relationship to delinquency, we must recognize that these topics are especially important. There is arguably no other time in life like the teenage years in terms of being "friendship intense"—there is

The teenage years are known as being the most "friendship intense" years of a person's life.

no other phase in life in which people spend as much time with their friends, think as often about their friends as central to their daily lives, and are influenced as strongly by their friends and peers.[1]

WHY DO PEERS MATTER TO DELINQUENCY?

There are a couple of ways that scholars assume that peers matter to delinquency. The first is the socialization hypothesis of delinquency—youth who socialize with friends who are highly delinquent will be more apt to be delinquent themselves.[2] It is often believed that the tighter the friendship group and the more time spent just "hanging out" with highly delinquent peers, the more likely a youth will act out delinquently. According to this perspective, this factor of socialization with "delinquents" is central—people learn to be delinquent from their peers.

The second is the opportunity hypothesis of delinquency—the idea that the most important factor that influences youth to engage in delinquency is not necessarily having friends who are highly delinquent but is, instead, the amount of time that youth spend with their friends away from parents, teachers, and other social control agents.[3] According to this hypothesis, when youth have free time on their hands, and are able to spend it out of the sight of authorities and with friends or with other youth, they will have an increased probability of engaging in delinquency even if their companions are not. It is almost as though their imaginations get inspired during this free time to try things that they might not otherwise try.

Research demonstrates that both hypotheses are supported. First of all, youth have been shown to be socialized by their peers over time.[4] According to Haynie and Osgood, "Peer socialization has a meaningful causal influence on delinquency contrary to claims that this association is entirely attributable to respondents choosing friends who are similar to themselves."[5] In addition, the ways in which youth use their time are significantly related to delinquency—if there are no structured plans for that time and no authority figures around, a young person will often decide to "do something wild" for the fun of it, even if those around her or him tend not to engage in delinquency.[6]

● ● ●
Socialization hypothesis of delinquency: The hypothesis about delinquency that states that youth who socialize with friends who are highly delinquent will be more apt to be delinquent themselves.

Opportunity hypothesis of delinquency: The hypothesis that the most important factor that influences youth to engage in delinquency is the amount of time that youth spend with their friends away from parents, teachers, and other social control agents.

Research shows that even youth who do not normally get into trouble will engage in minor acts of delinquency if they have free time and there is little adult supervision.

FRIENDSHIP AND DELINQUENCY: HOW GENDER MATTERS

One important issue to take into account when we think of the most important peer group in young people's lives, their friends, is gender. Studies have demonstrated that the gender of a youth's friends is an important factor to consider. Some research has indicated that when teenage boys have a greater proportion of friendships with teenage girls than expected, those friendships result in a decrease in the odds that the boys will take part in violence. The opposite has been shown to hold true as well: When teenage girls have a greater proportion of teenage boy friends than expected, they are more likely to engage in violence than they would be otherwise.[7] This finding about violence is in keeping with what has been observed about mixed-gender friendships and delinquency in general: Being friends with boys tends to increase the likelihood that girls will be involved in delinquency of all kinds.[8] Being friends with girls sometimes inhibits boys' delinquency, but that inhibition is never of the same magnitude of the influence that boys exert on girls.[9]

This is the case because mainstream gender socialization makes many girls focus on upholding norms and rules, and try to encourage their friends to do the same, which amounts to discouraging their friends from getting into trouble with the law or committing acts of violence.[10] Girls are taught that to be feminine is to be "ladylike" and to follow rules; to go against the rules will result in serious ostracism and stigmatization, so, unsurprisingly, girls often internalize the rules and act upon them. Because boys are encouraged to display "masculine" characteristics and behaviors, they tend to be different than girls are with their friends; boys are often competitive, encourage risk-taking, and tease one another in ways that ultimately encourage delinquency and violent behaviors.[11] Boys and men hold more social power in society, and thus the direction in which influence more powerfully flows—from boys to girls—is unsurprising.

THE KID IN THE CORNER: THE IMPACT OF A LACK OF FRIENDSHIPS

What about the youth who doesn't have many friends? Is being an isolated youth something that protects a child from delinquency by keeping him or her away from "bad" influences? The reality is that the isolated child who experiences a lack of friendships at school may soon be involved in delinquency. Children who experience rejection by their peers have been shown to have an increased likelihood of involvement in delinquent behavior in their teenage years.[12] Yet, as you will see in the box focusing on Nikki Jones's research,[13] some girls do use isolation in the teenage years to avoid delinquency, so the

A Focus on Research

Jones's "'It's About Being a Survivor'. . . African American Girls, Gender, and the Context of Inner City Violence"

"'It's About Being a Survivor' . . . African American Girls, Gender, and the Context of Inner City Violence" is a chapter in a book that Nikki Jones coedited with Meda Chesney-Lind (*Fighting for Girls: New Perspectives on Gender and Violence*). In it, she sheds light on the ways in which African American teenage girls negotiate violence in their neighborhoods.[14] Based on field research and interviews she conducted over several years in Philadelphia and San Francisco, Jones found that, like African American boys, African American girls have a hard-and-fast focus on surviving in the midst of frequent neighborhood violence. Their race, class, and gender uniquely shape their experiences of navigating the violence. To survive on the street, girls need to be tough and to adopt a street-smart attitude; but, at the same time, gender norms and norms of middle-class black culture (and white culture) make it easy for others to condemn teen girls who are vocal and assertive. African American girls in inner cities are often forced between choosing to be labeled as "good" (passive, and possibly a victim) or as "ghetto" (street smart, and on the defense). In order to get by, they develop what Jones calls "situated survival strategies." One of the strategies African American teens develop is to engage in relational isolation, which is to avoid building close friendships with other teen girls. By distancing themselves from their peers, girls can avoid having to fight to defend a friend if that friend were to be confronted or provoked. That way, girls do not have to worry about getting caught up in violence and can keep surviving. Jones concluded that by failing to create deep friendships during adolescence, African American girls from tough neighborhoods are running the risk of stunting their psychosocial development; she fears they may have difficulty as adults having meaningful relationships and states that this survival strategy should be of concern to others as well.

DISCUSSION QUESTION

1. Did you ever have to refrain from making friends as a way of avoiding violence in your neighborhood when you were growing up? If so, what did you find was the consequence of that strategy? If not, did you use another situational survival strategy? If you did not live in an area in which neighborhood violence was a consistent threat, how does understanding the findings of Jones's research affect your views about others' experiences and their potentially long-term consequences?

relationship between isolation and delinquency is complex. The difference is that when adolescents consciously choose to be isolated for delinquency prevention and safety, they do not experience the feelings of rejection that isolated children often do.

CONVENTIONAL ADOLESCENCE OR NEW FORMS OF DELINQUENCY? THE USE OF TECHNOLOGY AS A MEANS OF PEER INTERACTION

As technological advancements have been developed over time, cell phones and computers have become tools for youth and adults alike to communicate more and in new ways. Youth have come to engage in new types of behavior with their peers, and some

Relational isolation: The avoidance of friendships that is actively pursued by some youth to protect themselves from violence.

of the behaviors fall in the gray area of behavior that is sometimes not officially considered delinquent behavior but is also not condoned in some adult circles. According to research done by the Pew Research Center,[15] the changes in youth behavior are marked and are related to the fact that around 92% of teens aged 13–17 report daily online activity and 75% have access to a smartphone. The majority of Internet use by teens occurs via phones and other mobile devices. The use of cell phones has increased the availability of Internet access to youth whose families cannot afford a home computer and/or Internet access and has made the ability to take and mail photos and videos accessible to anyone with a smartphone. So, the vast majority of teens today are hooked into the digital culture in ways that teens in the generations before them simply were not (see Figure 9.1).

Unlike the days in which teens communicated primarily by talking on the phone, now teens report that their most frequent type of communication with their peers is text messaging. Most teens send and receive about 30 text messages a day. Black and Latino youth report the most frequent use of the Internet out of all groups of teens and the most use of specialized apps like Kik or WhatsApp to text as well.[16] Less used, but increasingly popular, are sharing apps (e.g., Yik Yak) or sites where posts, texts, and images can be posted anonymously, with about 11% of teens using them.[17] Often the popular types of online communication today are about speed and living in the moment, and young people are unsurprisingly draw to them for these reasons.[18]

A great deal of young people's online activity is spent on social networking sites, and the popularity of these sites waxes and wanes over the years. As illustrated in Figure 9.1, the Pew Research Center found that in recent years, approximately 71% of teens use Facebook, 52% use Instagram, and 41% use Snapchat.[19] Twitter, Google+, Vine, and

FIGURE 9.1 Top Social Media Platforms for Teens

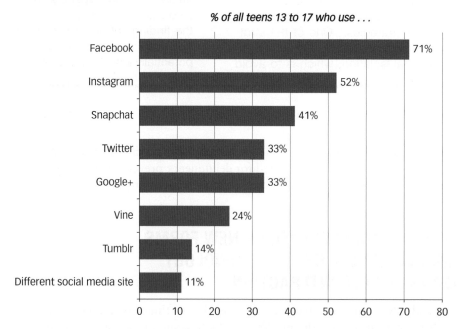

% of all teens 13 to 17 who use . . .

Source: Pew Research Center. (2015). *Teens, social media, & technology overview.* Retrieved from http://www.pewinternet.org/2015/04/09/teens-social-media-technology-2015/pi_2015-04-09_teensandtech_01/

Tumblr are all also noted as popular social media platforms for a number of adolescents. The pattern of social media use varies depending on the socioeconomic status of a teen's household, with teens from working-class households overwhelmingly relying on Facebook for their social networking and those from middle- and upper-income households using Instagram and Snapchat much more than other youth. Gender also influences social media use, with boys tending to be involved in online gaming more than girls and girls focusing their efforts more on social networking sites.

Teens often start romantic relationships by expressing interest in someone through a media site, and as adults do, they use social media to investigate information about people they like before (and after) getting involved with them.[20] Once they are involved in a romantic relationship, texting becomes the primary way of spending time with their partner over the course of a week.[21] The expectations for frequent communication are high among teens today because of their familiarity with different forms of technology; in one study by the Pew Research Center, the researchers found that 85% of teens expected communication with their romantic partners daily, and 11% of this group expected to have some form of communication with their romantic partners *every hour* of the day.[22] In the event that a relationship is not working out and a break-up is in order, the majority of teens do not think that the best way to do it is online or via text, in spite of the popularity of this misconception on the part of adults. Yet, the majority of youth note that when relationships end, there is often little privacy if they have a visible online presence.

Like romantic relationships, teen friendships are made, maintained, and broken through online interactions. The question of how friends' virtual interactions influence their actions off screen is an important one, especially when we think about delinquency and other risk-taking behaviors. There is conflicting evidence that online friendships and social networks are associated with increased delinquency. For example, Meldrum and Clark found in their school surveys of adolescents that the more virtual time that teens spend socializing with peers, the more frequently they engage in alcohol and marijuana use and some acts of delinquency, such as petty theft.[23] They concluded that when delinquency arises from virtual interactions, it is usually to help plan some sort of act of future delinquency offline, which is in contrast to the unstructured in-person socializing that is often hypothesized to lead to spontaneous delinquency.[24] On the other hand, Huang et al. found that the frequency of teen social networking involvement was not associated with increased risky behaviors.[25] What they did find was that being exposed to others' pictures of smoking and drinking alcohol was positively associated with teens' engagement in these behaviors. In addition, they found that teens who said their friends didn't drink alcohol were more likely to be affected by exposure to pictures of these same friends engaging in risky behavior than youth with friends they knew were alcohol drinkers. It appears that youth are especially influenced by the messages about what "normal" teenage behavior is as it is communicated through online pictures.[26]

Young people today live their lives in front of electronic devices, big and little, which allow them to communicate in ways that were not possible in previous generations.

It is important to note that although the accessibility of cell phones, computers, and tablets has given teens freedom to interact with peers in new ways, it has also provided parents and guardians with new ways of keeping tabs on what their children are doing at any given time. Youth can communicate with one another very frequently if they keep their phones or other electronic devices near them at all times, which they have been shown to do,[27] and parents can have the geographical tracking system activated on these devices to see where they are at nearly any point in the day. And, although it may not be the first reason for teens' love for their cell phones or computers, youth benefit by having ways to easily contact a loved one in the event that they are the victims of an act of delinquency or crime, or otherwise end up in trouble. Existing research demonstrates that parental social control plays a large role in minimizing online peer effects on delinquency.[28] The ever-increasing possibilities for youth surveillance that accompany the expanded use of technology must also be acknowledged as another factor influencing youth behavior.

In this section of the chapter, we will examine specific uses of technology that represent forms of peer communication and interaction that have garnered a lot of negative attention in recent years. As a result, there has been a desire on the part of some adults either to define the behaviors as delinquent or to otherwise assign disapproval and punishment to those who engage in them.

Sexting

In recent years, negative attention has been directed toward teens who engage in sexting—using their cell phones to send or receive sexually suggestive messages. The sending of such messages can involve a number of different methods, such as text messages, e-mail, and messaging on online social networks. Although some sexting is text-only messages, the majority of adult concern about these practices is directed toward teens who are involved in sending or receiving photographs or videos that are sexually suggestive. Recent research on sexting[29] estimated that about 4% of U.S. youth between the ages of 12 and 17 who have cell phones have sent a nude or nearly nude photo of themselves to someone else via cell phone. A much larger percentage, 15%–30% of U.S. youth of the same age range, are estimated to have received a sexually explicit image on their phone.[30] Youth who pay their own phone bills and, thus, have more control over their phone use and less oversight by an adult tend to engage in sexting more than youth who have adults who pay part or all of their bills. Boys and girls have been found to sext the same amount, and to be more likely to engage in the practice if they are near the end of their teen years and have an unlimited text messaging plan. Typically, teen sexting occurs within the following three types of scenarios:

1. Two people in a relationship are sexting instead of, or before, sexual interaction;

2. Someone forwards a picture or video sent to him or her to other people—either to brag about it or to shame a person after a breakup or fight; and

3. A girl or boy who wants to be in a relationship with someone sends the person a nude or nearly nude picture as a means of showing interest.[31]

● ● ●

Sexting: The use of cell phones or other electronic devices to send or receive sexually suggestive messages.

Many adults are worried about the social practice of teen sexting and its consequences. Concerns range from the need for youth to avoid stigmatization, particularly youth who send sexually explicit photos that may be disseminated to large numbers of people, to a concern that sexting is simply inappropriate sexual behavior for teens and needs to be stopped. Yet, given the cultural messages that abound in mainstream culture today, this is unlikely. As Hoffman states, "adults face a hard truth. For teenagers, who have ready access to technology and are growing up in a culture that celebrates body flaunting, sexting is laughably easy, unremarkable and even compelling: the primary reason teenagers sext is to look cool and sexy to someone they find attractive."[32]

Although the research on sexting is limited, a study by Wolfe, Marcum, Higgins, and Ricketts found that routine activities theory can be used to understand involvement in and exposure to sext messages.[33] Routine activities theory typically assumes that three factors must converge in space and time in order for an act of victimization to occur—a willing offender, an available target, and a lack of guardianship around that target.[34] In the case of sexting, the frequency with which youth use their cell phones and their use of their cell phones during school hours is related to their likelihood of receiving sexts. The probability is mediated by the supervision factors; teens who have cell phones that are part of a family cell phone contract are less likely to get sexts then teens who have prepaid phones or separate contracts. In addition, teens who go to schools with rules against cell phone use also increase the supervision or guardianship involved in their online activities and make it less likely they will receive sexts.

Sexting is not engaged in by most teens in the United States today, but the practice has been treated with the utmost seriousness. In several states, youth who have gotten caught sexting have been threatened with prosecution under child pornography laws (e.g., Pennsylvania, Ohio, Massachusetts). Many people disagree that sexting is the same as child pornography, however, and in some states teens who have been caught sexting have been tried under obscenity law or Internet crime law. Some argue that special "self-produced child pornography" laws for youth sexting need to be created[35] or a non–pornography-related sexting law specific to the practice. Given the nature of sexting and the fact it is a relatively new behavior for the law to address, one of the issues we should be aware of is the differential impact of the consequences on various groups. For example, girls are typically treated harsher than boys for their involvement in sexting. This is a classic example of unequal enforcement, where girls are held to a higher standard of behavior than boys.

The creation of a new category of delinquency or crime related to youth sexting is one that many critics state will simply widen the net of young people who are put into the juvenile justice system, unnecessarily give them records, and by extension, likely reduce their life opportunities. Yet, at least 20 states have created such laws and more than a dozen others are debating creating one in the near future.[36] Many states that are creating new targeted laws are making sexting a misdemeanor in lieu of a sex offense felony.[37] Proponents of these laws believe that rather than unnecessarily widening the net of social control, they are protecting adolescent sexters from the harsh consequences that they would face without them. Those who study sexting note that although both boys and girls engage in it, there is a double standard about the practice; boys are often laughed at for sending nude pictures of themselves, while girls are stigmatized as sexually available or without morals. In a world in which songs and videos promote sexting; youth, especially girls, are sexualized at a young age; pornography is widely available simply by clicking on the computer; and sexting is considered acceptable adult communication, it will be hard to prevent teens from engaging in the practice.[38]

Some young people today document their daily activities online, which can lead to trouble for them when the activities include acts of delinquency.

In the News

Snapchat Leads to Burglary Arrest

Although many teens like to use Snapchat because the pictures, videos, and other material that they send is said to only be accessible for a short amount of time, they often discover it still gets them into trouble. In April 2016, a 16-year-old in Appleton, Minnesota who allegedly broke into the local golf course clubhouse and stole their liquor became a suspect due to the use of Snapchat. The night began when he messaged his three friends on Snapchat and told them that he planned to burglarize the clubhouse. The other three friends, who ranged in age from 16 to 18 years of age, said that they waited outside the clubhouse in a car to see if he would do it. When he exited the clubhouse with a bunch of liquor bottles, they gave him a ride to one of their houses. Then, they took several pictures of the alcohol he stole and put it on Snapchat, along with a video showing two of them among the bottles (the other two could be heard on the video as well). Someone who saw the material on Snapchat reported his or her concerns to the police and provided the name of the Snapchat account used to post the material. The police followed up on the lead shortly after they heard that the golf course clubhouse had been broken into and went to the 16-year-old's house. They found many of the bottles there and charged him with second-degree burglary of a government building (because the clubhouse was owned by the city) and receiving stolen property. His friends also faced assorted charges.

DISCUSSION QUESTIONS

1. What are some other examples of young people using social media to advertise their delinquency?

2. Do you think social media apps encourage teens to engage in delinquency? Why or why not?

Source: Brown, G. (2016). Snapchat leads Appleton police to teen burglars. *West Central Tribune* (April 24). Retrieved from http://www.wctrib.com/news/local/4017095-snapchat-leads-appleton-police-teen-burglars.

Documenting Delinquency Online

Another technological shift related to how youth interact with their peers and others in the world is an increase in documenting their behavior in videos, pictures, and texts, and sharing this information with others both near and far. The use of online social media such as YouTube, Periscope, Instagram, Snapchat, and Yik Yak as a means of publicizing violent behavior and wrongdoing is garnering more attention each year.

Consider the following headlines as cases in point:

- Alabama teens charged with beheading puppies, posting video on Snapchat[39]

- Instagram rape video leads to juvenile arrests[40]

- Jeannette teen who took selfie with dead friend wants murder charge tossed[41]

- Two British girls post Snapchat selfie photo as they brutally murder 39-year-old woman—then get ride home from cops[42]

- Teenager is accused of live-streaming a friend's rape on Periscope[43]

Majid Yar pointed out that change in the face of online crime and delinquency is largely related to the act of *mediating oneself*—using social media to make oneself and one's acts publicly visible rather than having to get the mainstream media involved to do so.[44] Now people seeking attention do not have to call up a news reporter or journalist to get it—they can do it all by themselves with access to a cell phone or computer. In spite of the fact many of us may not understand the desire to do so, young people today often advertise their acts of wrongdoing on social media through pictures, videos. and texts. Even when they do so on apps and networks that guarantee that messages and posts will be quickly erased or are anonymous, increasingly there are cases in which others document them and report them to the authorities. After they are reported to the authorities, the mainstream news media gives them additional attention through their reporting on their alleged acts of delinquency. Often the publicized acts of delinquency are extreme and lead observers to overestimate how often they occur. There is not much research on this subject yet, but it is likely that in the next few years, researchers will study how the use of technology to publicize acts of delinquency impacts juveniles' relationships with one another, as well as the related legal and social consequences.

GANGS AND DELINQUENCY

Youth gang involvement has long been the form of peer delinquency that has gotten the most amount of attention among the general public. To study gang delinquency it is important to first ask, what is the difference between a friendship group that commits an occasional act of delinquency and a gang?

There is not always an agreement about the labels assigned to a given group. The police of the Southern California city mentioned in this chapter's opening scenario, Escondido, decided not to label the white youth who associate with a group called the Juggalos in spite of their acts of delinquency. They said that they did this because they did not want the teens to be discouraged from exploring the world. They also did not want them to escalate their delinquent activities, which they thought might occur if they were officially labeled as a gang. This thoughtful approach to the possible negative effects of labeling a group as a gang might seem to indicate that the Escondido police have a general policy and practice of being cautious with gang labeling and gang policy enforcement. Yet, this is not the case—several groups of Latino youth are labeled and actively monitored as gang members throughout the city. When law enforcement agents classify a youth group as a gang, it has an incredible impact on the lives of those youth—it stigmatizes the youth as hard-core delinquents, increases the negative responses of many people outside of their main friendship group, and decreases their opportunities for success in many of our mainstream institutions, especially in school and in the workplace. At the same time, if a group of young people have formed an official group that is threatening their fellow community members through the use of violence, it can be helpful to label the group to target efforts to stop their misbehavior. This is why it is important to consider how and to whom gang labels are applied.

Before we consider some of the interesting aspects of youth gang life and responses to perceived gang problems, let's begin by considering some popular definitions of gangs.

What Is a Youth Gang?

One of the persistent questions related to youth gangs is when does a friendship group cross

©iStockphoto.com/ericsphotography.

Young people who live in neighborhoods with heavy gang involvement can be faced with a double bind: They find themselves vulnerable to gang violence, as well as police suspicion, when they hang out with their friends outside.

According to critical scholars, graffiti or street art is a way for youth in gangs to express their opposition to capitalism and the status quo.

the line and enter into gang territory, so to speak? Scholars have offered up all sorts of definitions of gangs over the years, and disagreement remains.[45] One of the best known definitions of a gang was developed many years ago by Frederick Thrasher in his 1927 study of 1313 gangs in Chicago. He stated that a gang is

> an interstitial group originally formed spontaneously and then integrated through conflict. . . . The result of this collective behavior is the development of tradition, unreflective internal structure, *esprit de corps*, solidarity, morale, group awareness, and attachment to a local territory.[46]

As you can see by his definition, Thrasher focused on the development of gangs in the interstices, or the margins, of society. Traditionally, gangs have formed in cities where recent immigrants have settled, and these places have their own special dynamic. Immigrants are often torn between two cultures, and have challenges of adjustment with which they must contend. Thrasher came from a tradition in which he looked at how the social disorganization of the city affected the low-income people who must live in the areas most affected by social change. He theorized that gang activity resulted in the course of normal adolescent development, and when a friendship group began having overt conflicts with other groups, a gang developed. His definition emphasizes the social dynamics of a gang—the support provided from one youth to another—and what has come to be one of the enduring elements of many gang definitions, a focus on territory. Thrasher believed that most youth involved in gang activity will simply age out of it, and his work focused on the spirited attempts of youth to adapt to what were often very trying environments.

Another famous gang researcher, Malcolm Klein, developed a definition of a gang in the 1970s that has become one of the most accepted contemporary definitions.[47] This definition states that a gang is

> any identifiable group of youngsters who (a) are generally perceived as a distinct aggregation by others in their neighborhood, (b) recognize themselves as a denotable group (almost invariably with a group name), and (c) have been involved in a sufficient number of delinquent incidents to call forth a consistent negative response from neighborhood residents and/or law enforcement agencies.[48]

As you can see, Klein's definition stresses group identification and affiliation and delinquency. In addition, it considers a gang as an entity that inspires a negative reaction in others. This definition differs substantially from Thrasher's in that there is no discussion of the positive social dynamics between gang members and no consideration of gang members' social location in society. Nonetheless, the definition is seen as useful by some because it is practical and straightforward. It reflects the way that the mainstream member of society defines gangs today.

Yet another type of gang definition, although not as well-known as the two we just mentioned, comes out of a critical social science tradition, in which gang members are seen as actively resisting societal inequities.[49]

David Brotherton and Luis Barrios developed one such definition of a gang in 2004. According to their definition, a gang is

> a group formed largely by youth and adults of a marginalized social class which aims to provide its members with a resistant identity, an opportunity to be individually and collectively empowered, a voice to speak back to and challenge the dominant culture, a refuge from the stresses and strains of barrio or ghetto life and a spiritual enclave within which its own sacred rituals can be generated and practiced.[50]

This definition of a gang opens up yet another avenue of analysis for those who utilize it as a starting point. In some ways, it brings Thrasher's emphasis on the role of social support in the gang back to the forefront of discussion. Brotherton and Barrios make clear that gangs can serve as a means of bonding together with other peers who are in similar social locations and of resisting mainstream culture. Their definition of a gang stresses the role of gang members' agency, or ability to act, and their choice to carve out a safe space of peer interaction for themselves. This definition recognizes that it is important for youth to have a strong bond with others as a means of standing up against what is often experienced as a tough world. In addition, this definition places attention on the various ways that rituals, or systematic practices that hold significant shared meanings, play roles in youths' lives.[51]

A last definition to consider is one that broadens the scope of a gang. John Hagedorn, a well-known sociologist and gang researcher, defines a gang in the following way:

> Gangs are organizations of the street composed of either 1. the socially excluded or 2. alienated, demoralized, or bigoted elements of a dominant racial, ethnic, or religious group.[52]

By expanding his definition of a gang to include members of dominant racial, ethnic, or religious groups, Hagedorn allows for groups such as white youth who act out in hate against others to be included in serious discussions of gangs. It is often the case that groups of white youth, such as white supremacist youth, are ignored by law enforcement or the popular media, producing a particular notion of what gang life is about. In his work, Hagedorn argues that gangs are more than just "wild peer groups" and that in this globalized world that we live in the definition of a gang itself needs to be flexible and open.[53] He claims that the only thing that seems to hold true for a group that society identifies as a gang is the fact that the people involved feel alienated—left out and shut out—from society in some way, and are primarily socialized on the streets and in prisons. He states, as others have noted before him, that people who are thought to be in a gang often do not even call their peer group a gang, and simply use a number of different words, such as *clique* or *crew*, to refer to their friends. This is important to recognize because the groups are not usually as organized as the media would have us think, and people drift in and out of involvement with their gang depending on social circumstances. A definition of gangs such as this one can lead to investigations of different youth groups and their behaviors that might otherwise go unexplored.

In light of all of these definitions of gangs, which should a young scholar such as yourself use? It is indeed a complicated question. For the purposes of your introduction to this subject, we think that realizing that the question is an important one is in and of itself vital to understanding gangs. It is important because it shapes the research that scholars might pursue related to gang activity; the responses they might recommend on behalf of social service workers, juvenile justice workers, and possibly the police; and most importantly the manner by which youth who are gang involved, as well as their families and communities, are treated. As you will see later in this chapter, law enforcement agencies' definitions of gangs are central to the various social control efforts they use to fight gang involvement. Their definitions also tend to differ from those we have presented thus far.

How Common Is Youth Gang Activity?

When it comes to gang activity in the United States, the first thing that people want to know is the numbers. The National Gang Center (NGC), an entity of both the U.S. Bureau of Justice Assistance (BJA) and the Office of Juvenile Justice and Delinquency Prevention (OJJDP), gathers quantitative data on gangs and gang activity. Each year, the NGC looks into the question of how many gangs exist in the country and the degree to which gang violence is reported by law enforcement agencies, as well as other issues related to gangs. The NGC conducts surveys with a large, representative sample of law enforcement agencies around the country. Its data are considered the best estimate of law enforcement's cataloging of gang activity in the United States. The NGC reported that in 2012,[54]

- There were an estimated 30,700 gangs and 850,000 gang members throughout 3,100 jurisdictions nationwide

- Gangs were active in a little less than 30% of the responding jurisdictions

- About two-thirds of all gangs were located in large and small cities (see Figure 9.2)

- Eighty-three percent of the responding jurisdictions reported gang-related homicides, with a total of 2,363 gang homicides reported

- According to the report, gang violence was strongly related to drug issues and intergang (i.e., between-gang) conflict

The official numbers of gangs, gang involvement, and incidents of gang violence have been used by law enforcement entities to indicate that gang problems need a multifaceted governmental response. Because official gang data are considered hand in hand with research findings that demonstrate that gang involvement increases a young person's delinquency above and beyond what it would be had the youth only hung out with other delinquent peers,[55] experts in the field are convinced that gang problems are serious ones.

It is important to note that not all gang activity is violent, and it can be difficult to agree on accurate estimates of how common gang activity is. Some scholars, such as John Fagan, have categorized gangs according to the type of activities they participate in the most (see Table 9.1). Gangs that are primarily social gangs or party gangs are less likely to engage in violent behavior as serious delinquency and organization gangs. It is hard to know how often these common forms of gang or group activity occur.

FIGURE 9.2 Distribution of Gangs by Area Type in 2012

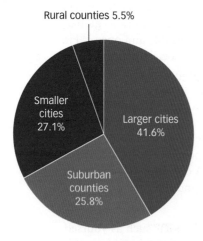

Rural counties 5.5%

Smaller cities 27.1%

Larger cities 41.6%

Suburban counties 25.8%

Source: National Gang Center. (2014). *2012 National Youth Gang Survey analysis*. Retrieved from https://www.nationalgangcenter.gov/Survey-Analysis/Measuring-the-Extent-of-Gang-Problems#distributiongangsarea

What Ethnic and Racial Groups Have Been Represented in Youth Gang Formation in the United States?

The creation of groups known as gangs has long occurred in the United States. Youth gangs began emerging along the East Coast at the end of the American Revolution.[56] In the late 1800s youth gangs in New York City included groups known as the Plug Uglies, the Roach Guards, and the Bowery Boys, among others.[57] The youth gangs of the 19th century were often of working-class or poor families of European ancestry—most often they were youth of Irish, Italian, and Jewish descent, but many other European groups were represented as well (e.g., Scotch-Irish, German, Dutch, and Welsh)[58]. In the early 20th century during Prohibition and then later during the Great Depression, U.S. society paid a good attention to the gangs of that time period. For example, the Forty Thieves gang and the Five Points gang (of which a young Alphonse, or Al, Capone was a member) gained notoriety as they grew out of the roughest areas in New York.

As black families from the southern United States moved to places with better economic (and social) opportunities in the mid-20th century, and immigration from Central and South America became more predominant, there was a rise in young male gangs of color in the low-income neighborhoods in urban areas, such as those in Chicago and Los Angeles. As we will discuss, this development can be seen as the result of many factors, such as a response to racism.[59] A similar pattern continued throughout the 20th century with a variety of different ethnic groups settling in different regions of the country including Chinese immigrant youth who arrived in San Francisco in the 1960s, Vietnamese immigrant youth, and Cambodian youth and youth from other South Asian countries who settled in Northern and Southern California.[60] In the 21st century, although Latino and black youth gangs receive the most public attention, there are gangs representing nearly every racial/ethnic group, along with gangs that are mixed in terms of ethnic and racial composition—what well-known gang scholar Diego Vigil describes as "a rainbow of gangs."[61]

Why Do Youth Gangs Form, and Why Does Gang Violence Occur? A Focus on Social Class, Race, Sexuality, and Social Inequality

Many theories of why gangs form have been forwarded over time. Traditionally, the most popular were similar to the two main pathways to delinquency discussed earlier in the chapter. In terms of gang development, people have referred to these two theories as subculture of violence theory and routine activities theory (also known as opportunity theory). The subculture of violence perspective[62] sees youth gangs as the result of a formation of a peer group that actively opposes middle-class mainstream norms of nonviolent behavior through the creation of a hypermasculine, aggressive subculture (most of this research has focused on boy gangs). According to this view, gang violence is simply the means by which members of a youth group decide to handle any sort of negative social interaction—someone looking the wrong way at them, insulting them while in their neighborhood or territory, or acting out violently against them or their friends. Violence is the expected response to offense or conflict, and to act differently is to risk being disrespected and to lose one's reputation. The routine activities[63] or opportunity perspective sees youth gangs as the result of youth having free time on their hands, and spending time in a location in which gang activity is an option. For gang violence to occur, three things have to be occurring at once: Youth must be motivated to participate in violence, people must be deemed to be suitable targets of the violence (i.e., there is someone—likely another member of a rival gang—who is in the vicinity and can be attacked), and there must be a

• • •

Subculture of violence theory: A perspective that characterizes youth gangs as the result of a formation of a peer group that actively opposes middle-class mainstream norms of nonviolent behavior through the creation of a hypermasculine, aggressive subculture.

Routine activities theory: A theory that states that gang involvement results because youth have too much free time on their hands and opportunities to join a gang.

TABLE 9.1 Types of Youth Gangs[64]

TYPE OF GANG	PRIMARY ACTIVITIES
Social gangs	use lots of alcohol and marijuana, but do not use many other drugs or engage in many acts of delinquency.
Party gangs	are heavily into drug use and drug sales, but few other types of delinquency.
Serious delinquency gangs	are not heavily involved in drug use and sales, but instead commit many other acts of delinquency.
"Organization" gangs	have a hierarchy that is linked to an adult criminal organization and that has members involved in all sorts of delinquency: drug use and sales, as well as other delinquent acts.

lack of "guardians" or authority figures, such as parents, law enforcement officers, and/or teachers, who might stop any acts of delinquency happening before they start. According to this perspective, a teenager who lives in a neighborhood in which gang-affiliated teenagers are hanging out on the streets outside all of the time is likely to be tempted to join in with the gang and engage in gang activities, violence included, because it is something this teen is faced with every day.

These perspectives on gang life and behavior have been shown to be part of the story, but many other factors need to be examined to consider why youth become part of a gang and engage in gang delinquency. For example, gay gang-involved youth sometimes seek protection and social capital in the form of a gang after they face homophobic bullying and harassment in school.[65] Another perspective on gang involvement examines the way that multiple forms of oppression affect youth behavior. This perspective sees the development of gangs as outgrowths of multiple marginalities or oppressions that affect residents of low-income communities. By seeing the gang as a group creation born out of specific structural, ecological, sociological, familial, and psychological factors,[66] the reason people take part in gang delinquency becomes complex.

According to Diego Vigil's **multiple marginality theory**[67] of gang development and involvement of youth in the United States, subcultural factors and opportunity come into play in neighborhoods where gangs emerge, but these occurrences need to be placed in a bigger context. Youth who experience several ways in which they are marginalized (i.e., treated as unimportant and shut out of mainstream opportunities) within society are more likely than others to engage in gang life as way of dealing with those stressors. Although less than 10% of youth in these marginal neighborhoods become gang members, Vigil states that it is important to look at the factors that influence the most vulnerable youth.[68]

First, it is important to consider the macro-historical and macro-structural factors that affect youths' lives—the large-scale overarching factors that affect many individuals' lives. Oftentimes, youth gang members are from groups of people who have immigrated to the United States or migrated from other areas of the country to a big city. Upon arriving in the city, many youth experience racism against their racial and/or ethnic group and are encouraged to ignore their cultural roots, ignore their language (if their first language is not English), and assimilate into mainstream Anglo culture. Girls deal with an extra dose of marginalization, as they must contend with sexism and gender role conflicts and sexual and other forms of violent victimization both from within and outside of their immediate communities. Regardless of gender, the youths' families do not have a lot of money, typically, and they find somewhere to live among others of their same ethnic, racial, and socioeconomic group. This dynamic holds true for a variety of ethnic and racial groups, such as Mexican Americans, Salvadoran Americans, Vietnamese Americans, and African Americans.

● ● ●

Multiple marginality theory: Vigil's theory that links the many ways that youth are marginalized in society (ranging from the macro level to the individual level) to their eventual involvement in a gang.

These ethnic enclaves are often in the least desirable areas of the city with the least amount of social resources being put into them—areas commonly called barrios or ghettos. Schools suffer from a lack of financial backing and materials, and children often fall between the cracks, often facing discriminatory practices and/or a lack of concern about their learning needs. Parents or adult guardians are often working multiple jobs to make ends meet and are very busy trying to put food on the table. Both at the school and in the home, there is often a breakdown in social control, or oversight of the youth, and these children turn to other youth on the streets to learn how to deal with the world around them. Youth feel the strain of wanting to have a lot of money and material goods, but few legitimate means of obtaining them. In the process of becoming street socialized, youth often bond with others who share a common background; at this stage, youth become part of a subcultural group in which they develop and share their own values. These values may be opposed to those of mainstream society in some ways, but often support popular notions of loyalty, honor, and friendship as well.

On an individual and psychosocial level, each youth goes through a process of developing a street identity as she or he grows closer to others in the group, complete with the creation of a gang name and a persona to go along with it. Boys go through their experience of maturing into manhood and trying to figure out what being a man looks like. Oftentimes, being a man is equated with being fearless, aggressive, and sometimes violent. Ideas of male dominance characterize gang life, and girls who are associated with a gang often also accept these ideas as their own. In spite of this, violent behavior is much less common in female gangs than in male gangs and tends to become more common in gangs that increase the ratio of male to female members.[69]

Once youth become street socialized their life chances start to be limited. They are labeled as undesirable, and it is hard for them to leave their neighborhood or change their lives. At the same time, they continue to be encouraged to act "crazy" (or "loco" depending on the group) and to demonstrate that they are representing their group and their territory by fighting and defending it against rival gang members and, possibly, by earning money through the sales of drugs or weapons.

Yet, it is also true that not all gang members actively pursue delinquent or violent behaviors.[70] Many youths who face multiple situations of marginality in their lives "slide into" gang life, and are drawn to gang affiliation simply because generations of their family have been associated with a particular gang. These youth are often happy to be part of the parties and socialization that go on around the gang, as well as to have respect and protection.[71] As many observers have noted, not all people in a gang are intensely involved in it—some are in it for the social aspects of it, and a smaller group of "hard-core" youth perpetrate the majority of the gang violence. The moral panics about gangs,[72] in which politicians, law enforcement officers, and social crusaders have created fear about gangs exploding into uncontrollable forces of mayhem and destruction, have not acknowledged the full picture of gang life.

Hautala, Sittner, and Whitbeck use Vigil's model of multiple marginality to understand the involvement of indigenous youth living on reservations and reserves in the Midwest United States and Canada.[73] They begin by noting that gang activity on reservations is a relatively new phenomenon, which began to be very apparent in the 1990s. In order to understand the unique context of indigenous youth gang involvement, several macro-historical factors related to cultural loss must be acknowledged. These include the forced relocation of indigenous people, the creation of boarding schools and attempts to destroy language and cultural ties, the creation of the reservations/reserves system, racial micro-aggressions and racism against indigenous people, continued assaults on tribal sovereignty, and long-term economic marginalization. Without understanding the macro-level context, the authors explain, it is impossible to truly understand the stressors that indigenous youth living on reservations or reserves face and how gang activity may appeal to them.

Visit edge.sagepub .com/bates2e to view a video clip about gang influence.

Street socialization: When youth bond with others who share a common background and become part of a subcultural group in which they develop and share their own values.

Girls in Gangs

Usually, when people think about youth gangs, they automatically think about young men. (How about you? What well-known gangs were you imagining when you began reading this part of the chapter about gangs? Were they male gangs?) For years, most scholars ignored the issues related to girls' involvement in gang activity, although juvenile girl gang experts, such as Meda Chesney-Lind, estimate that there is more female gang activity than the official numbers typically show. In-depth studies of girls' lives indicate that from 10% to 30% of gang members in the United States are young women.[74] In some cities in states with a large number of gangs, such as many in California, up to 40% to 50% of gang members are girls.[75] A recent nationwide survey of law enforcement agencies demonstrates that in at least nine states, female gang members either are considered equal in status to male gang members or have their own gangs.[76]

Traditionally, the types of gangs that young women were involved with were classified as one of three types:[77]

1. **Autonomous gangs**—female gangs that existed on their own, with no attachment to male gangs;

2. **Mixed-gender gangs**—gangs that had both boys and girls in their ranks (this is the most common one for girls to be involved in); and

3. **Auxiliary gangs**—female gangs that worked side-by-side with a male gang.

Autonomous gang: A type of female gang that exists on its own with no attachment to male gangs.

Mixed-gender gang: A type of female gang that has both boys and girls in its ranks.

Auxiliary gang: A type of female gang that works together with a male gang.

Girls face a number of societal challenges that sometimes compel them to look for a sense of security and family in a gang.

Beyond thinking about girls in gangs as accessories of male gangs, or just strange exceptions to the rule, not much analysis of girl gang members' experiences occurred until the 1980s.[78] Since that time, a growing body of research has looked at girls' experiences in gangs from their own points of view. It is clear that with the exception of all-girl gangs that are completely autonomous and working on their own, girls' gang activity is shaped by a gang structure dominated by young men, and reflects an emphasis on markers of masculinity. In other words, girls' gang involvement, like boys', is shaped by efforts to show "toughness."

Girls who join gangs typically join them for all of the reasons discussed earlier in the chapter related to social class, race and ethnicity, and social inequities in general. In addition, girls join gangs to help with stressors related to being a young woman in society today. Many girls who join gangs have been sexually and/or physically abused in their homes, often by family members, before joining. They feel powerless and fearful, and look at gang association as a way of finding another family—one in which they hope to find the safety and support that they don't find at home. Girls often have low self-esteem going into the gang, and when they enter a mixed-gender or auxiliary gang, they do not necessarily find the comfort they are looking for; they are often sexually objectified and abused once again.[79]

Yet, sometimes girls conceive of their own gang involvement in different terms and not as victimization, but as decisions of their own as autonomous beings.[80]

A few general findings about girls' involvement in gang activity and gang violence have emerged from studies of the topic:

- Young women in gangs are more violent than their female and male nongang peers.[81]

- Young women in gangs are less often involved in serious gang crimes than young men in gangs.[82] This is often because when they are in mixed-gender gangs, the young men don't allow them to participate in drive-bys or other sorts of shootings,[83] or girls themselves use their gender as a reason for not participating in violent activities.[84]

- Girls tend to serve as sources of intelligence for male gangs, as drug mules, and as transporters of weapons.[85]

- Girls are less likely to be the victims of violence caused by members of other gangs retaliating against them than boys are (because of their different degrees of involvement in gang violence).[86]

- Young women within gangs are at a greater risk of victimization, such as sexual assault, abuse, violence, and exploitation, than young men.[87] With the rise of prostitution as a money-making endeavor for many mixed-gender gangs, girls often are routed into prostitution, which proves to be dangerous to them on many levels.[88]

The involvement of young women in gangs, and their vulnerable roles in the power structure of gangs that also have young men in them or are linked to a male gang, are often cited as reasons why gang prevention and intervention efforts need to target their needs in a specific way. Yet, recent scholarship supports the idea that there are both gender differences and similarities among those who decide to leave or be less involved in a gang. O'Neal, Decker, Moule Jr., and Pyrooz studied teens and young adults who identified as former gang members and found that girls and women tended to exit gang life earlier than boys and men, but the most common reasons for doing so for both groups was because they were tired of it and/or because they started a family.[89] Both women and men noted that the biggest source of help for them when disengaging from the gang was other family members and that employment was the second-biggest source of help. The material consequences that emerged after stopping gang involvement were gendered: men and boys reported being treated like gang members by police significantly more than women and girls.

As we discuss in the next section of the chapter, many different methods have been used to address the delinquency of gangs. Many of them have a general focus on gang prevention and do not include a specialized focus on girls' experiences.

Responses to Youth Gangs

Given all of the concerns about youth gangs and how they may contribute to delinquency, many interested parties have attempted to stop youth gang involvement. In 2003, the OJJDP launched what is known as the Gang Reduction Program, which stems from the Comprehensive Gang Model. In 2008 and 2009 the OJJDP published reports on best practices for addressing community gang problems. The best practices focus on a model that advocates for a multipronged approach to gangs, which includes the following elements:

1. Gang prevention—stopping the formation of gangs and the involvement of youth in existing gangs;

2. Gang intervention—working to get gang-involved youth out of gangs once they are already in;

● ● ●

Gang prevention:
Concerted efforts to stop the formation of gangs and the involvement of youth in existing gangs.

Gang intervention:
Efforts to get youth out of gangs once they are already involved in them.

3. **Gang suppression**—cracking down on gang delinquency by using law enforcement powers to arrest and incarcerate youth; and

4. **Gang reentry**—providing resources to help youth who were incarcerated for gang delinquency find jobs, shelter, and help with schooling.

● ● ●
Gang suppression:
Attempts to crack down on gang delinquency by using law enforcement powers to arrest and incarcerate youth.

Gang reentry:
Efforts to provide resources to help youth who were incarcerated for gang delinquency find jobs, shelter, and help with schooling.

As you can see, if this multipronged approach to gang activity were to be applied, communities would need to have several different methods of addressing communities and youth. In this last section of the chapter, we will examine one of the most popular, and most controversial, mechanisms being used today to address youth and young adult gang involvement: the civil gang injunction.

Civil Gang Injunctions: A Suppression Method Rising in Popularity

Civil gang injunctions (CGIs) are used as part of a "get tough on crime" approach to delinquency. CGIs fall under the suppression arm of the Gang Reduction Program outlined above, and they are currently being used throughout the United States and in the District of Columbia. These injunctions were first used in the late 1980s in Los Angeles, California, and their use remains especially popular in their home state. (California has over 150 CGIs in effect, far surpassing any other state.) Unlike criminal legal measures, civil gang injunctions are court-issued restraining orders prohibiting members of enjoined criminal street gangs from activities that can be defined as public nuisances. To put it in simpler terms, young people who are suspected gang members are included

● ● ● *on the* **MEDIA**

Portrayals of Gay and Transgender Youth in Gangs

Very little attention is given to the topic of gay and transgender youth who are involved in gangs. According to scholar Vanessa Panfil, gay young men are involved in gang activity and other acts labeled as delinquent, yet people generally ignore this.[90] She states this occurs in part because "prevailing popular stereotypes of gay men as weak, effeminate, non-threatening pacifists provide no impetus to investigate their potential violence perpetuation or gang membership, precisely because they are perceived to pose no physical danger to society." She also explains that popular media stereotype gay boys and men as "infantilized, impotent, or clownish."[91]

The documentarians behind the film *Check It* (2016) attempted to challenge those stereotypes by focusing upon a group of black gay and transgender youth and young adults who decided to form a gang to defend themselves against homophobic bullying in the Trinidad neighborhood in Washington, D.C.

Over time, they have worked to change their lives by getting involved in the fashion industry—creating their own clothing line, working as models, and putting on fashion shows. Part of the contributions that the public made to the creation of the documentary went directly to the creation of the youths' clothing line.

DISCUSSION QUESTION

1. Although gay and transgender gang-involved youth are addressed by this documentary, lesbian gang-involved youth are not considered. What sorts of accurate media depictions and coverage of lesbian youth involved in gangs and/or delinquency are currently available? How might you find out about these media sources?

Sources: Indiegogo. (2016). *Check it: A documentary about an inner-city gay gang in Washington, DC.* Retrieved from https://www.indiegogo.com/projects/check-it#/; Panfil, V. (2014a). Better left unsaid? The role of agency in queer criminological research. *Critical Criminology, 22,* 99–111.

in a civil lawsuit against a particular gang for being public nuisances. Once a person is on an injunction, she or he is legally forbidden from being out in public with other members of her or his alleged group in a certain target area of the city (usually the part of the city in which she or he lives). Youth who violate the injunction can be faced with a variety of punishments, including fines, probation, and/or jail time. Let's look at the example of San Diego County in California to better understand CGIs and associated gang suppression techniques.

Visit edge.sagepub .com/bates2e to view a video about strategies for dealing with youth gangs.

Case Study: San Diego County, California. First, law enforcement officials and district attorneys work together to determine who is in a youth gang whose activity they would like to stop. In San Diego County, California, a law enforcement agent decides if someone is affiliated with a gang based on any of the following factors:

- A person admits being a member of a gang;

- A person has tattoos, clothing, and/or other possessions that are associated with a particular gang;

- A person has been arrested while participating in activities with a known gang;

- Information that places the person with a gang has been obtained from a reliable informant; or

- Close association with known gang members has been confirmed.

As you can see, this method of identifying gang-associated youth is pretty broad, and supporting evidence can be obtained from personal knowledge or through information submitted by other officers in field interviews, reports, or other sources. After a particular group has been identified by gang task force members, they work with the district attorney's office to put together a civil injunction against the people they have enumerated, which states they have violated California Civil Code Sections 3479 and 3480 and are acting as a public nuisance. What is a nuisance?

> Anything which is injurious to health, including, but not limited to, the illegal sale of controlled substances, or is indecent or offensive to the senses, or an obstruction to the free use of property, so as to interfere with the comfortable enjoyment of life or property, or unlawfully obstructs the free passage or use, in the customary manner, of any navigable lake, or river, bay, stream, canal, or basin, or any public park, square, street, or highway. (California Civil Code § 3479)

A nuisance that is public is said to affect either an entire neighborhood or community, or part of one, in a manner that takes away from residents' enjoyment of life (California Civil Code § 3480).

In San Diego County there have been 20 CGIs put into effect since 1997. Nineteen of these CGIs have been against Latino gangs, and one has been against a black gang. Although there are an increasing number of white youth groups that many consider gangs, no white gangs have been targeted under a gang injunction to date (please see the Juggalos example earlier in this chapter as a case in point). Research has demonstrated that civil gang injunctions in San Diego County, for all intents and purposes, mimic many of the racialized laws that we had early on in U.S. history in times of slavery and the Black Codes. They all target groups of people and define them as public nuisances, restrict their freedom of movement and assembly, criminalize ordinary behaviors, and fail to allow for legal protection or due process rights.[92]

● ● ●
Civil gang injunction: A court-issued restraining order prohibiting members of enjoined criminal street gangs from activities that can be defined as public nuisances.

A couple of concrete examples will demonstrate how this works. In general, behaviors not normally considered delinquent (or criminal) have serious consequences for enjoined people. Behaviors such as littering; fighting; possessing markers, spray paint, or nails; wearing certain clothing; and urinating in public in a designated area of the city are all evidence that can be used to say that a person violated a gang injunction. Alleged members of the Center Street gang in Oceanside, California, are enjoined from "making, or causing, loud noise of any kind, including, but not limited to, yelling and loud music at any time of day or night" in the target area, which generally is their own neighborhood (Oceanside Municipal Code § 38). In addition, those on the injunction are not allowed to be "standing, sitting, walking, driving, bicycling, gathering, or appearing anywhere in public view with any other defendant herein, or with any other Center Street gang member" (Permanent gang injunction against Center Street Gang, December 3, 2003).

Because many people on the injunction are brothers, cousins, close friends, and neighbors, it is very difficult not to quickly violate the injunction—so many of the behaviors prohibited are those that happen on a daily basis in the course of normal social interaction.

When a teenager or a young adult violates the injunction, it can have criminal consequences—jail time and a criminal record depending on one's past delinquent history—although the whole process is rooted in civil law. Because injunctions are civil legal measures, the alleged gang members are simply given a notice to appear in court to hear the complaints against them. They are not given the right to free legal representation, unless they are already serving parole time. Most alleged gang members do not have the financial resources to hire a lawyer, do not understand the legal language used on the court notice they receive, and do not go to court to address the charges. This makes for a troubling situation, because being placed on the injunction and one day violating the order can land a person in jail. This legal problem is not unique to California and is one that many lawyers and concerned residents have attempted to fight in court as a violation of due process and the Constitution,[93] usually to little avail.

Civil gang injunctions in San Diego County have been shown to complicate the daily lives of young people and adults on the CGIs, to make it very difficult for them to "go straight" by shutting down legitimate opportunities upon them, sometimes to result in the labeling of non–gang members as gang members, and to transform patterns of gang activity by moving gang activity from the enjoined area of the city to a nearby area.[94] In effect, suppression efforts against gangs are making it impossible for any of the three other elements of the Gang Reduction Program to take effect—it is difficult to prevent, intervene with, or reintegrate people who are likely to violate the injunction and be punished in ways that are highly stigmatizing.

The findings related to San Diego County CGIs are in keeping with the general critiques of civil gang injunctions. Many critics state that such injunctions shut down the opportunities for change that every youth needs[95] and that most people on CGIs are on them indefinitely and find it almost impossible to get removed from the gang lists years after aging out of gang involvement.[96]

Nevertheless, civil gang injunctions have been found by others to have a positive effect on communities—making them less vulnerable to violent delinquency and crime in target neighborhoods.[97] Other research has been mixed as to whether CGIs are an effective tool at stopping gang activity or reducing fear in a community.[98] It is clear that gang violence, or violence of any kind in a community, needs to be seriously addressed. Nobody wants to be a victim to violence, especially in his or her own neighborhood. The question becomes how to address the potential for gang violence without unnecessarily infringing upon the rights of groups of people.

from the CLASSROOM to the COMMUNITY

Homeboy Industries

Homeboy Industries (http://homeboy-industries.org) is a nonprofit organization created by Jesuit priest Father Gregory Boyle to address the multiple challenges that gang-affiliated and formerly gang-affiliated youth and adults are faced with daily. The nonprofit's mottoes "Nothing Stops a Bullet Like a Job" and "Jobs not Jails" point to their founder's understanding of the need for socioeconomic opportunities for youth. Homeboy Industries offers an assortment of services to individuals who want to move away from gang life—each geared at strengthening participants through increasing their social and cultural capital. These services included counseling, educational classes of all sorts, tattoo removal services, legal advice, addiction rehabilitation, job training and employment, and case management. In addition, the nonprofit runs various businesses such as Homeboy Bakery, Homeboy Silkscreen & Embroidery, Homegirl Café & Catering, Homeboy Farmers Market, and Homeboy Diner. Youth and adults are provided with jobs at these businesses, which help them build their skills and their résumés. Father Boyle travels around with homeboys and homegirls to different venues to discuss the successes and challenges of their efforts. He writes about them in his book *Tattoos on the Heart: The Power of Boundless Compassion*.[99] Although Homeboy Industries is based in downtown Los Angeles, other companies around the United States and the world have used its example as one to emulate.

DISCUSSION QUESTION

1. How do the many components of Homeboy Industries attempt to address the motto of the organization "Nothing Stops a Bullet Like a Job"? Are there any other components that you think would be helpful additions? If so, what?

The Justice Policy Institute,[100] a Washington, D.C.–based think tank, studied the existing research on responses to gang issues, and found that black and Latino communities as a whole suffer from failed gang enforcement and suppression measures. Aggressive antigang tactics often do not stop gang activity, and they additionally place other community members under heightened surveillance and an environment of fear. The Justice Policy Institute suggests the following measures for addressing gang violence, after studying evaluations of the most popular governmental and nonprofit gang programs in the country:

1. Expand the use of evidence-based practices in the health and human services to promote positive outcomes with use instead of using suppression practices (e.g., multisystemic therapy, which provides intensive services, counseling, and training to young people, their families, and the larger network of people engaged in young people's lives through schools and the community).

2. Promote jobs, education, and healthy communities, and lower barriers to the reintegration of former gang members; and

3. Redirect resources from failed gang enforcement efforts to proven public safety strategies.[101]

Once again, the idea is to give human service organizations with a proven record of success in helping people strategize ways to live happily and delinquency-free more financial backing to do their work. Many of the therapies proven to be successful take social, economic, and cultural issues into account and help provide clients with resources to change their lives. This has been shown to be the most helpful in allowing gang-involved youth to pursue legitimate opportunities and to allow their loved ones and community members to enjoy increased safety in the neighborhood and home.

Most youth will age out of gang involvement and delinquency as they mature and take on jobs and other life responsibilities, such as families. The less stigmatizing the societal responses to early youth and gang delinquency, the more likely that positive, prosocial behavior will be encouraged in the long run among the youth.

SUMMARY

It has long been a common observation that groups of teenagers are more likely to stir up trouble than a young person on his or her own. Scholars have different hypotheses about this, including the socialization hypothesis of delinquency and the opportunity hypothesis of delinquency. It indeed appears to be the case that young people influence the behavior of one another and that the more unstructured free time that they have, the more likely it is that they will pursue opportunities to misbehave. When we look at the forms that delinquency takes, we can see that gender figures prominently: Boys are involved in more delinquency in general than girls, and being friends with boys increases girls' likelihood of being involved in delinquency. Boys are socialized to be risk takers, and to be "macho" and/or violent, while girls are not—this, in part, explains these differences. The issues of what behaviors currently are labeled, or which ones should be labeled, as delinquent are important ones. As we see new forms of peer interaction and communication develop with young people's "creative" use of technologies such as the Internet and the cell phone, the question about where adults should draw the line between youth fun and youth delinquency gets raised. The labeling issue is also raised when we discuss the appropriateness of labeling a group of

teens a gang, rather than just a group of friends that occasionally engages in acts of delinquency.

There are many definitions of a gang, and experts disagree on which one is best. Nevertheless, based upon the definitions used by law enforcement agencies and governmental officials, we can see that youth gangs are more commonly found in cities than in rural areas, and although they include more boys than girls, the number of girls who identify as a gang member is rising. The multiple marginality model of gang involvement explains that numerous factors lead to the involvement of a young person in gang life. These issues range all the way from large-scale social issues, such as immigration, racism, and classism, to individual-scale issues, such as the desire to identify with a group as a family. Girl gang members typically have been exposed to violence and abuse in their homes, before turning to a gang for protection. If they are in a gang that is either mixed or affiliated with a male gang, it is very likely they will find more victimization after joining a gang. There are a variety of approaches being used to stop youth gang activity and violence. Research demonstrates that a combination of prevention, intervention, and reentry approaches is the most effective.

EYE ON DIVERSITY EXERCISE: GANGS AND TECHNOLOGY

Two of the themes related to peer interactions that were considered in this chapter are new forms of delinquency brought about by technological innovations, and youth gangs. For this activity, try your hand at each of the following:

1. Spend some time exploring the Internet and take notes on what you find and where you found it.

(Note: You may find some evidence of technological uses of the Internet itself, or you may find online materials explaining how gang-affiliated youth use technology.) Pay attention to the types of technology and the methods of communication being used. Consider what types of youth gangs are utilizing technology—are they from particular ethnic or racial groups? Are they from a particular region of the country? Or the world? What gender are the members of the gangs you observe? If you are able to examine materials being spread via technology on behalf of gang-affiliated youth, take note of the types of information being communicated and the format of the information.

2. Next, analyze your notes and write up a synopsis of what you found. End your paper with a consideration of how one might expect that the form or forms of peer communication that you uncovered would shape youth gang activity and identity.

DISCUSSION QUESTIONS

1. Discuss the two major hypotheses about why peers matter to delinquency and whether you have seen evidence to support either (or both) of them during your adolescent years. If you have, what sorts of examples can you provide as support?

2. The chapter discusses the important ways that the use of new technology changes the communication and interaction patterns of teenagers. Can you think of any recent examples of technology use not mentioned in the chapter that have led to behaviors adults are concerned about? Are these behaviors officially labeled as a form of delinquency? Why or why not?

3. Gender socialization and the different social experiences of boys and girls have been shown to impact delinquency in a number of ways. What are the main ways discussed in the chapter? Are

there other things about young men or women in today's society that influence the sort of delinquent acts that they do with their friends? If so, what are they?

4. As discussed in the chapter, African-American girls in inner cities characterized by violence often choose to isolate themselves from their peers in an effort to stay safe and survive. Are there any examples in which other teens avoid interacting with others their age to protect themselves?

5. Are there youth gangs in your city? How do you know? What definition of a gang are you drawing upon in your answers to these questions?

6. Youth gangs get the most public attention of nearly any youth peer group. What sorts of public attention do you observe gang members receiving? What do you see as the effect of the attention?

KEY TERMS

Autonomous gang 266

Auxiliary gang 266

Civil gang injunction 268

Gang intervention 267

Gang prevention 267

Gang reentry 268

Gang suppression 268

Mixed-gender gang 266

Multiple marginality theory 264

Opportunity hypothesis of delinquency 251

Relational isolation 253

Routine activities theory 263

Sexting 256

Socialization hypothesis of delinquency 251

Street socialization 265

Subculture of violence theory 263

1. True
4. False
7. False

2. False
5. True
8. True

3. True
6. True
9. False

STUDENT STUDY SITE

$SAGE edge™

edge.sagepub.com/bates2e
Sharpen your skills with SAGE edge!

SAGE edge for students provides a personalized approach to help you accomplish your coursework goals in an easy-to-use learning environment. You'll find action plans, mobile-friendly eFlashcards, and quizzes, as well as videos, web resources, and links to SAGE journal articles to support and expand on the concepts presented in this chapter. Check out the website for original videos of former offenders discussing their experiences as juveniles.

©iStockphoto.com/jpbcpa

DRUGS IN CONTEXT

After reading this chapter, you should be able to

- Discuss the reasons for youth drug use and societal understandings of substance use

- Provide illustrations of the role of legal products in youth substance use

- Analyze the general pattern and trends of youth drug use in the United States today, as well as patterns related to gender, race, and ethnicity

- Explain the effects of drug prohibition and the war on drugs

- Examine the relationship between drug and alcohol use and delinquency and how it can be affected by sexism, racism, homophobia, and transphobia

- Compare and contrast societal responses to youth drug use, including the use of culturally specific approaches

Kyle is an Italian-American 11th grader in a suburban school in Connecticut. He is a good student and a star athlete, and his lifelong goal is to get into a prestigious Ivy League university and, later, a high-ranking law school. He is serious about his plans, but he is finding it difficult to balance all of his demands—athletic practices and games, as well as studying for long hours in an attempt to earn top grades in his Advanced Placement classes, which are quite challenging. He is feeling worn down and is stressed about the pressure on him to keep up his hectic routine. Everyone at school and in his neighborhood are counting on him to lead his team to a winning season in football, and his parents are already bragging to all of their own lawyer colleagues about his academic future.

One day after practice, Kyle's friend Sebastian asks him if he is feeling okay, because he looks a little run-down. Kyle decides to tell him how stressed he is feeling and how tired he is; he states that he can't even imagine how he is going to do well on his SATs in a few weeks, and he knows that a high score on the exam is crucial to his entrance into Yale or Harvard. Sebastian tells him he was feeling the same way until he started taking some Adderall, and now he finds it easier to stay up all night and to study. Kyle knows several kids who have been prescribed Adderall because they were diagnosed with ADHD (attention deficit/hyperactivity disorder), but admits that he never thought of taking it because his concentration is quite good when he isn't tired. Sebastian explains that Adderall is an amphetamine that will keep him energized and that he can get some either by going to the doctor and telling him it is hard to concentrate, or through one of the many friends they know who already have a prescription. A last resort would be to get some through one of the dealers they know at school. Kyle feels scared to take the drugs, but Sebastian convinces him that it is not a big deal and that many of the kids they know who are trying to get into competitive schools are already taking them. Kyle begins taking Adderall regularly and justifies it to himself by thinking that it wouldn't be prescribed so much by doctors if it were really harmful.

CHAPTER PRETEST

Test your knowledge of this chapter's material by determining whether the following statements are true or false. Be sure to compare your answers with the answers on page 306.

1. Youth in Western industrialized countries today have grown up in a setting in which substance use is a regular part of daily life.

2. The reasons why people used alcohol and drugs historically mirror the primary reasons people use them today.

3. Young club drug users often study drug use and plan their use of drugs ahead of time.

4. Harmful legal products are everyday products that are used or consumed in an effort to get intoxicated or high.

5. The patterns of drug and alcohol usage in the United States among youth are the same across all racial and ethnic groups.

6. Youth who engage in serious substance use and have problems with it are less likely to engage in serious juvenile delinquency than those who do not.

7. Due to the multiple stressors that LGBT youth face, they are more likely than heterosexual teens to engage in high-risk drug use.

8. Juvenile drug courts in the United States are based on a harm reduction model similar to their counterparts around the world.

9. Research has demonstrated that, to be successful, drug-related programs need to be sensitive to ethnic and racial differences and community norms and consider the community characteristics of the youth being served.

The decision to use a substance to alter one's social and individual experiences has characterized youth (and adult) life throughout the ages. These decisions are impacted by a person's social surroundings and position in society. Because of this, young people are not equally likely to be exposed to the opportunity to engage in a given type of drug use. Kyle's experience reflects his *social location* as a young white teenager in a socioeconomically privileged setting. Although not all youth will have easy access to the "study drugs"[1] that Kyle and his friend Sebastian can easily obtain, they will likely have relatively easy access to some sort of substance that, if taken, can change their daily experience of the world.

Youth in Western industrialized countries today have grown up in a setting in which substance use of all types is a regular part of daily life for so many people (simply look at how much caffeine is being taken in the form of coffee and soda on your college campus to get a quick sense of this). Therefore, it is not surprising that young people often begin experimenting with alcohol and other drugs during their teens (or their tweens). Yet, unless prescribed for an approved purpose, such drug use is generally frowned upon by the adults around them, and labeled a form of delinquency, as well as a behavior that leads to other forms of delinquency and harm. In this chapter, we will consider the reasons for drug and alcohol use and the forms that adolescent use takes. We will look at data that show the general trends in teen drug use in the 21st century and take a look at the question that is perhaps the most central to a book on delinquency—how is drug and alcohol use related to other forms of delinquency? These findings are crucial to understanding the different programs and policies that have been created to prevent illegal youth drug use or to stop young people from using drugs if they have already started.

REASONS FOR AND SOCIETAL UNDERSTANDINGS OF DRUG USE

Substance use has been part of human society for millennia. According to drug researcher and criminologist James Inciardi, the reasons why people used drugs historically mirror their uses today.[2]

1. *In Celebrations:* Drugs, particularly in the form of alcohol, have long been used to celebrate accomplishments at the personal, group, or national level. The practice of imbibing a drink to "let loose" and to mark a special occasion is not a modern-day one, but one that has its roots in antiquity.

2. *In Rituals:* Drugs also have been used as a part of many institutions' rituals. For example, making a toast to someone with a glass of alcohol in hand in a social setting or political setting had its beginnings in the rituals of ancient nomads. Religious institutions have also used alcohol and other drugs in their rituals to better connect with their gods and goddesses. Popular examples include the use of wine in the rituals of the Catholic Church and the use of peyote or mushrooms in the Native American Church.

3. *For Coping Purposes:* The historical record shows that people have used drugs to help them get through the day in the face of hard times or challenges. These challenges can be related to emotional and psychological problems and/or to social problems that affect individuals. Indigenous people in South America have been known to chew coca leaves to help alleviate hunger and to give them energy.

4. *For Pain Relief:* Substances have also traditionally been used to relieve pain. The most famous historical example is the use of opium to do so.

It is important to note that another reason why some youth use substances is they are raised in a family in which intergenerational substance use is the norm.[3] This use may be for any of the reasons stated above as well.

Although the reasons for drug and alcohol use have stayed the same over the course of history, the ways in which various substances have been socially constructed have shifted over time—and will likely continue to shift. Mainstream messages about a particular drug change. As Richard Hammersley explains:

> At the start of the 21st century, tobacco is moving from being acceptable toward a "drug" to be excluded from acceptable behavior, while cannabis is moving away from being a drug, although movement is fitful. The illegitimate status of other drugs has fluctuated. For example, amphetamines seemed like medicines in the 1940s and 1950s, then became drugs. Cocaine was a not-so-bad drug for a while, then an even worse drug than heroin, in the form of crack anyway, and is perhaps now returning to being not quite as bad as heroin after all. MDMA (ecstasy) has been a beneficial adjunct to psychotherapy (Grob, 2000). Then it became a controlled drug but one not widely used, then as mass use has developed society has become quite confused as to whether it is a largely harmless substance taken by millions of people with very few misadventures, or an extremely dangerous substance that has killed people and may cause long-term brain damage.[4]

When we look back on history, we can see that some substances that were seen as relatively innocent at one time (such as the cocaine that was originally in Coca-Cola)[5] came to be seen as dangerous over time by mainstream society, and vice versa. But when it comes to youth substance use, there has always been less acceptance for it in general than for adult usage. Of course, in the 21st century, it is common knowledge that although most drug and alcohol use is illegal and forbidden for young people, it is almost a rite of passage for teens to engage in acts of alcohol and drug use at events such as football games, dances, and clubs. Popular culture, as expressed on television shows, movies, and music, glorifies young people getting drunk or high, and it is clear that adolescents (and preadolescents) do indeed engage in a lot of such activities. According to Hunt, Moloney, and Evans,[6] when many adults attempt to address why adolescents engage in substance use, they ignore some of the most important realities:

1. First, young people have *agency,* or the ability to choose whether or not to use drugs. Although drugs and drug dealers are often depicted as evil forces in public service messages and antidrug campaigns, human beings are making the decisions to use drugs or alcohol, and that activity holds a particular meaning for them, and often plays a significant role in their downtime or leisure time.

2. On a similar note, one of the primary reasons for youth consumption of drugs is the *pursuit of pleasure.* The enjoyment that youth are attempting to find through the use of substances typically takes place in the context of friendship groups and consists of finding ways to relax and have fun with others. Often, adults make it seem that all youth drug use occurs in an isolated manner—that it is driven by purely individualistic factors, such as psychological problems and addiction. In fact, much drug use is driven by social factors and group efforts to engage in "fun" with others.

In their research, Hunt et al. interviewed over 300 people—adolescents and young adults—to understand what their use of "club drugs" and other drugs meant to them. The researchers focused on young people who went to raves and clubs in San Francisco, Hong Kong, and Amsterdam in the 2000s, and how they went about deciding to use, and their experience with, the drugs. They found that unlike stereotypes of the

Teen drug use is often a social, rather than a purely individual, activity.

impulsive, and possibly ignorant, teenage drug user, young drug users engaged in the social activity of drug use by first *studying about it and planning for it*. In their effort to learn more about a drug before using it they did pay attention to negative accounts about drug effects that came from governmental agencies and nonprofits, but also searched drug and nightlife sources online that claimed to be more objective about drug use (e.g., the Erowid and DanceSafe websites). In addition, they *looked toward friends' experiences* as markers of what substance use looks like in the particular setting of a rave or club. When they noted that antidrug messages of governmental agencies ignored the qualities of drug use that their friends, and eventually they, perceived as pleasurable, they began to look more skeptically upon such messages. The young people Hunt et al. interviewed typically had regular weekly schedules, either as students or as workers, which they maintained while engaging in drug use on the nights they went out. They attempted to minimize the effects of their drug use by eating a particular type of diet during the day before the club or rave, and by taking vitamins and other substances to prepare themselves for the use of Ecstasy and other drugs. The majority of the young people would engage in the use of multiple substances over the course of a night out (which nearly always included marijuana and Ecstasy), and noted that they liked using the substances because it helped them let loose and focus only on that immediate moment and place in time.

If it is the case that adolescent drug use is often given more thought by teens than we typically give them credit for, then there are important implications for the ways we go about dealing with the issue of youth substance use, which we will consider at the end of the chapter. But, first, it is important to take a quick look at how youth use everyday legal products to attempt to escape from reality.

THE ROLE OF LEGAL PRODUCTS IN YOUTH SUBSTANCE USE

As you can see from perusing the National Institute on Drug Abuse's Commonly Abused Drugs Chart in Table 10.1, a number of illegal drugs tend to dominate adult discussions of teen drug misuse. But, as we will discuss throughout this chapter, the use of legal substances garners quite a bit of concern as well. For example, think about the consumption of caffeine, a legal drug that young people take by drinking sodas, teas, and coffees. Seems innocent enough, right? But what about when you amp up the caffeine in the form of the now popular energy drinks (e.g., Red Bull, Monster, Rockstar)—drinks that have come to represent a high-risk or extreme lifestyle? Should adults be concerned about that sort of caffeine intake on the part of teens? Research has demonstrated that energy drink usage by older teens and young adults is linked to identification with hypermasculine values, as well as a pattern of risk taking, problem drinking, and occasionally forms of delinquency and/or crime, especially among white students.[7] The number of emergency room visits for youth and adults related to the consumption of energy drinks doubled from 2007 to 2011.[8] Are these findings enough for us to restrict access to these drinks to teens?

The use of other **harmful legal products** (or HLPs) by young people is of particular concern because there is a seemingly endless number of ways that people find to get high. HLPs are readily available for inhalation or ingestion around one's home, school, or community or can be bought at a local store. Inhalable HLPs include airplane glue, paint thinner, gasoline, and model airplane glue, as well as aerosols, nitrates or "poppers," and anesthetics.[9] Ingestible HLPs, substances that are swallowed, include over-the-counter medications of all sorts, for example antihistamines, cough syrups, cold medications, and prescription drugs (discussed below), as well as products found around the house including mouthwash, disinfectants, and cooking extracts. Because these products are so accessible, sometimes they are the first a child uses before moving on to illegal drugs.

● ● ●

Harmful legal products: Legal products that are used or consumed in an effort to get intoxicated or high, and can have negative repercussions.

TABLE 10.1 Commonly Used and Abused Drugs

SUBSTANCES	EXAMPLES OF COMMERCIAL AND STREET NAMES	DEA SCHEDULE/HOW ADMINISTERED	EFFECTS/HEALTH RISKS
TOBACCO			
Nicotine	Found in cigarettes, cigars, bidis, and smokeless tobacco	Not scheduled/smoked, snorted, chewed	Increased blood pressure and heart rate/ chronic lung disease; cardiovascular disease; stroke; cancers of the mouth, pharynx, larynx, esophagus, stomach, pancreas, cervix, kidney, bladder, and acute myeloid leukemia; adverse pregnancy outcomes; addiction
ALCOHOL			
Alcohol (ethyl alcohol)	Found in liquor, beer, and wine	Not scheduled/swallowed	In low doses, euphoria, mild stimulation, relaxation, lowered inhibitions; in higher doses, drowsiness, slurred speech, nausea, emotional volatility, loss of coordination, visual distortions, impaired memory, sexual dysfunction, loss of consciousness/increased risk of injuries, violence, fetal damage (in pregnant women); depression; neurologic deficits; hypertension; liver and heart disease; addiction; fatal overdose
CANNABINOIDS			
Marijuana	Blunt, dope, ganja, grass, herb, joint, bud, Mary Jane, pot, reefer, green, trees, smoke, sinsemilla, skunk, weed	I/smoked, swallowed	Balance and coordination; increased heart rate and appetite; impaired learning, memory; anxiety; panic attacks; psychosis/cough; frequent respiratory infections
Hashish	Boom, gangster, hash, hash oil, hemp	I/smoked, swallowed	Possible mental health decline; addiction; euphoria; drowsiness; impaired coordination; dizziness; confusion; nausea; sedation

(Continued)

TABLE 10.1 (Continued)

SUBSTANCES	EXAMPLES OF COMMERCIAL AND STREET NAMES	DEA SCHEDULE/HOW ADMINISTERED	EFFECTS/HEALTH RISKS
OPIOIDS			
Heroin	Diacetylmorphine: smack, horse, brown sugar, dope, H, junk, skag, skunk, white horse, China white; cheese (with OTC cold medicine and antihistamine)	I/injected, smoked, snorted	Feeling of heaviness in the body; slowed or arrested breathing/constipation; endocarditis; hepatitis; HIV; addiction; fatal overdose
Opium	Laudanum, paregoric: big O, black stuff, block, gum, hop	II, III, V/swallowed, smoked	
STIMULANTS			
Cocaine	Cocaine hydrochloride: blow, bump, C, candy, Charlie, coke, crack, flake, rock, snow, toot	II/snorted, smoked, injected	Increased heart rate, blood pressure, body temperature, metabolism; feelings of exhilaration; increased energy, mental alertness; tremors; reduced appetite; irritability; anxiety; panic; paranoia; violent behavior; psychosis/weight loss; insomnia; cardiac or cardiovascular complications; stroke; seizures; addiction; nasal damage (cocaine); severe dental problems (meth)
Amphetamine/Methamphetamine	Biphetamine, Dexedrine: bennies, black beauties, crosses, hearts, LA turnaround, speed, truck drivers, uppers	II/swallowed, snorted, smoked, injected	
CLUB DRUGS			
MDMA (methylenedioxy methamphetamine)	Desoxyn: meth, ice, crank, chalk, crystal, fire, glass, go fast, speed Ecstasy, Adam, clarity, Eve, lover's speed, peace, uppers	II/swallowed, snorted, smoked, injected	MDMA—mild hallucinogenic effects; increased tactile sensitivity, empathic feelings; lowered inhibition; anxiety; chills; sweating; teeth clenching; muscle cramping/sleep disturbances; depression; impaired memory; hyperthermia; addiction
Flunitrazepam	Rohypnol: forget-me pill, Mexican Valium, R2, roach, Roche, roofies, roofinol, rope, rophies	I/swallowed, snorted, injected	sedation; muscle relaxation; confusion; memory loss; dizziness
GHB	Gamma-Hydroxybutyrate: G, Georgia home boy, grievous bodily harm, liquid ecstasy, soap, scoop, goop, liquid X unconsciousness; seizures; coma	IV/swallowed, snorted I/swallowed	drowsiness; nausea; headache; disorientation; loss of coordination; memory loss/unconsciousness; seizures; coma
DISSOCIATIVE DRUGS			
Ketamine	Ketalar SV: cat Valium, K, Special K, vitamin K	III/injected, snorted, smoked	Feelings of being separate from one's body and environment; impaired motor function/anxiety; tremors; numbness; memory loss; nausea
PCP and analogs	Phencyclidine: angel dust, boat, hog, love boat, peace pill	I, II/swallowed, smoked, injected	Also, for ketamine—analgesia; impaired memory; delirium; respiratory depression
Salvia divinorum	Salvia, Shepherdess's Herb, Maria Pastora, magic mint, Sally-D	Not scheduled/chewed, swallowed, smoked	Also, for PCP and analogs—analgesia; psychosis; aggression; violence; slurred speech; loss of coordination; hallucinations
Dextromethorphan (DXM)	Found in some cough and cold medications: Robotripping, Robo, Triple C	Not scheduled/swallowed	Also, for DXM—euphoria; slurred speech; confusion; dizziness; distorted visual perceptions

SUBSTANCES	EXAMPLES OF COMMERCIAL AND STREET NAMES	DEA SCHEDULE/HOW ADMINISTERED	EFFECTS/HEALTH RISKS
HALLUCINOGENS			
LSD	Lysergic acid diethylamide: acid, blotter, cubes, microdot, yellow sunshine, blue heaven	I/swallowed, absorbed through mouth tissues	Altered states of perception and feeling; hallucinations; nausea
Mescaline	Buttons, cactus, mesc, peyote	I/swallowed, smoked	Also, for LSD—flashbacks, Hallucinogen Persisting Perception Disorder
Psilocybin	Magic mushrooms, purple passion, shrooms, little smoke	I/ swallowed	Also, for psilocybin—nervousness; paranoia; panic
OTHER COMPOUNDS			
Anabolic steroids	Anadrol, Oxandrin, Durabolin, Depo-Testosterone, Equipoise: roids, juice, gym candy, pumpers	III/injected, swallowed, applied to skin	Liver cysts; hostility and aggression; acne; in adolescents—premature stoppage of growth; in males—prostate cancer, reduced sperm production, shrunken testicles, breast enlargement; in females—menstrual irregularities, development of beard and other masculine characteristics
Inhalants	Solvents (paint thinners, gasoline, glues); gases (butane, propane, aerosol propellants, nitrous oxide); nitrites (isoamyl, isobutyl, cyclohexyl): laughing gas, poppers, snappers, whippets	Not scheduled/inhaled through nose or mouth	Inhalants (varies by chemical)—stimulation; loss of inhibition; headache; nausea or vomiting; slurred speech; loss of motor coordination; wheezing/cramps; muscle weakness; depression; memory impairment; damage to cardiovascular and nervous systems; unconsciousness; sudden death

Source: National Institute on Drug Abuse. (2011, March). *Commonly abused drugs chart*. Retrieved from http://www.drugabuse.gov/drugs-abuse/commonly-abused-drugs/commonly-abused-drugs-chart

The recreational use of such substances is easily concealed, and a small amount of these products can lead to powerful effects that dissipate pretty quickly.[10]

As the numbers show, prescription drug misuse, often called nonmedical use of prescription drugs (NMUPD), is now a popular form of recreational drug use among teens. Since around 2005, a lot of adult attention has been given to activities such as "pharming" or "pharm" parties in which kids get together and exchange their prescription drugs. Young people get their hands on prescription drugs by a number of means, but the most popular ways include finding drugs in their own home (prescriptions that adults have not finished, for example) or using drugs that they have been prescribed for medical or psychological reasons.[11] Given that an assortment of drugs is widely prescribed to young people today, it is easy for them to gain access to them, and to share them with others. The predilection of many adults to use medication as a way of handling personal and social problems is central to the recreational use of prescription drugs.

There are class and race dimensions to the widespread prescription of stimulant drugs. Children who live in low-income areas and go to schools with inadequate resources and funding tend to be prescribed stimulants for the stated purpose of improving their academic performance even if it is not clear that they have ADHD or another disorder.[12] A child may be given a drug such as Adderall or Concerta in elementary school simply to help him or her compete academically with others. As school funding declines and programs are cut, these drugs are being increasingly prescribed to students. As alluded to in the scenario at the beginning of the chapter, another segment of the population whose members have increasingly been prescribed stimulants is older teens from middle- and upper-class backgrounds, but the nonmedical usage of such drugs is typically to help these users increase their already strong academic records in order to get accepted to an elite university. Some doctors who prescribe stimulant medications to children in poor and working-class neighborhoods who do not need them for medical reasons justify their actions as socially just and helping to level the playing field for young people in families that do not have the means to pay for tutoring or family counseling.[13] Critics believe that this is a dangerous practice with unknown health risks and often amounts to youth being prescribed multiple drugs (e.g., antipsychotic drugs and sleeping pills) to counteract some of the unwanted effects of the stimulants. The ultimate result of all this pharmaceutical prescribing, according to critics, is that there are more drugs in circulation, more opportunities to misuse these drugs, and more low-income youth and youth of color under social control. Indeed, underground markets of stimulants are said to exist at every level of the educational system, demonstrating the depth of the demand.[14] Let's turn to the data on the substance usage patterns of youth today to get a sense of this demand and the demand for other substances.

YOUTH SUBSTANCE USE PATTERNS TODAY

A government survey shows seniors in U.S. high schools are now smoking marijuana more than tobacco. Daily marijuana use among high school seniors has surpassed that of cigarettes for the first time, according to a new survey by the National Institute on Drug Abuse, *The Atlantic* reports. While the percentage of 12th graders who said they smoked marijuana daily did not change much from last year—jumping from 5.8% to 6%—the number of daily cigarette smokers dropped from 6.7% to 5.5%. Among sophomores, daily use of cigarettes and marijuana was at 3%.[15]

There are multiple ways to measure the shape that teen drug use takes today. Three well-regarded indicators of the types of substance use prevalent among teens in the United States are the numbers generated yearly by the Monitoring the Future study, the National Survey on Drug Use and Health, and the Drug Abuse Warning Network.

One way to look at the *frequency and type* of substance use by youth is by surveying them directly about these issues. As discussed in Chapter 3, researchers at the University of Michigan do this every year in their Monitoring the Future study. They survey around 45,000 students in middle and high schools in Grades 8, 10, and 12 across the United States, and then one more time the year after they graduate. The trends that could be seen in the United States related to substance use in 2015 included the following:

- Cigarette and alcohol use were at the lowest level *ever* in the history of the study (since 1975).

- Marijuana is, by far, the illicit drug that youth use the most (see Figure 10.1), with an annual prevalence rate of about 24%. The perceived risk of smoking marijuana decreased in 8th, 10th, and 12th graders.

FIGURE 10.1 Reasons for Use of Electronic Vaporizers, 2015

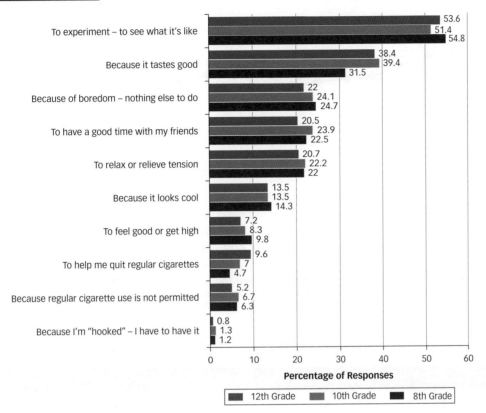

Source: Based on data from Reasons for Use of Electronic Vaporizers. University of Michigan, 2015, Monitoring the Future Study.

- The annual prevalence of use for several illicit drugs decreased, including synthetic marijuana (Spice or K2), heroin, MDMA (Ecstasy or Molly), sedatives, and the use of prescription drugs for nonmedical reasons.

- E-cigarettes or electronic vaporizers are used more often in the course of a month than regular cigarettes and, on the whole, they are not used as cigarette replacements (see Figure 10.2).

Another survey, the National Survey on Drug Use and Health (NSDUH), also adds to our picture of youth substance use today. This survey, which involves face-to-face interviews at respondents' homes by the Substance Abuse and Mental Health Services Administration (SAMHSA), an agency of the U.S. Department of Health and Human Services, considers substance use by people over 12 years of age. Each year the agency surveys around 70,000 randomly selected people. In addition to finding many of the same general trends for youth drug use that the Monitoring the Future study finds, this survey takes a look at the initiation age of substance use—the age at which teens first tried a substance—and finds that most people try alcohol and cigarettes before the age of 21 and that the average age for trying inhalants, PCP, marijuana, LSD, and Ecstasy for the first time also falls during the teenage years.

Another interesting finding from NSDUH is that trends in substance use correspond to trends in how risky young people think drug and substance use is. SAMHSA reports that after cigarette smoking began to be perceived as risky by young people, they began to

●●●

National Survey on Drug Use and Health (NSDUH): A yearly SAMHSA survey of drug use patterns of approximately 70,000 people 12 years of age and older that occurs through face-to-face interviews at respondents' homes.

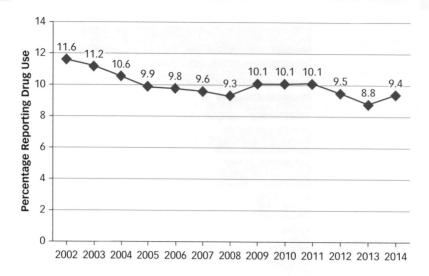

Source: U.S. Department of Health and Human Services, Substance Abuse and Mental Health Services Administration, Center for Behavioral Health Statistics and Quality (2015). Behavioral health trends in the United States [Figure 2 Table]. *Results from the 2014 National Survey on Drug Use and Health: Summary of National Findings.* Retrieved from http://www.samhsa.gov/data/

TABLE 10.2 Past Month Illicit Drug Use among People Aged 12 or Older, by Age Group: Percentages, 2002–2014

	2002	2003	2004	2005	2006	2007	2008	2009	2010	2011	2012	2013	2014
12 or Older	8.3+	8.2+	7.9+	8.1+	8.3+	8.0+	8.1+	8.7+	8.9+	8.7+	9.2+	9.4+	10.2+
12 to 17	11.6+	11.2+	10.6+	9.9	9.8	9.6	9.3	10.1	10.1	10.1	9.5	8.8	9.4
18 to 25	20.2+	20.3+	19.4+	20.1+	19.8+	19.8+	19.7+	21.4	21.6	21.4	21.3	21.5	22.0
26 or Older	5.8+	5.6+	5.5+	5.8+	6.1+	5.8+	5.9+	6.3+	6.6+	6.3+	7.0+	7.3+	8.3

Difference between this estimate and the 2014 estimate is statistically significant at the .05 level.

report smoking cigarettes less, and smoking rates have decreased ever since 2002. Youth who see binge drinking and marijuana use as very harmful to their health also report lower rates of those two activities than those who report that they perceive them as less of a health risk.

Gender, Race, Ethnicity, and General Drug Use Patterns

When we take into account the findings of both the Monitoring the Future study and the National Survey of Drug Use and Health, we can see the following broad patterns in drug use as it relates to gender and race/ethnicity.

- Boys tend to have higher rates of illegal substance use than girls in general, and they also tend to be more frequent users than girls. Boys have a much higher use rate of steroids and smokeless tobacco—findings that are not surprising considering gender ideals in contemporary U.S. society.[16]

- Among all ethnic and racial groups, white and Hispanic or Latino teens were significantly more likely than black or Asian teens to have engaged in binge drinking over the past month. (The differences between white and Latino/Hispanic teens and American

A Focus on Research

Kopak's Drug Use Among Latino Youth: Two Popular Criminological Perspectives Infused With Latino Culture

In his *Sociology Compass* article, "Drug Use Among Latino Youth: Two Popular Criminological Perspectives Infused With Latino Culture," Albert Kopak claims that two popular explanations for delinquency and drug use, social control theory and strain theory, help us understand the reasons why Latino youth do or do not use illicit drugs. In this Focus on Research feature, we will focus on his consideration of social control theory.

Hirschi's social control theory assumes that attachment to, commitment to, involvement in, and belief in conventional values, activities, and people help youth stay away from illicit drug use. Kopak states that attention to core elements of traditional Latino cultures can help us better understand the relevance of social control theory. He alludes to the following as key elements:

Familialism: A strong orientation toward both immediate and extended family creates a strong form of interdependence and feelings of youth attachment to adults. In families with little conflict and adult conformity, some subsets of youth are less likely to engage in drug use, such as Latinas who are close to their mothers and recent immigrants. On the other hand, if youth are connected to families in conflict-laden or especially conflictual households, they are more likely to engage in illicit drug use than they would be otherwise.

Personalismo: A preference for personalized attention and courtesy in interpersonal relations. Kopak explains that after-school programs and other activities that use culturally sensitive mentors and advisors help Latino youth to be more committed to conventional activities.

Respeto: Respect for others is a value that is traditionally emphasized in Latino families. If youth are in schools where there is respect between the teachers and the students, the youth are more likely to be involved in school and related activities,

and less involved in recreational drug use. Alternatively, if youth perceive that they are not respected by their teachers or school officials, they are apt to have less involvement in conventional activities.

Machismo: A cultural emphasis on the male gender role that emphasizes strength, patriarchy, and the control of most emotions. Kopak claims that many male youth believe it is important to show they are tough, and therefore they engage in drug use in front of their peers if encouraged by them to do so. Latino boys are traditionally given more independence and freedom than girls, so they are more likely to be exposed to situations in which others are using drugs.

Marianismo: A cultural emphasis on the female gender role as one that is giving, pure, and in need of protection. In many Latino families, girls are tasked with doing housework and other chores and are limited in their independence in the name of protection. Kopak states that a young woman who believes in this gender role is less likely to be involved in illicit drug use because it might cast shame upon her and her family.

He concludes his analysis by stating that the cultural factors related to Latino youth drug use are important and are in need of additional attention in prevention efforts and outreach.

DISCUSSION QUESTION

1. Based on Kopak's findings, what should a drug prevention program that addresses Latino youth entail? What do you see as the opportunities and challenges to the implementation of such a program?

Source: Kopak, A. (2014). Drug use among Latino youth: Two popular criminological perspectives infused with Latino culture. *Sociological Compass, 8*(3), 233–245.

Indian or Alaskan Native teens and Native Hawaiian or Other Pacific Islander teens were not statistically significant—the differences in percentages were not as extreme.)[17]

- Between 2009 and 2013, there were significant decreases in the use of illicit drugs for white and Latino/Hispanic youth, but not for black youth.[18] (These were the only racial/ethnic groups included in this particular analysis.)

- White adolescents were significantly more likely to smoke cigarettes than adolescents from any other racial or ethnic group.[19] Latino students, on the whole, report a mid-range level of drug use, but they have shown to be more likely than white and black students to use cocaine, crack, inhalants, and crystal methamphetamine in their senior year.[20]

- Asian adolescents report lower rates of cigarette use, alcohol use, marijuana use, and nonmedical use of prescription drugs than the national average. Yet, this varies depending on the Asian subgroup involved. Filipino youth are much more likely than Southeast Asian youth to drink alcohol, for example. Also, Asian and Pacific Islander teens who were born in the United States are much more likely to report past-month alcohol use than those who were born outside of the country.[21]

- Latino adolescents are reported to be below national averages on the whole for most drug use, but have demonstrated a recent increase in the use of marijuana and prescription drugs for recreational purposes. Latino youth born in the United States are more likely to use illegal drugs than those born outside of the country.[22]

- The need for substance use treatment for American Indians or Alaska natives 12 years of age or older is greater than for other populations. SAMHSA includes teens in their recommendation that special attention be paid to the needs of indigenous peoples.[23]

Rates of Serious or Risky Youth Substance Use

Many adolescents today can be labeled as having a substance use disorder, a label used among most drug experts and professionals and defined by the *Diagnostic and Statistical Manual of Mental Disorders* (DSM-IV-TR).[24] There are two types of substance use disorders. Those who display the characteristics of *drug abusers* continue to use drugs and/or alcohol in spite of the negative ways it affects their schooling, work, and relationships. Those who are *alcohol or drug dependent* are not able to control their use of a substance, develop a tolerance for it (i.e., they need more and more of it to feel the desired effect), and have symptoms of withdrawal if they attempt to end their usage. Studies have shown that serious juvenile delinquents are up to three times more likely to be labeled with one of these psychiatric labels than other youth their age.[25] In 2014, the NSDUH found that the percentage of youth between the ages of 12 and 17 who engaged in either drug or alcohol dependence or abuse was about 5%. This percentage is similar to 2013's percentage, but is still lower than the percentage of youth substance dependence from 2000–2012.[26]

Drug Abuse Warning Network (DAWN): A network that existed until 2011 that created yearly reports on the number of youth who ended up in emergency departments due to their use of alcohol and/or other drugs.

Another way we can get a sense of the *seriousness* of drug use among youth is to look at the information provided by the Drug Abuse Warning Network (DAWN), run by the Substance Abuse and Mental Health Services Administration. Each year until 2011, DAWN reported the number of youth who ended up in emergency rooms (or "departments") due to their use of alcohol and/or other drugs. (SAMHSA is working to develop a new data collection system, and until then, they are continuing to use the DAWN data as the best national estimate of drug emergencies.)[27] In 2010, people under the age of 21 constituted 18.8% of all recorded drug-related visits to emergency rooms in the United States (see Figure 10.3). Some of these visits were simply for help with negative reactions to prescribed pharmaceuticals or over-the-counter drugs (see Figure 10.4) and are not indicative

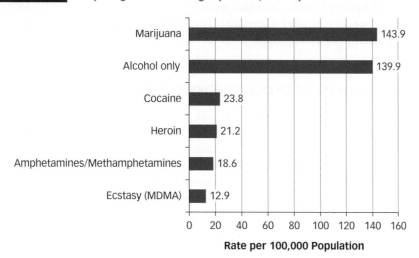

U.S. Rates of Emergency Department Visits Involving Illegal Drugs for People Aged 20 or Younger per 100,000 Population in 2010

Drug	Rate per 100,000 Population
Marijuana	143.9
Alcohol only	139.9
Cocaine	23.8
Heroin	21.2
Amphetamines/Methamphetamines	18.6
Ecstasy (MDMA)	12.9

Rate per 100,000 Population

Source: Substance Abuse and Mental Health Services Administration, Center for Behavioral Health Statistics and Quality. (2012, July 2). *The DAWN report: Highlights from the 2010 Drug Abuse Warning Network findings on drug-related emergency department visits*. Rockville, MD: Author.

FIGURE 10.4

U.S. Rates of Emergency Department Visits Involving Use or Abuse of Select Pharmaceuticals for People Aged 20 or Younger per 100,000 Population in 2010

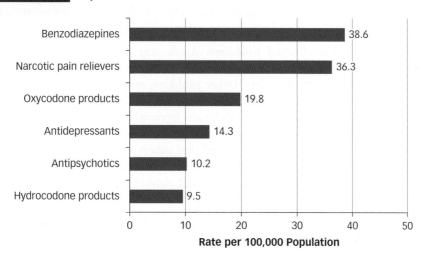

Drug	Rate per 100,000 Population
Benzodiazepines	38.6
Narcotic pain relievers	36.3
Oxycodone products	19.8
Antidepressants	14.3
Antipsychotics	10.2
Hydrocodone products	9.5

Rate per 100,000 Population

Source: Substance Abuse and Mental Health Services Administration, Center for Behavioral Health Statistics and Quality. (2012, July 2). *The DAWN report: Highlights from the 2010 Drug Abuse Warning Network findings on drug-related emergency department visits*. Rockville, MD: Author.

of the sort of drug use that most adults are concerned about. To get a better sense of the scale of the problematic use of drugs among youth, we can look at the DAWN estimate of the number of emergency room visits that involved drug misuse or abuse. For example, in 2010, 2.3 million visits involved such use, and of that total 3.8%, or 189,060 incidents, involved underage drinking of alcohol or drinking and taking drugs together.[28]

The data show that emergency room visits related to alcohol use and illegal drug use did not increase significantly for U.S. youth from 2004 to 2010. What did increase substantially during that period was the misuse or abuse of pharmaceuticals—reported emergency visits related to those substances increased by 45%. DAWN data demonstrate that 95% of emergency department visits for drug-related suicide attempts among adolescents aged 12–17 in 2010 involved such pharmaceuticals,[29] and girls made up the majority of the attempts. The category of pharmaceuticals found to be the most common in boys' and girls' suicide attempts was acetaminophen (found in products such as Tylenol).

The Repercussions of Serious Substance Use

As shown above, in any given year we can look to the most reliable large-scale studies of youth drug use and get a sense of the overall picture. But for the parents or adult relatives of a teen with a serious substance use problem, it sometimes matters little if the overall rate of teen drug abuse is going up or down—their major concern is the negative effects stemming from the drug use of their family member. When young people use drugs regularly and heavily, they often experience the following types of problems:

School-related problems: Teen drug use is associated with a lack of interest in school that might manifest in young people starting to skip school, to ignore classwork, and to drop out of school altogether. If they do stay in school, they may be disruptive or experience problems due to their substance use, which makes it harder for other students to learn in the classroom.[30]

Health-related problems: Teens abusing drugs and alcohol are more likely than other teens to accidentally injure themselves, find themselves with physical disabilities or illnesses, and overdose. In addition, substance-abusing youth have an increased risk of contracting HIV or a sexually transmitted infection if they are engaging in drug use that involves behaviors such as injecting themselves with psychoactive substances or if they have low impulse control after using a drug.[31]

Psychological and intellectual problems: Adolescent substance abusers have been shown to be at a higher risk for psychological problems such as depression, conduct disorder, and personality disorders. Other problems related to teen drug and alcohol abuse involve slower development than expected both socially and physiologically, and a general sense of apathy and withdrawal from others. For example, research has demonstrated that when youth become heavy users of marijuana before the age of 18, they may experience a long-term dip in IQ that others who begin smoking marijuana regularly after the age of 18 do not experience.[32] Young people's brains are in a vulnerable state of development, and heavy drug and alcohol use during the teen years may lead to damage or interrupted development.

Family/economic problems: Teenage drug abuse can lead to problems with other family members. Youth who are abusing drugs often create financial and psychological stressors within their families that make it difficult for their parents and siblings to have healthy relationships with one another. The parents have to spend so much time and energy on the child using drugs that they do not have as many financial and emotional resources to give to the child's siblings. This can lead to resentment all around.

In addition to the personal problems that may affect young drug users, many in society are concerned about the *social costs*, the costs that affect others outside of the young person's immediate family. Youth drug abuse often results in the need for service support in either medical or social form. If teens are seriously addicted, they may need help to get off the drugs or alcohol, they may be in the juvenile or adult justice system if their usage is linked to delinquency in some way, or they may be getting themselves back on their feet and finding a way to support themselves. All of these endeavors require financial and social investments by the greater community.[33]

Dope

The film *Dope* (2015) centers its story on three high school students of color (Malcolm and his friends, Jib and Diggy) who live in Inglewood, California in a neighborhood with a good deal of delinquency called "The Bottoms." The tagline for the film—It's hard out here for a geek—hints at how the main characters' interests and presentations of self differ from many of the others in the neighborhood—at least the teens and adults who hang out on the streets and are sometimes involved with drug sales. Malcolm runs into some trouble as he accidentally gets involved in a drug deal, and all sorts of twisted things happen as he attempts to get out of it with the help of Jib and Diggy. While he is contending with the mess he is in, he is also trying to successfully apply to Harvard University. Although the movie is a comedy, it is a unique look at the stressors young people who live in neighborhoods with serious delinquency and adult crime must navigate and the resilience that they often demonstrate in the process.

The film *Dope* focuses on youth who use their wits to reach their goals after unintentionally getting involved in a drug deal.

DISCUSSION QUESTION

1. What other films show teens making choices about how to interact with neighbors who are involved in drug dealing? How are these teens portrayed?

Source: *Dope*. (2015). Directed by Rick Famuyiwa. 103 minutes. Open Road Films.

THE RELATIONSHIP OF SUBSTANCE USE TO DELINQUENCY

Although people have long made assumptions that illicit drug and alcohol use goes hand in hand with delinquency, scientific researchers continue to work to clarify whether there are verifiable linkages between the two and, if so, what the connections are and how they may change over time. According to an overview of contemporary drug research,[34] a few things can be said about the relationship with some confidence:

1. *Youth who engage in serious substance use and have problems with it are more likely to engage in serious juvenile delinquency.* This finding has been supported in studies of youth in the community, studies of youth in juvenile court, and long-term studies of teens who have engaged in substance use at one point in time in order to see if they engage in serious offending in the future.

2. *The use of substances and involvement in delinquency change in a similar pattern over time.* The majority of research findings on the topic indicate that substance use and delinquency involvement are related over time, but there is no clear progression from one to the other. (In other words, it is not clear that early substance use always leads to delinquency, nor is it clear that early delinquency

always leads to drug use.) Some of the primary research findings that support this linkage is that aggressive conduct at a young age is linked to later illicit substance use, increasing substance use as the youth gets older, and future diagnoses of substance problems. Substance use has been shown to predict later criminal behavior in teens, and statistical analyses have shown that substance use and delinquency follow similar paths over time.

3. *There may be different forms of linkages between substance use and delinquency.* Substance use and delinquency appear to be linked to one another in a variety of ways (see Figure 10.5). First of all, heavy drug or alcohol use appears to affect some youth by delaying their physical, psychological, and social development. Substance use can hamper the development of adolescents' brains, and can be related to difficulties in making decisions that are in their best interest and in managing their emotions. In other words, youth using drugs and alcohol are more likely to make impulsive decisions that satisfy them immediately, but that will not benefit them in the long run. This pattern can be one that leads to involvement in delinquency.

Substance use and delinquency can also be linked through a number of other factors that interact with one another. A young person who uses drugs may get accustomed to being intoxicated and, to maintain his/her habit, may need money—money that she or he may try to obtain through delinquent activities such as theft or drug sales. Or a person may simply be intoxicated and make choices that lead to breaking the law, or may just use drugs recreationally but need money for the family and decide to engage in delinquency. A young person who uses drugs is also very likely to find friends or peers who also use drugs. This group of kids who are getting drunk and/or high may decide to get involved in delinquent behavior for any number of reasons, including the simple desire to break the rules and/or rebel against the system.

In many of the cases in which substance use and delinquency are linked, the outcome is delayed transition into adulthood. Serious drug-using teens often do not successfully accomplish the achievements typically found on the road to adult life, such as obtaining and holding down part-time jobs, having healthy relationships, and making mature decisions.

4. *Substance use and delinquency decrease in late adolescence.* Although there are variations, almost all studies show that substance use and delinquency become less common activities among youth in their late teens and young adult years. This is thought to occur because thrill-seeking seems less and less of a good idea as young people developmentally mature and begin to see the big picture of their lives more clearly. In addition, as youth begin to take on more responsibilities and more serious roles in society, they realize that antisocial or delinquent behaviors are not good for them, and could lead to the loss of things and people they value deeply (e.g., jobs, romantic partners, and possibly children for some).

Gender, Race, Ethnicity, and Sexuality Factors

In addition to the linkages between substance use and delinquency noted above, other factors related to a teen deciding to use, and possibly to continue to use, drugs or alcohol and get involved with other forms of delinquency are the ongoing stressors that young people face due to their gender, race/ethnicity, and sexuality.

Often, girls' substance use and delinquency follow experiences of physical and sexual abuse.[35] Cuellar and Curry found that gendered experiences of drugs and delinquency

FIGURE 10.5 Factors That May Link Substance Use and Offending in Adolescents

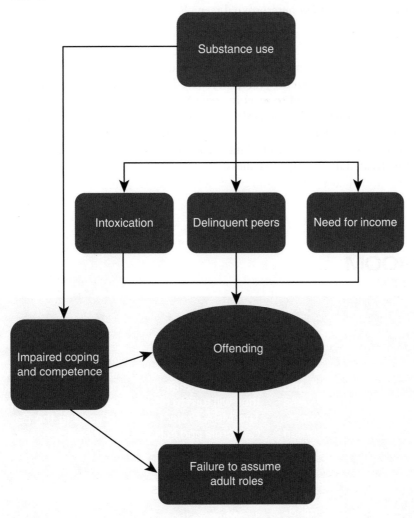

Source: Mulvey, Schubert, and Chassin (2010, p. 4).

interact with race, ethnicity, and class concerns so that girls of color are particularly vulnerable.[36] They studied the cases of Mexican American girls who had been adjudicated delinquent and were serving time on probation. These girls on the whole came from communities characterized by poverty and a lack of attention or investment by the government or other agencies. Cuellar and Curry found that Mexican American girls' drug use and delinquency was also often accompanied by cutting or self-mutilation, as well as suicide attempts. The girls' various behaviors were, in part, a means of reacting to and coping with the social and personal stressors they had experienced before and after their first experience with substance use.

Lesbian, gay, bisexual, and transgender (LGBT) youth have other types of stressors that need to be addressed when charting the possible relationship between their drug use and delinquency: heterosexism and genderism. Like youth of color and girls of all racial and ethnic backgrounds, LGBT youth are often harassed by other young people and, in addition, many adults. As a result they often become depressed, use drugs or alcohol as a coping mechanism, and/or commit delinquent acts related to survival. Many youth are kicked out of their homes when their parents realize they are LGBT and end up living on the street. Not surprisingly, gay, lesbian, and bisexual youth have been shown to engage in higher-risk drug use than heterosexual teens.[37]

Racism and discrimination affect both girls and boys of color and serve as stressors that can be linked to high-risk activities such as drug use and delinquency. Gibbons et al. found that when African American teens perceived discrimination early on in their lives and for over a period of several years, they were likely to experience a gradual wearing away of their self-control and to react in anger.[38] One way that the anger manifested was in risky behaviors such as drug and alcohol use. It is not unreasonable to think the same reaction to injustice might inspire youth who are facing it to act out in other delinquent behaviors, as might a reaction to feeling it does not matter what they do or do not do—they will be treated negatively regardless.

from the CLASSROOM to the COMMUNITY

The Mind Body Awareness Project

The Mind Body Awareness (MBA) Project is a non-profit that works to address youth drug use and other forms of delinquency through mindfulness meditation and emotional intelligence exercises. The program is designed for teens living in urban areas and is meant to reach the young people by speaking in a language that they understand and about concerns that matter the most to them. Its methods are based on "successfully helping teens to develop self-regulation, empathy, and mindful attention, gain impulse control, and relieve the extremely high levels of anxiety and stress they struggle with. These are the real tools youth today need—tools that bring an inner revolution of the heart and mind." The MBA Project has trained facilitators who deliver a curriculum that they developed to speak to both the issues incarcerated youth or youth in detention state are the most important to them, and the risk factors for delinquency that the research demonstrates are important. After studying the effects of an eight-week mindfulness program for incarcerated and at-risk youth, a program that involved meditation, group exercises, and modules about drug education, the project found that there was a significant decrease in youth impulsiveness and a significant increase in youth perceptions of the riskiness of drug use.[39] The program's founders believe that these changes will serve youth well throughout their lives and decrease the likelihood they will turn to drug use after finishing the program. The MBA Project is being used in the Bay Area of California and in Nashville, Tennessee, and there are plans to expand its usage to many other arenas.

DISCUSSION QUESTIONS

1. What are the benefits of mindfulness, or meditation training, according to the Mind Body Awareness Project?

2. How might familiarity with mindfulness techniques be helpful to youth both inside and outside of detention facilities?

3. What do you think the obstacles might be to getting kids who have gotten in trouble with the law to engage in a meditation-based program? What approach could an adult take to address those obstacles?

Sources: Himelstein, S. (2011). Mindfulness based substance abuse treatment for incarcerated youth. *International Journal of Transpersonal Studies, 30* (1–2), 1–10; Mind Body Awareness Project website (www.mbaproject.org).

RESPONSES TO AND PREVENTION OF YOUTH DRUG USE

Given what our experts know about youth substance use today, it is not surprising that the different methods used to address it range in scope from large-scale campaigns to small group exercises aimed at a particular group of young people. As you read about some of the most popular of these programs and practices, keep in mind some of the important things we know about teen drug use: that modern teens have access to a great deal of drug information that they can retrieve in seconds via the Internet; that a good portion of their drug use is planned ahead of time and is seen as a way to have fun with their friends; that some young people who are experiencing serious stressors related to abuse and discrimination are utilizing drugs and alcohol, in part, as a way of reacting to those experiences; and that others have developed habits that they are trying to find the money for, often through committing other acts of delinquency.

Media Campaigns

It has been a long time since former First Lady Nancy Reagan campaigned across the United States in the 1980s and early 1990s, spreading the message of her campaign, "Just Say No!" Other campaigns throughout history have included the famous commercial of an egg frying on a frying pan accompanied by the voice-over "This is your brain on drugs," which was made by the Partnership for a Drug-Free America in 1987. A few years after that campaign, the Federal Bureau of Investigation spread the antidrug message in a campaign in which 20 video game manufacturers put the message "Winners Don't Use Drugs." All video games imported into North America between 1989 and 2000 had the slogan showing on one of their screens during playing time.

Campaigns that encourage teens to stay away from using drugs are still being utilized. In 2005, the National Youth Anti-Drug Media Campaign launched an antidrug education campaign aimed at youth that utilizes both national and local approaches. This campaign is called Above the Influence (www.abovetheinfluence.com/influence), and the message that it advertises is that teens who are independent thinkers can distance themselves from the influences of their drug-using peers and stay drug free:

> In a matter of seconds, you could make a decision that will affect the rest of your life.
>
> Easy? No way. You won't always get it right.
>
> But here's the thing—it's your call. Your life.

At the height of its popularity, "Just Say No" supporters used a variety of methods to advertise their drug abstinence message. Do you think that putting the slogan on unexpected objects, such as athletic gear, might have influenced young people to reject offers to use drugs?

Your chance to define yourself. To stand up for who you are,

instead of letting others define you.

Every single day, we need to think about how we're going to live.

Above the influence? Or, under the influence?

I am above the influence. How about you?

Organizers believe that the message they are using appeals more to young people's desire for freedom and autonomy and conveys that they can be better than the average teen if they choose to be. Researchers who have studied the campaign claim that it has resulted in less marijuana use among junior high students exposed to the message than among junior high students reporting no exposure to the campaign message.[40]

Drug Abuse Resistance Education (D.A.R.E.)

There aren't many of us who went through our schooling in the 1980s, 1990s, or 2000s who don't remember the Drug Abuse Resistance Education or D.A.R.E. program! Police officers and sheriffs deliver the D.A.R.E. curriculum in schools. They start by talking to fifth-grade students about how to avoid being peer pressured into smoking cigarettes, drinking alcohol, and using other drugs. In middle school or junior high school, they typically target preteens and young teens with specialized lessons about methamphetamine and over-the-counter drugs. This is done in conjunction with lessons about bullying, navigating the Internet, and gangs. Then, in high school, D.A.R.E. programs attempt to teach students emotional management skills that will help them stay away from both drugs and violence.

The D.A.R.E. program is funded by various U.S. government agencies as well as state and federal agencies. It promotes zero tolerance—the approach that no drug usage whatsoever will be accepted without serious consequences and that all drugs are equally harmful. Although D.A.R.E. programs have been around since 1983, it is not clear if the lessons they teach prevent youth from exploring drug use. Most of the research fails to demonstrate a significant difference in the drug use of youth who were exposed to the D.A.R.E. curriculum and those who were not.[41] Critics of the D.A.R.E. program often point out that students are familiarized with drugs through the curriculum, which may actually do the opposite of what the officers involved intend—inspire these youth to try drugs. Critics of the approach also worry that many of the practices of the program work to use students as drug informants as they ask students to reveal the facts about drug use in their homes and then use that information to make arrests.[42]

Drug Testing

Another method used by some adults to stem adolescent drug use is drug testing. Drug testing kits can now be purchased and used by adults who hope to deter youth from using drugs through the analysis of bodily materials (urine, hair, saliva). Some parents use these tests at home with their children, but typically they are used in schools.

School drug testing has increased over time, in part, due to the strong support for drug testing by former President George W. Bush's administration.[43] The use of school drug tests is highly controversial as it raises the question of whether students should have the right to be free of unwanted drug testing and if drug tests are a violation of the Fourth Amendment protecting individuals against unlawful searches and seizures. The Supreme Court in the *Earls* decision said that it is okay for schools to do mandatory drug testing on public school students who are involved in sports and other extracurricular activities.[44]

D.A.R.E.: The Drug Abuse Resistance Education program, which uses anti–drug use curriculum delivered by law enforcement officers in school classrooms in an effort to deter kids from using drugs.

Zero tolerance: The ideology of most U.S. government–funded drug prevention programs that states that no drug usage whatsoever is acceptable without serious consequences and all drugs are equally as harmful.

Drug testing: A method used to deter drug use by means of testing bodily materials (e.g., urine, hair, saliva) for evidence of drug consumption.

The majority of the Supreme Court justices stated that when youth are involved in extra-curricular activities, they give up some of their rights to privacy. In addition, they stated that mandatory drug testing serves the important interest of the school to prevent student drug use.

Besides the issues of reliability of the test itself, there is also the concern kids can easily cheat on the home drug tests by a number of means, including switching their samples with someone else's and/or adding substances to the sample that will hide a given drug from being detected by the test. The National Institute on Drug Abuse states that it is not a good idea for parents to use home drug testing as the only way of dealing with their child's suspected drug use. Typically when parents resort to the home test, they are pretty concerned that their child has been using drugs, and then if they do get a positive result, they may not be equipped to deal with it. Issues such as whether to take their child to rehabilitation or counseling, or to punish him or her, can be difficult. The American Academy of Pediatrics agrees and takes the position that home drug tests should not be used unless there is a suitable assessment and treatment plan in the community. In addition, parents are cautioned to be careful about testing their children because it could damage their relationship. The children may feel they are not trusted at all, and as a result, they could act in their frustration and disappointment by using drugs. Even if that doesn't occur, experts warn that a damaged relationship is a high price to pay for a drug test.

In spite of the Supreme Court's thumbs-up for drug testing of students in certain contexts, a concern about drug tests still remains among some. One of the most commonly voiced concerns is that drug test results are not always accurate, yet they hold serious consequences for the youth who tests positive for using drugs, including suspension and expulsion from school. The drug tests purchased by most schools are affordable urine tests that are not as accurate as the much more expensive drug tests used by college athletic associations. These tests have been shown to be inaccurate a surprisingly high percentage of the time they have been taken[45] and often produce false positives when another medication (such as ibuprofen) is misidentified as an illegal drug. But the inaccuracies of drug tests are not limited to the mislabeling of drug users—they also often fail to detect actual drug use as well.[46]

●●●
Drug courts: Courts that deliver a series of services geared at helping youth using drugs to become rehabilitated and stop their usage.

Another concern is that scholarly studies of drug testing have tended to demonstrate that schools with drug testing do not have lower student drug use rates than those without drug testing.[47]

Drug Courts

Drug testing is used in another context as well—in juvenile **drug courts**. These drug courts were developed to attempt to deliver a series of services that will help youth who are accused of using drugs to get on the right track and stop their usage. The first juvenile drug courts in the United States were developed in the mid-1990s in Birmingham, Alabama, and Miami, Florida. More than 20 years later, there are now more than 450 juvenile drug courts operating

A teenage Hispanic defendant appears before a juvenile court in Orange, CA. Note African American judge, lawyers at table, and court reporter.

in the United States and many more around the world.[48] The major difference between juvenile drug courts in the United States and those in other countries around the world is that, in the United States, an **abstinence model of drug use** serves as the basis of the drug court program, and a harm reduction model serves as the basis of many programs outside of the United States.[49] This means that young people who go through juvenile court programs in the United States are thought to successfully complete the requirements of court only after stopping the usage of *all drugs*. In harm reduction juvenile drug courts youth may be deemed successful if they stop their usage of one drug (e.g., meth), but still occasionally smoke marijuana or drink alcohol.[50]

The typical drug court utilizes teamwork between a judge, a prosecutor, a defense attorney, a service treatment provider representative, and a probation officer or another law enforcement officer. The goal that the team players work toward is rehabilitation for youth with substance abuse issues. To that end, the adversarial framework that usually characterizes the courtroom is abandoned as the team works to have the defendant placed quickly on an appropriate treatment plan and monitored intensively while on the plan through frequent court visits and drug tests. The continued close involvement of the court in cases of drug-using youth is a move away from the conventional approach to such defendants, which often requires drug treatment as a condition of diversion, but cannot involve close monitoring of defendants due to the large caseloads that probation officers must manage.

● ● ●

Abstinence model of drug use: The model of drug use used by juvenile drug courts, which defines a young person's involvement in court-mandated programs as only when they completely stop all drug usage.

The first evaluation studies of juvenile drug courts lacked scientific rigor. It wasn't until the first decade of the 2000s that several rigorous evaluation studies were conducted. The findings of these studies tend to demonstrate support for the courts as a tool to help reduce both youth substance use and delinquency. In addition, they have been shown to save the state up to $5,000 per participant by keeping him or her out of detention.[51]

Drug Rehabilitation Programs

Another way of addressing adolescent substance use is through drug rehabilitation programs. This approach is looked upon very favorably among juvenile justice professionals; in fact, it has been ranked as the single most effective way to address youth delinquency in a study of over 500 individuals working in the U.S. juvenile justice system![52] Young people who are sent to these programs, usually either by their parents or by the juvenile court, are thought to have a serious problem with drugs and/or alcohol. (It should be noted that teens can refer themselves as well—it just is not nearly as common.) Usually the adults who refer the boys or girls to a drug rehabilitation program label their problem as a form of addiction or a disease. The rehabilitation programs are aimed to rid adolescent users of their addiction through one or all of the following methods: therapy, the use of drugs (e.g., methadone being subscribed

Drug rehabilitation programs, both residential and outpatient, are highly regarded by many juvenile justice professionals.

to block heroin addiction), and life skills training. These programs may involve a stay in an inpatient facility away from the youths' homes, or may be outpatient programs in which youth live at home and go to regular meetings and/or counseling sessions. In some cases, youth may live away from home in a program known as a **residential therapeutic community** for an extended period of time that lasts longer than a year.

For many years, rehabilitation programs for youth looked a lot like those for adults and modeled the well-known 12-step model of recovery that groups such as Alcoholics Anonymous use.[53] In this model of rehabilitation, the first step to recovery is for young people to admit they are powerless in the face of their addiction. This model has been shown to not always be the best one for teens, because they often take the message that they are powerless and have an addiction that they have no control over to mean that their situation is hopeless. This can lead to a self-fulfilling prophecy in which labeled teens continue to go on the same drug-using path they were on prior to rehabilitation. But, the model has been shown to reduce drug and alcohol use among teens who go into the programs voluntarily and who have labeled themselves as being unable to deal with their drug use on their own.[54]

In addition, experts on teen drug abuse note that the group therapy model can sometimes actually spark interest in future drug use among casual drug users who are forced to attend such programs. They learn about other "harder" drugs than those they may have experimented with from teens with more serious drug problems, and also become friends with many of these same teens—leading them to use the drugs together after the program ends. This has led some experts to say that group therapy acts as a form of drug, or **deviancy training**.[55] Yet, studies have demonstrated that for serious drug-using teens, group therapy with other teens who weren't serious users ended up reducing their drug use.[56]

Since the late 1990s, there have been innovations in drug rehabilitation programs for teens because leaders in the field began publicly acknowledging that the adult models of rehab were not working as well for them. In addition to the problem with the ways that treatment groups were being run, researchers and advocates began to emphasize that children were not benefiting from living away from their families in residential programs—they were instead experiencing a lack of social bonding and support with their parents that was not helping them refrain from substance use.[57] So, new programs have been developed that address those issues. These programs focus on treatment or therapy in the home or the community that explicitly strengthens the ties of the adolescents to their families in the hopes that they will make choices to stay away from drug and alcohol use. Unlike the 12-step programs, there is little or no group therapy with other drug-using youth. Instead, the therapy involved is often family therapy with the goal of increasing healthy communication and the family's ability to positively address the youth's needs. In addition, they often concentrate on teaching skills for adults and kids to deal with the ups and downs of the teen years, they make sure that interventions are culturally appropriate, they encourage family members and teens to set goals related to drug use reduction, and they help the families find concrete ways to translate those goals into action. Programs such as Vera Institute of Justice's Adolescent Portable Therapy, Cannabis Youth Treatment, multidimensional family therapy, and multidimensional therapeutic foster care all use this sort of multifaceted approach in an effort to bring about lasting change in a young person's substance use.[58] By considering the many factors that influence drug use, these types of programs are able to work more effectively to rehabilitate drug-using teens than more simplistic programs of rehabilitation.

● ● ●

Residential therapeutic community: Drug programs in which youth live away from home in a facility for an extended period of time to address their drug use.

Deviancy training: The idea that group therapy for youth drug use sometimes functions to spark interest in future drug use among casual users who participate.

In the News

The War on Drugs Is a War on Kids

Law professor Patricia J. Williams wrote an editorial for a news magazine in which she asserted that the war on drugs is a war on kids. She opened the piece by contrasting the experiences in different educational settings. She began by describing colleges across the U.S. during springtime—the smell of medical marijuana in the air and the widespread use of various amphetamines to give students that extra boost of energy and concentration for their exams. Williams then described the typical set-up for inner-city public schools throughout the nation: the daily presence of law enforcement agents and their drug sniffing dogs, routine searches of backpacks and bags, and a general surveillance culture in which students are assumed to be the carriers of illicit substances. She explains the dichotomy:

> Drugs are ubiquitous in this country, and yet we know that some people have the privilege of doctor-prescribed intoxication, while others are thrown into dungeons for seeking the same relief. We know that the war on drugs is heavily inflected with Jim Crow-ism, economic inequality, gun culture myths and political opportunism. . . . We divert resources from mental health or rehab, and allocate millions to militarize schools. The result: the war on drugs has metastasized into a war on children.

The war on drugs has resulted in the increased social control of kids and the school-to-prison pipeline.

Williams made the argument that the hypersurveillance of youth of color in poor and working class communities, in combination with zero-tolerance policies, results in the creation of the school-to-prison pipeline. Due to the social factors targeting these youth, it is much less likely they will experience college or university life. Yet, Williams asserted that the war on kids is not just on youth of color, but on all kids—because these policies eventually affect suburban kids as well. She concluded, "Criminalizing children will have constitutional implications for generations to come."

DISCUSSION QUESTIONS

1. Think about your high school experiences. Looking back, how did you see the war on drugs affect the way social control occurred at your school?

2. Did you make the connection between surveillance and social control measures at your school and the bigger context of the U.S. policy to have a "war" on drugs at the time? Explain why or why not.

Source: Williams, P. J. (2013). The war on drugs is a war on kids. *The Nation*, February 13. Retrieved from http://www.thenation.com/article/war-drugs-war-kids

Differing Policy Approaches: Drug Prohibition, Legalization, and Harm Reduction Strategies

Any approach we take to the use and misuse of drugs by juveniles is related to the overarching policies we have with respect to such use. In the United States today, **drug prohibition** remains the main approach to the disapproved drug use of adults and young people—the so-called **war on drugs** and the heavy punishment of drug users that still occurs is indicative of this approach. This view sees drug use as an immoral behavior and one that should be condemned. The war on drugs, which began under President Nixon in the late 1960s and hit its peak in the 1980s and 1990s, amped up punishments for drug offenses, and supporters encouraged long terms of incarceration as the answer to illicit drug use and sales. It disproportionately wreaked havoc on youth within these communities and, by extension, low-income communities of color as a whole.[59] This was done, in part, by the disproportionately harsh federal punishments given to users and dealers of crack cocaine, who were often people of color in low-income communities, compared to the lesser punishment given to powder cocaine users, who were typically well-off white people (a 100:1 disparity for more than two decades).[60] In recent years, as the use of drugs such as heroin has risen substantially among white youth and young adults, there has been a general trend away from the war on drugs driven by their parents and other concerned adults.[61] Yet, the war on drugs is by no means completely over.

Advocates of alternative drug policies who would like to decriminalize or legalize drug use cite the many downsides of prohibition as reasons why alternative policies should be pursued: the large number of people in the country who are imprisoned regardless of whether they have caused harm or posed any threat to others with their drug use, the costs that the public bears by paying for such high incarceration numbers, the infringement of individual rights, the creating and maintenance of a dangerous underground drug market, and the lack of logic involved in naming some harmful substances as legal (e.g., alcohol) while criminalizing substances that have been found to be associated with lesser harms (e.g., marijuana). There has not been widespread acceptance of alternative policies in the case of most illicit drugs, which is linked to the popular perception that widespread legalization of currently illicit drugs will only increase misuse and produce more social problems. Yet, since 1996, 25 U.S. states and the District of Columbia have passed medical marijuana laws, which legalize cannabis for certain medical uses.[62] Four states have legalized the use and sale of marijuana (Washington, Oregon, Colorado, and Alaska), and at least 15 states have decriminalized the possession and use of marijuana by adults.[63] Research demonstrates that after the decriminalization of marijuana in California, there was a 61% drop in youth arrests for drug possession.[64] There is evidence that living in a state that allows the use of medical marijuana leads to both adult and youth tolerance of marijuana use, but the law itself does not always result in increased youth marijuana use.[65]

As briefly alluded to earlier in the chapter, another approach often situated somewhere between those of the prohibitionists and the legalization advocates is the **harm reduction** approach. Harm reduction responses to drug use are popular, especially in countries outside of the United States. The harm reduction approach to drug use takes a public health angle and acknowledges that illegal and legal drug use are always going to occur, so they need to be addressed in a way that minimizes the harm associated with use. This is known as a realistic approach to substance use and one that takes more of a value-neutral view of drug use and the user.[66] Some of the best known programs to help adults who use illicit drugs include needle exchange programs (so clean needles can be used and hepatitis C and HIV can be avoided), and methadone maintenance programs for people

●●●

Drug prohibition: An approach to drug use that involves the harsh punishment of drug users.

War on drugs: An assortment of drug prohibition efforts implemented by the U.S. government since the early 1970s.

Harm reduction: An approach to drug use that takes a public health angle and acknowledges that illegal and legal drug use are always going to occur, so they need to be addressed in a way that minimizes the harm associated with use.

addicted to heroin—these programs have goals such as reducing crimes associated with drug use and keeping people as healthy as they can be.

Advocates of harm reduction with adolescent drug users state that instead of trying to look at measures of whether young people have reduced or stopped their drug use as a mark of a successful intervention or policy, social, economic, and health outcomes need to be the foci of concern. For example, alcohol harm reduction programs for teens usually involve exposing them to honest information about the consequences of alcohol use and a discussion of how to avoid falling into drinking patterns that cause negative health-related, social, and economic consequences. Such programs may include frank discussions of how to drink in the most responsible fashion possible if one is going to drink alcohol, depending upon the age group targeted (this is more likely with older teens than younger ones). Harm reduction programs for teens usually involve teaching social skills, resistance skills, and education components as well.[67] The Integrated School- and Community-Based Demonstration Intervention Addressing Drug Use Among Adolescents, or SCIDUA,[68] and the School Health and Alcohol Harm Reduction Project[69] are examples of harm reduction programs that demonstrated significant reductions in alcohol use among program-involved youth. In Chapter 14 we will address some more delinquency prevention programs that include harm reduction substance use components; this approach is possible and appears to be around for the long haul.

Cultural Issues and Drug Prevention and Rehabilitation Programs

Research has demonstrated that, to be successful, drug-related programs need to be sensitive to ethnic and racial differences and community norms, and consider the community characteristics of the people being served.[70] There are many examples of programs that are trying to do just that. Let's look at two of them to get a sense of how they operate.

Project Venture: An American Indian and Alaska Native Youth-Oriented Program

According to scholars, American Indian and Alaska Native (AIAN) youth in the United States are especially apt to get involved with substance use, to continue with substance use after their initial attempt to get drunk or high, and to use a number of substances together (which is known as polysubstance use).[72] These youth face serious social and environmental challenges at a higher rate than other ethnic and racial groups—poverty, lack of quality health care, and adult alcoholism—and the historical trauma that their communities have faced can lead youth to feel a sense of despair.[73] As a result, the suicide rate for AIAN youth has been estimated to be three times higher than the national rate.[74]

To minimize the substance use that often works as a way for youth to self-medicate or to numb their difficult feelings, the National Indian Youth Leadership Project developed a program called Project Venture. This project is developed and rooted in the AIAN community and thus is geared toward recognizing the challenges that AIAN youth have presently and have had historically. The aim is to connect young people with community role models, traditions, and nature as a means of building confidence and developing healthy ways of living. This approach reflects the increasingly popular idea that building upon youths' strengths is a more effective drug prevention approach than sending youth negative messages about drugs and telling them to stop using them.[75]

Project Venture uses adventure as the main theme of a yearlong curriculum that takes place not only in the wilderness, but also in everyday settings, such as school and in the communities in which the young people live. The youth in selected elementary and middle schools (Grades 5–9) engage in classroom sessions in which they engage in games and activities that

● ● ●

Polysubstance use: The use of multiple drugs or substances at the same time.

help them to develop social skills and self-esteem, as well as to take control of their own decisions and to make positive choices that will benefit not only themselves, but others in the community. Selected youth engage in other activities and challenges to build trust and confidence, such as white-water rafting, rock climbing, backpacking, rappelling, and learning survival skills that have been passed on by their ancestors. In addition, the youth take part in projects to help their communities, and in the summer they may participate in weeklong camping and hiking expeditions. Evaluations of Project Venture have demonstrated that youth in the program were less likely to drink alcohol than those who were not in the program. Two years after finishing the program, youth have shown increased use of alcohol, but significantly less of an increase than youth who have not gone through the program. The program is seen as largely successful and has been used in 19 states and Canada (www.niylp.org).

Amish Youth Vision Project: A Drug and Alcohol Intervention Program Aimed at Amish Teens

As explained in Weber, Cates, and Carey's study about Amish youth and drug interventions, the Old Order Amish people are Christians who live in a way that differs from many adolescents' ways of life in the United States.[76] Typically they are raised to live away from mainstream society and non-Amish people in enclaves in the United States, without modern technology. They speak a language that is a mixture of German and Swiss dialects ("Dutch") as well as English, and live in a strongly patriarchal society in which men and boys have more power than girls and women. Children are raised to be uncomfortable with lots of individual attention and are encouraged to be humble and modest. In their religion, adults choose to be baptized into the church after going through a period in their teenage years known as **Rumspringa**, in which they explore the world outside of the Amish community to make sure they want to make the commitment to the Amish religion. Rumspringa typically lasts one to two years but can last into adulthood. In the Elkhart-LaGrange Amish area of Indiana, Rumspringa has been associated with a lot of drug and alcohol use, which was highlighted in the documentary *The Devil's Playground* (2002).

Although many in the Amish community did not agree that the film was a completely accurate depiction of teenage life during their period of exploration, they were concerned that there might be too much drug use in the community. So, they developed a drug and alcohol intervention program for teens that was geared toward their particular sociocultural needs. This program was called the Amish Youth Vision Project, whose founders designed it to take the Amish distaste for individual attention, as well as psychology and counseling, into account. In the first stage of program development they asked members of the Amish community what their concerns were related to drug and alcohol use in their area. They found that there was a common concern about drug treatment groups mandated by the juvenile court that require Amish youth to discuss their usage with non-Amish youth

●●●
Rumspringa:
The period in Amish teenagers' lives in which they explore the world outside of their community to make sure they want to commit to their religion; it is known to involve experimentation with drugs and alcohol.

Special sociocultural interventions have been developed for Amish youth with drug and alcohol problems.

(whom they call "English"). The Amish youth were uncomfortable being mixed with the English because they often had to educate them about the Amish culture and practices, which was tiring and took away from their purpose in being there. They also expressed feeling a communication barrier when they spoke English because "Dutch" is the language they speak at home, and it is what they usually use to discuss important or emotional matters.

The program that was developed, and continues today, aimed to address these issues through the use of segregated classes with only Amish youth and allowed them to speak in their Dutch dialect. The groups were designed to be led by Amish young adults and non-Amish therapists or counselors. The therapists are trained to show respect for the distance that the Amish keep from mainstream U.S. society. Drug and alcohol classes are also segregated by gender in keeping with the ways in which girls and boys are segregated in Amish institutions, such as schools and churches. Parents are invited to attend as well. The eight-week program involves education about particular drugs (usually caffeine, alcohol, marijuana, and methamphetamine), weekly homework that asks the teens to discuss a topic with an adult of their choice, and group activities. The program has graduated hundreds of Amish youth, and is deemed successful, in large part due to the role of the Amish young adult leaders who help "translate" Amish culture and communication to the therapists.

Now that we have considered two examples of culturally focused drug programs, we can think about the importance of social factors to the example at the beginning of the chapter about Kyle and Sebastian. Their case was one in which they chose to use an amphetamine, Adderall, in order to do better in school and to reach the socially approved goal of getting good grades and being accepted into a prestigious university. Many adults express shock upon hearing that use of "study drugs" is very popular among young people today. Yet, given what you have learned in this chapter about the reasons why teens use substances to either manage or escape from the world around them, we can see that their substance use is not surprising or unexpected. Efforts to stop Kyle and Sebastian's drug use will be the most effective if they consider the pressures placed upon them to succeed, their social experiences as young white men with lots of money at their disposal, and the wide availability of study drugs at their school. In general, all efforts to prevent youth drug use may be more effective if they are tailored to populations of youth users based on their race, ethnicity, gender, religion, sexuality, and/or social class.

SUMMARY

Youth substance use (and overuse) has been an ever-present part of society. Adolescents, like adults, use drugs and alcohol in celebrations, in rituals, for coping purposes, and for pain relief. They often make the choice to use substances as a recreational activity with their friends—research demonstrates they do so with the goal to relax and have fun. Societal ideas about substance use fluctuate and vary according to time and place, but generally adults disapprove of illegal drug and alcohol use by young people.

As illustrated in this chapter, a variety of drugs are easily available to teens at this point in history. Young people use many of these drugs, and marijuana is by far the most popular illegal drug that teens use—in part because they perceive it to be a substance that has little risk involved. Patterns of substance use vary depending upon youths' race, ethnicity, and gender. Because of this, people who are interested in prevention efforts need to pay special attention to the sociocultural factors related to youth drug use.

Much of the concern about adolescent substance use is related to serious drug use, the problems it poses to the user and to society, and its relationship to other forms of delinquency. When teens use drugs heavily, they tend to experience a variety of problems: school-related problems, health-related problems, psychological and intellectual problems, and family and economic problems. The relationship between substance use and delinquency is not easy to make generalizations about, but most research does demonstrate that heavy substance users are more likely than other youth to engage in serious acts of juvenile delinquency. A number of factors are thought to link substance use with delinquency, including intoxication, delinquent peers, a need for income, and impaired coping and competence. Girls' experiences with both substance use and delinquency are commonly related to issues of sexism and sexual abuse, while the experiences of LGBT youth are related to homophobia, genderism, and harassment. Boys and girls of color also experience racism that can come to play a role in their drug use and delinquency. Media campaigns, educational programs, drug testing, drug courts, and drug rehabilitation programs are all efforts that have been used to either prevent or stop teen substance use. In addition, harm reduction approaches are growing in popularity. Efforts tailored to address the cultural issues of a given group of youth are shown to be the most appropriate and to have the most promise.

EYE ON DIVERSITY EXERCISE: FINDING CULTURALLY RELEVANT DRUG PREVENTION/TREATMENT PROGRAMS

To get a sense of the sorts of juvenile drug prevention and/or treatment programs that aim to be culturally relevant today, pick a dimension of your life with which you identify (e.g., religion, ethnicity/race, gender, class, or sexuality), and then find two programs for juveniles that focus on that social factor. When you pick among programs online, pick the two that are the closest to where you live. (In other words, if you are a New Yorker and you decide to focus on programs for Salvadoran American youth, and you find a program focusing on that group in California, do not use it unless you can't find any other such programs that are located closer to your state.) Examine the information that you find about each program and answer the following questions:

1. What do the founders of the program see as the cause(s) of juvenile drug use? How can you tell? Do they base their perspective on any research? If so, what studies do they cite?

2. What segment of the juvenile drug-using population is the program attempting to address?

3. In what ways do the program founders try to address the special needs of the population involved?

4. As you compare and contrast the different approaches of the two programs, which do you think best addresses the factors related to youth drug use as outlined in this chapter? What program do you think best addresses the factors related to the drug use of the particular group of youth you are researching? Why?

5. To conclude this exercise, discuss what you think might be a helpful component of each program that is not there based upon your own experience related to the group you are studying. Explain your answer and consider the possible drawbacks of attempting to incorporate your suggestion in a program. In addition, look at the location of the programs that you found and consider how available they are to youth in your area.

DISCUSSION QUESTIONS

1. Consider the patterns of youth drug use that are discussed in the chapter. Which finding surprises you the most, and why? Prior to reading this chapter, what was your impression of teen drug and alcohol use based upon?

2. Mainstream ideas about drugs and drug use fluctuate over time. Discuss current examples from popular culture (movies, songs, videos, popular websites, etc.) in which particular messages about teen drug use are evident. What messages are they sending?

3. The relationship between substance use and delinquency is a complicated one. Analyze the factors that can be related to both drug use and delinquency. In the event that you ever drank alcohol or used drugs as a teenager, consider how these various factors led (or did not lead) you to engage in delinquent behaviors. Or, did you find that engaging in delinquent behaviors led you to start using drugs and/or alcohol? Explain.

4. In a few places in the chapter, we explain that the United States tends to take an abstinence or zero-tolerance approach to adolescent drug use and that some other countries around the world focus on a harm reduction approach. What do you see as the benefits and drawbacks of each approach to dealing with teen substance use?

5. One thing that can be said for young people throughout history is that they are certainly creative when it comes to getting high or drunk. What other everyday substances besides those mentioned in detail in this chapter are used by teens today to get a different perspective on everyday reality?

6. Review the various responses to drug use detailed at the end of the chapter. Which do you see as holding the most potential for reaching youth today? Why?

KEY TERMS

Abstinence model of drug use 298

D.A.R.E. 296

Deviancy training 299

Drug Abuse Warning Network (DAWN) 288

Drug courts 297

Drug prohibition 301

Drug testing 296

Harm reduction 301

Harmful legal products 281

National Survey on Drug Use and Health (NSDUH) 285

Polysubstance use 302

Residential therapeutic community 299

Rumspringa 303

War on drugs 301

Zero tolerance 296

CHAPTER PRETEST ANSWERS

1. True

2. True

3. True

4. True

5. False

6. False

7. True

8. False

9. True

STUDENT STUDY SITE

$SAGE edge™

edge.sagepub.com/bates2e

Sharpen your skills with SAGE edge!

SAGE edge for students provides a personalized approach to help you accomplish your coursework goals in an easy-to-use learning environment. You'll find action plans, mobile-friendly eFlashcards, and quizzes, as well as videos, web resources, and links to SAGE journal articles to support and expand on the concepts presented in this chapter. Check out the website for original videos of former offenders discussing their experiences as juveniles.

PART 4:
RESPONSES TO
JUVENILE DELINQUENCY

©iStockphoto.com/Joe Potato Photo

WHY A SEPARATE JUVENILE JUSTICE SYSTEM?

I n 1960, Joseph was a 15-year-old boy who lived in Atlanta, Georgia. He hung out with the kids on the block, and eventually ended up skipping school quite a bit, drinking beers with his friends, and playing pranks on his neighbors. They were particularly fond of throwing raw eggs at people's mailboxes and cars. One early evening Joseph and his friends drank some beers, and when the sun went down they all got on their bicycles, and sped through the neighborhood throwing eggs wherever they felt like it. Right in the middle of one of his most powerful throws, Joseph's friends yelled that the cops were there and quickly biked away. Joseph was caught egging a neighbor's expensive car by the police. When the officer realized he had beer on his breath, he was especially enraged. He took him into the police station and kept him there for two days without any contact with the outside world. While he was in the holding cell of the jail, he was with adults who had been arrested as well. He was very frightened by a number of these men because they bragged about committing serious crimes, and there were a number of fights that broke out; Joseph just hoped he wouldn't soon be in the middle of one.

The police eventually took Joseph to another small room and conducted an interrogation of him. They asked him about his involvement in a line of home burglaries that had plagued the neighborhood and told him if he admitted that he was part of a gang of juvenile thieves he could go home and see his parents. Joseph was scared and lonely and went ahead and confessed to being a burglar, even though he wasn't one. He figured it would be better to lie and to get out of the jail physically unharmed than to stay there. Nevertheless, Joseph quickly discovered that he would not actually be going home, and the police told him he would likely have his case heard in the adult court rather than in a juvenile hearing. Joseph was also told it looked like he was bound to spend some time in an adult prison because he had confessed to the burglaries, and in fact they had evidence related to his drinking and vandalizing. The police finally called Joseph's parents, and they were shocked and appalled at what had transpired. They knew Joseph got involved in typical juvenile pranks now and again, but thought that teenage misbehavior should be thought of differently than adult crime and couldn't believe the police didn't treat Joseph more gently. Wasn't that why there was a juvenile justice system after all? Why didn't he have any protection under the law? Couldn't anyone see that he was scared and felt pressured to confess?

CHAPTER PRETEST

Test your knowledge of this chapter's material by determining whether the following statements are true or false. Be sure to compare your answers with the answers on page 329.

1. Retribution was a popular justification for juvenile punishment until the invention of adolescence.

2. Teens have the same cognitive and reasoning abilities as adults.

3. The concept of restoration is that punishment should ideally be the least restrictive form necessary and that it should be used to bring some sort of healing or closure to the people affected by an act of delinquency or harm.

4. When reformers started the first juvenile court, they used the same terms and concepts for the process as adult court, in order to show that juveniles were equal to adults in their eyes.

5. During the due process revolution of the 1960s, youth were given the right to a trial by jury in juvenile court proceedings.

6. The last three decades of the 20th century were characterized by measures to get tough on delinquency by harshly punishing youth.

7. The predictions of a "superpredator" explosion contributed to the panic over young men of color and their increased placement in institutions.

8. A number of U.S. Supreme Court cases in the 2000s have alluded to the need to protect youth from cruel and unusual punishment, and the Court has considered the ongoing development of the teenage brain in these decisions.

WHAT IS THE GOAL OF THE JUVENILE JUSTICE SYSTEM?

When we look back now at Joseph's situation and the point in history in which it happened—1960—we look back from a vantage point that is both similar to and different from the earlier one. On the one hand, as you saw in Chapter 2, the development of the first juvenile court in 1899 in Cook County, Illinois, was driven by one of the most important philosophical shifts that have influenced how we handle accusations of juvenile misbehavior under the law—the idea that young people are developing, and it is only right for adults to recognize this fact and to treat them differently from adults when they do wrong. At the time of Joseph's mischief there had been a separate system for dealing with juvenile delinquency in place for over six decades. Yet, as you can see, in practice the system did not fully protect youth from unwarranted coercion while under investigation by juvenile justice authorities. Teens were stuck in a legal limbo of sorts: They were not legally considered adults, but they were thought to be due a more compassionate approach to their misbehavior.

In this chapter we will discuss the shifting goals of juvenile justice systems in the United States by considering in detail some of the most important legal decisions that changed the face of contemporary juvenile justice, most markedly in the due process revolution of the 1960s. Had Joseph decided to egg his neighbors' houses 10 years later than he did, he would have had the legal right to a number of protections; these protections, if implemented, would have made his experiences with law enforcement officers transpire in a different way. Nevertheless, in spite of the legal changes that have occurred over time (including a number of important Supreme Court decisions in the 2000s that set boundaries on juvenile punishments), there are still instances today in which juveniles who are accused of acts of wrongdoing are denied their rights while being processed by juvenile justice workers. So, although on the books youth are allowed some due process rights, sometimes their realities are not as far from Joseph's as we might expect. We have state juvenile justice systems today that are still imagined to be separate from adult state and federal criminal justice systems, in spite of significant overlap in terms of handling juvenile cases. The debate about why we should punish young people is ongoing, and we will first explore the philosophical justifications for punishment in order to better understand them. Then, in Chapter 12, we will look closely at the way that the juvenile justice process operates.

JUSTIFICATIONS FOR PUNISHMENT

There are many different reasons people allude to when they speak about why they think punishing people who have broken the law is necessary. Although they may not always be using the philosophical terminology that corresponds with their points of view, it is usually pretty easy to determine which philosophical justification(s) for punishment they are addressing.

Retribution:
A justification for punishment that is based on the idea of just deserts; punishment that is proportionate to the act that a person has committed.

Retribution is one of the justifications used for the punishment of both juveniles and adults. The notion of "an eye for an eye," which originated from the Code of Hammurabi in Mesopotamia (1750 BCE) and was later incorporated into the belief systems of Judaism and Christianity, embodies the idea of retribution.[1] This is the idea of "you do this to me, so I do this to you." Or in other, more philosophical terms, if you engage in wrongdoing it is only proper that you receive your just deserts (pronounced like your favorite after-dinner treat in spite of its spelling)—punishment that is proportionate to the harm that you have caused. Retribution hinges upon the idea that punishment is merited or deserved.[2]

from the CLASSROOM to the COMMUNITY

The Equal Justice Initiative

The Equal Justice Initiative (EJI) is a nonprofit organization of lawyers who work on behalf of populations that do not always get adequate legal assistance due to their age, race, and/or socioeconomic status. One of EJI's campaigns focuses on children in adult prisons. As the organization explains it,

> Across the United States, thousands of children have been sentenced as adults and sent to adult prisons. Nearly 3000 nationwide have been sentenced to life imprisonment without the possibility of parole. Children as young as 13 years old have been tried as adults and sentenced to die in prison, typically without any consideration of their age or circumstances of the offense.[3]

Lawyers with EJI have campaigned to educate the public about the vulnerabilities of youth and what they see as unjust correctional practices that lump young people in with adults and treat them the same. Their main contribution is to litigate cases on behalf of juvenile offenders, and to prepare reports, newsletters, and manuals to inform policymakers and others who want to reform the juvenile justice system. Prior to the decisions about juveniles serving life without parole, EJI prepared a report, *Cruel and Unusual: Sentencing 13- and 14-Year-Old Children to Die in Prison*.[4] EJI lawyer, Bryan Stevenson, represented Joe Sullivan, a black man with a mental disability who was sentenced to life in prison for committing the rape of a 72-year-old white woman at the age of 13 in 1989. Sullivan admitted that he

had burglarized the woman's house, but denied that he went back and raped her later in the day. His two older friends who he was with blamed the act on him. The victim, who was visually impaired, couldn't see her assailant well and described him only as "a colored boy . . . who had kinky hair and was quite black and he was small." Although there was biological evidence, it was never tested, and years later when EJI lawyers went to retrieve the material to test it, they found it had been destroyed. Sullivan took his case all the way to the Supreme Court, but the justices decided to comment on the case not separately but as part of the *Graham v. Florida* decision.

DISCUSSION QUESTIONS

1. Listen to either the arguments or the decision of the court in the *Graham v. Florida* case (available online from The Oyez Project at IIT Chicago-Kent College of Law, 2013) to better understand the case EJI presented to the Supreme Court. What did you learn from listening to the case?

2. Quickly research Joe Sullivan's case on the Internet. What has happened to Joe Sullivan since *Graham v. Florida* was decided?

Sources: Equal Justice Initiative. (2007). *Cruel and unusual: Sentencing 13- and 14- year-old children to die in prison*. Retrieved from http://eji .org/childrenprison/deathinprison; Equal Justice Initiative. (2012a). *Children in adult prison*. Retrieved from http://www.eji.org/children prison; Equal Justice Initiative. (2012b). *Graham v. Florida*. (2013, May). The Oyez Project at IIT Chicago-Kent College of Law. Retrieved from http://oyez.com/cases/2000-2009/2009/2009_08_7412

Some people liken retribution to a more common term, *revenge*. The focus of retribution is *on the past*. Under this rationale, punishment should occur simply because a person engaged in wrongdoing in the past, not because of any concern with the future. Philosopher Immanuel Kant argued for retribution as the sole justification for punishment, stating that "punishment can never be administered merely as a grounds for promoting another good with regard to the criminal himself (rehabilitation) or to civil society (deterrence or incapacitation), but in all cases must be imposed only because the individual on whom it is inflicted has committed a crime."[5]

The decision to engage in a delinquent act is often an impulsive one that may reflect confused or illogical reasoning on the part of a young person.

Retribution is based on ideas that became prevalent during the times of the Enlightenment in the 16th and 17th centuries. At the heart of this justification for punishment is the supposition that all people are in possession of a free will and a rational mind. Thus we can freely make choices, and it is only logical that we be held responsible for them. As described in Chapter 2, historically children were thought to be capable of utilizing their abilities to logically reason by the age of 14 or so, and retribution was a popular justification for juvenile punishment until the invention of adolescence; after the invention of adolescence other justifications for punishment became increasingly popular for many years. Then, retributive discussions about youth accused of breaking the law enjoyed a resurgence in popularity in the last three decades of the 20th century in the United States.

Zimring, in his discussion of penal proportionality and *moral desert* for the young offender, discusses the three types of personal attributes that might influence the commission of teen acts of delinquency. He states that, in each example he provides, teens lack adult skills and thus necessarily lack full moral responsibility for their acts. The three points he makes are the following:[6]

1. There is a lack of cognitive capacity that youth experience. In other words, they typically do not have the ability to reason as a fully developed adult does. Older children and adolescents may lack the cognitive ability to understand the moral basis for rules and laws, and may not understand how to apply such rules to social situations. They may be able to recognize, if asked on a paper quiz for example, what the rules are but may not be able to translate that into how to follow them in the real world.

2. The ability to control impulses is essential to being able to translate an understanding of rules or laws into action. In large part, this kind of self-control is developed over time and strengthened each time a young person has the choice to act impulsively and consciously chooses not to do so. The mastery of impulse control also must occur in different circumstances, such as in temptation and in frustration. It is unlikely that teens can demonstrate a mastery over anger that is similar to that of an experienced adult due to a lack of life experience. As adolescents are allowed more and more freedom to try new experiences related to driving, dating, and socializing throughout their teen years, most people recognize that they cannot be held as morally responsible for their acts as adults who have already finished their stage of being exposed to the standard variety of impulse-testing experiences.

3. Resistance to peer pressure is a skill that is also being developed during the teen years. The social force of a group to encourage delinquency is one that a single teenager often has a difficult time staving off even if she or he has a solid grasp on right and wrong when alone. Because of this, adolescents are known for committing acts of group delinquency; it is much more rare for a young person to be acting completely on her or his own. Acts such as theft, rape, burglary, robbery, assault, and homicide are usually committed by lone adults, but the same acts, when committed by youth, are usually committed in groups. Research demonstrates

that challenges to youths' pride and courage are usually what motivate such acts, and it takes a long time, developmentally, to master the art of saying no in the face of ridicule and ostracism. Morally, it is difficult to argue that a child who has not had the opportunity to develop coping skills for such social situations should be held as legally and morally responsible for his or her behavior.

In sum, Zimring argues that when adults debate the moral responsibility of juveniles, it is important to decide what measure of youth abilities we want to use. If we decide to use written tests as the gauge of youths' moral abilities, we are bound to find that many more youth are capable of reasoning in a manner similar to adults. But, if we decide that looking at youth decision making in real-world contexts is a better indication of their cognitive and moral development, then we will find a more complicated picture that shows their immaturity.

Deterrence is a justification for punishment that is rooted in the assumption that human beings are rational and make free choices for which they should be responsible. To deter means to prevent, so this justification is focused upon *the future* and preventing crime through punishment. As explained by Packer, "punishment, as an infliction of pain, is unjustifiable unless it can be shown that more good is likely to result from inflicting than withholding it."[7]

The concept of deterrence is rooted in Jeremy Bentham's (1748–1832) utilitarian philosophy—one that stresses that the role of the government is to maximize the happiness of the greatest number of people.[8] According to the philosophy of deterrence, people are out to increase their own happiness, and sometimes this pursuit is not in the interest of the greater society (especially if it makes them happy to go out and harm others or commit crimes). So, they need to be influenced to perceive that although lawbreaking might be something that they see as bringing them pleasure in the future, the punishment that will follow that lawbreaking if they are caught will outweigh any personal benefits they derive from doing it. For crimes or acts of delinquency to be deterred, punishments that are known and that make people think twice about their choices are needed. According to the proponents of this rationale, punishment should be slightly more severe than the pleasure derived from a given act, certain, and delivered with celerity (i.e., swiftness), in order for it to effectively deter. Cesare Beccaria (1738–1794), an Italian scholar who influenced Bentham's utilitarianism and is known for his contributions to deterrence theory and the classical school of criminology, stated that swiftness was the most important factor:

> The promptness of punishment is more useful because when the length of time that passes between the misdeed is less, so much the strong and more lasting in the human mind is the association of these two ideas, crime and punishment.[9]

The following three examples highlight contemporary examples of retribution and shaming of young people across the United States. These acts are done by adults who are in positions of authority over the youth and they are quite controversial.

1. **Utah: Ponytail Cut Off.** The mother of a 13-year-old Utah girl chopped off her daughter's ponytail in court in order to reduce her community service sentence. The girl was in trouble for cutting the hair of a 3-year-old girl she met at a fast-food restaurant. The judge gave the mother an unusual choice: cut your daughter's ponytail off (as a form of retribution) or have your daughter serve a longer community service sentence. The mother chose to cut off her daughter's hair, but she later regretted doing so and said she felt intimidated by the judge. She expressed her concerns in a formal complaint against the court.

2. **Arizona: Boys Holding Hands as Punishment.** A 14-year-old boy, Charles Crockett, got in trouble at school for fighting with another boy during P.E. class. The principal of his school

What do you think are the strengths and weaknesses of this sort of stigmatizing punishment?

told them they could either be suspended or choose what he intended to be a shaming punishment: holding hands with each other in the middle of school for an hour. The boys didn't want to be suspended, so they opted for the handholding punishment, while other students taunted them and posted their picture on Facebook.

3. **Michigan: Holding a Lawn Sign as Punishment for Misbehavior.** A Michigan child got in trouble for talking back to his fourth-grade teacher. His parents decided to punish him by publicly shaming him. They required him to sit in front of his house with a sign that stated, "I don't want to behave at school."

There are two primary types of deterrence: specific and general. The idea behind specific deterrence, or **individual deterrence**, is that if people are punished for their crimes or acts of delinquency, then they will begin to think about the choices they made leading up to that act and will decide not to commit that same act in the future. For example, if Jazmin is punished for cheating on a test, then she will be less likely to cheat in the future if her punishment is appropriately severe and swift. The idea behind **general deterrence**, or deterrence aimed at the entire population, is that others will observe a person who is punished, and that person's crime becomes an example of what not to do. If you see your father go to prison for many years for committing a crime, you will observe that and decide not to do the same according to this rationale. Although many use the philosophy of deterrence to justify the use of extreme punishments, such as torture and the death penalty, its original proponents argued that the philosophy does not support these punishments because they are not useful or necessary.[10]

Incapacitation is yet another popular justification for punishment. The concept refers to making someone incapable of committing a crime, usually from either isolating or restricting his or her movement and/or choices within society. As with the concept of deterrence, incapacitation is oriented toward the future and is concerned with preventing crime and delinquency.[11] As Feeley and Simon explain,

> Incapacitation promises to reduce the effects of crime in a society, not by altering either offender or social context, but by rearranging the distribution of offenders in a society. If the prison can do nothing else, incapacitation theory holds, it can detain offenders for a time and thus delay their resumption of criminal activity. . . . if such delays are sustained for enough time and for enough offenders, significant aggregate effects in crime can take place although individual destinies are marginally altered.[12]

The concept of **selective incapacitation** is a variant of the incapacitation justification that states that high-risk offenders can be identified and incapacitated for long periods of time, while lower-risk offenders can be handled with less serious punishments and for shorter amounts of time.[13]

There are many ways that people have attempted to incapacitate through punishment practices. Whenever societies have attempted to stigmatize people who have committed acts of wrongdoing in ways that let the general public become aware of their acts,

Individual (specific) deterrence:
A justification for punishment that involves the goal of punishing an individual as a means of stopping her or him from doing the same act of delinquency or crime in the future.

General deterrence:
The goal of punishing an individual as a means of deterring others from participating in delinquency or crime.

Incapacitation:
Making someone incapable of committing a crime, usually through isolating and/or restricting movement and decision making.

they are working to make them less capable of doing those acts again particularly if they victimized others. Practices such as branding people, having thieves wear the letter *T* on their bodies to signify their offenses, and cutting off part of a person's body to prevent future wrongdoing (e.g., a thief might have a hand cut off as a means of dissuading him or her from future thieving) were attempts at incapacitation practiced in the United States that are no longer popular today. Instead, today various other forms are used, including databases of people convicted at any point of sex offenses, and the occasional punishments judges in the United States will mete out involving any range of sham-ing devices—signs in the front yard announcing offenses ("Watch out—I'm a convicted felon"), license plate holders announcing the crime of which a person was involved to the general public ("Call the police to tell them how I'm driving—I've been convicted of a DUI"), or license plates themselves for those convicted of driving under the influence.[14]

In the United States today, the best-known approach to incapacitation by far for adults is imprisonment. This is not surprising because the United States has had one of the highest imprisonment rates in the world since 2002. (The United States has been second to the Seychelles for a few years now, but this is because of the country's unique role in locking up alleged pirates.)[15] Imprisonment as incapacitation assumes that by locking people up, you are making them incapable of committing the illegal acts they committed on the out-side. Other means of incapacitation include different forms of probation, such as house arrest and the use of electronic tracking devices.[16] A controversial method of incapacita-tion is the chemical castration of some convicted sex offenders, which has been put into practice in states such as California since the mid-1990s.[17]

Rehabilitation is a justification for punishment that, like many others, is concerned with the future. The word can be understood by breaking it down into its two parts: *re* ("again") and *habilitate* ("to make fit"). According to this rationale, punishment is needed to help wrongdoers change their behavior so they can eventually thrive as healthy members of society. The rehabilitative philosophy found its way into discussions about crime, delin-quency, and punishment largely due to the influence of the Progressive movement at the turn of the 20th century (see Chapter 2 for more detail) and the rise of the scientific ideas of determinism (see also Chapter 5) and **positivism**. Some of the basics of the philosophy of rehabilitation involve the following ideas:

1. Human behavior is the product of causes often outside of one's conscious control (determinism) that can be scientifically examined (positivism) and then scientifi-cally controlled;

2. Offenders and delinquents should go through a form of treatment that gets at the factor or factors related to their behaviors; and

3. Any treatment conducted to treat a lawbreaking person should be done with the aim of benefiting his or her health and happiness, as well as benefiting the greater society as a whole.[18]

The use of rehabilitation as a justification for punishment was especially popular from the late 1800s through the 1960s. Fans of rehabilitation approach the subject in a variety of ways—touching upon issues of biology, psychology, sociology, and social work as a means of understanding lawbreaking. The actual methods by which the philosophy of rehabilitation has been implemented are similarly diverse—for those offenders thought to have a biochemical disorder, medication may be determined to be in order; for those thought to be reacting to some sort of psychological trauma, therapy and/or medicaliza-tion may be seen to be in order; for those who are thought to be affected by factors such as lack of access to jobs, quality education, and supportive communities, job training

• • •

Selective incapacitation: A variant of the incapacitation justification for punishment in which high-risk offenders can be identified and incapacitated for long periods of time, while lower-risk offenders can be handled with less serious punishments.

Positivism: An approach to the study of delinquency and other behaviors that involves the use of scientific observations and controls.

Job training programs are considered a form of rehabilitation that helps youth develop skills that can help them in and out of the work world.

programs, educational programs, and employment readiness might be encouraged; those with substance addictions might be placed in a therapeutic community or drug treatment facility. There are numerous ways this philosophy is translated into action depending upon what factors are believed to be driving the need for a change in behavior.

In the 1970s, a debate about the relevance of rehabilitation emerged, and the general public and politicians were swayed by the argument that "nothing works" to rehabilitate former offenders.[19] Nevertheless, the philosophy remains a popular one among criminologists and other scholars who cite evidence for the value of the philosophy in informing punishment as well as among large portions of the general public who agree with the humanistic angle of this approach.[20]

The last popular justification for punishment, restoration, is the least known, although its roots are in indigenous and religious belief systems that have been around for thousands of years.[21] The idea behind it is that punishment should ideally be the least restrictive form necessary and that it should be used to bring some sort of healing or closure to the people affected by a crime or a harm (the victim[s], the wrongdoer, and the community as a whole). This justification for punishment is in many ways similar to rehabilitation, in that punishment is thought to be necessary for adults and teenagers who have broken rules or law, and possibly injured others either physically or mentally in the process, to make some important changes. Yet, restorative justice advocates tend to focus beyond the individual as they consider what punishments or mechanisms can be used to create change that will prevent future acts of wrongdoing.

The philosophy of restoration stresses *accountability* as a desired outcome of punishment—not only accountability on the part of the individual who has broken the law, but accountability on the part of society as a whole. According to this rationale, communities also bear responsibility for crime, because we collectively create the conditions that motivate people to commit crime. The philosophy of restoration thus encourages punishments that differ from what many of us typically label as punishments as a means to increase accountability and strengthen relationships between people and institutions. Mandated mediation sessions or family group conferences are often used when restoration is the aim of punishment. In these a combination of victims, offenders, and interested community members get together in an effort to figure out an act of delinquency or a crime occurred and what can be done to address the underlying problem. Oftentimes, those who have engaged in acts of delinquency or crimes pay monetary restitution to the victims or the victims' families, or perhaps do some work for them to symbolically pay back the harm caused by their behavior. As we will discuss later in this book, restoration is a justification for punishment more commonly employed with juveniles than it is with adults.

● ● ●

Restoration:
A justification for punishment that focuses on dealing with delinquency as a harm and bringing healing in the aftermath of a harm.

JUVENILE JUSTICE AND SPECIALIZED TERMINOLOGY

When the first juvenile justice system was established in Cook County, Illinois, reformers wanted it to be clearly distinguished from the adult criminal system, so they used a different language to discuss the youth who entered the civil juvenile justice system, the primary issue at hand, and the stages of the process they encountered. This language was used to help young people rehabilitate and to avoid the stigmatizing terms of the adult system. When other juvenile courts were developed, they followed the model of the first juvenile court and used different terminology as well. Table 11.1 compares terms used for similar concepts or stages in the juvenile and adult systems.

Ritter raised the question of whether these terms are necessary in our current-day climate in which juveniles are often punished harshly as a means of satisfying the general public's desire for retribution.[22] He believes that it might be more useful to get rid of all of the different terms that describe the process of the juvenile system (in other words, to speak about youth being indicted, found guilty, and sentenced rather than hearing their charges on a petition, being adjudicated delinquent, and being given a disposition of delinquency) and to keep the one major distinction of referring to acts of youth lawbreaking as "delinquency." Indeed, Nell Bernstein, the author of *Burning Down the House, the End of the Juvenile Prison* (2014), stated that she uses the terms *children* instead of *juveniles* and *prison* instead of *detention facility, training school, juvenile camp,* or *reform school* because they are more accurate terms. Christopher Bickel also made a powerful argument against the traditional juvenile justice terms and what they obscure:

> Juvenile detentions centers are not simply places that regulate and control the behavior of children accused of crimes. Nor are they places that "rehabilitate" or "fix" children in need. Instead, juvenile detention centers provide the social location in which detained children, who are often working class and of color, are created unequal, and treated accordingly. I argue that inside juvenile detention centers, children are constructed as "captives," as members of a permanent, disreputable category.[23]

PHILOSOPHICAL SHIFTS AND THE LEGAL TREATMENT OF JUVENILES

The popularity of the various justifications for punishment ebbs and flows over time, and the U.S. Supreme Court leads the way in terms of giving official backing to some justifications for punishments over others.

TABLE 11.1 Juvenile Justice Terminology Versus Criminal Justice Terminology

JUVENILE JUSTICE SYSTEM	CRIMINAL JUSTICE SYSTEM
Delinquent	Criminal
Hearing	Trial
Order to appear/Charges on a petition	Warrant for arrest/Indictment
Adjudicated delinquent	Found guilty
Disposition	Sentence
Held in detention	Imprisoned

The Due Process Revolution

In the 1960s, the rehabilitation of juveniles was still the most popular justification among the general public for their punishment. During this period, a number of U.S. Supreme Court decisions were made that acknowledged that the experiences of many youth with law enforcement and juvenile justice officials, like those of Joseph in the opening scenario of the chapter, were fundamentally unfair. The Warren Court (known as such because the Chief Justice of the Supreme Court of the era was Earl Warren) ruled on a number of cases in which the due process rights of juveniles were increased. In *Kent v. United States* (1966), the U.S. Supreme Court stated that juveniles had the right to a hearing before having their cases transferred to adult court and an explanation as to why the juvenile court thought it necessary. The majority of the justices expressed concern about whether the juvenile courts had the necessary resources to do the job of which they were tasked, and agreed that "there may be grounds for concern that the child receives the worst of both worlds [in juvenile courts]: that he gets neither the protections accorded to adults nor the solicitous care and regenerative treatment postulated for children." The *Kent* decision was followed by what has become one of the most well-known juvenile decisions of this period, *In re Gault*. The *Gault* case was decided in 1967, and it required that alleged juvenile delinquents had the right to hearings in which formal procedures were followed. In addition, the Supreme Court stated that juveniles could not be institutionalized unless there was evidence that they had committed an act of delinquency. This decision inspired a shift in the popular concept of the juvenile delinquent yet again. Instead of the image of young people in need of care by the state to either protect them or teach them how to stay out of trouble, juvenile delinquents came to be seen simply as younger criminal defendants.[24]

The *In re Winship* (1970) case signaled another move on the part of the U.S. Supreme Court to treat juvenile defendants more like their adult counterparts. The justices ruled that the highest standard of proof, "beyond a reasonable doubt," needed to be used in juvenile proceedings to protect juveniles from the possibility of undeserved confinement in a juvenile institution. This decision meant a move away from the standard that had been used up until that point, the "preponderance of the evidence" standard, and from unquestioned use of the *parens patriae* philosophy (i.e., the state as a substitute parent) as a justification for placing youth into institutions.[25] It was also a legal acknowledgment that state intervention was not always working in the best interest of the child. Yet, due process rights for youth were not fully implemented. For example, in *McKeiver v. Pennsylvania* (1971), the Supreme Court ruled that youth were not entitled to a trial by jury in juvenile court proceedings.

Warren Court:
The Supreme Court during the leadership of Chief Justice Earl Warren that increased the due process rights of juveniles.

The due process revolution of the Supreme Court was in keeping with the social justice concerns that characterized the late 1960s and early 1970s.

The "Get Tough" Period: An Emphasis on Retribution, Incapacitation, and Deterrence

The majority of the 1970s, 1980s, and 1990s were characterized by efforts that countered the due process revolution for juveniles and emphasized getting tough on delinquency and those labeled as delinquents. The social construction of youth as mini-adults, which was in some ways reminiscent of the Middle Ages, began to take a firm hold in popular consciousness. This image was reinforced with scholarly claims that involuntary rehabilitation in treatment institutions was not consistently effective, as well as social panics about youth's descent into delinquency, such as those that we examined in Chapter 2.[26] Young people, particularly teenagers, were seen as scary and threatening people who had grown up too fast and needed to be treated accordingly. In addition, the U.S. Supreme Court chipped away at the anonymity of juvenile court proceedings—in *Oklahoma Publishing Company v. District Court* (1977) and *Smith v. Daily Mail Publishing Co.* (1979)—and allowed the preventative detention of juveniles in some circumstances—in *Schall v. Martin* (1984)—developments that signaled that the due process revolution was no longer in full swing (see Figure 11.1). As legal scholar Barry Feld stated from the vantage point of the late 1990s, the judges and politicians during this period used whatever image of children that would empower them to better control them: "Courts and legislatures choose between competing characterizations of young people as autonomous and self-determining or as immature and incompetent in order to maximize their social control."[27]

The notion of the youth "superpredator" was discussed frequently by well-known scholars who were looking at population forecasts and imagining a dim and scary future

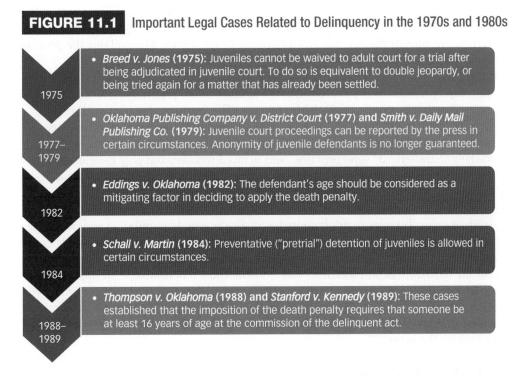

FIGURE 11.1 Important Legal Cases Related to Delinquency in the 1970s and 1980s

1975
- *Breed v. Jones* **(1975)**: Juveniles cannot be waived to adult court for a trial after being adjudicated in juvenile court. To do so is equivalent to double jeopardy, or being tried again for a matter that has already been settled.

1977–1979
- *Oklahoma Publishing Company v. District Court* **(1977) and** *Smith v. Daily Mail Publishing Co.* **(1979)**: Juvenile court proceedings can be reported by the press in certain circumstances. Anonymity of juvenile defendants is no longer guaranteed.

1982
- *Eddings v. Oklahoma* **(1982)**: The defendant's age should be considered as a mitigating factor in deciding to apply the death penalty.

1984
- *Schall v. Martin* **(1984)**: Preventative ("pretrial") detention of juveniles is allowed in certain circumstances.

1988–1989
- *Thompson v. Oklahoma* **(1988) and** *Stanford v. Kennedy* **(1989)**: These cases established that the imposition of the death penalty requires that someone be at least 16 years of age at the commission of the delinquent act.

Sources: *Oklahoma Publishing Company v. District Court* 430 U.S. 308 (1977); *Smith v. Daily Mail Publishing Co.* 443 U.S. 97 (1979); *Eddings v. Oklahoma* 455 U.S. 104 (1982); *Schall v. Martin* 467 U.S. 253 (1984); *Thompson v. Oklahoma* 487 U.S. 815 (1988); *Stanford v. Kennedy* 492 U.S. 361 (1989).

© Jamie Pham / Alamy Stock Photo

The last three decades of the 20th century were characterized by measures to get tough on delinquency by harshly punishing youth.

for law-abiding people living in the 2000s. James Q. Wilson predicted that there would be a million more people in their teens by the 2000s, and stated that of the half expected to be male, "six percent of them will become high rate, repeat offenders—30,000 more young muggers, killers, and thieves than we have now."[28] John DiIulio went with that idea and stated that the super-predators who would be running through U.S. communities in the 2000s would be upwards of 270,000 in number.[29] James Alan Fox stated that the population growth would be concentrated more among black youth than it would among white youth, and media attention fueled the flames of racist stereotypes—*superpredator* became widely recognized as a "code word for young black males."[30] Youth of color were disproportionately the object of police attention and subsequently placed in institutions of all types. In his law review article, "The End of Adolescence: The Child as Other—Race and Differential Treatment in the Juvenile Justice System," Kenneth Nunn states the concept of "othering" is what allowed the retributive turn in the juvenile justice system in the 1990s. He explains the process as one in which

> the "superpredator" was constructed as the ultimate other, as possessing all the characteristics that innocent young children do not. The "superpredator" was "brutally remorseless," incorrigible, and savage. And because the "superpredator" was the antithesis of childhood, it was slyly constructed as young, Black, and male. This racially characterized "superpredator" was in fact a monster, and only the most serious and determined efforts could address the threat that the "superpredator" posed.[31]

The superpredator panic amped up punitive responses to youth—in particular, responses to youth of color. Transfer to adult court became increasingly popular, as well as stricter sentences and a corresponding decrease in the level of confidentiality of juvenile court proceedings during this point in history, as the popular image of the delinquent became that of the hard-core delinquent who was "violent and irredeemable."[32] It appeared that juveniles were to have the punishment of adults, but without all of the legal rights given to adult defendants to protect themselves.[33] All of this occurred in spite of the fact that juvenile justice systems were still based on the idea of rehabilitation. A clash in philosophies became the norm.

The Federal Response to the "Get Tough" Trend: The Juvenile Justice and Delinquency Prevention Act

The U.S. Congress passed the federal Juvenile Justice and Delinquency Prevention Act (JJDP Act) of 1974, in an effort to address growing concerns among the general public related to juvenile delinquency.[34] At this time the Office of Juvenile Justice and Delinquency Prevention was created as a means of establishing a national entity that would focus on research and the dissemination of research related to juvenile delinquency and delinquency prevention. This act limited the powers of the juvenile court to handle not only delinquents, but troubled or neglected youth. Status offenders, nonoffenders, child delinquents, and dependent and neglected children were no longer seen as the primary concern of the juvenile courts.[35] Supporters of the act were also concerned that juvenile delinquents should, whenever possible, be **deinstitutionalized,** or taken out of prisons and jails. As in our scenario at the beginning of the chapter with Joseph, in spite of the desire for separate confinement that drove juvenile justice advocates in the late 1800s, youth were still being locked up with adults in jails and prisons in some places in the United States more than 75 years later, and many observers were upset about it.[36] This move toward **deinstitutionalization** of status offenders was evident in the JJDP Act. State juvenile justice systems were only to get funding from the OJJDP to support their efforts if they abided by the mandates of the JJDP Act and its subsequent reauthorizations, which mandated the following core requirements for juvenile justice systems (the latest being in 2002):

- *Deinstitutionalization of status offenders (DSO):* Juveniles who commit status offenses, those that only apply to children, such as running away, truancy (skipping school), drinking or possessing alcohol, and breaking curfew, should not be held for any period of time in adult facilities, and should not be held in juvenile facilities for any extended length of time. Exceptions to this rule can be made for some status offenders for up to 24 hours of detention time. Instead, youth should be given the opportunity to get services in the community such as mentoring, education, job support, counseling, and/or treatment of substance issues.

- *Adult jail and lockup removal:* To prevent psychological and physical abuse, young people are not supposed to be placed in adult jails or lockups. There are a few exceptions in which this is allowed: for up to 6 hours before and after a court hearing, up to 24 hours plus weekends and holidays in rural areas, or in what is deemed unsafe travel conditions.

- *Sight and sound separation:* When in an adult jail or lockup for the exceptions listed above, youth are supposed to be separated enough from the incarcerated adults to keep them safe. They should be protected from both hearing and seeing the adults. They shouldn't share any common spaces with the adults in the facility, including time in the dining hall or recreational areas, and shouldn't be housed next to the adults in their cells.

- *Reduction of disproportionate minority confinement (DMC):* Because data show that youth of color are more likely to be adjudicated delinquent and required to serve more time in secure facilities than their white counterparts, states must demonstrate that they are paying attention to this issue. They are supposed to assess the issue in their state and address the underlying reasons why it exists, ultimately reducing its occurrence.

As of mid-2016, the last time the JJDP Act was reauthorized was in 2002. It is set to expire in September 2016. Juvenile advocates would like to see a new version of the law that does the following:

1. Keeps youth out of the justice system.

2. Ensures equity and competence in legal representation and throughout the entirety of juvenile justice systems.

● ● ●

Deinstitutionalization: The act of moving a juvenile out of and/or avoiding the detention of a juvenile in an institution as a punishment for wrongdoing.

The majority of the Supreme Court justices in the 2000s have supported a return to the view that children and teens are significantly different from adults. (This is one of the last pictures of the Supreme Court prior to Justice Scalia's death in 2016.)

3. Guarantees developmentally appropriate responses to youth behavior including punishments that are based on youth's age and actions.

4. Creates more federal support for tribal, state, and local governments to implement in the JJDP Act in their juvenile justice systems.

Advocates who would like to see the JJDP Act updated cite the need for it to reflect contemporary research findings related to juvenile delinquency. In addition to recent sophisticated brain research that demonstrates the teenage brain is fundamentally different from a healthy adult brain, and less prepared to make skilled decisions (see A Focus on Research: Dobbs's Beautiful Brains, below), juvenile justice reformers stress that the needs of girls are being overlooked by juvenile justice systems today. It wasn't until 1992 that amendments to the JJDP Act required juvenile justice systems to provide gender-specific treatment, and prevention services to girls. Girls are often found to be victims of abuse both inside and outside of the system, and advocates stress the need for changes to the system to better protect girls held in detention. Advocates for a new JJDP Act authorization explain that funding needs to be made available for rigorous research into how gender-specific programming affects girls in the system, and how the effects are similar or different along racial, ethnic, and social class lines.[37] In addition, a concern of many advocates is that although juveniles are not supposed to be placed in juvenile detention centers for status offenses, a loophole in the act allows it if they have violated a VCO. Thousands of youth on any given day are held in detention for status offenses if they have violated a probation order or committed a status offense, such as being out past curfew, being truant, or missing a probation meeting.[38] Many of these young people do not pose a threat to the community, so their detention seems unnecessary, and even counterproductive, to many juvenile justice reformers, as they appear to be negatively influenced by exposure to those who have committed more serious acts of delinquency or adult crimes.

Turning Tides? The 2000s and the Reassertion of Youth Differences

Somewhat surprisingly, after the punitive turn of the mid-to-late 1990s, the tides have yet again shifted in the 2000s in terms of the construction of juvenile delinquency and its appropriate responses. Although the retributive and incapacitative aims of punishment are still very popular among a segment of the population, as well as the social construction of youth as violent and irrational, the U.S. Supreme Court has emphasized the original vision of youth as deserving of different treatment that informed the development of the juvenile court.[39] A number of U.S. Supreme Court cases have alluded to the need to protect youth from cruel and unusual punishment and have considered the ongoing development of the teenage brain in these decisions (see Figure 11.2). Once again, the legal construction of youth is swinging back to the idea that they are vulnerable and

Photo credit on left side: "Steve Petteway, Collection of the Supreme Court of the United States"

In the News

Why So Many Hawaiian, Samoan, and Filipino Youth in the Justice System?

In spite of the stated emphasis on rehabilitation in juvenile justice systems across the U.S., there is still plenty of evidence in the news that this philosophy does not always inform how juveniles are treated (as you will see in Chapters 12 and 13). The article "Why So Many Hawaiian, Samoan, and Filipino Youth in the Justice System?" published in the *Honolulu Civil Beat,* a source for news in the Hawaiian capital, highlighted one of the major themes that has come to characterize juvenile justice systems around the United States in recent decades: **disproportionate minority confinement**. The author of the article, Chad Blair, considered an Office of Youth Services report that found that mixed race youth, Native Hawaiians, and Pacific Islanders were disproportionately involved in the juvenile justice system of Hawaii. He explained that "race, ethnicity, class, and gender converge in the juvenile justice system to confine more youth of color than can be explained merely by criminal activity." Blair reported that Samoan, Filipino, and Native Hawaiian youth were treated more harshly than Caucasian and East Asian youth at the arrest stage of the juvenile justice process and at the subsequent stages of detention, probation, and protective services. He pointed out that the root of the problem "seems to be related to racism and discrimination and how mixed-race people are treated in society" and highlighted the study's findings that Hawaiian and Pacific Islander youth would likely fare much better if they were diverted into culturally based programs instead of being placed in juvenile detention facilities.

DISCUSSION QUESTION

1. The author of the news article drew from existing research to make the point that racism is linked to the disproportionate minority confinement of youth of Native Hawaiian, Filipino, and Samoan background in Hawaii. How do you think this root issue should be addressed? Why?

Source: Blair, C. (2012). Why so many Hawaiian, Samoan and Filipino youth in justice system? *Honolulu Civil Beat,* Oct. 24. Retrieved from http://www.civilbeat.org/2012/10/17448-why-so-many-hawaiian-samoan-and-filipino-youth-in-justice-system/

deserve the chance for rehabilitation or, at a minimum, an acknowledgment that they are not as fully culpable of their acts as the average mature adult.

Recent decisions of the Supreme Court have signaled a recommendation for more lenient directions in sentencing. In *Roper v. Simmons* (2005), the court surprised the international community as it joined the ranks of most nations in the world in forbidding the death penalty for those who committed their acts of crime while juveniles. The Eighth Amendment's proscription against cruel and unusual punishment was cited as the basis of the decision. In this decision the Court held that juveniles are less responsible for their actions, and less deserving of the most serious form of punishment. This decision was followed by *Graham v. Florida* (2010), a case in which the Supreme Court decided that juveniles who had not killed anyone should not be sentenced to life without parole. The decision stated that none of the four best known justifications for punishment—retribution, deterrence, incapacitation, and rehabilitation (restoration wasn't acknowledged)—were seen as adequate for sentencing juveniles who had not murdered to life without parole. As in the *Roper* decision, the Supreme Court noted that the United States was the only country that imposed life without parole for nonhomicidal youthful offenders,

● ● ●
Disproportionate minority confinement: Youth of color are more likely to be adjudicated delinquent and to serve more time in secure facilities than white youth.

FIGURE 11.2 Important Legal Cases Related to Juvenile Delinquency in the 2000s

2002
- U.S. Supreme Court decided in *Atkins v. Virginia* that executing people considered mentally retarded (with an IQ of under 70) is unconstitutional under the Eighth Amendment's prohibition of cruel and unusual punishment.

2005
- *Roper v. Simmons* decision, the U.S. Supreme Court abolished capital punishment for people who were juveniles when they committed their crimes based on the Eighth Amendment protection against cruel and unusual punishment. The majority of the court cited evolving national standards as the basis for looking at the issue again.

2010
- In *Graham v. Florida* (2010), the U.S. Supreme Court ruled that juveniles who have not killed anyone cannot be sentenced to life in prison without the possibility of parole. To do otherwise is unconstitutional because it constitutes cruel and unusual punishment under the Eighth Amendment.

2012
- In *Miller v. Alabama* (2012), which was linked with *Jackson v. Hobbs* (2012), the U.S. Supreme Court barred mandatory life sentences without parole for juveniles convicted of murder and stated they violate the Eighth Amendment's ban on cruel and unusual punishment.

2016
- In *Montgomery v. Louisiana* (2016) the U.S. Supreme Court decided that the ban on life without parole sentences for juveniles convicted of homicide in the *Miller* decision must be retroactively applied in each state.

Sources: *Atkins v. Virginia*, 536 U.S. 304, 316, 122 S. Ct. 2242, 2249 (2002); *Roper v. Simmons*, 543 U.S. 631 (2005); *Graham v. Florida*, 560 U.S. 48 (2010); *Miller v. Alabama*, 132 S. Ct. 2455 (2012); *Jackson v. Hobbs*, 132 S. Ct. 1733 (2012); *Montgomery v. Louisiana*, 577 U.S. ___(2016).

and that was further support that the practice was cruel and unusual under the Eighth Amendment. In 2012, in the combined cases of *Miller v. Alabama* and *Jackson v. Hobbs*, the Supreme Court decided that youths under the age of 18 who commit acts of murder should not be sentenced to a mandatory life sentence without the chance of parole. The *Miller* opinion noted that judges need to weigh an individual case to determine if life without parole would be a proportionate sentence for a youth who has committed murder. The majority opinion stated that young people have "diminished culpability and heightened capacity for change" and that, as a result, "appropriate occasions for sentencing juveniles to the harshest penalty will be uncommon." The Court also noted that it will be difficult for a judge to be able to tell when a young person who has committed murder was acting from an "unfortunate but transient immaturity" or is an example of "the rare juvenile offender whose crime reflects irreparable corruption." As you can see, the language employed in these decisions acknowledges that there is a place for both rehabilitation and retribution in the juvenile justice system, and gives juvenile judges the power to distinguish when one should inform a sentencing decision, rather than the other. In 2016, the U.S. Supreme Court decided in *Montgomery v. Louisiana* that the ban on life without parole sentences for juveniles convicted of homicide in the *Miller* decision must be retroactively applied in each state. This was an important decision because many states were trying not to apply the decision to those individuals who were convicted in the past, and hundreds of people who were sentenced to death across the United States may now have their sentences reconsidered in hearings or be released on parole.

THE FUTURE OF JUVENILE JUSTICE

In light of the conflicting visions of juvenile justice in the 21st century, it is unclear how long a separate juvenile justice system will be retained. Some sociolegal scholars advocate abolishing the juvenile court altogether and having only one system that processes youth, yet allows for more lenient sentencing due to age and lack of mental and social development.[40] According to this rationale, a single court would facilitate a move to give young people accused of lawbreaking all of the legal rights given to adults in a criminal court. As we will elaborate upon in the following chapter, youth are not given all of the due process protections that adult defendants are, and this is seen as a problem by many observers. As Barry Feld notes, "while the sanctions of the juvenile court may be less harsh than criminal sentences, the direct penalties (institutional confinement) and the collateral consequences (transfer to criminal court, use of delinquency convictions to enhance sentences, sex offender registration, and the like) share similar penal elements."[41] In addition, research has demonstrated that juveniles who get the assistance of lawyers in their cases typically receive harsher sentences than those with the same sentences who did not "lawyer up."[42] Youth of color with public defenders are especially negatively affected.

Most juvenile justice reformers are working within their current juvenile justice systems to change how the public and the formal system conceptualize youth and youth misbehavior. For example, there is a growing movement to abolish or minimize the punishments related to status offenses—acts that are only illegal because the people doing them are minors. In addition, several states (Arkansas, Georgia, Hawaii, Indiana, Kansas, Kentucky, Nebraska, New Hampshire, South Dakota, Utah, and West Virginia) have engaged in comprehensive reforms of their juvenile justice systems that avoid net-widening for low-level acts of delinquency and that finance the use of community-based resources for diverted youth.[43] Other states have engaged in realignment of their juvenile justice systems by closing some of their youth prisons and placing youth in facilities closer to their homes or in community-based rehabilitation programs, such as Ohio, Texas, New York, and Georgia or, in California, letting county-level agencies rather than state agencies supervise all youth involved in nonviolent and low-level delinquency.[44]

There is also a move to include 17-year-olds in the age of juvenile jurisdictions in the nine U.S. states that do not do so. Three states have recently done this (Connecticut, Illinois, and Massachusetts) and have reported positive results, and at least four others are attempting to raise the age as well.[45] Arguments for these changes are justified by the decline in U.S. juvenile delinquency overall in the United States, brain development research, and legal precedents. The Youth Education and Families Institute argues that counties around the country should draw upon insights from research to reform their juvenile justice systems, primarily that youth delinquency is related more to being a teenager than being a "criminal"; severe punishments for delinquency have not been shown to be more effective than certain, immediate light consequences; and matching services to young people's needs is the most direct path to positive outcomes.[46] These rationales also help fuel the campaigns to end the transfer of children to adult courts for prosecution and the housing of youth in adult prisons and jails where they are five times more likely to be sexually assaulted than they would be in juvenile detention (Equal Justice Initiative, n.d.).[47] They also are related to the federal government's move to forbid solitary confinement for juveniles in federal facilities beginning in 2016, the elimination of solitary confinement in 19 states and the District of Columbia, and the restriction of solitary confinement in cities like Los Angeles (in conjunction with the main argument that isolation of this sort can do serious psychological harm to vulnerable young people).[48]

U.S. Supreme Court decisions in the 2000s indicate that at the highest level of our judicial system, there is a shift in the majority's views of delinquency that mirror the original rehabilitative aims claimed by those who established the first juvenile justice systems. As we will examine in Chapter 14, these changes do appear to be indicative of a gradual philosophical shift at the state and local levels, as reflected in the comprehensive delinquency programs currently under way in the United States today.

A Focus on Research

Dobbs's Beautiful Brains: Scientific Discoveries About Adolescent Brain Development

U.S. Supreme Court decisions related to punishing juveniles in the 2000s have often alluded to the science of adolescent brain development. Scientists have found that teenage brains are different from adult brains in significant ways. As neuroscientist Laurence Steinberg points out, "the fact that there are significant changes in the brain during adolescence is no longer debatable—if indeed it ever was. Indeed, it appears that the brain changes characteristic of adolescence are among the most dramatic and important to occur during the human lifespan."[49]

As explained by David Dobbs, some of the traits of teenage behavior that are the most frustrating to their parents and other "more mature" people

are actually important to their future successes as adults.[50]

Brain imagery scanning now allows scientists to compare and contrast the brains of adults and children. The National Institutes of Health did the first series of scans of the brain over time and found that although the brain doesn't grow much after the age of 6, there is a lot going on in the brain starting at around age 12. Dobbs likens it to an "extensive remodeling, resembling a network and wiring upgrade." The speeds of transmission of signals between the neurons in the brain get faster; the outer layer of gray matter of the brain that handles most of our conscious thinking, the cortex, gets thinner and more efficient;

and the changes occur gradually from the back of the brain (which handles basic functions such as vision and movement) to the front of the brain (which handles complicated thinking and reasoning). In addition, the brain begins processing at a more advanced level and the corpus callosum, the connection between the left and right sides of the brain, is strengthened as well as the connections between the hippocampus, which is involved in memory, and the front of the brain, which helps us set goals and compare and contrast different choices. Aging is also related to the faster processing of information in the front of the brain that allows for more complex reasoning. But, as these connections develop, there is a period of time in which it is all getting worked out, and skilled decision making can be inconsistent. (In other words, sometimes teenager Fred may be making what appear to be well-reasoned decisions, and other times he seems to be completely out to lunch.)

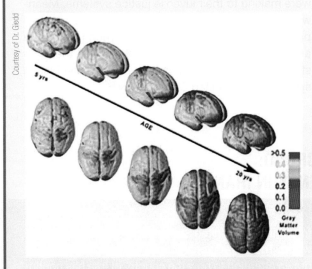

Courtesy of Dr. Giedd

Time lapse imagery tracks brain maturation ages 5 to 20. The brain develops over time, and from the ages of 5 to 20 significant decreasing of gray matter occurs, as neural connections in the brain are pruned.

Brain scans of teens asked to ignore stimuli that they view on a monitor demonstrate that they did not use often the regions of the brain that help adults resist temptation. Teens were much more likely to be impulsive instead. But, they did respond to the challenge better when they received an extra reward and, in turn, used those areas of the brain that could help them more

often. According to some scientists, adolescents are interested more in impulsivity (which peaks at around 15) and risk-taking (which is prevalent from 15 to 25 years of age) and other behaviors that sometimes just don't make any logical sense, but they are actually engaging in an adaptive process. As they find out which behaviors do not further their successful existence, those eventually get eliminated from their repertoire. Teen brains are especially influenced by social rewards at this time, and the large amounts of dopamine and oxytocin in the brain during the teen years prime them for sensitivity and sometimes dramatic reactions to the outcomes of their decision making. Dobbs notes,

> Some brain studies, in fact, suggest our brains react to peer exclusion much as they respond to threats to physical health for food supply. At a neural level, in other words, we perceive social rejection as a threat to existence. Knowing this might make it easier to abide the hysteria of a 13-year-old deceived by a friend or the gloom of a 15-year-old not invited to a party. These people! we lament. They react to the ups and downs as if their fates depended upon them! They're right. They do.[51]

DISCUSSION QUESTIONS

1. After reading the above material about brain development, can you summarize what takes place in the brain of a young person over time?

2. Did you realize that your own brain was developing well into your early 20s? Does that change the way you might behave in the future?

3. If you have passed that stage of development, think back to how this information may have changed the way you lived (e.g., what substances you put into your body) had you known about it before then.

Sources: Dobbs, D. (2011). Beautiful brains. *National Geographic, 4,* 1–8. Retrieved from http://ngm.nationalgeographic.com/2011/10/teenage-brains/dobbs-text; Steinberg, L. (2010). A behavioral scientist looks at the science of adolescent brain development. *Brain and Cognition, 72,* 160–164.

As explained in the historical overview in Chapter 2, the stated purpose of the first juvenile justice system, which was emulated by others around the United States, was for the rehabilitation of youth who had acted out delinquently. Nevertheless, a number of different philosophical justifications for punishment exist—retribution, deterrence, incapacitation, rehabilitation, and restoration—and at various times of history they have all been invoked as being the proper reason behind juvenile punishment. When we look at legal decisions of the due process revolution of the 1960s, we see that during that period the majority of people, as well as the majority of Supreme Court justices, accepted the rehabilitation of juveniles as a laudable goal for juvenile justice systems. This changed in the three decades that followed, as support for a model in which juveniles were treated as less culpable and in greater need of protection than adults waned significantly. It became popular to "get tough" on juveniles, and retribution, incapacitation, and deterrence became the most popular approaches taken by state juvenile justice systems. The Juvenile Justice and Delinquency Prevention Act was developed in 1974 as a means of reasserting some core protections for juveniles in the system, and has subsequently been reauthorized with new protections included several times.

The myth of the juvenile "superpredator," an image that was associated with low-income boys of color, particularly African American youth, fueled the popularity of get-tough approaches in the late 20th century. Juvenile justice scholars analyzed and debunked the superpredator myth, but it wasn't until the late 1990s and early 2000s that another shift began to occur. In the 2000s, the U.S. Supreme Court made a number of decisions that alluded to and supported a vision of youth as developing human beings who should be treated differently than their adult counterparts. Scientific research on brain development and the human life course was marshaled by the Supreme Court in their decisions about the death penalty and life imprisonment without parole. Many juvenile justice reformers in the last few years in the United States have drawn upon both the scientific evidence and the legal decisions of the Supreme Court to justify the changes they were making to their juvenile justice systems. Meanwhile, juvenile justice advocates continue to campaign for stronger protections for young people in a new reauthorization of the JJDP Act, as there are still a number of inequities built into juvenile justice systems in the United States today.[52]

EYE ON DIVERSITY EXERCISE: A LOOK ABROAD: THE TREATMENT OF JUVENILE DELINQUENCY IN IRAN

© REUTERS/Morteza Nikoubaz

Iran is one of the few countries in the world that still executes people for acts committed while juveniles.

The philosophical debate about how to treat youth who have allegedly broken the law is relevant not only to events in the United States but to actions around the world. The international human rights community has drawn attention to how the country of Iran has continued to execute children in spite of the fact it agreed to follow the Convention on the Rights of the Child (CRC) more than 20 years ago. The CRC included an agreement to abolish the youth death penalty and life imprisonment without release. According the United Nations and Amnesty International, there are almost 200 youth on death row in Iran, and many have been found to have spent at least seven years there. The Iranian government reformed their laws about juvenile delinquency in 2013 and gave judges the discretion to consider the maturity level of the child and assign a different punishment instead of the death penalty. The Supreme Court said that all juveniles on death row were eligible for a retrial. Yet, all evidence points to the fact that these formal legal changes haven't translated to real reform. For this eye on diversity exercise, examine the photos and captions on *The Guardian*'s webpage "Waiting to Die: The Iranian Child Inmates Facing Execution—in Pictures" (https://www.theguardian.com/artanddesign/gallery/2016/jan/08/inside-iran-jail-where-children-face-execution-in-pictures).

1. What are the factors related to the girls' presence on Iran's death row?

2. Which images do you find tell the most compelling story about life on death row for the inmates? Why?

DISCUSSION QUESTIONS

1. Consider the various justifications for punishment. Which do you think serve as the strongest basis for juvenile justice, and why? Do you think having different juvenile and adult justice systems serves the justification you have picked? Why or why not?

2. The myth of the superpredator fueled the punitive mood of the 1970s, 1980s, and 1990s. Can you see a similar myth or scare today that may be driving public concerns about delinquency?

If so, explain what it is and how you see it operating in your community or in the world at large.

3. The scientific research on brain development is compelling evidence that the teenage (and young adult) brain is in a state of flux and is not capable of the same degree of rationality as the adult brain. Do you understand why the Supreme Court decided to consider that research in its legal cases related to juveniles in the 2000s?

KEY TERMS

Deinstitutionalization 321

Disproportionate minority confinement 323

General deterrence 314

Incapacitation 314

Individual (specific) deterrence 314

Positivism 315

Restoration 316

Retribution 310

Selective incapacitation 314

Warren Court 318

CHAPTER PRETEST ANSWERS

1. True

2. False

3. True

4. False

5. False

6. True

7. True

8. True

$SAGE edge™

edge.sagepub.com/bates2e

Sharpen your skills with SAGE edge!

SAGE edge for students provides a personalized approach to help you accomplish your coursework goals in an easy-to-use learning environment. You'll find action plans, mobile-friendly eFlashcards, and quizzes, as well as videos, web resources, and links to SAGE journal articles to support and expand on the concepts presented in this chapter. Check out the website for original videos of former offenders discussing their experiences as juveniles.

JUVENILE DIVISION
TOW-AWAY
NO STOPPING
ANY
TIME
WHEN THESE DOORS
ARE LOCKED
PLEASE USE
MISSION STATION
ENTRANCE

CHAPTER

12

POLICING AND THE PROCESS OF THE JUVENILE COURT

CHAPTER OBJECTIVES ·······················

After reading this chapter, you should be able to

- Describe the roles of law enforcement

- Explain the stages of the juvenile justice system

- Explain cumulative disadvantage

- Analyze the relationship between race/ethnicity and unequal treatment in the juvenile justice process

- Analyze the relationship between gender and unequal treatment in the juvenile justice process

- Compare and contrast the juvenile justice process and the juvenile dependency process

I was at the small community park in my neighborhood with my husband and two kids. We come often because it is pretty close to our house and usually vacant. It isn't a city park, but it is part of our neighborhood, so while it isn't private—anyone can come use it—I don't think many people know about it. The park is in a circular drive, flanked on all sides by cookie-cutter, suburban, Southern California houses. There is no cross traffic, and everyone who drives into this part of the neighborhood has a reason to be here. They live here, or come to visit the park. The neighborhood is about 15 years old. The houses across the street have backyards that nestle up against the local golf course. I don't know the people who live on this street. We live about five streets over. Our block is somewhat ethnically diverse, but I would assume, given what I know about the price of the houses, that it is not class diverse. Most of the people living around me are middle to upper-middle class.

On this particular day, we had been at the park about 30 minutes. I was ready to go, but the kids were still going strong, alternating between playing in the sand, sliding down the slide, and finally figuring out that they could throw sand down the slide and then slide through it. My husband and I were sitting at the picnic table next to the play equipment, talking and playing with our phones.

Looking up, I noticed a group of teenagers amassing on the edge of the park. They were clearly in their early teens—I suspect they were middle schoolers. There were both boys and girls in the group, most looked to be Latino, and I would estimate there were at least 10 of them. They sat down at the edge of the park and watched us. They were fairly quiet, talking among themselves. It was clear to me that they wanted to come into the park, but no one made the move to walk across the small lawn to the play equipment while we were there. I finally leaned across to my husband and told him I thought we should leave. He looked up and asked quizzically if I was worried about the teens. I laughed. They were so remarkably well behaved it was hard to think of them as threatening, but, while middle school was a long time ago for me, I remember what it meant to get out after school and have a couple of hours to hang out with friends. I remember the rush of watching the boy I liked and wondering if he knew I liked him, of talking big, swearing, and laughing with friends before I had to go home to homework and the rules imposed on a 13-year-old.

CHAPTER PRETEST

Test your knowledge of this chapter's material by determining whether the following statements are true or false. Be sure to compare your answers with the answers on page 360.

1. Police have three roles that often conflict when dealing with juveniles.

2. Juveniles are treated differently than adults during police interactions.

3. The probation officer role is central to the juvenile justice system and sets it apart from the adult system.

4. One of the most important rules of the juvenile justice system is that juveniles must be handled in the juvenile system and cannot be seen in the adult system until they are 18.

5. Juveniles do not have a constitutional right to bail.

6. In order for states to get some of their juvenile justice funding, they must show they are trying to decrease disproportionate minority contact in the juvenile justice system.

7. The overrepresentation of youth of color in the juvenile justice system has been stopped due to careful attention at all stages to individual and institutional racism.

8. Crossover youth are those who have had success in the juvenile justice system and learned how not to break the law.

I told him no, I wasn't worried, but I thought we should take pity on them because they clearly weren't going to come into the park until we left and I figured we had had our time. My husband grew up in the punk era—he probably understands more than most the need for teens to hang out and express themselves. He smiled and picked up our youngest son and started to walk to the car. I called to our older son, smiled at the teenagers and moved to the car, too. I heard my husband tell a couple of the kids that the park was all theirs, and I watched as they slowly made their way to the play equipment. Two of them smiled and nodded at us, and at least half climbed up to the top of the jungle gym to sit on the bars. We continued to the car and put our kids in their car seats.

As we got in the car and my husband started it up, he looked in the rearview mirror. He shook his head and rolled his eyes at me, and I turned to look at what he saw. There was a cop car right behind us that hadn't been there while we were putting the kids in their car seats. Initially, I thought the car was there for us (amazing how quickly I always wonder if I have done something wrong). But the two police officers barely looked our way. Instead they got out, adjusted their belts, touched their guns, and walked up the grass toward the teenagers.

Teenagers have always been a group that has endured a fair amount of social control. This vignette illustrates one of the struggles for teens, especially in urban and suburban settings: the struggle to exist in a public setting. While my husband and I had been to that park with our kids hundreds of times, we had never been in contact with the police there. In fact, before this day, we had never seen the police on this street at all. But within 15 minutes of 10 teenagers walking into this neighborhood the police had arrived to talk to them.

The prior sections of this book have examined our understanding of juvenile delinquency as a behavior. How do we define juvenile delinquency? How much juvenile delinquency exists? How do we explain juvenile delinquency? And what correlates seem to predict juvenile delinquency? This last section of the book (starting with Chapter 11) focuses on our response as a society to juvenile delinquency specifically, and juveniles more generally—and this chapter focuses on our formal responses from the stage of policing to disposition, from the juvenile justice system to the dependency court.

POLICE AND JUVENILES

This chapter starts by discussing the role of policing and juveniles, then takes an extensive look at the juvenile court—which in most jurisdictions is broken down into two separate divisions, the juvenile justice system (handling delinquency cases) and the dependency court (handling issues of dependency and child welfare). We examine the stages and processes of the juvenile justice system and then end with a discussion of the processes of the dependency court (note that the dependency court goes by several names depending on the jurisdiction—two of the other most popular are family court and child welfare court).

Police are likely the first contact with both the adult and juvenile justice systems. It is estimated that over 80% of all cases referred to the juvenile court are referred by the police (Office of Juvenile Justice and Delinquency Prevention, n.d.). The remainder are referred by parents, schools, victims, and probation officers. Police are the most visible actors in the justice system, responsible for three main roles and responsibilities—law enforcement, order maintenance, and service—although there are some who would dispute whether each of these duties holds equal importance.[1]

Roles of the Police

Law enforcement: The role most often thought of for police involves detecting, investigating, and arresting offenders. During the course of these duties, police are often also responsible for interrogating suspects, collecting evidence, and presenting evidence in court. The law enforcement role includes detecting felony and misdemeanor crimes, as well as traffic violations. In this role, police often come in contact with juveniles. Given the relative lack of sophistication and maturity for juveniles as compared to adults, juvenile bad behavior is often easier to detect. Any of this behavior that is considered delinquent (or in some instances a status offense) and is addressed by the police falls under the role of law enforcement.

Order maintenance: This role is much less defined, although its presence has been increasing. Police are tasked with maintaining the order at public events—concerts, rallies, parades. In addition, they are tasked with maintaining order at more private events, such as private parties that may become loud and disturbing to neighbors. The largest difference between this role and that of law enforcement is that order maintenance relies on the discretionary observation of police officers even more than law enforcement. The behaviors being controlled are less clearly defined and in most instances are not considered to be deviant or delinquent at their outset. Our opening vignette is an example of police engaging in order maintenance. The teenagers at the park were not engaging in delinquent behavior. In fact they were using the park as it was expected to be used. But given the characteristics and size of the group, the expectation was that they may engage in disorderly behavior.

Service: The final role of the police seems to be the least well defined. While most police cars are stenciled with the motto "Serve and Protect," the definition of service is not always clear. In addition, the role of service is often overlapped by the role of law enforcement. For example, police are often expected to shuttle children who are victims of abuse to child protective services. In this scenario, the police may be engaging in law enforcement when they respond to a call of abuse, if they arrest a suspect, and in the process of gathering evidence. The police engage in the role of service when they take the child out of the home and transport him or her to a different setting. Other types of service the police might engage in may be helping a stranded motorist or a child who has been lost. It is this role for the police that is most likely to generate a case for a juvenile in dependency court.

Visit edge.sagepub .com/bates2e to view a video about working in the juvenile justice system.

Police-Juvenile Interactions

The police roles of law enforcement, order maintenance, and service can often be in conflict when dealing with juveniles. Given that juveniles are seen as needing more protection but also more help learning how to become upstanding citizens than adults need, the use of police discretion during police-juvenile interactions becomes significant.[2] Research that examines the police-juvenile interaction views the age of the juvenile as a characteristic that impacts police decision making.[3] More specifically, the suggestion is that juveniles are perceived as less respectful, more prone to noncompliance, and more irrational than adults.[4] And Allen argues that bad behavior committed by a juvenile is seen as, symbolically, more serious than bad behavior committed by an adult; thus, police may believe that juveniles are more in need of formal police attention than adults.[5]

Brown, Novak, and Frank studied the difference between police interactions with juveniles and adults and found that police were more likely to arrest juveniles than adults for similar behavior.[6] In addition to this general finding, they also found that juveniles in "distressed communities" (measured by poverty level, racial composition, proportion of renter-occupied households, and proportion of single-family households) were more likely to be arrested than adults, while adults in "nondistressed communities" were more likely to be arrested than juveniles. This means that for juveniles, being from a working-poor community of color means they are more likely to be arrested when they come in contact with the police. In addition, the race of the officer was found to impact police-juvenile interactions. White officers were found to exercise significantly more authority when interacting with juveniles than when interacting with adults.

Given the research placing greater emphasis on the developmental stages of youth, especially the reasoning skills related to brain development (see Chapter 4, Biosocial Theories) and the connection to our understanding of juvenile delinquency, some argue that we should treat juveniles differently than adults. According to Steinberg, "Research on adolescent brain, cognitive, and psychosocial development supports the view that adolescents are fundamentally different from adults in ways that warrant their differential treatment in the justice system."[7]

The International Association of Chiefs of Police, in collaboration with the OJJDP, took this research into account, providing for police an overview of the research and how this might affect policing interactions with youth.[8] Figure 12.1 offers the 10 strategies that may improve law enforcement interactions with youth.[9]

When Is a Juvenile in Custody? The Cases of Yarborough v. Alvarado (2004) and J. D. B. v. North Carolina (2011)

The question of when a juvenile is considered in custody has been one the courts have struggled with for several years. In general, an individual is considered in custody if he or she is not allowed to leave the presence of the police (at a police station or in a public setting such as a park, an airport, or a street corner). If a person willingly comes to a police station for questioning, for example, the courts generally do not consider the person to be in the custody of the police. This is important because in *Miranda v. Arizona* (1966), the Supreme Court determined that when individuals have been taken into custody, they must be informed of their rights—specifically, the right to an attorney and the right to remain silent and not incriminate themselves.[10] The question the courts have struggled with over the years, then, is whether juveniles have the same capacity to understand whether or not they are in custody when they are in the presence of the police.

There have been several recent Supreme Court rulings on how juveniles should be handled during questioning. The Supreme Court has found that age should be a consideration when questioning juveniles, but only a consideration, which means that there is still a large degree of discretion in how police may choose to question juveniles.

Yarborough v. Alvarado (2004):[11] Michael Alvarado was a 17-year-old who was questioned about his involvement in a crime at a police station. His parents had brought him to the police station but were not present for the questioning. Alvarado was not Mirandized and during the questioning admitted to his involvement in an attempted robbery that had ended in the death of the victim. Based in large part on his statements, he was convicted of second degree murder and attempted robbery. Alvarado appealed his conviction arguing that, because of his age, he had understood himself to be in custody and had not been read his *Miranda* rights, so the statements were not admissible in court. While the lower courts did not agree, the Ninth Circuit Court of Appeals agreed that Alvarado should have been read his *Miranda* rights because as a juvenile he would feel more compelled in the presence of the police and more likely to consider himself in custody and not able to leave. In a 5-4 decision, the Supreme Court disagreed with the appellate court and upheld the conviction. The justices argued that whether an individual was in custody had always been based on objective criteria, such as whether the individual had come in voluntarily or had been brought in by the police; to introduce personal characteristics of the individual would be to introduce nonobjective criteria into the decision-making process. Therefore, an individual's age could not be taken into consideration when deciding whether

FIGURE 12.1 Ten Strategies for Improving Law Enforcement Interactions With Youth

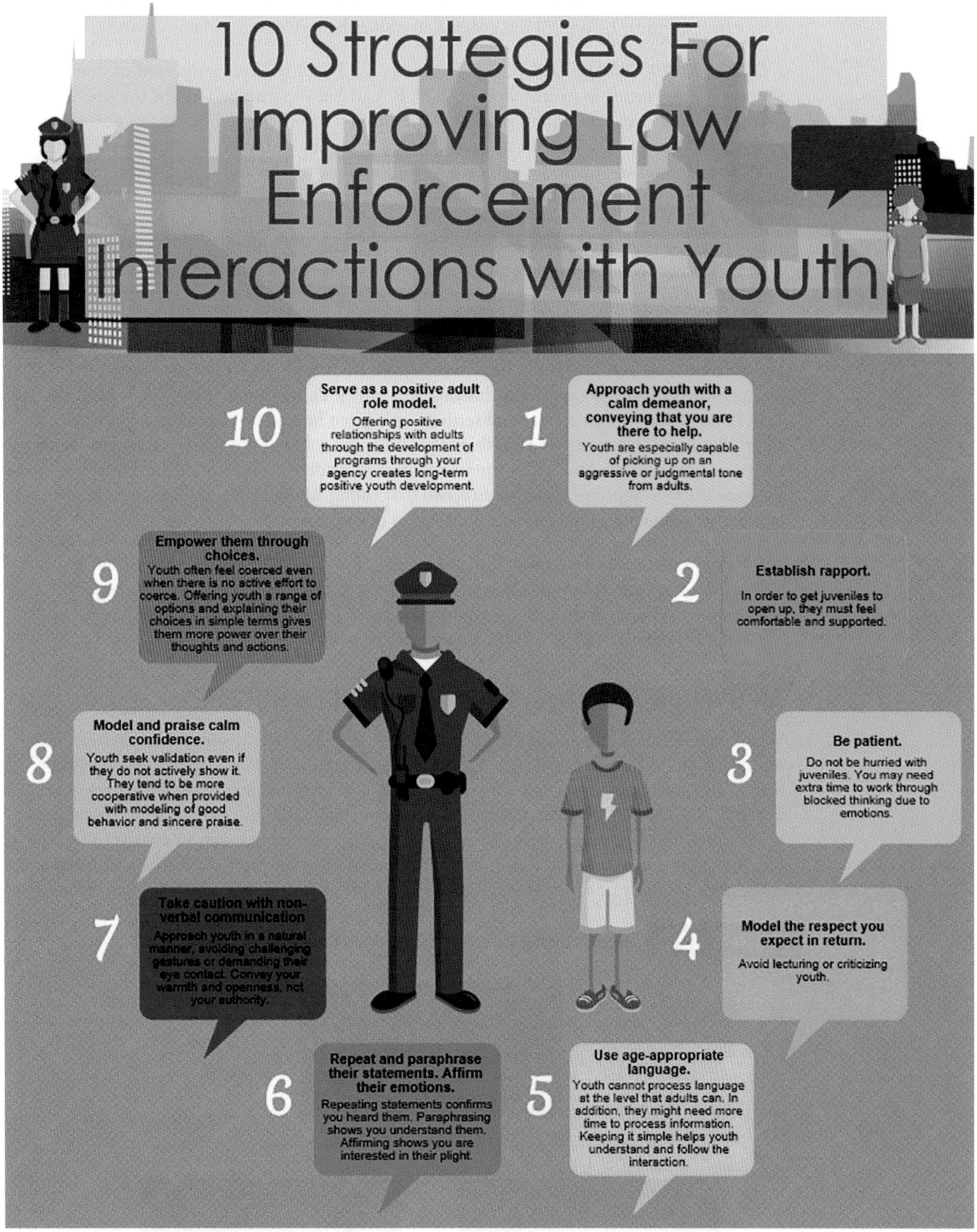

Created using Piktochart.com

Miranda should be read. In other words, even though one might argue that a juvenile does not understand that he or she can leave the questioning, it is still up to juveniles in this position to understand their rights and whether they are in custody or not, and *Miranda* does not need to be read until the police determine the individual to be in custody.

J. D. B. v. North Carolina (2011):[12] J. D. B. was a 13-year-old boy suspected of committing several break-ins in nearby homes. J. D. B. had been questioned about the break-ins because he had been seen in the vicinity of the homes. After learning he was in possession of a digital camera that was like a camera stolen from one of the homes, the police officer in charge of the case went to J. D. B.'s school and spoke with the uniformed officer assigned to the school and members of the administration. The uniformed officer pulled J. D. B. out of one of his classes, and the investigating officer, school officer, and administrators were all present in a room while J. D. B. was questioned for at least 30 minutes about his activities. J. D. B. was not read his Miranda rights, was not told he could leave, and was not given an opportunity to speak with his guardian. After being confronted about the stolen camera and at the urging of an administrator, J. D. B. confessed to the crime. It was at this time that the investigator informed J. D. B. that he was allowed to refuse to answer questions and that he was free to leave if he wanted. J. D. B. indicated he understood, but stayed and provided further details about his involvement. J. D. B.'s public defender argued that J. D. B. had been held in a custodial setting, and, given he had not been read his Miranda rights, his initial statements and anything that followed could not be used against him. Both the trial court and the North Carolina Supreme Court denied this argument. However, in this case the U.S. Supreme Court overturned that ruling, allowing age to be a consideration in whether individuals understand if they are in custody, writing:

> To hold, as the State requests, that a child's age is never relevant to whether a suspect has been taken into custody—and thus to ignore the very real differences between children and adults—would be to deny children the full scope of the procedural safeguards that *Miranda* guarantees to adults.[13]

AN OVERVIEW OF THE JUVENILE JUSTICE PROCESS

When we talk about the juvenile justice system, we often make it sound like there is one uniform system. But the truth is that there are 50 separate systems, because each state is responsible for maintaining its own structure. And, in fact, one might argue that there are nearly 3,000 separate juvenile justice systems, since in most states courts are established at the county (borough/parish) level, meaning that daily operations even in a state can vary by the number of counties in that state. For this reason, when we describe juvenile justice processing we must be fairly general in our description (see Figure 12.2). We can explain

FIGURE 12.2 Organizational Structure of Juvenile Court

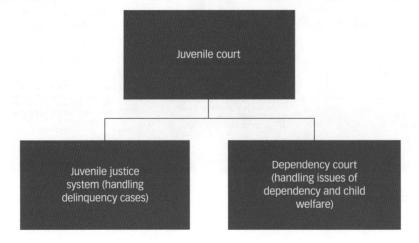

the stages or decision-making points in the process, but how a county or state acts within that stage varies. For example, a large county will have intake officers whose sole job is to process juveniles as they enter the system. In a small county, the intake officer is probably also the probation officer, meaning that the same person who processes the juvenile into the system is also the person responsible for gathering the information that the court needs during the hearing, and is also responsible for following the success of the juvenile if the court requires probation or other rehabilitation (see Table 12.1).

TABLE 12.1 Key Personnel in the Juvenile Justice System

ROLE	DUTIES
Probation Officer	The probation officer role is one of the central roles of the juvenile justice system, and the one that sets it apart from the adult criminal justice system. The probation officer has a broad range of tasks to perform in the system: (1) conducting investigations into family history, education, friends of the juvenile, and juvenile attitude for the reports to be used in the various stages of the system; (2) meeting with and supervising juveniles at various stages in the system; (3) assessing the juvenile for compliance with probationary duties; (4) presenting reports at adjudication and disposition hearings; and (5) engaging in a variety of administrative tasks (e.g., in some jurisdictions, probation officers may actually pick the juvenile up and transport him or her to court. If a juvenile is referred to the court again, in most jurisdictions it is likely his or her case will go back to the same probation officer).
Intake Officer	In some jurisdictions, the probation officer is also the intake officer, and a single person engages in the duties of initially assessing the individual to determine whether the case should be dismissed, diverted, or moved formally into the system. But in large jurisdictions, the intake officer is often a separate role. In these jurisdictions, the intake officer is the initial screening officer, determining the initial path of the juvenile through the system. Once that path has been started, the intake officer passes the juvenile's file to a probation officer, who is assigned to the case for the rest of the stages.
Guardian *ad litem*	A person, often an attorney, who is appointed by the court to represent the "best interest" of the juvenile while that juvenile is involved in court proceedings. This person is not a prosecuting or defense attorney (and thus representing a due process position); the person is less focused on the legal aspects of the proceedings and more focused on juvenile concerns.
Prosecuting Attorney	The prosecuting attorney is usually responsible for deciding which cases go forward into the system. This person decides which cases to petition (charge) and which will be prosecuted and is responsible for plea bargain negotiations. The prosecuting attorney can set the tone of the juvenile court by focusing on certain types of behaviors over others. For example, the prosecuting attorney can focus on drug crimes or curfew laws and, thus, set a tone and send a message to the community about what will and will not be tolerated. Given the immense extent of behaviors that can be considered status offenses or delinquent activity, most jurisdictions will require that prosecuting attorneys make discretionary decisions about what delinquent behaviors will be focused on and how to use plea bargains to manage resources.
Defense Attorney	The role of the defense attorney is to advocate for the due process rights of the juvenile as he or she moves through the juvenile justice system. Ideally, the defense attorney works closely with the juvenile and his or her family to help them navigate the court process; however, in large jurisdictions where there are numerous cases, defense attorneys often meet their clients right before they enter the court. It is not unusual for the probation officer to have spent more time than the defense attorney with the juvenile and his or her family. While the defense attorney should follow the wishes of his or her client (the juvenile), the attorney still has a fair amount of discretion to decide whether to pursue a hearing or suggest a plea bargain for his or her client.
Judge or Magistrate	While the role of judge varies across juvenile courts, there are two general jobs that the judge is responsible for: (1) the management of the court, which might include decisions about resource management and personnel decisions, and (2) judicial decision making in the courtroom, which includes both the micro decision making of who is adjudicated delinquent and nondelinquent and what types of cases are focused on in the courtroom. In most states judges are elected, although some jurisdictions make judicial appointments instead. In jurisdictions where the workload for judges is unmanageable, the court may employ magistrates to make many of the decisions that the judge does not have time to make. These might include decisions about preadjudication detention, adjudication, or dispositions. The decisions of the magistrate are considered binding, just like the decisions of judges, but magistrates are not given the scope of responsibility that judges are given. Judges have considerable power and discretion in and outside of the courtroom to mold both the focus of the court and the decisions made in that court.

Figure 12.3 shows the general process through the juvenile justice system. As shown, juveniles can progress through or leave the system at several stages. Juveniles are referred to the court from two general groups: law enforcement or non–law enforcement entities such as school, parents, or probation officers. Even at this first stage, there is enough discretion in the system that juveniles can be diverted out to be handled more informally by community agencies or family.

FIGURE 12.3 Case Flow Diagram of Juvenile Justice System

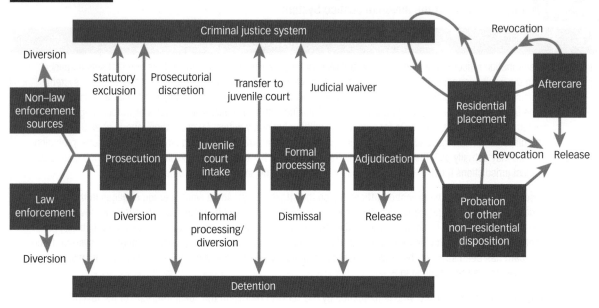

Source: Office of Juvenile Justice and Delinquency Prevention. (n.d.). Case flow diagram. *Statistical briefing book.* Retrieved from http://www.ojjdp.gov/ojstatbb/structure_process/case.html

Jurisdiction: Transfer to the Criminal Court or Remain in the Juvenile Court?

One of the decisions that may be made very early in the juvenile justice process for a juvenile, if the juvenile is not diverted out of the system at the law enforcement stage, is whether or not the case will be handled by the juvenile court or the criminal (adult) court. This process is usually called a certification, remand, transfer, or **waiver to adult court.** Different jurisdictions have different procedures for how this decision is made, but in general it can happen in one of several ways.

Waiver to adult court: The process by which it is decided whether a juvenile will be handled in the juvenile justice system or the adult justice system.

Automatic waiver: A list of offenses for which a juvenile is automatically moved to the adult system.

• **Automatic waiver:** (also known as *legislative waiver* or *statutory exclusion*): Many jurisdictions have a list of offenses for which a juvenile is automatically moved to the adult system. For example, in many states homicide and some sex crimes require a mandatory filing in the adult court. In Figure 12.3, this is shown to happen very early in the process at the prosecution stage.

• **Prosecutorial waiver:** (also known as concurrent jurisdiction or direct file): Many jurisdictions also have a second list of offenses for which the prosecuting attorney has the discretion to file in either juvenile or adult court. In Figure 12.3 this is shown to happen at the prosecution stage, although it would happen later in that stage than an automatic waiver.

- **Judicial waiver:** The most common type of waiver to the adult court, the judicial waiver gives the discretion to the judge or magistrate of the juvenile court to transfer a juvenile to the adult criminal court. Judges must consider several criteria while considering a transfer to adult court: (1) the level of sophistication exhibited by the juvenile, (2) whether the juvenile seems amenable to rehabilitation, (3) the juvenile's previous delinquent history, (4) whether the juvenile court has successfully rehabilitated the juvenile prior to this offense, and (5) the circumstances and seriousness of the current offense. In Figure 12.3 this is shown to happen later in the process at the formal processing stage.

In addition to there being several ways in which juveniles can be waived to the adult system, depending on the jurisdiction there is also varying minimum ages for which a juvenile can be waived to the adult system. This ranges from the age of 10 in Kansas and Vermont to several states with a minimum age of 14. Many states do not specify a minimum age (see Figure 12.4).

●●●
Prosecutorial waiver: A list of offenses for which the prosecuting attorney has the discretion to file in either the juvenile or the adult court.

Judicial waiver: The most common type of waiver to the adult court in which a judge or magistrate has the discretion to transfer a juvenile to adult criminal court.

FIGURE 12.4   Judicial Waiver Offense and Minimum Age Criteria, 2014

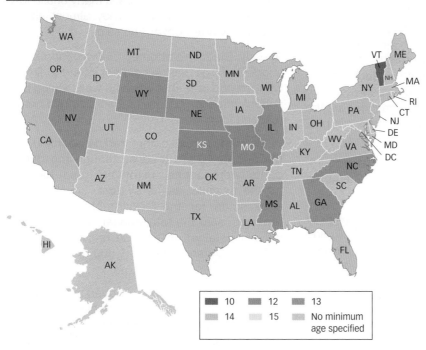

Source: OJJDP. (2015). *Statistical Briefing Book*. Retrieved from http://www.ojjdp.gov/ojstatbb/structure_process/qa04110.asp?qaDate=2014

Notes:

a. Ages in the minimum age column may not apply to all offense restrictions, but represent the youngest possible age at which a juvenile may be judicially waived to criminal court.

b. All states have provisions for trying certain juveniles as adults in criminal court. This is known as *transfer to criminal court*. There are three basic transfer mechanisms: *judicial waiver*, *statutory exclusion*, and *concurrent jurisdiction*.

c. Under judicial waiver provisions, the juvenile court judge has the authority to waive juvenile court jurisdiction and transfer the case to criminal court.

d. Waiver provisions vary in terms of the degree of flexibility allowed. Some waiver provisions are entirely *discretionary*. In other provisions there is a rebuttable *presumption* in favor of waiver, and in others waiver is *mandatory* once the juvenile court judge determines that certain statutory criteria have been met.

e. As of the end of the 2014 legislative session, 45 states and the District of Columbia allow juvenile court judges to waive jurisdiction over certain cases and transfer them to criminal court.

f. Age and offense criteria are common components of judicial waiver provisions, but other factors come into play as well. For example, most state statutes limit judicial waiver to juveniles who are "no longer amenable to treatment." The specific factors that determine lack of amenability vary, but they typically include the juvenile's offending history and previous dispositional outcomes.

g. Many (18) states with judicial waiver provisions establish 14 as the minimum age for waiver, but there is variation across states. The provision in Vermont, for example, permits 10-year-olds to be waived.

In the News

Charging Juveniles as Adults Not Unusual: Law Requires Prosecutors to Charge Many Teens as Adults for Specific Set of Crimes

Fifteen-year-old Robert Gladden has been charged as an adult with attempted first-degree murder in connection with last week's shooting at Perry Hall High School, an aggressive measure by prosecutors in response to a high-profile crime.

Despite his youth, Gladden is one of many being treated like a legal adult in Maryland courts—forgoing a juvenile justice system that focuses on rehabilitation and limits confinement.

Since 1994, the General Assembly has drawn up a growing list of crimes for which Maryland prosecutors must charge children as adults. Teenagers as young as 14 can be charged as adults in violent or sexual crimes that could be punishable by life in prison or death. (Even though those are the qualifications, juveniles aren't eligible for capital punishment.)

The list for older juveniles, between 16 and 18, is longer and includes carjacking and attempted robbery.

In Baltimore County on Thursday, 21 juveniles were being held on adult charges, including two on murder and three on attempted murder. Eleven were held on armed-robbery charges and five on gun allegations.

In 2011, 771 juveniles were charged as adults in Maryland, according to statistics collected at the request of a House of Delegates subcommittee investigating whether to provide juveniles charged as adults with a separate jail. No information was available about incarceration rates of juveniles convicted as adults.

As the default for many crimes has shifted to charging juveniles as adults, Byron Warnken, associate professor at the University of Baltimore School of Law, said the law has become "more pro-prosecution." Juveniles charged as adults bear the burden of convincing a judge that their cases should not be handled in adult courts by asking for a waiver.

Attorneys push hard to win waivers, Warnken said, because cases heard in juvenile courts do not result in a criminal record, and a person convicted cannot be imprisoned with adults and has to be released at the age of 21.

"If you are the defense counsel, even if you lose everything else, if you win the jurisdictional issue, today was a winning day," Warnken said.

Scott Shellenberger, the state's attorney for Baltimore County, said he sees many challenges to the adult designation. "They almost always ask to be waived down," he said.

Already, Gladden's attorney, George Psoras, has suggested that Gladden did not intend to fire his weapon and only shot when he was tackled by a school guidance counselor. Psoras could not be reached for comment.

While many crimes committed by people under the age of 18 are tried as though the defendants were adults, many are also handled by the juvenile justice system. Jay Cleary, a spokesman for the Department of Juvenile Services, said the total annual number of individuals detained in juvenile facilities is probably somewhere between 1,000 and 2,000, he said.

In normal circumstances, Gladden might make a good candidate for a waiver, Warnken said, given his age and lack of previous criminal history. But the high profile of the case could work against Gladden, Warnken said.

"A judge would not want to look like he's not taking this seriously," he added.

DISCUSSION QUESTIONS

1. What are the implications of the quote, "A judge would not want to look like he's not taking this seriously"?

2. Make an argument for and against the following three scenarios: (a) all juveniles under the age of 18 must be tried in juvenile court, (b) if juveniles are tried and convicted in an

Diversion

Just as transfer to the adult system can happen at more than one stage, diversion is also a condition that can happen at more than one stage. We have chosen to put both conditions at the beginning of this discussion of the juvenile court process, but it is probably more accurate to think about both transfer to adult court and diversion as "opportunities" that lead a juvenile out of the juvenile court process altogether. These opportunities may happen so early in the process that a juvenile has not even made it to intake (see the next stage), or they may happen as the juvenile moves formally into the system. While transfer to adult court is designed to paint the juvenile as an adult with adult awareness and responsibility (and thus ready for adult punishments), diversion is designed to keep the juvenile from being stigmatized by even the juvenile system. The philosophy behind diversion is that a formal experience in the juvenile justice system may not be in the best interest of some juveniles. Diversion allows the juvenile justice system to offer juvenile programs designed to help the juvenile without having to go formally through the system. These programs can include the following:

- Basic counseling services
- Family intervention programs
- Drug and alcohol programs
- Educational services
- Teen courts
- Conflict resolution
- Mediation

While a number of studies show that diversion programs can be more useful than formal case processing, there are several general concerns with such programs.[14] One of the biggest concerns with diversion is the possibility of net-widening. Net-widening is the concept that more juveniles will get drawn into the juvenile justice system than need to be because the repercussions do not seem to be something from which children need protection. In other words, given that diversion is designed to keep juveniles from a formal trip through

●●●

Diversion:
A process that allows the juvenile justice system to offer programs designed to help a juvenile without the young person having to go formally through the system.

Net-widening:
The concept that more juveniles will get drawn into the juvenile justice system than necessary because actions once determined to be legal become illegal.

Kirk McKoy/Los Angeles Times via Getty Image

Juveniles may be diverted out of the formal stages of the juvenile justice system and into programs such as drug and alcohol counseling or teen courts where the youth agrees to have a group of their peers decide their case.

the system, it can be seen as a way to "help" juveniles without needing to worry about the due process of proving that the juvenile has engaged in a delinquent act. In fact, research has found that some programs may actually increase the percentage of juveniles in the juvenile justice process by up to 49%.[15] This leads to the second large concern about diversion, which is that it circumvents *due process* rights because it requires the juvenile to engage in required activities without the court needing to prove the case against the juvenile.[16] Many consider that this exchange is also coercive in that juveniles are told if they engage in these diversion programs they will not end up being formally petitioned (charged) by the juvenile justice system.

Preadjudication Stage

The preadjudication stage is actually several smaller stages, including intake screening and an intake hearing, a detention hearing, and often an opportunity for a plea bargain. Those stages are discussed below.

The Intake Process

When a juvenile is arrested or referred to the juvenile court, most might assume this means that juveniles are physically arrested and taken to detention. This happens for some juveniles, but many are released to their parents without ever being taken into custody. The police finish an arrest report, and this report is forwarded to an intake officer for further screening. This intake screening is, then, another place for discretion, as an intake officer makes a determination about what should happen to the juvenile. Given that the behaviors or conditions for which juveniles can get into trouble are much broader than those adults can get into trouble for, it is the job of the intake officer during the intake screening to determine the most appropriate way to handle the juvenile's case. During the intake screening, the intake officer determines whether a juvenile's case should be dismissed from the system or should be referred to the system for either informal or formal services. To determine the handling of a case, the intake officer takes into account such criteria as the following:

- The age of the juvenile

- The seriousness of the crime

- The prior record of the juvenile

- The cooperation of the juvenile and parents

- School records/performance

- Whether the juvenile admits to the behavior

- Attitude of the juvenile

- Family history

- Employment history

If the seriousness of the crime is severe enough, the intake officer has very little discretion in his or her decision. For some offenses it is mandatory that a formal petition be filed. However, there are many cases in which the intake officer has a lot of discretion. In these instances, an intake officer may determine that it is in the best interest of the child to handle the case informally or dismiss it altogether. An intake officer can base these decisions on information in the police report (for example, the police report may indicate that the victim does not want formal action taken) or on legal (for example, the seriousness of the offense is so trivial that the intake officer does not believe court resources should be wasted) or

Intake: An initial screening stage at which the intake officer determines whether a juvenile's case should be dismissed from the system or should be referred to the system.

Petition: A short statement of the facts of an alleged crime that are filed in the juvenile court.

Preadjudication detention: The stage at which a juvenile can be kept in detention prior to his or her adjudication hearing.

Preventive detention: The expanded use of detention to include the consideration of whether a juvenile will engage in delinquent offenses while awaiting his or her hearing.

extralegal characteristics (for example, the juvenile's attitude is contrite, or the intake officer believes that the juvenile's family can handle the matter informally).

Detention Intake and Detention Hearing

In some instances a juvenile can be kept in detention prior to his or her adjudication hearing. This is known as **preadjudication detention**. The decision to place the juvenile in detention prior to his or her hearing is the responsibility of the intake officer, who weighs many factors, including the severity of the crime, the likelihood of the juvenile to appear for the hearing, and the likelihood of the juvenile to hurt him- or herself or someone else prior to the hearing. At this stage, a detention hearing is scheduled at which the formal process of deciding whether a juvenile should be held in detention, and where that custody should take place, occurs. While the adult system uses pretrial detention as a means to make sure that alleged offenders show up for their court date (and in all but the most serious cases, adults have the right to bail, in order to avoid pretrial detention), in the juvenile system the use of preadjudication detention is broader, including the consideration as to whether the juvenile will engage in delinquent offenses while awaiting the hearing. This expanded use of detention is called **preventive detention**.

●●●
Plea bargain:
The process by which the juvenile agrees to plead guilty to a crime in exchange for a lower charge or lesser disposition (sentence).

Detention hearings must be scheduled within 72 hours of the juvenile being detained. Most states also require that the juvenile's hearing be scheduled within a certain time frame if the juvenile is held in preadjudication detention, although the time frame varies by state, between 10 and 180 days.[17] This is obviously quite a range in time, and it might seem like 180 days is incredibly long (and, if you are in detention, it is incredibly long), but a relatively short time frame can also have its problems because it leaves very little time for defense attorneys to plan their case.

One of the largest differences between adult and juvenile detention at this stage is that juveniles do not have a constitutional right to bail, while adults do. This is very important because it means that if an intake officer determines that a juvenile should be held in detention prior to the hearing and this is the formal decision at the detention hearing, there is no recourse for the juvenile to get out of detention. While there is no constitutional right to bail, some states do allow bail in certain instances, but other states have no allowances for bail under any circumstances.

Plea Bargaining

If a juvenile and prosecuting attorney are going to agree to a **plea bargain**, it is more likely to happen in the preadjudication stage. As with all processes, the use of the plea bargain varies across states. Some states rely heavily on the plea bargain, while other states rarely engage in plea deals. The benefits of a plea bargain can be numerous. In jurisdictions that have a large number of cases, plea bargains help manage the caseload and resources for the court, since a plea bargain means that the juvenile does not need to go to an adjudication hearing and can skip right to the disposition hearing stage. Juveniles can also benefit from having their charges reduced or have charges removed for pleading to some of the most serious (it is traditional in a plea bargain agreement for the juvenile to agree to plea if the prosecuting attorney agrees to reduce the

While many initially see the benefits of a plea bargain, there are still many drawbacks, too. What might be the drawbacks for a youth admitting guilt to a crime?

from the CLASSROOM
to the COMMUNITY

The Juvenile Collateral Consequences Project

Often, pleading to a charge in juvenile or adult court can be thought of as an expedient and useful way to manage a charge in the justice system. Those who plead are often offered less time, or a lesser charge, in exchange for their guilty plea. In the juvenile justice system where many of the dispositions (sentences) are not detention based, pleading guilty may hold a particular appeal. However, the American Bar Association (ABA) is involved in the Juvenile Collateral Consequences Project, designed to emphasize many of the extralegal consequences (those beyond the punishment) of pleading guilty.

The Juvenile Collateral Consequences Project is an endeavor undertaken by the American Bar Association to document and analyze the significant hardships experienced by youth who have come in contact with the juvenile justice system. These hardships,

known as collateral consequences, affect youth who have successfully completed a sentence imposed by the court. The hardships include barriers to education, employment, and public benefits.[18]

The project is a web-based Wiki created to detail the consequences of pleading guilty in the juvenile justice system in all 50 states and the federal system. It is designed to bring awareness to individuals about the consequences of agreeing to a juvenile sentence and, therefore, a juvenile record without the benefit of a hearing.

DISCUSSION QUESTION

1. What are the pros and cons of pleading guilty in juvenile court?

number or severity of the charges). However, there are serious drawbacks to plea bargaining, too. For the state, a plea bargain means that the state is reducing charges that had initially been considered representative of the offense (some might argue this means that the state is "going easy" on the juvenile offender). For the juvenile, there are a number of drawbacks to a plea deal, including the fact that the juvenile has given up his or her right to a hearing, and that a plea bargain creates a record for the juvenile that under certain circumstances can follow him or her into adulthood (see the Box "The Juvenile Collateral Consequences Project" to see the American Bar Association's warnings to juveniles about engaging in plea bargains).

Adjudication Stage

●●●

Adjudication:
The stage at which a juvenile goes before the court for a hearing in which it is determined whether the juvenile did or did not engage in the alleged crimes.

The adjudication hearing is the equivalent of the adult criminal trial. If a juvenile does not plea and the case is not dismissed, this hearing is where the decisions about whether the juvenile is *adjudicated delinquent or not delinquent* will be made. The adjudication hearing follows many of the same rules about due process that an adult trial must follow. A juvenile has the right to an attorney, to confront the witness against him or her, and to not self-incriminate. But a juvenile does not have the right to have his or her case heard by a jury of peers (although some states allow it in some cases). Instead, every case at the adjudication hearing stage (and our later stage the disposition hearing) is heard by a judge or magistrate of the court.

••• *on the* MEDIA

Juvenile Injustice: The "Cradle to Prison Pipeline" Zine Series

Some argue the Internet is nothing more than a wasteland of loud voices and cat videos. And it is the case that opinions and events can get grossly amplified by the echo chamber of the web. In addition, the digital divide suggests that there are huge numbers of people who do not have systematic access, or access at all, to the everyday technology that other people have, which means they end up even further behind in access to opportunities. But the Internet can also offer opportunities to many who would not have been heard prior to Twitter and WordPress. In other words, social media can facilitate work, social movements, or just getting the word out about something that is important to a group of people. This is how we got the rapper Russ, Markiplier, and the Rich Kids of Instagram. But it is also how we can hear the voices of juveniles who are in correctional facilities. The "Cradle to Prison Pipeline" zine series is four

stories put out in a partnership between Chicago-area artists, the Chicago Freedom School, and juveniles in the Cook County Juvenile Temporary Detention Center. We suggest you check out "Youth Stories of the Incarcerated" and "Girls in the System," both powerful zines illustrating the stories of youth who are in Chicago-area detention facilities.

DISCUSSION QUESTION

1. What can you imagine producing a zine about? How would you put one together to integrate the stories of young people and the research you are learning in this class?

Source: Adapted from Juvenile Injustice. (2011). The "Cradle to Prison Pipeline" Zine Series. Retrieved from https://juvenileinjustice.wordpress.com/

Probably the biggest difference in adjudication hearings as opposed to adult criminal trials is the role of the probation officer. While the adjudication hearing is similar to the adult trial on many of the due process requirements and in many instances can look almost identical to an adult trial, unlike the adult trial, a probation officer is a central figure in adjudication hearings in most states. The general role of the probation officer is to collect as much information as possible on the juvenile in all aspects of his or her life, including attitude, family history, employment, and education. How are the juvenile's relationships with family and friends? Has the juvenile been abused? How is he or she doing in school? Does the juvenile engage in extracurricular activities? Does he or she show remorse for the alleged offenses? Does the juvenile show responsibility in his or her actions, for example, holding down a job or completing all of his or her coursework? While such extralegal factors would not be allowed in an adult trial, in an adjudication hearing, a broader profile of the juvenile can be presented.

Disposition Stage

Most juvenile courts have **bifurcated hearings**, meaning that the adjudication hearing and the disposition hearing are separate. The **disposition** hearing (similar to sentencing in the adult court) is considered one of the more unique aspects of the juvenile justice experience because the juvenile court has a broader scope than the adult system. The adult system is focused on punishing those found guilty, but the juvenile system is focused on rehabilitating the juvenile and protecting the community. This means that part of the consideration during this hearing is "the best interest of the child," which allows for more discretion when making decisions about correctional outcomes for the juvenile. Although the probation officer has been gathering information for this report throughout the juvenile's court experience, from intake to the disposition hearing, and the information gathered has been used to determine the need for preadjudication detention, the information is relied on most heavily during the disposition hearing

•••
Bifurcated hearing: The division of a trial into two parts, for example, an adjudication hearing and a disposition hearing.

Disposition: The stage at which it is determined what punishment a juvenile will receive for his or her alleged acts of delinquency.

to make sure that the juvenile receives "individualized" justice. In addition to information on attitude, family history, employment, and education, the juvenile report by the probation officer may include victim statements, substance abuse assessments, family financial statements, letters from the juvenile's friends and family, psychological evaluations, and the probation officer's observations concerning the juvenile. Jurisdictions vary as to how much they rely on these probation officer reports when determining the dispositions for the juvenile. Some reports are extremely detailed and are the basis for court recommendations while others are much briefer, but in most instances, the recommendations contained in the report are followed by the court.[19] Figure 12.5 shows the percentage of cases that are adjudicated delinquent or not delinquent and their final dispositions. An extended discussion explaining the range of disposition will be offered in Chapters 13 and 14. Table 12.2 summarizes the differences between the juvenile system and the adult system.

THE JUVENILE JUSTICE PROCESS AND RACE, CLASS, AND GENDER

Research has shown that youth of color are disproportionately confined to state correctional facilities, and over the course of several decades this research has added to a growing concern about the unequal experiences of youth of color and white youth in the correctional system. Chapter 13 focuses specifically on the correctional stage of the juvenile justice system and will focus on the disparate experiences of youth based on race, ethnicity, class, and gender while in confinement. However, these experiences at the end stage are based on disparate experiences at every stage in the juvenile justice system. This process of unequal treatment is referred to as cumulative disadvantage—the idea, introduced in Chapter 6, that the experiences at one stage in the system/process have an effect on or add to the experiences at a later stage (see Table 12.3). Remember,

Cumulative disadvantage is a real worry for youth of color who see small individual disadvantages pile up in the juvenile justice system. Imagine a white youth and youth of color standing next to each other, each told they are to take 10 steps. The white youth has a stride of 12 inches, while the youth of color has a stride of 18 inches. At the end of the first step, the youths are still fairly close to each other (6 inches apart), but after 10 steps the youths are 60 inches (5 feet) apart. Small differences (disadvantages) in the juvenile justice system can add up to significant differences over stages and time.

Depending on local practices and traditions, states and communities can differ in the way that they process juvenile law violators. However, a common set of critical decision points—arrest, intake, detention, adjudication, and disposition—have become the basis for research on system overrepresentation of youth of color.[20]

These disparities may be because the ability for discretion in the juvenile system is greater than that in the adult system.[21]

These disparities are linked to one of two forms of racism, classism, and sexism. Chapter 1 explained the differences between individual and institutional racism, classism, and sexism, but a reminder is probably useful. Individual racism, individual sexism, and individual classism occur when

FIGURE 12.5 Case Processing Overview, 2013

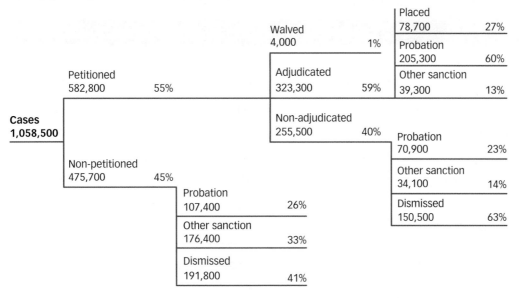

Source: OJJDP. (2015). *Statistical Briefing Book*. Retrieved from http://www.ojjdp.gov/ojstatbb/court/JCSCF_Display.asp?ID=qa06601&year=2013&group=1&estimate=2

Note: Cases are categorized by their most severe or restrictive sanction. Detail may not add to totals because of rounding.

TABLE 12.2 Differences Between the Juvenile and Adult Justice Systems

JUVENILE JUSTICE SYSTEM	ADULT JUSTICE SYSTEM
Rehabilitation is the goal of the system because juveniles are considered developmentally different from adults and, therefore, still "savable."	*Deterrence* in the form of punishment is the goal of the system because adults are assumed to be rational actors who are unlikely to engage in bad behavior if the punishment is commensurate with the crime.
There is limited public access to juvenile records and court proceedings to avoid stigmatizing the juvenile.	There is public access to criminal records, and court proceedings are open to the public.
Both legal factors (such as severity of the offense) and extralegal factors (such as family history, attitude, and school) are taken into consideration during the juvenile justice process.	Only legal factors can be considered during the pretrial and trial stages. Victim impact statements may be taken into consideration during the sentencing stage.
Juveniles do not have the right to bail, although in some jurisdictions bail is allowed.	Adults have the right to be considered for bail (although in some instances it can be denied).
Juveniles do not have a constitutional right to a jury trial, although some states, in some circumstances, have allowed a jury trial.	Adults have the constitutional right to a jury trial.
Indeterminate dispositions (sentences) are common. Juveniles often need to prove they are rehabilitated before their dispositions are considered finished.	While adult sentences are often in a range (for example, 18–24 months), it is more common for them to be determinate (have an end date).
The probation officer has a central role in all stages in the system.	The probation officer has the job of monitoring those adults who receive probation as a sentence.

TABLE 12.3	The Cumulative Disadvantage for Black Youth: Percentage of Black Youth at Various Stages in the Juvenile and Adult Justice Systems, 2013*			
STAGE	PERSON CRIMES	PROPERTY CRIMES	DRUG CRIMES	ALL CRIMES
Juvenile arrests	38.7	29	30.4	28.3
Referrals to juvenile court	42.1	35.5	21.3	35.3
Detained population	47	44.6	28.6	42
Youth formally processed by the juvenile court	46.1	39.5	24.4	39
Adjudicated youth	43.7	36.5	21.4	35.9
Youth judicially waived to criminal court	51.8	40.3	29.9	45
Youth in residential placement	46.9	41.4	27.5	40.1
Youth admitted to state adult prison	–	–	–	73**

Source: Sickmund, M., Sladky, A., & Kang, W. (2015). *Easy Access to Juvenile Court Statistics: 1985–2013.* Retrieved from http://www.ojjdp.gov/ojstatbb/ezajcs/

*Black youth population is 15% of total population.

**Estimate based on the 2011 statistics found in Carson, E. A., & Sabol, W. J. (2012). *Prisoners in 2011.* Washington, DC: U.S. Department of Justice, Office of Justice Programs. Retrieved from http://bjs.ojp.usdoj.gov/content/pub/pdf/p11.pdf

individuals hold *personal* attitudes of prejudice based on race, class, or gender and act on these attitudes in a discriminatory fashion.[22] For example, a police officer who believes that girls should not engage in sex (but does not hold the same strong belief about boys engaging in sex) may be more likely to pursue a formal arrest for a girl caught engaging in acts that are sexual or make sex more likely—even if the police officer argues that the reason for this differential treatment is because girls are in need of more protection than boys, and this is the reason for harsher treatment for girls at the arrest stage, it stems from an individual sexist belief in the differences between girls and boys. Or a police officer who has classist beliefs about who is most likely to use drugs (she believes that working-class juveniles use drugs more than wealthy juveniles) might focus her policing in poor neighborhoods or handle teens from rich neighborhoods informally by taking them home to their parents if they get in trouble, while handling poorer teens formally and arresting them for their bad behavior.

Individual racism, classism, and sexism are important aspects of the juvenile experience in the United States, but institutional racism, classism, and sexism probably have a far greater impact on the juvenile experience. Institutional racism, institutional sexism, and institutional classism occur when individuals are disadvantaged because of their race, class, or gender because of the routine workings of institutions, such as the juvenile justice system, in the United States.[23]

For example, it is generally the case that an institutional policy exists in most juvenile justice systems that the parent or guardian meet with an intake officer in order for a juvenile to be considered for an informal processing decision. Bishop and Frazier found that youth of color are often less likely than white youth to have parents or guardians who can take time off of work to meet with intake officers.[24] For this reason, fewer youth of color can be considered for informal processing than white youth, leaving more youth of color to be formally processed by the system.[25] The intake officer need not hold racist thoughts for the experiences of youth of color to differ from those of white youth at the intake stage—the institutional rule sets up the disadvantage.

Given that the structure and the nature of the juvenile justice system vary across counties and states, it stands to reason that evidence of unequal treatment in the juvenile justice system would also vary across jurisdictions. Both the decision-making practices of individual workers and the rules and regulations of different jurisdictions will have an effect on the experiences of those going through the various juvenile justice systems. As we go through this next section in which we examine the likelihood of discrimination in stages of the juvenile justice system, remember that there is no uniform system in the United States. We will see studies that offer evidence of unequal treatment in the system based on race/ethnicity, class, gender, and sexual orientation and studies that suggest that personal demographic characteristics play little part in juvenile experiences in the system. It is less likely that this research contradicts or calls into question research with contradictory findings, and more likely that it suggests we must understand the importance of institutionalized discrimination and individual racist, classist, sexist, and homophobic beliefs on the experiences of juveniles in the juvenile justice system. While, to some extent, race/ethnicity, class, gender, and sexual orientation have been studied in relation to unequal treatment in the juvenile justice system, by far the most studied relationship is race/ethnicity and unequal treatment. In fact, the level of minority over-representation in the juvenile justice system must be monitored by states according to the Disproportionate Minority Confinement Initiative.[26] This means most research on unequal treatment focuses on race.

The Disproportionate Minority Confinement Initiative started as a requirement of the Juvenile Justice and Delinquency Prevention Act (JJDPA; previously discussed in Chapter 11) for states to address disproportionate minority confinement by developing plans to reduce minority confinement in detention and correctional facilities, if the proportion exceeded that of the general population. Then, in 2002, the JJDPA changed the focus from confinement to contact, thus expanding the focus to all stages of the juvenile justice system. In these later amendments, a portion of state funding was tied to states' showing they were complying with efforts to decrease **disproportionate minority contact (DMC)**. According to the OJJDP, two major lessons have been learned over the years as states monitor and address DMC:[27]

1. In most jurisdictions, disproportionate juvenile minority representation is not limited only to secure detention and confinement; it is evident at nearly all contact points on the juvenile justice system continuum, and

2. Contributing factors to DMC are multiple and complex; reducing DMC requires comprehensive and multipronged strategies that include programmatic and systems change efforts.

Figure 12.6 illustrates the five phases of the DMC reduction cycle: identification, assessment/diagnosis, intervention, evaluation, and monitoring. The identification phase is descriptive; it provides a preliminary answer to the question, are there differences in the race and ethnicity of youth who have contact with the juvenile justice system? This first stage does not offer reasons for differences in levels of youth contact by race or ethnicity. It merely points out whether differences exist. The assessment/diagnosis phase is designed to ask questions about the mechanisms and reasons for these racial and ethnic differences in contact, if they exist. It is in this phase that the in-depth examination of DMC occurs. The intervention phase is the stage at which state or local entities prepare and implement intervention strategies to decrease DMC at whatever stages in the system the assessment phase has identified. The evaluation phase involves assessing the performance of the interventions

●●●
Disproportionate minority contact:
The disproportionate number of minority youth who come into contact with the juvenile justice system.

FIGURE 12.6 The DMC Reduction Cycle

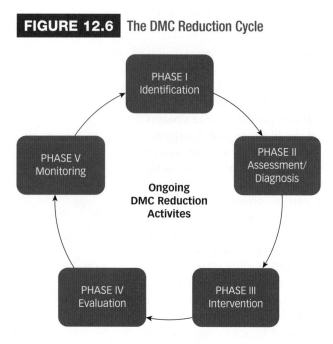

Source: Hsia, H. (2009). Introduction. *DMC Technical Assistance Manual* (4th ed.). Washington, DC: Office of Juvenile Justice and Delinquency Prevention.

that were implemented in the previous phase. This involves evaluating both their implementation and whether they are achieving their desired outcomes. Finally, the monitoring phase continues the collection of data (like the identification phase) in order to determine how trends from year to year illustrate the level of DMC in targeted areas. Ideally, interventions will solve DMC; if not, the identification stage starts all over again, as the problem is addressed and interventions are improved.[28]

Race/Ethnicity and Unequal Treatment

The overrepresentation of youth of color in the juvenile justice system is extensively documented (see Tables 12.4 and 12.5 for example rates and relative rates).[29] The research does not always agree on how race affects decision-making practices—some research suggests a direct relationship (decision makers are racially biased), some research suggests an indirect relationship (institutional decisions, such as focusing on family type, disproportionately affect one race over another), and some research focuses on contextual factors (characteristics of a jurisdiction or geographic area have more or less effect on the relationship). Whatever the reasons are, there is substantial evidence that race does impact the experience in the juvenile justice system.

When it comes to policing and arrests, race and class are closely linked in the experience of juveniles. Some research suggests that there is little race or class bias in arrest decisions[30]—for example, most juveniles who come in contact with police because of felony crimes are arrested, independent of the juvenile's race, class, or gender. However, under 10% of all police encounters with juveniles are because of felonies. A majority of the research does highlight a connection between race, class, and likelihood of arrest. Lower-class youth of color are more likely to be arrested than their middle- and upper-class white counterparts.[31] However, as Elrod and Ryder point out, this is probably less from individual racist behavior among the police (although racist and classist behavior exists, as it does everywhere) but more about institutional decisions, the most important being the decision on where and how to distribute police resources, which are often concentrated in urban areas most likely populated by the lower class and communities of color.[32]

In California, for example, both African American and Latino youth are overrepresented at every stage in the juvenile justice system.[33] And this is a trend that exists nationally, too. Youth of color are overrepresented at the arrest stage.[34] African American and Latino youth are more likely to be transferred to the adult criminal court than white youth.[35] Youth of color are also more likely to be detained preadjudication, no matter what the charge, and are more likely to be formally charged for some offenses (most notably drug charges).[36]

Gender and Unequal Treatment

Research on gender and unequal treatment in the juvenile justice system is much less prevalent than the research on race. Much of the research has been historical in nature, documenting the treatment of girls at the creation of the juvenile justice system in the

TABLE 12.4 · 2013 Case Processing Summary Rates for Delinquency Offenses, by Race

RATE	ALL	WHITE	MINORITY	BLACK	AMERICAN INDIAN OR ALASKAN NATIVE	ASIAN, HAWAIIAN, OR PACIFIC ISLANDER
Juvenile arrests per 1,000 person in population	37.7	32.2	55.4	73.8	28.7	10.7
Cases referred per 100 juvenile arrests	84.7	80.6	92.3	93.4	98.9	65.2
Cases diverted per 100 cases referred	26.8	29.8	21.9	21.7	23.8	26.9
Cases detained per 100 cases referred	20.9	18.6	24.7	24.9	24.4	21.2
Cases petitioned per 100 cases referred	55.1	51.8	60.4	60.7	55.3	58.2
Cases adjudicated per 100 cases petitioned	55.5	58.1	51.8	51.1	65.0	56.7
Probation cases per 100 adjudicated cases	63.5	64.8	61.6	61.1	61.4	74.4
Placement cases per 100 adjudicated cases	24.3	22.8	26.7	27.2	24.0	18.5
Cases judicially waived per 100 cases petitioned	0.7	0.6	0.8	0.8	0.8	*0.3

Source: Puzzanchera, C., & Hockenberry, S. (2015). *National Disproportionate Minority Contact Databook.* Developed by the National Center for Juvenile Justice for the Office of Juvenile Justice and Delinquency Prevention. Retrieved from http://www.ojjdp.gov/ojstatbb/dmcdb/

*Interpret data with caution; rates and RRI's are based a small of cases.

early 1900s. This research found that girls were held to higher moral standards, the focus being on turning questionably behaving girls into properly behaving wife and mother material.[37] There is much less research focusing on the current impact of gender on unequal treatment. This research argues that paternalism still exists and that, much like the experiences of girls at the beginning of the 1900s, currently girls are still held to gender norms and a higher standard of morality, with harsher outcomes especially for status offenses.[38] However, a second set of research finds that girls are actually treated less harshly under some circumstances, especially when legal characteristics like prior record or severity of offense are controlled.[39] This research argues that girls are treated chivalrously because they are seen as less threatening than boys.

Gender appears to influence police decision making and arrest in a number of ways. Some research suggests that girls who are caught for status offenses are treated more harshly (formally) than boys who are caught for similar behaviors, while other research suggests that boys may be arrested more for delinquent offenses than girls (controlling for offense characteristics).[40] Much of the research suggests that the demeanor of girls is particularly important during the arrest process. Girls who engage in gender-appropriate behavior (behavior that is approved for and expected of girls) are treated less harshly than girls who break gender norms.

TABLE 12.5	2013 Case Processing Summary, Relative Rate Indices For Delinquency Offenses, by Race			
RELATIVE RATES	MINORITY	BLACK	AMERICAN INDIAN OR ALASKAN NATIVE	ASIAN, HAWAIIAN, OR PACIFIC ISLANDER
Arrest rate	1.7	2.3	0.9	0.3
Referral rate	1.1	1.2	1.2	0.8
Diversion rate	0.7	0.7	0.8	0.9
Detention rate	1.3	1.3	1.3	1.1
Petitioned rate	1.2	1.2	1.1	1.1
Adjudicated rate	0.9	0.9	1.1	1.0
Probation rate	1.0	0.9	0.9	1.1
Placement rate	1.2	1.2	1.1	0.8
Waiver rate	1.3	1.3	1.4	*0.6

Source: Puzzanchera, C., & Hockenberry, S. (2015). *National Disproportionate Minority Contact Databook.* Developed by the National Center for Juvenile Justice for the Office of Juvenile Justice and Delinquency Prevention.

*Interpret data with caution; rates and RRI's are based a small number of cases.

FAMILY COURT

As with the delinquency side of the juvenile court, the dependency side differs depending on the state/jurisdiction. For this reason, we will be fairly general about the processes on this side of the court system, too (see Figure 12.7).

There are several basic reasons that a juvenile might end up in the dependency court:

- The juvenile has experienced serious physical harm inflicted non-accidentally by the parent or guardian.

- The juvenile has experienced serious physical harm because the parent has not adequately supervised or protected the juvenile. This includes not providing food, clothing, shelter, or medical treatment. This may occur because of general neglect or because the parent suffers from addiction, mental illness, or a developmental disability.

- The juvenile has experienced serious emotional harm inflicted nonaccidentally by the parent or guardian.

Juvenile dependency process: The process by which it is determined whether a juvenile is safe in his or her home with his or her guardians or parents.

- The juvenile has experienced sexual abuse by the parent, or the parent has failed to protect the juvenile from sexual abuse.

- The juvenile is without parental protection because the parent refuses or is unwilling to provide care, or cannot provide care (for example, because the parent is incarcerated or institutionalized).

The Juvenile Dependency Process

A juvenile comes into the juvenile dependency process when the state believes that the juvenile may be in danger of serious harm or neglect that may lead to serious harm.

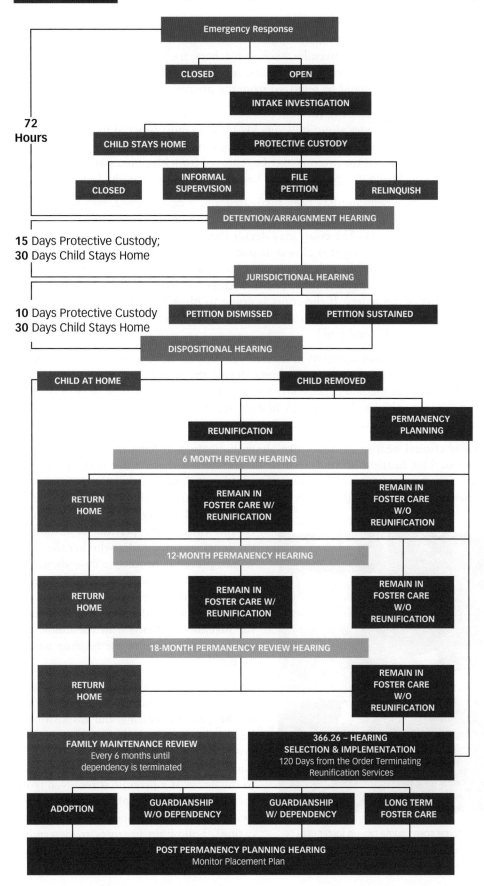

Source:http://www.sdcourt.ca.gov/pls/portal/docs/PAGE/SDCOURT/JUVENILE3/JUVENILEFAQ3/
Dependency_Process.pdf

In most jurisdictions everyone has a legal obligation to report a suspicion of neglect or abuse of a minor (or the elderly), although those with the most likelihood of reporting cases are those nearest to the juveniles, such as teachers, friends or family, or neighbors, and the police when called into situations (like domestic violence) in which it becomes obvious that a juvenile should be removed from the premises.

Both cases that go through the juvenile justice system and those that go through the dependency court have rules about how quickly the case must proceed to the next stage. Dependency hearings, especially, have a short timeline because the ramifications in the dependency court are that the juvenile may be removed from his or her parents and, in its most extreme conclusion, the parents could lose their rights to their children.

Once an emergency response has been instigated and a case opened, an investigation into the allegations of abuse and/or neglect is started. There are several initial outcomes for a dependency case: (1) The court may decide that there is no evidence for a case to move forward, in which case it is closed or dismissed; (2) the court may decide that a juvenile can remain with his or her parent or guardian but needs to be supervised in this situation for some length of time; or (3) the juvenile may be taken into protective custody for his or her safety. If the court is going to file a formal petition, it must be filed in the first 72 hours after the case has been opened, at which time a detention/ arraignment hearing is conducted.

The detention hearing is conducted to determine whether the juvenile will be placed in protective custody or can remain in the home during the rest of the process. If the juvenile is removed from the home, the court has 15 days to commence the next hearing; if the child can stay at home, the court has 30 days to commence the next hearing, at which stage a jurisdictional hearing is conducted.

The jurisdictional hearing is much like the adjudication hearing in the juvenile justice system. This hearing is conducted to determine whether or not there is enough evidence for the state to conclude that the child is indeed in jeopardy in the home. If the petition is sustained (found to be true), it is similar to the parent or guardian being found "guilty" of neglect or abuse. At this time, if the petition is sustained, the court, again, decides whether the child will be placed in protective custody or can remain in the home. If the child is to be placed in protective custody, the court has 10 days to commence the next hearing; if the juvenile can remain in the home, the court must commence the hearing within 30 days.

This next hearing is the dispositional hearing, and is the last hearing in this first stage of the process. During the dispositional hearing it is determined whether or not the juvenile is going to be removed from the home for some length of time or can return to the home. If a juvenile is removed from the home, he or she is placed in foster care (with or without the possibility of reunification). Follow-up hearings to determine whether the child can be reunified with his

Many youth who are having trouble at home spend some time in foster care or a group home if the dependency court rules that they are in danger at home.

or her parent or guardian are conducted at spaced intervals (in many jurisdictions, at 6, 12, and 18 months).

The dependency court makes the dispositional decision concerning the final outcome of dependency cases:

- Remove children from their home to be cared for by relatives, foster care, or group homes.

- Cancel or create new parental rights.

- Work with agencies to coordinate and implement services the juvenile may need.

Crossover Youth: From Dependency Court to the Juvenile Justice System

Why would we spend time discussing the dependency court in detail, given there is never much emphasis placed on this court system in juvenile delinquency classes? There are two reasons: (1) some argue that group homes represent another type of total institution, like detention and correctional facilities, in which juveniles are more likely to be controlled and even abused, rather than helped; and (2) research suggests that there are more connections between these two courts than just that they are housed under a single juvenile court.[41] Youth who start in the dependency court often end up in the juvenile justice system. These juveniles are often referred to as **crossover youth** (those who have experienced abuse or neglect and engaged in delinquency whether they are formally in either system), **dually involved youth** (crossover youth who are receiving services from both the juvenile justice and dependency courts simultaneously), or **dually adjudicated youth** (dually involved youth who have actually been adjudicated by both the juvenile justice and dependency courts).[42]

Chapter 7 discussed the link between juveniles who have been neglected or abused and their likelihood of engaging in delinquent behavior and/or ending up in the juvenile justice system. There is an increasing body of research on crossover youth.[43] We know from this research that crossover youth have spent longer-than-average periods of time in the dependency system, being placed out of the home, often in multiple placements. Being a crossover youth predicts the likelihood of being truant, doing poorly in school, being detained prior to adjudication, being perceived as high risk by juvenile justice workers, and receiving harsh punishments.[44] Both girls and youth of color are overrepresented in the crossover population, as Lutz and Stewart explain

According to the 2007 GAO report, African American children were more likely to be placed in foster care than their white and Hispanic counterparts. While disproportionality is severe for African American children, Native American children experience a higher rate than other races and ethnicities. These startling statistics parallel what occurs in the juvenile justice system. In 1997, African American juveniles represented 15% of the U.S. population ages 10 to 17 years, but accounted for 26% of juvenile arrests and 45% of pre-adjudication decisions in the juvenile court. Over-representation is also found for Latinos and Native Americans involved in the juvenile justice system. The disproportionality is greater when youth cross over from one system and engage with the second system of care simultaneously. A study conducted in Los Angeles and Alameda County, California, found that of the crossover population, 63% and 75% respectively were African American youth, much higher than their representation in the population generally or in the child welfare or juvenile justice systems individually.[45]

●●●

Crossover youth: Any youth who has experienced abuse or neglect and engaged in delinquency whether formally in either system or not.

Dually involved youth: Crossover youth who are receiving services from both the juvenile justice and dependency courts simultaneously.

Dually adjudicated youth: Dually involved youth who have actually been adjudicated by both the juvenile justice and dependency courts.

A Focus on Research

Victory's Structured Abuse: Life in a Group Home

In the foster care system, youth experience the structured abuse of a total institution when they live in group homes.[46] Although there are various types of group homes, these facilities are different than traditional family-like settings found in foster care placements. Group homes are considered to be a total institution because of the common institutional aspects: the control and surveillance, separation from the outside world, a prearranged set of daily activities and requirements, and a constricted schedule based on a formal set of rules.[47]

Inside this total institution, a system of control is created that aims to keep youth complacent and docile until they are no longer the responsibility of the state. When youth fail to comply with institutional control, they are further criminalized and punished.[48] Jessica reflects on her experiences with this control in a group home:

> I had found out my brother had died in February. This is nine years ago. I was really upset. I asked to go out of my room and go into this spare room they had where kids could go to express themselves. Well I went there, I was really angry, I was crying. I was so [pause] I ended up getting put on restriction because I was out of my room after curfew hours even though I was told it was okay to go in there to get away from my roommate and just let steam out. I got put on restriction. I wasn't allowed to call anybody on my phone list. The only person I could talk to was my social worker. But again, some social workers are really hard to get to because they are busy.
>
> Then two months later I found out my brother got stabbed 17 times and was in the hospital. I was again, really upset and this was in the same year. I asked to go into this room and went off and I got put on [pause]. Not restriction. I got put on a higher level because I was at risk of hurting myself, because I was punching the wall. And again, I wasn't allowed to talk to anybody. And that just made me more angry. And I would make comments

saying I am going to hurt myself. And then my social worker actually ended up picking me up that night because he had found out that my brother was in the hospital. And he basically went over their rules and said I am taking her.

> And took me to go see my brother. So obviously, when I got back I was in a lot of trouble, because I left the premises without having permission to leave. Even though I left with my county worker. Then from there I wasn't allowed to go outside. I was in my room 24 hours a day. Eating in my room. There would be times when I would be really depressed and I didn't want to eat. And I get in trouble for not eating and wasting money. And then in that same year, I found out my dad died. And again, it was the same thing. I mean you have something big like that happen to you and they punish you for it. And I'm like, how is that? You should be comforting someone. How are those rules okay to have when someone is dealing with something that is so major in their life?[49]

Rather than helping Jessica through a terrible time in her life, the group home tried to control her emotional reactions through isolation and punishment. Jessica questions the use of such rules and shows the inhumanity in punishing someone during such a hard time in her life rather than consoling and helping her. This structured abuse found in group homes can be seen in the policies and rules that dehumanize and criminalize youth such as Jessica. The group home is able to maintain complete control by treating Jessica as the problem. Youth's resistance to the total institution is further identified as reasons for their confinement.[50]

Group homes create policies and rules that maintain managerial ease, rather than supporting the needs and well-being of youth.[51] Ariana shares how relationships are not allowed in group homes:

Because I made a relationship with another staff she had to move. She had to quit working at PB-18 where I was at. And she had to get a totally different job. And that was their way of separating the bond that we had. Because she was the only person that I would talk to that understood me, and that actually took the time. And that's what I'm saying, like how do they expect us to succeed if we don't have anybody? Or if they don't teach us, or if they're not there for us? How do they expect us to succeed? I don't understand. Cause they take us away from our family.[52]

As Ariana shows, social relationships are not allowed or supported within group homes. Staff members must remain detached from youth in order to make it easier to enforce the rules of the institution.[53] Ariana argues that such abusive institutional practices harm youth and prevent them from having lasting and supportive relationships that are pivotal to their future success. Once youth enter into the institutional confines of group homes, they are automatically treated as a criminal in need of isolation and control.[54]

DISCUSSION QUESTIONS

1. How do youth experience structured abuse in group homes and what function does it serve for the institution?

2. How are youth criminalized and dehumanized in group homes?

Source: Victory, O. (2016). *"All I wanted was someone to be there": Surviving the structured abuse in group homes.* Unpublished master's thesis, Department of Sociology, California State University, San Marcos.

SUMMARY

This chapter has focused on the structure and process of the juvenile court, examining both the delinquency side referred to as the juvenile justice system and the family court side referred to as the juvenile dependency process. Studies have shown us that a significant amount of discretion can happen at all of the stages in both court systems. This discretion means that juveniles often have very different experiences in these systems based on their race/ethnicity, class, and gender.

We can see that this discretion can add to a cumulative disadvantage for juveniles, and some are more likely to be treated formally throughout all stages of the system. This cumulative disadvantage can exist for youth of color, but it can also exist for youth who find themselves in situations in which they come to the attention of police or the system even if they have not necessarily engaged in delinquent behavior. We see this of young people who start on the dependency side of the court and are drawn into delinquency. These juveniles also experience a cumulative disadvantage in the system.

We will see in Chapter 13 how these processes lead to the correctional stage of the juvenile justice system.

EYE ON DIVERSITY EXERCISE: JUVENILE INTAKE SCREENING

During the intake screening process, intake officers must determine which juveniles should be detained prior to their hearings and which do not need to be formally detained. Over the years the process of determining who will be detained has become more routinized, but each jurisdiction has its own intake screening procedures.

1. In a group, discuss the criteria that you would use to determine whether someone should be detained preadjudication. Examine each of your criteria. Are all of these criteria neutral? Are any of your criteria likely to create an unfair disadvantage to anyone based on race/ethnicity, class, or gender?

DISCUSSION QUESTIONS

1. Explain the three roles of law enforcement.

2. Explain, according to the Supreme Court, when a juvenile is considered in custody of the police.

3. How might it be that diversion can contribute to the process of net-widening?

4. What are the pros and cons of plea bargaining for a juvenile?

5. Describe the percentage breakdown of dispositions.

6. How does the process of cumulative disadvantage work in the juvenile justice process?

7. What is the relationship between race/ethnicity and unequal treatment during the juvenile justice process?

8. What is the relationship between gender and unequal treatment during the juvenile justice process?

9. Explain the juvenile dependency process. How does it interact with the juvenile justice (court) process?

KEY TERMS

Adjudication 346

Automatic waiver 340

Bifurcated hearing 347

Crossover youth 357

Disposition 347

Disproportionate minority contact 351

Diversion 343

Dually adjudicated youth 357

Dually involved youth 357

Intake 344

Judicial waiver 341

Juvenile dependency process 354

Net-widening 343

Petition 344

Plea bargain 345

Preadjudication detention 345

Preventive detention 345

Prosecutorial waiver 340

Waiver to adult court 340

CHAPTER PRETEST ANSWERS

1. True

2. True

3. True

4. False

5. True

6. True

7. False

8. False

edge.sagepub.com/bates2e

Sharpen your skills with SAGE edge!

SAGE edge for students provides a personalized approach to help you accomplish your coursework goals in an easy-to-use learning environment. You'll find action plans, mobile-friendly eFlashcards, and quizzes, as well as videos, web resources, and links to SAGE journal articles to support and expand on the concepts presented in this chapter. Check out the website for original videos of former offenders discussing their experiences as juveniles.

JUVENILE CORRECTIONS

After reading this chapter, you should be able to

- Describe the correctional alternatives

- Explain the difference between secure and open correctional facilities

- Analyze the current problems that characterize juvenile correctional facilities

- Compare and contrast the impact of gender, race and ethnicity, and sexual orientation on the experiences of youth in the correctional system

spent six months observing juvenile court hearings. The following notes are from one of those observations:

The courtroom doesn't look like the type you see on TV. It is a smallish room with a raised desk on the far wall. It is the most imposing piece of furniture in the room, but it is still small compared to what a judge sits behind in the adult court. The magistrate is sitting at this desk now. Off to his right is a desk with the court administrator sitting behind it. She has a stack of cases sitting in front of her and the necessary equipment to record the hearings, but she doesn't seem to always do this. In front of the large desks are three regular office desks; in fact, they look rather cheap. At the left one sits the defense attorney, at the middle one sits the probation officer, and at the right one sits the prosecuting attorney. Behind these three tables is a single row of chairs that have several teenagers sitting in them. And behind those chairs are two more rows of chairs that house various individuals—probation officers waiting for one of their cases before the judge or occasional family members who come in for a juvenile hearing. The room is quiet. In comparison to an adult courtroom, which seems to always have a low hum rushing through it—people coming and going for their cases and court workers quietly conferring about an upcoming case—the juvenile court has almost none of this bustle. The next case brought before the court is that of Rachel, a 16-year-old girl.

Rachel has been adjudicated delinquent for possessing meth. She has received three days in detention and been put on probation. Her probation conditions were the standard conditions, but in addition, she had received an earlier curfew of 7 p.m. and been forbidden to see her boyfriend because, as her mom put it, "I know they are sleeping together and that's just not right." Now she stands before the juvenile court judge, again. She has been brought back in because her mother called to complain she had violated her probation. According to her mother, Rachel had not gotten home until 7:15 p.m. one night, and her mom knew it was because "she was with that boy." Rachel doesn't deny she got home after curfew. She works at the local Burger King, and the bus she was waiting for didn't come when she got off work. Her mother took away her cell phone in an attempt to make sure Rachel didn't meet up with her boyfriend, so Rachel says she couldn't call her mom and tell her the bus never came. She was going to go back in

CHAPTER PRETEST

Test your knowledge of this chapter's material by determining whether the following statements are true or false. Be sure to compare your answers with the answers on page 388.

1. Probation is the most popular correctional alternative used by the juvenile court.

2. The federal government requires that all probation programs be the same across states.

3. Electronic monitoring, such as the ankle monitor, can be an efficient way to socially control juveniles without having to keep them in a detention facility.

4. Research on foster homes suggests they might be detrimental to stopping delinquency.

5. Long-term secure detention facilities are linked to higher rates of recidivism.

6. Boot camps are the most effective correctional program for reducing recidivism.

7. Girls in correctional facilities who are characterized as overly sexual, aggressive, or incorrigible are more likely to be punished.

8. Controlling for type of offense, youth of color are more likely to be transferred to adult court than white youth.

9. Correctional facilities are required to have training and policies in place addressing support and resources for LGBTQ youth.

between the probation officer and the juvenile, but the level of resources. In some jurisdictions, a probation officer can have between 100 and 200 youth to supervise every month. There is little time in these situations for meaningful interactions.

Given that probation is the most likely disposition for a juvenile to receive, it is surprising how few studies have been conducted on the success of these programs.[4] One of the reasons that research on probation programs may be rather scarce is that probation programs are not uniform across jurisdictions. In other words, while the general conditions of probation (go to school, be home by curfew) might be similar in different areas, once we move beyond these general conditions, juvenile experiences can be very different. Research that compared the types of probation (standard, moderate, and intensive) found no difference in incidence, frequency, nature, or timing of subsequent arrests.[5] Lane et al. found no difference between juveniles randomly assigned to an intensive probation program in Ventura County, California, and those assigned to routine probation, with most of the youth being rearrested though not receiving a sustained petition or incarceration.[6] Those studies that compared probation programs to detention also found no difference in the likelihood to reoffend.[7] And research that compared multiagency juvenile justice centers (one-stop shops) to traditional probation units also found little difference in recidivism between the two groups.[8] While most of the research suggests that there may be little difference between types of probation, several studies suggest that the type of treatment or resources available may have an effect on likelihood to reoffend.[9]

Restitution

Restitution programs are designed to compensate the crime victim for the harm done to him or her. Restitution can come in several forms: monetary, victim service, or community service. Monetary restitution requires that the juvenile pay the victim for monetary damages that the juvenile created, for example from property damage or damage to a victim's car. Monetary restitution is designed to show the juvenile that his or her actions have economic consequences. Victim service restitution requires that the juvenile perform services for the victim, for example repairing private property or perhaps running errands. This form of restitution is designed to emphasize the humanity of the victim to the juvenile. Finally, community service restitution requires that the juvenile perform some sort of service for the community, for example volunteering for a community organization or cleaning up a park. The goal of community service restitution is to teach the juvenile that the community can also be harmed by the bad behavior of the juvenile. At its most basic, restitution comes from the restorative justice model, which will be discussed in Chapter 14. However, while their philosophy may not stem from the correctional philosophy of deterrence and punishment, restitution programs are coordinated by the juvenile court and are part of the corrections stage.

Restitution, like all other correctional options, seems to show mixed success at rehabilitating juveniles. When success is measured at completing the requirement of restitution (paying the victim back or completing the service to the victim or community), some programs show a success rate as high as 95%.[10] However, this success appears to be in programs where juveniles are monitored in structured, well-managed environments.[11] Programs that did not properly supervise juveniles or were poorly managed did not have good compliance rates. When success is measured by the recidivism rate, restitution is found to have an effect under some conditions. Juveniles who were required to give restitution early in their juvenile court process (as early as the preadjudication stage) were less likely to reoffend than other juvenile offenders, and in another study restitution was found to be more successful than probation or incarceration for lowering recidivism rates.[12]

• • •

Restitution:
The act of "paying back" the victim of an act of delinquency or his or her family by means of money, volunteer labor, community service, or some other agreed-upon method.

Monetary restitution:
A sanction in which the juvenile offender is required to pay the victim for monetary damages that the juvenile created.

Victim service restitution:
A sanction in which the juvenile is required to perform services for the victim such as repairing private property.

Community service restitution:
A sanction in which the juvenile offender is required to perform some sort of service for the community.

FIGURE 13.1

Example Standard Probation Agreement (Example From Utah and the Second District Juvenile Court)

STATE OF UTAH, in the interest of

PROBATION ORDER

[Minor's name]

CASE NUMBER: [Case number]

A person under eighteen years of age.

IT IS HEREBY ORDERED that the above named be placed on probation under the supervision of the Probation Division of the Court under the following conditions:

I, [Minor's name], understand that I have been placed on probation by order of the Second District Juvenile Court. I recognize that throughout my probation term I may be returned to the court for violation of any of the following conditions. I further acknowledge that the Court has jurisdiction to amend or modify the conditions of probation. I understand that the length of time on probation will be determined by the Court and termination of probation will not become effective until an order of the Court is issued. In consideration of this grant of probation, I will comply with all of the following conditions:

1. I will obey all local, state, and federal laws and ordinances, and will report all contacts with law enforcement personnel to my Probation Officer within two days of occurrence.

2. I will obey the lawful and reasonable requests of the Probation Division, and my parent(s) or custodian(s) with whom I am living.

3. I understand that Probation staff may contact me at my place of residence, my school, my place of employment, or elsewhere as deemed appropriate.

4. I will be subject to search of my person, auto, or any area of my residence under my control at any time as determined necessary by the Probation Division.

5. I will attend school as required by law, or will obtain and maintain gainful employment.

6. I will participate in any treatment/program ordered by the Court, or directed by my Probation Officer.

7. I will not use any intoxicating agents and I will submit to random tests for such agents as directed by the Probation Division.

8. I will not receive, possess, transport, or have under my control any dangerous instrument, weapon, or firearm except with the consent of the Probation Division for legitimate recreational purposes.

9. I will obtain permission from the Probation Division before leaving the State of Utah. If I leave the State of Utah without permission, or if I am arrested outside of the State of Utah, I hereby consent to voluntarily return from the state in which I may be found, to the State of Utah.

10. I will obtain permission from my Probation Officer before I marry, change employment, change my residence, enter the military service, purchase a motor vehicle, or enter into any installment purchases.

11. I will pay all fines and restitution as ordered by the Court and/or outlined by a Probation Officer.

12. I will comply with the requirements noted in Appendix A, and with the following special conditions of probation:

My signature on this document indicates that I understand and will comply with the requirements. If I fail to comply with the terms of probation, I understand that I may be placed in detention, or on electronic monitoring.

Dated _____

_____

Probationer

Source: http://www.utcourts.gov/courts/juv/juvsites/2nd/pro_ord.htm

Home Confinement: Electronic Monitoring

A growing trend in community corrections is **home confinement**. Home confinement uses intensive supervision by a probation officer and electronic monitoring to control juveniles. There are several levels of home confinement: curfew, home detention, and lockdown. Curfew home confinement requires that the juvenile be home at set times of the day. Home detention requires that juveniles remain at home except for preapproved absences such as for school, work, church, treatment, court appearances, and doctor/dentist appointments. Lockdown requires that juveniles be in the home 24 hours a day, except usually for medical visits and court appearances.[13]

Usually **electronic monitoring** plays a role in home confinement. Electronic monitoring can be either passive or active. For home confinement, electronic monitoring devices are usually either ankle or wrist bracelets, or voice recognition programs in which the juvenile is required to call or be available to answer the phone at certain times of the day. An ankle or wrist bracelet is considered an active monitoring system because it emits a continuous signal, while a system that involves the juvenile calling in or answering a phone is considered passive because the juvenile is not being monitored continuously. In addition to ankle and wrist devices, electronic monitoring can include field monitoring devices, alcohol and drug testing devices, voice verification systems, and global positioning systems.[14]

While juveniles have been electronically monitored since the 1980s, there has been little systematic research on the success of home confinement and electronic monitoring.[15] The research that has been conducted suggests that electronic monitoring and home confinement can reduce costs and detention overcrowding and do not seem to increase recidivism when compared to other dispositions.[16]

Foster Homes/Group Homes/Halfway Houses

While we discussed foster care in our last chapter (Chapter 12) on the dependency court, foster care can also be a dispositional alternative on the juvenile court side. If the court believes that a child who has engaged in delinquency is not receiving good care from his or her parents and that that negligent care may have contributed to his or her bad behavior, the court may decide to remove the juvenile from the home as part of the disposition. Children removed from the home under these conditions can end up in a **foster home, group home**, or **halfway house**. In 2014, 653,000 children were served by the foster care system, which was down from a high of 800,000 in 2006 (see Figure 13.2).[17]

While, ideally, foster homes strive to recreate the family-based atmosphere and structure of a "traditional" family, group homes and halfway houses do not have the structure of family life, it is likely more juveniles live under one roof in this setting, and the adults in charge do not take on the traditional "parental" role.[18] Group homes and halfway houses are often used either as a last resort before choosing to send a child to a detention facility or as a stepping-stone to independence once a juvenile

Electronic monitoring such as the ankle monitor can be an efficient way to socially control juveniles without having to keep them in a detention facility.

● ● ●

Home confinement: Intensive supervision by a probation officer and electronic monitoring to control juveniles.

Electronic monitoring: The process by which an offender is monitored in the community through the use of technology/ electronic devices.

Foster home: A household, designed to replicate a home environment, in which a delinquent or neglected child may be placed when he or she cannot be sent back home.

gets out of a detention facility.[19] Neither group homes nor halfway houses are meant to be permanent placements for juveniles.

Research on the success of foster homes, group homes, and halfway houses is limited. The research on foster homes suggests that it may actually be detrimental in stopping delinquency, which should not be surprising given our discussion in Chapter 12 concerning the links between the dependency and juvenile courts.[20] While it is obvious that some juveniles need to be removed from their family situations to be kept physically, mentally, and emotionally safe, the drawback of the foster care system is that placements are often short (meaning that juveniles have little time or opportunity to make emotional connections that are important for their development), multiple placements are not unusual, and often the care in foster homes is not much better than in the juvenile's original family.[21] While traditional foster care settings do not have much support from the research, treatment foster care has shown more success. In treatment foster care settings the foster parents receive extensive training to address the individual strengths and challenges of the juvenile who will be placed with them. Foster care settings that limit the number of children who can be placed and offer training to focus on the specific juvenile needs have shown much more success in reducing delinquency.[22]

Research on group homes and halfway houses also does not offer very positive reviews. While some research suggests that group homes are no worse than other placements, research that has compared group homes to treatment foster care has found that the treatment foster care programs are more successful at helping juveniles. While group homes and halfway houses are cheaper than many of these other alternatives, one of the reasons that they may not be very successful is that they are only a stopping point for juveniles, giving them little time to make connections or take advantage of treatment programs; staff are not paid very well; and there is little ability to focus on individual juveniles given the number of children in a single facility (in comparison to treatment foster homes).[23]

●●●

Group home: An alternative to the traditional in-home foster care for children in which a number of children live for various amounts of time with a single set of house parents or rotating staff.

Halfway house: A rehabilitative center or house in which juveniles are helped to readjust to the outside world after incarceration.

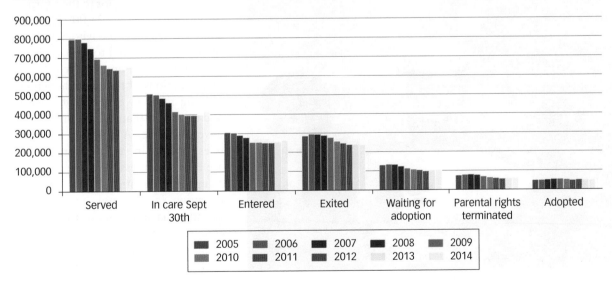

| FIGURE 13.2 | Trends in Foster Care and Adoption, 2005–2014

2005 2006 2007 2008 2009
2010 2011 2012 2013 2014

Source: U.S. Department of Health and Human Services, Administration for Children and Families. (2015). *Trends in Foster Care and Adoption.* Retrieved from http://www.acf.hhs.gov/sites/default/files/cb/trends_fostercare_adoption2014.pdf

INSTITUTIONAL CORRECTIONS

The most restrictive disposition that a juvenile can receive is placement in an institution or another residential setting. These placements mean a juvenile has lost the freedom to live in his or her community. Juveniles have been subjected to institutional settings since long before the official start of the juvenile court (in 1899). While these early placements were often abusive and harmful to juveniles, the juvenile facilities that have replaced them have their share of problems, too. While there are many criticisms that we will discuss, the two most general are the lack of systematic treatment available for juveniles in the institutional setting and the lack of evidence that the institutional setting rehabilitates juveniles or, in the end, keeps communities safe.[24]

Detention Facilities: Preadjudication

Detention facilities, also known as juvenile hall, are centers in which juveniles are housed while awaiting their adjudication hearing or, in some instances, their disposition hearing. Not all juveniles are detained prior to their hearings (remember some are sent home to their families to await their hearings and others are sent to other places, such as foster homes). Those who are deemed harmful to themselves or their community can be put in "protective custody," though, and these juveniles are most likely to end up in a detention facility. While this suggests that only the most serious offenders will be detained prior to their hearings, data suggest this is not the case. Fewer than 40% of those detained are put in custody for what most would consider to be "serious" delinquency (offenses involving the harm or threat of harm of other persons).[25] In fact, about 4% of detention cases are status offenses, even though, according to the Juvenile Justice and Delinquency Prevention Act of 1974, status offenders are prohibited from being held in detention. However, as the vignette at the beginning of this chapter shows, there are ways to get around holding youth for behaviors that are considered status offenses. In the case of Rachel, her "status offense" of being with her boyfriend became a delinquent offense when it was added to her probation conditions. Technically, she was detained for violating her probation, not missing her curfew or seeing her boyfriend.

●●●

Detention facilities: Centers in which juveniles are housed while awaiting their adjudication hearing, or in some instances their disposition hearing.

AP Photo/The Post-Crescent, WM. Glasheen

Youth can be detained prior to the adjudication hearing if it is determined they may be a danger to themselves or the community. What does detention mean for the daily experiences of youth, most specifically their education?

Detention facilities are primarily used to house juveniles prior to their formal disposition—roughly 25,000 juveniles a day are held.[26] Those who have been sentenced are moved to various facilities designed to house juveniles for longer periods of time and, hopefully, offering more in the way of services and treatment than detention facilities have available. A majority of juveniles housed in a detention facility are housed for less than one month.[27] Many large counties have at least one detention facility, and some smaller counties have facilities, too. Those counties that do not have their own facilities contract out with regional centers.

Just as with all parts of the juvenile justice system, the experience of juvenile detention varies by jurisdiction.

There are no strict standards that guide how a detention facility is used or what the experiences are in that facility. This means that one of the elements that guides the experience that a juvenile will have at this stage in the process is the jurisdiction that the juvenile is petitioned and adjudicated in.[28]

Research on preadjudication detention shows that one of the most pressing issues with this stage is the level of resources available and overcrowding that often exists in these facilities. Overcrowding leads to a variety of problems for both staff and juvenile detainees—it increases stress, anger, and hostility and leads to a greater likelihood of violence and escapes. It causes juveniles to feel less safe in the detention setting, and staff to focus their efforts on control and confinement. Ironically, lack of resources may also increase overcrowding at this stage. Lack of alternative placements in such facilities as drug treatment centers means that some juveniles end up placed in detention because it is the only available alternative even though it is not the placement the intake officer wants to make.[29] In addition, being detained preadjudication has a significant impact on the later stages in the juvenile justice process—youth who are detained preadjudication are treated more harshly in these later stages (even when controlling for severity of offense).[30]

••• on the MEDIA

They Call Us Monsters

The shifting philosophies about how adults should define and punish youth misbehavior relies on conceptualizations about who we think they are (remember Chapter 1 and 2's discussion of these changing social constructions of youth over the course of history?). A documentary by Ben Lear, *They Call Us Monsters* (2016), explores the stories of three boys between the ages of 14 and 16, Antonio, Juan, and Jared, who have been sentenced to adult prison for potentially all of their lives.[31] According to Lear, the purpose of the movie is to give these kids a place to tell their unique story, one of having committed horrible crimes and now living under a sentence that means they may never leave prison. But during the documentary, Lear not only asks the boys to tell their story of how they got to this place in their lives, he explores that complicated place where children have committed acts that society finds unforgivable. And he asks many questions that we are asking in this book: Can kids always be redeemed? When has a child gone too far? What do we achieve by locking up children forever? What about the victims and their families? Who should be in charge of navigating the answers to these questions? And does it say something about U.S. society that we are one of the few countries in which juveniles can be sentenced to life in prison?

DISCUSSION QUESTION

1. The Supreme Court has concluded that juveniles are fundamentally different from adults and that there are several stages in the justice process in which their age and individual characteristics must be taken into consideration. But while the Supreme Court has determined that juveniles must be considered on an individual basis, the court has not given guidelines as to what should be considered. What do you think should be considered while making the determination to try someone as an adult? Explain what the individual characteristics would have to be for a juvenile to be kept in the juvenile system. What would the characteristics have to be for the juvenile to be tried in the adult system and potentially receive a sentence of life without parole?

Source: Maleszka, J. (2016). "They call us monsters": A powerful new documentary on juveniles tried as adults. *Mass Appeal.* Retrieved from http://massappeal.com/they-call-us-monsters-documentary-ben-lear-interview/

Juvenile Correctional Institutions: Postadjudication

Juvenile **correctional institutions**, also known as training schools and reformatories, are the most popular institutional (residential) facilities in use for the juvenile justice system. The facilities can be categorized in several ways: secure versus open, and public versus private, facilities.[32] *Secure facilities* are the most restrictive of the facilities. They have locked doors, fencing and high walls, surveillance devices, and guards to monitor the youth. The most restrictive and harsh of these facilities look remarkably like adult prisons, and other than some requirements including access to schooling, juveniles have similar experiences in these facilities. Other facilities, while secure, may more likely resemble a cottage system—they are still secure facilities, but there is more emphasis on treatment and less on the harshness of punishment. An *open facility* is one in which security is based on staff involvement. Doors are often not locked, and there is no perimeter fencing or walls. Many of the farms and camps, and some of the private facilities, are run as open facilities. In addition to a facility being secure or open, it is publicly or privately run. *Public facilities* are run by the state, mostly likely at the county or regional level, although many states run facilities that often house serious offenders. Public facilities are more likely than private facilities to house serious offenders.[33] *Private facilities* are often smaller, and because they are privately run they have a bit more freedom to choose who is housed in them. While there is a common misconception that private facilities are better managed and safer than public facilities, this is actually not the case.[34] While there are many different types of institutional facilities (boot camps, wilderness programs, secure correctional facilities), the largest group (40%) of juveniles are confined in secure, long-term facilities.[35]

The United States relies heavily on incarceration of youth as a response to juvenile delinquency. While probation is the strongest response, more than 70,000 youth were in residential placement in the year 2010, although this was down from more than 107,000 in 1999.[36] In fact, the United States has the highest incarceration rate of any nation (336 out of every 100,000 juveniles in 2008—the next highest country was South Africa, with 69 out of 100,000 juveniles; see Figure 13.3).

• • •

Correctional institution: An institution, also known as a training school or reformatory, that is the most popular type of residential facility in use in the juvenile justice system.

FIGURE 13.3 Youth Incarceration Rate: United States Versus Other Nations

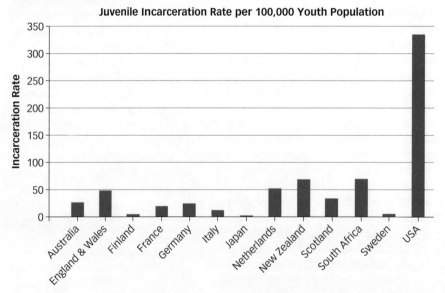

Source: Mendel, R. (2011). *No place for kids: The case for reducing juvenile incarceration.* Baltimore, MD: The Annie E. Casey Foundation. Copyright The Annie E. Casey Foundation.

Research does not show that these secure, long-term facilities (the ones that 40% of incarcerated juveniles are confined in) reduce delinquency. In fact, research suggests that there are high rates of recidivism in youth who are housed in these facilities.[37] The Annie E. Casey Foundation funded a report that highlighted what research has found about the effects of incarceration on juveniles.[38] Mendel reports what's wrong with America's juvenile correctional facilities:

1. Dangerous: America's juvenile corrections institutions subject confined youth to intolerable levels of violence, abuse, and other forms of maltreatment.[39]

2. Ineffective: The outcomes of correctional confinement are poor. Recidivism rates are almost uniformly high, and incarceration in juvenile facilities depresses youths' future success in education and employment.[40]

3. Unnecessary: A substantial percentage of youth confined in youth correctional facilities pose minimal risk to public safety.[41]

4. Obsolete: Scholars have identified a number of interventions and treatment strategies in recent years that consistently reduce recidivism among juvenile offenders. None require—and many are inconsistent with—incarceration in large correctional facilities.[42]

5. Wasteful: Most states are spending vast sums of taxpayer money and devoting the bulk of their juvenile justice budgets to correctional institutions and other facility placements when nonresidential programming options deliver equal or better results for a fraction of the cost.[43]

6. Inadequate: Despite their exorbitant daily costs, most juvenile correctional facilities are ill-prepared to address the needs of many confined youth. Often, they fail to provide even the minimum services appropriate for the care and rehabilitation of youth in confinement.[44]

●●●

Boot camp:
A correctional alternative in which juveniles participate in a program with military structure focused on physical activity and strict rules.

Boot Camps

In the 1990s, **boot camps** surged in popularity as a correctional alternative for juveniles. Boot camps were seen as a way to reduce recidivism, while also lowering costs and correctional populations.[45] While boot camp programs vary, the basic premise of military training and discipline is at the core of each program. The programs usually have a military structure: Groups of juveniles (platoons) move through the program to graduation; there is a heavy focus on physical activity, with strict rules about conduct and appearance; and infractions are dealt with immediately with physical punishments, such as push-ups that increase in severity if the juvenile continues to break the rules.[46] The first boot camps focused heavily on the military discipline; however, later camps introduced educational and treatment programs in addition to, or in place of, some of the military emphases.[47]

Once a popular alternative to detention, juvenile boot camps have declined in popularity since the 1990s. There is little research that suggests boot camps reduce recidivism when compared to other detention alternatives.

The idea has remained popular in many parts of the general public, but research shows that boot camps are not very effective at reducing recidivism, although some studies show an effect on juvenile attitudes.[48] Studies examining boot camps in California and Illinois found that there was no difference in recidivism among juveniles participating in boot camps versus other correctional programs. Some research found that boot camp participants were actually more likely to recidivate.[49] Parent suggests that one of the most likely ways to reduce recidivism in the boot camp setting would be to increase the program time for boot camps, and offer more intensive treatment as well as postrelease supervision.[50] However, these changes would increase the costs of such programs.

In the News

Hemorrhaging Florida Teen Dies in Custody Because Guards Think He Is Faking

A system that was created to keep children safe has more than once "neglected a youth to death."[51] July 10, 2011, is one example of a youth entering the juvenile justice system (this time in Florida) only to die while in custody. Eric Perez screamed in his cell, banged his head against a wall, and complained of hearing voices, but was ignored for more than six hours because the guard on duty did not believe that taking Perez to the hospital was worth the paperwork hassle. It turned out Perez was slowly dying from a cerebral hemorrhage. Perez had just recently turned 18 and was scheduled to be released.

In response to the incident, the Florida Department of Juvenile Justice made several decisions:

- The agency reiterated to all employees that 911 must be called immediately when a health situation appeared urgent

- Meetings were conducted with juvenile justice stakeholders (judges, prosecutors, public defenders, advocates, and clergy) in the area to hear concerns that could be addressed in a plan to reform the system

- Staff at the detention facility in question (West Palm Beach) received additional training on the importance of calling 911 when the situation appeared urgent

- Nine staff found to be involved in the incident were fired

The Palm Beach County grand jury investigated Eric Perez's death concluding that "no criminal charges could be filed against any of the guards because Florida law does not address a death caused by neglect in a juvenile jail."[52]

DISCUSSION QUESTIONS

1. The adaptation above describes the death of Eric Perez in the Palm Beach Regional Juvenile Detention Center. The articles show that nine people were fired, but no one was indicted for the crime of his death because "Florida law does not address a death caused by neglect in a juvenile jail." Discuss these decisions. Should a law have to detail the physical place that neglect occurred? Why might the law be interpreted this way?

2. If detention employees could be indicted, who should be held responsible? Only the medical worker? The guard(s)? The director of the detention facility? Every worker who came in contact with Perez while he was hurt? Why?

Sources: Adapted from Miller, C. M. (2012). As Florida teen lay dying, jail guards refused to call help, believed he was faking. *The Miami Herald,* October 19. Retrieved from http://www.miamiherald.com/2012/10/19/3057693/as-florida-teen-lay-dying-jail.html#storylink=cpy and Franceschina, P. (2012). Man died of brain injuries after 6 hours of neglect in juvenile jail, Palm Beach County grand jury says. *Sun Sentine,* March 9. Retrieved from http://articles.sun-sentinel.com/2012-03-09/news/fl-detention-death-grand-jury-20120309_1_grand-jury-juvenile-jail-juvenile-justice

Private Institutions

There has been a long history of the private sector offering services in the juvenile justice system. The very first juvenile institutions (the houses of refuge, described in Chapter 2) were privately run. Privatization runs the gamut from public institutions contracting with private agencies for services like food, to private rehabilitation programs, private construction for public facilities or lease-purchasing agreements between the state and private facilities, and private correctional facilities that take over full responsibility from state facilities.[53]

The current push for the privatization of correctional programs was primarily driven by an argument that corrections could be run more efficiently and cost-effectively by private organizations than the state. Pratt and Winston found that when smaller programs such as shelters, ranches, or halfway houses were privatized, there was a likelihood to save money, but the privatization of larger facilities did not seem to relieve budgetary problems.[54]

The research on the success of private institutions versus public institutions offers contradictory evidence of the success of such facilities. A large focus of this research is on quality of care, and this research shows that quality of care runs the spectrum from excellent and well above that of public facilities to care that brought about the threat of legal action because it was so inadequate.[55] In addition, while many private facilities have been shown to reduce recidivism better than their public counterparts, there is a real worry about net-widening (drawing more juveniles into these institutions than need be; see Chapter 12), especially in those facilities focused on mental health or chemical dependency.[56]

Jail/Prison

Juveniles may end up incarcerated in an adult jail or prison in several ways. One, in some states it is legal to house juveniles in adult jails while awaiting transfer or a judicial hearing. Two, in some states it is legal to house juveniles in an adult prison if it is deemed that they are too developed or sophisticated to remain with the juvenile population, even though legally they are still considered juveniles themselves. Finally, in almost all states there is a provision to waive juveniles to the adult court and consider them adults for the purposes of charging and trying them. In this instance, if juveniles are waived to the adult court for their trial, they give up their juvenile status in the eyes of the law and are housed in adult facilities.

At any one time there are more than 7,000 juveniles being held in adult prisons, and more than 2,500 of those juveniles are in for life without parole (LWOP). While there has been a push by the federal government to not house juveniles in adult facilities, this push is at odds with the "get tough" philosophy that advocates for becoming tougher and tougher on youth. This philosophy argues that younger and younger juveniles should be treated as adults, especially for person crimes, although in some states (such as California), the mere label of gang member can mean that a juvenile is waived to the adult court for any number of crimes that are not considered violent.

In 2010, the Supreme Court decided in the case *Graham v. Florida* that juveniles could no longer be sentenced to life without parole for non-homicide cases. Then in 2012, the Supreme Court decided in the joint cases, *Miller v. Alabama* and *Jackson v. Hobbs*, that states could not sentence juveniles to mandatory life without parole. Although juveniles can still be sentenced to life without parole, each case must be decided on an individual basis based on the characteristics of the juvenile defendant and the case. However, following the decision, some states chose to apply the decision retroactively (thus reviewing the cases that had already been sentenced to life without parole), while other states decided that they would not apply the decision retroactively. Finally, in 2016, the Supreme Court ruled in *Montgomery v. Louisiana* that its 2012 ruling would be retroactive, and all states needed to review all juvenile cases that had a sentence of life without parole.

These rulings are especially important because it turns out that juveniles sentenced to life without parole are similar in a variety of ways:

- 79% witnessed violence in their homes regularly

- 32% grew up in public housing

- 40% had been enrolled in special education classes

- Fewer than half were attending school at the time of their offense

- 47% were physically abused

- 80% of girls reported histories of physical abuse and 77% of girls reported histories of sexual abuse[57]

And there are racial disparities in life without parole sentences:

> While 23.2% of juvenile arrests for murder involve an African American suspected of killing a white person, 42.4% of JLWOP sentences are for an African American convicted of this crime. White juvenile offenders with African American victims are only about half as likely (3.6%) to receive a JLWOP sentence as their proportion of arrests for killing an African American (6.4%).[58]

Reentry

An irony of the juvenile justice system and juvenile corrections in particular is the lack of systematic knowledge about juvenile **reentry** into society once an offender's correctional term is completed. It is estimated that between 100,000 and 200,000 juveniles leave institutional correctional programs every year.[59] While the system holds a philosophy of treatment and rehabilitation, very little emphasis is placed on helping these juveniles once their sentences are over. Within several years after leaving correctional programs, approximately two thirds of juveniles will be rearrested and one third reincarcerated.[60]

Mears and Travis offer seven pathways to reentry.[61] These pathways are a combination of how and where a youth is incarcerated (which affects the experiences the youth has while incarcerated) and the age and status of the youth when released (is the youth still legally considered a juvenile, or is he or she now considered an adult?).

- Juveniles incarcerated in juvenile facilities as juveniles and then released while still legally defined as juveniles (under the age of 18 in most states).

- Juveniles incarcerated in juvenile facilities as juveniles and then released as young adults (age 18 or older). In many states, juveniles can be held until the age of 21.

- Juveniles incarcerated with a blended sentence in which they are considered juveniles but spend part of their incarceration in a juvenile facility and part in an adult facility, while still being considered juveniles, and then released while still legally defined as juveniles (under age 18).

Reentry:
The term used for the process of ending incarceration and reestablishing one's life after incarceration.

from the CLASSROOM
to the COMMUNITY

The Juvenile Justice Information Exchange: Stop Solitary for Kids: A National Campaign for Change

There are many problems associated with placing juveniles in adult correctional facilities. The most compelling is probably that juveniles incarcerated in adult facilities were found to be up to *seven times* more likely to commit suicide than juveniles incarcerated in a juvenile facility.[62] In addition to this alarming statistic, juveniles housed in adult facilities are at greater risk than other juvenile offenders for physical and sexual assault and psychological abuse. This victimization takes place even though, by law, juveniles are supposed to be segregated from the adult population in jails and prisons. This segregation (while necessary to keep juveniles safe) leads to more problems, isolation, and depression caused by spending so much time alone or with limited human interaction.

President Obama ordered new rules for solitary confinement for federal prisoners in January 2016, which included banning solitary confinement for juveniles in federal prisons.[63] While these changes are significant for the federal prison system, the majority of juveniles who are held in solitary confinement are at the state level, where the practice still exists. Thousands of juveniles each year (one estimate is more than 100,000 juveniles) are placed in solitary confinement (also known as seclusion, isolation, or segregation) for a variety of reasons, ranging from safety issues if the juveniles are being housed in adult prison, to mental health reasons if they are deemed a risk to themselves or others, or as punishment for bad behavior. Research has found that juveniles *and* adults who are placed in solitary confinement are more likely to become depressed, anxious, and suicidal over time. Given

the vulnerabilities of youth, the added strain of solitary confinement can be particularly harmful.

According to the Juvenile Justice Information Exchange "a number of national organizations, including the Center for Children's Law and Policy, the Center for Juvenile Justice Reform, the Council of Juvenile Correctional Administrators and the Justice Policy Institute are engaged in developing a strategy to bring others to the table on this critical issue."[64]

It is encouraging that the federal government has so drastically changed its solitary confinement policy and that so many organizations are focused on seeing many of these changes implemented for juveniles at the state level.

DISCUSSION QUESTION

1. As part of a class assignment at George State University, students were challenged to spend 24 hours in an 8′ by 8′ box, to simulate the experience of solitary confinement. What other assignments could help people understand the psychological harms that accompany solitary confinement? Do you think you could spend 24 hours in an 8′ by 8′ box, if you knew you were getting out the next day? What if you had to spend 7 days? 60? 365?

Sources: Adapted from JJIE. (2016). *Locked in the Box: Student Assignment—24 Hours in Solitary*. Retrieved from http://jjie.org/locked-in-the-box-student-assignment-24-hours-in-solitary/251186/; Lutz, J. (2016). *Stop Solitary for Kids: A National Campaign for Change*. The Juvenile Justice Information Exchange. Retrieved from http://jjie.org/stop-solitary-for-kids-a-national-campaign-for-change/163440/

- Juveniles incarcerated with a blended sentence, spending part of their incarceration in a juvenile facility and part in an adult facility, but released as young adults (age 18 or older).

- Juveniles waived to the adult system, tried in the adult court, incarcerated in an adult prison, and then released while still a juvenile (under the age of 18).

- Juveniles waived to the adult system, tried in adult court, incarcerated in adult prison, and then released as an adult (age 18 or older).

©STEPHEN SHAVER /UPI /Newscom

Juveniles who have an opportunity for aftercare services postincarceration are much better prepared to reenter society. However, there is little systematic regulation of or policy for services across states.

- Young adults incarcerated in adult facilities, and released. While this group is not part of the juvenile population, many are incarcerated just into young adulthood and are released while still young adults, and thus they face many of the same reentry challenges as those who enter the system under the age of 18.

The facility juveniles are housed in and the age at which they are released have an impact on their likely success once they have returned to their community. Many juveniles have little in the way of support or resources when they leave the correctional facility and, depending on the facility they were housed in, received little in the way of treatment or preparation for their life after incarceration.[65] Many have weak family support. Those under 18 may end up in a foster home or group home if their family is not a viable option, but those over 18 do not even have this option unless it is part of their conditions of release.

Most end their sentences wanting to succeed when they leave their correction facility. For this reason, many spend the last part of their sentences planning their lives on the outside, reaching out to friends, finding places to live, and hoping to find jobs or go to school.[66] But Inderbitzin documents how difficult, even with planning and hope for a new future, it can be for juveniles to "reenter" their communities and have a real chance at a life without worry of reincarceration:

As much as the emerging adults from the cottage may have looked forward to getting out of the institution, their own observations and experiences suggested that some of their number would become dependent on the structure that is so much a part of being incarcerated. A clear example was provided when I spoke to Alex a few weeks after his release back into the community. In a telephone conversation, he said that he was finding life "on the outs" extremely difficult as he fought continuously with his live-in girlfriend and was repeatedly turned down for even low-skill jobs. In voicing his frustration, Alex added that maybe he belonged in jail, saying, "maybe I was more at peace when I was locked up." When reminded of how much he had hated the institution and complained about it when he was there, he laughed sheepishly and agreed, but it seemed that he was already forgetting what life in the institution had been like. . . .

[T]he five young men in this study—Alex, Tony, Marco, Kody, and T.J.—were clearly written off by their families, their communities, and by the juvenile justice system charged with raising them into emerging adulthood. The individuals in this study walked out of the juvenile institution full of excitement, hope, trepidation, and fear, and within a matter of months, each was overcome by the frustration of trying to find their way in a world that made no place for them. The potential in each of them withered during their time in the institution, and they keenly felt the lack of opportunities upon their release. These emerging adults who had survived difficult childhoods and endured the pains of imprisonment (Inderbitzin, 2006; Sykes, 1958) with admirable resilience during their adolescence faced the biggest challenge of their young lives when they left the institution. . . .

In watching the five individuals of this study make the transition from the institution to their first months back in the community, it became clear that they were truly lost when left on their own and expected to behave as responsible adults. As representatives of a much larger group of incarcerated adolescents, their experiences suggest that emerging adults leaving juvenile correctional facilities will have a particularly hard time changing the trajectories of their lives. Equipped with few resources, they face enormous challenges and the highest stakes of their young lives: Mistakes made at this precarious juncture will have effects long into adulthood.[67]

CORRECTIONS AND GENDER, RACE, UNDOCUMENTED YOUTH, AND LGBTQ INTERSECTIONS

This book has documented the diversity of experiences juveniles face based on their race, class, gender, and sexual orientation. These diverse experiences have led us to the final stage of the juvenile justice system—corrections. We have seen that boys and girls may have different pathways to their delinquency, that society has different expectations and different assumptions about youth of color than white youth, and that this has an impact on how we label their behavior—that our institutions, education, family, and law, can serve as systems of social control that treat different groups unequally. And, in Chapter 12, we documented the unequal treatment in the processes of the juvenile justice system based on race and ethnicity, class, and gender. Those unequal processes bring us to the stage of corrections, where Schaffner argues several related trends are emerging:

> First, a growing, disproportionate representation of a minority population of African American, Latino/Chicano, Native American, and Asian/Pacific Islander children became apparent in the juvenile court system. Second, an influx of girls into the legal system required the delivery of some kind of gender-responsive programming. Third, a slow but increasing necessity for attending to the urgent and unmet needs of GLBTQ youth in the juvenile court system became apparent.[68]

Sedlak and Bruce report that 85% of juveniles in residential placement are male, which means that the custody rate for boys is much higher than that for girls (370 males per 100,000 population, 70 females per 100,000 population).[69] White youth are the largest percentage of the residential population (35%) with black juveniles a close second at 32%. Twenty-four percent of the population is Latino youth, while 3% are either American Indian/Alaska Native, Asian, or Native Hawaiian/Other Pacific Islander. Finally, 6% of the residential population reports that they are multiracial. However, while white juveniles make up the largest overall percentage, given their numbers in the population, they make up the smallest rate of youth housed in a correctional facility per 100,000 youth in the general population (this statistic takes into account the relative number of youth in any given racial category; see Figure 13.4).

Corrections and Gender

Just as the first theories of delinquency and criminal behavior ignored the experiences of women and girls, concentrating, instead, on explaining the behaviors of men and boys, so does most of the research on corrections ignore the experiences of incarcerated women and girls. In addition, much of the research we do have in this area focuses on women in prison, not girls in juvenile correctional facilities. The first studies were comparative in

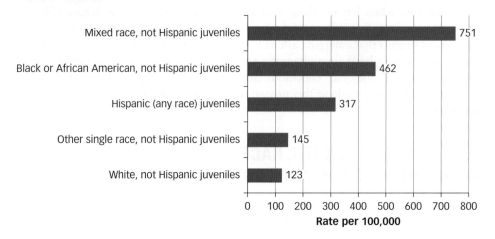

FIGURE 13.4 Rate of Juveniles in Residential Placement by Race/Ethnicity

nature, focusing on how women versus men adapted to life in prison, and how men and women's prisons differed in resources and programming.[70]

One of the most compelling themes about the experience of girls in correctional facilities was how much of their experience was dependent upon their ability to successfully "do gender."[71] Girls were characterized according to their physical characteristics and attractiveness, and those who were seen as overly sexual, aggressive, or incorrigible were more likely to be punished.[72] "Girls' court files contain an inordinate amount of gendered and sexualized references ('she is a very loud' or 'big' or 'defiant' girl, or 'she has many sexual partners')."[73] This extended to other experiences in correctional facilities, including vaginal exams to determine whether a girl had been sexually active, and the control of such resources as sanitary napkins, which in some facilities were counted when handed out and then counted again when handed back soiled.[74]

Dobash, Dobash, and Gutteridge found that these differences in gender also extended to how often men and women were punished for similar offenses while in correctional facilities.[75] Women were punished more often than men for breaking prison rules and regulations. It was not that women engaged in more rule-breaking behavior or that their behavior was more severe; it appeared to be a greater willingness for those in authority to write up women for behavior that was tolerated in male correctional facilities.

Corrections and Race

As we previously mentioned, the federal government has mandated that state juvenile justice systems address disproportionate minority confinement, showing that not only are they aware (by studying the problem), but they have policies in place to address the problem. Even with this mandate, research shows us that youth of color are still more likely to be locked up than white youth (see Table 13.1 for state-by-state differences). In fact, several studies have shown that the rate of minority youth confinement has been increasing over time.[76] Controlling for type of offense, youth of color are more likely to be transferred to adult court than white youth; this means that youth of color are also disproportionately housed in adult prisons. Black youth are 9 times more likely than white youth to be incarcerated in an adult prison. Latino youth are 1.4 times more likely to be incarcerated in adult prison than white youth, and American Indian and Alaska Native youth are 1.84 times more likely to be incarcerated in adult prison than white youth.[77]

TABLE 13.1 Residential Custody Rates by State and Race/Ethnicity, 2013

STATE OF OFFENSE	TOTAL	WHITE	MINORITY	BLACK	HISPANIC	AMERICAN INDIAN	ASIAN
U.S. total	173	100	268	464	173	334	28
Alabama	184	110	304	356	80	*80	*41
Alaska	241	150	361	413	228	414	*82
Arizona	122	94	144	203	123	200	*27
Arkansas	215	100	434	588	215	*104	*51
California	107	91	242	748	227	180	20
Colorado	107	136	200	223	106	251	61
Connecticut	74	17	172	306	122	*0	*17
Delaware	178	65	314	504	*26	*0	*0
District of Columbia	560	*144	638	671	406	*0	*0
Florida	152	100	100	366	81	700	33
Georgia	150	67	247	321	80	*121	*8
Hawaii	60	*12	71	*77	*40	*0	32
Idaho	238	217	308	628	278	578	*0
Illinois	134	65	218	388	116	628	*10
Indiana	219	164	306	545	146	*140	*62
Iowa	227	160	557	273	273	1,203	*78
Kansas	278	178	534	1,079	329	411	*07
Kentucky	170	122	416	405	152	*0	*41
Louisiana	180	65	314	362	60	*84	*40
Maine	130	106	307	825	*107	*528	*0
Maryland	127	43	206	280	84	*0	*8
Massachusetts	60	25	143	206	157	*0	*7
Michigan	183	24	404	550	114	105	*20
Minnesota	166	80	400	706	134	1,171	02

(Continued)

TABLE 13.1 (Continued)

STATE OF OFFENSE	TOTAL	WHITE	MINORITY	BLACK	HISPANIC	AMERICAN INDIAN	ASIAN
Mississippi	74	23	120	142	*0	*0	*0
Missouri	121	128	402	510	140	*26	*0
Montana	151	116	316	*681	234	312	*0
Nebraska	204	116	463	837	232	254	*62
Nevada	201	148	238	507	170	306	50
New Hampshire	68	20	302	1,052	285	*0	*0
New Jersey	95	17	187	450	87	*0	*0
New Mexico	179	132	197	422	206	85	*0
New York	116	58	180	344	97	*93	14
North Carolina	70	29	125	166	60	*82	*13
North Dakota	253	160	715	727	*323	837	*0
Ohio	188	100	447	550	140	*100	*12
Oklahoma	125	75	252	458	25	119	*0
Oregon	281	229	390	913	338	934	118
Pennsylvania	282	90	556	856	318	*0	35
Rhode Island	158	67	342	721	230	*0	*0
South Carolina	150	88	250	218	302	830	*88
South Dakota	378	211	936	713	204	1,264	*193
Tennessee	90	45	220	274	61	*347	*23
Texas	161	100	103	434	145	*33	14
Utah	160	84	427	2,162	204	417	*72
Vermont	45	38	*135	*195	*0	*1,010	*0
Virginia	188	93	329	506	114	*0	*16
Washington	144	106	216	427	163	422	47
West Virginia	204	256	750	712	*92	*1,017	*0
Wisconsin	158	50	461	946	115	434	*17
Wyoming	279	225	506	*276	425	1,113	*0

Source: OJJDP. (2015). *Statistical Briefing Book.* Retrieved from http://www.ojjdp.gov/ojstatbb/corrections/qa08203.asp?qaDate=2013

Notes: The information in this table is based on the state where the offense was committed. However, the state of offense is not always reported. Youth for whom state of offense was unknown are included in U.S. totals (2,648 in 2013). These instances are not evenly distributed across states.

U.S. total includes a small number of offenders (5) who committed their offense in a U.S. Territory, but excludes youth in tribal facilities.

The residential placement rate is the number of juvenile offenders in residential placement on October 23, 2013, per 100,000 juveniles age 10 through the upper age of original juvenile court jurisdiction in each state.

Minorities include blacks, Hispanics, American Indians/Alaskan Natives, Asians/Pacific Islanders, and those identified as other race.

While legal variables (such as severity of offense) account for much of the differences in offending, there is still ample evidence that not all of the difference can be attributed to a greater likelihood of youth of color to engage in bad behavior.[78] In addition to the likelihood of a direct effect of race on correctional outcomes, there appears to be a contextual effect through geography. Urban courts are more formal and so are more likely to sentence juveniles, in general, severely, but because youth of color are more likely to live in urban settings than white youth, this general likelihood to sentence severely has a disproportionate impact on those youth of color.[79]

When examining institutional placements, studies have found that in 41 of 42 states examined youth of color were overrepresented in secure detention facilities, and in the 13 states that examined placements after adjudication youth of color were disproportionately confined.[80] And Poe-Yamagata and Jones found that youth of color were more likely to be given out-of-home placements and serve longer sentences than white youth adjudicated guilty of similar offenses.[81]

Corrections and Undocumented Youth

One area that has a significant impact on racial and ethnic experiences in the juvenile justice system is that of undocumented youth who find themselves in the juvenile justice system. It is estimated that about 1,000 juveniles are apprehended by Immigration and Customs Enforcement (ICE). While the official message from the federal government is that ICE should focus its efforts on those engaging in violent crime, many of these juveniles end up in ICE custody after coming in contact with the juvenile justice system for such status offenses as underage drinking and truancy.[82]

There are several ways that the juvenile justice system and ICE work together to capture youth. There are formal programs such as Secure Communities, in which ICE can receive automatic record checks. But, informally, information is also passed on. In some jurisdictions ICE works directly with probation officers. Probation officers call ICE officers when they come in contact with someone they believe is undocumented, even though in these instances it often means that probation officers are sharing private information that should require the child's or parent's consent to divulge.

If it is determined by ICE that a juvenile in question is undocumented, then two procedures are immediately started: (1) The juvenile is placed in an immigration detention facility, and (2) removal proceedings are initiated. Unlike those in the juvenile justice system, juveniles in ICE custody have no right to have an attorney appointed for them during these removal proceedings. If they can afford their own attorney, they may have representation.[83] Because there is usually lack of representation at these crucial hearings, there is not much accountability if legal violations occur.[84] In

Youth of color are more likely to be held in juvenile and adult facilities.

Immigration and Customs Enforcement, working with police and the juvenile justice system, have a significant impact on the experiences of youth suspected to be undocumented. Should there be stronger federal and state policies concerning the relationship that ICE can have with the juvenile justice system? What should this policy be?

addition, immigration detention has no set release.

This focus on youth and non-violent youth, at that, is considered by many to be a misuse of scarce resources because all it does is increase the numbers of "noncriminal aliens" in custody. Frankel wonders whether "it is worth considering whether detaining youth who pose no threat to the community is worth the cost—both in terms of the monetary cost and in terms of the chilling effect that such policies have on victims reporting crimes and the impact on families."[85]

We wonder, beyond a question of resources and due process (which Frankel argues well), what are the implications of the juvenile justice system—a system with a philosophy to help juveniles, to offer them rehabilitation and treatment, and to be working with a government agency that does not protect due process and therefore cannot be working "in best interest of the child"?

Corrections and LGBTQ Youth

There is almost no research directed specifically at the experiences of lesbian, gay, bisexual, transgender, and queer (LGBTQ) youth in the juvenile justice system. As we have seen in other chapters, LGBTQ youth experience higher levels of bullying than other youth, and this bullying often leads to survival strategies that schools, police, and the courts deem delinquent (for example, running away). We know that LGBTQ youth end up in correctional facilities then, but policies and research do not systematically acknowledge this reality. An exception in the research is Schaffner who, in examining the experiences of girls in the juvenile justice system, acknowledges the fact that, given the strong focus on female sexuality in the juvenile justice system, the system implicitly assumes a heterosexual bias:

> In another controversial policy arena, gender-specific proponents consider it crucial to protect girls from boys. Unfortunately, this approach shores up the false assumption that all girls are heterosexual. For example the training module on safety suggests to juvenile justice personnel that "rerouting girls so they do not have to walk by the boys' facilities may reduce. . . excessive primping. . . . [Girls] will feel emotionally safer if [their] spaces are free from the demands for attention from adolescent males." Although these kinds of directives appear, at first glance, benign and even helpful, the underlying message about girls' beauty habits, girls' safety with boys, and their sexual attraction to adolescent males does the cultural work of constructing heterosexuality and femininity as the norm. Boys may be dangerous for all girls, but not all girls engage in "excessive primping" for boys. Furthermore, the solution of rerouting girls instead of challenging boys' behavior contributes to the problem in the first place.[86]

A Focus on Research

Sharma's Contesting Institutional Discourse to Create New Possibilities for Understanding Lived Experience: Life-Stories of Young Women in Detention, Rehabilitation, and Education

Sharma explored the stories of girls, aged 15–19, who were housed in a private detention facility.[87] Using autobiographies (and self-portraits drawn in oil and watercolor) written in an English composition course taught in the detention facility, Sharma examined the difference between the institutional story, the instructor story, and autobiographical stories of the girls residing at the facility.

Sharma found that the institution often constructed an identity for the girls that the girls disagreed with. For example, homosexuality is not an acceptable identity according to the detention facility; it is considered deviant. Because of this, girls who identify as lesbian in the facility have a certain "story" according to the institution:

Retrieved from the facility's records on March 27, 2007:

Chantia: Age 17, female African American, fourth placement in corrections, lived with foster parents before living on the run. Victim of sexual abuse, in group counseling to be able to speak about herself so that therapy can resume. Refuses interaction with male staff and has requested isolation from other students. School record shows habitual substance abuse and truancy. Sexual predator who refuses to take responsibility for her actions.[88]

Chantia knows how the staff at the institution have characterized her, she knows that her sexual orientation is considered a sexual disorder, and even though she is aware of the stigma at the facility she is open about her sexual choices and talks about being a lesbian. She is aware that the staff members have told the other girls that they need to stay away from her because she is considered a predator. She chooses to spend time in the isolation room rather than sit with the other girls. She responds to the institutional story of herself by saying that she is not a predator, but a proud African American lesbian. In other words, she refuses to accept the normative definition that the institution has tried to place on her.

Sharma concludes:

Life histories and life stories need to be told—what happens to young women in detention needs to be brought into the public space that is education. Young women in detention are capable of powerful refusals . . . that appear to permit them to reclaim agency, however temporally, in a system that consistently deprives them of autonomy and the right to privacy. In disrupting the categories used to define and discriminate, students are not denying identity per se; rather, they are questioning the terms on which identity has been coded and inscribed for young women in detention as a priori narrative. Opening ways to question . . . the construction of identity . . . are necessary conversations to provide the means to construct the terms by which identity is both represented and subverted.[89]

DISCUSSION QUESTION

1. The ability to construct an identity for oneself or others is a powerful thing. To put this into context, think about your own life and the identity you have for yourself. Does this identity come into conflict with others' identity for you? Your family or friends? Work? School? How do you negotiate how you define yourself with how some of these others do? Are there consequences for these differing definitions?

Source: Sharma, S. (2010). Contesting institutional discourse to create new possibilities for understanding lived experience: Life-stories of young women in detention, rehabilitation, and education. *Race Ethnicity and Education, 13*(3), 327–347.

Community groups such as the National Center for Lesbian Rights (NCLR) agree that there is little systematic focus on supporting LGBTQ juveniles while in custody. Few facilities have formal policies prohibiting discrimination based on sexual orientation or gender identity.[90] In addition, there is little training provided to staff for how to support LGBTQ youth.[91] This lack of awareness for LGBTQ juveniles is echoed by an e-mail that Schaffner received concerning the lack of awareness for LGBTQ youth in policy and program materials:

> What if I told you that there is a little boy (age 15) who was born female and has acted and been treated as a little boy and lived and gone to school as a little boy since the age of three? Further, what if I told you that HE was caught up in the juvenile justice system and was being warehoused in the female section of the Juvenile Detention Center, complete with bras, panties, and female pronouns? How would he fit into your Gender Specific Resource Manual? . . . It appears that the facility and the people working there (I have not been allowed to go talk to them) have no gender skills that allow them to help him to become strong and happy. They cannot even find it in their hearts to use the appropriate pronouns. . . . It may be a new concept to some people, but little girls who want to be boys cannot be cured nor do they need to be. They need to be nurtured and loved just exactly like your manual suggests for "regular girls."[92]

SUMMARY

In our opinion there are two important points to take away from this examination of juvenile corrections. The first is that the United States puts a lot of time, effort, and resources (even though we note that we still have more juveniles in the system that our resources can handle) into trying to deter juveniles from crime. And yet, given our focus on correctional methods to address juvenile misbehavior, there is little concrete support that most of these methods successfully reduce recidivism, and in several instances there are indications that our correctional methods may actually be harming youth.

Second, while there has been an acknowledgment of discriminatory experiences in the correctional stage based on race, class, gender, and sexual orientation, there is still no easy answer for what research is telling us about the problem of unequal treatment. We have focused most of our public policy attention on

disproportionate minority contact, and yet we still see that youth of color are more likely to be confined and more harshly confined than their white counterparts. There is no systematic effort from the federal government on down to address the unequal treatment based on gender and sexual orientation (although at least there are some data to be able to build a case); class differences are so little understood we do not even have systematic data to examine the issue.

Finally, while the correctional stage in the juvenile justice system is legally compelled to offer treatment in the form of educational opportunities and safety from harm (for example, in the form of segregating adults and juveniles who are housed in the same facility), it is important to note that the correctional stage does not systematically hold to the philosophy of treatment that is supposed to be central to the juvenile justice system.

EYE ON DIVERSITY EXERCISE: A LOOK AT JUVENILE INSTITUTIONS AND POLICIES

This chapter has examined the end stages of the juvenile justice system and the sometimes unequal treatment that exists in some of these stages. One of the ways to address issues of discrimination is to have specific policies in place to shape how institutions and staff in those institutions behave.

1. Identify the nearest juvenile detention center, juvenile correctional facility, and juvenile treatment center in your area.

2. Research these facilities online. What can you find out about these facilities from their online presence? Do they outline their policies for keeping juveniles safe while in their custody? What is their definition of safe?

3. Determine whether or not these facilities have policies concerning discrimination/disproportionality based on race/ethnicity, gender, and sexual orientation. You may have to contact these facilities for this information if it does not exist on their website.

4. How easy or hard was it to get this information? Did the facilities direct you to someone who had responsibility for these issues, or did you talk to someone more general?

5. Critique the facilities' policies. Do they have policies for all three: race/ethnicity, gender, and sexual orientation? Do they have one policy that they say covers all types of discrimination/disproportionality?

DISCUSSION QUESTIONS

1. Explain community corrections. According to research, which community correction alternatives are most successful? Which are least successful? Why?

2. Explain institutional corrections. According to research, which institutional correction alternatives are most successful? Which are least successful? Why?

3. How are foster homes/group homes/halfway houses used at the correctional stage?

4. Discuss the impact of race/ethnicity on the experiences of juveniles in the corrections stage.

5. How does gender impact the experiences of juveniles in correctional facilities?

6. Explain the experience of LGBTQ youth in correctional facilities.

KEY TERMS

Boot camp 373

Community service restitution 366

Correctional institution 372

Detention facilities 370

Electronic monitoring 368

Foster home 368

Group home 368

Halfway house 368

Home confinement 368

Monetary restitution 366

Reentry 376

Restitution 366

Victim service restitution 366

1. True

2. False

3. True

4. True

5. True

6. False

7. True

8. True

9. False

STUDENT STUDY SITE

$SAGE edge™

edge.sagepub.com/bates2e

Sharpen your skills with SAGE edge!

SAGE edge for students provides a personalized approach to help you accomplish your coursework goals in an easy-to-use learning environment. You'll find action plans, mobile-friendly eFlashcards, and quizzes, as well as videos, web resources, and links to SAGE journal articles to support and expand on the concepts presented in this chapter. Check out the website for original videos of former offenders discussing their experiences as juveniles.

Christian Science Monitor/Getty Images

PREVENTATIVE, REHABILITATIVE, AND RESTORATIVE APPROACHES TO DELINQUENCY

After reading this chapter, you should be able to

- Describe examples of delinquency prevention methods and programs

- Explain how specific types of youth rehabilitation programs operate

- Discuss the most popular forms of restorative justice used with young people

- Analyze race, class, and gender concerns related to prevention, rehabilitation, and restoration

- List the components of a comprehensive juvenile delinquency program

- Outline possible future directions in preventative, rehabilitative, and restorative justice approaches to youth and delinquency

Chantal is a recent university graduate who has just earned her bachelor's degree in a general social science program. She graduated with honors and wrote her thesis on racial, gender, and class inequities in the juvenile justice system in her home state of Louisiana. Now that she has left college, she is faced with the issue of what to do next. Chantal knows that she would like to make a positive impact on the problems that she studied, but feels overwhelmed and does not know what can be done or what is being done to change the status quo.

So, Chantal decides to go back to her university to talk to the juvenile delinquency experts on campus and ask for some guidance. She imagines they might give her a few books to read or websites to check out. To her surprise, they explain to her that in spite of the get-tough-on-crime stance that the federal, state, and local governments took with respect to juvenile delinquency in recent decades, at the same time there have been many people both inside and outside of juvenile justice systems attempting to help young people change their lives around. Programs to prevent delinquency, rehabilitate youths who have already engaged in delinquency, and restore youths' relationships with others (and themselves) are common. They are based on a number of different theories and range from very basic programs focused on the individual to complicated, multistage models of reform that involve many experts, researchers, and practitioners from multiple fields. Chantal's former professors note that the Supreme Court decisions of the 2000s have been encouraging people who previously only conceived of adolescents as "mini adults" to embrace the idea that teens are young people in the midst of their development as human beings. The idea that juveniles are capable of change, if encouraged and given the proper resources and support, is becoming part of popular and professional considerations of delinquency once again. In addition, they tell her that some advocates of juvenile justice support large overarching changes to the laws and juvenile justice practices to address the disproportionately negative treatment of marginalized youth in the system and are actively lobbying for them, and that Louisiana is actually one of the states making great strides in that regard.

Chantal leaves her meeting with her professors feeling encouraged. She still needs to spend some time by herself thinking about her personal goals, but she knows that she has a lot of options to consider, such as applying to a graduate school program in criminology, sociology, social work, or criminal justice; getting a job in the system as a probation officer or in another position to get some on-the-ground experience; or working for a nonprofit organization focused on juvenile justice reform or resources for youth. All of these different paths, and many others, could allow her to help influence the changes that she sees as necessary.

The experience that Chantal had following her undergraduate thesis is typical of a student who has spent any extended amount of time studying the realities of juvenile delinquency and juvenile justice. There may be moments when you read about research findings and data on the topic and are left feeling depressed, either because you are concerned about the conditions related to the production of delinquency and the treatment of youth or because you simply are worried about whether society as a whole is doing anything effective to address the problem of delinquency. We have attempted to spare you that experience of wondering if anything positive or innovative is being done by highlighting issues of prevention, rehabilitation, and/or restorative justice throughout each chapter of the book thus far. We have done this by pointing out specific examples of advocacy and reform in our boxes titled "From the Classroom to the Community," in discussions about the application of some of the delinquency theories, and in additional discussions about areas that have a great deal of literature on preventative or rehabilitative efforts that couldn't possibly be covered in detail in this one chapter, such as drug use and gang activity. So, if you have been reading through the book chronologically, you are already familiar with not only the philosophy of rehabilitation, prevention, and restoration, but also several examples about how those philosophies have been put into practice.

In this last chapter, we will focus on these general approaches to delinquency as a means of organizing our consideration of what is being done besides punishing youth for the sake of retribution or incapacitation goals. Because it is impossible to include a discussion of every sort of program or policy that has been implemented in the name of prevention and rehabilitation, we have chosen to include a sample of programs and approaches that have been recently evaluated either as models for others to emulate or as highly promising approaches. In addition, we will focus a good deal of our chapter on restorative justice practices in an effort to shed light on these innovative responses to juvenile delinquency that don't garner much mainstream attention in the United States. Efforts to find programs and policies that reduce delinquency by helping strengthen youth and communities are important ones. A great deal of research demonstrates that when programs or practices focus only upon punishment through means such as boot camps or basic detention, they are generally not successful in helping young people desist from delinquency, and they actually waste money.[1] As you will see later in the chapter, the development of comprehensive programs that attempt to address multiple factors, including laws and institutional practices that funnel the most vulnerable youth in our society into the juvenile justice system, are the most effective and cost-saving over the long run. We provide a detailed example of one such program, Models for Change, as a means of demonstrating the breadth of a program of its type.

It is important to note at the outset of this chapter that many of the approaches to delinquency that we have categorized as coming from either a preventative, a rehabilitative, or a restorative framework could be subsumed under more than one of those categories. For example, many programs address both prevention and rehabilitation, and many programs known primarily as oriented to restorative justice are also focused on prevention and rehabilitation.

PREVENTION

As we begin to consider some practices and programs that have proven themselves useful in preventing delinquency or stopping delinquency before it occurs, we can first stop and recall the opening scenario and Chantal's experiences. Although she was disillusioned with the juvenile justice system in her state, she was happy to learn that a wide variety of efforts were being put into juvenile delinquency prevention. Many times punishments not actually based in prevention are labeled as such, which leads to misconceptions about what prevention efforts really are. Large-scale efforts to address economic disparities, unjust laws, and the lack of resources in communities are often not labeled as juvenile delinquency efforts, but these sorts of changes are necessary first steps to support youth.

As we examine preventative efforts deemed among the most effective by experts, which include screening and early intervention practices and programs, early education and skills-based approaches, and after-care programs and mentoring, remember that their effectiveness is maximized in a society that minimizes inequities.

In the News

Attorney Dismisses Injunctions Against Two Oakland Gangs

One of the institutional changes that can be made to help prevent the quick closing off of opportunities for youth who are alleged to be associates or members of gangs is to change the laws that target them. As discussed in Chapter 9, civil gang injunctions (CGIs) work to limit the daily lives of youth and adults who are listed on them as a means of restricting their activity in what are labeled "target" or "safety" areas—areas that law enforcement deem to have a lot of gang activity. CGIs work in tandem with other laws to restrict the ability of young people to get work, housing, and employment, as well as to socialize with friends, family, and neighbors. In California, these laws are extremely common and ensure that people listed on them cannot associate with one another in public in the target area, which is typically a low-income or working class community of color. Yet, occasionally there is a shift in the tide. In Oakland

in 2015, the City Attorney, Barbara Parker, eliminated the civil gang injunctions for two gangs and stated that the Oakland Police Department was interested in other preventative measures. Community activists were pleased and noted that their attempts to get the authorities to eliminate the injunctions were successful.

DISCUSSION QUESTION

1. What are some other legal changes that could reduce the number of youths who are formally labeled as delinquents and/or criminals?

Source: Andersen, A. (2015). Attorney dismisses injunctions against two Oakland gangs. *KRON4*. Retrieved from http://kron4.com/2015/03/06/attorney-dismisses-injunctions-against-two-oakland-gangs/

Screening and Early Intervention

One approach implemented in a number of different settings, including schools, community programs, and juvenile justice settings, is the use of screening tools. Those who use this type of approach are often coming from a social-psychological or life course–based perspective on deviance; the idea is that risk factors and tendencies toward deviance can be identified by means of properly constructed screening tools and then addressed before a young person acts out in delinquency. Savignac explains that the main objectives of **risk assessment** include the following:[2]

- To produce a profile of a young person's current and past situation and measure his or her level of risk of offending or reoffending.

- To evaluate the significant relationships between the young person's risk factors and behaviors and to distinguish between those that are the most closely related to delinquency and those that seem the least influential.

- To identify the factors or people in a young person's life that are the most protective and positive in order to emphasize them in intervention efforts.

- To collect, through multiple sources, information about a young person and his or her family.

- To develop a plan based on the assessment results to meet the needs of a young person and to develop a program based on that information.

Clinicians and others who conduct risk assessments often list the following factors as ones that they believe to be the most predictive of future delinquency and antisocial behavior: a history of acting out in either antisocial or delinquent ways, such as stealing, vandalizing, or fighting; experience of abuse, neglect, and/or trauma; having antisocial or delinquent friends; and growing up in a family with involvement in criminal or delinquent activity.[3]

We can look to the categories found in the Early Assessment Risk List[4] as a typical risk assessment model. The subcategories of items it includes touch upon different factors that researchers have found can be associated with delinquency and/or antisocial behavior: family-related items (household circumstances, familial supports and stressors, parenting style, antisocial values and conduct, caregiver-daughter interaction); child-related items (developmental problems, onset of behavior difficulties, abuse/neglect/trauma, hyperactivity/impulsivity, likability, peer socialization, academic performance, neighborhood, authority contacts, antisocial attitude and behavior, emotional coping ability, and sexual development); and responsivity items (family denial of problems and need for intervention and child's unwillingness to cooperate or engage in an intervention). Risk assessment tools are utilized in a number of preventative programs among young children. According to Farrington, early invention is key to preventing children with delinquent tendencies from delving deeply into the world of delinquency.[5] **Early intervention programs** are focused on childhood and early adolescence, a period during which young people are receptive to nurturing and supportive environments.[6] Practitioners behind such efforts believe that the earlier intervention efforts are made, the more likely antisocial habits and tendencies can be eliminated due to children's impressionability.[7] The most effective early intervention programs address multiple risk factors at school, in the community, related to the child himself or herself, and related to parents.[8] Risk factors are thought to indicate the possibility of future delinquency, but practitioners acknowledge that the way these different risk factors interact is the most important, which makes it difficult to make completely accurate predictions. The more risk factors that are impacting a child, the more probable that these interactions will eventually result in delinquent

Risk assessment: The practice of using properly constructed screening tools to identify risk factors for delinquency in order to address them before a young person engages in misbehavior.

Early intervention programs: Delinquency prevention programs that are focused on the time during childhood and early adolescence when youth are receptive to nurturing and supportive environments.

behaviors.[9] Several programs have been designed to provide early intervention, and many of the most successful ones were designed by researchers addressing child well-being in general, rather than delinquency.[10]

Nurse-Family Partnerships

One type of prevention that has been garnered a great deal of support is known today as the Nurse-Family Partnership.[11] The original longitudinal study on which other programs today are based ("the Olds Model") involved nurse visits to the homes of a subset of low-income teens who became pregnant before the age of 19 and agreed to participate in the program. Nurses made monthly visits to the young mothers' homes during their pregnancies and the first two years of their children's lives. During these home visits, nurses were attempting to help the teens give birth to healthy babies by providing them with health education to help them become informed and competent parents and to assist them with long-term life planning as it related to education, work, and family issues.[12] Nurses also worked to get fathers, extended family, and friends involved in supporting the pregnancy and the early stages of the baby's life.

Follow-up studies of children born to the mothers in the Nurse-Family Partnership have been shown to be promising, particularly for girls. Nineteen years after their births, girls born in the nurse-visitation group to low-income, unmarried mothers were less likely to be involved with the juvenile justice system than girls born to similarly situated mothers who did not receive the visitations. Other outcomes included that the visitation group mothers were likely to have fewer children during their teen years than those who didn't experience nurse visitations, they were found to come from homes characterized by less neglect and abuse than the no-visitation mothers, and their families were less in need of economic assistance than those in comparison groups.[13] There are now over 200 sites in which the Nurse-Family Partnership model is being implemented both in the United States and abroad.[14]

Early Education

Preschool enrichment programs have been found to be effective means of helping children develop in a positive manner and avoid involvement in delinquency.[15] When preschool programs aimed at 3- and 4-year-olds have an element of collaboration with parents as well, they are shown to be the most effective.[16] The Perry Preschool in Ypsilanti, Michigan, is one of the most studied examples of this sort of education program. It was started in 1962 to include a randomly selected sample of low-income black youth who scored low on standardized IQ tests. The preschool provided them with opportunities for active learning, as well as monthly visits to the parents during the eight-month preschool year. There were four qualified teachers for every 25 students. A longitudinal study of the program that is ongoing shows the

When early education schools are equipped with highly skilled teachers and have multifaceted programs, they are associated with a reduced risk of delinquency.

results of the preschooling over the course of the participants' lives. Researchers found that compared to the control sample of students who did not experience preschool, those who did demonstrated big initial jumps in performance on standardized IQ tests (compared to their scores prior to the test). Although their scores did not remain as high in years after the first testing, researchers did notice a remarkable difference in young people who had been through the preschool—they were more motivated to do well in school, and thus more successful. This sort of attitudinal difference is a life skill that researchers found is related to positive life outcomes. In terms of delinquency, more than half of the students who didn't go to the Perry Preschool got in trouble for delinquent acts and were detained before they were 19. Follow-up studies of the youth when they were 40 demonstrated that the odds of being arrested were cut in half for the students who had gone to the preschool; this effect was especially pronounced among the male participants.[17]

Other programs that were inspired by the Perry Preschool and that involved both education and home visit components were the Houston Parent-Child Development Center,[18] the Syracuse Family Development Research Program,[19] and the Yale Child Welfare Research Program.[20] Preschool programs that include both of these components, as well as have highly trained and compensated teachers, with a low student-to-teacher ratio, are found to be the most successful.[21] The best known program that followed in the general tradition of the Perry Preschool is the Head Start program. Head Start is a federal program that has been in effect since 1965 and for most of that period has had an emphasis on the educational component of the early intervention approach, rather than a fully implemented multicomponent approach. In recent years it has been expanded to better address the need for family support, staff training, parental involvement, and more teachers per classroom. There are now centers or schools that children attend for part of the day or the entire day, family child care homes, and home visits, in which staff provide services to children and families.[22] Head Start has shown to be particularly effective in having immediate and positive effects on children's social and cognitive development, as

President Obama showed his support for Head Start programs by visiting a long-standing program in Lawrence, Kansas.

well as demonstrating some sleeper effects on well-being that may not show themselves outwardly until students enter mid-adolescence and high school.[23] Long-term studies show that boys who participated in Head Start are significantly less likely than others to repeat a grade. All participants are less likely to struggle with a learning disability, and more likely to graduate high school and to have tried to go to college.[24] Head Start programs are not as generously funded as the original Perry Preschool Project was, and this impacts practitioners' ability to provide multiple services. The long-term budget problems of the U.S. federal government continue to threaten the long-term financial support of Head Start and its future.

School- or Community-Based Education and Skill-Based Programs

A number of classroom- or school-based programs are used to sway youth toward prosocial, nondelinquent behavior and away from antisocial and delinquent behaviors. Many of them teach the same skills that are taught in many rehabilitation programs, as you will see later in this chapter.

The Blueprints for Healthy Youth Development project, run out of the Center for the Study and Prevention of Violence at the University of Colorado–Boulder, periodically reviews the evidence on prevention programs and identifies a number of school-based programs as models for others to emulate. Three programs have earned the highest distinction based on their efficacy and the fact they have been evaluated scientifically:

- LifeSkills Training (LST): LifeSkills Training is a classroom curriculum originally designed to prevent middle school children and adolescents from using tobacco, alcohol, and marijuana. In addition, LST targets reduction of violence and other risky behaviors. Students are taught to develop their personal self-management skills, to develop their social skills, and to resist drugs through drug education. Instructors include teachers, peer leaders, and health professionals. Studies of the middle school program have demonstrated that alcohol, marijuana, and cigarette use decreases during the program, and the students show reduced use throughout high school. In addition, it has been shown to be associated with steep reductions in physical aggression, verbal aggression, delinquency, and fighting.[25] There are now LST programs at both the elementary and high school levels, as well as a transition program for youth about to graduate from high school.

- Promoting Alternative Thinking Strategies (PATHS): Another model education program cited by Blueprints as one that positively influences youth behavior and emotional health is Promoting Alternative Thinking Strategies. PATHS is a program in which students from preschool to sixth grade are exposed to curriculum in their classrooms that teaches them developmentally based lessons on emotional intelligence, positive peer interactions, self-control, problem-solving skills, and social competence as a means of helping them avoid emotional and behavioral problems. The PATHS curriculum is taught by teachers two or three times a week for 20–30 minutes. Randomized and controlled studies of the PATHS program with students who are deaf/hearing impaired, students in regular education, and students classified as having special education needs found that the PATHS curriculum was associated in all cases with increasing protective factors and prosocial behavior and reducing aggression, depression, anxiety, withdrawal, and sadness in the classroom.[26]

- Project Toward No Drug Abuse (TND): A final education program considered by Blueprints to be a model for others to emulate is the Project Toward No Drug Abuse. This program was originally developed for students in alternative or continuation high schools who were deemed to be at high risk of abusing drugs but has since

● ● ●
Sleeper effects: Effects of a program or intervention that may not show themselves until several years after its completion.

been expanded to traditional high schools. It is based on research conducted at the University of Southern California and is focused on three factors that predict violence—tobacco, alcohol, and other drug use—and delinquent behaviors—motivation factors (attitudes, beliefs, expectations, and desires related to drug use); social, coping, and self-control skills; and decision making that promotes healthy behaviors. There are 12 classroom sessions each 40–50 minutes in length over the course of either a four- or six-week session. The sessions are interactive and are taught by the teachers with a great deal of student-teacher interaction, small-group work, and classroom discussion. Controlled evaluation studies of alternative school students in Project TND showed all of the following:

- A 27% prevalence reduction in 30-day cigarette use
- A 22% prevalence reduction in 30-day marijuana use
- A 26% prevalence reduction in 30-day hard drug use
- A 9% prevalence reduction in 30-day alcohol use among baseline drinkers
- A 25% prevalence reduction in one-year weapon carrying among males[27]

After-school programs: Delinquency prevention programs that aim to involve young people in organized social behaviors, learning activities, and/or recreational activities after school.

After-School Programs

Another type of program that studies have shown to be promising in terms of preventing delinquency are after-school programs.[28] After-school programs (ASPs) address the well-known finding that delinquency is most apt to be a pastime of children who aren't busy doing something else with their time.[29] As is the case when youth are involved in sports or other extracurricular activities in their free time, when young people spend their time in after-school programs, they are busy engaging in social behaviors, learning activities, and/or recreational activities and have less unsupervised time. Advocates of after-school programs believe that this may lessen children's chances of acting out delinquently. After-school programs are held on school campuses or off campus in community centers. There is an assortment of after-school programs, and they are popular recipients of support by local, state, and federal funders. It is difficult to fully understand how well ASPs prevent delinquency, because the children who volunteer to participate and continue to participate may be inclined to benefit from the program, whereas the young people who do not choose to participate or drop out quickly are often the young people thought to be at the highest risk of delinquency.[30] Nevertheless, researchers have done their best to research across programs to see what works best in ASPs. Programs that are of small size, and that are highly structured and emphasize social skills, education, and character development, have been shown to be the most effective.[31] There are also indications that having college-educated staff involved in delivering the after-school programs, a preexisting curriculum (such as the LifeSkills Training curriculum addressed previously in this chapter), and

After-school programs that have structured activities and adequate supervision help young people thrive.

men represented on the staff is associated with decreased delinquency and victimization.[32] A recent meta-analysis of 17 well-known evaluations of after-school programs indicated that after-school programs had a modest effect on delinquency, but it was statistically nonsignificant. Nevertheless, the authors suggest additional research is needed, and after-school programs should not be done away with because they serve other important purposes besides delinquency prevention, such as helping parents with child care.[33]

Mentoring Programs

Mentoring programs have also been shown to be useful in preventing delinquency.[34] When young people are matched up in schools or communities with adults who volunteer to mentor them, the experience often results in emotional bonding between the pair. If a strong relationship develops between a young person and a mentor, it serves as a prosocial reinforcement that may increase self-esteem and confidence and help youth succeed in conventional ways—all factors that decrease the likelihood of delinquency in the future.[35] Mentoring is based on the notion that the stable, positive attachment between a youth and an adult who demonstrates an interest in the youth's development can serve as an experience that spills over into the young person's expectations about relationships with others; this is the case even if the youth hasn't had the best of experiences with adults prior to the mentoring.[36] Ultimately, the young person being mentored may become more socially and emotionally skilled through the process, which leads to resilience. In addition, mentors may be able to provide those they are mentoring with information about and access to financial resources, cultural resources, and knowledge about topics with which the young people were previously unfamiliar.

Millions of adults and young people in the United States are involved in mentoring relationships,[37] such as those involved in Big Brothers Big Sisters, an organization linked to mentors all over the world. Community-based mentoring programs have been found to be more effective along multiple measures than school-based programs (which have benefits that are mostly academic).[38] Community-based mentoring has been shown to help youth improve parental relationships, as well as peer relationships, and the more frequent the interaction between the mentor and the young person, the better.[39] It is best for mentors to have training and support, parental involvement, expectations to have frequent and longer meetings between the youth and the mentor, and supplemental services.[40] It has been shown that mentoring relationships that end prematurely negatively influence youths' self concepts, so it is important that mentors recruited into programs take the responsibility seriously and commit to it in order to avoid such a result.[41]

●●●
Rehabilitation programs: Programs that are focused on changing juveniles' behavior after they have already engaged in an act of delinquency.

REHABILITATION

Rehabilitation programs in juvenile detention facilities, or those that take place in conjunction with conditions of diversion and/or probation in the community, are concerned with changing juveniles' behavior after they have already engaged in an act of delinquency. Like preventative approaches, rehabilitation is about making sure that a young person is likely and able

Research demonstrates that community-based mentoring is a powerful way of creating positive bonding experiences between a young person and a caring adult.

Visit edge.sagepub
.com/bates2e to
view a video about
programs available to
foster youth.

to follow society's conventions and rules following punishment. Rehabilitation tends to be focused on the individual level and is heavily influenced by psychological and social-psychological theories of human development. As we have mentioned frequently in this book, the creation of separate juvenile justice systems around the turn of the 20th century in the United States was based on the ideal of rehabilitation. Although it is arguable that the punishments that most youth experience today are not rehabilitative or are inadequately so, researchers have found that some programs are effective in helping young people change their lives. Some of the factors found to be especially important to the creation of effective rehabilitation programs are the involvement of mental health personnel in program delivery, in-depth programming that lasts a sufficient amount of time to be useful, and behavior- or skill-based content (shown to be the most useful in reducing recidivism).[42]

Therapeutic Approaches

Experts who have studied rehabilitation and intervention programs recognize a number of therapy programs as the most successful means of discouraging young people from reengaging in delinquency and other undesirable behaviors. The Blueprints evaluation cited the following therapies as model programs for others to use if they want to effectively prevent recidivism: Functional Family Therapy (FFT), Multisystemic Therapy (MST), and Multidimensional Treatment Foster Care (MTFC). All of these programs have been shown to be the most effective rehabilitative approaches across an ethnically and racially diverse range of youth.[43]

Functional Family Therapy (FFT):
A short-term program that is typically 30 hours long, in which a therapist, a social worker, or a trained probation officer works with a young person and her or his family after the youth has engaged in wrongdoing.

Functional Family Therapy (FFT) is used in a variety of settings after a young person gets in trouble with the law, signaling that some sort of change is needed. It is a short-term program, typically 30 hours long, in which a therapist, social worker, or trained probation officer works with the young person and her or his family to address any communication problems and negative or violent behaviors.[44] The idea is to facilitate a supportive environment for the young person and the family as a whole that will encourage positive change. Parenting skills are addressed in the curriculum as well as the youth's behavior, and the therapist considers the family members' thoughts, behaviors, and emotions as a means of helping them develop healthy family dynamics. Studies have demonstrated that FFT has been especially helpful in reducing teenage marijuana use and has resulted in the reduction of recidivism among seriously delinquent youth.[45] The program is most effective when the professional delivering the curriculum adheres to the program guidelines as variations in the delivery of the program have a significant impact on the results.[46]

Multisystemic Therapy (MST):
A therapy that engages a youth's entire family in the hopes of reducing aggressive, delinquent, and other undesirable behaviors.

Multisystemic Therapy (MST), like FFT, is a program that engages a youth's entire family in the hopes of reducing aggressive, delinquent, and other undesirable behaviors. Therapists with master's degrees in counseling provide the treatment, and sessions are often conducted in homes, schools, or community centers.[47] The content of the program addresses stress, parenting, and familial relationships, as well as the techniques that can be used to enhance family life and serve as protective factors against youth misbehavior. The program lasts approximately four months, and families have contact with the therapist about four times a week and are available 24 hours a day to help out with crisis situations. MST is more intense than FFT and more expensive.[48] It is also broader in its approach as therapists work with families to create a support network of families, friends, teachers, and adult authority figures to help them guide their child. Evaluations demonstrate that MST is effective in reducing recidivism among a wide variety of youth involved in the juvenile justice system.[49]

Multidimensional Treatment Foster Care (MTFC):
A specialized foster care program in which community families are recruited, trained, and closely supervised as they take a teenager into their homes.

Another form of effective program for a subset of juveniles who have engaged in delinquency, and a less expensive alternative than detention or residential treatment, is Multidimensional Treatment Foster Care (MTFC). In MTFC, community families are recruited, trained, and closely supervised as they take a teenager into their homes. They are paid to do the job, and are compensated much more than typical foster parents are because of the intensity of the job. A parent must be at home whenever the young person is, and a behavior modification system is in place in which the foster parent must tally points earned daily by the child for good behavior and adjust the freedom given to the child accordingly. Supervision and support are also provided to MTFC parents during daily telephone calls. Individual therapy and family therapy for the biological family is provided, and a case manager keeps in touch with the foster families daily.[50] The program typically lasts for six months and allows for up to a year of follow-up services. Studies have demonstrated that MTFC participation is associated with reduced youth drug use, recidivism and detention, status offenses, and adolescent pregnancies.[51]

Prevention and Rehabilitation: Race, Ethnicity, Gender, and LGBT Intersections

Although some analyses suggest that prevention and rehabilitation programs are similarly effective for youth of all social locations,[52] prevention and rehabilitation efforts that directly address youths' life experiences can be powerful tools for change.

Prevention and Rehabilitation and Race, Ethnicity, and Class

Prevention and rehabilitation efforts that meaningfully address race and ethnicity, and community needs as a whole (e.g., socioeconomic issues), are often ones that youth relate to more than others. Such approaches acknowledge the unique experiences that young people have due to their social locations and the challenges and opportunities available

A Focus on Research

Salisbury, Dabney, and Russell's Diverting Victims of Commercial Sexual Exploitation From Juvenile Detention

The Journal of Interpersonal Violence published a study called "Diverting Victims of Commercial Sexual Exploitation From Juvenile Detention: Development of the InterCSECt Screening Protocol" by Salisbury, Dabney & Russell. This study addressed an important need, which is to find youth victims of commercial sex trafficking and other forms of exploitation and to protect them, rather than process them through the juvenile justice system as delinquents. In Washington state, people started noticing that youth engaged in prostitution were often not identified during their arrest, and then they were charged with related acts such as curfew violations, possessing alcohol, loitering, or running away (i.e., they were basically victimized twice). Clark County Detention Center in Vancouver, Washington developed a screening tool to identify youth victims as part of the juvenile detention intake process. In this study, six girls were identified and confirmed as the victims of sexual exploitation and/or sex trafficking by using the

diagnostic tool. The overwhelming majority of the victims were white, 14–17 years of age, and were in detention for a probation violation or warrant. These girls were given access to community resources and advocates and diverted from juvenile detention.

DISCUSSION QUESTIONS

1. How prevalent is the commercial sex trafficking of juveniles in your area? Do some online research to help you answer this question.

2. What can be done to prevent the exploitation and victimization of young people in the sex trade?

Source: Salisbury, E. J., Dabney, J. D. & Russell, K. (2015). Diverting victims of commercial sexual exploitation from juvenile detention: Development of the InterCSECt Screening Protocol. *Journal of Interpersonal Violence, 30*(7), 1247–1276.

in their communities.[53] As we have discussed previously in the book (e.g., in Chapters 9 and 10), to adequately support youth and help them develop their strengths, programs that incorporate familial, community, and cultural components are successful in reducing delinquencies ranging from substance use and abuse to gang involvement. Programs that target a particular racial or ethnic demographic typically include curricular elements that validate youths' life experiences, while providing them with resources and helping them develop skill sets that will facilitate success by conventional means.

An example of a culturally targeted program is the Prodigy program, which focuses on the reduction of delinquency among Latinos in Tampa Bay, Florida.[54] Prodigy is a community-based cultural arts program in South Florida designed to keep young people tied to their community while receiving services geared to helping them develop their skill sets and better navigate the word around them. It is particularly aimed at developing **self-regulation skills**, which enable youths to control their behavior by aiming for positive goals. This, in turn, is thought by Prodigy founders to ultimately serve the community as well because less delinquency will occur as a result. The Prodigy program offers youth who are currently being held in the juvenile justice system as well as youth in the community an eight-week course that focuses on visual, musical, media, performing, and theater arts as a means of teaching self-regulation skills. Trained artists teach the students problem-solving skills, social skills, and anger management. They also become mentors to the young people. Rapp and her colleagues evaluated the program and discovered that Latino youth were significantly healthier mentally, that they acted out less in problem behaviors, that they felt better equipped to succeed academically, and that their family functioning improved during the length of the course.

It is important to note that prevention efforts such as risk assessments that isolate youth from a particular racial or ethnic group as particularly apt to engage in delinquency are risky in and of themselves. Although this research may find that certain risk factors for delinquency make a bigger impact, for example, on low-income black youth than low-income white youth, predictions of future delinquency is an imperfect science and can result in the disproportionate social control of low-income youth of color.[55]

Prevention, Rehabilitation, and Gender

According to the Juvenile Justice and Delinquency Prevention Act Reauthorization of 1992, programs geared at preventing and rehabilitating delinquency should focus also on the specific needs of youth that are related to their gender. This is considered necessary because of the lack of programs that address the social experiences of girls who end up in

● ● ●

Self-regulation skills: Skills that help young people control their own behavior and aim for positive goals.

©iStockphoto.com/miodrag gajlatovic

Juvenile delinquency prevention and rehabilitation programs must be designed carefully in order to avoid further oppression of LGBT youth.

the juvenile justice system—experiences based in race, class, and gender inequality.[56] As we examined in our discussion of research and programs informed by feminist theories and other theories of delinquency in Part 2 of this book, the multiple marginalities that affect girls, and the likelihood that their lives have been characterized with abuse, trauma, poor health, and residential instability of some sort, make gender-specific programming especially important. The OJJDP stated that **gender-responsive programming** is needed for girls, and should have the following qualities:[57] Programs should be all female, wherever possible; girls should be treated in the least restrictive environment, whenever possible; programs should be close to girls' homes to maintain family relationships; programs should be consistent with female development and stress the role of relationships between staff members and girls; and programs should address the needs of parenting and pregnant teens. Nonetheless, as discussed by Watson and Edelman in their report *Improving the Juvenile Justice System for Girls,* because girls are considered at lower risk for delinquency than boys, whenever cuts to publicly funded programs need to be made, typically gender-responsive programs are the first to go.[58] Nevertheless, as we will examine in the next section of this chapter, forays into the use of restorative justice are some of the ways that community agencies create preventative and rehabilitative approaches that manage to take gender into account.

Prevention, Rehabilitation, and LGBT Youth

Due to the homophobia that lesbian, gay, and bisexual youth face and the transphobia that transgender youth face in society as a whole, prevention and rehabilitation efforts can replicate those oppressions if program designers do not address them directly. Juvenile detention programs can be especially counterproductive for LGBT youth.[59] As scholar Jeffrey Dennis explained, "The impact of heterosexist erasure on those LGBT individuals who are introduced into the criminal justice system is severe."[60] As Irvine notes, juveniles in juvenile detention, always assumed to be heterosexual, are given advice about heterosexual courtship and marriage, enrolled in homophobic faith-based programs, and punished severely for gender transgressions."[61] School-based prevention efforts are often occurring in schools in which people are hostile toward LGBT youth. LGBT youth are punished for public displays of affection and for challenging gender norms.[62] They often resort to fighting to protect themselves and are easily pushed out of school and into the

●●●
Gender-responsive programming: Delinquency prevention program that takes into account gendered experiences of youth (e.g., delinquency programming aimed at girls).

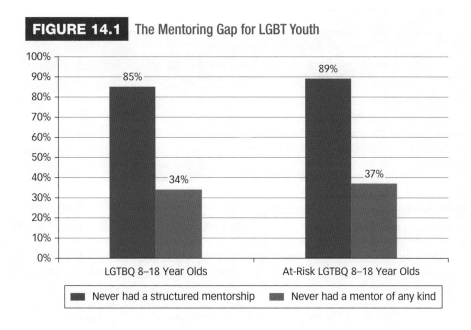

FIGURE 14.1 The Mentoring Gap for LGBT Youth

LGTBQ 8–18 Year Olds: Never had a structured mentorship 85%, Never had a mentor of any kind 34%
At-Risk LGTBQ 8–18 Year Olds: Never had a structured mentorship 89%, Never had a mentor of any kind 37%

Legend:
■ Never had a structured mentorship ■ Never had a mentor of any kind

school-to-prison pipeline[63] or into living on the streets.[64] Mentoring programs that welcome LGBT youth and that involve mentors who are willing to discuss the challenges that these young people face are especially crucial to their resilience.[65] Research demonstrates that only a fraction of LGBT youth have ever had a mentor, and for LGBT youth who are considered "at risk," fewer than one in five have had a formal mentor (see Figure 14.1).[66] Mentoring programs that have policies and programs that enforce nondiscrimination rules, antiharassment policies, confidentiality policies, and identity-confirming language can go a long way in meeting the needs of LGBT youth.[67] Similarly, programs and services related to LGBT youth involvement in the juvenile justice system must also be set up to address the multiple injustices they face on a daily basis.[68]

RESTORATIVE JUSTICE APPROACHES

As discussed in Chapter 11, restorative justice, or restoration, is based on the philosophy that good relations between people and their communities should be central to our focus on dealing with crimes and delinquency. Restorative justice is both a theory and a practice advocating the involvement of offenders, victims, and community members in dealing with the harm of a crime or delinquent act. *Accountability* or taking responsibility for delinquency is thought to be necessary on the part not only of the young people who commit acts of delinquency, but of *society as a whole*, as we all collectively create the social conditions that facilitate crime. Usually restorative justice methods are closely linked to those labeled preventative or rehabilitative—so much so that oftentimes the terms are used interchangeably.

Many practices are placed under the umbrella of "restorative justice" at this point in time. Usually they work as alternatives to the formal processing of juveniles, and youth who come in contact with school or law enforcement authorities because of their questionable behavior get recommended to programs that implement restorative justice. In these cases, restorative justice involvement is being used as a diversion from formal processing, and if a young person completes a restorative justice program successfully, a delinquency petition is not filed against her or him. In other cases, involvement in a restorative justice process is part of a juvenile's disposition or probation in a case in which she or he has

••• *on the* MEDIA

Online Tools to Expunge Juvenile Records

An online development that is in line with the philosophy of restorative justice is the creation of websites that allow people to get help expunging (which is usually equivalent to sealing) their juvenile records. (Note: some of these resources also help expunge adult records). For example, http://www.expunge.io/about helps people in Illinois request help with expunging their juvenile records, and http://www.expungemaryland.org allows requests related to both juvenile and adult records in Maryland. These websites clearly spell out the steps to expunging one's record, provide access to free legal advice about the process, and explain why it is so important to do so. These online resources are very

helpful because there is very little understanding on the part of most youth about how often a juvenile record might be able to be accessed in the future and the negative impacts that record could have on their life chances.

DISCUSSION QUESTION

1. Do you know people who would benefit from having their juvenile records expunged? If so, would you feel comfortable pointing out that they should look for online resources or legal aid to help them seal their records? Why or why not?

admitted guilt already. Many restorative justice practices are informed by the concept of **reintegrative shaming**,[69] the idea that shaming someone who has done wrong followed by reintegration of the wrongdoer into the fabric of her or his family or greater community is a powerful way of influencing her or his future behavior. This type of shaming is thought to work best in settings in which the people being shamed are generally treated in positive and encouraging ways most of the time, and then when they face disapproval about their acts, they are ashamed and feel bad about it. The shaming does not go on indefinitely, though, because the community demonstrates that reintegration and positive change are possible with some effort, even for people who have done something that has harmed others. Ultimately, restorative justice advocates generally believe that the experience of reintegrative shaming cuts down on recidivism of juveniles (and adult offenders) in the long run. Many studies back up this claim as well.[70]

Well-known restorative justice practices used with young people include Victim-Offender Mediation, Family Group Conferencing, and restorative circles. Advocates of these practices cite research that has found that restorative justice interventions are more effective at guiding young people away from their previous misbehavior than tradition juvenile court intervention.[71]

Victim-Offender Mediation

Victim-Offender Reconciliation Programs (VORP), or **Victim-Offender Mediation (VOM)**, are among the most popular restorative justice practices used to address acts of delinquency. The potential for these programs to generate meaningful change among youth started getting a lot of attention in the 1970s, and the programs have increased in popularity in the United States and other countries ever since that time.[72] The basic mechanics of a mediation session are simple: A young person who has committed an act of delinquency will meet with the person or persons who were directly affected by the act. The youth will also meet with a mediator who is trained to be as neutral as possible and to help the parties involved work out a mutually satisfying agreement that deals with the harm emanating from the conflict. Often this agreement involves some form of restitution, or paying the victim back for the offending either with money (usually earned on the part

of the young person over time) or in terms of volunteer labor or community service (see also Chapter 13). Mediation is often used as a diversionary measure within the criminal justice system and is thought to save time and money—precious commodities in an overloaded system.

Jung Jin Choi, Diane Green, and Michael Gilbert looked at the ways in which restorative justice processes affected the perceptions of juveniles who had committed acts of delinquency and the victims of those acts.[73] They found that their perceptions of the delinquent act (which they refer to as a crime in Table 14.1) changed as a result of the process. In one particular case, three teens played a game they called

●●●
Reintegrative shaming:
The shaming of someone who has done wrong that is followed by reintegration of the wrongdoer into the fabric of his or her family or greater community.

Victim-Offender Mediation (VOM):
A restorative justice process in which a young person who has committed an act of delinquency will meet with the victim of her or his act, as well as a mediator, in the hopes of arriving at a mutually satisfying agreement.

At the end of a Victim-Offender Mediation, various forms of restitution might be agreed upon as a means of paying someone back for an act of delinquency.

"mailbox baseball" and damaged the mailboxes of eight families. Three of the victims participated in a Victim-Offender Mediation with the three boys and the boys' parents. Table 14.1 demonstrates how the boys and the victims changed their thoughts about one another and the event over time and, ultimately, how everyone affected by the act of delinquency was able to find some common ground. The victims were not as fearful or angry about what had happened to them and were able to experience an apology from those who harmed them. The boys who committed the vandalism were able to see that what they originally thought of as a game actually caused some psychological damage to the victims' families, who felt vulnerable and targeted. Choi et al. found that meeting with the people whose property they harmed helped the boys to put a human face on their acts of delinquency by means of the VOM and, ultimately, to become more empathetic.

Research demonstrates that VOM programs for young people often result in high levels of satisfaction related to the process and the outcomes for young people and those victimized by their acts of delinquency.[74] In addition, VOM programs are often effective in reducing the prevalence and severity of juvenile delinquency among young people who participate.[75] Although sometimes upon hearing about restorative justice methods for the first time people think they are an easy way out for those who have committed acts of delinquency, juveniles often find the process to be a difficult one. As Choi et al. discovered in their analysis of interviews with VOM youth participants, young people often state that VOM is "not an easy punishment to take."[76] Yet youth participants often benefit by learning important lessons, which include learning to better communicate with others, learning how their delinquency affected the people and communities they victimized, and developing empathy for the people around them. In addition, the victims of the acts of delinquency may benefit from the processes of talking with the young people who harmed them and/or their property.

TABLE 14.1 Perceptions of Delinquency: Mailbox Baseball Case

SITUATION	MAILBOX BASEBALL CASE	
	JUVENILE OFFENDERS	VICTIMS
Definitions of the crime	A game among friends It is a culture	Ongoing vandalism in the community It is a violation of basic human right (privacy and property)
CHANGES IN SITUATION		
Prior to the VOM	Having fun and looking cool, unless getting caught Grabbing a bat and smashing mailboxes Getting caught	Considering moving out Taking a stand: installing security camera Being vigilant and watching and taking pictures of them Calling the police
At the VOM	Being afraid of meeting the victims Being able to apologize sincerely	Finally being able to confront the offenders Having difficulty believing them
After the VOM	Being able to see the effect of their behavior Realizing the game is "not fun" "not cool" anymore Being able to be empathetic for victims	Being able to disapprove the behavior in a respectful way Being able to be empathetic for other victims

Source: Choi, J., Green, D., & Gilbert, M. (2011). Putting a human face on crimes: A qualitative study on restorative justice processes for youths. *Child & Adolescent Social Work Journal, 28*(5), 349.

Family Group Conferencing

Family Group Conferencing (FGC) is a variation on the VOM structure that includes a larger number of people in its processing of conflict. This method has its roots in New Zealand and has adopted many of the traditional values of conflict resolution practiced by the Maori people, such as the inclusion of family and extended family members.[77] In 1989, New Zealand passed the Children, Young Persons, and Their Families Act, which established a youth court that handles almost all acts of delinquency by allotting decision-making power to participants in family group conferences. This is considered by many to be the first major move in the institutionalization of restorative justice as a mainstream method.[78] Other countries, including Australia, Canada, and the United States, began to utilize the method in various forms following its development in New Zealand. In a family group conference, the circle of individuals drawn into the resolution of a conflict is widened beyond the circumscribed group of VOM to include individuals indirectly affected by a given incident. This may include the victim(s), the offender(s) and their families, police officers, a youth advocate if desired on the part of the offender, the occasional social worker, the youth justice coordinator, the individual who facilitates the conference, and invited community members.[79] The number of people participating in FGC can be as many as 50, although that size of conference is rare.[80] As in VOM, the two primary parties discuss the event that transpired, how it affected them, and what should be done to amend the situation. The process differs from its predecessor in the involvement of other concerned individuals. **Secondary victims** of an act of delinquency, such as family members who are impacted negatively by the victimization of a member of their family, or community members who are frightened for their own safety because of an act of delinquency, are acknowledged if they participate in the process. All members of the family group conference, including the youth who offended, must agree to the terms of the agreement made in the conference. In most cases, diversionary mechanisms of rectification (apology, restitution, service agreements, community service, and other agreements) are preferred to formal processing of the cases and custodial sentences; rarely are informal means of handling conflicts overridden by the youth court in favor of imprisonment.[81] The family group conferences are used for youth who are placed both in and out of custody before a disposition is made.

Research indicates that FGC generally leads to a high amount of participant satisfaction and completion of youth agreements to make restitution and/or amends.[82] Calhoun and Pelech found that youth who experienced restorative conferencing in response to their acts of delinquency were significantly more likely to be accountable for their behavior (defined as assuming responsibility, experiencing empathy, experiencing remorse, and making a commitment to redress wrongdoing) and to experience relationship repair with their victims (defined as understanding the impact of the crime, and experiencing respect) than youth who were processed in conventional ways.[83]

Although family group conferences are quite popular and have often been demonstrated to be effective, there are some potential hazards of their use. If the parties involved and the facilitator are not adequately trained prior to the conference, if there is insensitivity to the victim's needs, if young offenders feel intimidated by adults, and if the process is characterized by a lack of neutrality by the facilitator (e.g., when police make it very clear throughout the process that they are approaching the conflict as law enforcement officers rather than as people who are striving to be objective and neutral), there can be problems with the use of FGC. In addition, a scripted dialogue may not allow for the flexibility needed to address the unique cultural needs of the actual people involved in the process.[84]

Restorative Justice Circles

Additional practices that are used with juveniles in the name of restoration (and ultimately also in the name of rehabilitation and prevention) are different types of circles, which

● ● ●

Family Group Conferencing (FGC): A means of handing acts of juvenile delinquency in line with restorative justice aims, involving a conference between victims, offenders, and their families, as well as police, youth advocates, community members, and other interested parties who decide what should be done in the aftermath of harm.

Secondary victims: Indirect victims of an act of delinquency such as family members who are impacted negatively by the victimization of a member of their family, or community members who are frightened for their own safety because of an act of delinquency.

Family group conferences include a large group of community members who discuss why an act of delinquency occurred, what the consequences should be for the young person involved, and any resources that can help the child be accountable.

go by a variety of names, including restorative circles, peacemaking circles, healing circles, and sentencing circles. In a circle, people who are meeting together for some sort of dialogue sit in a circular formation. This design is purposive and is based on the concept that circular arrangement of people allows for a sharing of power and a more equitable space. Circles are also considered symbols of healing and completion in many cultures, and this is additionally considered significant in the restorative justice movement because it is informed by indigenous traditions of communication and conflict resolution.[85] In all circle processes, the process is geared to allowing an equitable dialogue between the people involved. A facilitator, or a peacemaker, helps guide the process, and a talking piece is passed around to each person in the circle. When a person receives the talking piece it is his or her time to speak and to be heard without any interruptions. This approach can minimize any potential conflict or debate in the course of discussion of difficult topics that arise around issues of delinquency and harm.[86] In addition, circle processes address the big picture that surrounds an act of delinquency rather than only focusing on the incident itself. The underlying reasons for why a young person committed an act of delinquency are raised in the course of the circle process.[87]

Restorative justice advocates make use of a number of different practices that utilize the circle both symbolically and pragmatically. These practices range from the sentencing circle, a variation of the family group conference that occurs postadjudication or posthearing in the case of juveniles, to separate healing circles for victims and offenders. The latter two types of processes allow victims and offenders to get support from interested members of the community and support service professionals without confronting the other party involved in a conflict. Circles typically include even more people than the standard family-group conference and are thus seen as facilitating community building in a way that other methods do not. Victim circles are said to promote psychological healing, and offender circles, often known as circles of support, help provide guidance in terms of getting a person back on his or her feet and reintegrating him or her back into the community. Interaction between an offender-oriented circle and a victim-oriented circle might occur to facilitate a better understanding of the other group's role in the processing of harm; this interaction does not necessarily involve parties involved in the same conflict and often entails the meeting of victims and offenders from different incidents in an effort for participants to understand by proxy the other side of the coin.

Restorative Justice and Institutional Change

As Braithwaite has noted, restorative methods such as the use of conferencing, circles, and mediation can be used to address not only people, but institutions.[88] Sometimes restorative processes are used in a given institution to promote healthier ways of dealing

●●●

Circles of support: Offender-oriented circles that help people get back on their feet after detention or incarceration and facilitate their community reintegration.

with conflict. For example, Ted Wachtel and Paul McCold of the International Institute for Restorative Practices in Bethlehem, Pennsylvania, provide a number of services to schools ("SaferSaner Schools") in which variations on the conferencing approach are taught to members of those institutions in the hopes of transforming relationships to healthier ones.[89] In addition, as we have discussed in previous chapters of this book, innovations such as drug courts, and teen courts, often draw upon a restorative justice perspective.

Juvenile Restorative Justice and Race, Ethnicity, Class, and Gender Intersections

Abrams et al. note the difficult questions that need to be asked about VOM and other restorative justice programs that bring together victims and offenders from different walks of life, many of which hinge upon issues of social privilege and social marginalization:[90]

- Is appropriate translation provided for offenders and their families?

- Do mediators carry cultural assumptions that might bias the process from the beginning?

- Is training in cultural competence provided and followed?

- Are sexist, racist, and/or homophobic assumptions or accusations permitted?

- When young people victimize adults, can mediations actually be on a level playing field? Or is it impossible because of the large power differential between the two parties due to their ages?

Juvenile Restorative Justice and Race, Ethnicity, and Class

Many observers of restorative justice programs and processes worry that because they are often recommended at the discretion of a judge or juvenile probation officer, young people from some walks of life will be more likely to have the chance to participate than others. Another concern is that the involvement of community members and volunteers in restorative justice programs often amounts to severe consequences for youth of color that harm them and may lead them down the path to future delinquency.[91] Nancy Rodriguez found that in Maricopa County, Arizona, black and Latino juveniles were less likely than white juveniles to be placed in a restorative justice program by juvenile court officials.[92] In addition, young people who were from predominantly Spanish-speaking communities or communities that were racially and ethnically diverse were less likely than youth from other communities to be chosen for a restorative justice program. She believed that one of the reasons this might be the case is additional financial resources are needed to incorporate community members into restorative justice processes when translators must be present. Because those youth who participated in restorative justice programs were significantly less likely to recidivate than those in a comparison group, it can be argued that it is important to open up access to restorative alternatives to people from all racial and ethnic groups.

Restorative justice programs implemented in low-income communities and/or communities of color have been shown to positively influence the behavior of youth and keep them off the path to delinquency. For example, after Cole Middle School in West Oakland, California, began implementing a restorative justice approach to address children's misbehavior, suspensions and expulsions decreased dramatically.[93] The students, who were mostly African American, Latino, Asian, and Pacific Islander, the majority of whom came from low-income families, learned how to navigate conflicts with others at the school more peacefully, and staff and parents learned how to as well. Such programs have been cited as an important piece of the dismantling of the school-to-prison pipeline that has long characterized the West Oakland community.

On the other hand, wary observers of restorative justice claim that caution is needed when restorative justice options are framed as a way for officials to help "empower" people from marginalized communities, as is particularly evidenced in use of restorative justice with indigenous populations in the United States and around the world.[94] When Native youth are encouraged to go through restorative processes rather than the traditional system, it is possible for their families to be tasked with the responsibility of figuring out how to resolve their children's challenges with very few resources to do so.

Juvenile Restorative Justice and Gender

Many of the restorative justice efforts that address gender stress that many girls and women are socialized to focus on relationships with others and connections to other people. Restorative justice methods are seen as potentially very helpful because juvenile girls who have gotten in trouble have often been subjected to abuse and pain both before and during their involvement with the juvenile justice system.[95] True restorative programs that address girls' needs are rare and are in their early stages of development. An example of a program in Minnesota that attempts to provide gender-based restorative justice programming is the Amicus Radius. The program is run by a nonprofit, Amicus, Inc., a program of Volunteers of America Minnesota, for youth referred by the Hennipen County juvenile probations office.[96] The philosophy of the program is grounded in the understanding that because most girls who end up in the juvenile justice system have experienced a number of harms, and those harms are related to their subsequent acts of delinquency, a restorative justice approach focused on healing the harms related to an act of delinquency is ideal (see Figure 14.2).[97] A diverse group of services are available to

FIGURE 14.2 The Components of Amicus's Strength-Based Program for Girls

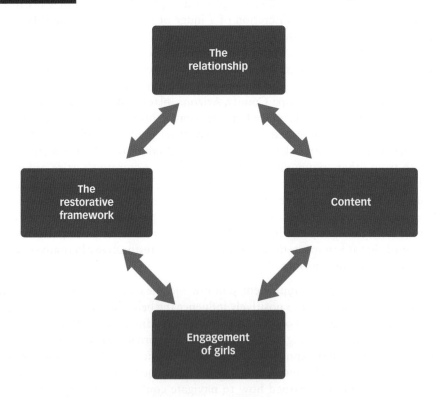

Source: Reprinted with permission of Amicus, Inc., a program of Volunteers of America, Minnesota.

Amicus's Radius Program is aimed specifically at addressing the roots of girls' delinquency through the formation of rich relationships, restorative justice programming, and content that aims to motivate them to work through complex challenges in healthy ways.

the girls including what they call Girls Group—a weekly group meeting over 14 weeks in which there are discussions about trauma and victimization, dealing with emotional pain, managing anger, accountability for choices, developing healthy relationships, and making choices to remain safe. The Amicus Group offers individual counseling, support for finding services and direct referrals to girls and their families, and restorative justice support circles, which focus on the girls' healing and futures by involving them in a dialogue with their families and other supportive individuals. In addition, the staff members are available to consult and train other professionals in the juvenile justice field who want to include gender-responsive programming.[98]

Evaluation research of Amicus's programs indicates that an older iteration of the program, based in a long-term residential facility for the most seriously delinquent girls (a collaboration with the Minnesota Department of Corrections that was discontinued due to budget constraints), was an especially effective program that met the needs of the girls.[99] This program allowed some girls to participate in circles in which they met their victims and also gave them a greater deal of time and focus to experience the programming Amicus had to offer.[100] In order for gendered programming to be restorative in the traditional sense, these factors are necessary.

Other concerns about restorative justice processes that involve girls include the fact that a large amount of preparation is needed for girls who have been involved in violent fights with other girls before a restorative meeting.[101] The possibility for revictimization is thought by some to be a real concern when girls do not admit responsibility for their actions, either due to the fact that the stigma against aggression by girls is such a serious one it is hard to discuss, or because they don't want to discuss the intricacies of their lives in front of their parents (who are typically present in many restorative justice conferences, for example).[102] In addition, restorative processes can allow some participants to reinforce stereotypes about girls that are harmful to them and double standards related to their behavior, particularly sexual behavior.[103] Yet, some studies indicate that girls are more positively affected by restorative justice participation than boys are in the long run, as boys are more likely to recidivate in the future.[104]

Juvenile Restorative Justice and LGBT Youth

Although there is a serious lack of social science research on the relationship between restorative justice practices and programs for LGBT youth and delinquency, there is a small body of research that has considered it indirectly. Miller and Endo explained that LGBT youth are considered a *silent minority* because teachers and administrators generally do not speak about their sexuality and/or gender identities, and the totality of their lives are not acknowledged by the curriculum.[105] The result of such an experience includes feeling insecure, experiencing bullying, and often skipping school to avoid harassment. Eventually, many LGBT youth are pushed out of school and their likelihood of engaging in delinquency increases. A few schools in the United States are known for using restorative practices to address the needs of youth before that happens, which decreases the likelihood of delinquency. These schools include the Harvey Milk High School in New York City and The Alliance School in Milwaukee, Wisconsin. Miller and Endo focused upon The Alliance School (a gay-friendly charter school for Grades 6–12) and its embrace of a restorative justice philosophy in their analysis. The Alliance School treats issues of homophobic bullying as an offense against the whole community rather than just an offense against one person or a breaking of the rules. This changes the dynamic that LGBT students usually experience in other schools and makes all students at the school feel welcomed and safe. This prevents LGBT youth from ending up out of school and on the streets, which increases their likelihood of engaging in acts of survival delinquency (acts that they do in order to get food, shelter, or money). Additional research is needed to understand the strengths and weaknesses of a restorative justice approach to LGBT youth and their involvement in delinquency.

A COMPREHENSIVE APPROACH:
THE MODELS FOR CHANGE PROGRAM

The techniques of prevention, rehabilitation, and restoration that we have touched upon above are only some of the most positively regarded and evaluated responses to juvenile delinquency. In order for large-scale transformation of juvenile justice systems to occur, coordination between multiple entities and a comprehensive overhaul of individual states' justice models is needed. In the 2000s, a great deal of effort has been made to develop and implement such changes, through the restructuring of juvenile justice systems and creating complex, multifaceted programs. Although many of these changes are driven by the fiscal reality that early intervention, prevention, and rehabilitation efforts are cost-effective alternatives to the long-term detention of juveniles, many are also informed by a belief that juveniles deserve the chance to develop to the best of their abilities. Let's take a close look at one program that has garnered international praise for its approach, the Models for Change program.

Models for Change

Since 2004, a program called Models for Change has been underway as a method of bringing juvenile justice advocates, government officials, lawyers, educators, families, and community leaders from across the United States together to address the issue of juvenile delinquency and reform of justice systems. The program is funded by the John D. and Catherine T. MacArthur Foundation, is based primarily at the National Center for Juvenile Justice in Pittsburgh, Pennsylvania, and focuses on a number of key areas that researchers determined are crucial to policy and practice reform. These include mental health services, juvenile indigent defense, racial and ethnic disparities, community-based alternatives, evidence-based practices, dual status youth, and status offense reform. They started by focusing on reform in four core states (Louisiana, Pennsylvania, Washington, and Illinois). They expanded to create an action network with an additional 12 states as a means of sharing information and tips with one another about juvenile justice reform, a Resource Center Partnership that provides people working in the juvenile justice system with tools and resources to work on creating positive change, and projects with federal agencies such as the OJJDP and SAMHSA. As you can see, the scope of this project is enormous, but as the information in this book has demonstrated, addressing youth behavior is a complex and multifaceted endeavor!

One of the approaches that Models for Change has initiated is developing improved screening practices. In Pennsylvania, the group helped introduce expanded screening processes by juvenile probation departments (the Juvenile Probation Massachusetts Youth Screening Instrument, Version 2—known as MAYSI-2). The goal of this approach was to screen with a reliable and valid instrument that could be used at the beginning of the processes—at intake or prior to adjudication in most cases. This way youth who indicate that they may be struggling with serious mental health concerns, such as having suicidal thoughts, can be given special attention and perhaps mental health assistance. In addition, participating probation departments in the state all began using the same screening tool (the Youth Level of Service/Case Management Inventory), rather than their own independent judgment as they did in the past, to assess delinquency risk and needs of the young people entering the system. In Louisiana, the implementation of another risk assessment tool, the Structured Assessment of Violence Risk in Youth (SAVRY), drastically changed the procedures of the probation and juvenile justice offices. The analysis of the assessment data is run nightly, and then probation officers and other professionals can keep on top of the needs and challenges that the youth they are dealing with face.

● ● ●
Models for Change Program: One of the best known evidence-based delinquency programs in the United States today, involving numerous states and parties in its complex implementation and design; it is based primarily at the National Center for Juvenile Justice in Pittsburgh, Pennsylvania, but involves a large network of justice professionals based across the country.

from the CLASSROOM *to the* COMMUNITY

The Community Youth Center and Support Services for Asian and Pacific Islander Youth

Originally formed in 1970 in the Chinatown area of San Francisco, California, the Community Youth Center[106] was established to address problems of youth gang violence and juvenile delinquency in the Asian American and Pacific Islander community as well as issues of immigration, housing, language, and unemployment. CYC has expanded over time, and now has a number of programs and services available to help youth develop their potential and to stay out of trouble with the law. To best reach the community, staff members speak multiple languages including Bahasa, Cambodian, Cantonese, English, Korean, Laotian, Mandarin, Tagalog, Toishanese, and Vietnamese. Two examples of programs and services that CYC offers that are aimed at prevention, intervention, and restoration of young people are The Community Assessment and Referral Center and the Asian Pacific Islander Youth Violence Prevention Network.[107]

The Community Assessment and Referral Center (CARC)

- Serves arrested youth ages 11–17 in San Francisco by providing assessment, service integration, referral, booking, crisis intervention, and case management.

- Works with youth to reintegrate them into school, complete community service and probation requirements, and engage in positive social, arts, athletic, and youth development programs.

- Provides guidance, opportunity, and support to youth and their families in order to reduce the rate of being rearrested.

Asian Pacific Islander Youth Violence Prevention Network (APIYVPN)

- Provides wrap-around services and youth development activities to young people at risk of involvement in the juvenile justice system, particularly Asian immigrants.

- Conducts weekly support group at Youth Guidance Center for Asian male detainees.

- Offers school-based violence prevention workshops and community-based outreach to reduce violence and promote productive lifestyles.

DISCUSSION QUESTION

1. Are the needs of Asian and Pacific Islander youth addressed by community agencies in your area? Take a few minutes to research this online and see what you discover.

Sources: Community Youth Center. (2016). *Who we are.* Retrieved from http://cycsf.org/about.php; National Council on Crime and Delinquency. (2007). *Promising approaches: A nationwide resource guide to Asian/Pacific Islander youth organizations and programs* (pp. 54–55). Reprinted with permission from the National Council on Crime and Delinquency.

When Models for Change participants utilize assessment tools, they can make informed decisions about what sorts of **evidence-based programs**, which social science research has demonstrated are among the most effective, should be recommended for a given person. These programs often have a psychosocial emphasis and include many forms of therapy, including two we addressed earlier in the chapter, Functional Family Therapy and Multisystemic Therapy, along with cognitive behavioral therapy, anger replacement therapy, and substance use therapy. Another approach that Models for Change has utilized is a combination of improved mental health screening and a number of restorative justice programs that divert youth out of formal processing in the system. In Ogle County, Illinois, the probation department examines youth's social history in conjunction with the results of the MAYSI-2 to determine who might be well suited

Evidence-based programs:
Prevention-based programs that social science research has demonstrated are among the most effective.

to engaging in alternatives such as victim-offender conferencing, volunteer-staffed community impact panels, or accountability contracts with youth rather than facing adjudication and its possible consequences.[108] The results of this sort of approach, and many others practiced in Models for Change states and counties, is that custody rates of juveniles decreased in the first decade of the 2000s. Nationally, this was the pattern for all states, but Louisiana in particular showed a decrease in custody rate that was more marked than the average across the United States.[109]

Models for Change states have also focused on reducing the number of youth who are formally processed for committing status offenses. Washington is one of the states that have made the most progress diverting truant youth from the system. Petition rates of truant youth per 1,000 in Washington decreased 22% statewide from 2007 to 2011.[110] The efforts to assess youth using appropriate tools and to divert youth into alternatives to formal adjudication and detention, when possible, are about fairness of both juvenile justice procedures and outcomes. Another focus of the Models for Change initiative is to reduce ethnic and racial disparities in the system. This focus acknowledges the role of environmental factors and social inequities that a number of youth of color experience in their schools and communities—some of the institutional and macro-level influences on juvenile behavior that are the hardest to transform. The Berks County, Pennsylvania, Reducing Racial and Ethnic Disparities project has done particularly well in chipping away at the racial and ethnic inequities in the juvenile justice system by using a number of approaches. In addition to the emphasis on using data to make decisions and using appropriate screening tools to help divert youth from formal processing, they have also worked to address accountability to the population of Spanish speakers that they serve by increasing Spanish language capabilities throughout the system and the cultural competence of people working within the system, recruiting nontraditional service providers, and developing workforce opportunities for the youth. They have also established an Evening Reporting Center, which allows youth to stay in their homes and out of detention facilities after getting in trouble with the law. Every day from 3 to 9 p.m. youth who have been referred to the program must report to the facility, and staff people give the teens rides. They are required to bring homework to do, and if they don't have any they are provided with some. Snacks and dinner are also provided. Probation officers conduct urinalysis weekly, and staff members keep in weekly contact with their youths' families. Program employees also attempt to provide alternatives to out-of-home residential placements.[111] In Berks County, the overall detention rate of all youth, as well as that of youth of color, decreased over the span of the Models for Change program.

In Louisiana, Models for Change partners work to reduce the school-to-prison pipeline, which disproportionately affects poor youth and youth of color, by diverting status offense referrals to community programs or support services. The idea behind this interruption of the funneling of children with behavioral problems into the juvenile justice system is that children's problems in school (learning problems and behavior problems) are best addressed by experts in the schools, not in the detention facilities. Family members and support systems that can be engaged as well in addressing a young person's challenges are also crucial.

In Illinois, Models for Change associates conducted research used to show that a law on the books was having a disproportionately negative impact on youth of color and needed to be changed. The law, which allowed youth who were 15 or older to be automatically tried as adults if they were charged with drug offenses that took place within 1,000 feet of a public housing development or school, seriously impacted youth of color in cities such as Chicago. The Models for Change research demonstrated that in Cook County, which contains Chicago, 99% of the youth transferred were black or Latino. Due to national concern with these findings, Illinois changed the law, and now juveniles are processed through the juvenile court for such acts.[112]

THE FUTURE OF PREVENTION, REHABILITATION, AND RESTORATIVE JUSTICE APPROACHES TO DELINQUENCY

Based on the analysis of U.S. Census Bureau data, fewer youth in the United States than at any time since 1975 are locked up in juvenile detention institutions, and there has been a 41% decrease in the rate of youth confinement since 1995.[113] Nevertheless, children in the United States are significantly more likely to be held in an institution after committing an act of juvenile delinquency than are children in many other countries,[114] and youth of color and low-income youth (particularly Native American and black youth) are still disproportionately confined in juvenile institutions in spite of reductions across all demographics. The National Juvenile Justice Network's analysis of advances in juvenile justice reform in a mere two-year period lists *50 pages* of examples, signaling a large shift toward prevention and rehabilitation.[115] Several states in the late 1990s and early 2000s, in some cases inspired by lawsuits related to inadequate juvenile justice systems and in other cases inspired by a shift of juvenile justice responsibilities from the state to local levels, have changed their emphases from juvenile adjudication and detention to evidence-based prevention and rehabilitation practices. Five states that have relied heavily on evidence-based practices are Connecticut, Tennessee, Louisiana, Minnesota, and Arizona, and they have all reduced their juvenile confinement by more than half as a result.[116] As a whole, fewer youth are being held for less serious offenses such as property- and drug-related delinquency.

Although there appears to be a trend of support for increasing comprehensive approaches in the United States in the 2010s, which has been bolstered by the Supreme Court decisions about juvenile justice in the 2000s (see Chapter 11),[117] the necessity for prevention, rehabilitation, and restorative efforts still remains. The complex lives that young people live today warrant investment in their education and development as a means of helping them develop their potential and avoid involvement in potentially harmful delinquent activities. The National Juvenile Justice Network explains that the type of successful youth advocacy needed in the future depends on building awareness about the juvenile and justice in the community; finding scholars, activists, and other experts who get things done; amplifying the voices of those who are the most affected—children and teens; monitoring outcomes; and working with legislators, policymakers, practitioners, and funding agencies to make change.[118] Given the fact that many young people are similar to Chantal in this chapter's opening scenario—young people who are educated about juvenile delinquency and juvenile justice and ready to work for change—the challenges of the juvenile justice system will undoubtedly continue to be met with enthusiasm in the future. If these efforts are paired with adequate financial investment and intellectual commitment by society as a whole, they are likely to make a significant impact.

Although approaches to crime that are not solely punitive may not appear to be the most popular, as we move deeper into the 21st century, visible indications that methods for dealing with youth misbehavior give young people room to change and to turn their lives around—that allow them to be seen as people full of potential—are gaining an appreciation among researchers, judges, and practitioners. The various preventative, rehabilitative, and restorative methods that have been shown to be particularly effective, and that are highlighted in this chapter and throughout the book, are similar in that they all hold the possibility for change as a real one, and recognize (at least in part) that young people need social, familial, emotional, psychological, and financial resources to thrive.

Programs to prevent delinquency often utilize screening processes to identify youth in need of such resources. Traditionally these youth are labeled "at risk" (although many advocates now prefer "at promise"), and they are enrolled in programs that may be able to provide tools, skills, and resources to facilitate their development. Early intervention programs, such as Nurse-Family Partnerships and early education programs for preschoolers, have been shown to be related to positive outcomes that are preventative. Programs for older children and teens that researchers have found to be effective include a wide array of school- and community-based programs, such as LifeSkills Training, Project Toward No Drug Abuse, and PATHS. After-school programs and mentoring programs are also considered promising if they are structured in a particular manner. Efforts to dismantle the school-to-prison pipeline are large-scale efforts to change the policies and practices in schools and in the juvenile justice system that funnel marginalized

students from one institution to the other. Although this level of prevention and rehabilitation is harder to implement than the therapeutic approaches, it is a crucial part of any significant reduction of the disproportionate minority confinement that has long occurred in state juvenile justice systems. Many of the most positively evaluated youth rehabilitation programs are therapeutic in design and include Functional Family Therapy, Multisystemic Therapy, and Multidimensional Treatment Foster Care. Rehabilitation programs are used both inside of and as alternatives to formal processing of delinquent youth. Volunteer-run programs include an array of support and educational services that can help youth as well.

Restorative justice approaches to juvenile delinquency prevention and rehabilitation are increasingly popular. Victim-Offender Mediation, Family Group Conferencing, support circles, and restorative justice circles are four of the many types of restorative justice methods used to get to the root of why delinquency occurred; to facilitate the healing of the relationships between the person who committed harm, the victim(s), and the community; and to help people involved change their lives for the better. As is the case with prevention and rehabilitation programs, there is no one-size-fits-all formula to address the needs of all youth, as their particular social experiences need to be addressed. Many programs are tailored to youth based on their race, ethnicity, class, gender, and/or sexuality, and these programs tend to address delinquency more powerfully than programs that ignore such factors. Comprehensive programs that integrate a number of different programs into a delinquency reduction approach, such as the Models for Change program, are the most promising in terms of long-lasting transformation of the status quo.

EYE ON DIVERSITY EXERCISE: GLOBAL APPROACHES TO DELINQUENCY

Now that you have likely just finished reading this chapter's overview of a sample of the many approaches to prevention, rehabilitation, and restorative justice currently being used in the United States and around the globe, you are well equipped to think about what other approaches are promising.

1. Pick a country outside of your own, and find a scholarly article written in the last year that discusses programs that are the most successful at inspiring young people to stay out of trouble with the law there. Take some notes on what the approaches consist of and jot down whether they are classified as restorative, rehabilitative, and/or preventative.

2. Consider whether these approaches take into account the diversity of the youth of the country you have chosen and what has been done in your chosen country to address any social inequities that are present in that country (e.g., race or ethnicity based, or based on gender, sexuality, or class disparities).

3. Analyze the program and think about any additional components that might make the program more effective at addressing these inequities. Write a short paper that synthesizes all of your responses.

DISCUSSION QUESTIONS

1. In this chapter, we have highlighted some of the most effective methods of prevention and rehabilitation. Others that researchers have deemed to be ineffective have not been included, but may include some of the methods of punishment that you have heard about in popular discussions about juvenile delinquency. What are some other approaches to juvenile misbehavior that you thought might be classified as rehabilitative or preventative? Analyze what you know about these approaches. Are they actually aimed more at getting tough on juvenile delinquency than on bringing about meaningful change?

2. Restorative justice advocates frequently discuss the concept of accountability as a means of preventing and reducing juvenile delinquency and crime in general. Accountability is seen not just as accountability on behalf of juvenile offenders, but as accountability on behalf of the greater communities that create the conditions that encourage delinquency and crime. How does broadening the concept of accountability affect the ways that we should go about pursuing delinquency prevention and rehabilitation?

3. Many of the methods and programs that researchers have found to be the most effective for individual youth who have engaged in delinquency are therapy based. Pick one of the types of therapies discussed and consider its breadth. How does it attempt to influence change on the individual level? Does it attempt to address the familial level? What about the community level? Are there social or legal factors that affect these types of change as well? Discuss the implications of your answers and what they mean for juvenile delinquency prevention and rehabilitation efforts.

4. Consider how laws and policies shape juvenile prevention, rehabilitation, and restorative justice efforts. How can youth advocates and juvenile justice reformers best influence change at that level?

5. In this book as a whole, we have focused upon juvenile delinquency in a diverse society. Consider your own social location—race, ethnicity, social class, gender, sexuality, ability levels, age, and nationality—and think about what type of program or practice would have best addressed the reasons why you engaged in an act of delinquency, or a series of acts of delinquency, in your teenage years. (If you are the rare person who *never* did anything that could have been labeled delinquent if discovered, think about someone else's social location and life experiences instead.) How did your social world affect your choices? What would you have liked to have known back then, or what resources would you have liked to have had that might have made a difference to your decision making?

KEY TERMS

After-school programs 398

Circles of support 408

Early intervention programs 394

Evidence-based programs 413

Family Group Conferencing (FGC) 407

Functional Family Therapy (FFT) 400

Gender-responsive programming 403

Models for Change program 412

Multidimensional Treatment Foster Care (MTFC) 400

Multisystemic Therapy (MST) 400

Rehabilitation programs 399

Reintegrative shaming 405

Risk assessment 394

Secondary victims 407

Self-regulation skills 402

Sleeper effects 397

Victim-Offender Mediation (VOM) 405

CHAPTER PRETEST ANSWERS

1. False

2. False

3. True

4. True

5. True

6. False

7. True

8. False

9. True

STUDENT STUDY SITE

$SAGE edge™

edge.sagepub.com/bates2e

Sharpen your skills with SAGE edge!

SAGE edge for students provides a personalized approach to help you accomplish your coursework goals in an easy-to-use learning environment. You'll find action plans, mobile-friendly eFlashcards, and quizzes, as well as videos, web resources, and links to SAGE journal articles to support and expand on the concepts presented in this chapter. Check out the website for original videos of former offenders discussing their experiences as juveniles.

Abstinence model of drug use The model of drug use used by juvenile drug courts, which defines a young person's involvement in court-mandated programs as only when they completely stop *all* drug usage (10).

Abuse Overt aggression that can be categorized in three ways: physical, emotional, and/or sexual abuse (7).

Academic achievement The extent to which students achieve their academic goals (8).

Achieved category A flexible category that individuals may be able to move in and out of (1).

Adaptations to strain The five ways that Merton theorized that people adjust to the strain created by the societal goals and the legitimate means by which to achieve those goals: conformity, innovation, ritualism, retreatism, and rebellion (5).

Adjudication The stage at which a juvenile goes before the court for a hearing in which it is determined whether the juvenile did or did not engage in the alleged crimes (12).

After-school programs Delinquency prevention programs that aim to involve young people in organized social behaviors, learning activities, and/or recreational activities after school so that they have less unsupervised time to engage in delinquency (14).

Alienation A low degree of integration or high degree of isolation or distance between an individual and another individual, group, community, or institution (8).

Androcentrism An approach that places boys' and men's experience at the center of scholarly examination, thereby neglecting or ignoring aspects of girls' and women's experience (6).

Anomic suicide One of the types of suicide that Durkheim theorized, which was more likely to occur in societies experiencing rapid social change and a lack of social norms (5).

Anomie theory Durkheim's theory that proposes that rapid social change often results in a state of normlessness that results in the deregulation of people and their behavior (5).

Appeal to higher loyalties A neutralization technique in which a youth who has committed a delinquent act justifies it on the basis of a higher calling or purpose (4).

Arrest rate The number of arrests per 100,000 in the population (3).

Ascribed category A category that an individual is born into and cannot change (1).

Attachment The "emotional" component of the social bond that signifies that individuals care about what others think (4).

Automatic waiver A list of offenses for which a juvenile is automatically moved to the adult system (12).

Autonomous gang A type of female gang that exists on its own with no attachment to male gangs (9).

Auxiliary gang A type of female gang that works together with a male gang (9).

Behavioral coping According to strain theory, a type of coping strategy that focuses on actions that might help to reduce the strain itself (4).

Belief The component of the social bond that suggests the stronger one's awareness of, understanding of, and agreement with the rules and norms of society, the less likely one will be to deviate (4).

Bifurcated hearing The division of a trial into two parts, for example, an adjudication hearing and a disposition hearing (12).

Biological determinism The view that biology is responsible for criminal behavior (4).

Boot camp A correctional alternative in which juveniles participate in a program with military structure focused on physical activity and strict rules (13).

Bullying The use of physical strength or emotional influence to intimidate another individual (8).

Child maltreatment The general term for child abuse that includes both abuse and neglect (7).

Circles of support Offender-oriented circles that help people get back on their feet after detention or incarceration and facilitate their community reintegration (14).

Civil gang injunction A court-issued restraining order prohibiting members of enjoined criminal street gangs from activities that can be defined as public nuisances (9).

Class conflict The conflict between owners and workers that Marx and Engels stated was built into the workings of a capitalist economy (6).

Class struggle The outward manifestation of discontent that arises after workers realize that their class interests are being oppressed in a capitalist system; it may be expressed in forms such as protests and strikes (6).

Clearance rate The rate at which a certain crime category is closed because of arrest or exceptional means (3).

Coercive mobility The removal of people from a poor neighborhood as a result of incarceration. A formerly incarcerated youth or adult re-enters the neighborhood with the added socialization of the prison or detention center subculture, which is said to increase the heterogeneity of community values and lead to further disorganization (5).

Cognitive coping According to strain theory, a type of coping strategy that involves trying to reinterpret the strain to lessen the impact of that strain (4).

Collective conscience Society's shared moral sense or sense of right and wrong according to Durkheim (5).

Collective efficacy Social cohesion among neighbors that is characterized by efforts to make positive changes in their neighborhoods (5).

Commitment The "rational" component of the social bond that signifies that individuals weigh the costs and benefits of their behavior (4).

Community service restitution A sanction in which the juvenile offender is required to perform some sort of service for the community (13).

Concentric zone model A model used by social disorganization theorists in which they map an urban area from its urban center, or downtown, to the zone of transition, multiple-family zone, single-family zone, and suburban or commuter zone and measure the degree of social disorganization in each (5).

Condemnation of the condemners A neutralization technique in which a person tries to turn the tables on those who condemn or disapprove of his or her behavior by condemning them (4).

Conflict delinquent subculture A subculture in which youth oppose the mainstream through violence, underground economies, and/or gang activity because of a lack of opportunities to succeed (5).

Conflict theorist A theorist who assumes that society is based on class conflict and that laws tend to reflect the interests of the powerful (6).

Consensus theorist A theorist who assumes that society is based upon consensus and that laws generally reflect agreed-upon societal expectations (5).

Correctional institution An institution, also known as a training school or reformatory, that is the most popular type of residential facility in use in the juvenile justice system (13).

Criminal delinquent subculture A subculture in which youth commit acts of delinquency as a means to an end—usually to obtain something material or monetary to gain status in the group (5).

Critical conception of delinquency A conception that critiques the existing social system that creates norms of oppression (1).

Crossover youth Any youth who has experienced abuse or neglect and engaged in delinquency whether formally in either system or not (12).

Cumulative disadvantage Disadvantage that a labeled delinquent youth experiences due to stigmatization in society's primary social institutions: family, school, peers, and the government-run juvenile justice system; it may result in a narrowing of positive life options and encourage delinquency (6).

Cyberbullying The use of technology such as social media sites or texting to intimidate another individual (8).

D.A.R.E. The Drug Abuse Resistance Education program, which uses anti–drug use curriculum delivered by law enforcement officers in school classrooms in an effort to deter kids from using drugs (10).

Deductive reasoning Reasoning from general ideas (theory) to more specific observations (data). Deductive reasoning is often used in quantitative research (3).

Deinstitutionalization The act of moving a juvenile out of and/or avoiding the detention of a juvenile in an institution as a punishment for wrongdoing; this movement has been aimed in recent years at status offenders (11).

Denial of injury A neutralization technique in which the person denies that anyone has been harmed by her or his actions (4).

Denial of responsibility The belief that outside forces compel a person's behavior, and thus the person refuses to take responsibility for his or her actions (4).

Denial of the victim A neutralization technique in which a person justifies his or her behavior by stating that the person who was victimized deserved it, or that because of circumstances, the delinquent act committed needed to occur (4).

Detention facilities Centers in which juveniles are housed while awaiting their adjudication hearing, or in some instances their disposition hearing (13).

Determinism The concept that factors *outside of* the conscious control of individuals, chiefly the social organization of society and/or the environment, influence or determine behavior (5).

Deviancy training The idea that group therapy for youth drug use sometimes functions to spark interest in future drug use among casual users who participate (10).

Deviant career Delinquency, crime, or deviance that an individual pursues over the span of his or her life (6).

Differential association The learning of behaviors and norms from the groups with which we have contact (4).

Differential opportunity theory Cloward and Ohlin's theory that builds upon Merton's strain theory by focusing on access to illegitimate means (5).

Dignity in Schools Campaign A national coalition of grassroots organizations that advocate

for human dignity in our schools and are focused on the detrimental impact of what they call "push out" in these schools (8).

Discipline A process that includes punishment for wrongdoing (7).

Disposition The stage at which it is determined what punishment a juvenile will receive for his or her alleged acts of delinquency (12).

Disproportionate minority contact The disproportionate number of minority youth who come into contact with the juvenile justice system (12).

Diversion A process that allows the juvenile justice system to offer programs designed to help a juvenile without the young person having to go formally through the system (12).

Dropping out The act of quitting school before graduating (8).

Drug Abuse Warning Network (DAWN) A network that existed until 2011 that created yearly reports on the number of youth who ended up in emergency departments due to their use of alcohol and/or other drugs (10).

Drug courts Courts that first emerged in the 1990s in the United States and deliver a series of services geared at helping youth using drugs to become rehabilitated and stop their usage (10).

Drug prohibition An approach to drug use that involves the harsh punishment of drug users (10).

Drug testing A method used to deter drug use by means of testing bodily materials (e.g., urine, hair, saliva) for evidence of drug consumption (10).

Dually adjudicated youth Dually involved youth who have actually been adjudicated by both the juvenile justice and dependency courts (12).

Dually involved youth Crossover youth who are receiving services from both the juvenile justice and dependency courts simultaneously (12).

Early intervention programs Delinquency prevention programs that are focused on the time during childhood and early adolescence when youth are receptive to nurturing and supportive environments (14).

Ecological fallacy The mistake of making an inference about an individual based on aggregate data for the group (3).

Ectomorphic A body type that is fragile, thin, and delicate, with poor muscles and weak bones (4).

Educational neglect Neglect characterized by the failure to meet a child's educational needs, such as neglecting to enroll him or her in school or allowing chronic truancy (7).

Egalitarian household A household in which both partners (for example, mother and father) have similar levels of power (7).

Electronic monitoring The process by which an offender is monitored in the community through the use of technology/electronic devices (13).

Emotional abuse The constant criticism, rejection, or demeaning of a person (7).

Emotional coping According to strain theory, a type of coping strategy that is an attempt to lessen the negative emotions that might arise from the strain (4).

Emotional neglect Ignoring a child's need for affection or engaging in the abuse of others, such as spousal abuse, in front of a child (7).

Endomorphic A body type that is soft and round with small bones, short limbs, and soft smooth skin (4).

Environmental determinism The view that one's environment or experiences are responsible for criminal behavior (4).

Ethnography A qualitative method that is the scientific description of the customs of a group (3).

Evidence-based programs Prevention-based programs that social science research has demonstrated are among the most effective (14).

Family conflict Considered a family process in which there is unrest or bad feelings between either the juvenile in question and his or her parents or siblings, or the juvenile's parents (7).

Family Group Conferencing (FGC) A means of handing acts of juvenile delinquency in line with restorative justice aims, involving a conference between victims, offenders, and their families, as well as police, youth advocates, community members, and other interested parties who decide what should be done in the aftermath of harm (14).

Family process The interactions and social exchanges that happen within a family (7).

Family structure The compositional makeup of the family, such as parental type

(for example, single parent or stepparent) or number of children in the household (7).

Feminisms The many theories that center on gender and the ways it is constructed and reinforced through laws and social practices (6).

Folkways Everyday norms that do not generate much uproar if they are violated (1).

Foster home A household, designed to replicate a home environment, in which a delinquent or neglected child may be placed when he or she cannot be sent back home (13).

Functional Family Therapy (FFT) A short-term program that is typically 30 hours long, in which a therapist, a social worker, or a trained probation officer works with a young person and her or his family after the youth has engaged in wrongdoing to address any communication problems and negative or violent behaviors (14).

Gang intervention Efforts to get youth out of gangs once they are already involved in them (9).

Gang prevention Concerted efforts to stop the formation of gangs and the involvement of youth in existing gangs (9).

Gang reentry Efforts to provide resources to help youth who were incarcerated for gang delinquency find jobs, shelter, and help with schooling (9).

Gang suppression Attempts to crack down on gang delinquency by using law enforcement powers to arrest and incarcerate youth (9).

Gender-responsive programming Delinquency prevention program that

takes into account gendered experiences of youth (e.g., delinquency programming aimed at girls) (14).

Gendered pathways Pathways to delinquency that are influenced by one's gender (6).

General deterrence A justification for punishment that involves the goal of punishing an individual as a means of deterring others from participating in delinquency or crime (11).

Group home An alternative to the traditional in-home foster care for children in which a number of children live for various amounts of time with a single set of house parents or rotating staff (13).

Halfway house A rehabilitative center or house in which juveniles are helped to readjust to the outside world after incarceration (13).

Harm reduction An approach to drug use that takes a public health angle and acknowledges that illegal and legal drug use are always going to occur, so they need to be addressed in a way that minimizes the harm associated with use (10).

Harmful legal products Legal products that are used or consumed in an effort to get intoxicated or high, and can have negative repercussions (e.g., airplane glue, gasoline, and over-the-counter drugs) (10).

Heterogeneity Difference and diversity; in a neighborhood context heterogeneity often reduces informal social control (5).

Heterosexism The institutionalized favoritism toward heterosexual people and bias against others (6).

Home confinement Intensive supervision by a probation officer and electronic monitoring to control juveniles (13).

Houses of refuge Institutions developed in the United States in the early 19th century to house children who were poor and steer them away from pursuing a life of crime through hard labor and a strict system of punishment (2).

Hypothesis A testable supposition or tentative explanation for a phenomenon (3).

Incapacitation A justification for punishment that believes it is useful for making someone incapable of committing a crime, usually through isolating and/or restricting movement and decision making (11).

Incarceration rate The number of prisoners per 100,000 population (also known as imprisonment rate) (7).

Individual classism Prejudice or discrimination based solely on someone's class (1).

Individual racism The belief in the inferiority of certain racial or ethnic groups, often accompanied by discrimination (1).

Individual sexism Prejudice or discrimination based solely on someone's sex (1).

Individual (specific) deterrence A justification for punishment that involves the goal of punishing an individual as a means of stopping her or him from doing the same act of delinquency or crime in the future (11).

Inductive reasoning Reasoning that moves from specific observations (data) to broader generalizations (theory) based on those observations. Qualitative research often uses inductive reasoning (3).

Informal social control The means by which ordinary people exert control over others' behavior through enforcing traditions or norms and by informally punishing those who break such norms through the use of gossip, stigmatization, and disapproval (5).

Institutional classism: Classism that occurs when individuals are disadvantaged or oppressed because of their class because of the routine workings of social institutions (1).

Institutional racism Racism that occurs when individuals are disadvantaged or oppressed because of their race because of the routine workings of social institutions (1).

Institutional sexism Sexism that occurs when individuals are disadvantaged or oppressed because of their sex or gender because of the routine workings of social institutions (1).

Intake An initial screening stage at which the intake officer determines whether a juvenile's case should be dismissed from the system or should be referred to the system for either informal or formal services (12).

Intersectionality The ways in which race, ethnicity, class, gender, age, sexuality, and ability (and other social factors) interact to shape a person's social experience (6).

Intervening variables Variables that change the relationships between other variables because of their existence (e.g., Sampson and Groves stated that sparse friendship networks, unsupervised peer groups, and low organizational participation intervened in the relationship between social disorganization and delinquency) (5).

Involvement The component of the social bond that suggests the more time one spends engaged in conforming activities, the less time one has available to deviate (4).

Judicial waiver The most common type of waiver to the adult court in which a judge or magistrate has the discretion to transfer a juvenile to adult criminal court (12).

Juvenile dependency process The process by which it is determined whether a juvenile is safe in his or her home with his or her guardians or parents (12).

Laws The strongest norms because they are backed by official sanctions (or formal responses) (1).

Life course theory A theoretical perspective that considers the entire course of human life (from childhood, adolescence, and adulthood to old age) as social constructions that reflect the broader structural conditions of society (4).

Looking-glass self The idea that a person imagines how others perceive her or him and then internalizes that idea as her or his own (6).

Macro-level theories Theories of delinquency that focus on the social structure or the big picture of society (5).

Master status A status or label that comes to be held as more powerful than others (e.g., "delinquent") (6).

Mechanical society Durkheim's concept of preindustrial societies that shared a strong collective conscience and had high levels of informal social control (5).

Mens rea A Latin term meaning "guilty mind," which is central to determinations of criminal responsibility for adults (2).

Mesomorphic A body type that is muscled and strong, with an upright, hard, sturdy physique (4).

Micro-level theories Theories of delinquency that focus on the individual level (4).

Mixed-gender gang A type of female gang that has both boys and girls in its ranks (9).

Models for Change Program One of the best known evidence-based delinquency programs in the United States today, involving numerous states and parties in its complex implementation and design; it is based primarily at the National Center for Juvenile Justice in Pittsburgh, Pennsylvania, but involves a large network of justice professionals based across the country (14).

Monetary restitution A sanction in which the juvenile offender is required to pay the victim for monetary damages that the juvenile created (13).

Monitoring the Future study One of the best known sources of data related to teen drug use today; a University of Michigan study that surveys around 50,000 youth about their drug use patterns in middle and high schools in Grades 8, 10, and 12 across the United States, and then one more time the year after they graduate (3).

Moral entrepreneurs People who work to garner attention toward a social issue or group that they have decided amounts to a social problem, which is followed by negative labeling of the targeted behaviors and/or actors (6).

Moral panic Heightened concern over an issue that is not in line with its seriousness or frequency of occurrence in the world (2).

Mores "Moral" norms that may generate more outrage if broken (1).

Multidimensional Treatment Foster Care (MTFC) A specialized foster care program in which community families are recruited, trained, and closely supervised as they take a teenager into their homes; it involves behavior modification, therapy, and intense interaction as a means of supporting youth (14).

Multiple marginality theory Vigil's theory that links the many ways that youth are marginalized in society (ranging from the macro level to the individual level) to their eventual involvement in a gang (9).

Multisystemic Therapy (MST) A therapy that engages a youth's entire family in the hopes of reducing aggressive, delinquent, and other undesirable behaviors through education and tips related to stress, parenting, and familial relationships and the creation of supportive family networks (14).

National Crime Victimization Survey The primary U.S. source of data on criminal victimization (3).

National Incident-Based Reporting System A reporting system that houses data on incidents, both crimes known to police and arrests, on 46 specific crimes (expanded categories over the UCR) (3).

National Survey on Drug Use and Health (NSDUH) A yearly SAMHSA survey of drug use patterns of over 65,000 people 12 years of age and older that occurs through face-to-face interviews at respondents' homes (10).

Negative punishment Something that is taken away, instead of introduced, as a punishment (4).

Negative reinforcement An event that strengthens behavior because the behavior stops a negative event that an individual wants to stop (4).

Neglect The act of depriving or failing to provide for a child's basic needs (7).

Net-widening The concept that more juveniles will get drawn into the juvenile justice system than necessary because, for example, the repercussions do not seem to be something from which children need protection or actions once determined to be legal become illegal (12).

Normative conception of delinquency A conception that assumes that there is a general set of norms of behavior, conduct, and conditions with which we can agree (1).

Normative theory A theory that assumes that there is a standard or agreed-upon set of societal norms that everyone knows and can, therefore, live by (4).

Opportunity hypothesis of delinquency The hypothesis that the most important factor that influences youth to engage in delinquency is not necessarily having friends who are highly delinquent, but is, instead, the amount of time that youth spend with their friends away from parents, teachers, and other social control agents (9).

Organic society Durkheim's concept of industrial societies that are fragmented due to the division of labor, yet maintain a sense of collective conscience (although weaker than in mechanical society) (5).

Parens patriae A Latin term signifying the philosophical concept that the state should serve as a substitute parent in cases in which children's actual parents either neglect or abuse them, or simply cannot control their behavior. The doctrine was adopted from English common law and serves as the rationale for juvenile justice systems in the United States (2).

Parental rights The rights of a parent to have a say in a child's legal and physical custody (7).

Participant observation A qualitative method of data collection in which the researcher studies a group by sharing in its activities and daily life (3).

Patriarchy A social system that is based on "the rule of the father" and a male-dominated power structure that is evident in the majority of social institutions (6).

Petition A short statement of the facts of an alleged crime that are filed in the juvenile court (12).

Physical abuse Abuse that includes kicking, hitting, throwing, burning, stabbing, biting, shaking, or otherwise physically accosting another individual (7).

Physical neglect Deprivation that results in physical harm for a child (7).

Plea bargaining The process by which the juvenile agrees to plead guilty to a crime in exchange for a lower charge or lesser disposition (sentence) (12).

Polysubstance use The use of multiple drugs or substances at the same time (10).

Positive punishment A punishment that is introduced or added to decrease a behavior (4).

Positive reinforcement A reward for behavior, for example the pleasurable feeling that people might feel they get from doing drugs (4).

Positivism An approach to the study of delinquency and other behaviors that involves the use of scientific observations and controls (11).

Power The ability to make things happen and to exert your will or wishes upon others (6).

Preadjudication detention The stage at which a juvenile can be kept in detention prior to his or her adjudication hearing (12).

Prevention Any number of programs and policies geared at keeping youth on the conventional path and out of delinquency involvement (5).

Preventive detention The expanded use of detention to include the consideration of whether a juvenile will engage in delinquent offenses while awaiting his or her hearing (12).

Primary deviance The initial act of deviance or delinquency that a person engages in according to labeling theorists (6).

Property crime index Measure of property crime comprising four offenses: arson, larceny, burglary, and motor vehicle theft (3).

Prosecutorial waiver A list of offenses for which the prosecuting attorney has the discretion to file in either the juvenile or the adult court (12).

Qualitative data Data that are descriptive in nature that can be observed rather than measured (3).

Quantitative data Data that are measured or identified on a numerical scale (3).

Racism The systematic subordination of people of color based on and maintained by stereotypes of inferiority (6).

Random sample When each individual in the group (population) has the same chances of making it into the sample as the next individual (3).

Reentry The term used for the process of ending incarceration and reestablishing one's life after incarceration (13).

Rehabilitation The original philosophical justification for punishment that served as the basis for the creation of a separate juvenile justice system; the idea that youth who engage in delinquency and misbehavior should be taught how to change their ways in order to develop prosocial behaviors (2).

Rehabilitation programs Programs that are focused on changing juveniles' behavior after they have already engaged in an act of delinquency; these programs tend to be focused on the individual level and heavily influenced by psychological and social-psychological theories of human development (14).

Reintegrative shaming The shaming of someone who has done wrong that is followed by reintegration of the wrongdoer into the fabric of his or her family or greater community as a means of reducing recidivism and promoting restorative justice (14).

Relational isolation The avoidance of friendships that is actively pursued by some youth to protect themselves from violence (9).

Residential therapeutic community Drug programs in which youth live away from home in a facility for an extended period of time to address their drug use (10).

Restitution The act of "paying back" the victim of an act of delinquency or his or her family by means of money, volunteer labor, community service, or some other agreed-upon method (13).

Restoration A justification for punishment that focuses on dealing with delinquency as a harm and bringing healing in the aftermath of a harm (11).

Retreatist delinquent subculture A subculture of youth who join together after failing to find a place in either the criminal or the conflict delinquent subculture (5).

Retribution A justification for punishment that is based on the idea of just deserts; punishment that is proportionate to the act that a person has committed (11).

Risk assessment The practice of using properly constructed screening tools to identify risk factors for delinquency in order to address them before a young person engages in misbehavior (14).

Routine activities theory A theory that states that gang involvement results because youth have too much free time on their hands and opportunities to join a gang (9).

Rumspringa The period in Amish teenagers' lives in which they explore the world outside of their community to make sure they want to commit to their religion; it is known to involve experimentation with drugs and alcohol (10).

Sample A smaller group that is representative of the whole (3).

School failure A process by which a student falls farther and farther behind his friends and expected level in his or her educational development, gradually disengaging from the school system (8).

School-to-Prison Pipeline An argument that overly harsh rules, security enhancements, and punishments mean that for many students school becomes a preparation ground for prison (8).

Secondary deviance An act of deviance or delinquency that follows the labeling of a person as a delinquent or troublemaker (6).

Secondary victims Indirect victims of an act of delinquency such as family members who are impacted negatively by the victimization of a member of their family, or community members who are frightened for their own safety because of an act of delinquency (14).

Selective incapacitation A variant of the incapacitation justification for punishment in which high-risk offenders can be identified and incapacitated for long periods of time, while lower-risk offenders can be handled with less serious punishments and for shorter amounts of time (11).

Self-concept A concept that refers to the way in which a person views her- or himself (6).

Self-regulation skills Skills that help young people control their own behavior and aim for positive goals (14).

Self-report survey A data collection method in which respondents select the responses themselves, usually in questionnaire format (3).

Sexism The systematic subordination of girls and women based on and maintained by stereotypes of inferiority (6).

Sexting The use of cell phones or other electronic devices to send or receive sexually suggestive messages (9).

Sexual abuse Abuse that consists of rape, molestation, incest, and other sexual assaults (7).

Sleeper effects Effects of a program or intervention that may not show themselves until several years after its completion, making it difficult to judge the program or intervention's effectiveness (14).

Social bonds Bonds to conformity that keep us from engaging in socially unacceptable activities (4).

Social constructions of youth and delinquency Popular ideas about delinquency that are created and influenced by social, political, and economic factors and that change over time (2).

Social differentiation The process by which we define, describe, and distinguish people based on different categories (1).

Social disorganization theory The theory of delinquency that posits that neighborhoods may become so disorganized that delinquent behavior occurs as a result (5).

Social ecology The study of relationships between individuals, social groups, and the environment (5).

Social exclusion Youth who are negatively labeled as delinquents may later find themselves shut out or excluded from conventional or beneficial opportunities (6).

Social facts Dimensions of social life that are external to the individual and that restrain individuals, including values, cultural norms, and social structures (5).

Social inequality Unequal distribution of resources, services, and positions (1).

Social inequity A concept that refers to unfair distributions of power and social control (6).

Socialization hypothesis of delinquency The hypothesis

about delinquency that states that youth who socialize with friends who are highly delinquent will be more apt to be delinquent themselves (9).

Sociological positivist theories Social theories that have been created by scholars using scientific methods (i.e., observation, measurement, and empirical verification) (5).

Spoiled identity Goffman's term for what happens when a person has been labeled as delinquent, criminal, or deviant, and the negative identity sticks, leaving him or her in a perpetual state of stigmatization (6).

Status offenses Acts that are considered problematic because of the age of the person carrying them out (e.g., truancy and curfew violations); acts that are not considered crimes and for which adults cannot get in trouble, but that society does not want juveniles doing (1).

Stigmatization The process by which a person is marked or labeled as a deviant or disgrace, which can spoil a person's normal identity and reduce his or her life chances (6).

Strain theory Merton's idea of what happens when social norms of conventional success (i.e., the American Dream) are not accompanied by equally strong or available legitimate means of achieving that success; strain can often lead to delinquency and/or deviance (5).

Street socialization When youth bond with others who share a common background and become part of a subcultural group in which they develop and share their own values (9).

Subcultural delinquency theory The theory that involvement in small groups of youth in marginalized neighborhoods or social groups arises in the face of limited legitimate opportunities and often leads to delinquency (5).

Subculture of violence theory A perspective that characterizes youth gangs as the result of a formation of a peer group that actively opposes middle-class mainstream norms of nonviolent behavior through the creation of a hypermasculine, aggressive subculture (9).

Supervision A family process in which the juvenile's actions are either directly known or indirectly known by a parent or guardian (7).

Symbiosis A state of interdependence that social disorganization theorists state characterizes the social world (5).

Symbolic interactionism A framework that examines the way that people make meaning out of symbols, words, and other forms of communication to make sense of the world (6).

Techniques of neutralization Rationalizations used by individuals in order for individuals to engage in delinquency even though they understand it is wrong (4).

Throwaways The term used for youth whose parents have kicked them out of the house (7).

Tracking A practice that occurs when juveniles are placed in classrooms or groups within the classroom based

28. Krisberg, B., & Austin J. (1993). *Reinventing juvenile justice*. Thousand Oaks, CA: Sage.

29. Feld, B. (1993). Juvenile (in)justice and the criminal court alternative. *Crime and Delinquency, 39*, 403–424.

30. Feld, Juvenile (in)justice and the criminal court alternative; Harris, A. (2007). Diverting and abdicating judicial discretion: Cultural, political, and procedural dynamics in California juvenile justice. *Law & Society Review, 41*, 387–427.

31. Feld, B. (1998). Juvenile and criminal justice systems' responses to youth violence. *Crime and Justice, 24*, 189–261.

32. Harris, Diverting and abdicating judicial discretion.

CHAPTER 2

1. Matsell, G. W. (1970). Report of the Chief of Police concerning destitution and crime among children in the city. In W. B. Sanders (Ed.), *Juvenile offenders for a thousand years* (pp. 378–383). Chapel Hill, NC: North Carolina Press see p. 14. (Original work published 1849)

2. Bosman, J. (2010, January 20). City signals intent to put fewer teenagers in jail. *The New York Times*. Retrieved from http://www.nytimes.com/2010/01/21/nyregion/21juvenile.html

3. Ibid.

4. Ibid.

5. Feld, B. (1999). *Bad kids: Race and the transformation of the juvenile court*. New York, NY: Oxford University Press.

6. Mennel, R. (1973). *Thorns and thistles: Juvenile delinquents in the United States, 1825–1940*. Hanover, NH: University Press of New England, p. xii.

7. Garland, R. (1991). Juvenile delinquency in the Graeco-Roman world. *History Today, 41*(10), 12–19, especially p. 13.

8. Ibid.

9. Ibid.

10. Ariès, P. (1962). *Centuries of childhood: A social history of family life*. New York, NY: Vintage Books; de Mause, L. (1974). *The history of childhood*. New York, NY: Harper Books; Feld, *Bad kids*.

11. de Mause, *The history of childhood*.

12. Feld, *Bad kids*; Kett, J. (1977). *Rites of passage: Adolescence in America 1790 to present*. New York, NY: Basic Books.

13. Blackstone, W. (1795). *Commentaries on the laws of England* (12th ed., Vol. IV). London, UK: Clarendon Press.

14. Pintard, J. (1827). *Report of the committee appointed by the Board of Guardians for the Poor of the City and Districts of Philadelphia to visit the cities of Baltimore, New York, Providence, Boston, and Salem*. Philadelphia, PA: Samuel Parker, p. 338.

15. Mennel, *Thorns and thistles*; Platt, A. M. (2009). *The child savers: The invention of delinquency* (expanded 40th anniversary edition) with an introduction and critical commentaries compiled by Miroslava Chávez-García. New Brunswick, NJ: Rutgers University Press. (Original work published 1969)

16. Feld, *Bad kids*; Postman, N. (1994). *The disappearance of childhood*. New York, NY: Vintage Books.

17. Quoted in Sanders, W. B. (Ed.). (1970). *Juvenile offenders for a thousand years: Selected readings from Anglo-Saxon times to 1900*. Chapel Hill, NC: University of North Carolina Press, p. 40.

18. Mennel, *Thorns and thistles*, p. xxvi.

19. Bush, B. (2006). The rediscovery of juvenile delinquency. *The Journal of the Gilded Age and the Progressive Era, 5*(4), 393–402; Mennel, *Thorns and thistles*.

20. Fox, S. J. (1970). Juvenile justice reform: An historical perspective. *Stanford Law Review, 22*, 1187–1239.

21. Young, V. D. (1994). Race and gender and the establishment of juvenile institutions. *The Prison Journal, 73*, 244–265.

22. *Ex parte Crouse*, 4 Wharton (Pa.) 9 (1838).

23. Mennel, *Thorns and thistles*.

24. Ibid.

25. Fox, Juvenile justice reform; Pisciotta, A. W. (1985). Treatment on trial: The rhetoric and reality of the New York House of Refuge, 1857–1935. *The American Journal of Legal History, 29*(2), 151–181.

26. Chávez-García, M. (2007). Intelligence testing at Whittier State School, 1890–1920. *Pacific Historical Review, 76,* 193–228; Ward, G. (2006). The "other" child savers: Racial politics of the parental state. In A. Platt (Ed.), *The child savers: The invention of delinquency* (expanded 40th anniversary edition) with an introduction and critical commentaries compiled by Miroslava Chávez-García (pp. 225–241). New Brunswick, NJ: Rutgers University Press; Young, Race and gender, 244–265.

27. Mennel, R. (1971). Juvenile delinquency in perspective. *History of Education Quarterly, 13,* 275–281; Odem, M. (1995). *Delinquent daughters: Protecting and policing adolescent female sexuality in the United States, 1885–1920.* Chapel Hill, NC: University of North Carolina Press; Pickett, R. (1969). *House of refuge: Origins of juvenile reform in New York state, 1815–1857.* Syracuse, NY: Syracuse University Press.

28. Shelden, R. (1979). From slave to case society: Penal changes in Tennessee, 1830–1915. *Historical Quarterly, 38,* 462–478.

29. Frey, C. (1981). The house of refuge for colored children. *Journal of Negro History, 66,* 1–28; Mennel, *Thorns and thistles*.

30. Frey, The house of refuge for colored children, 1–28.

31. Ibid., especially p. 13.

32. Brenzel, B. (1985). *Daughters of the state: A social portrait of the first reform school for girls in North America: 1856–1905.* Cambridge, MA: MIT Press; Freedman, E. (1981). *Their sisters' keepers: Women's prison reform in America, 1830–1930.* Ann Arbor: University of Michigan Press; Schlossman, S., & Wallach, S. (1978). The crime of precocious sexuality: Female juvenile delinquency in the progressive era. *Harvard Educational Review, 48,* 65–94.

33. Schlossman & Wallach, The crime of precocious sexuality, 65–94.

34. Ibid.

35. Brenzel, *Daughters of the state*.

36. Clement, P. F. (1985). The city and the child, 1860–1885. In J. Hawes & N. R. Hiner (Eds.), *American childhood* Westport, CT: Greenwood; Feld, *Bad kids*.

37. Kett, *Rites of passage*.

38. Feld, *Bad kids*; Platt, *The child savers*.

39. Wiebe, R. H. (1967). *The search for order, 1877–1920.* New York, NY: Hill and Wang.

40. Feld, *Bad kids*.

41. Hall, G. S. (1904). *Adolescence: Its psychology and relations to physiology, anthropology, sociology, sex, crime, religion, and education* (Vols. I & II). New York, NY: Appleton, as cited in Arnett, J. J. (2006). G. Stanley Hall's adolescence: Brilliance and nonsense. *History of Psychology, 9*(3), 186–197, especially p. 188.

42. Mennel, Juvenile delinquency in perspective, 275–281.

43. Chávez-García, Intelligence testing at Whittier State School, 193–228.

44. Mennel, *Thorns and thistles*.

45. Most famously Platt, *The child savers*; Trost, J. (2005). *Gateway to justice: The juvenile court and progressive child welfare in a southern city.* Athens: University of Georgia Press; Ward, The "other" child savers.

46. Feld, *Bad kids*.

47. Lemann, N. (1992). *The great black migration and how it changed America.* New York, NY: Vintage Books.

48. Richie, B. (2005). Queering antiprison work: African American lesbians in the juvenile justice system. In J. Sudbury (Ed.), *Global lockdown: Race, gender, and the prison industrial complex* (pp. 73–85). New York, NY: Routledge; Ware, W. (2015). "Rounding up the homosexuals": The impact of juvenile court on queer and trans/gender non-conforming youth. In E. A. Stanley & Nat Smith (Eds.), *Captive genders: Trans embodiment and the prison industrial complex* (2nd ed., pp. 97–104). Chico, CA: AK Press.

49. Cohen, S. (1972). *Folk devils and moral panics*. London, UK: MacGibbon & Kee; Goode, E., & Ben-Yehuda, N. (2009). *Moral panics: The social construction of deviance* (2nd ed.). Malden, MA: Wiley-Blackwell. See also Chapter 6 in this book.

50. Ferguson, C. J., & Olson, C. K. (2010, July). The Supreme Court and video game violence: Will regulation be worth the costs to the First Amendment? *The Criminologist, 35*(4), 18–24; Gauntlett, D. (1995). *Moving experiences: Understanding television's influences and effects*. Luton, UK: John Libbey.

51. Smith, W. (1778). *Mild punishments sound policy: Or observations on the laws relative to debtors and felons*. London, UK: J. Bew, pp. 44–45.

52. Brown, J. P. (1833). *Fifth annual report of the House of Refuge of Philadelphia*. Philadelphia, PA: William Brown, p. 14.

53. Park, D. (2002). The Kefauver comic book hearings as show trial: Decency, authority, and the dominated expert. *Cultural Studies, 16*(2), 259–288.

54. Travis, T. (1908). *The young malefactor: A study in juvenile delinquency, its causes, and treatment*. New York, NY: T. Y. Crowell.

55. Gilbert, J. B. (1986). *A cycle of outrage: America's reaction to the juvenile delinquency in the 1950s*. New York, NY: Oxford University Press.

56. Faulkner, A. S. (1921). Does jazz put the sin in syncopation? *Ladies Home Journal*, 16–34.

57. McMahon, J. R. (1921). Unspeakable jazz must go. *Ladies Home Journal, 38,* 116.

58. Gilbert, *A cycle of outrage*; Goode & Ben-Yehuda, *Moral panics*.

59. Goode & Ben-Yehuda, *Moral panics*.

60. Scott, M. (2014). My looking-glass self. *Represent: The Voice of Youth in Care*. Retrieved from http://representmag.org/issues/FCYU116/My_Looking-Glass_Self.html?story_id=FCYU-2014-04-05

61. Binder, A. (1993). Constructing racial rhetoric: Media depictions of harm in heavy metal and rap music. *American Sociological Review, 58*(6), 753–767.

62. Mann, P. (1988, July). How shock rock harms our kids. *Readers Digest*, p. 101.

63. Binder, Constructing racial rhetoric.

64. Ibid.

65. Ibid.

66. Quinn, M. (1996). "Never shoulda been let out of the penitentiary": Gangsta rap and the struggle over racial identity. *Cultural Critique, 34* (Autumn), 65–89; Quinn, E. (2005). *Nuthin' but a "g"thang*. New York, NY: Columbia University Press.

67. Leeds, J. (2007, September 26). Hearing focuses on language and violence in rap music. *The New York Times*. Retrieved from http://www.nytimes.com/2007/09/26/washington/26rap.html

68. Tepper, S. J. (2009). Stop the beat: Quiet regulation and cultural conflict. *Sociological Forum, 24*(2), 276–306.

69. Leonard, D. (2009). Young, black (& brown) and don't give a fuck . . . virtual gangstas in an era of state violence. *Critical Methodologies, 9,* 248–272.

70. Brown, Governor of California, et al. v. Entertainment Merchants Association et al. 131 S. Ct. 2279.11 (2011).

71. Barron, J. (2012, December 15). Children were all shot multiple times with a semiautomatic, officials say. *The New York Times*, A1. Retrieved from http://www.nytimes.com/2012/12/16/nyregion/gunman-kills-20-children-at-school-in-connecticut-28-dead-in-all.html?_r=0

72. See, for example, Henderson, B. (2012). Connecticut school massacre: Adam Lanza "spent hours playing Call of Duty." *The Telegraph*. Retrieved from http://www.telegraph.co.uk/news/worldnews/northamerica/usa/9752141/Connecticut-school-massacre-Adam-Lanza-spent-hours-playing-Call-Of-Duty.html; Kleinfeld, N. R., Rivera, R., & Kovaleski, S. F. (2013, March 28). Newtown killer's obsessions, in chilling detail. *The New York Times*, A1. Retrieved from http://www.nytimes.com/2013/03/29/nyregion/search-warrants-reveal-items-seized-at-adam-lanzas-home.html

73. Lichtblau, E. (2013, January 11). Makers of violent videogames marshal support to fend off regulation. *The New York Times,* A10. Retrieved from http://www.nytimes.com/2013/01/12/us/politics/makers-of-violent-video-games-marshal-support-to-fend-off-regulation.html

74. Sasso, B., & Kasperowicz, P. (2013, January 17). Dem lawmaker introduces bill to ban sales of violent video games to minors. *The Hill.* Retrieved from http://thehill.com/policy/technology/277781-dem-bill-would-ban-sale-of-violent-games-to-minors

75. Lichtblau, Makers of violent videogames marshal support.

76. Bennett-Smith, M. (2013, March 13). Nathon Brooks, teen who allegedly shot parents over video games, charged with attempted murder. *Huffpost Crime.* Retrieved from http://www.huffingtonpost.com/2013/03/13/nathon-brooks-teen-shot-parents-video-games_n_2868805.html

77. Probert, C. (2015). Nathon Brooks sentenced to 15 years for shooting his parents. *iFiberOne News.* Retrieved from http://www.ifiberone.com/news/nathon-brooks-sentenced-to-years-for-shooting-his-parents/article_5aeb92e4-bd2b-11e4-86b6-53352b65eee5.html

78. Ferguson, C. J. (2014, January 3). Lanza's violent video game play overblown. Op Ed. *Hartford Courant.* Retrieved from http://www.courant.com/opinion/hc-op-ferguson-violent-video-games-blamessless-for-20140103-story.html

79. Ferguson & Olson, The Supreme Court and video game violence; Ferguson, C. J. (2015). Clinicians' attitudes toward video games vary as a function of age, gender and negative beliefs about youth: A sociology of media research approach. *Computers in Human Behavior 52,* 379–385.

80. Adachi, P. J. C., & Willoughby, T. (2013). More than just fun and games: The longitudinal relationships between strategic video games, self-reported problem solving skills, and academic grades. *Journal of Youth and Adolescence, 42*(7), 1041–1052.

81. Adachi, P. J. C., & Willoughby, T. (2013). Demolishing the competition: The longitudinal link between competitive video games, competitive gambling, and aggression. *Journal of Youth and Adolescence, 42*(7), 1090–1104.

82. Roy, J. (2014, June 3). Behind creepypasta, the Internet community that allegedly spread a killer meme. *Time.* Retrieved from http://time.com/2818192/creepypasta-copypasta-slender-man/

83. Wagstaff, K. (2014, June 4). "Slender Man" creator speaks on stabbing: "I am deeply saddened." *NBCnews.com.* Retrieved from http://www.nbcnews.com/storyline/slender-man-stabbing/slender-man-creator-speaks-stabbing-i-am-deeply-saddened-n122781

84. Miller, L. (2015, August 24). Slender Man is watching. *New York Magazine.* Retrieved from http://nymag.com/daily/intelligencer/2015/08/slender-man-stabbing.html#

85. Ibid.

86. Sanchick, M. (2015, November 23). Indiana girl accused in "Creepypasta" stabbing case; how it's different from the "Slenderman" case. *Fox6 News.* Retrieved from http://fox6now.com/2015/11/23/indiana-girl-accused-in-creepypasta-stabbing-case-how-its-different-from-the-slenderman-case/

87. Hoffman, C. (2015). Preteen girls says "Laughing Jack" told her to stab stepmother to death. *Inquisitr.* http://www.inquisitr.com/2580433/preteen-girl-says-laughing-jacktold-her-to-stab-stepmother-to-death/

88. Sanchick, Indiana girl accused in "Creepypasta" stabbing case.

89. Altheide, D. L. (2002). Children and the discourse of fear. *Symbolic Interaction, 25*(2), 229–250; Best, J. (1990). *Threatened children: Rhetoric and concern about child victims.* Chicago, IL: University of Chicago Press; Best, J. (1994). *Troubling children: Studies of children and social problems.* Hawthorne, NY: Aldine de Gruyter; Sommerville, C. J. (1982). *The rise and fall of childhood.* Beverly Hills, CA: Sage; Zelizer, V., & Rotman, A. (1985). *Pricing the priceless child: The changing social value of children.* New York, NY: Basic Books.

90. Altheide, Children and the discourse of fear; Altheide, D. L. (2009). The Columbine shootings

and the discourse of fear. *American Behavioral Scientist, 52,* 1354–1370.

91. Leonard, Young, black (& brown) and don't give a fuck; Males, M. (1999). *Framing youth: Ten myths about the next generation.* Monroe, ME: Common Courage Press.

92. Cox, P. (2003). *Gender, justice and welfare: Bad girls in Britain, 1900–1950.* New York, NY: Palgrave.

93. Ware, "Rounding up the homosexuals."

94. Giroux, H. (2012). *Disposable youth: Racialized memories and the culture of cruelty.* New York, NY: Routledge, p. xv.

95. Gutman, M. (2012, March 16). Trayvon Martin neighborhood watch shooting: 911 tapes send mom crying from room. *ABC News.* Retrieved from http://www.abcnews.go.com/US/treyvon-martin-neighborhood-watch-shooting-911-tapes-send/story?id=15937881#.T2vBicyyzQo

96. Tienabesco, S., Gutman, M., & Wash, S. (2013, July 13). George Zimmerman found not guilty and goes free. *ABC News.* Retrieved from http://abcnews.go.com/US/george-zimmerman-found-guilty-free/story?id=19653300

97. Amnesty International. (2015). *Deadly force: Police use of force in the United States.* New York, NY: Author.

98. Associated Press. (2014, August 22). Racial and gender makeup of grand jury revealed in Ferguson case. *CBS News.* Retrieved from http://www.cbsnews.com/news/ferguson-case-racial-and-gender-makeup-of-grand-jury-revealed/

99. Lee, J. (2015, October 28). Outrage is growing over the Tamir Rice investigation. Is the grand jury process stacked in favor of the cop that killed the 12-year-old? *Mother Jones.* Retrieved from http://www.motherjones.com/politics/2015/10/tamir-rice-leaked-reports-grand-jury

100. Fantz, A., Almasy, S., & Shoichet, C. E. (2015, December 28). Tamir Rice shooting: No charges for officers. *CNN News.* Retrieved from http://www.cnn.com/2015/12/28/us/tamir-rice-shooting/

101. Sandy, E., & Grzegorek, V. (2016, January 20). The grand jury in the Tamir Rice case did not take a vote on charges. *Scene.* Retrieved from http://www.clevescene.com/scene-and-heard/archives/2016/01/20/the-grand-jury-in-the-tamir-rice-case-did-not-take-a-vote-on-charges

102. Swaine, J., Laughland, O., & Lartey, J. (2016, January 2). *Young black men killed by police at highest rate in year of 1,134 deaths.* Retrieved from http://www.alternet.org/civil-liberties/young-black-men-killed-us-police-highest-rate-year-1134-deaths

103. Amnesty International, *Deadly force: Police use of force in the United States.*

104. Mann, C. R., Zatz, M., & Rodriguez, N. (Eds.). (2006). *Images of color, images of crime* (3rd ed.). Los Angeles, CA: Roxbury.

CHAPTER 3

1. Twohey, M. (2004, August 25). Violent crimes by girls rising, but the reason remains unclear. *The International Child & Youth Care Network.* Retrieved from http://www.cyc-net.org/features/ft-violentgirls.html

2. Ibid.

3. Huff, D. (1954/1993). *How to lie with statistics.* New York, NY: Norton.

4. Best, J. (2004). *More damned lies and statistics: How numbers confuse public issues.* Berkeley, CA: University of California Press.

5. Huff, *How to lie with statistics.*

6. Howell, J. C. (2009). *Preventing and reducing juvenile delinquency: A comprehensive framework.* Thousand Oaks, CA: Sage; Omaji, P. O. (2003). *Responding to youth crime: Towards radical criminal justice partnerships.* Sydney: Hawkins Press; Snyder, H. N., Sickmund, M., & Poe-Yamagata, E. (1996). *Juvenile offenders and victims: 1996 update on violence.* Washington, DC: Office of Juvenile Justice and Delinquency Prevention.

7. Children's Defense Fund. (2012). *Cradle to prison pipeline campaign: Take action.* Retrieved from http://www.childrensdefense .org/programs-campaigns/cradle-to-prison-pipeline/take-action.html

8. See, for example, Rios, V. (2011). *Punished: Policing the lives of black and Latino boys.* New York, NY: NYU Press; Zatz, M., & Portillos, E. (2000). Voices from the barrio: Chicano/a gangs, families and communities. *Criminology, 38*(2), 369–402.

9. See Ferrell, J., & Hamm, M. S. (1998). *Ethnography at the edge: Crime, deviance and field research.* Boston, MA: Northeastern University Press.

10. U.S. Department of Justice. (2004). *The Uniform Crime Reporting handbook.* Retrieved from http://www.fbi.gov/about-us/cjis/ucr/addi tional-ucr-publications/ucr_handbook.pdf

11. United States Department of Justice, Federal Bureau of Investigation. (2015, September). *Crime in the United States, 2014.* Retrieved from https://www.fbi.gov/about-us/cjis/ucr/crime-in-the-u.s/2014/crime-in-the-u.s.-2014/ offenses-known-to-law-enforcement/clear ances/main

12. Howell, *Preventing and reducing juvenile delinquency.*

13. U.S. Department of Justice, *The Uniform Crime Reporting handbook,* p. 19.

14. Federal Bureau of Investigation. (2009). *NIBRS general, frequently asked questions.* Retrieved from http://www.fbi.gov/about-us/cjis/ucr/frequ ently-asked-questions/nibrs_faqs

15. United States Department of Justice, Federal Bureau of Investigation. (2013, January). *National Incident-Based Reporting System (NIBRS) user manual.* Retrieved from https:// www.fbi.gov/about-us/cjis/ucr/nibrs/nibrs-user-manual

16. United States Department of Justice, Federal Bureau of Investigation. (2012). *NIBRS partici-pation by state.* Retrieved from https://www.fbi .gov/about-us/cjis/ucr/nibrs/2012/resources/ nibrs-participation-by-state

17. Center for Court Innovation. (2012). *Angela Irvine interview: Improving youth programming: The role of research.* Retrieved from http:// www.courtinnovation.org/research/improving-youth-programming-role-research-0?url=resea rch%2F9%2Fall&mode=9&type=all&page=4

18. Howell, *Preventing and reducing juvenile delinquency.*

19. National Archive of Criminal Justice Data. (2010). *National Crime Victimization Survey resource guide.* Retrieved from http://www .icpsr.umich.edu/icpsrweb/NACJD/NCVS/

20. Ibid.

21. Blumstein, A., Cohen, J., Roth, J. A., & Visher, C. A. (Eds.). (1986). *Criminal careers and career criminals.* Washington, DC: National Academy Press; Hindelang, M. J., Hirschi, T., & Weis, J. (1981). *Measuring delinquency.* Beverly Hills, CA: Sage; Thornberry, T. P., & Krohn, M. D. (2000). The self-report method for measur-ing delinquency and crime. In D. Duffee (Ed.), *Criminal justice 2000* (pp. 33–84). Washington, DC: U.S. Department of Justice, the National Institute of Justice.

22. Regents of the University of Michigan. (2016). *Monitoring the future: Purpose and design.* Retrieved from http://monitoringthefuture.org/ purpose.html

23. Bureau of Labor Statistics. (2011). *National longitudinal surveys: The NLSY97.* Retrieved from http://www.bls.gov/nls/nlsy97.htm

24. Piquero, A., Macintosh, R., & Hickman, M. (2002). The validity of a self-reported delin-quency scale: Comparisons across gender, age, race, and place of residence. *Sociological Methods and Research, 30,* 492–529; Bachman, J., & O'Malley, P. M. (1984). Yea-saying, nay-saying, and going to extremes: Black-White differences in response style. *Public Opinion Quarterly, 48,* 491–509; Huizinga, D., & Elliott, D. S. (1986). Reassessing the reliability and validity of self-report delinquent measures. *Journal of Quantitative Criminology, 2*(4), 293–327; Lauritsen, J. (1998). The age-crime debate: Assessing the limits of longitudinal self-report data. *Social Forces, 77,* 127–155.

25. Elliott, D. S., & Huizinga, D. (1989). Improving self-report measures of delinquency. In M. Kelin (Ed.), *Cross-national research in self-reported crime and delinquency* (pp. 155–186). Boston,

MA: Kluwer Academic; Farrington, D., Loeber, R., Stouthamer-Loeber, M., Van Kammen, W., & Schmidt, L. (1996). Self-reported delinquency and a combined delinquency seriousness scale based on boys, mothers and teachers: Concurrent and predictive validity for African-Americans and Caucasians. *Criminology, 34,* 501–525; Huizinga & Elliott, Reassessing the reliability and validity of self-report delinquent measures, 293–327.

26. Kingery, P. M., Biafora, F. A., & Zimmerman, R. S. (1996). Risk factors for violent behaviors among ethnically diverse urban adolescents: Beyond race/ethnicity. *School Psychology International, 17*(2), 171–186.

27. Hindelang, Hirschi, & Weis, *Measuring delinquency.*

28. Hagan, J., & McCarthy, B. (1992). Streetlife and delinquency. *The British Journal of Sociology, 43*(4), 533–561.

29. Sampson, R. J. (2008). Rethinking crime and immigration. *Contexts, 7,* 28–33.

30. Ibid., 28–33, especially p. 29.

31. Ibid.; Martinez, R., Jr., & Valenzuela, A., Jr. (Eds.). (2006). *Immigration and crime: Race, ethnicity, and violence.* New York, NY: New York University Press.

32. Snyder, H. N., & Sickmund, M. (1999). *Juvenile offenders and victims: A national report.* Washington, DC: Office of Juvenile Justice and Delinquency Prevention; DiIulio, J. J., Jr. (1995). The coming of the super-predators. *Weekly Standard,* November 27, pp. 23–28.

33. Zimring, F. E. (1998). *American youth violence.* New York, NY: Oxford University Press.

34. Ibid.

35. Howell, *Preventing and reducing juvenile delinquency.*

36. Beckett, K., & Sasson, T. (2003). *The politics of injustice: Crime and punishment in America.* Thousand Oaks, CA: Sage.

37. Huff, *How to lie with statistics.*

38. Zahn, M., Hawkins, S., Chiancone, J., & Whitworth, A. (2008). *The girls study group: Charting the way to delinquency prevention for girls.* Washington, DC: Office of Juvenile Justice and Delinquency Prevention.

39. Slowikowski, J. (2010). *OJJDP in focus.* Washington, DC: Office of Juvenile Justice and Delinquency Prevention.

40. Zahn, M., Brumbaugh, S., Steffensmeier, D., Feld, B. C., Morash, M., Chesney-Lind, M., . . . Kruttschnitt, C. (2008). *Violence by teenage girls: Trends and context.* Washington, DC: Office of Juvenile Justice and Delinquency Prevention.

41. Ibid.

42. Morenoff, J. D. (2005). Racial and ethnic disparities in crime and delinquency in the United States. In M. Rutter & M. Tienda (Eds.), *Ethnicity and causal mechanisms* (pp. 139–173). Cambridge, MA: Cambridge University Press.

43. Tonry, M. (1995). *Malign neglect: Race, crime, and punishment in America.* New York, NY: Oxford University Press; Zimring, F. E., & Hawkins, G. (1997). *Crime is not the problem: Lethal violence in America.* New York, NY: Oxford University Press.

44. Morenoff, Racial and ethnic disparities in crime and delinquency; Reiss, A. J., & Roth, J. A. (Eds.). (1993). *Understanding and preventing violence.* Washington, DC: National Academy Press.

45. Farrington et al., Self-reported delinquency, 501–525; Paschall, M. J., Ornstein, M. L., & Flewelling, R. L. (2001). African American male adolescents' involvement in the criminal justice system: The criterion validity of self-report measures in a prospective study. *Journal of Research in Crime and Delinquency, 38,* 174–187; Thornberry, T. P., & Krohn, M. D. (2002). Comparisons of self-report and official data for measuring crime. In J. V. Pepper & C. V. Petrie (Eds.), *Measurement problems in criminal justice research: Workshop summary* Washington, DC: National Academies Press.

CHAPTER 4

1. Sellin, T. (1942). Youth and crime. *Law and Contemporary Problems, 9,* 581–587.

2. Brown, S. E., Esbensen, F., & Geis, G. (2013). *Criminology: Explaining crime in its context* (8th ed.). New York, NY: Routledge.

3. Schram, P. J., & Tibbets, S. G. (2014). *Introduction to criminology.* Thousand Oaks, CA: SAGE.

4. Beccaria, C. (1819). *Of crimes and punishments* (Dei delitti e delle pene). Philadelphia, PA: Philip H. Nicklin. (Original work published 1764); Bentham, J. (1789). *An introduction to the principles of morals and legislation.* South Australia: University of Adelaide. (Original work published 1780)

5. Beccaria, C. (1963). *On crimes and punishment* (H. Paloucci, trans.). Englewood Cliffs, NJ: Prentice Hall p. 43. (Original work published 1764)

6. Becker, G. (1968). Crime and punishment: An economic approach. *Journal of Political Economy, 76,* 169–217; Cornish, D., & Clarke, R. (1986). Introduction. In D. B. Cornish & R. V. Clarke (Eds.), *The reasoning criminal: Rational choice perspectives on offending* (pp. 1–16). New York, NY: Springer-Verlag.

7. Cornish & Clarke, Introduction.

8. Paternoster, R. (1989). Decisions to participate and desist from four types of common delinquency: Deterrence and the rational choice perspective. *Law and Society Review, 23,* 7–40.

9. Morton, S. G. (1849). Observations on the size of the brain in various races and families of man. *Proceedings of the Academy of Natural Sciences (Philadelphia), 4,* 221–224.

10. Schram & Tibbets, *Introduction to criminology.*

11. Ibid.

12. Lombroso, C. (1911). *Criminal man* (L'Uomo delinquents) (G. Lombroso-Ferrero, trans.). Montclair, NJ: Patterson Smith.

13. Burfeind, J. W., & Bartusch, D. J. (2011). *Juvenile delinquency: An integrated approach* (2nd ed.). Boston, MA: Jones and Bartlett.

14. Sheldon, W. H. (1940). *The varieties of human physique: An introduction to constitutional psychology.* New York, NY: Harper; Sheldon, W. H. (1949). *Varieties of delinquent youth.* New York, NY: Harper.

15. Glueck, S., & Glueck, E. (1956). *Physique and delinquency.* New York, NY: Harper.

16. Freud, S. (1964). *New introductory lectures on psycho-analysis.* New York, NY: W.W. Norton.

17. Aichhorn, A. (1935). *Wayward youth.* New York, NY: World.

18. The August Aichhorn Center. (2015). *An introduction: Who we are and what's in this site.* Retrieved from http://www.aichhorn.org/index.html

19. NPR. (2016, April 24). *How talking openly against stigma helped a mother and son cope with bipolar disorder.* Weekend Edition Sunday. Retrieved from http://www.npr.org/sections/health-shots/2016/04/24/475461959

20. Ibid.

21. Brennan, P. A., & Raine, A. (1997). Biosocial bases of antisocial behavior: Psychophysiological, neurological, and cognitive factors. *Clinical Psychology Review, 17,* 589–604.

22. Andrews, D. A., & Bonta, J. (2006). *The psychology of criminal conduct* (4th ed.). Cincinnati, OH: Anderson; Fishbein, D. (2001). *Biobehavioral perspectives in criminology.* Belmont, CA: Wadsworth; Rowe, D. C. (2003). *Biology and crime.* Los Angeles, CA: Roxbury; Wright, J. P., Boisvert, D., Dietrich, K., & Douglas Ris, M. (2009). The ghost in the machine and criminal behavior: Criminology for the 21st century. In A. Walsh & K. M. Beaver (Eds.), *Biosocial criminology: New directions in theory and research* (pp. 73–89). New York, NY: Routledge.

23. Andrews & Bonta, *The psychology of criminal conduct,* p. 170.

24. Murata, K., Weihe, P., Budtz-Jorgensen, E., Jorgensen, P. J., & Grandjean, P. (2004). Delayed brainstem auditory evoked potential latencies in 14-year-old children exposed to methylmercury. *Journal of Pediatrics, 144,* 177–183; Richardson, A., & Montgomery, P. (2005). The Oxford-Durham study: A randomized controlled trial of dietary supplementation with fatty acids in children with developmental coordination disorder. *Pediatrics, 115,* 1360–1366.

25. Jacobson, K., & Rowe, D. C. (2000). Nature, nurture and the development of criminality. In J. F. Sheley (Ed.), *Criminology* (3rd ed., pp. 323–347). Belmont, CA: Wadsworth.

26. Jacobson & Rowe, Nature, nurture and the development of criminality; Mazur, A. (2009). Testosterone and violence among young males. In A. Walsh & K. M. Beaver (Eds.), *Biosocial criminology: New directions in theory*

and research (pp. 190–204). New York, NY: Routledge.

27. Dabbs, J. M., & Morris, R. (1990). Testosterone, social class and antisocial behavior in a sample of 4462 men. *Psychological Science, 1,* 209–211.

28. Beaver, K. (2008). *Biosocial criminology: A primer.* Dubuque, IA: Kendall/Hunt.

29. Sutherland, E. H. (1947). *Principles of criminology* (4th ed.). Philadelphia, PA: Lippincott.

30. Ibid., pp. 4–9.

31. See Akers, R. L. (1996). Is differential association/social learning cultural deviance theory? *Criminology, 34*(2), 229–247; Burgess, R. L., & Akers, R. L. (1966). A differential association reinforcement theory of criminal behavior. *Social Problems, 14,* 128–147.

32. See Rowe, *Biology and crime*; Walsh, A. (2000). Behavior genetics and anomie/strain theory. *Criminology, 38*(4), 1075–1107.

33. Sheldon, *The varieties of human physique*; Sheldon, *Varieties of delinquent youth*.

34. Okie, S. (2009, January 29). The epidemic that wasn't. *New York Times.* Retrieved from http://www.nytimes.com/2009/01/27/health/27coca.html

35. Warr, M. (2002). *Companions in crime: The social aspects of criminal conduct.* Cambridge, UK: Cambridge University Press.

36. For a recent overview of the issues, see Kubrin, C. E., Stucky, T. D., & Krohn, M. D. (2009). *Research theories of crime and deviance.* New York, NY: Oxford University Press.

37. Akers, R. L. (1973). *Deviant behavior: A social learning approach.* Belmont, CA: Wadsworth; Burgess & Akers, A differential association reinforcement theory of criminal behavior.

38. Akers, R. (1979). Social learning and deviant behavior: A specific test of a general theory. *American Sociological Review, 44,* 635–655.

39. Sutherland, *Principles of criminology*; Sutherland, E. H., & Cressey, D. R. (1978). *Criminology* (10th ed.). Philadelphia, PA: Lippincott.

40. Reinarman, C., & Fagan, J. (1988). Social organization and differential association: A research note from a longitudinal study of violent juvenile offenders. *Crime and Delinquency, 34,* 307–327.

41. Mears, D., Ploeger, M., & Warr, M. (1998). Explaining the gender gap in delinquency: Peer influence and moral evaluations of behavior. *Journal of Research in Crime and Delinquency, 35*(3), 251–266; Simons, L. R., Miller, M. G., & Aigner, S. M. (1980). Contemporary theories of deviance and female delinquency: An empirical test. *Journal of Research in Crime and Delinquency, 17,* 42–57; Mears et al., Explaining the gender gap in delinquency.

42. Mears et al., Explaining the gender gap in delinquency.

43. Gabbidon, S. L. (2010). *Criminological perspectives on race and crime* (2nd ed.). New York, NY: Routledge.

44. Matsueda, R., & Heimer, K. (1987). Race, family structure, and delinquency: A test of differential association and social control theories. *American Sociological Review, 52,* 826–840.

45. Berger, A. S., & Simon, W. (1974). Black families and the Moynihan Report: A research evaluation. *Social Problems, 22,* 145–161; Matsueda & Heimer, Race, family structure, and delinquency.

46. Vold, G., Bernard, T., & Snipes, J. (1998). *Theoretical criminology.* Oxford, UK: Oxford University Press.

47. Ibid.

48. Traub, S. H., & Little, C. B. (1985). *Theories of deviance* (3rd ed.). Itasca, IL: Peacock, p. 241.

49. Nye, F. I. (1958). *Family relationships and delinquent behavior.* New York, NY: Wiley.

50. Hirschi, T. (1969). *Causes of delinquency.* Berkeley, CA: University of California Press.

51. Kubrin et al., *Research theories of crime and deviance.*

52. Hirschi, *Causes of delinquency*, p. 187.

53. Kubrin et al., *Research theories of crime and deviance*, p. 172.

54. Sampson, R. J., & Laub, J. H. (1993). *Crime in the making: Pathways and turning points through life.* Cambridge, MA: Harvard University Press; Sampson, R. J., & Laub, J. H. (1995). Understanding variability in lives through time: Contributions of life-course criminology. *Studies in Crime and Crime Prevention, 4,* 143–158.

55. Burfeind & Bartusch, *Juvenile delinquency,* p. 99.

56. Hirschi, *Causes of delinquency*; Gottfredson, M., & Hirschi, T. (1990). *A general theory of crime.* Palo Alto, CA: Stanford University Press.

57. Sampson & Laub, *Crime in the making.*

58. Ibid., p. 8. See also Sampson & Laub, Understanding variability in lives through time.

59. Sampson & Laub, *Crime in the making*; Sampson & Laub, Understanding variability in lives through time.

60. Sampson & Laub, Understanding variability in lives through time, p. 146.

61. Moffitt, T. E. (1993). "Life-course-persistent" and "adolescence-limited" antisocial behavior: A developmental taxonomy. *Psychological Review, 100,* 674–701; Moffitt, T. E. (2003). Life-course-persistent and adolescence-limited antisocial behavior: A 10-year research review and research agenda. In B. B. Lahey, T. E. Moffitt, & A. Caspi (Eds.), *Causes of conduct disorder and juvenile delinquency* (pp. 49–75). New York, NY: Guilford; Moffitt, T. E. (2006). Life-course-persistent versus adolescence-limited antisocial behavior. In D. Cicchetti & D. Cohen (Eds.), *Developmental psychopathology* (2nd ed., pp. 570–598). New York, NY: Wiley.

62. Piquero, A. R., Daigle, L. E., Gibson, C. L., Piquero, N. E., & Tibbetts, S. G. (2007). Are life-course-persistent offenders at risk for adverse health outcomes? *Journal of Research in Crime and Delinquency, 44,* 185–207.

63. See Farrington, D. (1986). Age and crime. *Crime and Justice, 7,* 189–250. For a discussion, see Piquero et al., Are life-course-persistent offenders at risk for adverse health outcomes?

64. Steffensmeier, D. J., Allan, E. A., Harer, M. D., & Streifel, C. (1989). Age and the distribution of crime. *American Journal of Sociology, 94,* 803–831.

65. Hagan, J., Gillis, A. R., & Simpson, J. (1985). The class structure of gender and delinquency: Toward a power-control theory of common delinquent behavior. *American Journal of Sociology, 90,* 1151–1178; Hagan, J., Simpson, J., & Gillis, A. R. (1987). Class in the household: A power-control theory of gender and delinquency. *American Journal of Sociology, 92,* 788–816.

66. Hagan et al., Class in the household.

67. Bonger, W. A. (1916). *Criminality and economic conditions.* Boston, MA: Little, Brown.

68. Grasmick, H. G., Hagan, J., Blackwell, B. S., & Arneklev, B. J. (1996). Risk preferences and patriarchy: Extending power-control theory. *Social Forces, 75*(1), 177–199.

69. For example, Morash, M., & Chesney-Lind, M. (1991). A reformulation and partial test of the power-control theory of delinquency. *Justice Quarterly, 8,* 347–377.

70. McCarthy, B., Hagan, J., & Woodward, T. S. (1999). In the company of women: Structure and agency in a revised power-control theory of gender and delinquency. *Criminology, 37,* 761–788.

71. Sykes, G., & Matza, D. (1957). Techniques of neutralization: A theory of delinquency. *American Sociological Review, 22*(6), 664–670.

72. Ibid., especially p. 667.

73. Ibid., especially p. 668.

74. Ibid., especially p. 668.

75. Ibid., especially p. 668.

76. Cullen, F. T., & Agnew, R. (2006). *Criminological theory past to present: Essential readings* (3rd ed.). New York, NY: Oxford University Press.

77. Agnew, R. (1992). Foundation for a general strain theory of crime and delinquency. *Criminology, 30*(1), 47–87.

78. Ibid.

79. Agnew, R. (2006). *Pressured into crime: An overview of general strain theory.* Los Angeles, CA: Roxbury.

80. Ibid.

81. Agnew, Foundation for a general strain theory of crime and delinquency; Agnew, R. (2001). Building on the foundation of general strain theory: Specifying the types of strain most likely to lead to crime and delinquency. *Journal of Research in Crime and Delinquency, 38,* 319–361.

82. Kaufman, J. M., Rebellon, C. J., Thaxton, S., & Agnew, R. (2008). A general strain theory of racial differences in criminal offending. *The Australian and New Zealand Journal of Criminology, 41,* 421–437.

83. Gabbidon, *Criminological perspectives on race and crime.*

84. Simons, R. L., Chen, Y. F., Stewart, E. A., & Brody, G. H. (2003). Incidents of discrimination and risk for delinquency: A longitudinal test of strain theory with an African American sample. *Justice Quarterly, 20,* 827–854.

85. Perez, D. M., Jennings, W. G., & Gover, A. R. (2008). Specifying general strain theory: An ethnically relevant approach. *Deviant Behavior, 29,* 544–578.

86. Ibid. As cited in Gabbidon, *Criminological perspectives on race and crime*, p. 75.

87. Moon, B., Hays, K., & Blurton, D. (2009). General strain theory, key strains, and deviance. *Journal of Criminal Justice, 37,* 98–106.

88. For example, Piquero, N. L. &, Sealock, M. D. (2004). Gender and general strain theory: A preliminary test of Broidy and Agnew's gender/GST hypotheses. *Justice Quarterly, 21,* 125–158; Manasse, M. E., & Ganem, N. M. (2009). Victimization as a cause of delinquency: The role of depression and gender. *Journal of Criminal Justice, 37,* 371–378.

89. Broidy, L., & Agnew, R. (1997). Gender and crime: A general strain theory perspective. *Journal of Research in Crime and Delinquency, 34*(5), 275–306.

90. Mirowsky, J., & Ross, C. E. (1995). Sex differences in distress: Real or artifact? *American Sociological Review, 60,* 449–468.

91. Ibid.

92. Eitle, D., & Eitle, T. (2016). General strain theory and delinquency: Extending a popular explanation to American Indian youth. *Youth & Society, 48*(4), 470–495.

93. Andrews & Bonta, *The psychology of criminal conduct.*

CHAPTER 5

1. Moyer, I. L. (2001). *Criminological theories: Traditional and nontraditional voices and themes.* Thousand Oaks, CA: Sage.

2. Durkheim, E. (1933). *The division of labor in society.* New York, NY: Free Press. (Original work published 1893)

3. Ibid., p. 368.

4. Durkheim, E. (1938). *The rules of sociological method.* New York, NY: Free Press. (Original work published 1895)

5. Durkheim, E. (1951). *Suicide.* New York, NY: Free Press. (Original work published 1897)

6. Pfohl, S. (2009). *Images of deviance and social control: A sociological history* (2nd ed.). New York, NY: McGraw-Hill.

7. Merton, R. K. (1938). Social structure and anomie. *American Sociological Review, 3*(5), 672–682.

8. Ibid., especially p. 672.

9. Ibid., especially p. 680.

10. Cohen, A. (1955). *Delinquent boys.* New York, NY: Free Press.

11. Cernkovich, S. A., Giordano, P. C., & Rudolph, J. L. (2000). Race, crime, and the American Dream. *Journal of Research in Crime and Delinquency, 37*(3), 131–170.

12. Ibid., especially p. 162.

13. Walters, M. A. (2011). A general theories of hate crime? Strain, doing difference, and self-control. *Critical Criminology, 19,* 313–330.

14. Cernkovich, S. A., & Giordano, P. C. (1979). Delinquency, opportunity, and gender. *The Journal of Criminal Law & Criminology, 70,* 145–151; Datesman, K. S., Scarpitti, F. R., & Stephenson, R. M. (1975). Female delinquency: An application of self and opportunity theories.

Journal of Research in Crime and Delinquency, 12, 107–123; Leiber, M. J., Farnworth, M., Jamieson, K. M., & Nalla, M. K. (1994). Bridging the gender gap in criminology: Liberation and gender-specific strain effects on delinquency. *Sociological Inquiry, 64,* 56–68; Özbay, O., & Özcan, Y. Z. (2006). Classic strain theory and gender: The case of Turkey. *International Journal of Offender Therapy and Comparative Criminology, 50*(1), 21–38; Segrave, O. J., & Hastad, D. N. (1985). Evaluating three models of delinquency causation for males and females: Strain theory, subcultural theory, and control theory. *Sociological Focus, 18,* 1–17; Simons et al., Contemporary theories of deviance and female delinquency; Simpson, S. S., & Elis, L. (1995). Doing gender: Sorting out the caste and crime conundrum. *Criminology, 33,* 47–81; Smith, A. D. (1979). Sex and deviance: An assessment of major sociological variables. *The Sociological Quarterly, 20,* 183–195; Smith, A. D., & Paternoster, R. (1987). The gender gap in theories of deviance: Issues and evidence. *Journal of Research in Crime and Delinquency, 24,* 140–172.

15. For example, Datesman et al., Female delinquency; Simpson & Elis, Doing gender; Leiber et al., Bridging the gender gap in criminology.

16. Smith & Paternoster, The gender gap in theories of deviance.

17. Özbay & Özcan, Classic strain theory and gender.

18. Antonaccio, O., Smith, W. R., & Gostjev, F. A. (2015). Anomic strain and external constraints: A reassessment of Merton's anomie/strain theory using data from Ukraine. *International Journal of Offender Therapy and Comparative Criminology, 59*(10), 1079–1103.

19. Kubrin, C. E., & Weitzer, R. (2003). New directions in social disorganization theory. *Journal of Crime and Delinquency, 40*(4), 374–402.

20. Shaw, C., & McKay, H. (1942). *Juvenile delinquency and urban areas: A study of delinquents in relation to differential characteristics of American cities.* Chicago, IL: University of Chicago Press. (Original work published 1931)

21. Bursik, R. J. (1988). Social disorganization and theories of crime and delinquency: Problems and prospects. *Criminology, 26*(4), 519–551, especially p. 520.

22. Moyer, *Criminological theories.*

23. Platt, A. (1991). *E. Franklin Frazier reconsidered.* New Brunswick, NJ: Rutgers University Press.

24. Moyer, *Criminological theories.*

25. Bursik, Social disorganization and theories of crime and delinquency.

26. Sampson, R. J., & Groves, W. B. (1989). Community structure and crime: Testing social disorganization theory. *American Journal of Sociology, 94*(4), 774–802, especially p. 777.

27. For example, Lowenkamp, C. T., Cullen, F. T., & Pratt, T. C. (2003). Replicating Sampson and Groves' test of social disorganization theory. *Journal of Research in Crime and Delinquency, 40*(4), 351–373; Sun, I. Y., Triplett, R., & Gainey, R. R. (2004). Neighborhood characteristics and crime: A Test of Sampson and Groves' model of social disorganization. *Western Criminology Review, 5*(1), 1–16; Veysey, B. M., & Messner, S. F. (1999). Further testing of social disorganization theory: An elaboration of Sampson and Groves' "community structure and crime." *Journal of Research in Crime and Delinquency, 36*(2), 156–174.

28. Sampson, R. J., & Laub, J. H. (1997). A life-course theory of cumulative disadvantage and the stability of delinquency. In T. P. Thornberry (Ed.), *Developmental theories of crime and delinquency* (pp. 133–161). New Brunswick, NJ: Transaction, p. 918.

29. Chen, X., & Zhong, H. (2013). Delinquency and crime among immigrant youth—An integrative review of theoretical explanations. *Laws, 2,* 210–232.

30. See Rose, D., & Clear, T. (1998). Incarceration, social capital, and crime: Implications for social disorganization theory. *Criminology, 36*(3), 441–480; Clear, T. R., Rose, D. R., Waring, E., & Scully, K. (2006). Coercive mobility and crime: A preliminary examination of concentrated incarceration and social disorganization, *Justice Quarterly, 20*(1), 441–480; Clear, T. R. (2007). *Imprisoning communities.* New York, NY: Oxford University Press.

31. Rose & Clear, Incarceration, social capital, and crime, especially p. 441.

32. Roberts, D. (2004). The social and moral cost of mass incarceration in African American

Communities. *Faculty Scholarship. Paper 583*, p. 1281. Retrieved from http://scholarship.law .upenn.edu/faculty_scholarship/583

33. Bursik, R. J., Jr., & Grasmick, H. G. (1993). *Neighborhoods and crime: The dimensions of effective community control.* New York, NY: Lexington Books; Wilson, W. J. (1987). *The truly disadvantaged, the inner city, the underclass, and public policy.* Chicago, IL: University of Chicago Press.

34. Clear et al., Coercive mobility and crime; Frost, N., & Gross, L. A. (2012). Coercive mobility and the impact of prison-cycling on communities. *Crime, Law, & Social Change, 57,* 459–474.

35. Rose & Clear, Incarceration, social capital, and crime; Clear et al., Coercive mobility and crime; Clear, *Imprisoning communities.*

36. Burch, T. (2014). The old Jim Crow: Racial residential segregation and neighborhood imprisonment. *Law & Policy, 36*(3), 223–255; Frost & Gross, Coercive mobility and the impact of prison-cycling on communities.

37. Osgood, D. W., & Chambers, J. M. (2000). Social disorganization outside the metropolis: An analysis of rural youth violence. *Criminology, 38*(1), p. 81.

38. Kingston, B., Huizinga, D., & Elliott, D. S. (2009). A test of social disorganization theory in high-risk urban neighborhoods. *Youth & Society, 41,* 53–79.

39. Ibid., p. 75.

40. Kroneman, L., Loeber, R., & Hipwell, A. E. (2004). Is neighborhood context differently related to externalizing problems and delinquency for girls compared to boys? *Clinical Child and Family Psychology Review, 7,* 109–122; Zahn, M. A., & Browne, A. (2009). Gender differences in neighborhood effects and delinquency. In M. A. Zahn (Ed.), *The delinquent girl* (pp. 164–181). Philadelphia, PA: Temple University Press.

41. Beyers, J. M., Bates, J. E., Pettit, G. S., & Dodge, K. A. (2003). Neighborhood structure, parenting processes, and the development of youths' externalizing behaviors: A multilevel analysis. *American Journal of Community Psychology, 31,* 35–53; Jacob, J. C. (2006). Male and female youth crime in Canadian communities: Assessing the applicability of social

disorganization theory. *Canadian Journal of Criminology and Criminal Justice, 48,* 31–60; Karriker-Jaffe, K. J., Foshee, V. A., Ennett, S. T., & Suchindran, C. (2009). Sex differences in the effects of neighborhood socioeconomic disadvantage and social organization on rural adolescents' aggression trajectories. *American Journal of Community Psychology, 43,* 189–203; Molnar, B. E., Cerda, M., Roberts, A. L., & Buka, S. L. (2008). Effects of neighborhood resources on aggressive and delinquent behaviors among urban youths. *American Journal of Public Health, 98,* 1086–1093; Mrug, S., & Windle, M. (2009). Mediators of neighborhood influences on externalizing behavior in preadolescent children. *Journal of Abnormal Child Psychology, 37,* 265–280; Simons, R. L., Johnson, C., Beaman, J., Conger, R., & Whitbeck, L. B. (1996). Parents and peer group as mediators of the effect of community structure on adolescent problem behavior. *American Journal of Community Psychology, 24,* 145–171.

42. Fagan, A. A., & Wright, E. M. (2012). The effects of neighborhood context on youth violence and delinquency. Does gender matter? *Youth Violence and Juvenile Justice, 10,* 64–82.

43. Graif, C. (2015). Delinquency and gender moderation in the Moving to Opportunity intervention: The role of extended neighborhoods. *Criminology, 53*(3), 366–398.

44. Kling, J. R., Ludwig, J., & Katz, L. F. (2005). Neighborhood effects on crime for female and male youth: Evidence from a randomized housing voucher experiment. *The Quarterly Journal of Economics, 120*(1), 87–130; Ludwig, J., Duncan, G. J., Gennetian, L. A., Katz, L. F., Kessler, R. C., Kling, J. R., & Sanbonmatsu, L. (2012). Neighborhood effects on the long-term well-being of low-income adults. *Science, 337,* 1505–1510.

45. Einstadter, W. J., & Henry, S. (2006). *Criminological theory: An analysis of its underlying assumptions* (2nd ed.). Oxford, UK: Rowman & Littlefield, p. 177.

46. Ibid.

47. Davis, N. J. (1975). *Social constructions of deviance: Perspectives and issues in the field.* Dubuque, IA: William C. Brown, pp. 48–49.

48. Bortner, M. A. (1988). *Delinquency and justice: An age of crisis.* New York, NY: McGraw-Hill.

49. Schlossman, S., & Sedlak, M. (1983). *The Chicago area project revisited.* Santa Monica, CA: Rand Corporation.

50. Kingston et al., A test of social disorganization theory in high-risk urban neighborhoods.

51. Toro, P. A., Dworsky, A., Fowler, P. J. (2007). *Homeless youth in the United States: Recent research findings and intervention approaches.* National Symposium on Homelessness Research.

Retrieved from http://aspe.hhs.gov/hsp/home lessness/symposium07/toro/

52. Bantchevska, D., Bartle-Haring, S., Dashora, P., Glebova, T., & Slesnick, N. (2008). Problem behaviors of homeless youth: A social capital perspective. *Journal of Human Ecology, 23*(4), 285–293.

53. Majd, K., Marksamer, J., & Reyes, C. (2009). *Hidden injustice: Lesbian, gay, bisexual, and transgender youth in Juvenile courts.* San Francisco, CA: Legal Services for Children, National Center for Lesbian Rights.

CHAPTER 6

1. Domhoff, G. W. (2005). *Basics of studying power.* Retrieved from http://www2.ucsc.edu/ whorulesamerica/methods/studying_power .html

2. Paternoster, R., & Lovanni, L. (1989). The labeling perspective and delinquency: An elaboration of the theory and assessment of the evidence. *Justice Quarterly, 6,* 359–394.

3. Aesop. (1835). *Fables of Aesop and others* (S. Croxall, trans.). Philadelphia, PA: Desiliver, Thomas.

4. Becker, H. S. (1963). *Outsiders: Studies in sociology of deviance.* Glencoe, IL: Free Press.

5. Lemert, E. M. (1951). *Social pathology.* New York, NY: McGraw-Hill; Lemert, E. M. (1972). *Human deviance, social problems, and social control.* Englewood Cliffs, NJ: Prentice-Hall; Becker, *Outsiders*; Goffman, E. (1963). *Stigma: Notes on the management of spoiled identity.* New York, NY: Prentice-Hall.

6. Tannenbaum, F. (1938). *Crime and the community.* Boston, MA: Ginn.

7. Lemert, *Social pathology;* Lemert, *Human deviance.*

8. Lemert, *Human deviance,* p. 63.

9. Goffman, *Stigma.*

10. Becker, *Outsiders.*

11. Garfinkel, H. (1956). Conditions of successful degradation ceremonies. *American Journal of Sociology, 61,* 420–424.

12. Becker, *Outsiders,* p. 17.

13. Ibid., p. 20.

14. Ibid.

15. Gusfield, J. (1955). Social structure and moral reform: A study of the Women's Christian Temperance Union. *American Journal of Sociology, LXI,* 221–232, especially p. 223.

16. Cohen, *Folk devils and moral panics.*

17. Chambliss, W. J. (1995). Crime control and ethnic minorities: Legitimizing racial oppression by creating moral panics. In D. Hawkins (Ed.), *Ethnicity, race and crime: Perspectives across time and place* (pp. 235–258). Albany: State University of New York.

18. Ibid.; Miller, J. (2011). *Search and destroy: African-American males in the criminal justice system* (2nd ed.). Cambridge, UK: Cambridge University Press.

19. Hirschi, T. (1980). Labeling theory and juvenile delinquency: An assessment of the evidence. In W. R. Gove (Ed.), *The labeling of deviance: Evaluating a perspective* (pp. 181–204). New York, NY: Wiley; Tittle, C. (1980). Labeling and crime: An empirical evaluation. In W. Gove (Ed.), *The labeling of deviance* (pp. 241–263). Beverly Hills, CA: Sage.

20. Bernburg, J. G., & Krohn, M. D. (2003). Labeling, life chances, and adult crime: The direct and indirect effects of official intervention in adolescence on crime in early adulthood. *Criminology, 41,* 1287–1318.

21. Paternoster, Decisions to participate and desist from four types of common delinquency.

22. Ibid.

23. Liska, A. E., & Messner, S. (1999). *Perspectives on crime and deviance*. Englewood Cliffs, NJ: Prentice Hall.

24. Cooley, C. H. (1902). *Human nature and the social order*. New York, NY: Scribners; Mead, G. H. (1934). *Mind, self and society*. Chicago, IL: University of Chicago Press.

25. Adams, M., Robertson, C., Gray-Ray, P., & Ray, M. C. (2003). Labeling and delinquency. *Adolescence, 38,* 171–186; Jensen, G. F. (1980). Labeling and identity: Toward a reconciliation of divergent findings. *Criminology, 18,* 121–129; Matsueda, R. L. (1992). Reflected appraisals, parental labeling, and delinquency: Specifying a symbolic interactionist theory. *The American Journal of Sociology, 97,* 1577–1611.

26. Adams et al., Labeling and delinquency.

27. Matsueda, Reflected appraisals.

28. Bartusch, D. J., & Matsueda, R. L. (1996). Gender, reflected appraisals, and labeling: A cross group test of an interactionist theory of delinquency. *Social Forces, 75,* 145–177.

29. Bernburg, C. G., Krohn, M. D., & Rivera, C. J. (2006). Official labeling, criminal embeddedness, and subsequent delinquency: A longitudinal test of labeling theory. *Journal of Research in Crime and Delinquency, 43,* 67–88.

30. Sampson, R. J., & Laub, J. H. (1997). A life-course theory of cumulative disadvantage. In T. P. Thornberry (Ed.), *Developmental theories of crime and delinquency* (pp.133–161). New Brunswick, NJ: Transaction.

31. Morenoff, J. D., Sampson, R. J., & Raudenbush, S. W. (2001). Neighborhood inequality, collective efficacy, and the spatial dynamics of urban violence. *Criminology, 39*(3), 517–559; Sampson, R. J., Morenoff, J. D., & Gannon-Rowley, T. (2001). Assessing "neighborhood effects": Social processes and the new directions in research. *Annual Review of Sociology, 28,* 443–478.

32. Bernburg & Krohn, Labeling, life chances, and adult crime.

33. Johnson, L. M., Simons, R. L., & Conger, R. D. (2004). Criminal justice system involvement and continuity of youth crime: A longitudinal analysis. *Youth & Society, 36,* 3–29.

34. Brezina, T., & Aragones, A. (2004). Devils in disguise: The contribution of positive labeling to "sneaky thrills" delinquency. *Deviant Behavior, 25,* 513–535.

35. Ibid., especially p. 527.

36. Ibid.

37. Adams et al., Labeling and delinquency.

38. Hirschfield, P. J. (2008). The declining significance of delinquent labels in disadvantaged urban communities. *Sociological Forum*, *23,* 575–601.

39. Ibid., especially pp. 596, 597.

40. Holsinger, K., & Hodge, J. P. (2016). The experiences of lesbian, gay, bisexual, and transgender girls in juvenile justice systems. *Feminist Criminology, 11*(1), 23–47.

41. Marx, K. (1912). *Capital* (Vol. 1). Chicago, IL: Kerr; Marx, K., & Engels, F. (1848). *The communist manifesto.* London.

42. Ibid.

43. Moyer, *Criminological theories*.

44. Du Bois, W. E. B. (1889). The Negro and crime. *The Independent, 51,* 1355–1357; Du Bois, W. E. B. (1899). *The Philadelphia Negro: A social study*. New York, NY: Shocken Books; Du Bois, W. E. B. (1901). *The spawn of slavery: The convict lease system in the South.* Atlanta, GA: Atlanta University Press; Du Bois, W. E. B. (1904). *Some notes on Negro crime, particularly in Georgia*. Atlanta, GA: Atlanta University Press.

45. Du Bois, The Negro and crime, especially p. 1356.

46. Bonger, *Criminality and economic conditions.*

47. Chambliss, W. J. (1964). A sociological analysis of the law of vagrancy. *Social Problems, 12*(1), 67–77; Chambliss, W. J. (1969). *Crime and the legal process.* New York, NY: McGraw-Hill; Chambliss, W. J. (1975). Toward a political economy of crime. *Theory and Society, 2,* 149–170; Chambliss, W. J., & Seidman, R. (1971).

Law, order, and power. Reading, MA: Addison-Wesley; Hall, S., Critcher, C., Jefferson, T., Clarke, J., & Roberts, B. (1978). *Policing the crisis.* London, UK: Macmillan; Platt, T. (1974). Prospects for a radical criminology in the United States. *Crime and Social Justice, 1,* 2–10; Schwendinger, H., & Schwendinger, J. (1970). Defenders of order or guardians of human rights? *Issues in Criminology, 5,* 123–157; Spitzer, S. (1975). Toward a Marxian theory of deviance. *Social Problems, 22,* 638–651; Taylor, I., Walton, P., & Young, J. (1973). *The new criminology.* New York, NY: Harper Torchbooks; Turk, A. T. (1969). *Criminality and the legal order.* Chicago, IL: Rand McNally; Turk, A. T. (1976). Law, conflict and order: From theorizing toward theories. *Canadian Review of Sociology and Anthropology, 13*(3), 282–294; Turk, A. T. (1977). Class, conflict, and criminalization. *Sociological Focus, 10,* 209–220.

48. Quinney, R. (1970). *The problem of crime.* New York, NY: Dodd and Mead; Quinney, R. (1970). *The social reality of crime.* Boston: Little & Brown; Quinney, R. (1974). *Critique of legal order: Crime control in capitalist society.* Boston, MA: Little, Brown; Quinney, R. (1977). *Class, state, and crime: On the theory and practice of criminal justice.* New York, NY: Harper and Row.

49. Quinney, R. (1979). Crime and the development of capitalism. In R. Quinney (Ed.), *Capitalist society: Readings for a critical sociology* (pp. 319–332). Homewood, IL: The Dorsey Press, especially p. 325. (Original work published 1977)

50. Messner, S. F., & Krohn, M. D. (1990). Class, compliance structures, and delinquency: Assessing Integrated Structural-Marxist Theory. *The American Journal of Sociology, 96*(2), 300–328.

51. Greenberg, D. F. (1977). Delinquency and the age structure of society. *Contemporary Crises, 1,* 189–224.

52. Colvin, M., & Pauly, J. (1983). A critique of criminology: Toward an Integrated Structural-Marxist Theory of delinquency production. *American Journal of Sociology, 89*(3), 513–551, especially p. 536.

53. Following the lead of Cloward, R., & Ohlin, L. (1960). *Delinquency and opportunity: A theory of delinquent gangs.* New York, NY: Free Press.

54. Messner & Krohn, Class, compliance structures, and delinquency; Paternoster, R., & Tittle, C. R. (1990). Parental work, control and delinquency: A theoretical and empirical critique. In W. S. Laufer & F. Adler (Eds.), *Advances in criminological theory* (Vol. 2, pp. 39–65). New Brunswick, NJ: Transaction.

55. Simpson, S., & Elis, L. (1994). Is gender subordinate to class? An empirical assessment of Colvin and Pauly's Structural Marxist Theory of Delinquency. *Journal of Criminal Law & Criminology, 85,* 453–480.

56. Barak, G., Flavin, J. M., & Leighton, P. S. (2001). *Class, race, gender and crime: Social realities of justice in America.* Los Angeles, CA: Roxbury; Cole, D. (1999). *No equal justice: Race and class in the American criminal justice system.* New York, NY: The New Press; Mauer, M., & Chesney-Lind, M. (2002). *Invisible punishment: The collateral consequences of mass imprisonment.* New York, NY: The New Press; Pfohl, S. (1994). *Images of deviance and social control.* New York, NY: McGraw-Hill; Sudbury, J. (Ed.). (2005). *Global lockdown: Race, gender, and the prison-industrial complex.* New York, NY: Routledge.

57. Burgess-Proctor, Intersections of race, class, gender and crime.

58. Daly, K., & Chesney-Lind, M. (1988). Feminism and criminology. *Justice Quarterly, 5,* 497–538, especially p. 504.

59. Burgess-Proctor, Intersections of race, class, gender and crime.

60. Baca Zinn, M., & Thornton Dill, B. (1996). Theorizing difference from multiracial feminism. *Feminist Studies, 22,* 321–331.

61. Collins, *Black feminist thought*; Crenshaw, K. (1989). Demarginalizing the intersection of race and sex: A Black feminist critique of antidiscrimination doctrine, feminist theory, and antiracist politics. *University of Chicago Legal Forum, 14,* 538–554; Crenshaw, K. (1993). Mapping the margins: Intersectionality, identity politics, and violence against women of color. *Stanford Law Review, 43,* 1241–1299.

NOTES

62. Burgess-Proctor, Intersections of race, class, gender and crime.

63. Adler, F. (1975). *Sisters in crime: The rise of the new female criminal.* New York, NY: McGraw-Hill.

64. Adler, F. (1977). The interaction between women's emancipation and female criminality: A cross-cultural perspective. *International Journal of Criminology and Penology, 5,* 101–112.

65. Daly & Chesney-Lind, Feminism and criminology.

66. Chesney-Lind, M. (2006). Patriarchy, crime and justice: Feminist criminology in an era of backlash. *Feminist Criminology, 1,* 6–26; Daly & Chesney-Lind, Feminism and criminology.

67. Smart, C. (1976). *Women, crime and criminology: A feminist critique.* Boston, MA: Routledge and Kegan Paul.

68. Chesney-Lind, M. (1989). Girls' crime and woman's place: Toward a feminist model of female delinquency. *Crime & Delinquency, 35*(10), 5–29.

69. Daly & Chesney-Lind, Feminism and criminology.

70. Ibid.

71. Cain, M. (1990). Towards transgression: New directions in feminist criminology. *International Journal of the Sociology of Law, 18,* 1–18.

72. Ibid., especially p. 6.

73. Daly, K. (2006). Feminist thinking about crime and justice. In S. Henry & M. Lanier (Eds.), *The essential criminology reader* (pp. 205–213). Boulder, CO: Westview Press.

74. Crenshaw, Demarginalizing the intersection of race and sex; Crenshaw, Mapping the margins.

75. Chesney-Lind, Patriarchy, crime and justice.

76. Chesney-Lind, M., Morash, M., & Stevens, T. (2008). Girls' troubles, girls' delinquency, and gender responsive programming: A review. *Australian & New Zealand Journal of Criminology, 41,* 162–189, especially p. 194.

77. Belknap, J. (2001). *The invisible woman: Gender, crime, and justice* (1st ed.). Belmont, CA: Wadsworth; Gaarder, E., & Belknap, J. (2002). Tenuous borders: Girls transferred to adult court. *Criminology, 40*(3), 481–517; Pasko, L. (2008). The wayward girl revisited: Understanding the gendered nature of juvenile justice and delinquency. *Sociology Compass, 2/3,* 821–836; Salisbury, E. J., & Van Voorhis, P. (2009). Gendered pathways: A quantitative investigation of woman probationers' paths to incarceration. *Criminal Justice and Behavior, 36,* 541–566; Daly, K. (1992). Women's pathways to felony court: Feminist theories of lawbreaking and problems of representation. *Southern California Review of Law and Women's Studies, 2,* 11–52; Jones, N. J., Brown, S. L., Wanamaker, K. A., & Greiner, L. E. (2014). A quantitative exploration of gendered pathways to crime in a sample of male and female juvenile offenders. *Feminist Criminology, 9*(2), 113–116.

78. Chesney-Lind et al., Girls' troubles, girls' delinquency.

79. Salisbury & Van Voorhis, Gendered pathways.

80. Jones et al., A quantitative exploration of gendered pathways to crime in a sample of male and female juvenile offenders.

81. Messerschmidt, J. W. (2011). The struggle for heterofeminine recognition: Bullying, embodiment, and reactive sexual offending by adolescent girls. *Feminist Criminology, 6*(3), 203–233.

82. Currie, E. (1989). *Crime and punishment in the United States.* New York, NY: Picador.

CHAPTER 7

1. Parenting Inside Out. (2012). *Children of incarcerated parents bill of rights.* Retrieved from http://www.parentinginsideout.org/the-children-of-incarcerated-parents-bill-of-rights/

2. Cohn, D., Passel, J. S., Wang, W., & Livingston, G. (2011). *Barely half of U.S. adults are married: A record low. Social and demographic trends.* Washington, DC: Pew Research Center.

3. Mathews, T. J., & Hamilton, B. E. (2016). Mean age of mothers is on the rise: United States, 2000–2014. *NCHS Data Brief, No. 232.* Hyattsville, MD: National Center for Health

Statistics. Retrieved from http://www.cdc.gov/nchs/data/databriefs/db232.pdf

4. Stevenson, B., & Wolfers, J. (2007). Marriage and divorce: Changes and their driving forces. *Journal of Economic Perspectives, 21,* 27–52.

5. Federal Interagency Forum on Child and Family Statistics, *America's children.*

6. Hamilton, B. E., Martin, J., Osterman, M. J. K., Curtin, S. C., & Mathews, T. J. (2015). Births: Final data for 2014. *National Vital Statistics Reports, 64*(12). National Center for Health Statistics. Retrieved from http://www.cdc.gov/nchs/data/nvsr/nvsr64/nvsr64_12.pdf

7. Federal Interagency Forum on Child and Family Statistics, *America's children.*

8. See Glueck, S., & Glueck, E. (1950). *Unraveling juvenile delinquency.* Cambridge, MA: Harvard University Press; Nye, *Family relationships and delinquent behavior.*

9. Wells, L. E., & Rankin, J. H. (1986). The broken homes model of delinquency: Analytic issues. *Journal of Research in Crime and Delinquency, 23,* 68–93.

10. Rankin, J. H., & Kern, R. M. (1994). Parental attachments and delinquency. *Criminology, 32,* 495–515; Spohn, R. E., & Kurtz, D. L. (2011). Family structure as a social context for family conflict: Unjust strain and serious delinquency. *Criminal Justice Review, 36,* 332–356.

11. Spohn & Kurtz, Family structure as a social context for family conflict; Rankin, J. H. (1983). The family context of delinquency. *Social Problems, 30,* 466–479.

12. Cernkovich, S. A., & Giordano, P. C. (1987). Family relationships and delinquency. *Criminology, 20,* 149–167; Van Voorhis, P., Cullen, F. T., Mathers, R. A., & Chenoweth Garner, C. (1988). The impact of family structure and quality on delinquency: A comparative assessment of structural and functional factors. *Criminology, 26,* 235–261.

13. Van Voorhis et al., The impact of family structure and quality on delinquency.

14. Bradbury, K., & Katz, J. (2002). Women's labor market involvement and family income mobility when marriages end. *New England Economic Review, Q4,* 41–74.

15. Heck, C., & Walsh, A. (2000). The effects of maltreatment and family structure on minor and serious delinquency. *International Journal of Offender Therapy and Comparative Criminology, 44,* 178–193; Leiber, M. J., Mack, K. Y., & Featherstone, R. A. (2009). Family structure, family processes, economic factors, and delinquency. *Youth Violence and Juvenile Justice, 7*(2), 79–99; Juby, H., & Farrington, D. P. (2001). Disentangling the link between disrupted families and delinquency. *British Journal of Criminology, 41,* 22–40; Rebellon, C. J. (2002). Reconsidering the broken homes/delinquency relationship and exploring mediating mechanisms. *Criminology, 40*(1), 103–136; Sampson, R. J., & Laub, J. H. (1994). Urban poverty and the family context of delinquency: A new look at structure and process in a classic study. *Child Development, 65,* 523–541; Spohn & Kurtz, Family structure as a social context for family conflict.

16. Farnsworth, M. (1984). Family structure, family attributes, and delinquency in a sample of low-income, minority males and females. *Journal of Youth and Adolescence, 13,* 349–363; Leiber et al., Family structure, family processes, economic factors, and delinquency; Van Voorhis et al., The impact of family structure and quality on delinquency; Sokol-Katz, J., Dunham, R., & Zimmerman, R. (1997). Family structure versus parental attachment in controlling adolescent deviant behavior: A social control model. *Adolescence, 32,* 199–216.

17. Juby & Farrington, Disentangling the link between disrupted families and delinquency; Matsueda & Heimer, Race, family structure, and delinquency; Spohn & Kurtz, Family structure as a social context for family conflict.

18. Nye, *Family relationships and delinquent behavior;* Van Voorhis et al., The impact of family structure and quality on delinquency.

19. Glueck & Glueck, *Unraveling juvenile delinquency;* Gove, W., & Crutchfield, R. (1982). The family and juvenile delinquency. *Sociological Quarterly, 23,* 301–319; Klein, K., Forehand, R., Armistead, L., & Long, P. (1997). Delinquency during the transition to early adulthood: Family and parenting predictors from early adolescence. *Adolescence, 32,* 61–81.

20. Klein et al., Delinquency during the transition to early adulthood.

21. Gove & Crutchfield, The family and juvenile delinquency.

22. Bates, K. A., Bader, C. D., & Mencken, F. C. (2003). Family structure, power-control theory, and deviance: Extending power-control theory to include alternative family forms. *Western Criminology Review, 4*(3), 170–190; Kierkus, C. A., & Baer, D. (2002). A social control explanation of the relationship between family structure and delinquent behaviour. *Canadian Journal of Criminology, 44,* 425–458.

23. Apel, R., & Kaukinen, C. (2008). On the relationship between family structure and antisocial behavior: Parental cohabitation and blended households. *Criminology, 46,* 35–70.

24. Apel & Kaukinen, On the relationship between family structure and antisocial behavior.

25. Johnson, R. E. (1986). Family structure and delinquency: General patterns and gender differences. *Criminology, 24,* 65–84; Matlack, M. E., McGreevey, M. S., Jr., Rouse, R., Flatter, C., & Marcus, R. F. (1994). Family correlates of social skill deficits in incarcerated and non-incarcerated adolescents. *Adolescence, 29,* 117–132.

26. Johnson, Family structure and delinquency.

27. Cernkovich & Giordano, Family relationships and delinquency; LeFlore, L. (1988). Delinquent youths and family. *Adolescence, 23,* 629–642.

28. Bates et al., Family structure, power-control theory, and deviance.

29. Leiber et al., Family structure, family processes, economic factors, and delinquency. For a review, see Hoeve, M., Stams, G., van der Put, C., Dubas, J., van der Laan, P., & Gerris, J. (2012). A meta-analysis of attachment to parents and delinquency. *Journal of Abnormal Child Psychology, 40,* 771–785.

30. Bates, K. A. (1998). *Family matters: Theoretical and methodological issues surrounding family and juvenile delinquency.* Available from UMI, Ann Arbor, MI. Order No. DA9836138.

31. Broidy, L. (1995). Direct supervision and delinquency: Assessing the adequacy of structural proxies. *Journal of Criminal Justice, 23,* 541–554; Hay, C. (2001). Parenting, self-control, and delinquency: A test of self-control theory. *Criminology, 39,* 707–736; Jang, S. J., & Smith, C. A. (1997). A test of reciprocal causal relationships among parental supervision, affective ties, and delinquency. *Journal of Research in Crime and Delinquency, 34,* 307–337; Junger, M., & Marshall, I. H. (1997). The interethnic generalizability of social control theory: An empirical test. *Journal of Research in Crime & Delinquency, 34,* 79–112.

32. Bates, *Family matters.*

33. Spohn & Kurtz, Family structure as a social context for family conflict.

34. Klein et al., Delinquency during the transition to early adulthood; Shek, D. (1997). Family environment and adolescent psychological well-being, school adjustment, and problem behavior: A pioneer study in a Chinese context. *Journal of Genetic Psychology, 158,* 113–129.

35. Rowe, D. C., & Gully, B. L. (1992). Sibling effects on substance abuse and delinquency. *Criminology, 30,* 217–233.

36. Klein et al., Delinquency during the transition to early adulthood.

37. Shek, Family environment and adolescent psychological well-being, school adjustment, and problem behavior.

38. Rowe & Gully, Sibling effects on substance abuse and delinquency.

39. Dornfeld, M., & Kruttschnitt, C. (1992). Do the stereotypes fit? Mapping gender-specific outcomes and risk factors. *Criminology, 30,* 397–419; Hay, C., Fortson, E. N., Hollist, D. R., Altheimer, I., & Schaible, L. M. (2006). The impact of community disadvantage on the relationship between the family and juvenile crime. *Journal of Research in Crime and Delinquency, 43,* 326–356; Sampson & Laub, *Crime in the making;* Sampson & Laub, Urban poverty and the family context of delinquency; Sampson, R. J., & Laub, J. H. (2005). A life-course view of the development of crime. *The Annals of the American Academy of Political and Social Science, 602,* 12–45; Straus, M. A. (1991). Discipline and deviance: Physical punishment of children and violence and other crime in adulthood. *Social Problems, 38,* 133–155.

40. Gorman-Smith, D., Tolan, P. H., Zelli, A., & Huesmann, L. R. (1996). The relation of family functioning to violence among inner-city minority

youth. *Journal of Family Psychology, 10,* 115–130; Larzelere, R. E., & Patterson, G. R. (1990). Parental management: Mediator of the effect of socioeconomic status on early delinquency. *Criminology, 28,* 301–324; Seydlitz, R. (1993). Complexity in the relationships among direct and indirect parental controls and delinquency. *Youth and Society, 24,* 243–276.

41. Hay et al., The impact of community disadvantage on the relationship between the family and juvenile crime; Peiser, N. C., & Heaven, P. (1996). Family influences on self-reported delinquency among high school students. *Journal of Adolescence, 19,* 557–569; Sampson & Laub, Urban poverty and the family context of delinquency.

42. Alarid, L. F., Burton, V. S., Jr., & Cullen, F. T. (2000). Gender and crime among felony offenders: Assessing the generality of social control and differential association theories. *Journal of Research in Crime and Delinquency, 37,* 171–199; Canter, R. J. (1982). Family correlates of male and female delinquency. *Criminology, 20,* 149–167.

43. Alarid et al., Gender and crime among felony offenders; Blum, J., Ireland, M., & Blum, R. W. (2003). Gender differences in juvenile violence: A report from Add Health. *Journal of Adolescent Health, 32,* 234–240; Laundra, K. H., Kiger, G., & Bahr, S. J. (2002). A social development model of serious delinquency: Examining gender differences. *The Journal of Primary Prevention, 22,* 389–407.

44. Daigle, L. E., Cullen, F. T., & Wright, J. P. (2007). Gender differences in the predictors of juvenile delinquency. *Youth Violence and Juvenile Justice, 5,* 254–286; Fagan, A. A., Van Horn, M. L., Hawkins, J. D., & Arthur, M. (2007). Gender similarities and differences in the association between risk and protective factors and self-reported serious delinquency. *Prevention Science, 8,* 115–124.

45. Bronte-Tinkew, J., Moore, K. A., & Carrano, J. (2006). The father-child relationship, parenting styles, and adolescent risk behaviors in intact families. *Journal of Family Issues*, 27, 850–881.

46. Cernkovich & Giordano, Family relationships and delinquency; Crosnoe, R., Erickson, K. G., & Dornbusch, S. M. (2002). Protective functions of family relationships and school factors on the deviant behavior of adolescent boys and

girls: Reducing the impact of risky friendships. *Youth and Society, 33,* 515–544; Keenan, K., & Shaw, D. (1997). Developmental and social influences on young girls' early problem behavior. *Psychological Bulletin, 121,* 95–113.

47. Blitstein, J. L., Murray, D. M., Lytle, L. A., Birnbaum, A. S., & Perry, C. L. (2005). Predictors of violent behavior in an early adolescent cohort: Similarities and differences across genders. *Health Education and Behavior, 32,* 175–194.

48. Heimer, K., & De Coster, S. (1999). The gendering of violent delinquency. *Criminology, 37,* 277–318.

49. Fagan, A. A., Van Horn, M. L., Antaramian, S., & Hawkins, J. D. (2010). How do families matter? Age and gender differences in family influences on delinquency and drug use? *Youth Violence and Juvenile Justice, 9,* 150–170.

50. Hay, C. (2003). Family strain, gender, and delinquency. *Sociological Perspectives, 46*(1), 107–135.

51. Ibid.

52. Hadjar, A., Baier, D., Boehnke, K., & Hagan, J. (2007). Juvenile delinquency and gender revisited: The family and power-control theory reconceived. *European Journal of Criminology, 4,* 33–57.

53. Ibid.

54. Mack, K. Y., & Leiber, M. J. (2005). Race, gender, single-mother households, and delinquency: A further test of power-control theory. *Youth and Society, 37,* 115–144.

55. Hagan et al., Class in the household.

56. Mack & Leiber, Race, gender, single-mother households, and delinquency.

57. Child Welfare Information Gateway. (2007). *Recognizing child abuse and neglect: Signs and symptoms.* Retrieved from http://www.childwelfare.gov/pubs/factsheets/signs.cfm

58. Finkelhor, D., Turner, H., Shattuck, A., Hamby, S., & Kracke, K. (2015). Children's exposure to violence, crime, and abuse: An update. *Office of Juvenile Justice and Delinquency Prevention*. Retrieved from http://www.ojjdp.gov/pubs/248547.pdf

59. Goldman, J., Salus, M., Wolcott, D., & Kennedy, K. (2003). *A coordinated response to child abuse and neglect: The foundation for practice.*

Washington, DC: Office on Child Abuse and Neglect, Health and Human Services.

60. Curtis, G. C. (1963). Violence breeds violence: Perhaps? *American Journal of Psychiatry, 120,* 386–387.

61. McGloin, J. M., & Widom, C. S. (2001). Resilience among abused and neglected children grown up. *Development and Psychopathology, 13,* 1021–1038.

62. Mersky, J. P., Topitzes, J., & Reynolds, A. J. (2012). Unsafe at any age: Linking childhood and adolescent maltreatment to delinquency and crime. *Journal of Research in Crime and Delinquency, 49*(2), 295–318, p. 296.

63. See Maas, C., Herrenkohl, T., & Sousa, C. (2008). Review of research on child maltreatment and violence in youth. *Trauma, Violence, and Abuse, 9*(1), 56–67.

64. Yun, I., Ball, J. D., & Lim, H. (2010). Disentangling the relationship between child maltreatment and violent delinquency: Using a nationally representative sample. *Journal of Interpersonal Violence, 26,* 88–110.

65. Mersky et al., Unsafe at any age.

66. Thornberry, T. P., Henry, K. L., Ireland, T. O., & Smith, C. A. (2010). The causal impact of childhood-limited and adolescent maltreatment on early adult adjustment. *Journal of Adolescent Health, 46,* 359–365.

67. Van der Put, C., Lanctot, N., de Ruiter, C., & van Vugt, E. (2015). Child maltreatment among boys and girl probationers: Does type of maltreatment make a difference in offending behavior and psychosocial problems? *Child Abuse and Neglect: The International Journal, 46,* 142–151.

68. Greene, J., Ringwalt, C., Kelley, J., Iachan, R., & Cohen, Z. (1995). *Youth with runaway, throwaway, and homeless experiences: Prevalence, drug use, and other at-risk behaviors.* Washington, DC: Administration for Children and Families, Family and Youth Services Bureau.

69. Hammer, H., Finkelhor, D., & Sedlak, A. (2002). *Runaway/thrownaway children: National estimates and characteristics.* Washington, DC: National Incidence Studies of Missing, Abducted, Runaway, and Thrownaway Children;

Office of Juvenile Justice and Delinquency Prevention.

70. Office of Applied Studies, Substance Abuse and Mental Health Services Administration. (2004). *Substance use among youths who had run away from home.* National Survey on Drug Use and Health. Rockville, MD: SAMHSA.

71. Jencks, C. (1994). *The homeless.* Cambridge, MA: Harvard University Press; Tyler, K. A., Hoyt, D. R., Whitbeck, L. B., & Cauce, A. M. (2001). The impact of childhood sexual abuse on later sexual victimization among runaway youth. *Journal of Research on Adolescence, 11*(2), 151–176.

72. Kaufman, J. G., & Widom, C. S. (1999). Childhood victimization, running away, and delinquency. *Journal of Research in Crime and Delinquency, 36*(4), 347–371; Kempf-Leonard, K., & Johansson, P. (2007). Gender and runaways: Risk factors, delinquency, and juvenile justice experiences. *Youth Violence and Juvenile Justice, 5,* 308–327.

73. Janus, M., Burgess, A., & McCormack, A. (1987). Histories of sexual abuse in adolescent male runaways. *Adolescence, 22,* 405–417; McCormack, A., Janus, M., & Burgess, A. W. (1986). Runaway youths and sexual victimization: Gender differences in adolescent runaway populations. *Child Abuse & Neglect, 10,* 387–395.

74. Chesney-Lind, M. (1988). Girls and status offenses: Is juvenile justice still sexist? *Criminal Justice Abstracts, 20,* 144–165; Chesney-Lind, M. (1997). *Female offenders: Girls, women, and crime.* Thousand Oaks, CA: Sage.

75. Chesney-Lind, Girls and status offenses: Is juvenile justice still sexist?

76. Kaufman & Widom, Childhood victimization, running away, and delinquency.

77. Chesney-Lind, M., & Shelden, R. (1998). *Girls, delinquency, and juvenile justice* (2nd ed.). Pacific Grove, CA: Brooks/Cole; Kempf-Leonard & Johansson, Gender and runaways.

78. Rosario, M., Schrimshaw, E. W., & Hunter, J. (2011). Homelessness among lesbian, gay, and bisexual youth: Implications for subsequent internalizing and externalizing symptoms. *Journal of Youth and Adolescence, 41,* 544–560.

79. Ibid., p. 557.

80. Nickel, J., Garland, C., & Kane, L. (2009). *Children of incarcerated parents: An action plan for federal policymakers*. New York, NY: Council of State Governments Justice Center.

81. Ibid.; Simmons, C. W. (2000). Children of incarcerated parents. *California Bureau Research Reports*. Retrieved from https://www.library.ca.gov/crb/00/notes/v7n2.pdf

82. Simmons, Children of incarcerated parents.

83. Glaze, L. E., & Maruschak, L. M. (2010, revised). *Parents in prison and their minor children*. Washington, DC: U.S. Government Printing Office. Retrieved from http://bjs.gov/content/pub/pdf/pptmc.pdf

84. Western, B., & Wildeman, C. (2009). The black family and mass incarceration. *Annals of the American Academy of Political and Social Science, 621,* 221–242.

85. Braman, D. S. (2004). *Doing time on the outside: Incarceration family life in urban America.* Ann Arbor, MI: University of Michigan Press.

86. Sabol, W. J., & Lynch, J. P. (1998). *Assessing the longer-run consequences of incarceration: Effects on families and unemployment.* Paper presented at the 20th annual conference of the Association for Public Policy and Analysis, New York, NY.

87. Glaze & Maruschak, *Parents in prison and their minor children.*

88. Phillips, S. D., Costello, J., & Angold, A. (2007). Differences among children whose mothers have a history of arrest. *Women and Criminal Justice, 17*(2/3), 45–63.

89. Nickel et al., *Children of incarcerated parents;* Phillips et al., Differences among children whose mothers have a history of arrest; Phillips, S. D., & Dettlaff, A. J. (2009). More than parents in prison: The broader overlap between the criminal justice and child welfare systems. *Journal of Public Child Welfare, 3,* 3–22.

90. Phillips & Dettlaff, More than parents in prison.

91. Seymour, C. (1996, September/October). Children with parents in prison: Child welfare policy, program, and practice issues. *Child Welfare Special Issue, 77*(5), 469–493.

92. Simmons, Children of incarcerated parents.

93. Parenting Inside Out, *Children of Incarcerated Parents' Bill of Rights.*

94. Child Welfare Information Gateway. (2013). *Grounds for involuntary termination of parental rights.* Retrieved from https://www.childwelfare.gov/pubPDFs/groundtermin.pdf

95. Center for the Future of Teaching and Learning. (2008). *Ready to succeed: Changing systems to give California's foster children the opportunities they deserve to be ready for and succeed in school.* Retrieved from https://www.wested.org/project/center-for-the-future-of-teaching-and-learning/

96. Victory, O. (2016). *"All I wanted was someone to be there": Surviving the structured abuse in group homes* (Unpublished master's thesis). California State University, San Marcos.

97. Center for the Future of Teaching and Learning, *Ready to succeed.*

98. Berrick, J. D., Courtney, M., & Barth, R. P. (1993). Specialized foster care and group home care: Similarities and differences in the characteristics of children in care. *Children and Youth Services Review, 15*(6), 453–473; Parrish, T., Dubois, J., Delano, C., Dixon, D., Webster, D., Berrick, J. D., & Bolus, S. (2001). *Education in foster group home children, Whose responsibility is it? Study of the educational placement of children residing in group homes.* Palo Alto, CA: American Institute of Research.

99. Blome, W. W. (1997). What happens to foster kids: Educational experiences of a random sample of foster care youth and a matched group of non-foster care youth. *Child and Adolescent Social Work, 14,* 41–53.

100. Center for the Future of Teaching and Learning, *Ready to succeed.*

101. Barth, R. (1990). On their own: The experiences of youth after foster care. *Child and Adolescent Social Work, 7,* 419–440.

102. Taylor, C. (2006). *Young people in care and criminal behaviour.* London, UK: Jessica Kingsley Publishers.

103. Barn, R., & Tan, J.-P. (2012). Foster youth and crime: Employing general strain theory to promote understanding. *Journal of Criminal Justice, 40,* 212–220.

CHAPTER 8

1. Rampey, B. D., Dion, G. S., & Donahue, P. L. (2009). *NAEP 2008 trends in academic progress* (NCES 2009–479). Washington, DC: U.S. Department of Education, National Center for Education Statistics. Retrieved from http://nces.ed.gov/nationsreportcard/pdf/main2008/2009479.pdf

2. Kelly, D., Xie, H., Nord, C. W., Jenkins, F., Chan, J. Y., & Kastberg, D. (2013). *Performance of U.S. 15-year-old students in mathematics, science, and reading literacy in an international context: First look at PISA 2012 (NCES 2014-024).* Washington, DC: U.S. Department of Education, National Center for Education Statistics. Retrieved from http://nces.ed.gov/pubsearch

3. Center on Budget and Policy Priorities. (2013). *Policy basics: Where do our federal tax dollars go?* Retrieved from http://www.cbpp.org/files/4-14-08tax.pdf

4. Oakes, J. (2005). *Keeping track: How schools structure inequality* (2nd ed.). New Haven, CT: Yale University Press.

5. Kelly, S. P. (2007). Social class and tracking within schools. In L. Weis (Ed.), *The way class works: Readings on school, family and economy* (pp. 210–224). New York, NY: Routledge; Kozol, J. (1992). *Savage inequalities: Children in America's schools.* New York, NY: Harper Perennial; Macleod, J. (2008). *Ain't no makin' it: Aspirations and attainment in a low-income neighborhood* (3rd ed.). Denver, CO: Westview Press.

6. Oakes, *Keeping track.*

7. McNeely, C. A., Nonnemaker, J. M., & Blum, R. W. (2002). Promoting school connectedness: Evidence from the National Longitudinal Study of Adolescent Health. *Journal of School Health, 72*(4), 138–146.

8. Hirschi, *Causes of delinquency.*

9. Wilson, D. (2004). The interface of school climate and school connectedness and relationships with aggression and victimization. *Journal of School Health, 74*(7), 293–299.

10. Corrigan, P. (1979). *Schooling the smash street kids.* London, UK: Macmillan; Lacey, C. (1970). *Hightown grammar.* Manchester, UK: Manchester University Press; Willis, P. E. (1977). *Learning to labour.* Farnborough, UK: Saxon House.

11. Bourdieu, P. (1977). *Outline of a theory of practice.* Cambridge, UK: Cambridge University Press; Bourdieu, P., & Passeron, J. (1990). *Reproduction in education, society, and culture* (2nd ed.). London, UK: Sage; Connolly, P. (2004). *Boys and schooling in the early years.* Abingdon, UK: Routledge Falmer; Ingram, N. (2011). Within school and beyond the gate: The complexities of being educationally successful and working class. *Sociology, 45,* 287–302; Reay, D. (2004). "Mostly roughs and toughs": Social class, race, and representation in inner city schooling. *Sociology, 38*(5), 1005–1023.

12. Cohen, *Delinquent boys*; Toby, J. (1957). Orientation to education as a factor in the school maladjustment of lower class children. *Social Forces, 35,* 259–266.

13. Polk, K., Frease, D., & Richmond, F. L. (1974). Social class, school experience, and delinquency. *Criminology, 12,* 84–95.

14. Hannon, L. (2003). Poverty, delinquency, and educational attainment: Cumulative disadvantage or disadvantage saturation? *Sociological Inquiry, 73,* 575–595.

15. Liazos, A. (1978). School, alienation, and delinquency. *Crime & Delinquency, 24,* 355–370.

16. Greene, J., & Winters, M. (2005). *Public high school graduation and college-readiness rates: 1991–2002.* New York, NY: Manhattan Institute for Policy Research.

17. Stillwell, R., Sable, J., & Plotts, C. (2011). *Public school graduates and dropouts from the common core of data: School year 2008–09 (NCES 2011-312).* Washington, DC: U.S. Department of Education, National Center for Education Statistics. Retrieved from http://nces.ed.gov/pubsearch

18. Ibid.

19. For reviews, see Natriello, G. (Ed.). (1986). *School dropouts: Patterns and policies.* New York, NY: Teachers College Press; Rumberger, R. W.

(1987). High school dropouts: A review of issues and evidence. *Review of Educational Research, 57,* 101–121.

20. For reviews, see Delgado-Gaitan, C. (1988). The value of conformity: Learning to stay in school. *Anthropology and Educational Quarterly,* 19(4), 354–381; Fine, M. (1991). *Framing dropouts: Notes on the politics of an urban public high school.* Albany: State University of New York Press.

21. Finn, J. D. (1989). Withdrawing from school. *Review of Educational Research, 59,* 117–142; Finn, J. D. (1993). *School engagement and students at risk.* Washington, DC: National Center for Education Statistics; Rumberger, R. W. (1995). Dropping out of middle school: A multilevel analysis of students and schools. *American Educational Research Journal, 32*(3), 583–625.

22. Harlow, C. (2003). *Education and correctional populations.* Bureau of Justice Statistics Special Report. Washington, DC: U.S. Department of Justice.

23. Aloise-Young, P. A., Cruickshank, C., & Chavez, E. L. (2002). Cigarette smoking and self-reported health in school dropouts: A comparison of Mexican American and non-Hispanic white adolescents. *Journal of Pediatric Psychology, 27,* 497–507; Thornberry, T. P., Moore, M., & Christenson, R. L. (1985). The effect of dropping out of high school on subsequent criminal behavior. *Criminology, 23,* 3–18.

24. Sweeten, G., Bushway, S. D., & Paternoster, R. (2009). Does dropping out of school mean dropping into delinquency? *Criminology, 47*(1), 47–91.

25. Payne, A. (2008). A multilevel analysis of the relationships among communal school organization, student bonding, and delinquency. *Journal of Research in Crime and Delinquency, 45,* 429–455.

26. Liljeberg, J., Eklund, J., Fritz, M., & af Klinteberg, B. (2011). Poor school bonding and delinquency over time: Bidirectional effects and sex differences. *Journal of Adolescence, 34,* 1–9.

27. Fredricks, J. A., Blumenfeld, P. C., & Paris, A. H. (2004). School engagement: Potential of the concept, state of the evidence. *Review of Educational Research, 74,* 59–109.

28. Hirschfield, P. J., & Gasper, J. (2011). The relationship between school engagement and delinquency in late childhood and early adolescence. *Journal of Youth Adolescence, 40,* 3–22.

29. Ibid.

30. Muschert, G. W. (2007). Research in school shootings. *Sociology Compass, 1,* 60–80.

31. Zhang, A., Musu-Gillette, L., & Oudekerk, B.A. (2016). *Indicators of school crime and safety: 2015* (NCES 2016-079/NCJ 249758). Washington, DC: U.S. Department of Education, National Center for Education Statistics. Retrieved from http://www.bjs.gov/content/pub/pdf/iscs15.pdf

32. Leavy, P., & Maloney, K. P. (2009). American reporting of school violence and "people like us": A comparison of newspaper coverage of the Columbine and Red Lake school shootings. *Critical Sociology, 35,* 273–292.

33. Ibid.

34. Moon, B., Hwang, H., & McCluskey, J. D. (2011). Causes of school bullying: Empirical test of a general theory of crime, differential association theory, and general strain theory. *Crime & Delinquency, 57*(6), 849–877.

35. Dussich, J., & Maekoya, C. (2007). Physical child harm and bullying-related behaviors: A comparative study in Japan, South Africa, and the United States. *International Journal of Offender Therapy and Comparative Criminology, 51,* 495–509.

36. Olweus, D. (1993). *Bullying at school: What we know and what we can do.* Cambridge, MA: Blackwell.

37. Thornberg, R. (2010). Schoolchildren's social representations on bullying causes. *Psychology in the Schools, 47,* 311–327.

38. Thornberg, R. (2011). "She's weird!" The social construction of bullying in school: A review of qualitative research. *Children and Society, 25,* 258–267.

39. Lessert, M. (2012). *Cyberbullying: Analyzing the role of gender identity and general strain theory.* Unpublished manuscript, California State University San Marcos.

40. Hong, J. S., & Garbarino, J. (2012). Risk and protective factors for homophobic bullying in

schools: An application of the social-ecological framework. *Education Psychology Review, 24,* 271–285.

41. Kosciw, J. G., Greytak, E. A., Diaz, E. M., & Bartkiewicz, M. J. (2010). *The 2009 National School Climate Survey: The experiences of lesbian, gay, bisexual and transgender youth in our nation's schools.* New York, NY: GLSEN.

42. Hong & Garbarino, Risk and protective factors for homophobic bullying in schools.

43. U.S. Department of Education. (1997). Sexual harassment guidance: Harassment of students by school employees, other students, or third parties. *Federal Register, 62*(March 13), 12033–12051. Retrieved from http://www2.ed .gov/legislation/Fed Register/announcements/ 1997-1/031397b.html

44. Gruber, J. E., & Fineran, S. (2007). The impact of bullying and sexual harassment on middle and high school girls. *Violence Against Women, 13,* 627–643.

45. Ibid.

46. Nansel, T. R., Overpeck, M., Pilla, R. S., Ruan, W. J., Simons-Morton, B., & Scheidt, P. (2001). Bullying behaviors among U.S. youth: Prevalence and association with psychosocial adjustment. *Journal of the American Medical Association, 285,* 2094–2100.

47. Kochenderfer, B. J., & Ladd, G. W. (1996). Peer victimization: Cause or consequence of school maladjustment? *Child Development, 67,* 1305–1317.

48. Hinduja, S., & Patchin, J. W. (2009). *Bullying beyond the schoolyard: Preventing and responding to cyberbullying.* Thousand Oaks, CA: Corwin Press.

49. Hoff, D., & Mitchell, S. N. (2009). Cyberbullying: Causes, effects and remedies. *Journal of Educational Administration, 47*(5), 662–665.

50. Patchin, J., & Hinduja, S. (2011). Traditional and non-traditional bullying among youth: A test of general strain theory. *Youth & Society, 43,* 727–751.

51. Vanderbosch, H., & Van Cleemput, K. V. (2009). Cyberbullying among youngsters: Profiles of bullies and victims. *New Media & Society, 11,* 1349–1371.

52. Hinduja, S., & Patchin, J. (2007). Offline consequences of online victimization: School violence and delinquency. *Journal of School Violence, 6*(3), 89–112; Hoff & Mitchell, Cyberbullying.

53. Li, Q. (2006). Cyberbullying in schools: A research of gender differences. *School Psychology International, 27,* 157–170; Wade, A., & Beran, T. (2011). Cyberbullying: The new era of bullying. *Canadian Journal of School Psychology, 26*(1), 44–61.

54. Baldry, A. C. (2004). The impact of direct and indirect bullying on the mental and physical health of Italian youngsters. *Aggressive Behavior, 30,* 343–355; Beran, T. N., & Tutty, L. (2002). Children's reports of bullying and safety at school. *Canadian Journal of School Psychology, 17*(2), 1–14; Ma, X. (2002). Bullying in middle school: Individual and school characteristics of victims and offenders. *School Effectiveness and School Improvement, 13,* 63–89.

55. Hinduja, S., & Patchin, J. (2008). *Cyberbullying by race.* Retrieved from http://www.cyber bullying.us/research.php

56. Patchin & Hinduja, Traditional and non-traditional bullying among youth.

57. Hinduja, S., & Patchin, J. W. (2010). Bullying, cyberbullying, and suicide. *Archives of Suicide Research, 14*(3), 206–221.

58. Live Science. (2010, March 10). *Cyberbullying rampant for lesbian and gay teens.* Retrieved from http://www.livescience.com/6199-cyber bullying-rampant-lesbian-gay-teens.html

59. Willard, N. (2011). School response to cyberbullying and sexting: The legal challenges. *Brigham Young University Education and Law Journal,* pp. 75–125.

60. Ibid.

61. Blumenfeld, W. J., & Cooper, R. M. (2010). LGBT and allied youth responses to cyberbullying: Policy implications. *International Journal of Critical Pedagogy,* 114–133.

62. American Civil Liberties Union. (n.d.). *The School to Prison Pipeline.* Retrieved from http:// www.aclu.org/racial-justice/school-prison- pipeline

63. Nicholson-Crotty, S., Birchmeier, Z., & Valentine, D. (2009). Exploring the impact of school discipline on racial disproportion in the juvenile justice system. *Social Science Quarterly, 90,* 1003–1018.

64. Dignity in Schools. (2012). *Mission statement.* Retrieved from http://www.dignityinschools.org/about-us/mission

65. Ibid.

66. Dignity in Schools. (2012). *A Model code on education and dignity: Presenting a human rights framework for schools.* Retrieved from http://www.dignityinschools.org/files/DSC_Model_Code.pdf

67. Conan, N. (2012, September 11). Corporal punishment in schools: Does it work? *Talk of the Nation.* Retrieved from http://www.npr.org/2012/09/11/160952356/corporal-punishment-in-schools-does-it-work

68. U.S. Department of Education. (2016). *Civil rights data collection: A first look* [press release]. Office of Civil Rights. Retrieved from http://www2.ed.gov/about/offices/list/ocr/docs/2013-14-first-look.pdf

69. Skiba, R. J. (2000). *Zero tolerance, zero evidence: An analysis of school disciplinary practice.* Indiana Educational Policy Center: Policy Research Report #SRS2. Retrieved from http://www.indiana.edu/~safeschl/ztze.pdf

70. Villaruel, F. A., & Dunbar, C. (2006). Culture, race, and zero tolerance policy: The implications. *Journal of Forensic Psychology Practice, 6*(2), 53–63.

71. Dunbar, C., Jr., & Villaruel, F. A. (2002). Urban school leaders and the implementation of zero tolerance policy: An examination of its implications. *Peabody Journal of Education, 77,* 82–104.

72. Schwartz, R., & Rieser, L. (2001). Zero tolerance as mandatory sentencing. In W. Ayers, B. Dohrn, & R. Ayers (Eds.), *Zero tolerance: Resisting the drive for punishment in our schools* (pp. 126–135). New York, NY: New Press.

73. Miller, C. D. (2010, February 4). Two-inch LEGO gun gets 4th-grader Patrick Timoney in trouble: Where's the NRA? *CBS News.* Retrieved from http://www.cbsnews.com/8301-504083_162-6173526-504083.html

74. Masterson, T., & Chang, D. (2011, February 3). Cops charge 7-year-old for bringing toy gun to class: Kid charged with possession of a fake firearm after shooting Nerf-style gun. *NBC 10 Philadelphia.* Retrieved from http://www.nbcphiladelphia.com/news/local/Cops-Charge-7-Year-Old-for-Bringing-Toy-Gun-to-Class-115125844.html

75. Fox News. (2008). *Texas school suspends student for answering call in class from dad in Iraq.* Retrieved from http://www.foxnews.com/story/0,2933,350988,00.html#ixzz28Mnncy00

76. Monahan, R. (2010, February 4). Queens girl Alexa Gonzalez hauled out of school in handcuffs after getting caught doodling on desk. *New York Daily News.* Retrieved from http://www.nydailynews.com/new-york/education/queens-girl-alexa-gonzalez-hauled-school-handcuffs-caught-doodling-desk-article-1.194141#ixzz28MnMlrpj

77. Urbina, I. (2009, October 11). It's a fork, it's a spoon, it's a . . . weapon? *New York Times.* Retrieved from http://www.nytimes.com/2009/10/12/education/12discipline.html?_r=0

78. Zero tolerance. (2005). *West's Encyclopedia of American Law.* Retrieved from http://www.encyclopedia.com/doc/1G2-3437704780.html

79. Kupchik, A. (2010). *Homeroom security: School discipline in an age of fear.* New York, NY: NYU Press.

80. Ibid.

CHAPTER 9

1. Giordano, P., Longmore, M., & Manning, W. (2006). Gender and the meanings of adolescent romantic relationships: A focus on boys. *American Sociological Review*, 71(2), 260–287; Haynie, D. L., Steffensmeier, D., & Bell, K. E. (2007). Gender and serious violence: Untangling the role of friendship sex composition and peer violence. *Youth Violence and Juvenile Justice, 5,*

235–253; Warr, M. (1993). Age, peers, and delinquency. *Criminology, 31,* 17–40; Warr, *Companions in crime.*

2. Agnew, R. (1991). The interactive effect of peer variables on delinquency. *Criminology, 29,* 47–72; Akers, R. (1985). *Deviant behavior: A social learning approach.* Belmont, CA: Wadsworth; Haynie, D. L., & Osgood, W. (2005). Reconsidering peers and delinquency: How do peers matter? *Social Forces, 84*(2), 1109–1130; Mead, *Mind, self and society*; Newcomb, T. M. (1950). *Social psychology.* New York, NY: Dryden; Sutherland, E. H., & Cressey, D. R. (1955). *Principles of criminology* (5th ed.). Chicago, IL: J. B. Lippincott.

3. Cohen, L. E., & Felson, M. (1979). Social change and crime rate trends: A routine activity approach. *American Sociological Review, 44,* 588–608; Felson, M., & Gottfredson, M. (1984). Social indicators of adolescent activities near peers and parents. *Journal of Marriage and the Family, 46*(3), 709–714; Gold, M. (1970). *Delinquent behavior in an American city.* Belmont, CA: Brooks/Cole; Osgood, W., Wilson, J. K., O'Malley, P. M., Bachman, J. G., & Johnston, L. D. (1996). Routine activities and individual deviant behavior. *American Sociological Review, 61,* 635–655; Warr, M. (2005). Making delinquent friends: Adult supervision and children's affiliations. *Criminology, 43,* 77–106.

4. Akers, Social learning and deviant behavior; Elliott, D. S., Huizinga, D., & Ageton, S. S. (1985). *Explaining delinquency and drug use.* Beverly Hills, CA: Sage; Matsueda, R. L. (1982). Testing control theory and differential association: A causal modeling approach, *American Sociological Review, 47,* 489–504.

5. Haynie & Osgood, Reconsidering peers and delinquency, p. 1120.

6. Haynie & Osgood, Reconsidering peers and delinquency; Osgood et al., Routine activities and individual deviant behavior.

7. Haynie et al., Gender and serious violence; McCarthy, B., Felmlee, D., & Hagan, J. (2004). Girl friends are better: Gender, context, and crime. *Criminology, 42,* 805–836; Miller, J., & Brunson, R. (2000). Gender dynamics in youth gangs: A comparison of male and female accounts. *Justice Quarterly, 17*(3), 801–830.

8. Agnew, R., & Brezina, T. (1997). Relational problems with peers, gender, and delinquency. *Youth and Society, 29*(1), 84–111; Caspi, A., Lynam, D., Moffitt, T., & Silva, P. (1993). Unraveling girls' delinquency: Biological, dispositional, and contextual contributions to adolescent misbehavior. *Developmental Psychology, 29,* 29–30; Covington, J. (1985). Gender differences in criminality among heroin users. *Journal of Research in Crime and Delinquency, 22,* 329–353; Inciardi, J., Lockwood, D., & Pottieger, A. (1993). *Women and crack cocaine.* New York, NY: Macmillan; Magnusson, D., Stattin, H., & Allen, V. (1985). Biological maturation and social development: A longitudinal study of adjustment processes from mid-adolescence to adulthood. *Journal of Youth and Adolescence, 14,* 267–283; Miller, E. (1986). *Street woman.* Philadelphia, PA: Temple University; Miller, J. (1998). Up it up: Gender and the accomplishment of street robbery. *Criminology, 36*(1), 37–66; Steffensmeier, D., & Ulmer, J. (2005). *Confessions of a dying thief: Understanding criminal careers and illegal enterprise.* New Brunswick, NJ: Transaction-Aldine.

9. Haynie et al., Gender and serious violence.

10. Mears et al., Explaining the gender gap in delinquency.

11. Giordano et al., Gender and the meanings of adolescent romantic relationships.

12. Coie, J. D., Terry, R. A., Lenox, K., Lochman, J. E., & Hyman, C. (1995). Childhood peer rejection and aggression as predictors of stable patterns of adolescent disorder. *Development and Psychopathology, 7,* 697–713; Kreager, D. A. (2004). Strangers in the halls: Isolation and delinquency in school networks. *Social Forces, 83*(1), 351–390; Kupersmidt, J. B., Coie, J. D., & Dodge, K. A. (1990). The role of poor peer relationships in the development of disorder. In S. R. Asher & J. D. Coie (Eds.), *Peer rejection in childhood* (pp. 274–305). Cambridge, MA: Cambridge University Press; Lochman, J. E., & Wayland, K. (1994). Aggression, social acceptance, and race as predictors of negative adolescent outcomes. *Journal of the American Academy of Child and Adolescent Psychiatry, 33,* 1026–1035; Sampson & Laub, *Crime in the making.*

13. Jones, N. (2010). "It's About Being a Survivor" . . . African American girls, gender, and the context of inner city violence. In M. Chesney-Lind &

N. Jones (Eds.), *Fighting for girls: New perspectives on gender and violence* (pp. 203–218). Albany: State University of New York Press.

14. Ibid.

15. Lenhart, A. (2015, April). *Pew research center: Teen, social media and technology overview 2015.* Retrieved from http://www.pewinternet.org/files/2015/04/PI_TeensandTech_Update2015_0409151.pdf

16. Ibid.

17. Ibid.

18. Lockhart, J. (2014). *How safe are apps like Kik, Yik Yak, and Snapchat for kids?* Retrieved from http://www.makeuseof.com/tag/author/jlockhart/

19. Pew Research Center. (2015). *Teen voices: Dating in the digital age.* Retrieved from http://www.pewinternet.org/online-romance/

20. Ibid.

21. Ibid.

22. Ibid.

23. Meldrum, R. C., & Clark, J. (2015). Adolescent virtual time spent socializing with peers substance use, and delinquency. *Crime & Delinquency, 61*(8), 1104–1126.

24. Osgood et al., Routine activities and individual deviant behavior.

25. Huang, G. C., Unger, J. B., Soto, D., Fujimoto, K., Pentz, M. A., Jordan-Marsh, M., & Valente, T. W. (2014). Peer influences: The impact of online and offline friendship networks on adolescent smoking and alcohol use. *Journal of Adolescent Health, 54*, 508–514.

26. Dolcini, M. (2014). A new window into adolescents' worlds: The impact of online social interaction on risk behavior. *Journal of Adolescent Health, 54,* 497–498.

27. Lenhart, A. (2010, April 20). Teens, cell phones, and texting. *Pew Research Center.* Retrieved from http://pewresearch.org/pubs/1572/teens-cell-phones-text-messages

28. Meldrum & Clark, Adolescent virtual time spent socializing with peers substance use, and delinquency.

29. Lenhart, A. (2009, December 15). Teens and sexting. *Pew Research Center.* Retrieved from http://pewinternet.org/Reports/2009/Teens-and-Sexting.aspx

30. Rice, E., Rhoades, H., Winetrobe, H., Sanchez, M., Montoya, J., Plant, A., & Kordic, T. (2012). Sexually explicit cell phone messaging associated with sexual risk among adolescents. *Pediatrics, 130,* 667–673; Wolfe, S. E., Marcum, C. D., Higgins, G. E., & Ricketts, M. L. (2016). Routine cell phone activity and exposure to sext messages: Extending the generality of routine activity theory and exploring the etiology of a risky teenage behavior. *Crime & Delinquency, 62*(5), 614–644.

31. Lenhart, Teens and sexting.

32. Hoffman, J. (2011, March 26). A girl's nude photo and altered lives. *New York Times.* Retrieved from http://www.nytimes.com/2011/03/27/us/27sexting.html

33. Wolfe et al., Routine cell phone activity and exposure to sext messages.

34. Felson, M. (1987). Routine activities and crime prevention in the developing metropolis. *Criminology, 25,* 911–931.

35. Duncan, S. H. (2010). A legal response is necessary for self-produced child pornography: A legislator's checklist for drafting the bill. *Oregon Law Review, 89,* 645–699.

36. Wyatt, K. (2016, March 17). Teen sexting prompts efforts to update child-porn laws. *NBC San Diego.* Retrieved from http://www.nbcsandiego.com/news/national-international/Teen-Sexting-Prompts-Efforts-to-Update-Child-Porn-Laws-372466922.html

37. Ibid.

38. Hoffman, A girl's nude photo and altered lives.

39. Associated Press. (2015). Alabama teens charged with beheading puppies, posting video on Snapchat. *Alabama Media Group.* Retrieved from http://www.al.com/news/index.ssf/2015/03/alabama_teens_charged_with_beh.html

40. Robin, N. (2016, April 8). Instagram rape video leads to juvenile arrests. *Fox54.* April 8. Retrieved from http://www.wfxg.com/story/31679992/instagram-rape-video-leads-to-juvenile-arrests

41. Cholodofsky, R. (2016, January 17). Jeanette teen who took selfie with dead friend wants murder charge tossed. *Tribune Review.* Retrieved from http://triblive.com/news/westmoreland/9825775-74/morton-mangan-police

42. Boroff, D. (2016, February 18). Two British girls post Snapchat selfie photo as they brutally murder 39-year-old woman-then get a ride home from the cops. *New York Daily News.* Retrieved from http://www.nydailynews.com/news/crime/british-girls-post-snapchat-photo-kill-woman-article-1.2536387

43. McPhate, M. (2016, April).Teenager is accused of live-streaming a friend's rape on Periscope. *New York Times.* Retrieved from http://www.nytimes.com/2016/04/19/us/periscope-rape-case-columbus-ohio-video-livestreaming.html

44. Yar, M. (2012). Crime, media and the will-to-representation: Reconsidering relationships in the new media age. *Crime, Media, Culture*, 8(3), 245–260.

45. Hagedorn, J. (2008). *A world of gangs: Armed young men and gangsta culture.* Minneapolis, MN: University of Minnesota; Short, J. (2009). Gangs, law enforcement, and the academy. *Criminology & Public Policy, 8*(4), 723–730.

46. Thrasher, F. (1927). *The gang: A study of 1,313 gangs in Chicago.* Chicago, IL: University of Chicago Press, p. 46

47. Brotherton, D. (2008). Beyond social reproduction: Bringing resistance back in gang theory. *Theoretical Criminology, 12*(1), 55–77.

48. Klein, M. (1971). *Street gangs and street workers.* Englewood Cliffs, NJ: Prentice Hall, p. 13.

49. Kontos, L., Brotherton, D., & Barrios, L. (Eds.). (2003). *Gangs and society: Alternative perspectives.* New York, NY: Columbia University Press; Morash, M. (1983). Gangs, groups and delinquency. *British Journal of Criminology, 23,* 309–331.

50. Brotherton, D., & Barrios, L. (2004). *The Almighty Latin King and Queen Nation: Street politics and the transformation of a New York gang.* New York, NY: Columbia University Press, p. 23.

51. Mendoza-Denton, N. (2008). *Homegirls: Language and cultural practice among Latina youth gangs.* Malden, MA: Blackwell.

52. Hagedorn, J. (n.d.). *Gang research online.* Retrieved from http://www.gangresearch.net

53. Hagedorn, *A world of gangs.*

54. Egley, A., Jr., Howell, J. C., & Harris, M. (2014). Highlights of the 2012 National Youth Gang Survey. *Office of Juvenile Justice and Delinquency Prevention.* Retrieved from http://www.ojjdp.gov/pubs/248025.pdf

55. Battin, S. R., Hill, K. G., Abbott, R. D., Catalano, R. F., & Hawkins, J. D. (1998). The contribution of gang membership to delinquency beyond delinquent friends. *Criminology, 35,* 93–116; Melde, C., & Esbensen, F. (2011). Gang membership as a turning point in the life course, *Criminology, 49*(2), 513–552; Thornberry, T. P., Krohn, M. D., Lizotte, A. J., & Chard-Wierschem, D. (1993). The role of juvenile gangs in facilitating delinquent behavior. *Journal of Research in Crime and Delinquency, 30,* 75–85.

56. Sante, L. (1991). *Low life: Lures and snares of old New York.* New York, NY: Aldine de Gruyter.

57. Asbury, H. (1927). *The gangs of New York: An informal history of the underworld.* New York, NY: Vintage; Howell, J. C. (2012). *Gangs in America's communities.* Thousand Oaks, CA: Sage.

58. Haskins, J. (1974). *Street gangs: Yesterday and today.* Wayne, PA: Hastings Books; Howell, J. C. (1998). *Youth gangs: An overview.* Juvenile Justice Bulletin. Washington, DC: Office of Juvenile Justice and Delinquency Prevention; Sante, *Low life.*

59. Shelden, R. G., Tracy, S. K., & Brown, W. B. (2013). *Youth gangs in society* (4th ed.). Belmont, CA: Wadsworth, Cengage Learning.

60. Toy, C. (1992). A short history of Asian gangs in San Francisco. *Justice Quarterly, 9*(4), 647–665; Vigil, J. D. (2002). *A rainbow of gangs: Street cultures in the mega-city.* Austin: University of Texas Press.

61. Vigil, *A rainbow of gangs.*

62. Cloward & Ohlin, *Delinquency and opportunity;* Horowitz, R. B. (1983). *Honor and the American Dream.* New Brunswick, NJ: Rutgers University Press; Miller, W. B. (1958). Lower class culture as generating a milieu of gang delinquency. *Journal of Social Issues, 14*(3), 419–435; Wolfgang, M. E., & Ferracuti, F. (1967). *The subculture of violence.* London, UK: Tavistock.

63. Felson, Routine activities and crime prevention in the developing metropolis; Felson, M., & Cohen, L. E. (1980). Human ecology and crime: A routine activities approach. *Human Ecology, 4,* 389–406.

64. Fagan, J. (1989). The social organization of drug use and drug dealing among urban gangs. *Criminology, 27,* 633–669.

65. Dennis, J. P. (2014). The LGBT offender. In D. Peterson & V. R. Panfil (Eds.), *Handbook of LGBT communities, crime and justice* (pp. 87–101). New York, NY: Springer-Verlag; Panfil, V. (2014). Better left unsaid? The role of agency in queer criminological research. *Critical Criminology, 22,* 99–111; Panfil, V. (2014). Gay gang and crime involved men's experiences with homophobic bullying and harassment in schools. *Journal of Crime and Justice, 37*(1), 79–103.

66. Moore, J. W. (1978). *Homeboys: Gangs, drugs, and prison in the barrios of Los Angeles.* Philadelphia, PA: Temple University Press; Moore, J. (1991). *Going down to the barrio: Homeboys and homegirls in change.* Philadelphia, PA: Temple University Press; Vigil, J. D. (1988). *Barrio gangs: Street life and identity in Southern California.* Austin: University of Texas Press; Vigil, *A rainbow of gangs.*

67. Vigil, *Barrio gangs;* Vigil, *A rainbow of gangs.*

68. Vigil, J. D. (2003). Urban violence and street gangs. *Annual Review of Anthropology, 32,* 225–242.

69. Miller & Brunson, Gender dynamics in youth gangs; Peterson, D., Miller, J., & Esbensen, F. (2001). The impact of sex composition on gangs and gang member delinquency. *Criminology, 39*(2), 411–439.

70. Bortner, M. A., & Williams, L. M. (1997). *Youth in prison: We the people of Unit Four.* New York, NY: Routledge.

71. Bortner & Williams, *Youth in prison;* Zatz & Portillos, Voices from the barrio.

72. Chesney-Lind, M., & Jones, N. (2010). Introduction. In M. Chesney-Lind & N. Jones (Eds.), *Fighting for girls: New perspectives on gender and violence* (pp. 1–8). Albany: State University of New York Press; DeKeseredy, W. (2010). Moral panics, violence and the policing of girls: Reasserting patriarchal control in the new millennium. In M. Chesney-Lind & N. Taylor (Eds.), *Fighting for girls: New perspectives on gender and violence* (pp. 242–254). Albany: State University of New York Press; Hagedorn, J. (1998). *People & folks: Gangs, crime, and the underclass in a Rustbelt City* (2nd ed.). Chicago, IL: Lakeview Press; Zatz, M. (1987). Chicano youth gangs and crime: The creation of a moral panic. *Contemporary Crises,* 129–158.

73. Hautala, D. S., Sittner, K. J., & Whitbeck, L. B. (2015). Prospective childhood risk factors for gang involvement among North American indigenous adolescents. *Youth Violence and Juvenile Justice,* 1–21.

74. Macabasco, L. W. (2005). Girls in gangs. *Mother Jones.* Retrieved from http://www.motherjones.com/politics/2005/12/girls-and-gangs

75. Glesmann, C., Krisberg, B., & Marchionna, S., (2009). *Youth in gangs: Who is at risk?* Washington, DC: National Council on Crime and Delinquency.

76. National Gang Intelligence Center. (2013). *2013 National Gang Report.* Washington, DC: National Gang Intelligence Center. Retrieved from https://www.fbi.gov/stats-services/publications/national-gang-report-2013

77. Miller, W. B. (1975). *Violence by youth gangs and youth groups as a crime problem in major American cities.* Washington, DC: U.S. Government Printing Office.

78. Macabasco, Girls in gangs.

79. Anthony, A. (2012). Girls in gangs. *The Crime Report.* Retrieved from http://www.thecrimereport.org; Wolf, A., & Gutierrez, L. (2012). *It's about time: Prevention and intervention services for gang-affiliated girls.* Washington, DC: National Council on Crime and Delinquency.

80. Castañeda Rossman, L. (2013). *Transcending gangs: Latinas story their experience.* New York, NY: Hampton Press.

81. Miller & Brunson, Gender dynamics in youth gangs.

82. Ibid.

83. Bowker, L. H., Gross, G. S., & Klein, M. W. (1980). Female participation in delinquent gang activities. *Adolescence, 15,* 509–519.

84. Miller, J. (1998). Gender and victimization risk among young women in gangs. *Journal of Research in Crime and Delinquency, 35,* 429–453.

85. National Gang Intelligence Center, *2013 National Gang Report.*

86. Hagedorn, *People & folks;* Lauritsen, J. L., Sampson, R. L., & Laub, J. H. (1991). The link between offending and victimization among adolescents. *Criminology, 29,* 265–292.

87. Miller, Gender and victimization risk among young women in gangs; Fleisher, M. S. (1998). *Dead end kids: Gang girls and the boys that they know.* Madison: Wisconsin University Press.

88. Anthony, Girls in gangs.

89. O'Neal, E., Decker, S., Moule, R., Jr., & Pyrooz, D. (2014, September). Girls, gangs, and getting out: Gender differences and similarities in leaving the gang. *Youth Violence and Juvenile Justice,* 1–18.

90. Panfil, Better left unsaid?

91. Ibid., p.102.

92. Bates, K., & Swan, R. (2009). *The more things change, the more they stay the same.* Paper presented at 2009 Pacific Sociological Association Meeting, San Diego, CA.

93. Barajas, F. (2007). An invading army: A civil gang injunction in a California Chicana/o community. *Latino Studies, 5*(4), 393–471; Stewart, G. (1998). Black codes and broken windows: The legacy of racial hegemony in antigang civil injunctions. *Yale Law Journal, 107,* 2249–2279; Wang, C. (2008). Gang injunctions under heat from equal protection: Selective enforcement as a way to defeat discrimination. *Hastings Constitutional Law Review, 35,* 287–308.

94. Swan, R. S., & Bates, K. A. (in press). Loosening the bonds that tie: The hidden harms of civil gang injunctions in San Diego County. *Contemporary Justice Review.*

95. Barajas, An invading army; Rodriguez, L. (2009). Keeping at-risk kids out of jail–it's an art. *Los Angeles Times.* Retrieved from latimes.com/news/opinion/commentary/la-oe-rodriguezluis3-2009sep03,0,2748207; Swan & Bates, Loosening the bonds that tie; Wang, Gang injunctions under heat from equal protection.

96. Crawford, L. (2009). No way out: An analysis of exit processes for gang injunctions. *California Law Review, 97,* 161–193.

97. Allan, E. L. (2004). *Civil gang abatement: The effectiveness and implications of policing by injunction.* New York, NY: NFB Scholarly; Grogger, J. (2002). The effects of civil gang injunctions on reported violent crime: Evidence from Los Angeles County. *Journal of Law and Economics, 45*(1), 69–90.

98. Maxson, C. L., Hennigan, K. M., & Sloane, D. C. (2005). It's getting crazy out there: Can a civil gang injunction change a community? *Criminology & Public Policy, 4,* 577–606.

99. Boyle, G. (2010). *Tattoos on the heart: The power of boundless compassion.* New York, NY: Free Press.

100. Greene, J., & Pranis, K. (2007). *Gang wars: The failure of enforcement tactics and the need for effective public safety strategies.* Washington, DC: Justice Policy Institute.

101. Ibid., pp. 6–7.

CHAPTER 10

1. Schwarz, A. (2012, October 9). Attention disorder or not, pills to help in school. *New York Times.* Retrieved from http://www.nytimes .com/2012/10/09/health/attention-disorder-or-not-children-prescribed-pills-to-help-in-school .html?_r=0; Schwarz, A. (2012, June 9). Risky rise of the good grade pill. *New York Times.* Retrieved from http://www.nytimes.com/2012/06/10/education/seeking-academic-edge-teenagers-abuse-stimulants

2. Inciardi, J. A. (2008). *The war on drugs IV: The continuing saga of the mysteries and miseries of intoxication, addition, crime and public policy.* Boston, MA: Pearson, pp. 2–3.

3. Carbone-Lopez, K., Owens, J. G., & Miller, J. (2012). Women's "storylines" of methamphetamine initiation in the Midwest. *Journal of Drug Issues, 42*(3), 226–246; Mui, H. Z., Sales, P., & Murphy, S. (2014). Everybody's doing it: Initiation into prescription drug use. *Journal of Drug Issues, 44*(3), 236–253.

4. Hammersley, R. (2008). *Drugs and crime: Theories and practices.* Cambridge, UK: Polity Press.

5. Inciardi, *The war on drugs IV.*

6. Hunt, G., Moloney, M., & Evans, K. (2010). *Youth, drugs, and nightlife.* New York, NY: Routledge

7. Miller, K. E. (2008). Energy drinks, race, and problem behaviors among college students. *Journal of Adolescent Health, 43*(5), 490–497.

8. Substance Abuse and Mental Health Services Administration (SAMHSA). (2013, January 10). Update on emergency department visits involving energy drinks: A continuing public concern. *The DAWN Report*. Retrieved from http://www.samhsa.gov/data/sites/default/files/DAWN126/DAWN126/sr126-energy-drinks-use.htm

9. Johnson, K. W., Grube, J. W., Ogilvie, K. A., Collins, D., Courser, M., Dirks, L. G., ... Driscoll, D. (2012). A community prevention model to prevent children from inhaling and ingesting harmful legal products. *Evaluation and Program Planning, 35,* 113–123.

10. Ibid.

11. Zosel, A., Bartelson, B. B., Bailey, E., Lowenstein, S., & Dart, R. (2013). Characterization of adolescent prescription drug abuse and misuse using the researched abuse diversion and addiction-related surveillance (radars®) system. *Journal of the American Academy of Child & Adolescent Psychiatry, 52*(2), 196–204.

12. Schwarz, Attention disorder or not, pills to help in school; Schwarz, Risky rise of the good grade pill.

13. Schwarz, Risky rise of the good grade pill.

14. Bousquet, M. (2008). Ritalin generation 1. *Chronicle of Higher Education*. Retrieved from http://chronicle.com/blogs/brainstorm/ritalin-generation-1/6287

15. Blistein, J. (2015, December 17). Teens now smoke marijuana more than cigarettes, study says. *Rolling Stone*.

16. Substance Abuse and Mental Health Services Administration, Center for Behavioral Health Statistics and Quality. (2011). *Results from the 2010 National Survey on Drug Use and Health: Summary of national findings*. Rockville, MD: Author.

17. Substance Abuse and Mental Health Services Administration (SAMHSA). (2015). *Behavioral health barometer: United States 2014*. Rockville, MD: Substance Abuse and Mental Health Services Administration.

18. Ibid.

19. Ibid.

20. Substance Abuse and Mental Health Services Administration, *Results from the 2010 National Survey on Drug Use and Health*.

21. Substance Abuse and Mental Health Services Administration, Center for Behavioral Health Statistics and Quality. (2011, October 4). *Substance use among Asian adolescents*. Rockville, MD: Author.

22. Substance Abuse and Mental Health Services Administration, Center for Behavioral Health Statistics and Quality. (2011, October 4). *Substance use among Hispanic adolescents*. Rockville, MD: Author.

23. Substance Abuse and Mental Health Services Administration, Center for Behavioral Health Statistics and Quality. (2012, July 2). *The DAWN report: Highlights of the 2010 Drug Abuse Warning Network findings on drug-related emergency department visits*. Rockville, MD: Author.

24. American Psychiatric Association. (2000). *Diagnostic and statistical manual of mental disorders* (4th ed., text rev.). Washington, DC: Author.

25. Mulvey, E. P., Steinberg, L., Fagan, J., Cauffman, E., Piquero, A. R., Chassin, L., . . . Lasoya, S. H. (2004). Theory and research on desistance from antisocial activity among serious adolescent offenders. *Youth Violence and Juvenile Justice, 2*(3), 213–236.

26. Substance Abuse and Mental Health Services Administration, *Behavioral health barometer*.

27. Substance Abuse and Mental Health Services Administration (SAMHSA). (2016). *About emergency department data*. Retrieved from http://www.samhsa.gov/data/emergency-department-data-dawn/about

28. Substance Abuse and Mental Health Administration, *The DAWN report*.

29. Ibid.

30. Dickinson, T., & Crowe, A. (1997, December). Capacity building for juvenile substance abuse treatment. *OJJDP Juvenile Justice Bulletin*, 1–12.

31. Ibid.; Elkington, K. S., Teplin, L. A., Mericle, A. A., Welty, L. J., Romero, E. G., & Abram, K. M. (2008). HIV/sexually transmitted infection risk behaviors in delinquent youth with psychiatric

disorders: A longitudinal study. *Journal of American Academic Child Adolescent Psychiatry, 47*(8), 901–911; Teplin, L. A., Elkington, K. S., McClelland, G. M., Abram, K. A., & Mericle, A. A. (2005). Major mental disorders, substance use disorders, comorbidity, and HIV-AIDS risk behaviors in juvenile detainees. *Psychiatric Services, 56*(7), 823–828.

32. Associated Press. (2012, August 27). Teen pot use linked to later declines in IQ. *NPR News.* Retrieved from http://www.npr.org/templates/story/story.php?storyId=160126401; Meier, M. H., Caspi, A., Ambler, A., Harrington, H., Houts, R., Keefe, R. S. E., . . . Moffitt, T. (2012, August 27). Persistent cannabis users show neuropsychological decline from childhood to midlife. *Proceedings of the National Academy of Sciences of the United States of America.* Retrieved from http://www.pnas.org/content/early/2012/08/22/1206820109.abstract

33. Dickinson & Crowe, Capacity building for juvenile substance abuse treatment; Gropper, B. A. (1985, February). *Probing the links between drugs and crime.* Washington, DC: U.S. Department of Justice, Office of Justice Programs, National Institute of Justice.

34. Mulvey, E. P., Schubert, C. A., & Chassin, L. (2010, December). Substance use and delinquent behavior amongst serious adolescent offenders. *Juvenile Justice Bulletin.* Washington, DC: Office of Juvenile Justice and Delinquency Prevention.

35. Dembo, R., La Voie, L., Schmeidler, J., & Washburn, M. (1987). The nature and correlates of psychological/emotional functioning among a sample of detained youths. *Criminal Justice and Behavior, 14,* 311–324; Friedman, A. S. (1998). Substance use/abuse as a predictor to illegal and violent behavior: A review of the literature. *Aggression and Violent Behavior, 3,* 339–355; Hartwell, S. (2001). Female mentally ill offenders and their community reintegration needs: An initial examination. *International Journal of Law and Psychiatry, 24,* 1–11; Locke, T. F., & Newcomb, M. D. (2005). Psychosocial predictors and correlates and suicidality in teenage Latino males. *Hispanic Journal of Behavioral Sciences, 27,* 319–336.

36. Cuellar, J., & Curry, T. (2007). The prevalence and comorbidity between delinquency, drug abuse, suicide attempts, physical and sexual abuse, and self-mutilation among delinquent Hispanic females. *Hispanic Journal of Behavioral Science, 29,* 68–82.

37. Grafsky, E. L., Letcher, A., Slesnick, N., & Serovic, J. M. (2011). Comparison of treatment response between GLB and non-GLB street living youth. *Children and Youth Services Review, 33,* 569–574.

38. Gibbons, F. X., O'Hara, R. E., Stock, M. L., Gerrard, M., Weng, C.-Y., & Wills, T. A. (2012). The erosive effects of racism: Reduced self-control mediates the relation between perceived racial discrimination and substance use in African American adolescents. *Journal of Personality and Social Psychology, 102*(5), 1089–1104.

39. Himelstein, S. (2011). Mindfulness-based substance abuse treatment for incarcerated youth: A mixed method pilot study. *International Journal of Transpersonal Studies, 30*(1–2), 1–10.

40. Slater, M. D., Kelly, K. J., Lawrence, F. R., Stanley, L. R., & Comello, M. L. (2011). Assessing media campaigns linking marijuana non-use with autonomy and aspirations: "Be Under Your Own Influence" and ONDCP's "Above the Influence." *Prevention Science, 12,* 12–22.

41. Clayton, R., Cattarello, A., & Johnstone, B. (1996). The effectiveness of drug abuse resistance education (Project D.A.R.E.): 5-year follow-up results. *Preventative Medicine, 25,* 307–318; Lynam, D., Milich, M., Zimmerman, R., Novak, S., Logan, T. K., Martin, C., . . . Clayton, R. (1999). Project D.A.R.E.: No effects at 10-year follow-up. *Journal of Consulting and Clinical Psychology, 67,* 590–593; Rosenbaum, D., & Hanson, G. (1998). Assessing the effects of school-based drug education: A six-year multilevel analysis of Project D.A.R.E. *Journal of Research in Crime and Delinquency, 35,* 381–412.

42. Bovard, J. (1994). DARE scare: Turning children into informants? *Schaffer Library of Drug Policy.* Retrieved from http://www.druglibrary.org/schaffer/library/dare4.htm

43. Finley, L. L. (2007). Our drugs are better than yours: Schools and their hypocrisy regarding drug use. *Contemporary Justice Review, 10*(4), 365–381.

44. Board of Education v. Earls., 536 U.S. 822 (2002).

45. Hawkins, D. (1999, May 31). Trial by vial. *U.S. News and World Report, 126,* 70–73.

46. Finley, Our drugs are better than yours.

47. Goldberg, L., Elliot, D., MacKinnon, P., Moe, E. L., Kuehl, K. S., Yoon, M., . . . Williams, J. (2008). Outcomes of a prospective trial of student-athlete drug testing: The Student Athlete Testing Using Random Notification (SATURN) study. *Journal of Adolescent Health, 41,* 421–429; Yamaguchi, R., Johnston, L. D., & O'Malley, P. M. (2003). Relationship between student illicit drug use and school drug testing policies. *Journal of School Health, 73,* 159–164.

48. Schiller, W. (2012, July). The proliferation of juvenile drug courts. *National Council of Juvenile and Family Court Judges.* Retrieved from http://www.ncjfcj.org/proliferation-juvenile-drug-courts; Van Wormer, K., & Lutze, F. (2011). Exploring the evidence: The value of juvenile drug courts. *Juvenile and Family Justice Today,* 17–20.

49. Holst, K. (2010). A good score? Examining twenty years of drug courts in the United States and abroad. *Valparaiso University Law Review, 45*(1), 73–106.

50. Ibid.

51. Van Wormer & Lutze, Exploring the evidence.

52. Butts, J. A. (2008). Most effective juvenile justice policy? Practitioners say it's drug treatment. *Reclaiming Futures.* Retrieved from http://reclaimingfutures.org/most-effective-juvenile-justice-policy-adolescent-drug-treatment

53. Szalavitz, M. (2010, July 16). Does teen rehab cure addiction or create it? *Time.* Retrieved from http://www.time.com/time/printout/0,8816,2003160,00.html

54. Kelly, J. F., Dow, S. J., Yeterian, J. S., & Kahler, C. W. (2010). Can 12-step participation strengthen and extend the benefits of adolescent addition treatment? A prospective analysis. *Drug and Alcohol Dependence, 110*(1–2), 117–125.

55. Dishion, T. J., McCord, J., & Poulin, F. (1999). When interventions harm: Peer groups and problem behavior. *American Psychologist, 54*(1), 755–764.

56. Szalavitz, Does teen rehab cure addiction or create it?

57. Elkin, E. (2010, July 20). What *Time* didn't tell about teen treatment programs. Retrieved from http://www.vera.org/content/what-time-didn't-tell-about-teen-treatment-programs

58. Elkin, E. (2005). *Adolescent portable therapy: A practical guide for service providers.* New York, NY: Vera Institute of Justice. Retrieved from www.vera.org/aptmanual

59. Alexander, M. (2012). *The New Jim Crow: Mass incarceration in the age of colorblindness.* New York, NY: The New Press; Coates, R. D. (2015). A perfect storm. *Critical Criminology,* 1–11; Rios, *Punished: Policing the lives of black and Latino boys.*

60. Karakatsanis, A. (2013, July 23). The trial that is the Obama administration's greatest shame. *Alternet.* http://www.alternet.org/civil-liberties/trial-obama-admins-greatest-shame; Reinarman, C., & Levine, H. G. (1997). *Crack in America: Demon drugs and social justice.* Berkeley: University of California Press.

61. Retro report: Heroin and the war on drugs [video]. (2015). *The New York Times.* Retrieved from http://www.nytimes.com/video/us/100000004052651/heroin-and-the-war-on-drugs.html

62. NORML. (2016). *Medical marijuana.* Retrieved from http://norml.org/legal/medical-marijuana-2

63. Ibid.

64. Varjacques, L. (2013, January 16). Looking back and casting forward: An emerging shift for juvenile justice in America. *Juvenile Justice Information Exchange.* Retrieved from: http://jjie.org/looking-back-casting-forward-emerging-shift-for-juvenile-justice-america/102591/

65. Friese, B., & Grube, J. W. (2013, February 1). Legalization of medical marijuana and marijuana use among youths. *National Center for Biotechnology Information, 20*(1), 33–39. Retrieved from http://www.ncbi.nlm.nih.gov/pmc/articles/PMC3638722; Hasin, D. S., Wall, M., Keyes, K. M., Cerda, M., Schulenberg, J., O'Malley, P. M., . . . Feng, T. (2015). Medical marijuana laws and adolescent marijuana use in the USA from 1991 to 2014: Results from annual, repeated cross-sectional surveys. *The Lancet Psychiatry.* Retrieved from http://www.ncbi.nlm.nih.gov/pubmed/26303557

66. Cheung, Y. W. (2000). Substance abuse and developments in harm reduction. *Canadian Medical Association Journal, 162*(12), 1697–1700.

67. Logan, D. E., & Marlatt, G. A. (2010). Harm reduction therapy: A practice-friendly review of research. *Journal of Clinical Psychology in Session, 66*(2), 201–214.

68. Poulin, C., & Nicholson, J. (2005). Should harm minimization as an approach to adolescent substance use be embraced by junior and senior high schools? Empirical evidence from an integrated school- and community-based demonstration intervention addressing drug use among adolescents. *International Journal of Drug Policy, 16,* 403–414.

69. McBride, N., Farringdon, F., Midford, R., Meuleners, L., & Phillips, M. (2004). Harm minimization in school drug education: Final results of the School Health and Alcohol Harm Reduction Project (SHAHRP). *Addiction, 99,* 278–291.

70. Stevens, S., Leybas-Amedia, V., Bourdeau, B., McMichael, L., & Nytitray, A. (2006). Blending prevention models: An effective substance use and HIV prevention program for minority youth. *Child and Adolescent Social Work, 23*(1), 4–23.

71. Sanchez-Way, R., & Johnson, S. (2000). Cultural practices in American Indian prevention programs. *Juvenile Justice Journal, 7*(2), 20–30.

72. Association for Experiential Education. (2011). Adventure therapy with American Indian youth. *White paper.* Retrieved from http://www.aee .org/whitepapers

73. Ibid.; Fox, K., Becker-Green, J., Gault, J., & Simmons, D. (2005). *Native American youth in transition: The path from adolescence to adulthood in two Native American communities.* Portland, OR: National Indian Child Welfare Association.

74. Coalition for Juvenile Justice. (2000). *Enlarging the healing circle: Ensuring justice for American Indian children.* Retrieved from http://juvjustice.njjn.org/ media/resources/public/resource_135.pdf

75. Carter, S., Straits, K., & Hall, M. (2007). Project Venture: Evaluation of an experiential, culturally based approach to substance abuse prevention with American Indian youth. *Journal of Experiential Education, 29,* 397–400.

76. Weber, C., Cates, J. A., & Carey, S. (2010). A drug and alcohol intervention with Old Order Amish Youth: Dancing on the devil's playground. *Journal of Groups in Addiction and Recovery, 5,* 97–112.

CHAPTER 11

1. Weisheit, R., & Morn, F. (2004). *Pursuing justice.* Belmont, CA: Wadsworth.

2. Shichor, D. (2006). *The meaning and nature of punishment.* Long Grove, IL: Waveland Press.

3. Equal Justice Initiative. (2012). *Children in adult prison.* Montgomery, AL: Equal Justice Initiative. Retrieved from http://www.eji.org/ childrenprison

4. Equal Justice Initiative. (2007). *Cruel and unusual: Sentencing 13- and 14-year-old children to die in prison.* Retrieved from http://eji .org/childrenprison/deathinprison

5. Cited by Van den Haag, E. (1975). *Punishing criminals.* New York, NY: Basic Books, p. 26.

6. Zimring, F. E. (2005). *American juvenile justice.* New York, NY: Oxford.

7. Packer, H. (1968). *The limits of the criminal sanctions.* Stanford, CA: Stanford University Press, p. 39.

8. Shichor, *The meaning and nature of punishment.*

9. Beccaria, On crimes and punishment, p. 56.

10. Pfohl, *Images of deviance and social control* (2nd ed.).

11. Shichor, *The meaning and nature of punishment.*

12. Feeley, M. M., & Simon, J. (1992). The new penology: Notes on the emerging strategy of corrections and its implications. *Criminology, 30*(4), 449–474, especially p. 458.

13. Greenwood, P. (1982). Selective incapacitation. Santa Monica, CA: Rand; Moore, M. H., Estrich, S., McGillis, D., & Spelman, W. (1984). *Dangerous offenders: The elusive target of justice.* Cambridge, MA: Harvard University Press.

14. Bavely, S. (2012, November 9). *A DUI could mean a "scarlet letter" license plate.* Retrieved from http://www.lifesafer.com/blog/dui-scarlet-letter-license-plate/

15. International Centre for Prison Studies. (2016). Highest to lowest prison population rate. *World Prison Brief*. Retrieved from http://www.prisonstudies.org/highest-to-lowest/prison_population_rate?field_region_taxonomy_tid=All

16. Cotter, R., & De Lint, W. (2009). GPS-electronic monitoring and contemporary penology: A case study of US GPS-electronic monitoring programmes. *The Howard Journal, 48*(1), 76–87.

17. Stinneford, J. F. (2006). Incapacitation through maiming: Chemical castration, the Eighth Amendment, and the denial of human dignity. *University of St. Thomas Law Journal, 3*(3), 569–599.

18. Allen, F. (1964). *The borderland of criminal justice: Essays in law and criminology*. Chicago, IL: The University of Chicago Press.

19. See Martinson, R. (1974). What works? Questions and answers about prison reform. *The Public Interest, 35*, 22–54; Palmer, T. (1975). Martinson revisited. *Journal of Research in Crime and Delinquency, 12*, 133–152; Palmer, T. (1978). *Correctional intervention and research: Current issues and future prospects*. Lexington, MA: Lexington Books.

20. Cullen, F. T. (2005). The twelve people who saved rehabilitation: How the science of criminology made a difference. The American Society of Criminology 2004 Presidential Address. *Criminology, 43*(1), 1–42; Cullen, F. T., & Gendreau, P. (2000). Assessing correctional rehabilitation: Policy, practice, and prospects. *Criminal Justice, 3*, 109–175; Cullen, F. T., & Gilbert, K. E. (1982). *Reaffirming rehabilitation*. Cincinnati, OH: Anderson; Gendreau, P., & Ross, R. R. (1987). Revivification of rehabilitation: Evidence from the 1980s. *Justice Quarterly, 4*, 349–407; Lipsey, M. W., & Wilson, D. B. (1993). The efficacy of psychological, educational, and behavioral treatment: Confirmation from meta-analysis. *American Psychologist, 48*, 1181–1209; Cullen, F. T. (2001). From nothing works to what works: Changing professional ideology in the 21st century. *The Prison Journal, 81*, 313–338; Cullen, F. T., Skovron, S. E., Scott, J. E., & Burton, S., Jr. (1990). Public support for correctional rehabilitation: The tenacity of the rehabilitative ideal. *Criminal Justice and Behavior, 17*, 6–18.

21. Sullivan, D., & Tifft, L. (2005). *Restorative Justice: Healing the foundations of our everyday lives*. Monsey, NY: Willow Tree Press; Yazzie, R., & Zion, J. W. (1996). Navajo restorative justice: The law of equality and justice. In B. Galaway & J. Hudson (Eds.), *Restorative justice: International perspectives* (pp. 157–173). Monsey, NY: Criminal Justice Press; Zehr, H. (1990). *Changing lenses: A new focus for crime and justice*. Scottsdale, PA: Herald Press.

22. Ritter, M. J. (2010). Just (juvenile justice) jargon: An argument for terminological uniformity between the juvenile and criminal justice systems. *The American Journal of Criminal Law, 37*, 221–239.

23. Bickel, C. (2010). From child to captive: Constructing captivity in a juvenile institution. *Western Criminology Review, 11*(1), 37–49.

24. Feld, *Bad kids*.

25. Ibid. See also Chapter 2 in this book.

26. Allen, F. (1981). *The decline of the rehabilitative ideal*. New Haven, CT: Yale University Press; Lipton, D., Martinson, R., & Wilks, J. (1975). *The effectiveness of correctional treatment*. New York, NY: Praeger; Martinson, What works?

27. Feld, *Bad kids*, p. 108.

28. Wilson, J. Q. (1995). Crime and public policy. In J. Q. Wilson & J. Petersilia (Eds.), *Crime* (pp. 619–630). Ithaca, NY: ICS Press.

29. Zimring, *American juvenile justice*.

30. Nunn, K. B. (2002). The end of adolescence: The child as other—Race and differential treatment in the juvenile justice system. *DePaul Law Review, 51*, 679–714, especially p. 712.

31. Nunn, The end of adolescence, p. 713.

32. Bortner & Williams, *Youth in prison*, p. 175; Chamberlin, C. (2001). Not kids anymore: A need for punishment and deterrence in the juvenile justice system. *Boston College Law Review, 41*, 391–419.

33. Feld, *Bad kids*; Feld, B. (2013). *Kids, cops, and confessions: Inside the interrogation room*. New York, NY: NYU Press.

34. MacDonald, J. M., & Chesney-Lind, M. (2001). Gender bias and juvenile justice revisited: A multi-year analysis. *Crime and Delinquency, 47*, 173–195.

35. Farrington, D. P. (2012). Should the juvenile justice system be involved in early intervention? *Criminology & Public Policy, 11*(2), 265–273.

36. Zimring, *American juvenile justice.*

37. Soler, M., Shoenberg, D., & Schindler, M. (2009). Juvenile justice: Lessons for a new era. *Georgetown Journal on Poverty Law & Policy, XVI,* 483–541.

38. Austin, J., Johnson, K. D., & Weitzer, R. (2005, September). Alternatives to the secure detention and confinement of juvenile offenders. *Juvenile Justice Bulletin.* Washington, DC: Office of Juvenile Justice and Delinquency Prevention.

39. Myers, R. R. (2012). "Society must be protected from the child": The construction of U.S. juvenile detention as necessary and normal. *Critical Criminology, 20,* 395–407.

40. See Butts, J. A. (2000, May 1). *Can we do without juvenile justice?* American Bar Association. Retrieved from http://www.urban.org/url.cfm?ID=1000232; Feld, *Bad kids.*

41. Feld, *Kids, cops, and confessions,* p. 3.

42. Armstrong, G. S., & Kim, B. (2011). Juvenile penalties for "lawyering up": The role of counsel and extralegal case characteristics. *Crime and Delinquency, 57,* 827–848.

43. Brown, S. A. (2015). *Trends in juvenile justice state legislation 2011–2015.* Washington, DC: National Conference of State Legislatures.

44. Ibid.; Prison Legal News. (2014). *California auditor: Data hinders effectiveness of juvenile "realignment."* Retrieved from https://www.prisonlegalnews.org/news/2014/oct/3/california-auditor-data-hinders-effectiveness-juvenile-realignment/

45. LSU Health New Orleans, Institute for Public Health and Justice. (2016). *A legislated study of raising the age of juvenile jurisdiction in Louisiana.* New Orleans, LA: Author.

46. National League of Cities. (n.d.). *Research to practice memo: How city leaders can draw upon adolescent development research findings to provide a framework for juvenile justice reform.* Washington, DC: Author. Retrieved from http://www.nlc.org/Documents/Find%20City%20Solutions/IYEF/Research%20Supporting%20Reforms%20Memo.pdf

47. Equal Justice Initiative. (n.d.). *Children in prison.* Retrieved from http://www.eji.org/childrenprison

48. Sewell, A., & Therolf, G. (2016, May 3). L.A. County severely restricts solitary confinement for juveniles. *Los Angeles Times.* Retrieved from http://www.latimes.com/local/lanow/la-me-ln-juvenile-solitary-20160503-story.html; Shear, M. (2016, January 25). Obama bans solitary confinement of juveniles in federal prisons. *Los Angeles Times.* Retrieved from http://www.nytimes.com/2016/01/26/us/politics/obama-bans-solitary-confinement-of-juveniles-in-federal-prisons.html?login=email&_r=0

49. Steinberg, L. (2010). A behavioral scientist looks at the science of adolescent brain development. *Brain and Cognition, 72,* 160–164.

50. Dobbs, D. (2011). Beautiful brains. *National Geographic, 4,* 1–8. Retrieved from http://ngm.nationalgeographic.com/2011/10/teenage-brains/dobbs-text

51. Ibid.

52. Morales, L. (2015). *Reports: Juvenile justice systems fails Native youth.* Retrieved from http://www.fronterasdesk.org/content/10062/reports-juvenile-justice-system-fails-native-youth

CHAPTER 12

1. Wilson, J. W. (1968). *Varieties of police behavior: The management of law and order in eight communities.* Cambridge, MA: Harvard University Press.

2. Walker, S., & Katz, C. M. (2013). *Police in America: An introduction* (8th ed.). Boston, MA: McGraw-Hill.

3. Brown, R. A., Novak, K. J., & Frank, J. (2009). Identifying variation in police officer behavior between juveniles and adults. *Journal of Criminal Justice, 37,* 200–208.

4. Black, D. (1976). *The behavior of law.* New York, NY: Academic Press; McCluskey, J. D., Mastrofski, S. D., & Parks, R. B. (1999). To

acquiesce or rebel: Predicting citizen compliance with police requests. *Police Quarterly, 2,* 389–416; Muir, W. K. (1977). *Police: Streetcorner politicians.* Chicago, IL: University of Chicago Press.

5. Allen, T. T. (2005). Taking a juvenile in to custody: Situational factors that influence police officers' decisions. *Journal of Sociology and Social Work, 32,* 121–129.

6. Brown et al., Identifying variation in police officer behavior.

7. Steinberg, L. (2009). Adolescent development and juvenile justice. *Annual Review of Clinical Psychology, 5,* 459–485.

8. International Association of Chiefs of Police (2015). *The effects of adolescent development on policing.* Retrieved from http://www.theiacp.org/Portals/0/documents/pdfs/IACPBriefEffectsofAdolescentDevelopmentonPolicing.pdf

9. Ibid., p. 5.

10. Miranda v. Arizona, 10 Ohio Misc. 9 (1966).

11. Yarborough v. Alvarado, 541 U.S. 652 (2004).

12. J. D. B. v. North Carolina, No. 09-11121 (2011).

13. Ibid., p. 18.

14. Butts, J. A., & Buck, J. (2000). Teen courts: A focus on research. *Juvenile Justice Bulletin.* Washington, DC: Office of Juvenile Justice and Delinquency Prevention; Butts, J. A., Buck, J., & Coggeshall, M. B. (2002). *The impact of teen court on young offenders.* Washington, DC: Urban Institute Press.

15. Blomberg, T. G. (1979). Diversion from juvenile court: A review of the evidence. In F. L. Faust & P. J. Brantingham (Eds.), *Juvenile justice philosophy: Readings, cases and comments* (2nd ed., pp. 415–430). St. Paul, MN: West; Palmer, T., & Lewis, R. V. (1980). *Evaluation of juvenile diversion.* Cambridge, MA: Oelgeschlager, Gunn, and Hain.

16. Fischer, B., Wortley, S., Webster, C., & Kirst, M. (2002). The socio-legal dynamics and implications of "diversion": The case study of the Toronto "John School" diversion programme for prostitution offenders. *Criminal Justice, 2*(4), 385–410.

17. Snyder, H. N., & Sickmund, M. (1995). *Juvenile offenders and victims: A national report.* Washington, DC: Office of Juvenile Justice and Delinquency Prevention.

18. American Bar Association. (n.d.). *Before you plea: The Juvenile Collateral Consequences Project.* Retrieved from http://www.beforeyouplea.com/home

19. Jacobs, M. D. (1990). *Screwing the system and making it work: Juvenile justice in the no-fault society.* Chicago, IL: University of Chicago Press; Siegel, L. J., & Senna, J. J. (1997). *Juvenile delinquency: Theory, practice, and law* (6th ed.). St. Paul, MN: West Group; Siegel, L. J., Welsh, B. C., & Senna, J. J. (2003). *Juvenile delinquency: Theory, practice, and law* (8th ed.). Belmont, CA: Wadsworth.

20. Hartney, C., & Silva, F. (2007). *And justice for some: Differential treatment of youth of color in the justice system.* Oakland, CA: The National Council on Crime and Delinquency. Retrieved from http://www.nccdglobal.org/sites/default/files/publication_pdf/justice-for-some.pdf

21. Kempf, K. (1992). *The role of race in juvenile justice processing in Pennsylvania.* Shippensburg: Center for Juvenile Justice Training and Research and Pennsylvania Commission on Crime and Delinquency.

22. Neubeck, Neubeck, & Glasberg, *Social problems: A critical approach.*

23. Ibid.

24. Bishop, D. M., & Frazier, C. E. (1996). Race effects in juvenile justice decision making: Findings of a statewide analysis. *Journal of Criminal Law and Criminology, 86*(2), 392–414.

25. Ibid.

26. Devine, P., Coolbaugh, K., & Jenkins, S. (1998). *Disproportionate minority confinement: Lessons learned from five states.* Washington, DC: U.S. Department of Justice; Guevara, L., Herz, D., & Spohn, C. (2006). Gender and juvenile justice decision making: What role does race play? *Feminist Criminology, 1,* 258–282; Hsia, H., Bridges, G., & McHale, R. (2004). *Disproportionate minority confinement: 2002*

update. Washington, DC: U.S. Department of Justice.

27. Hanes, M. (2012). *In focus: Disproportionate minority contact.* Office of Juvenile Justice and Delinquency Prevention, p. 1. Retrieved from http://www.ojjdp.gov/pubs/239457.pdf.

28. Office of Juvenile Justice and Delinquency Prevention. (2009). *Disproportionate minority contact technical assistance manual.* Retrieved from http://www.ojjdp.gov/compliance/dmc_ta_manual.pdf

29. Bishop & Frazier, Race effects in juvenile justice decision making: Findings of a state-wide analysis. Bridges, G., & Steen, S. (1998). Racial disparities in official assessments of juvenile offenders: Attributional stereotypes as mediating mechanisms. *American Sociological Review, 63,* 554–570; Conley, D. (1994). Adding color to a black and white picture: Using qualitative data to explain racial disproportionality in the juvenile justice system. *Journal of Research in Crime and Delinquency, 31,* 135–148; Engen, R., Steen, S., & Bridges, G. (2002). Racial disparities in the punishment of youth: A theoretical and empirical assessment of the literature. *Social Problems, 49,* 194–220; Feld, B. (1991). Justice by geography: Urban, suburban and rural variations in juvenile justice administration. *Journal of Criminal Law and Criminology, 82,* 156–210; Frazier, C., & Bishop, D. (1995). Reflections on race effects in juvenile justice. In K. Kempf-Leonard, C. Pope, & W. Feyerherm (Eds.), *Minorities in juvenile justice* (pp. 16–46). Thousand Oaks, CA: SAGE; Sampson, R., & Laub, J. (1993). Structural variations in juvenile court processing: Inequality, the underclass, and social control. *Law and Society Review, 27*(2), 285–311.

30. Lundman, R. J., Sykes, R. E., & Clark, J. P. (1990). Police control of juveniles: A replication. In R. Weisheit & R. G. Culbertson (Eds.), *Juvenile delinquency: A justice perspective* (2nd ed.). Prospect Heights, IL: Waveland Press; Weitzer, R. (1996). Racial discrimination in the criminal justice system: Findings and problems in the literature. *Journal of Criminal Justice, 24,* 309–322.

31. Fagan, J., Slaughter, E., & Hartstone, E. (1987). Blind justice? The impact of race on the juvenile justice process. *Crime and Delinquency, 33,* 224–258.

32. Elrod, P., & Ryder, R. S. (2011). *Juvenile justice: A social, historical, and legal perspective* (3rd ed.). Boston, MA: Jones and Bartlett.

33. Leiber, M. (2002). Disproportionate minority confinement (DMC) of youth: An analysis of state and federal efforts to address the issue. *Crime and Delinquency, 48*(1), 3–45.

34. Engen, Steen, & Bridges, Racial disparities in the punishment of youth: A theoretical and empirical assessment of the literature. Males, M., & Macallair, D. (2000). *The color of justice: An analysis of juvenile adult court transfers in California.* Washington, DC: Justice Policy Institute; Poe-Yamagata, E., & Jones, M. A. (2000). *And justice for some: Differential treatment of minority youth in the justice system.* Washington, DC: Building Blocks for Youth.

35. Clarke, E. (1996). A case for reinventing juvenile transfer: The record of transfer of juvenile offenders to criminal court in Cook County, Illinois. *Juvenile and Family Court Journal, 47*(3), 3–22.

36. Poe-Yamagata & Jones, *And justice for some.*

37. Odem, M. (1995). *Delinquent daughters: Protecting and policing adolescent female sexuality in the United States, 1885–1920.* Chapel Hill, NC: University of North Carolina Press; Odem, M., & Schlossman, S. (1991). Guardians of virtue: The juvenile court and female delinquency in early 20th century Los Angeles. *Crime & Delinquency, 372,* 186–203.

38. Chesney-Lind, M. (1977). Judicial paternalism and the female status offender. *Crime & Delinquency, 23,* 121–130; Chesney-Lind, M., & Shelden, R. (2004). *Girls, delinquency, and juvenile justice.* Belmont, CA: West/Wadsworth.

39. Bishop, D., & Frazier, C. (1992). Gender bias in the juvenile justice system: Implications of the JJDP act. *Journal of Criminal Law and Criminology, 82,* 1162–1186; Johnson, D. R., & Scheuble, L. K. (1991). Gender bias in the disposition of juvenile court referrals: The effects of time and location. *Criminology, 29*(4), 677–699.

40. Elliott, D. S., & Voss, H. L. (1974). *Delinquency and dropout.* Lexington, MA: Lexington Books; Krohn, M. D., Curry, J. P., & Nelson-Kilger, S. (1983). Is chivalry dead? An analysis of changes in police dispositions of males and females. *Criminology, 21,* 417–437; Morash, M. (1984). Establishment of a juvenile police record: The influence of individual and peer group characteristics. *Criminology, 22,* 97–111.

41. Goffman, E. (1961). *Asylums: Essays on the social situation of mental patients and other inmates.* Garden City, NY: Anchor Books; Victory, *"All I wanted was someone to be there": Surviving the structured abuse in group homes.*

42. Lutz, L., & Stewart, M. (2011). *Crossover youth practice model.* Center for Juvenile Justice Reform. Washington, DC: Georgetown Public Policy Institute. Retrieved from http://cjjr .georgetown.edu/pdfs/cypm/cypm.pdf

43. Ibid.

44. Herz, D. C., & Ryan, J. P. (2008). *Exploring the characteristics and outcomes of 241.1 youths in Los Angeles county.* San Francisco: California Courts, The Administrative Office of the Courts; Ryan, J. P., Herz, D., Hernandez, P., & Marshall, J. (2007). Maltreatment and delinquency: Investigating child welfare bias in juvenile justice processing. *Children and Youth Services Review, 29,* 1035–1050.

45. Lutz & Stewart, *Crossover youth practice model,* p. 34.

46. Goffman, *Asylums;* Victory, *"All I wanted was someone to be there."*

47. Ibid.

48. Victory, *"All I wanted was someone to be there."*

49. Ibid.

50. Goffman, *Asylums;* Victory, *"All I wanted was someone to be there."*

51. Mohr, W. K., Martin, A., Olson, J. N., Pumariega, A. J., & Branca, N. (2009). Beyond point and level systems: Moving toward child-centered programming. *American Journal of Orthopsychiatry, 79,* 8–18; Rauktis, M., Fusco, R. A., Cahalane, H. G., Bennett, I. K., & Reinhart, S. (2011). "Try to make it seem like we're regular kids": Youth perceptions of restrictiveness in out-of-home care. *Children and Youth Services Review, 33,* 1224–1233; Rauktis, M. (2016). "When you first get there, you wear red": Youth perceptions of point and level systems in group home care. *Child and Adolescent Social Work Journal, 33*(1), 91–102; Victory, *"All I wanted was someone to be there."*

52. Victory, *"All I wanted was someone to be there."*

53. Goffman, *Asylums;* Lipsky, M. (2010). *Street-level bureaucracy: Dilemmas of the individual in public services.* New York, NY: Russell Sage Foundation; Victory, *"All I wanted was someone to be there."*

54. Victory, *"All I wanted was someone to be there."*

CHAPTER 13

1. Torbet, P. M. (1996). *Juvenile probation: The workhorse of the juvenile justice system.* Washington, DC: Office of Juvenile Justice and Delinquency Prevention.

2. Puzzanchera, C., & Adams, B. (2012). *National disproportionate minority contact databook.* Developed by the National Center for Juvenile Justice for the Office of Juvenile Justice and Delinquency Prevention. Retrieved from http:// www.ojjdp.gov/ojstatbb/dmcdb/

3. Elrod P. & Ryder, *Juvenile justice: A social, historical, and legal perspective.*

4. Lane, J., Turner, S., Fain, T., & Sehgal, A. (2005). Evaluating an experimental intensive juvenile probation program: Supervision and official outcomes. *Crime and Delinquency, 51,* 26–52.

5. Austin, J., Joe, K., Krisberg, B., & Steele, P. A. (1990). *The impact of juvenile court sanctions: A court that works.* San Francisco, CA: National Council on Crime and Delinquency.

6. Lane et al., Evaluating an experimental intensive juvenile probation program.

7. Barton, W. H., & Butts, J. A. (1990). Viable options: Intensive supervision programs for

juvenile delinquents. *Crime & Delinquency, 36,* 238–256; Barton, W. H., & Butts, J. A. (1991). Intensive supervision alternatives for adjudicated juveniles. In T. L. Armstrong (Ed.), *Intensive interventions with high risk youths: Promising approaches in juvenile probation and parole* (pp. 317–340). Monsey, NY: Criminal Justice Press.

8. Zhang, S. X. (1996). The efficiency of working under one roof: An evaluation of Los Angeles County juvenile justice centers. *Crime & Delinquency, 42,* 257–268.

9. Altschuler, D. M. (1998). Intermediate sanctions and community treatment for serious and violent juvenile offenders. In R. Loeber & D. P. Farrington (Eds.), *Serious & violent juvenile offenders: Risk factors and successful interventions* (pp. 367–385). Thousand Oaks, CA: Sage; Palmer, T. (2002). *Individualized intervention with young multiple offenders.* New York, NY: Routledge.

10. Schneider, P. R., & Finkelstein, M. C. (Eds.). (1998). *RESTTA national directory of restitution and community service programs.* Bethesda, MD: Pacific Institute for Research and Evaluation. Retrieved from http://www.ojjdp .ncjrs.gov/pubs/restta/index.html

11. Schneider, A. L., & Schneider, P. R. (1984). A comparison of programmatic and "ad hoc" restitution in juvenile courts. *Justice Quarterly, 1,* 529–547.

12. Butts, J. A., & Snyder, H. N. (1992). *Restitution and juvenile recidivism: OJJDP update on statistics.* Washington, DC: Office of Juvenile Justice and Delinquency Prevention; Ervin, L., & Schneider, A. (1990). Explaining the effects of restitution on offenders: Results from a national experiment in juvenile courts. In B. Galaway & J. Hudson (Eds.), *Criminal justice, restitution, and reconciliation.* Monsey, NY: Criminal Justice Press.

13. Office of Juvenile Justice and Delinquency Prevention. (n.d.). *Home confinement/electronic monitoring.* Washington, DC: U.S. Department of Justice, Office of Justice Programs.

14. National Law Enforcement and Corrections Technology Center. (1999). *Keeping track of electronic monitoring.* Washington, DC: U.S.

Department of Justice, National Institute of Justice.

15. Ford, D., & Schmidt, A. K. (1985). Electronically monitored home confinement. *NIJ Reports.* Washington, DC: National Institute of Justice; Renzema, M., & Skelton, D. T. (1990). Use of electronic monitoring in the United States: 1989 update. *Research in Brief.* Washington, DC: National Institute of Justice.

16. Roy, S. (1997). Five years of electronic monitoring of adults and juveniles in Lake County, Indiana: A comparative study of factors related to failure. *Journal of Crime and Justice, 20,* 141–160.

17. U.S. Department of Health and Human Services, Administration for Children and Families. (2015). *Trends in foster care and adoption: FY 2005–FY 2014.* Retrieved from http://www.acf.hhs .gov/sites/default/files/cb/trends_fostercare_ adoption2014.pdf

18. Finckenauer, J. O. (1984). *Juvenile delinquency and corrections: The gap between theory and practice.* Orlando, FL: Academic Press.

19. Ibid.

20. McCord, J., McCord, W., & Thurber, E. (1968). The effects of foster-home placement in the prevention of adult antisocial behavior. In J. R. Stratton & R. M. Terry (Eds.), *Prevention of delinquency: Problems and programs.* New York, NY: Macmillan.

21. Rubin, H. T. (1985). *Juvenile justice: Policy, practice, and law* (2nd ed.). New York, NY: Random House.

22. Chamberlain, P. (1990). Comparative evaluation of specialized foster care for seriously delinquent youths: A first step. *Community Alternatives: International Journal of Family Care, 2,* 21–36; Chamberlain, P., Leve, L. D., & DeGarmo, D. S. (2007). Multidimensional treatment foster care for girls in the juvenile justice system: 2-year follow up of a random clinical trial. *Journal of Consulting and Clinical Psychology, 75,* 187–193; Chamberlain, P., & Reid, J. B. (1998). Comparison of two community alternatives to incarceration for chronic juvenile offenders. *Journal of Consulting and Clinical Psychology, 66,* 624–633; Eddy, J. M., Whaley, R. B., & Chamberlain, P. (2004). The

prevention of violent behavior by chronic and serious male juvenile offenders: A 2-year follow-up of a randomized clinical trial. *Journal of Emotional and Behavioral Disorders, 12,* 2–8.

23. Chamberlain et al., Multidimensional treatment foster care for girls in the juvenile justice system; Chamberlain & Reid, Comparison of two community alternatives to incarceration for chronic juvenile offenders; Empey, L. T., & Lubeck, S. G. (1971). *The Silverlake experiment: Testing delinquency theory and community intervention.* Chicago, IL: Aldine.

24. Elrod & Ryder, *Juvenile justice.*

25. National Center for Juvenile Justice. (2011). *Easy access to the census of juveniles in residential placement 1997–2010 (online tool).* Retrieved from http://www.ojjdp.gov/ojstatbb/ezacjrp/asp/selection.asp

26. Mendel, R. A. (2011). *No place for kids: The case for reducing juvenile incarceration.* Baltimore, MD: The Annie E. Casey Foundation.

27. Elrod & Ryder, *Juvenile justice.*

28. Frazier, C. E. (1989). Preadjudicatory detention. In A. R. Roberts (Ed.), *Juvenile justice: Policies, programs, and services* (pp. 143–168). Chicago, IL: Dorsey Press.

29. Lerman, P. (1977). Discussion of "differential selection of juveniles for detention. *Journal of Research in Crime and Delinquency, 14,* 166–172; Poulin, J. E., Levitt, J. L., Young, T. M., & Pappenfort, D. M. (1977). *Juveniles in detention centers and jails: An analysis of state variations during the mid 1970s.* Washington, DC: Office of Juvenile Justice and Delinquency Prevention.

30. Henretta, J. C., Frazier, C. E., & Bishop, D. M. (1986). The effect of prior case outcomes on juvenile justice decision making. *Social Forces, 65,* 542–562.

31. Maleszka, J. (2016). "They call us monsters": A powerful new documentary on juveniles tried as adults. *Mass Appeal.* Retrieved from http://massappeal.com/they-call-us-monsters-documentary-ben-lear-interview

32. Thornberry, T. P., Tolnay, S. E., Flanagan, T. J, & Glynn, P. (1991). *Children in custody 1987: A comparison of public and private juvenile custody facilities.* Washington, DC: Office of Juvenile Justice and Delinquency Prevention.

33. Elrod & Ryder, *Juvenile justice.*

34. Ibid.

35. Hazel, N. (2008). *Cross-national comparison of youth justice.* London: Youth Justice Board.

36. National Center for Juvenile Justice. *Easy access to the census of juveniles in residential placement 1997–2010.*

37. Mendel, *No place for kids.*

38. Ibid.

39. Ibid., p. 5.

40. Ibid., p. 9.

41. Ibid., p. 13.

42. Ibid., p. 16.

43. Ibid., p. 19.

44. Ibid., p. 22.

45. Parent, D. G. (2003). *Correctional boot camps: Lessons from a decade of research.* Washington, DC: U.S. Department of Justice Office of Justice Programs.

46. Elrod & Ryder, *Juvenile justice*; Parent, *Correctional boot camps.*

47. Parent, *Correctional boot camps.*

48. Meade, B., & Steiner, B. (2010). The total effects of boot camps that house juveniles: A systematic review of the evidence. *Journal of Criminal Justice, 38,* 841–853.

49. Austin, J. (2000). *Multisite evaluation of boot camp programs: Final report.* Washington, DC: George Washington University, Institute on Crime, Justice, and Corrections; Bottcher, J., & Isorena, T. (1994). *LEAD: A boot camp and intensive parole program: An implementation and process evaluation of the first year.* NCJ 150513. Washington, DC: California Youth Authority and U.S. Department of Justice, National Institute of Justice; Peters, M., Thomas, D., & Zamberlan, C. (1997). *Boot camps for juvenile offenders.* Program Summary, NCJ 164258. Washington, DC: U.S. Department of Justice, Office of Juvenile Justice and Delinquency Prevention; Zhang, S. C. (1999). *An evaluation of the Los Angeles County Juvenile Drug Treatment*

Boot Camp. Final Report, NCJ 189787. San Marcos: California State University and the U.S. Department of Justice, National Institute of Justice.

50. Parent, *Correctional boot camps.*

51. Miller, C. M. (2012). As Florida teen lay dying, jail guards refused to call help, believed he was faking. *The Miami Herald,* October 19. Retrieved from http://www.miamiherald.com/2012/10/19/3057693/as-florida-teen-lay-dying-jail.html

52. Franceschina, P. (2012). Man died of brain injuries after 6 hours of neglect in juvenile jail, Palm Beach County grand jury says. *Sun Sentinel,* March 9. Retrieved from http://articles.sun-sentinel.com/2012-03-09/news/fl-detention-death-grand-jury-20120309_1_grand-jury-juvenile-jail-juvenile-justice

53. Cikins, W. I. (1986). Privatization of the American prison systems: An idea whose time has come? *Notre Dame Journal of Law, Ethics and Public Policy, 2,* 445–464; Cullen, F. T. (1986). The privatization of treatment: Prison reform in the 1980s. *Federal Probation, 50*(1), 8–16; Joel, D. C. (1992). Containing costs through privatization. In E. Hudgins & R. Utt (Eds.), *How privatization can solve America's infrastructure crisis* (pp. 149–170). Washington, DC: The Heritage Foundation; Burger, W. E. (1992). More warehouses, or factories with fences? In G. Bowman, S. Hakim, & P. Seidenstat (Eds.), *Privatizing the United States justice system: Police adjudication, and corrections services from the private sector* (pp. 330–335). Jefferson, NC: McFarland; Durham, A. M. (1993). The future of correctional privatization: Lessons from the past. In G. Bowman, S. Hakim, & P. Seidenstat (Eds.), *Privatizing correctional institutions* (pp. 33–49). New Brunswick, NJ: Transaction.

54. Pratt, T. C., & Winston, M. R. (1999). The search for the frugal grail: An empirical assessment of the cost-effectiveness of public versus private correctional facilities. *Criminal Justice Policy Review, 10,* 447–471.

55. Schwartz, I. M. (1989). *(In)justice for juveniles: Rethinking the best interests of the child.* Lexington, MA: Lexington Books.

56. Schwartz, I. M., Jackson-Beeck, M., & Anderson, R. (1984). The "hidden" system of juvenile control. *Crime and Delinquency, 30,* 371–385.

57. Rovner, J. (2016). Juvenile life without parole: An overview. *The Sentencing Project.* Retrieved from http://sentencingproject.org/wp-content/uploads/2015/12/Juvenile-Life-Without-Parole.pdf

58. Ibid.

59. Snyder, H. N. (2004). An empirical portrait of the youth reentry population. *Youth Violence and Juvenile Justice, 2,* 39–55; Mears, D. P., & Travis, J. (2004). Youth development and reentry. *Youth Violence and Juvenile Justice, 2,* 3–20.

60. Krisberg, B. A., Austin, J., & Steele, P. (1991). *Unlocking juvenile corrections.* San Francisco, CA: National Council on Crime and Delinquency; Krisberg, B., & Howell, J. C. (1998). The impact of the juvenile justice system and prospects for graduated sanctions in a comprehensive strategy. In R. Loeber & D. P. Farrington (Eds.), *Serious and violent juvenile offenders: Risk factors and successful interventions* (pp. 346–366). Thousand Oaks, CA: Sage.

61. Mears & Travis, Youth development and reentry.

62. Schwartz, *(In)justice for juveniles.*

63. Eilperin, J. (2016, January 26). Obama bans solitary confinement for juveniles in federal prisons. *The Washington Post.* Retrieved from https://www.washingtonpost.com/politics/obama-bans-solitary-confinement-for-juveniles-in-federal-prisons/2016/01/25/056e14b2-c3a2-11e5-9693-933a4d31bcc8_story.html

64. Lutz, J. (2016). Stop solitary for kids: A national campaign for change. *The Juvenile Justice Information Exchange.* Retrieved from http://jjie.org/stop-solitary-for-kids-a-national-campaign-for-change/163440/

65. Inderbitzin, M. (2009). Reentry of emerging adults: Adolescent inmates' transition back into the community. *Journal of Adolescent Research, 24,* 453–476.

66. Arnett, J. J. (2000). Emerging adulthood: A theory of development from the late teens through

the twenties. *American Psychologist, 55,* 469–480; Arnett, J. J. (2004). *Emerging adulthood: The winding road from the late teens through the twenties.* New York, NY: Oxford University Press.

67. Inderbitzin, Reentry of emerging adults, pp. 468–473.

68. Schaffner, L. (2006). *Girls in trouble with the law.* New Brunswick, NJ: Rutgers University Press, p. 152.

69. Sedlak, A. J., & Bruce, C. (2010). *Youth's characteristics and backgrounds: Findings from the survey of youth in residential placement.* Bulletin. Washington, DC: U.S. Department of Justice, Office of Justice Programs, Office of Juvenile Justice and Delinquency Prevention.

70. Giallombardo, R. (1966). *Society of women: A study of a women's prison.* New York, NY: Wiley; Baskin, D., Sommers, I., Tessler, R., & Steadman, H. (1989). Role incongruence and gender variation in the provision of prison mental health services. *Journal of Health and Social Behavior, 30,* 305–314; Morash, M., Haarr, R., & Rucker, L. (1994). A comparison of programming for women and men in U.S. prisons since the 1980s. *Crime & Delinquency, 40,* 197–221.

71. Rosenbaum, J., & Chesney-Lind, M. (1994). Appearance and delinquency: A research note. *Crime & Delinquency, 40*(2), 250–261.

72. Ibid.

73. Schaffner, *Girls in trouble with the law,* p. 20.

74. Ibid.

75. Dobash, R. P., Dobash, R. E., & Gutteridge, S. (1986). *The imprisonment of women.* New York, NY: Basil Blackwell.

76. Krisberg, B., Schwartz, I., Fishman, G., Eisikovits, Z., Guttman, E., & Joe, K. (1987). The incarceration of minority youth. *Crime & Delinquency, 33,* 173–204.

77. Arya, N., & Augarten, I. (2008). *Critical condition: African-American youth in the justice system.* Washington, DC: Campaign for Youth Justice; Arya, N., & Rolnick, A. A. (2008). *Tangled web of justice: American Indian and Alaska Native youth in federal, state, and tribal justice systems.* Washington, DC: Campaign for Youth Justice; Arya, N., Villarruel, F., Villanueva, C., & Augarten, I. (2009). *America's invisible children: Latino youth and the failure of justice.* Washington, DC: Campaign for Youth Justice.

78. Kempf-Leonard, K., & Sontheimer, H. (1995). The role of race in juvenile justice in Pennsylvania. In K. Kempf-Leonard, C. E. Pope, & W. Feyerherm (Eds.), *Minorities in juvenile justice* (pp. 98–127). Thousand Oaks, CA: Sage.

79. Feld, *Bad kids: Race and the transformation of the juvenile court.*

80. Pope, D. E. (1994). Racial disparities in juvenile justice system. *Overcrowded Times, 5,* 1–4.

81. Poe-Yamagata, & Jones, *And justice for some: Differential treatment of minority youth in the justice system.*

82. McKinley, J. (2009, June 13). San Francisco at crossroads over immigration. *New York Times,* p. A12.

83. Frankel, E. (2011). Detention and deportation with inadequate due process: The devastating consequences of juvenile involvement with law enforcement for immigrant youth. *Duke Forum for Law and Social Change, 63,* 1–43.

84. Ibid.

85. Ibid., p. 18.

86. Schaffner, *Girls in trouble with the law,* p. 61.

87. Sharma, S. (2010). Contesting institutional discourse to create new possibilities for understanding lived experience: Life-stories of young women in detention, rehabilitation, and education. *Race Ethnicity and Education, 13*(3), 327–347.

88. Ibid., p. 341.

89. Ibid., p. 345.

90. National Center for Lesbian Rights. (2006). *LGBTQ youth in the juvenile justice system.* San Francisco, CA: Author.

91. Ibid.

92. Schaffner, *Girls in trouble with the law,* p. 149.

CHAPTER 14

1. Butts, J. A., & Mears, D. P. (2001). Reviving juvenile justice in a get-tough era. *Youth and Society, 33,* 169–198; Cullen & Gendreau, Assessing correctional rehabilitation.

2. Savignac, J. (2010). *Tools to identify and assess the risk of offending among youth.* Ottawa, Canada: National Crime Prevention Centre.

3. Koegel, C. J., Farrington, D. P., & Augimeri, L. K. (2009). Clinician perceptions of childhood risk factors for future antisocial behavior. *Journal of Clinical Child & Adolescent Psychology, 83*(4), 564–575.

4. Ibid., p. 566.

5. Farrington, Should the juvenile justice system be involved in early intervention?

6. Greenwood, P. (2008). Prevention and intervention programs for juvenile offenders. *Future of Children, 18*(2), 185–210. Retrieved from http://www.futureofchildren.org; Welsh, B. C., & Farrington, D. P. (2007). Save children from a life of crime. *Criminology & Public Policy, 6*(4), 871–879.

7. Zagar, R. J., Busch, K. G., & Hughes, J. R. (2009). Empirical risk factors for delinquency and best treatments: Where do we go from here? *Psychological Reports, 104*(1), 279–308.

8. Koffman, S., Ray, A., Berg, S., Covington, L., Albarran, N., & Vazquez, M. (2009). Impact of a comprehensive whole child intervention and prevention program among youths at risk of gang involvement and other forms of delinquency. *Children & Schools, 31*(4), 239–345; Nation, M., Crusto, C., Wandersman, A., Kumpfer, K. L., Seybolt, D., Morrissey-Kane E., & Davino, K. (2003). What works in prevention. *American Psychologist, 58*(6–7), 449–457.

9. Zigler, E., & Muenchow, S. (1992). *Head Start: The inside story of America's most successful educational experiment.* New York, NY: BasicBooks.

10. Greenwood, Prevention and intervention programs for juvenile offenders.

11. Eckenrode, J., Campa, M., Luckey, D., Henderson, C., Jr., Cole, R., Kitzman, H., . . . Olds, D. (2010). Long-term effects of prenatal and infancy nurse home visitation on the life course of youths: 19-year follow-up of a randomized trial. *Archives of Pediatric and Adolescent Medicine, 164,* 9–15; Olds, D., Hill, P., Mihalic, S., & O'Brien, R. (1998). Prenatal and infancy home visitation by nurses. In D. S. Elliot (Series Ed.), *Blueprints for violence prevention* (Book 7). Boulder: University of Colorado, Boulder, Center for the Study and Prevention of Violence; Olds, D. L., Kitzman, H. J., Hanks, C., Cole, R. E., Anson, E., Sidora-Arcoleo, K., . . . Bondy, J. (2007). Effects of nurse home-visiting on maternal and child functioning: Age 9 follow-up of a randomized trial. *Pediatrics, 120,* 832–845; Olds, D. L., Robinson, J., Pettitt, L., Luckey, D., Holmberg, J., Ng, R. K., . . . Henderson, C. R., Jr. (2004). Effects of home visits by paraprofessionals and by nurses: Age-four follow-up of a randomized trial. *Pediatrics, 114*(6), 560–568.

12. Eckenrode et al., Long-term effects of prenatal and infancy nurse home visitation on the life course of youths.

13. Ibid.

14. Nurse-Family Partnership. (2011). *Nurse-family partnership international.* Boulder, CO. Retrieved from http://www.nursefamilypartnership.org/communities/NFP-Abroad

15. Welsh & Farrington, Save children from a life of crime.

16. Greenwood, Prevention and intervention programs for juvenile offenders.

17. Hanford, E. (2009). *Early lessons.* American Radioworks. Retrieved from http://americanradioworks.publicradio.org/features/preschool/index.html

18. Johnson, D. L., & Walker, T. (1987). Primary prevention of behavior problems in Mexican-American children. *American Journal of Community Psychology, 15*(4), 375–385.

19. Lally, J. R., Mangione, P. L., & Honig, A. S. (1988). The Syracuse University Family Development Research Project: Long-range impact of an early intervention with low-income

children and their families. In D. R. Powell (Ed.), *Parent education as early childhood intervention: Emerging directions in theory, research, and practice* (Vol. 3, pp. 79–104). Norwood, NJ: Ablex.

20. Seitz, V., & Apfel, N. (1994). Parent-focused intervention: Diffusion effects on siblings. *Child Development, 65*(2), 677–683.

21. Parks, G. (2000). The High/Scope Perry Preschool Project. *Juvenile Justice Bulletin.* Washington, DC: Office of Juvenile Justice and Delinquency Prevention.

22. Office of Head Start. (2013). *Head Start services.* Washington, DC: Office of the Administration for Children & Families. Retrieved from http://www.acf.hhs.gov/programs/ohs/about/head-start

23. Deming, D. (2009). Early childhood intervention and life skill development: Evidence from Head Start. *American Economic Journal: Applied Economics, 1*(3), 111–134.

24. Ibid.

25. Blueprints for Healthy Youth Development. (2013). *All programs.* Boulder: University of Colorado Boulder, Institute of Behavioral Science, Center for the Study and Prevention of Violence. Retrieved from http://www.blueprintsprograms.com/allPrograms.php

26. PATHS. (2011). *Research overview: Evidence of program effectiveness.* Retrieved from http://www.pathstraining.com/pages/research_overview.html

27. USC Institute for Prevention Research. (2013). *Project toward no drug abuse: USC program evaluation research.* Retrieved from http://tnd.usc.edu/overview_research.php

28. Sherman, L. W. (1997). Communities and crime prevention. In L. W. Sherman, D.C. Gottfredson, D. L. MacKenzie, J. E. Eck, P. Reuter, & S. D. Bushway (Eds.), *Preventing crime: What works, what doesn't, what's promising* (pp. 3–49). Washington, DC: National Institute of Justice, U.S. Department of Justice; Welsh & Farrington, Save children from a life of crime; Welsh, B. C., & Hoshi, A. (2002). Communities and crime prevention. In L. W. Sherman, D. P. Farrington, B. C. Welsh, & D. L. MacKenzie (Eds.), *Evidence-based crime prevention* (pp. 165–197). New York, NY: Routledge.

29. Gottfredson, D. C., Gottfredson, G. D., & Weisman, S. (2001). The timing of delinquent behavior and its implications for ASPs. *Criminology & Public Policy, 1,* 61–80.

30. Gottfredson, D. C., Cross, A., & Soule, D. A. (2007). Distinguishing characteristics of effective and ineffective after-school programs to prevent delinquency and victimization. *Criminology & Public Policy, 6*(2), 289–318.

31. Gerstenblith, S. A., Soulé, D. A., Gottfredson, D. C., Lu, S., Kellstrom, M. A., Womer, S. C., & Bryner, S. L. (2005). ASPs, antisocial behavior, and positive youth development: An exploration of the relationship between program implementation and changes in youth development. In J. L. Mahoney, R. W. Larson, & J. S. Eccles (Eds.), *Organized activities as contexts of development: Extracurricular activities, after-school and community programs* (pp. 457–478). Mahwah, NJ: Lawrence Erlbaum; Gottfredson et al., Distinguishing characteristics of effective and ineffective after-school programs to prevent delinquency and victimization; Weisman, S. A., Womer, S. C., Kellstrom, M. A., Bryner, S. L., Kahler, A., Slocum, L., & Gottfredson, D. C. (2002). *Maryland After School Community Grant Program: Report on the 2001–2002 school year evaluation of the Phase 3 After School Programs.* College Park: University of Maryland.

32. Gottfredson et al., Distinguishing characteristics of effective and ineffective after-school programs to prevent delinquency and victimization.

33. Taheri, S. A., & Welsh, B.C. (2015). After-school programs for delinquency prevention: A systematic review and meta-analysis. *Youth Violence and Juvenile Justice, 14*(3), 272–290.

34. Howell, J. C. (Ed.). (1995). *Guide for implementing the comprehensive strategy for serious, violent, and chronic juvenile offenders.* Washington, DC: Office of Juvenile Justice and Delinquency Prevention, U.S. Department of Justice; Welsh & Farrington, Save children from a life of crime; Welsh & Hoshi, Communities and crime prevention.

35. Rhodes, J. E. (2002). *Stand by me: The risks and rewards of mentoring today's youth.* Cambridge, MA: Harvard University Press; Rhodes, J. E. (2005). A theoretical model of youth mentoring. In D. L. DuBois & M. J. Karcher (Eds.), *Handbook of youth mentoring* (pp. 30–45). Thousand Oaks, CA: Sage.

36. Koball, H., Dion, R., Gothro, A., Bardos, M., Dworsky, A., Lansing, J., . . . Manning, A. E. (2011). *Synthesis of research and resources to support at-risk youth.* OPRE Report #OPRE 2011-22. Washington, DC: Office of Planning, Research and Evaluation, Administration for Children and Families, U.S. Department of Health and Human Services.

37. MENTOR. (2013). *MENTOR's mission.* Retrieved from http://www.mentoring.org/about_mentor/mission

38. Koball et al., *Synthesis of research and resources to support at-risk youth.*

39. Slicker, E. K., & Palmer, D. J. (1993). Mentoring at-risk high school students: Evaluation of a school-based program. *The School Counselor, 40,* 327–334.

40. Jolliffe, D., & Farrington, D. P. (2007). *A rapid evidence assessment of the impact of mentoring on re-offending: A summary.* Cambridge University Online Report. Retrieved from http://www.crimereduction.gov.uk/workingoffenders/workingoffenders069.html

41. Slicker & Palmer, Mentoring at-risk high school students.

42. Lipsey, M. W., Wilson, D. B., & Cothern, L. (2000). *Effective intervention for serious juvenile offenders.* Washington, DC: U.S. Department of Justice, Office of Justice Programs, Office of Juvenile Justice and Delinquency Prevention.

43. Blueprints for Healthy Youth Development, *All programs.*

44. Office of Juvenile Justice and Delinquency Prevention. (2011). *OJJDP model programs guide: Functional Family Therapy.* Retrieved from http://www.ojjdp.gov/mpg/Functional%20Family%20Therapy-MPGProgramDetail-29.aspx

45. Gordon, D. A., Arbuthnot, J., Gustafson, K. E., & McGreen, P. (1988). Home-based behavioral-systems family therapy with disadvantaged juvenile delinquents. *American Journal of Family Therapy, 16*(3), 243–255; Sexton, T. L., & Alexander, J. F. (2004). Functional family therapy for at-risk adolescents and their families. In F. W. Kaslow & T. Patterson (Eds.), *Comprehensive handbook of psychotherapy, cognitive-behavioral approaches* (pp. 117–140). New York, NY: Wiley; Sexton, T. L., & Turner, C. W. (2010). The effectiveness of functional family therapy for youth with behavioral problems in a community practice setting. *Journal of Family Psychology, 24*(3), 339–348.

46. Office of Juvenile Justice and Delinquency Prevention, *OJJDP model programs guide.*

47. Koball et al., *Synthesis of research and resources to support at-risk youth.*

48. Greenwood, Prevention and intervention programs for juvenile offenders.

49. Ibid.; Henggeler, S. W., Melton, G. B., & Smith, L. A. (1992). Family preservation using multisystemic therapy: An effective alternative to incarcerating juvenile offenders. *Journal of Consulting and Clinical Psychology, 60,* 953–961; Henggeler, S. W., Melton, G. B., Smith, L. A., Schoenwald, S. K., & Hanley, J. H. (1993). Family preservation using multisystemic treatment: Long-term follow-up to a clinic trial with serious juvenile offenders. *Journal of Child and Family Studies, 2,* 283–293.

50. Greenwood, Prevention and intervention programs for juvenile offenders.

51. Blueprints for Healthy Youth Development, *All programs.*

52. de Vries, S. L. A., Hoeve, M., Assink, M., Stams, G. J. J. M., & Asscher, J. J. (2015). Practitioner review: Effective ingredients of prevention programs for youth at risk of persistent juvenile delinquency—recommendations for clinical practice. *Journal of Child Psychology and Psychiatry, 56*(2), 108–121.

53. National Council on Crime and Delinquency. (2007). *Promising approaches: A nationwide guide to Asian/Pacific Islander youth organizations and programs.* Oakland, CA: National Council on Crime and Delinquency. Retrieved from http://www.nccdglobal.org/sites/default/files/publication_pdf/promising-approaches.pdf

54. Rapp-Paglicci, L., Stewart, C., Rowe, W., & Miller, J. M. (2011). Addressing the Hispanic delinquency and mental health relationship through cultural arts programming: A research note from the Prodigy evaluation. *Journal of Contemporary Criminal Justice, 27*(1), 110–121.

55. Maldonado-Molina, M. M., Piquero, A. R., Jennings, W. G., Bird, H., & Canino, G. (2009). Trajectories of delinquency among Puerto Rican children and adolescents at two sites. *Journal of Research in Crime and Delinquency, 46,* 144–181.

56. Gaarder, E., & Hesselton, D. (2012). Connecting restorative justice with gender-responsive programming. *Contemporary Justice Review, 15*(3), 239–264.

57. Office of Juvenile Justice and Delinquency Prevention. (1998). *Female offenders: A status of the states report.* Retrieved from http://www.ojjdp.gov/pubs/gender/oview-3.html

58. Watson, L., & Edelman, P. (2012). *Improving the juvenile justice system for girls: Lessons from the states.* Washington, DC: Georgetown Center on Poverty, Inequality and Public Policy. Retrieved from http://www.law.georgetown.edu/academics/centers-institutes/poverty-inequality/upload/JDS_V1R4_Web_Singles.pdf

59. Curtin, M. (2002). Lesbian and bisexual girls in the juvenile justice system. *Child and Adolescent Social Work Journal, 19*(4), 285–299.

60. Dennis, The LGBT offender.

61. Irvine, A. (2010). "We have had three of them": Addressing the invisibility of lesbian, gay, bisexual and gender nonconforming youths in the juvenile justice system. *Columbia Journal of Gender and the Law, 19*(3), 675–699, p. 694.

62. Snapp, S. D., Hoenig, J. M., Fields, A., & Russell, S. T. (2015). Messy, butch, and queer: LGBTQ youth and the school-to-prison pipeline. *Journal of Adolescent Research, 30*(1), 57–82.

63. Himmelstein, K. E. W., & Bruckner, H. (2011). Criminal justice and school sanctions against non-heterosexual youth: A national longitudinal study. *Pediatrics, 127*(1), 48–57; Snapp et al., Messy, butch, and queer.

64. The Urban Institute. (2015). *Surviving the streets of New York: Experiences of LGBTQ youth, YMSM, and YWSW engaged in survival sex.* New York, NY: Author.

65. Mallory, C., Sears, B., Hasenbush, A., & Susman, A. (2014). *Ensuring access for LGBTQ youth.* The Williams Institute, UCLA School of Law. Retrieved from http://williamsinstitute.law.ucla.edu/wp-content/uploads/Access-to-Youth-Mentoring-Programs.pdf

66. Ibid.

67. Ibid.

68. Majd et al., *Hidden injustice,* pp. 137–144.

69. Braithwaite, J. (1989). *Crime, shame, and reintegration.* New York, NY: Cambridge University Press.

70. Rodriguez, N. (2007). Restorative justice at work: Examining the impact of restorative justice resolutions on juvenile recidivism. *Crime and Delinquency, 53,* 355–379; Sherman, L. W., & Strang, H. (2000). *Restorative justice: The evidence.* London, UK: Smith Institute.

71. Bergseth, K. J., & Bouffard, J. A. (2007). The long-term impact of restorative justice programming for juvenile offenders. *Journal of Criminal Justice, 35,* 433–451; Bergseth, K. J., & Bouffard, J. A. (2012). Examining the effectiveness of a restorative justice program for various types of juvenile offenders. *International Journal of Offender Therapy and Comparative Criminology, 57,* 1054–1075; Bouffard, J., Cooper, M., & Bergseth, K. (2016). The effectiveness of various restorative justice interventions on recidivism outcomes among juvenile offenders. *Youth Violence and Juvenile Justice,* 1–16.

72. Bazemore, G., & Schiff, M. (2005). *Juvenile justice reform and restorative justice: Building theory and policy from practice.* Portland, OR: Willan; Umbreit, M. S., Vos, B., & Coates, R. B. (2005). Restorative justice dialogue: A review of evidence-based practice. *Offender Programs Report, 9*(4), 49–64; United Nations Office on Drugs and Crime. (2006). *Handbook on restorative justice programmes. Criminal justice handbook series.* New York, NY: United Nations.

73. Choi, J., Green, D., & Gilbert, M. (2011). Putting a human face on crimes: A qualitative study

on restorative justice processes for youths. *Child & Adolescent Social Work Journal, 28*(5), 335–355.

74. Abrams, L. S., Umbreit, M., & Gordon, A. (2006). Young offenders speak about meeting their victims: Implications for future programs. *Contemporary Justice Review, 9*(3), 243–256; Umbreit, M., Coates, R., & Vos, B. (2002). *The impact of restorative justice conferencing: A review of 63 empirical studies in 5 countries.* St. Paul, MN: Center for Restorative Justice and Peacemaking.

75. See Nugent, W., Umbreit, M., & Williams-Hayes, M. (2003). The relationship between participation in victim-offender mediation and the prevalence and severity of subsequent delinquent behavior. *Utah Law Review, 1,* 173–166; Nugent, W. R., Williams, M., & Umbreit, M. (2004). Participation in victim-offender mediation and the prevalence of subsequent delinquent behavior: A meta-analysis. *Research on Social Work Practice, 14,* 408–416; Umbreith, M., & Coates, R. (1993). Cross-site analysis of victim-offender mediation in four states. *Crime and Delinquency, 39*(4), 565–585.

76. Choi et al., Putting a human face on crimes.

77. Maxwell, G., & Morris, A. (2002). Restorative justice and reconviction. *Contemporary Justice Review, 5*(2), 133–146.

78. McElrea, F. (1996). The New Zealand Youth Court: A model for use with adults. In B. Galaway & J. Hudson (Eds.), *Restorative justice: International perspectives* (pp. 69–84). Monsey, NY: Criminal Justice Press; Pratt, J. (1996). Colonization, power, and silence: A history of indigenous justice in New England society. In B. Galaway & J. Hudson (Eds.), *Restorative justice: International perspectives* (pp. 137–155). Monsey, NY: Criminal Justice Press.

79. McElrea, The New Zealand Youth Court.

80. Umbreit, M. (2000). *Family group conferencing: Implications for crime victims.* Washington, DC: U.S. Department of Justice.

81. McElrea, The New Zealand Youth Court.

82. Umbreit, M., & Stacy, S. (1996). Family group conferencing comes to the U.S.: A comparison with victim offender mediation. *Juvenile and Family Court Journal, 47*(2), 29–39; Umbreit, M., & Zehr, H. (1996). Restorative family group conferences: Differing models and guidelines for practice. *Federal Probation, 60*(3), 24–29.

83. Calhoun, A., & Pelech, W. (2010). Responding to young people responsible for harm: A comparative study of restorative and conventional approaches. *Contemporary Justice Review, 13*(3), 287–306.

84. Umbreit, *Family group conferencing.*

85. Stuart, B. (1996). Circle sentencing: Turning swords into ploughshares. In B. Galaway & J. Hudson (Eds.), *Restorative justice: International perspectives* (pp. 193–206). Monsey, NY: Criminal Justice Press.

86. Umbreit, M. (2008). *Peacemaking circles.* St. Paul, MN: Center for Restorative Justice and Peacemaking.

87. Stuart, B., & Pranis, K. (2006). Peacemaking circles: Reflections on principal features and primary outcomes. In L. Tifft & D. Sullivan (Eds.), *Handbook of restorative justice: A global perspective* (pp. 121–133). Abingdon, UK: Routledge.

88. Braithwaite, J. (2002). *Restorative justice and responsive regulation.* Oxford, UK: Oxford University Press.

89. International Institute for Restorative Practices. (2013). *SaferSaner Schools: Whole-school change through restorative practices.* Retrieved from http://www.safersanerschools.org

90. Abrams et al., Young offenders speak about meeting their victims.

91. Feld, B. (1999). Rehabilitation, retribution, and restorative justice: Alternative conceptions of juvenile justice. In G. Bazemore & L. Walgrave (Eds.), *Restorative juvenile justice: Repairing the harm of youth crime* (pp. 17–44). Monsey, NY: Criminal Justice Press; Karp, D. (2002). The offender/community encounter: Stakeholder involvement in the Vermont community reparative boards. In D. Karp & T. Clear (Eds.), *What is community justice? Case studies of restorative justice and community supervision* (pp. 61–86). Thousand Oaks, CA: Sage; Roberts, J., & LaPrairie, C. (1996). Sentencing circles: Some unanswered questions. *Criminal Law Quarterly, 39,* 69–83.

92. Rodriguez, N. (2005). Restorative justice, communities, and delinquency: Whom do we reintegrate? *Criminology and Public Policy, 4*(1), 103–130.

93. Sumner, M. D., Silverman, C. J., & Frampton, M. L. (2010). *School-based restorative justice as an alternative to zero-tolerance policies:*

Lessons from West Oakland. Berkeley, CA: University of Berkeley School of Law.

94. Brown, M., & Bloom, B. E. (2008). Colonialism and carceral motherhood: Native Hawaiian families under corrections and child welfare control. *Feminist Criminology, 4,* 151–169; Richards, K. (2011). Restorative justice and "empowerment": Producing and governing active subjects through "empowering" practices. *Critical Criminology, 19,* 91–105.

95. Chesney-Lind et al., Girls' troubles, girls' delinquency, and gender responsive programming; Goodenough, K. (2000). *AMICUS: Restorative justice for girls.* Minneapolis, MN: Amicus.

96. Gaarder & Hesselton, Connecting restorative justice with gender-responsive programming.

97. Gordon, K. G. (2004). *From corrections to connections: A report on the Amicus Girls Restorative Program.* St. Paul, MN: Amicus.

98. Amicus, Inc. (2013). *Amicus Radius strength-based services for girls.* Minneapolis, MN: Author.

99. See Gaarder & Hesselton, Connecting restorative justice with gender-responsive programming.

100. Ibid.

101. Daly, K. (2008). Girls, peer violence, and restorative justice. *The Australian and New Zealand Journal of Criminology, 41,* 109–137.

102. Ibid.

103. Elis, L. (2006). Restorative justice programs, gender & recidivism. *Public Organization Review: A Global Journal, 5,* 375–389.

104. Ibid.; Hayes, H., & Daly, K. (2003). Youth justice conferencing and reoffending. *Justice Quarterly, 20,* 725–746; Hayes, H., & Daly, K. (2004). Conferencing and re-offending in Queensland. *The Australian and New Zealand Journal of Criminology, 37,* 167–191; Rodriguez, Restorative justice at work.

105. Miller, P. C., & Endo, H. (2012). Restorative justice: A model for meeting the needs of LGBT youth. In A. Honigsfeld & A. Cohen (Eds.), *Breaking the mold of education for culturally and linguistically diverse students* (pp. 31–38). Lanham, MD: R&L Education.

106. Community Youth Center San Francisco. (2016). *Who we are.* Retrieved from http://cycsf.org/about.php

107. National Council on Crime and Delinquency, *Promising approaches: A nationwide guide to Asian/Pacific Islander youth organizations and programs.*

108. Hurst, H. (2012). *Modules for change: Update 2012: Headlines.* Pittsburgh, PA: National Center for Juvenile Justice.

109. Ibid.

110. National Center for School Engagement. (2013). *Washington state's models for truancy interventions: A cost-benefit analysis.* Denver, CO: The Partnership for Families & Children. Retrieved from http://www.naco.org/sites/default/files/documents/10%20Washington_States_Models_for_Change_Truancy_Interventions_A_CostBenefit_Analysis.pdf

111. Hurst, *Modules for change: Update 2012.*

112. Ibid.

113. Annie E. Casey Foundation. (2013). *Infographic: Youth incarceration in the United States.* Retrieved from http://www.aecf.org/KnowledgeCenter/Publications.aspx?pubguid={EC9F363E-43A6-45F9-B0B8-2709D084C412}

114. Paulson, A. (2013, February 27). Why juvenile incarceration reached its lowest rate in 38 years. *Christian Science Monitor.* Retrieved from http://www.csmonitor.com/layout/set/print/USA/Justice/2013/0227/Why-juvenile-incarceration-reached-its-lowest-rate-in-38-years

115. Balck, A. (2012). *Advances in juvenile justice reform: 2009–2011.* Washington, DC: The National Juvenile Justice Network.

116. Justice Policy Institute. (2013). *Common ground: Lessons learned from five states that reduced juvenile confinement by more than half.* Washington, DC: Justice Policy Institute.

117. Scott, E., Grisso, T., Levick, M., & Steinberg, L. (2015). The Supreme Court and the transformation of Juvenile sentencing. *Models for Change.* New York: Trustees of Columbia University.

118. Balck, *Advances in juvenile justice reform,* pp. 2–3.

INDEX

Above the Influence campaign, 295
Abrams, L. S., 409
Abuse and neglect. *See* Child maltreatment
Academic achievement, 219–221
  See also Educational settings
Accountability, 316, 404
Adachi, P. J. C., 50
Adjudication, 346–347
Adler, Freda, 172, 174
Administration for Children's Services, 34
Adoption and Safe Families Act, 210
af Klinteberg, B., 228
After-school programs, 398–399
Age-delinquency correlation, 72, 108–110, 110 (figure)
Aggression and video games, 50
Agnew, Robert, 115, 116, 117
Aichhorn, August, 98
Akers, Ronald, 103
Alcoholics Anonymous, 299
Alcohol use. *See* Substance use
Alienation, 224–225
Allan, E. A., 110
Alvarado, Michael, 336
American Academy of Pediatrics, 297
American Association of University Women, 234
American Bar Association, 346 (box)
American Civil Liberties Union, 217, 237
American Dream concept, 128–130, 145–146
"American Reporting of School Violence and 'People Like Us'" (Leavy and Maloney), 232–233 (box)
America's Children in Brief (Federal Interagency Forum on Child and Family Statistics), 8
Amicus Radius program, 410–411, 410 (figure)
Amish youth and drug interventions, 303–304
Amish Youth Vision Project, 303–304
Amnesty International, 328 (box)
Andrews, D. A., 100
Androcentrism, 174
Annie E. Casey Foundation, 373

Annual Media for a Just Society Awards, 47 (box)
Anomic suicide, 127
Anomie theory
  differential opportunity, 130–131
  Durkheim's, 126–128
  gender and, 133–134
  overview, 145 (table)
  public policy and, 145–146
  race and, 133
  socioeconomic status and, 134
  strain theory and, 128–130, 130 (table)
  subcultural delinquency theory, 131
Apel, R., 192
Appeal to higher loyalties, 114
Aragones, A., 161
Aria, Bianca, 111–112 (box)
Arthur, M., 194
Asian Pacific Islander Youth Violence Prevention Network, 413 (box)
Atkins v. Virginia, 324 (figure)
Attachment, 108
Attorneys, 339 (table)

Baglivio, M. T., 202
Baier, D., 195, 197
Ball, J. D., 202
Barrios, Luis, 261
Beccaria, Cesare, 95, 105, 313
Becker, Howard, 155
Behavior, criminal
  anomie theory and, 127
  differential association theory and, 100–105, 103 (figure)
  rewards and punishments, effects of, 103
Belief component of social bond, 108
Bentham, J., 95, 313
Bernburg, J. G., 160
Bernstein, Nell, 317
Bickel, Christopher, 317
Biden, Joseph, 50
Big Brothers Big Sisters organization, 399
Biological theories
  craniometry, 97
  eugenics, 97
  phrenology, 97
  stigmata, 97–98
Biosocial theories, 99–100
Birchmeier, Z., 237

Bisexual youth. *See* Lesbian, gay, bisexual, transgender youth
Bishop, D., 350
Black Lives Matter movement, 52–53 (box)
Blair, Chad, 323 (box)
Bloomberg, Michael, 34
Blueprints for Healthy Youth Development project, 397, 400
Blurton, D., 117
Body types, 97–98
Boehnke, K., 195, 197
Bonger, W. A., 113, 164
Bonta, J., 100
Boot camps, 373–374
Boyle, Gregory, 271 (box)
Boys. *See* Gender
Brain research, 322, 326–327 (box)
Braithwaite, J., 408
Breed v. Jones, 319 (figure)
"Brendan Dassey" (Nirider & Drizin), 166 (box)
Brennan, John, 169 (box)
Brezina, T., 161
Brody, G. H., 116
Broidy, L., 117
Brooks, Nathan, 50
Brotherton, David, 261
Brown, Michael, 52–53 (box)
Brown, R. A., 335
Brown v. Entertainment Merchants Association, 49
Bruce, C., 379
Bullying, 121 (box), 233–234
  See also Cyberbullying
Burgess, Ernest, 135–136, 140
Burgess-Proctor, Amanda, 16, 170
Burning Down the House, the End of Juvenile Prison (Bernstein), 317
Bursik, R. J., 137
Bush, George W., 296
Bushway, S. D., 227

Cain, Maureen, 175
Calhoun, A., 407
Call of Duty video game, 49, 50
Campaign for Youth Justice, 49 (box)
"Capitalism, Class, and Crime in America" (Gordon), 165
Capital punishment, 323–324, 324 (figure), 328 (box)
Carey, S., 303

480 Index

ABOUT THE AUTHORS

Kristin A. Bates is Professor of Sociology and Criminology and Justice Studies at California State University, San Marcos. She earned her Ph.D. in sociology from the University of Washington where she concentrated in criminology and social control. She has been teaching juvenile delinquency in both large and small sections for more than 20 years. Her research is in the area of inequality and social justice, with a specific focus on issues of race and social control. Her current research project with Richelle Swan looks at gang injunctions' impact on the community in Southern California. She is the co-editor, with Richelle Swan, of *Through the Eye of Katrina: Social Justice in the United States* (2nd ed.) and co-author of *Deviance and Social Control: A Sociological Perspective* (2nd ed.) and *Perspectives in Deviance and Social Control* (with Michelle Inderbitzin and Randy Gainey).

Richelle S. Swan is Professor of Sociology and Criminology and Justice Studies at California State University, San Marcos. She earned her Ph.D. in criminology, law, and society from the University of California, Irvine, and her M.S. in justice studies from Arizona State University. She teaches a number of classes related to delinquency, crime, law, and social justice. Her ongoing research projects focus on gang injunction laws in Southern California (with Kristin Bates) and the intersection between law, undocumented immigration, and society (with Marisol Clark-Ibáñez). Past research has included problem-solving courts, welfare fraud diversion, restorative justice, and social justice movements. She is the co-editor of *Through the Eye of Katrina: Social Justice in the United States* (2nd ed.) and co-author of *Spicing Up Sociology: The Use of Films in Sociology Courses.*